Turkey, Islam, Nationalism, and Modernity

TURKEY, ISLAM,
NATIONALISM, AND
MODERNITY

A History, 1789–2007

Carter Vaughn Findley

Yale
UNIVERSITY
PRESS
New Haven & London

Published with assistance from the Louis Stern Memorial Fund.

Yale University Press books may be purchased in quantity for educational, business, or promotional use. For information, please e-mail sales.press@yale.edu (U.S. office) or sales@yaleup.co.uk (U.K. office).

Set in Postscript Electra type by diacriTech
Printed in the United States of America.

Library of Congress Cataloging-in-Publication Data

Findley, Carter V., 1941–
Turkey, Islam, nationalism, and modernity / Carter Vaughn Findley.
p. cm.
Includes bibliographical references and index.
ISBN 978-0-300-15260-9 (clothbound : alk. paper) 1. Turkey–History–19th century. 2. Turkey–History–20th century. 3. Turkey–Politics and government–19th century. 4. Turkey–Politics and government–20th century. 5. Nationalism–Turkey–History–19th century. 6. Nationalism–Turkey–History–20th century. 7. Secularism–Turkey–History–19th century. 8. Secularism–Turkey–History–20th century. 9. Islam and state–Turkey–History–19th century. 10. Islam and state–Turkey–History–20th century. I. Title.
DR557.F56 2010
956.1–dc22   2010013169

A catalogue record for this book is available from the British Library.

This paper meets the requirements of ANSI/NISO Z39.48–1992 (Permanence of Paper).
10 9 8 7 6 5 4 3 2 1

Frontispiece: An Ottoman school, 1885, site for the expansion of literacy that made possible the rise of print media. The teachers include both ulema (in turbans) and non-ulema (in fezes). The globe, books, and maps proclaim the school's modernity. (By Sebah and Joaillier, 1885; courtesy of Pierre de Gigord.)

For my children
Madeleine Vaughn Findley
and
Benjamin Carter Findley

CONTENTS

Maps and Illustrations   ix

Acknowledgments   xi

Note on Usage   xiii

Introduction   1

ONE The Return Toward Centralization   23

TWO The Tanzimat   76

THREE The Reign of Abdülhamid   133

FOUR Imperial Demise, National Struggle   192

FIVE The Early Republic   247

SIX Turkey's Widening Political Spectrum   305

SEVEN Turkey and the World   350

Conclusion   405

Abbreviations Used in the Notes and Bibliography   423

Notes   425

Bibliography of Published Sources   457

Index   489

Maps and Illustrations

Note about Illustration Sources: Where known, the source of each illustration is identified in its caption. If an illustration is still under copyright, permission to publish has been obtained from that source. In the case of some photographs, the identity of the photographer or other source of the photograph is not known. These photographs are identified as from the collection of the author, who would like to hear from anyone holding rights to these photographs.

Map 1. The Ottoman Empire, 1774–1912   5
Map 2. Provisions of the Treaty of Sèvres, 1920   220
Map 3. The Republic of Turkey   225

An Ottoman school, 1885   ii
Ahmed İhsan Bey printshop   11
An Ottoman writer at his stand-up desk   12
Ebüzziya printers   14
Janissaries, late eighteenth century   32
A provincial notable's mansion   56
The Sublime Porte   77
Crimean War, British troops camped at Üsküdar, Istanbul   81
Ömer Paşa, commander of Ottoman troops in the Crimea   82
Fuad, Âli, and Midhat Paşas   89
Bosphorus ferry at Beykoz   96
Family life in photographs   119
Abdülhamid II as a young man   134
The Ottoman Imperial Bank and the Régie des tabacs   140
School building under Abdülhamid   152
Ottoman schoolgirls   155

Railroads   167

Silk spinning mill at Bursa   172

Small size of Ottoman towns: Bethlehem in 1857, Ankara in 1888   176

A neighborhood in Istanbul   179

The Imperial Military Medical Academy   180

An Ottoman family reading the newspapers   195

Young Turk Leaders   198

Mustafa Kemal in the trenches   213

Foreign troops occupy Istanbul   216

Turkish women support the war effort   232

Ziya Gökalp   236

Halide Edib [Adıvar]   242

Gazi Mustafa Kemal, president of the republic   249

The alphabet reform   254

The alphabet reform in cartoons   255

Physical culture for modern Turkish girls   260

Sabiha Gökçen   263

İsmet İnönü and his family, 1940   269

Bediüzzaman Said Nursi, 1918   285

Istanbul by night   299

Prime Minister Adnan Menderes with President Celâl Bayar   307

Prime Minister Bülent Ecevit welcomes Justice Party head Süleyman Demirel   317

May Day, 1977, Taksim Square, Istanbul   319

Tractors become widespread in Anatolia   326

Personal automobile ownership comes to Turkey   328

The 1980 coup   352

Turgut Özal   355

Fethullah Gülen   385

"America go home!"   396

Kars   406

Color illustrations follow pages 80 *and* 272

ACKNOWLEDGMENTS

I first thought about writing a book of this type as a beginning graduate student, and I began preparing to do so about 1990. My research in Ankara and Istanbul was aided by Fulbright fellowships from the U.S. Department of Education and the Council on International Exchange of Scholars. While writing, I have benefited especially from the support of the National Endowment for the Humanities and the Mershon Center for International Security Studies at Ohio State University, as well as from the College of Humanities and the Department of History at Ohio State. The individuals who have helped me are legion. Long ago, Gaddis Smith guided my first steps in historical research. Among those who have helped make this a better study I am supremely indebted to Irvin Schick for both ideas and practical assistance. Adalet and Halim Ağaoğlu have become family friends. Metin Heper and Donald Quataert have both shared their expertise with me. So have Virginia Aksan, Randi Deguilhem, Edhem Eldem, Müge Göçek, Kemal Karpat, Philip Khoury, Ussama Makdisi, and Şevket Pamuk. Valuable assistance with the illustrations has come from Irvin Schick, Erdeniz Şen, Günsel Renda, İnci and Mine Enginün, Nilüfer İsvan, Oya Soner, Halim Ağaoğlu, Edhem Eldem, Frédéric Hitzel, William Ochsenwald, Nicole van Os, Ali Aslan of *Zaman*, Fahri Aral, and many others. Dona Straley and Patrick Visel have provided state-of-the-art library support with unfailing alacrity and good cheer. Anthony Baker and Kevin Fitzsimons have performed miracles with graphics and illustrations. Yiğit Akın, Ayşe Baltacıoğlu, Zekeriya Başkal, Ahmet Bozbey, Snjezana Buzov, Benzion Chinn, Nathan Citino, Mehmet Uğur Ekinci, Boğaç Ergene, Özgen Felek, James Helicke, Catalina Hunt, Steven Hyland, Asım Karaömerlioğlu, Ayşe Koçoğlu, George Lywood, Serdar Poyraz, Safa Saraçoğlu, Patrick Scharfe, Gülşah Şenkol, Ayfer Karakaya

Stump, Georges Tamer, Ufuk Ulutaş, Charles Wilkins, Vincent Wilhite, and Yücel Yanıkdağ have all contributed in important ways. Karolyn Beery, Theresa Kyeremeh, Theresa Obeng, Felicia Sampah, Sara Shuherk and many others have provided support that helped me stay focused on my research when other demands loomed up. My children, Madeleine and Benjamin, and other family members have done more than their share to make completion of this project possible. Above all, in sickness and in health, my wife, Lucia, has always supported my research. Completion of this book is another testimony to her love and constancy.

NOTE ON USAGE

The rendering of Ottoman and Turkish names and terms reflects modern Turkish usage, including the following features:

c, C   like "j" in English

ç, Ç   like "ch" in English

ğ   the "soft g." Depending on the adjoining letters, this is either dropped, pronounced like "y" in English, or treated as lengthening the preceding vowel. Soft g does not appear at the beginning of words in Turkish. Thus, in loanwords from Arabic, while "ğ" is used to represent medial "gh" (the Arabic letter *ghayn*), initial *ghayn* becomes "g" in Turkish, whence Turkish *gazi* for Arabic *ghazi*.

ı, I   has no consistent orthographic representation in English. Spreading the lips as if to say "easy" and then trying to say "cushion" produces the Turkish word *kışın*, "in winter."

i, İ   like "i" in English "bit"

ö, Ö   like "ö" in German or "eu" in French *peur*

ş, Ş   like "sh" in English

ü, Ü   like "ü" in German or "u" in French

Turkish spellings have been checked first against the *Redhouse Çağdaş Türkçe-İngilizce Sözlüğü, Contemporary Turkish-English Dictionary* (Istanbul: Redhouse Yayınevi, 1983) and secondarily against *Redhouse Yeni Türkçe-İngilizce Sözlük, New Redhouse Turkish-English Dictionary* (Istanbul: Redhouse Press, [1968]).

A note is also in order about surnames in brackets in the names of individuals active in the years leading up to 1935. Turkish law required Turks to adopt surnames in 1935. As a result, the names of individuals whose active careers began before that date but continued afterward appear differently in sources of different dates. In an effort to avoid ambiguity without introducing anachronisms, historians commonly refer to such individuals as Halide Edib [Adıvar] or İsmet [İnönü] before 1935 and then drop the brackets around the surnames in referring to them from 1935 on. Examples of this practice appear in chapters 4 and 5.

Ottoman cultural diversity challenges efforts to achieve consistency in the rendering of names and terms. Generally speaking, Turkish spellings will prevail in this book. Where the context has to do with the Arab lands or Islam in a general rather than a specifically Turkish frame of reference, the spellings appropriate to the context will take precedence. For example, *Kur'an* will be the spelling preferred in most parts of the book; in a general discussion of Islam, however, *Qur'an* will appear instead to avoid inconsistency with other terms in such a discussion. *Islam* will appear without the dotted uppercase "I" used in Turkish; however, the hero of an Ottoman play discussed in chapter 2 will take the stage as *İslam* Bey. One of the major religious movements discussed in the book will be referred to as the Khalidiyya-Naqshbandiyya in the discussion of its roots in Islamic history and its early history in Ottoman Iraq and Syria; discussions of its later history in Turkey will refer to the same order, Turkish style, as the Halidiye-Nakşibendiye. Some personal names will vary correspondingly. Individuals named Ibrahim and Ismail do not have dotted upper-case initial "I" in their name if they are Arabs or appear in an Arab context; they appear as İbrahim and İsmail if they are Turkish or figure in Turkish context. Stalin's attack on Islam in Central Asia was referred to in the regional languages by the term *hujum* (attack); that spelling has been retained in referring to that event, rather than the spelling of the same term now used in Turkey, *hücum*.

Turkey, Islam, Nationalism, and Modernity

INTRODUCTION: TURKEY, ISLAM, NATIONALISM, AND MODERNITY

The scholarly study of Ottoman and Turkish modernity was launched by a cluster of important books published between 1959 and 1964.[1] All of them reflected the modernization theory of the period, explicitly or implicitly. Their greatest flaw, consequently, was their teleological vision of an upward march from Islamic empire to secular republic. The title of Niyazi Berkes's book, *The Development of Secularism in Turkey*, epitomized this understanding. Of these books, Bernard Lewis's *Emergence of Modern Turkey* influenced thousands of readers among students, politicians, government officials, and the general public; that book remains in print. For students entering the field when Lewis's *Emergence* was new, it was natural to ask: "What does it take to write a book like that?" The result was a generation of archivally based, revisionist scholarship, which cast shopworn images of the late Ottoman Empire as the "sick man of Europe" onto the ash heap of historiography and replaced them with proofs of reformist dynamism—powerful heartbeats, albeit within a multiethnic imperial superstructure doomed by the rising forces of nationalism.[2]

When the foundational studies of the early 1960s appeared, the official triumph of laicism in the Turkish republic made Turkey look, in fact, like an exemplar of the secularism that social science theory then associated with modernization. As it turns out, Turkey's conformity to the theory was no accident: several of the scholars most active in developing 1960s modernization theory were experts on Turkey and theorized with Turkey in mind.[3] Already by the 1970s, however, new developments made the inadequacies of teleological secularizing visions obvious. The triumphalism of Turkey's official laicism proved premature, then, long before the circular relationship between the Turkish case and modernization theory came to light. The Islamic resurgence was gaining momentum, as was the global trend toward identity politics, and modernization theory was falling into discredit. Scholars interested in the Ottoman and Turkish experience of modernity adjusted to these changes with difficulty. The volume of their scholarly production was growing rapidly; indeed, this study would have been impossible without their work. However, as the literature grew, what it gained in specialization it often lost in breadth of vision. The politicization of culture in Turkey meant, as well, that many scholars wrote to promote partisan positions and therefore lacked the detachment required to replace linear visions of either secularization or Islamization with a nonpartisan consideration of the interaction between forces of both types. At the same time, the old practice of leaving the Ottoman Empire to historians and the Turkish republic to social scientists was creating problems of a different order as the history of the republic lengthened. The synchronic approach generally preferred by social scientists no longer sufficed for the study of the republican experience. As it evolved over time, it required the attention of historians, whose primary concern is change over time. One recent assessment has noted with reason that few scholars have "stepped up to study the real history" of modernity in Turkey "in all its aspects."[4]

Now facing a larger task, the scholar aspiring to do for the early 2000s what Bernard Lewis's book did for the 1960s might almost ask what it would take to write *The Emergence of Postmodern Turkey.*[5] That might make a good title for this book, were it not for a critical fact to which Edward Said called attention. However great the fascination that ideas of postmodernity have created among Western philosophers and artists, most of their counterparts in developing countries "are still preoccupied with modernity itself."[6] The premise of this book is that both advocates of rapid change and religious and cultural conservatives share that preoccupation.

My initial goal was to write a panoramic history of the late Ottoman Empire and modern Turkey. Chronologically, the book would cover the period from 1789 to the present. Topically, the study would consider political, economic, social, and cultural history. At first, I pictured this as a work of synthesis. Research soon revealed, however, that the scholarly literature would not support synthesis on some topics. Political, economic, and the demographic side of social history had been relatively well studied. Both the quality-of-life side of social history and cultural history, however, would require original research. This realization defined the first of several senses in which this book moves beyond synthesizing others' work to present original findings.

As I began to read literary works of different periods in my search for cultural history, a revelation rewarded me. Ottoman and Turkish writers of imaginative literature most often wrote about their own times, at least until very recently; and their insights into the society around them are far richer than those of historians and social scientists. That discovery offered me a way to escape the dry lists of authors and books that pass for cultural history in many large-scale histories. It would enrich my study, I realized, to focus on one or a few works from each period, using them to open a window on life at the time. "The writer," an otherwise unnamed character in a novel discussed in chapter 7, makes this point in his own vivid terms: "How must one explain the cosmic fact of the novel to them? To plot a novel means starting out with a world planned out into the finest details. We can only get these details from the life to which we are bound, which we have lived."[7] Placed at the end of each chapter, I concluded, short essays exploring different writers' worlds would reflect not only on cultural production but also on political, social, and economic issues discussed throughout that chapter. To the chronological structures and propositional arguments of historical scholarship, these essays would add harmonic resonances from the literary language of symbol and allusion.

Seeking these richer resonances for my study, I chose ten writers, from the 1790s to 2000, and began to study their works. Many of my recent publications have taken the form of preparatory studies on the works of imaginative literature discussed in this book. Two of the ten are living authors, and one of the rewards of my research has been to become acquainted with them. Readers who know a great deal about Turkish literature may find the approach taken here unsatisfactory. However, readers who cannot read Turkish may appreciate the chance to gain insights into what makes these works so illuminating. Having read all these works in their original versions, I share that feeling: as my reading in recent theoretical works on nationalism and modernity deepened, my literary studies gained in salience for my book, thanks to the theorists' emphasis on the imaginative realm as the primary site for the construction of new images of modernity, images that inspire efforts to reshape workaday reality accordingly.

This primacy of the imaginative realm applies as much to religious as to secular trends. My aspirations to overcome the secularist biases of the foundational studies on Ottoman and Turkish modernity therefore necessitated identifying influential religious movements and thinkers to emphasize in my study. Recent publications gradually made me realize that three religious movements have exerted exceptional influence. These movements were founded successively by Mevlana Halid (1776–1827, known in Arabic as Shaykh Khalid al-Baghdadi or al-Naqshbandi), Said Nursi (1873–1960), and Fethullah Gülen (b. 1938). The religious landscape is broad and diverse, but these three tower over it.

The biggest challenge presented itself next: how to bring everything together. As my research progressed, musing about what to call the book made me realize what might be its largest claim to originality. By proving unexpectedly difficult, the search for the best title pointed to the largest sense in which this study could achieve originality. The title needed to express the book's main point; and to do that required discovering the organizing interpretation or thesis that best fitted the evidence offered by the historical panorama of the past two centuries. The book's title had to evoke its key concepts. Their interaction over time defined the book's thesis.

TURKEY, ISLAM, NATIONALISM, AND MODERNITY

After much experimentation, the title that proved to match the subject best and most concisely consisted of these four terms. Each term, however, evokes another term or concept. Inasmuch as these alternative terms could not be included in the title without making it unwieldy, they need to be introduced here to define the context of the study completely.

Turkey. Not just today's Turkey, the book's geographical subject area consists of first the late Ottoman Empire and then the Turkish republic. Despite their differences of scale, they correspond to each other as the geopolitical structures in which Ottomans and Turks staked their place in the modern world. The Turkish republic is not the only Ottoman successor state. It is the one built most directly on the Ottoman foundation. Moreover, the spatial transformation from empire to republic did not occur all at once after 1918. Rather, Ottoman frontiers contracted and populations shifted over time in stages that defined critical continuities and discontinuities. Later chapters will have a great deal to say about these crises, which map 1 displays graphically. Today, some scholars object to studies that picture a continuity between the Ottoman Empire and the Turkish republic. An even greater problem is that many Turkish scholars look back on the Ottoman Empire as if it consisted only of Anatolia before 1923—a consequence of Turkish nationalism and the limits of Turkish historical curricula. The consequences could not be graver. As late as the Balkan Wars of 1912–1913, the real homeland of many Turks, especially those in leadership positions, was not Anatolia but Rumelia, the Ottoman Balkans. For many of them, the sudden necessity to rethink Anatolia as their homeland was a wrenching, unwelcome change. And that is to say nothing so far about the dire consequences of the destruction of Ottoman cosmopolitanism.

Important though it is to emphasize the spatial differences of the empire and republic, cultural factors underscore their coherence across time as units of analysis. In Turkish political culture, the sacralization of the institutions of rule and the concentration of power at the top and the center go back to the Turks'

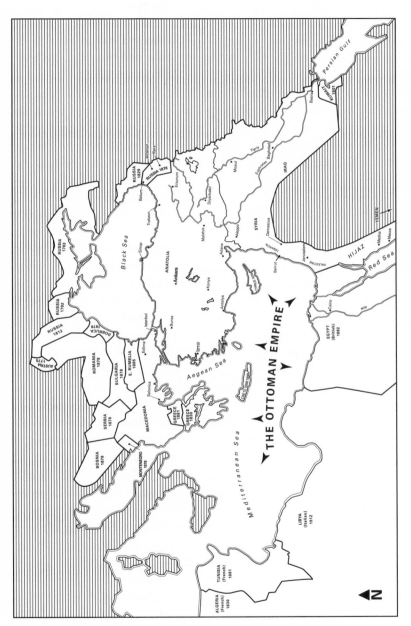

The Ottoman Empire, 1774–1912, showing territorial losses from the Treaty of Küçük Kaynarca (1774) to the eve of the Balkan Wars (1912–1913).

pre-Islamic origins. The shrinking borders of the later Ottoman period helped project these patterns into postimperial times. As the definition of boundaries and populations grew more and more contested, the ideal of the state retained its clarity and purity in Ottoman reformers' minds. Becoming the rulers of the Turkish republic, they transferred to it their loyalty to their ideal of the state. Moreover, the minds to whom this ideal meant most thought and verbalized in Turkish, as the language evolved with time. The political, social, and cultural succession from the Ottoman Empire to the Turkish republic is fundamental to questions of Ottoman and Turkish identity, which form one of the most important determinants of Turks' sense of their place in the world. Other Ottoman successor states inherited a great deal from the Ottoman Empire, but not this kind of continuity.

Islam. The mention of Islam in the title obviously implies secularism as Islam's "other" in the period studied here. Many forms of diversity within Islam are salient for this study. The topic of secularism or laicism also needs contextualization.

Islam is simple in its basics and complex in its manifestations. Islam means "submission" to God, and a Muslim is "one who submits." Most basically, Islam is monotheism, in Arabic *tawhid*, "affirming the oneness [of God]." This Kur'an verse summarizes Islam's most basic beliefs: "O believers, believe in God and His Messenger and the Book He has sent down and the Books which He sent down before. Whoever disbelieves in God and His Angels and His Books, and His Messengers, and the Last Day, has surely gone astray into far error" (4.136).

Believers are members of a worldwide community (*umma*) that expresses its beliefs through certain essential practices. The most basic are the "five pillars" of Islam: profession of faith (*shahada*), prayer (*salat* in Arabic, *namaz* in Persian and Turkish), almsgiving (*zakat*), fasting (*sawm*) during Ramadan, and the pilgrimage (*hajj*). All of these act out equal participation in the community in varied ways and with different frequencies: five times a day in the case of the ritual prayer, one month a year in the case of the Ramadan fast, once a year in the case of the pilgrimage, which occurs annually but is obligatory only once in a lifetime for adult Muslims who are financially and physically capable of it. Struggle (*jihad*) is sometimes cited as a sixth pillar, with meanings ranging from the struggle for spiritual mastery to "holy war" to defend Islam.

The five pillars are defined in Islamic law, the *sharia* ("way"), which early religious scholars elaborated from the basic texts of Islam, primarily the Kur'an and the *hadith* ("reports") about the sayings and practice (*sunna*) of the Prophet Muhammad. As a result, Islam is a religion of law observance, resembling

Orthodox Judaism closely in that sense. Islamic rulers cannot change the sharia or "legislate" about it; they can at best try to gain legitimacy by enforcing it. In the sense that the sharia exists independent of their authority, Muslim rulers have no legislative function, except in matters ancillary to the sharia, a function that the Ottoman sultans were famous for exercising. Not a law code, the sharia is more nearly a field of disputation and practice among religious scholars; and Islamic jurisprudence (*fiqh*, literally "understanding") is one of the disciplines taught in a Muslim seminary (*madrasa*). Sunnis acknowledge four "schools" of Islamic jurisprudence as equally legitimate; Shi'is have their own schools. Imprinted on Islamic lifeways through the five pillars and prescriptions about the basics of life, starting with ritual cleanliness, dress, and gender relations, sharia observance creates uniformities across the Islamic world. It also creates a universe of values that Muslims can expect to find honored by their coreligionists everywhere. So deep is the imprint of Islam on Turkish society that it and the Turkish language form the two primary markers of Turkish identity.

Alongside the factors that give it uniformity, a religion that has meant so much to so many for so long also displays internal diversity. Sectarian differences developed early in Islamic history. The best known sectarian difference, between Sunnis and Shi'is, is the biggest. The Ottomans were officially Sunnis of the Hanafi legal school. Their subjects included Sunnis of other legal schools, Shi'is, and members of other smaller sects. One of these, historically disdained by both Sunnis and Shi'is, is now the largest religious minority in the Turkish republic: the Alevis. Religious brotherhoods, whose members met to engage in distinctive rites to deepen their religious experience, were extremely widespread during the Ottoman centuries and have survived, despite the Turkish republic's efforts to suppress them. Across history, Islam has also pulsated with renewal movements, three of which, as noted, prove especially significant for late Ottoman and modern Turkish history.

Emphasizing the relationship between the believer and God, Islam is pervaded by a strong ethical egalitarianism. Through frequent exhortations to "Muslim men and Muslim women" (*al-Muslimin wa'l-Muslimat*) and analogous phrases, the Kur'an addresses the faithful in gender-inclusive language, in a way not found in Jewish and Christian scripture.[8] At the same time, Kur'an and sharia recognize three status disparities, regulating them in ways that improved on pre-Islamic norms but not eliminating them. These are the difference between male and female, free and slave, Muslim and non-Muslim. The Kur'an also states that God has "exalted some in rank above others" (6.165 and 43.32). On this basis, one would expect Islamic societies to combine a strong ethos of equality with hierarchical orderings. Paradoxical though that might sound, it is true of Ottoman and Turkish society, as will become abundantly clear.

The advent of modernity, particularly the idea of secular law that could assign equal rights to all, challenged all three of the status disparities that the sharia accommodated, as later chapters will demonstrate. In the case of gender relations, Islamic norms define them in terms of complementarity, not equality, assigning rights and duties to both sexes. Among other entitlements, married Muslim women historically had rights to own property, at a time when married Christian women in Europe still did not. In this and other respects, Westernizing change confronted Muslim women with jarring choices between Ottoman and European versions of patriarchy. Perhaps it is not surprising, then, that the beginnings of an Ottoman women's movement date back as far as 1868, the period when bourgeois self-consciousness and demands for greater freedom of spousal choice were beginning to emerge.

In the case of slavery, international opposition gradually wore away at Ottoman slaveholding in the nineteenth century. Ottoman slavery had a variety of forms, some of them closer to surrogate kinship. The sharia likewise moderated slavery in various ways. The sharia encouraged manumission, for example. It permitted concubinage and legitimated children of slave concubines. The Ottoman dynasty historically relied on slavery for elite recruitment and particularly for dynastic reproduction. Later chapters will provide evidence of how hard such practices died.

Traditional interfaith relations were also destabilized by new ideas of equality backed by international pressure. The historical Islamic norms of interfaith relations were based on the Kur'anic vision of sacred history. The Kur'an identifies Islam as the religion of Abraham, presenting him as both the first Muslim ("one who submitted" to God, a monotheist) and the ancestor of the Arabs. The prophetic revelations that came to the Prophet Muhammad (570–632CE) from 610 on were compiled after his death, becoming the written text of the Kur'an. It does not textually incorporate earlier scripture in the way the Christian Bible incorporates the Hebrew Bible, but the Kur'an includes many biblical elements and frequently mentions Jews and Christians. All these scriptures are akin because all of God's prophets (*nabi*) and messengers (*rasul*) received the same message. All of them form a series including many biblical figures, some non-biblical ones, Jesus as a prophet (nothing more), and finally Muhammad, the "seal" of the prophets. Islamic sacred history thus generated an understanding of Jews and Christians as "peoples of the book" (*ahl al-kitab*), not the Muslims' equals, but worthy to be accommodated under a system of protection (*dhimma*) defined by the sharia. This gave Jews and Christians communal semiautonomy under their religious leaders on condition that they accept their subaltern position; non-Muslims had to pay a special tax, the *jizya*, but were exempt from military service, a heavy burden on Muslims.[9] As long as states were assumed to have religious identities and law fundamentally meant religious law, this system effectively accommodated religious difference, as the millennial survival of Middle Eastern Jewish and Christian communities proves. Later, the idea that all should have equal rights, something possible only under a secular legal system, challenged all three of the inequalities tolerated within sharia law; but demands for gender equality and abolition of slavery produced far less explosive consequences in late Ottoman times than the challenges to the Islamic system of intercommunal relations.

Even limited exposure to secular ideas from Europe challenged Islamic societies in ways that required a response. Islamic thought began to undergo a transformation from something that encompassed the world of knowledge to one part of a world of knowledge, much of it alien in origin. Although it is clear today that secularism cannot eliminate religion, many people have thought that it would, and powerful intellectual and political movements have espoused that belief. Such ideas began to circulate in the late Ottoman Empire. Although they had multiple sources, the ideological hard core that shaped the official secularism of the Turkish republic derived from nineteenth-century European scientific materialism, which became entrenched in the academies that trained the Ottoman civil and military elites.

Even if secularism does not sweep religion away, it turns religion into a problem, no longer the all-encompassing reality but something whose place must be determined. This fact has had ironic consequences for modern Turkey. The religion that Turkish secularists do not practice is Sunni Islam. Consequently, the institutions set up to control Islam propagate Sunni Islam. The situation is fertile in irony, not the least being its unwelcome consequences for the Alevis, non-Sunnis who form a significant percentage of the population and have generally supported the secular republic. The ironies of this situation will become apparent in chapter 7.

Nationalism. The "nationalism" in the title competes with imperialism. Paradoxically, the late Ottoman Empire was doubly "imperial." It was a multinational empire that was endangered by both separatist nationalism and European imperialism. Ottoman and Turkish forms of nationalism developed in response to that untenable situation. The Ottoman Empire never lost its sovereignty, although it lost territories to colonialism. The threat of imperialism was, however, pervasive. Ottoman sovereignty was eroded systemically in addition to the loss of outlying provinces; and the struggle to establish the Turkish republic really was a struggle for national survival.

In recent decades, the study of nationalism has been reinvigorated by the study of nationalism outside the major powers. The label "postcolonial" is often applied to these nationalisms, but they had to be "anticolonial" before they could be post-colonial. Consequently, although Turks are reluctant to accept "postcolonial" theory as applicable to the Ottoman Empire, as "anticolonial" theory it illumi-nates their experience significantly. Following on several significant studies on post- or anticolonial nationalism, a more recent study, has moved beyond them to reintegrate the study of nationalism globally. The result has been to show that even many European nations, not only small ones but also a large power like Germany, faced many of the same problems as did less advantaged peoples. All of these studies are part of the larger reorientation from materialist to culturalist modes of theorization. The series of noteworthy authors on nationalism begins with Benedict Anderson, continues with Partha Chatterjee's and Prasenjit Duara's works on anticolonial nationalism, and concludes with Gregory Jusdanis's reinte-grative, global study.

Although often spoken of as an ideology, nationalism is not an ideology like others. The two fundamental questions in modern government are: Who are the people, and how are they to be governed? Questions about how to govern the nation can be formulated in terms of abstract principles, such as those of liberalism or Marxism, which can be applied in different countries. Questions about national identity are formulated in terms of cultural uniqueness. Dif-ferent nationalisms bear generic resemblances to one another, reinforced by emulation and competition. The idea of the nation resembles kinship or reli-gion more than it resembles liberalism or fascism. As a social body, a nation is therefore an "imagined community" most of whose members never have direct contact with one another but who share common experiences and media of communication and hold ideas of shared identity.[10]

The pioneer nineteenth-century sociologists already noted the tight connec-tion between nationalism and the rise of mass-circulation newspapers, a phe-nomenon of which they were contemporary observers. Anderson's concept of "print capitalism" elaborates on this perception. In itself, the phrase alludes to the connections between cultural and economic production. Publishing was a business, "the book was the first modern-style mass-produced industrial commodity," and the newspaper was a variation of that, a "one-day best-seller," with the built-in obsolescence of modern consumer goods.[11] Although printing had been invented centuries earlier, even in Europe its significance and its market expanded vastly with the nineteenth-century spread of nationalism.

Ahmed İhsan Bey printshop advertised that it offered its customers the latest advances, including color printing. (Courtesy of Alpay Kabacalı; Kabacalı, *Matbaa*, 108.)

Consequently, the idea of print capitalism implies much more than the term expresses. The rise of mass print media required the triumph of vernacular languages, in place of other classical or elite languages. With the vernacular language rose a new reading public that spread to encompass new segments of society, such as women or merchants, who usually lacked education in classical languages. The expansion of the reading public presupposed increased literacy in the modern vernacular, better access to education, and often also changes to adapt the language for effective mass communication. New readers' tastes and desires created opportunities for writers and publishers who knew how to respond to them. Consequently, new literary forms, such as the novel and modern theater, spread globally. Novels were often published initially as newspaper serials. Awareness that others were waiting breathlessly for the next installment of the same story became another factor in reinforcing the imagined national community. With the added idea that this community inhabited a specific territory and was entitled to sovereignty over it, "print capitalism" became a symbolic name for a reality that interlinked politics, society, economy, and culture. Anderson's idea of print capitalism proves fruitful in illuminating the connections among a number of notable phenomena in late Ottoman history.[12]

Partha Chatterjee delves deeper into what is imagined among peoples threatened or subordinated by imperialism and who does the imagining. For him, "anticolonial nationalism creates its own domain of sovereignty within colonial society, well before it begins its political battle with the imperial power. It does this by dividing the world of social institutions and practices into two domains—the material and the spiritual." The material domain is an outer one, where the technical triumphs of the West are conceded. The spiritual domain is an inner one. There, "nationalism launches its most . . . creative . . . project: to fashion a 'modern' national culture that is nevertheless not Western. If the nation is an imagined community, then this is where it is brought into being . . . [and] is already sovereign."[13]

An Ottoman writer at his stand-up desk, book cover,
"The Corrected, Perfected, and Detailed *Gülşen-i Muharrerat*"
(Rose garden of good writing), a guide to "official, unofficial,
and commercial writing, Sun Bookstore, Seyyid Hasan and
Hüseyin Brothers, price 10 kuruş." (Courtesy of Irvin Schick.)

Colonial power presented a model of modern statehood to those it threatened or colonized but simultaneously thwarted their realization of that model. Their tasks, then, were first to achieve independence first in the inner cultural domain—and inside the fortress of their own language—and then to win independence in the outer domain of material power relations. How does the situation of a people who were in the doubly "imperial" situation of the Ottomans, rulers over others now threatened in their sovereignty, resemble or differ from that of nationalists in a colonial environment?

In the title of Chatterjee's 1993 book, *The Nation and Its Fragments,* "the nation" refers initially to the nationalist intellectual elite who create this inner domain of cultural sovereignty and start the political struggle for independence. "The fragments" whom the elite must mobilize consist of all their relevant "others," the cultural and human resources for the nation-building project. In colonial Bengal, Chatterjee's geographical focus, as in the Ottoman Empire, the nationalist vanguard initially consisted of elite males. The "fragments" they had to mobilize consisted in human terms of women and all the nonelite male segments of society. Among these, women hold a position of special significance because they include the elite males' wives and daughters: New Man cannot build the nation without New Woman. And their numbers must increase. In many ways, the Turkish nation-building project was dominated for a century or more, through the 1960s, by the effort to form and politically mobilize a national bourgeoisie. After that, it was the mobilization of the entire population that made the 1960s into the start of a new era. In cultural terms, the nationalist elite must also "mobilize" the past by refashioning existing understandings of history to create a worthy past for the nation. Spending much of their time writing poems, plays, and novels and not only ideological tracts, the nationalist elite will try to furnish all the accessories of a modern culture. At the successful conclusion of the national struggle, the elites will also have to "mobilize" the national future by setting the course for political and economic development.

Inevitably, not everyone and everything can be included in the nationalist project, or not without reform and reeducation. As true as this is of social groups that do not fit into the nationalist identity construct, so it is also true of culture. Prasenjit Duara has studied the inclusions and exclusions required to rework China's millennial, imperial history into a historical canon acceptable as politically correct for a modern nation.[14] The Ottoman and Turkish elites did no less.

Gregory Jusdanis's *The Necessary Nation* reintegrates the study of nationalism in a global perspective, emphasizing its constructive as well as destructive potentials. For Jusdanis, nationalism has been a vehicle of resistance from the

Ebuzziya printers, advertisement announcing its high-
quality printing services for both Ottoman and French. This
press produced perhaps the most elegant Ottoman typography
and design. (Courtesy of Alpay Kabacalı; Kabacalı, ed., *Tokgöz*,
illustrations at the back of the book.)

beginning, and not only in the colonial context. Nationalism has "always given
priority to cultural survival," and the nation-state has been idealized everywhere
politically "as a vehicle to modernity." To the extent that it is an ideology,
nationalism has been the dominant ideology of the twentieth century, coexist-
ing with governmental systems of every kind. "The singularity of nationalism
rests in its tenet that a marriage must take place between culture and politics

and that this union must be sanctified on a native land"; nationalism thus "added the prerogative of collective difference to the already established list of individual franchises." As this occurred, differences of language, ethnicity, and religion acquired new political significance. Nationalism turned ethnicity into "a political project," and the nation-state became self-evidently the political form for the organization of modernity. Through the development of national culture, the idea of the nation acquired the emotional force that motivated people to sacrifice their own lives and deprive others of theirs in its defense. "Ultimately, nationalism is a form of self-worship, the adoration by the nation of its own uniqueness." Only under modern conditions could even the most advanced countries make national unification more than a political fact.[15]

As they strove to do so, continues Jusdanis, the irony persisted that many nations had the internal "heterogeneity of an empire while claiming the homogeneity of a village."[16] Creating a sense of unity to transcend those differences was largely a project in propagating a national culture, as the history of modern education illustrates. As long ago as the partition of Poland (1772), Jean-Jacques Rousseau noted that the Poles' culture was the "only rampart" that could make it impossible for Russia to subjugate them. Clearly, then, it was not only in the colonial world that peoples politicized culture to create an autonomous realm and gain future unity and freedom. Even in Europe, the sense of backwardness in relation to others who are more advanced bedeviled many countries, especially those that had to struggle for unity or independence, from Italy to Germany, from Greece to Norway. During the wars following the French Revolution, reactions against Napoleonic empire-building sharpened the sense of backwardness and the desire to assert difference across most of Europe, intruding into Ottoman lands as well.

Modernity. Independent of the modernization theory of the 1960s, recent analyses of modernity provide essential insights for understanding the global context of national histories. The simplest historical definition of modernity is as "an epoch turned toward the future," characterized by the expectation that the world of the future will be better.[17] This expectation follows from the idea of progress in its modern meaning: not just forward spatial motion, but qualitative improvement through reason and scientific experimentation. With the industrial revolution, scientific and technological advances began for the first time to continue in a self-compounding way. Accelerating and proliferating change began to shrink time and space. Change also produced a profusion of manifestations that complicate the analysis of modernity: new fields of knowledge to classify and organize, political revolutions, new techniques of production, new weapons of destruction, new media of communications, new social interactions, new senses of self-awareness, new forms of cultural creativity.

Amid this profusion, one of the most significant features of modernity was that ultimately no one belief system prevailed overall. Old religions and value systems persisted, but accelerating innovation eroded their capacity to offer all-encompassing explanations. The secular character of many modern innovations also gave them a value neutrality that facilitated their cross-cultural adoption. Secularism and materialism emerged as belief systems in their own right. So did the expectation in some quarters that religion would eventually dwindle and vanish. Many thinkers realized that would not happen. Still, encroaching secularism challenged the authority of religion and made an issue of it as never before.

The advent of modernity created transformations at all levels of political and social organization, and discords among the effects of transformations on different scales have defined some of the tensions most distinctive of the modern condition. To a striking extent, however, the literature on modernity focuses on two levels, the macrosocietal and the individual.[18] The political organization of Europe and the Ottoman lands into states, and particularly the momentum over time to replicate the nation-state as *the* modern form of polity, meant that most people experienced the impact of modernity largely through demands their governments made on them. On the one hand, states attempted to transform their subjects or citizens collectively. The idea of the nation-state presupposed a collective homogeneity that the governed population almost never displayed without radical social engineering. On the other hand, governments' desires to transform individuals into dutiful citizens also reached into their innermost lives as individuals. Modern state policy imposed its own standards of rationality on every individual while ignoring that modernity transformed subjectivity in terms not only of reason and duty but also of will, desire, even faith. Consequently, "the stormy relationship" between "rationalization" and "subjectivization" has defined the "tragic history of modernity," and the construction of more humane and pluralistic social orders has emerged as the cardinal need of late modernity.[19]

What does it mean, however, to talk about the individual and subjectivization in environments where political, social, and cultural forces limit the scope for individualism? Anglo-American liberal thought idealizes an egalitarian concept of individual freedom that certainly does not prevail everywhere. Subjectivity cannot mean democracy and egalitarianism without universality, mutual recognition among individuals of one another's subjectivity, a mutuality that depends on equality before the law.[20] Otherwise, the only individual subject with any freedom of action will be an autocrat or a dictator, and the result of his overthrow may be "a quest for a collective subject, thereby negating the very principle of subjectivity."[21] Such collectivism is clearly one reason why Marxism had so much appeal to Turkish intellectuals of the 1960s. In the preference for collective subjectivity, more is likely to be in play than political culture. The "fear of freedom" in times of insecurity is one such factor. The communal egalitarianism of Islamic ethics and the communalism of Turkish social norms, rooted in the heritage of kinship society, may also reinforce these collective political preferences. Later chapters will, indeed, illustrate how the modern tension between rationalization and subjectivization played out in the mind of an autocrat or among a narrow ruling elite, and how their subjects' aspirations to personal fulfillment competed with desires to belong to a strong collectivity. As a result, the construction of more humane and pluralistic societies also implies allowing scope for "autonomous, self-willing subjects" and mutual acceptance among them of that autonomy.[22] To the extent that nationalism is a collective "form of self-worship," the waning of its virulence must be a prerequuisite for achieving greater individual autonomy.[23]

The European origins of modernity raise important questions as well about whether the Western way is the only way. Some scholars prefer to posit the existence of alternative modernities in other cultural settings.[24] Others emphasize differences in the vernacularization of modernity in different settings. As intriguing as these lines of argument are, one could argue that they err in focusing on the local and neglecting the global. Empirically, historians can certainly trace how European modernity spread first to "neo-Europes" like North America and Australasia and then globally, provoking myriad appropriations and resistances as it did. Ultimately, alternative or vernacularized modernities are part of the global phenomenological profusion of modernity. As this developed, many phenomena that started out as peculiarly Western—whether the Western Christian calendar or the rules of European football—gained global appropriation as matters of convenience. More recently, many standards that facilitate participation in global modernity have been created from the start with a considerable degree of value neutrality. More and more, it is difficult to identify these innovations with any single part of the world. Consequently, this study does not attempt to define a "Turkish modernity." It does talk about many modern Turkish phenomena, but their context is greater than national. They are all part of the Turkish experience of modernity, which is European in its origins but ever more global in its scope.

At the transition from empire to republic—the moment most critical in determining whether an Ottoman or Turkish polity would survive—pioneer Turkish sociologist Ziya Gökalp debated the Turks' place in the world in a book on "Becoming Turkish, Islamic, and Modern" (*Türkleşmek, İslamlaşmak,*

Muasırlaşmak, 1918). He adapted his triad from the Azeri intellectual Hüseyinzade Ali, whose third term was "European." The fact that Gökalp put "modern" where Hüseyinzade Ali put "European" is noteworthy. Social science theorists distinguish between "Europeanization" and "modernization," but Ottoman thinkers usually equated the two. Today, the challenges of accession to European Union membership still keep European standards central to Turkish understandings of modernity. Gökalp, however, realized that modernity was ultimately not just European but global. In contrast to many other Turkish intellectuals, Gökalp's goal was not to choose among Turkish, Islamic, and modern identities. Rather, he sought to combine ethnicity and religion on the level of national "culture" with modernity on the level of international "civilization."[25] Although the early Turkish republican leadership tried to sacrifice Islam to nationalism and produce a secular future, the possibility of other choices about how to configure Turkish and Islamic identity with global modernity provides the starting point for an analysis of developments since 1789, not as "the development of secularism," but as the dynamic interaction between religious and secular approaches to modernity.

THESIS: TWO CURRENTS OF CHANGE
IN DIALECTICAL INTERACTION

This book advances a new argument about how two major currents of change interacted to shape Ottoman and Turkish history over the past two centuries. Gökalp showed profound insight in recognizing that both ethnolinguistic and religious identity shaped the Turks' engagement with modernity. The challenges of triangulating among these three reference points led to the development of two alternative approaches to the choices they represented: a comparatively radical, secularizing current and a more conservative, Islamically committed current. This is not a simplistic binarism. Gökalp's triad suggests that both currents formed in relation to a larger array of choices. Like political parties or other large sociocultural formations, both currents also included divergent tendencies or movements. Moreover, many Ottomans and Turks identified with both currents and resisted choosing between them. At critical moments, however, the choices embodied by the two currents became unavoidable and polarized opinion. At such moments, binary opposition between radical and conservative approaches organized the field of contestation in the same way that binary opposition of parties or teams optimizes contests in politics or sports. At such moments, the opposition between the two currents could become starkly antagonistic. Still, exponents of both shared common interests. The differences among the two currents of change are more matters of emphasis within Gökalp's triad than of excluding one of its components. As time went by, both currents interacted dialectically, alternately clashing and converging, transforming themselves and flowing toward a future whose imagined contours shifted as global modernity continued to evolve.

To site the radical current, Anderson's concept of "print capitalism" suggests a starting point. Launched earlier (1789–1839) by government efforts to create new institutions and elites, the secularizing trend expanded beyond government control with the rise (1840–1860) of privately owned Ottoman print media. The "print capitalism" image, as noted, evokes new linkages among cultural production, economic enterprise, society, and politics. With the florescence of the print media and attendant changes in language and literacy, new literary forms opened imaginative realms in which to envision alternative futures; and the elite males who propounded those visions assumed vanguard roles in mobilizing others to pursue their dreams. Political controversy intensified as competing visions proliferated, and old forms of personality-centered factionalism clashed with a new politics of issues and ideologies. Among the Ottomans, most elements of this complex existed by the 1860s. It took another generation, however, for the cutting edge of the Western-oriented intelligentsia to become doctrinaire materialists. During the terminal crisis of the empire, they provided the leadership for first the *constitutional* (1908) and then the *national* (1919–1922) phases of the political restructuring that replaced empire with republic. Secularists governed Turkey from 1908 until at least 1950 and still retain great power and prestige.

If phenomena associated with print culture gave radical modernizers their forum, symmetrical logic suggests that manuscript culture must have served conservatives analogously. In fact, a more narrowly defined phenomenon, albeit one identified at first with manuscript production, served this purpose: Islamic religious movements, and not just any of them. The Islamic movements of the period varied widely, and anti-Ottomanism or otherworldliness prevented some of them from stimulating Ottoman revitalization. So much greater was the significance, then, of a shaykh from Ottoman Iraq, who introduced the reformist Mujaddidi form of the Naqshbandiyya from India and won recognition even from other orders as "the Renewer" of his century. Khalid al-Naqshbandi founded the Khalidiyya. In Turkish, he and his order became known as Mevlana Halid and the Halidiye-Nakşibendiye. His teaching and example made it into the dominant branch of its order in the Western Islamic world and a movement of enduring importance.[26]

Emerging on the empire's periphery, the Halidiye sparked a great awakening in center and periphery alike. Among the Muslim protobourgeoisie, if progressives with intellectual capital (the new official and literary elites) rallied around the emerging print media, people with economic assets (merchants, landowners) generally espoused more conservative views and sought their cultural outlet in religious movements, particularly the Halidiye and its branches.[27] Under the early republic, the fact that the Nakşibendis performed their essential ritual silently and could do so in private houses helped them to survive the 1925 ban on sufi brotherhoods. Although Kurdish Nakşibendis rebelled against the early republic, the order's historically positive orientation toward the state led other Nakşibendis to take jobs within the state-controlled Directorate of Religious Affairs and so "colonize" one bastion of the secular republic. In recent decades, organizations of other forms—mosque congregations, foundations, business firms, media ventures, political parties—also evolved out of the Halidiye. As secularists and Islamists came to compete in the same arenas, Turgut Özal (prime minister 1983–1989, president 1989–1993) openly proclaimed himself a Nakşibendi.

Turkey's two other leading religious movements did not derive directly from the Halidiye but reacted to its stimulus, among others, and led the way in generating new organizational forms. These movements began with Said Nursi, known as *Bediüzzaman*, "the wonder of the age."[28] He sought to fill the spiritual void of republican secularism by founding, not a sufi order, but rather a text-based movement that people would join by studying his writings. Advocating both modern science and religious studies, he produced sophisticated refutations of the European materialists esteemed by Turkish secularists. Nursi embodied both the transition in religious teaching from orality to textualism and religious activists' adoption of the modern media. In the same period, the rise of Islamic "print capitalism" was evidenced not only by the slow transition from manuscript to print production of Nursi's treatises but also by Islamist journals like *Sırat-ı Müstakim* (later *Sebilürreşad*) and by the role model for the Islamist man of letters defined by Necip Fazıl Kısakürek (1904–1983).

The branches into which Nursi's movement divided after his death include that of Fethullah Gülen, now Turkey's most influential religious leader.[29] More interested in acting on their beliefs than in reading, Gülen's followers founded schools in many countries and sponsored print and electronic media, among other, diverse forms of social action. With Gülen, Turkish Islamists have adapted to the new era of globalization.

The institutions, economic interests, sociabilities, and modes of cultural production associated with the launching of the modern print media in the secularists' case and with the three great religious waves in the conservatives' case collectively site the two competing currents of change in which Turks have lived out their stormy struggle for nationhood and modernity. The two currents' historical chronologies differed markedly. The radicals emerged during the Tanzimat (1839–1870s), engineered the Young Turk Revolution (1908) and National Struggle (1919–1922), ruled the republic for two generations, consolidated power positions they still retain, and made secularism into a lasting "belief system." Powerful under the empire, religious conservatives ran afoul of the early republic's secularism and nationalism, struggled to reorganize and create their own modern media, and could again compete successfully in the political arena only by the 1980s. They have since reestablished themselves as part of the mainstream, no longer the objects of state policy but among its makers. The conclusion of my book considers the factors that governed the interaction among these two currents of change across time.

Thinking about how best to interpret the interaction between these two approaches to change, I first thought of them as occurring at different rates of speed. In the early stages of this project, I defined the secularizing, Westernizing current in terms of fast change and the more conservative, Islamically grounded current in terms of slower change. In the background of my thoughts was the multiscalar analysis of change over time that Fernand Braudel borrowed from economic historians and applied to the study of societies and cultures. My Braudelian musings eventually made me realize that the "radical" and "conservative" trends in late Ottoman history, far from having different rates of change, both combined phenomena of long, medium, and short duration. However much religious conservatives might have preferred gradual change, not only were abrupt transformations thrust upon them, but they themselves generated disruptive change. All three of the most influential religious awakenings of the past two centuries burst on the scene in compressed time spans. The most active phase of Mevlana Halid's career dates from 1811 to 1827. Said Nursi produced most of the treatises on which his movement is based between 1925 and 1944. Fethullah Gülen began to expand his movement beyond local scale only in 1983. Conversely, although secularist modernists attach unique importance to the alphabet reform of 1928 as revolutionizing Turkish culture, that is only the sharpest turning point in a wave of revolutionary cultural change that was secular in the older sense of lasting a century or more, a wave that began with the rise of the modern print media (roughly 1840–1860) and—as far as language reform is concerned—has still not fully stopped.

When both trends are compared, it becomes apparent not only that each results from phenomena operating on multiple time scales but also that the two trends' periodizations differ from each other. Consequently, it will not work to periodize the chronology of this entire book in terms of the two currents. Instead, an organization in which each chapter takes a topically inclusive approach to one of the periods in the rather clearly defined chronology of the Ottoman and Turkish political economy provides both the analytical grid and the supporting evidence for an analysis of the dialectical interaction across time of the two macrohistorical trends, in each of which cultural, social, economic, and political forces converge.

1

THE RETURN TOWARD CENTRALIZATION

During the late eighteenth century, the Ottoman Empire lived through wars and defeats that opened a new epoch in the empire's history. Simultaneous with revolutionary change in Europe and the Americas, these crises expressed, at the regional level, global forces that tightened spatial interlinkages and accelerated change. Studies focusing on the Middle East see the crisis that opened this new era in the Napoleonic invasion of Egypt (1798). Studies examining all the Ottoman lands, including the Balkans and Black Sea region, see the Ottoman-Russian war of 1768 as the new era's opening crisis. That war ended in 1774 with the Treaty of Küçük Kaynarca and had as its sequels the Ottoman loss of the Crimea (1783) and Austrian and Russian wars extending through 1792. Both interpretations are right: 1768 and 1798 were both "opening shots" of the new era of crisis and change, signifying that the threats to the empire were not localized on its frontiers but might make themselves felt anywhere.

The impact of 1768 and 1798 precipitated long-demanded changes and opened the Ottoman reform era (roughly 1789–1922). Although outsiders came to think of the Ottoman Empire as "the sick man of Europe," that image captures only one side of a paradoxical contrast between internal reformist dynamism and a superstructure of multinational empire that could not survive in an age of nationalism. During the Ottoman reform era, this contrast developed across several distinct periods. This chapter examines the first period, characterized by the two decisive reigns of Selim III (1789–1807) and Mahmud II (1808–1839). In reaction to the crises of 1768–1798, they turned away from two centuries of decentralization, toward a new centralization and defensive modernization of the empire. While Selim's efforts appeared to have failed by the time he was overthrown, Mahmud prepared carefully and revived them lastingly. Among many reasons for the eventual success of this turn toward centralization and reform, perhaps the most fundamental is often overlooked. In the Ottoman polity, three sources of legal authority existed: Islamic law, custom, and the sultan's power to issue laws and decrees. Decentralization had divided the sultan's powers in fact but not diminished them in principle. Of the three sources of legal authority, the only one that could serve to implement innovative policies was the sultan's decree power. Reforming the empire required bringing practice and principle back into alignment by reasserting his authority and projecting it throughout the empire.

In order to understand this period, this chapter will first examine political and military events. An examination of the economy will then illustrate important issues in state finance, manufacturing, trade, and agriculture. Ottoman society underwent important changes, too, even while preserving conservative characteristics that are essential for the understanding of later developments. The two great currents of change that would interact dialectically to shape Ottoman Muslims' responses to modernity were only beginning to differentiate in this period. However, Ottoman diplomats were already making eye-opening discoveries about the implications of European modernity. As they did, Mevlana Halid emerged from Ottoman Kurdistan to found the most influential late Ottoman Islamic movement.

WAR AND THE TURN TOWARD CENTRALIZATION

Selim III assumed the throne in 1789 amid a military crisis that threatened the empire's survival as nothing had before. When Mahmud II died in 1839, the empire was caught in another war that threatened its survival. Both European imperialism and the spread of separatist nationalism in the Balkans endangered the empire. Yet Selim and Mahmud produced a greater impact than any sultans had in centuries.

EUROPE'S "EASTERN QUESTION" BEGINS: THE CRISES OF 1768 AND 1798

What nineteenth-century diplomats knew as the "Eastern Question" pertained specifically to the Ottoman lands and their future. Eastern Question diplomacy began with the dual crises of the Ottoman-Russian war of 1768 and the Napoleonic invasion of Egypt in 1798.

In the eighteenth century, Russia replaced Austria as the principal European threat to the Ottomans. Not until the 1768 war, however, did the extent of the menace of Russian expansionism become fully clear. After thirty years at peace, the war showed the Ottomans how much their military forces, especially the Janissary infantry, had lost in effectiveness. Even the famous Ottoman supply system collapsed. In contrast, Russia reaped the payoff of a century of efforts to develop a conscript army with a firm chain of command and professional commanders.[1] The Ottomans imprudently declared war first. The main theater of war lay in the Ottoman Balkans, along the lower Danube, with the siege of Hotin (1769) and the Battle of Kartal (1770) as critical Ottoman defeats. The Russians opened another front by sending a fleet into the Mediterranean in 1770, defeating the Ottoman navy at Çeşme near Izmir, and raising a rebellion in the Morea (or Peloponnesus, the southern peninsula of mainland Greece). The Ottomans suppressed that rebellion. Russian efforts were hindered by plague, bad harvests, the military demands of the partition of Poland (1772), and the most serious peasant uprising in Russian history, the Pugachev Rebellion (1773–1775), a reaction against Russia's efforts to integrate its southern borderlands. Peace negotiations began in 1772, but fighting continued until the 1774 campaign left the Ottomans no alternative to the dictated Treaty of Küçük Kaynarca, "Little Hot Spring" in Turkish, a place near Silistria on the Danube.

The Treaty of Küçük Kaynarca (1774) imposed an unprecedented setback on the Ottomans. It made the Crimea independent, a precarious and short-lived status. Under its dynasty descended from Chinggis Khan, the Crimean khanate had been an honored satellite of the Ottomans; it was no more than an obstacle to Russia's expansion.[2] The Russians acquired control of the northern Black Sea littoral between the Dnieper and Bug rivers. The two empires reciprocally guaranteed each other freedom of navigation in all the seas washing their shores; and the Ottomans guaranteed Russian subjects all the commercial privileges granted to the most favored nation, including the right to station consuls throughout the empire (art. 11). The treaty authorized the Russians to build a church in Beyoğlu, the part of Istanbul where the embassies were located, and required the Ottomans to protect Christian worship (arts. 7, 14). The Russian ambassador was to have a right of remonstrance on behalf of the principalities of Wallachia and Moldavia (art. 15). A major concession in protocol, the Ottomans thenceforth had to refer to the Russian sovereign in Turkish as *padişah*, the same title used for the Ottoman sultan (art. 13). In defining the independence of the various peoples of the Crimea, Black Sea steppes, and adjacent parts of the Caucasus (art. 3), the treaty referred to the Ottoman sultan as the "Imam of the Faithful and Caliph of the Monotheists."[3] As Muslims, the Tatars should regulate their religious affairs in respect of him (or for his sake) as required by the Islamic sharia (*taraf-ı hümayunum hakkına şeriat-i islamiye muktezasınca tanzim edeler*). The laborious wording, perhaps made up in Russia, poorly camouflaged what was about to happen to the "independent" Tatars. For Muslims, any thought of the caliphate as a purely spiritual authority divorced from sovereignty was ahistorical. To the extent that the caliphate gained importance in late Ottoman history, this treaty launched the process. The treaty further required Ottoman payment of an indemnity to Russia, 7.5 million kuruş (4.5 million rubles) within three years.

Muslims in the Crimea, Ukraine, and northern Caucasus were now "independent," deprived of any but spiritual help from their former Ottoman overlord, and left to await the Russians. The Black Sea, for centuries an Ottoman lake, was now open to the Russians, who had acquired rights to trade, establish consulates, and protest on behalf of certain Ottoman subjects. For the first time, the Ottomans had been forced to grant trading privileges to an unfriendly power. The Russians also acquired the right to have not only a chapel at the Russian legation but a public "Russo-Greek" church (art. 14).[4] Later interpretation expanded this clause into Russian protection over all the Ottomans' Orthodox Christian subjects. The indemnity compounded the costs of defeat. Indemnities demanded after repeated defeats by Russia must have materially weakened the Ottoman economy over the next century.

The 1774 treaty did not end the crisis in Russo-Ottoman relations. To spell out the details of the Russians' new commercial and legal privileges (referred to by Europeans as capitulations), another treaty had to be concluded (1783). Catherine II annexed the Crimea in 1783. Unable to resist, the Ottomans had to accept the loss by treaty in 1784.[5] These were so many steps toward the tsarina's vision of re-creating an Orthodox empire, centered at Istanbul, with a Romanov on the throne. The Ottomans again went to war against Russia (and Austria) in 1787, hoping to push back Russian expansion. Events in Poland and the French Revolution (1789) enabled the Ottomans to get through that war without further losses, but not without recognizing Russian annexation of the Crimea and Georgia.

Even if the Crimean khanate was a small, remote part of the Muslim world, its loss could not be overlooked. The Ottomans had lost territories in eastern Europe before, but this was the first time they had lost Muslim territory. Ottoman claims as preeminent defenders of the faith (*ghazis*) were suddenly in jeopardy, a fact noticed by Muslims everywhere. European encroachment was not isolated on a distant frontier but threatened the "heart of Islam" (*beyza-i islamiye*) and the "entire Muslim community" (*cümle-i ümmet-i Muhammedi*).[6]

The Napoleonic invasion of Egypt confirmed that point. As the effects of the French Revolution and Napoleonic wars spread, Napoleon campaigned into the Mediterranean in 1797. Annexing the Ionian islands and nearby coastal towns, France acquired a border adjoining the Ottoman Empire. Napoleon invaded Egypt in July 1798, defeating the Egyptian warlords. Loosely called *mamluks* (slaves) because they commanded and emerged from household retinues made up largely of slave soldiers, the mamluk *beys* (commanders) embodied the distinctive form that warlordism had assumed in Ottoman Egypt.[7] Although Napoleon defeated them in the Nile Delta and at Cairo, pushing them into upper (southern) Egypt, the British navy under Horatio Nelson quickly destroyed the French fleet at Abukir in August. Dreaming of India but blockaded by the British, Napoleon campaigned as far as Palestine but failed to take the fortress at Acre (March–May 1799), thanks to local warlord Cezzar Ahmed Paşa, with help from Ottoman troops and British ships. Napoleon returned to Egypt, abandoned his army, and sailed back to France in August 1799 to pursue his political ambitions. The French forces remained behind until an Ottoman-British expeditionary force evacuated them in 1801.[8]

Compared to the Ottoman-Russian wars, the French invasion of Egypt was a flash in the pan.[9] Neither did Napoleon's assertions that he had come to restore the sultan's authority and support Islam carry conviction, nor did his French Republic of Egypt make it a modern place. The French displayed aspects of modernity, and not only in their military superiority. The French expedition included about a hundred scholars, organized as the Institut d'Égypte. With them came presses, used to publish periodicals and proclamations. Their attempts to translate revolutionary ideas of "liberty" (*hurriya*, which heretofore had meant "freedom" as opposed to slavery) and "equality" (*taswiya*, which actually means "leveling") clumsily anticipated the new political vocabulary that Muslim thinkers would later develop. The scholars' reports about Egypt, later published in many volumes as the *Description de l'Égypte*, gave the outside world unprecedented information about the country. French scholars also gave Egyptian ulema their first exposure to modern scientific experiments. Napoleon set up councils (*diwans*) and appointed ulema to them. He employed Coptic Christians extensively. This reliance on native Egyptians enlarged their role in governing, but in disruptive ways. Napoleon asked the ulema in his divans to legislate; yet God's law, the sharia, on which they were experts, was not a matter of human legislation, unlike the rules proclaimed by worldly rulers. Rulers of Egypt had historically employed Copts as financial experts, but the French expanded non-Muslims' roles in ways that inverted Egypt's social hierarchy. The French soldiers' behavior toward women of all religions compounded the disorder. Having disrupted Egyptian politics, violated social norms, and used armed force to back up aggressive taxation, the French unwittingly provoked a tax revolt against the "Great Satan" (Napoleon), who repressed it with great violence in October 1798. The Egyptian response to the French was not positive; yet things would never again be the way they were before.[10]

Once the French left, the question was who would control Egypt. By 1805, the answer was clear: Mehmed Ali, destined to become the biggest Ottoman warlord. In his governorship of Egypt (1805–1848), the warlord challenge assumed a new magnitude in competition with the drive for centralization in Istanbul.

Two shocks—the Ottoman-Russian wars of 1768–1792 and the Napoleonic invasion of Egypt in 1798—had turned the imperialist threat to the Ottomans into European diplomacy's Eastern Question, which defined Ottoman international relations until the empire's demise in 1922. The Napoleonic invasion also set a pattern that has continued ever since in the international relations of the Middle East, the pattern of the outside power that intervenes to create or restore "order" and then cannot withdraw without seeing its idea of order collapse.[11] A related pattern began to appear in Egypt and developed fully later. In Egypt, the French invasion disturbed intercommunal equilibria; in later cases, the politicization of such differences generated new forms of conflict and led to demands to "separate the warring parties," even grant them independent nation-states. Many more chapters remained to be written in this history of foreign intervention. The Ottomans also made strides in learning to resist such assaults.

PROVINCIAL WARLORDS

The internal pendant to the assaults of 1768 and 1798 was an expansion of warlordism that endangered the empire. The Ottoman Empire was not the first Islamic state that had gone through a period of decentralization, in which regional power brokers assumed much of the nominal sovereign's power. The Abbasid caliphate (750–1258) displayed an *"ayan-amir* system" during its last three centuries.[12] Under both empires, given the principle that the Muslim community (*umma*) should be united both spiritually and politically, most local power holders preferred to operate as nominal subordinates of the ruler, deriving legitimation from him without following orders. It made no sense to take oneself out of the shadow of the legitimate sovereign's sacrosanct aura, at least not without a rival claim to Islamic legitimacy. Over the centuries, the history of Islamic polity displayed long waves of centralization and decentralization. As the age of European imperialism dawned, the Ottoman Empire had to overcome its decentralization or risk disintegration.

The Ottoman age of decentralization (1600–1800) was characterized by a proliferation of powerful intermediaries between the central government and its subjects. Generically, these are known in Arabic as *ayan*, "notable," and in Turkish as *derebey*, "lord of the valley." The term *ayan* has an extremely wide range of use, including leaders of different types and sizes, who often performed needed roles for both the local populace and the state. For this reason, a term like *warlord* seems useful to identify the extreme cases in which overmighty magnates with private armies defied the sultan and jeopardized the empire's integrity.[13]

The roots of warlordism lay in changes in local administration and tax collection. Over several centuries Ottoman governance had come to assume that a man had to have a large household retinue, including armed men, in order to hold provincial governorships. Growing reliance on tax-farming (the contracting out of the right to collect a given tax in a given place) led to combining governorships with tax-farms. Provincial tax-farmers whose origins lay outside the ruling elites gradually began to acquire these governorships and with them the ruling elites' titles (both high, *bey*, and highest, *paşa*). In an effort to improve conditions, the central government began to change from auctioning revenue-collection rights for several years at a time (*iltizam*) to auctioning life-term tax-farms (*malikâne*, 1695). A decree of 1726 ended the requirement that district governors (*sancak beyi*) be appointed from Istanbul and permitted provincial notables' appointment to those posts. These two measures turned the local notables into the central government's chief interlocutors in the provinces. Istanbul's hold over the countryside loosened; conversely, by investing in state finance and assuming public office, a wider range of people acquired a stake in "being Ottoman."

The great ayan of the 1700s governed districts and provinces, supported large retinues, provisioned armies on campaign, even maintained post-coach systems in their territories. These capabilities hinged on huge fortunes built up by investing in state finance and local financial operations like money lending. The 1768 Ottoman-Russian war greatly increased the sultan's dependence on the warlords to fight and to provide troops and provisions. In the Morea, the Russian attempt to raise a rebellion also activated the local Greek notables, with some supporting the rebellion and others aiding in its suppression. Security in the provinces was deteriorating in many places, and violence was increasing. The local contestants might include Janissary garrisons, perhaps factionalized among themselves, like Trabzon's "Fives" and "Twenty-fives," so-called after the numbers of two of the three regiments involved.[14] In the Balkans, alongside older types of banditry, a new type, referred to by the term *kırcalı*, appeared from 1785 on. These were gangs of professional soldiers, combining Muslims and non-Muslims, who attacked villages and towns, killing hundreds of people at a time. By that date, rising violence, by warlords and kircalis alike, expressed opposition to military reforms in Istanbul. The rising warlord violence was linked over time both to the outbreak of separatist nationalist movements in the Balkans and to the Janissary rebellion that toppled Selim III in 1807. As

European interest in the Balkans grew, some warlords became the object of diplomatic attention or even conducted their own foreign relations; examples include Ali Paşa of Tepelen, based in Albania and Greece, and Osman Pasvanoğlu of Vidin in western Bulgaria.

Against a backdrop that included smaller local notables, variations of this pattern of warlordism extended across most of the empire by the late 1700s. Variations appeared especially in outlying regions not fully integrated into the Ottoman system of local governance, such as the Danubian principalities (Moldavia and Wallachia), provinces bordering Iran (especially Mosul, Baghdad, and Basra), much of the Arabian Peninsula, or Libya, Tunisia, and Algeria. The resources and methods used to create a great ayan's power base define a pattern that to some degree crosscuts these spatial variations.

Provincial warlords and notables organized their power in emulation of the imperial household in Istanbul. Metaphorically, the entire empire was one great patrimonial household; the sultan and the dynasty constituted the family, the imperial palace was their residence and power center, the ruling elites were their slaves (*kul*), the subjects were their "flocks" (*reaya*), the lands under Ottoman rule constituted the dynastic patrimony, and hereditary succession within the dynasty perpetuated the empire through time. Whatever their origins, provincial warlords consolidated their power by emulating this patrimonial model. Aspiring to found local dynasties, they acquired imposing, often fortlike mansions, with public (*selamlık*) and private (*harem*) parts, vast stables and many outbuildings.

To expand the size and strength of their family, notables emulated the sultans' strategies in reproduction and retinue-formation. They took advantage of polygyny and concubinage to increase their number of offspring. Under prevailing gender norms, they needed able sons or surrogate sons to perpetuate their power. This implied maximizing the number and training of their sons, marrying their daughters to promising men who could be integrated into the household, recruiting other able young men through patronage relationships (*intisab*), or buying slave boys and educating them like sons to assume leadership roles in the household. As in the sultan's household, young men who started out as a warlord's protégés or slaves might marry one of his daughters and acquire multiple ties to the household. For the warlords as for the sultan, slavery offered the greatest potential for expanding the household numerically. Georgian mamluks from the Caucasus were particularly in demand and became prominent in warlord households in this period. Egypt's mamluk warlord households were a mixed phenomenon, including both Muslim freebooters and Caucasian slaves. The so-called mamluk regime that ruled Baghdad and Basra in the 1700s was more like an ayan household, in which leadership passed from founder Hasan Paşa to his son, then successively to two slaves married to the founder's remarkable daughters.[15] Normally family-centered, the ayan household and its political entourage also had to be surrounded by a larger following: servants or slaves to do menial work, clerks, regiments of mercenaries, and a patronage network with wide social roots.

After the crises of 1768 and 1798, the time had come for Selim III and Mahmud II to reassert their power against these warlords. Mahmud II succeeded in this by the 1830s to the extent that he is still remembered—paradoxically—for having "destroyed" families that still ran things in some places a century later.[16] In the form of warlords with huge armies, ayans challenged reforming sultans to cut them down to size. That done, ayans as local notables still performed useful functions in mediating between the central government and the populace.

SELIM AND CENTRALIZATION: THE NEW ORDER

Mustafa III (1757–1774) and Abdülhamid I (1774–1789) had already improved the navy and created a rapid-fire artillery corps, a new cannon foundry, and a Naval Engineering School (Mühendishane-i Bahri-i Hümayun).[17] State-sponsored economic enterprises and printing, which had been introduced for Ottoman books briefly in 1726–1746 and was permanently revived by the 1780s, extended the reformist initiative beyond the military sphere.

Selim's more extensive initiatives opened a new era, even if they failed in the short run. Before his accession, through secret correspondence he sought French aid for his intended reforms. Becoming sultan in the midst of war with Austria and Russia (1787–1792) and just as France's Revolution began, he made further preparations by sending envoys to Austria and Prussia and commissioning reports from twenty-odd advisers, who presented their wide-ranging ideas for reform. After peace was reestablished, policy implementation began. The first priority was to reform the existing military corps, upgrade the technical services, and create a European-style infantry known as the Nizam-ı Cedid (New Order). By extension, that became the name of Selim's whole reform program.

Selim's reforms included measures to improve the organization and discipline of the major historical land forces, both the Janissary infantry and the cavalry (*sipahis*).[18] For the Janissaries, he introduced hierarchies of command and organization (battalions and companies) and required two days of drill a week, a low requirement that implies no drill previously. Powerful vested interests, the traditional forces resisted, especially the Janissaries. Efforts to upgrade technical forces or create new services yielded some results. These began with the artillery

JANISSAIRE,
en habit d'Ordonnance.

JANISSAIRE ARMÉ.

JANISSAIRE ARME

POMPIER.

Janissaries, late eighteenth century. Upper left, a Janissary in dress uniform;
lower right, a sapper; upper right and lower left, armed Janissaries, front and side
views. (d'Ohsson, *Tableau,* 3:394, pls. 208–11.)

and mortar corps. Improvements were made in gunpowder production, in the artillery foundry, navy, and naval arsenal, and in ship construction. The Army Engineering School (Mühendishane-i Berri i Hümayun) was founded in 1795.

The major military initiative was the new infantry (Nizam-ı Cedid), supported by its own treasury (İrad-ı Cedid, "new revenue").[19] After initial experimentation, the formation of the new corps, equipped, uniformed, and trained in European style, was announced in 1794. The number of regiments gradually grew, and cooperative provincial governors founded several. Elements of the new force proved their effectiveness against the French in Gaza and in Egypt. The old forces, the Janissary infantry and sipahi cavalry, refused to serve with the new forces and revolted when they had the chance, overthrowing the New Order and deposing Selim III in 1807.

Ottoman experience recapitulated that of other states in showing that it was impossible to create new and better armed forces without raising the efficiency of government throughout, especially in finance. The creation of the "New Treasury" to serve the "New Order" infantry testifies to the dependence of military reform on finance; yet matters did not stop there. From the moment Selim III commissioned a score of memoirists to submit their reform proposals, almost any facet of the imperial system could come up for revision. Selim's reforms and attempted reforms ranged widely beyond the military, and some produced lasting results. Istanbul's grain supply system was upgraded, replacing contractors with a Supervisorate of Grain (Zahire Nezareti, 1793). Supplying a third to a half of the city's grain and operating for decades (1793–1839), this was essentially a large state enterprise.[20]

Selim also made changes in the central and local governance. In Istanbul, he issued new regulations aimed at greater functional specialization and higher recruitment standards in the grand vezir's chancery. In the provinces, to improve relations between government agents and the populace, he called for election of the local notables (ayan) by the populace and for separating the judicial and administrative functions of the religious court judges (kadıs).[21] The central government's limited ability to make its writ run in the provinces blunted the impact of these measures. Undeterred, Selim also acted to strengthen his subjects' competitiveness in international trade. He created a privileged category of "Europe merchants" (Avrupa tüccarı, 1802), who were to be non-Muslim Ottoman subjects; a similarly privileged category for Muslims was later created under the name "auspicious merchants" (hayriye tüccarı). The reason for extending this benefit first to non-Muslims was to counteract their desire for foreign citizenship, which enabled them to trade on the privileged terms that the capitulations gave foreign merchants.

Selim III's most innovative nonmilitary reform was to inaugurate permanent diplomatic representation in European capitals in 1793. Hitherto, the empire had followed diplomatic practices at odds with European norms, sending out embassies only temporarily for special missions. For the Ottomans, creating permanent embassies and later consulates was a critical step in developing peaceful relations with Europe. Officially, the embassies represented the empire to Europe. They also represented Europe to the Ottomans by collecting information about the countries where they served and training Ottomans in European languages.[22]

Scholars have long debated whether Selim III's reforms marked a real turn toward innovation. Such discussions overlook the fact that this was the first time the imperial system had been held up for comprehensive scrutiny with the idea of "giving order to everything"—a recurrent phrase in documents on the period.[23] Not all the proposals were implemented. In the short run, few outlasted Selim's overthrow. However, the mere thought that the old order, which ran on custom and routine, should be replaced by a new order based on plans and regulations crystallized the difference between the reform era and times past. Selim's New Order was innovative in some of its parts—the new infantry, the embassies—and *in totality* as a turn away from deferring to past custom toward planning for the future. Selim's spiritual adviser, the mystical poet Şeyh Galip, sought to justify innovation through perpetual creation; but perhaps his poems on the perpetual re-creation of all things were too mystical to sway opinion widely.[24] In any event, as the leading reformist statesmen's writings prove, the Enlightenment's "spirit of system" (*esprit de système*) intruded into Ottoman thinking in these very years. Selim's New Order started the Ottoman turn toward the rationalization that is of the essence of modernity.

Selim's misfortune was in having to make this turn without adequate external or internal support. France's revolution was extremely destabilizing for an empire that regarded France as its closest European ally. France's invasion of Egypt in 1798 was only one bad turn in a series of reversals in Ottoman-French relations. Domestic vested interests also opposed reform in the provinces and in the capital. A revolt among the Janissaries' *yamak* auxiliaries, who thought they were going to have to adopt Nizam-ı Cedid uniforms, led to Selim's fall on 29 May 1807.[25] A successful reformer would have to neutralize such opponents.

MAHMUD II PREPARES

Upon Selim's overthrow and confinement in the palace, his cousin Mustafa IV was enthroned, Selim's New Order was abolished, and the Janissaries launched a reign of terror in Istanbul. Amid the confusion, a critical new alignment formed. A leading warlord, Bayrakdar Mustafa, broke with Mustafa IV's partisans and returned home to Rusçuk in Bulgaria. Others rallied to him and formed a secret committee to restore Selim and the Nizam-ı Cedid. This group had to maneuver carefully: to restore Selim III, they had to depose Mustafa IV, but Selim was Mustafa's prisoner in the palace. The Rusçuk committee had nearly succeeded when Mustafa IV, trying to make himself indispensable, ordered the execution of his brother Mahmud and Selim. Mustafa's servants did kill Selim, but Mahmud's servants helped him escape. At a critical moment, a palace slave woman, Cevri, hurled hot coals into the eyes of Mahmud's pursuers to gain time while others helped him escape onto the palace roof. Bursting into the palace, Bayrakdar Mustafa was grief-stricken to discover the bloody corpse of Selim, whom he had hoped to restore. With the survival of the dynasty in danger, Mahmud made his way down from the roof and was proclaimed sultan.[26]

During Mustafa IV's fourteen-month reign, Selim and Mahmud were both confined in the imperial harem. It is fascinating to imagine discussions they might have had. Mahmud seems to have learned a great deal from Selim's mistakes. Eventually, he revived and perpetuated Selim's reforms. First, he had to prepare carefully. One of the greatest warlords, Bayrakdar Mustafa Paşa, had brought him to the throne and was now his grand vezir.

During his five months as Mahmud's grand vezir, Bayrakdar (or Alemdar, both meaning "standard-bearer") tried to satisfy all the interests associated with him.[27] He tried to re-create something like Selim's new troops under a different name, *sekban-ı cedid* ("new houndsmen"). Trying to make a compact between the central government and the warlords, he invited all the great notables to assemble at Istanbul, although some of the biggest—Ali Paşa of Yanina, Mehmed Ali Paşa of Egypt—did not come. Those who came brought large forces, reportedly totaling seventy thousand. In October 1808, a "deed of agreement" (*sened-i ittifak*) was concluded by which the signatories became co-guarantors of state interests defined in the document.

Although some scholars look back on the "deed of agreement" as a step toward an Ottoman constitutional tradition, it had little lasting significance.[28] Mahmud did not sign it. He thought it conceded too much to the notables. Most of the warlords also did not sign; they thought the agreement limited their powers. Ultimately, while the notables wielded power as a matter of fact, sovereignty belonged to the sultan in principle. Decentralization and warlordism had eroded the sultan's power in practice but had not changed the principles of Ottoman polity. Rather than founding a constitutional tradition for the Ottomans, the "deed of agreement" violated the Ottomans' historical, unwritten constitution by making its signers co-guarantors of powers that were not theirs. A forceful sultan could reassert those powers. For another century, as often as not, the modern tension between rationalization and subjectivization manifested itself in reasserted autocracy.

In the fall of 1808, Bayrakdar's reforms provoked a Janissary revolt, whose failure cost him and ex-sultan Mustafa IV their lives. The fact that Mahmud II was now the sole surviving Ottoman prince safeguarded him. Forced to sacrifice military reform, he set to work to build support and neutralize opposition. Success required expanding his control both in the provinces and at the center while defending the empire from external enemies.

In the border district of Belgrade, the decentralization and militarization of politics had boiled over into a Serbian uprising. The Serbs still professed loyalty to the sultan but sought help from Russia, with which the Ottomans were again at war in 1806.[29] Facing Napoleon's invasion of Russia, the Russians made peace with the Ottomans in 1812. The Serbs were crushed in 1813 but revolted again. After Napoleon's final defeat in 1815, Russia forced Mahmud to make Serbia an autonomous vassal principality. Although the Ottomans retained a governor at Belgrade and some garrisons, this was an ominous step toward losing a province.

The end of the Russian and Napoleonic wars offered Mahmud a chance to expand his control internally by eliminating some warlords in the Balkans, parts of Anatolia, and northern Syria (roughly 1812–1820). In Iraq, the restoration of rule from Istanbul occurred only with military campaigns of 1831–1834. In different parts of the empire, defeated warlords' fates varied. Some were executed. Others died peacefully and were replaced by governors from Istanbul; the deceased notable's heirs might receive appointments, but only in other provinces. Reducing warlord autonomy also helped reduce brigandage and secure the countryside.

Mahmud proved adroit in reasserting his power. Provincial opinion supported this trend. Some provincial opponents, never having seen any justification for the warlords except as the sultan's agents, turned against the warlords when they challenged state authority, instead demanding active rule by the sultan.[30] Outcomes differed in different places. Tepelenli Ali Paşa had created an autonomous domain based at Yanina in Epirus. An Albanian-born Muslim and adept in regional politics, he ran his administration in Greek, and Greek schools were founded in his domains; in those ways, he laid bases for Greek nationalism.[31] Mahmud's campaign against him (1819–1822) did help precipitate the Greek Revolution (1821–1827). Becoming the biggest crisis of the 1820s, it forced Mahmud to call on the biggest warlord of all, Egypt's Mehmed Ali Paşa.

Mahmud strove to expand his control at the center at the same time as in the provinces. He used his powers of appointment astutely. Leading figures of his reign included Halet Efendi, who helped restore Istanbul's authority in the provinces until he was dismissed and executed after the campaign against Ali Paşa of Yanina (1822). In the bureaucracy, Mahmud's collaborators included Mehmed Said Galib Paşa, who had supported Selim's reforms; Galib's protégé Pertev Paşa, who held important positions in the chancery and foreign affairs; and Pertev's protégé, Mustafa Reşid Paşa, prominent as a diplomat in the 1830s. Among Mahmud's military supporters, Husrev Paşa was the dominant figure. The upper ranks of Ottoman officialdom were still politically divided among factions that powerful men formed to outmaneuver rivals for the sultan's favor, often at terrible costs to state interests. Pertev Paşa lost his life as a result of factional conflict in 1837; Husrev Paşa had a hand in that. His even bigger rivalry with his nemesis, Egypt's Mehmed Ali Paşa, caused turmoil for decades.[32]

At the same time that factionalism complicated his preparations for reform, Mahmud also cultivated Islamic religious scholars, not only the aristocratized higher ulema but also the lower ranks and the medrese students. These students numbered several thousand in Istanbul, forming a disadvantaged interest group, whose relations with the Janissaries were tense. Mahmud's later reforms got him denounced as the "infidel sultan." While preparing to abolish the Janissaries, however, he cultivated the image of a proper Muslim sovereign. He was preparing for the day when he would need a *fetva* from the Şeyhülislam (head of the religious hierarchy) in favor of military reform and supportive sermons from the mosque preachers.

Without confronting the Janissaries for the time being, Mahmud strengthened military forces, like the artillery and navy, that earlier reforms had made more disciplined and efficient. He upgraded strategic fortifications and arsenals, increased gunpowder production, and imported muskets. Among the Janissaries, he used his powers of appointment to banish troublemakers to remote provinces, where the executioner often awaited. He advanced men who supported restoring discipline, notably Ağa Hüseyin Paşa, commander (*ağa*) of the Janissaries and later a key actor in their suppression. Ultimately, Janissary unwillingness to campaign played into Mahmud's hands, proving the dangers of having no regular infantry at his command.[33]

MEHMED ALI AND OTTOMAN-EGYPTIAN RIVALRY THROUGH 1826

The intersection of Egyptian and Greek affairs clinched the case. Mehmed Ali Paşa, or Muhammad Ali Pasha in Arabic, had gone to Egypt in 1801 with the Ottoman expedition that evacuated the French. By 1805, he had bested Husrev

Paşa for control of Egypt; their lifelong rivalry sprang from that fact. Selim III reluctantly appointed Mehmed Ali governor of Egypt. Mehmed Ali's efforts to create a power base for himself turned him into the empire's biggest warlord and, for a time, its most successful centralizing reformer.

Mehmed Ali tightened Cairo's control over the Egyptian countryside, carried out a cadastral survey, abolished tax-farming, and canceled the tax immunity of religious foundations. He expanded irrigation and the land area under cultivation, and he set up a monopoly system, requiring many crops to be sold to state warehouses at set prices. These measures increased his revenues more than sixfold by 1821. Sometimes regarded as the "father of modern Egypt," he was culturally Ottoman, not Egyptian. The Egyptian people, whom he ruthlessly exploited in his and his family's interests, had little reason to think of him as a father.[34]

Two measures of 1821–1822 greatly expanded Mehmed Ali's scale of endeavor. He introduced the cultivation of long-staple cotton, for which Egypt became famous. He also founded a modern army based on conscription.[35] The army's needs in turn required other innovations: new factories, schools, hospitals, all intended for the army's good, not the people's. Mehmed Ali's thinking had been influenced by the French forces still in Egypt when he arrived there in 1801. Yet in 1822 he rejected a plan based on the Napoleonic model and chose one based on Selim III's New Order as better suited to a country with a small army in an early state of development. Already subject to demands for taxes and labor demands for projects like canal-building, Egypt's peasants now also had to bear the burden of mass conscription.

Mehmed Ali conscripted Egyptians only as a last resort, however. The Mamluks, who had dominated Egypt before 1798, reemerged after the French withdrew. Realizing from Selim III's fate that reform could not succeed with such an old guard on hand, in 1811 Mehmed Ali invited the Mamluk commanders to a festivity where more than four hundred were massacred, following which thousands of their followers were hunted down. The Albanian military retainers whom Mehmed Ali had brought with him to Egypt had their turn in 1815, when they rebelled against his effort to impose New Order discipline on them. Sultan Mahmud II had ordered Mehmed Ali Paşa to fight the anti-Ottoman Wahhabi religious movement in Arabia. Otherwise reluctant, the paşa seized his chance to send troublesome groups like the Albanians to meet death in Arabia for a good cause. His next experiment in recruitment was campaigning into the Sudan to capture slaves for use as soldiers. So high were captive death rates, however, that the campaign tied up more men than it produced; one of Mehmed Ali's own sons died in the Sudan. Only after all else failed did Mehmed Ali issue orders, in 1822, to recruit Egyptian peasants. By the early 1830s, more than 130,000 had been conscripted. Inasmuch as Mehmed Ali's ruling elite was non-Egyptian and operated in Ottoman Turkish, not Arabic, native Egyptians were confined to the ranks below about captain, while the command structure was reserved for the elite, including several French Napoleonic veterans employed in high commands.

Egyptian peasants resisted recruitment every way they could, maiming themselves, abandoning their villages, rebelling.[36] Recruits disappeared into the army for life, and conditions of service were brutal. The impact of recruitment on rural economy and society was drastic. Women and children followed husbands and tried to set up camps near military installations; some women disguised themselves as men and followed their husbands as far as Syria. The birthrate fell from fear that sons would be taken as soldiers. The government responded by applying new forms of regimentation, not just to the troops, but to society in general. Examples include new record-keeping requirements such as individual identification papers (*tezkere*), inspection missions, quarantines, regulations, and punishments for violating them.

Despite the recruits' resistance and inertness to appeals to religious zeal, modern methods of drill and discipline wrought their proverbial miracle in forming armies from the lower rungs of society. At least, Mehmed Ali's army became the best in the region. Unable to suppress the Greek Revolution with his own forces, Mahmud II again turned to his governor of Egypt, Mehmed Ali.[37] Under Mehmed Ali's son Ibrahim Paşa, the Egyptians took the island of Crete in 1825, then invaded Morea. With the fall of Missolonghi and the occupation of Athens in 1826, they seemed to have defeated the Greek Revolution. European—especially English—philhellenism kept that from happening. But first, Egypt's triumphs in Greece provided the momentum for decisive change in Istanbul. Any eye could see the danger if the governor of Egypt's forces could defeat Greek rebels, but the sultan's could not.

DESTROYING THE JANISSARIES, MAKING REFORM IRREVERSIBLE

Seizing the moment, Mahmud II secured agreement from key figures, including top Janissary commanders, to create modern companies known as *eşkenci*s, "campaigners," within the Janissaries. On 14 June 1826, two days after the new force's first drill, the Janissaries rebelled. In a consultation at Topkapı Palace about what to do, Mahmud hesitated, until a fiery speech by one of the ulema moved him to rush into the hall where relics of the Prophet were kept, bring out the Prophet's banner (*sancak-ı şerif*), and symbolically declare war on the Janissaries.[38] They barricaded themselves inside their compound at Et Meydanı, unwisely making themselves an easy target for Mahmud's artillery, which destroyed them that afternoon. Of the leaders whom Mahmud had cultivated, only a few Janissary commanders reverted to old loyalties; the rest stood firm. Janissaries who escaped the bombardment were hunted down. In the provinces, Janissaries were killed by the thousands. The corps was officially abolished, and the closely associated Bektaşi dervish order was also suppressed. Many of its meeting halls and its shrine at Kırşehir were turned over to the Nakşibendi order, raising its influence.[39] The formation of a new army, headed by a new commander in chief (*serasker*), was announced.

The "auspicious incident" (*vak'a-i hayriye*) of the Janissaries' destruction precipitated revolutionary change. Recruitment and training began for the new army, the Trained Victorious Soldiers of Muhammad (Muallem Asakir-i Mansure-i Muhammediye). The regulations of Selim's Nizam-ı Cedid were reimplemented with slight revisions.[40] Systematization of recruitment did not really begin before 1846. Consequently, after brief initial enthusiasm, recruitment became a problem. The duration of service was initially unlimited, and soldiers could request discharge only after twelve years. The resistances that confronted Mehmed Ali's recruiters soon appeared, including self-mutilation, desertion, and village abandonment. Forcible impressment provoked complaints, as did the unequal impact of recruitment, from province to province, and across ethnoreligious lines. Non-Muslims were historically exempt from military service with limited exceptions. Many Muslims—ulema, villagers performing services of military value—were exempt; paid substitution was permitted for Muslims. Ottoman commanders regarded some Muslim groups as unreliable (bedouin, Kurds, Albanians) and quickly established a preference for "Turkish lads" (*Türk uşağı*). In this period, that implied recruitment across parts of the Ottoman Balkans (Rumelia) and Anatolia. The Gülhane decree of 1839 cited the harmful consequences of regional disparities in recruiting and the unlimited term of service. The preference for Turks did not mean that other Muslims did not serve in the military. Yet when time came to face the Russians, the Ottomans were handicapped by unsystematic recruitment limited to parts of a smaller populace.

Mahmud's reforms spread through the military and far beyond. The adoption of European-style military uniforms started a dress revolution that extended to the civilian population in 1829, anticipating the republic's dress revolution of 1925. The new troops' initial military headgear (*şubara*) was soon replaced by the fez; two of the color illustrations show New Army uniforms both before and after the adoption of the fez. Appointed serasker in 1827, Husrev Paşa expanded that role from commander to minister of war. Military organization, drill, command and control were aligned with Napoleonic patterns. The old palace guard, known as *bostancıs* ("gardeners"), were reorganized as a guard regiment (*hassa*). The historically separate artillery (*topçu*), artillery transport (*arabacı*), bombardier (*humbaracı*), and sapper (*lağımcı*) corps were combined in the 1830s under a single command. The mounted artillery (*suvari topçusu*) force, which Mahmud had raised and trained in preparation for 1826, was more modern to start with. An effort was made to reorganize what remained of the provincial cavalry (*timarlı sipahis*) as a semiregular cavalry to serve along with the new forces.[41] The navy was strengthened. A provincial militia (*redif*) was created in 1834. For officer training, the Army and Navy Engineering schools were upgraded, and a new Military Medical School (1827) and Military Academy (*Harbiye*, 1834) were added. Most officers were still not academy men at all. Tensions between "school men" (*mektepli*) and often illiterate "regimentals" (*alaylı*) plagued the officer corps from then on.

In the 1830s, the scope of reform expanded to include the entire government. The central agencies were reorganized into European-style ministries. Selim's embassies were revived for good in 1833. In the same year, the Translation Office of the Sublime Porte (Bab-ı Âli Tercüme odası) was expanded to become a key support for Ottoman diplomacy and modernization. The training ground for the civil elite of the next period, the Translation Office was actually founded in 1821, when the outbreak of the Greek Revolution forced the government to abandon its old reliance on Greek translators. Along with the ministries, councils proliferated, including the Council of Ministers (Meclis-i Hass-i Vükelâ). With these councils, historical Islamic forms of consultation (*şura, meşveret*) assumed new forms—a trend with which new ideas of representation and parliamentary government later became associated.

To make these new organizations serve his purposes, Mahmud needed more and better civil officials and new ways to project the reformist message. The 1830s consequently marked the critical turning point from an old scribal corps, made up of secretaries (*katib*) who kept records, toward a civil official corps (*mülkiye memurları*), who implemented policies as well as kept records and actually governed the empire. Major changes in personnel policy created a hierarchy of civil ranks; defined the equivalencies among civilian, military, and religious ranks; substituted monthly salaries for the fees and perquisites that had compensated most officials before; implemented disciplinary codes for civil and religious functionaries; and reduced the disabilities of officials' historic legal status as the rulers' slaves.[42] Mahmud also needed new means to communicate with his subjects. Not to speak of earlier precedents, including gazettes published in Istanbul or Cairo by the French as early as 1795, Mehmed Ali launched the first Ottoman journal, *Vekayi-i Misriye* (Egyptian events, 1829). Mahmud II responded with his *Takvim-i Vekayi* (Calendar of events, 1831). Both these official journals soon also had their French-language editions, the *Moniteur ottoman* (1831) and *Moniteur égyptien* (1833).[43]

Using his new elites in his efforts to clip overmighty warlords' wings, Mahmud gave civil functionaries, as opposed to military officers or *kadıs*, primary responsibility over local administration for the first time in Ottoman history. The project of creating a modern system of local administration, manned by civil officials, continued long after Mahmud. The reforms that improved the status of civil officialdom helped to provide essential human resources. Other measures created new roles and offices for them to fill. In 1829, he began to appoint headmen (*muhtars*), chosen among local residents, to provide neighborhood governance, first in Istanbul, and then in provincial towns and villages. With time, muhtars became the key intermediaries between the populace and the government, expanding their influence at the expense of the neighborhood religious leaders. This humble but useful innovation survived the empire in numerous successor states; Turkish neighborhoods still have *muhtars*. Following the creation of the provincial militia (*redif*), the militia units (*tabur*) were regrouped in 1836 into province-sized units headed by a *müşir* (the term later used for a field marshal), instead of a *vali* (governor), as previously.[44] However, the tax reforms prescribed in the Gülhane decree soon shifted reliance back to civil officials for provincial governance.

The reorganization of provincial administration included both new services and new social controls. With military recruitment in mind, the census of 1830–1831 served chiefly to count the male population of Anatolia and Rumelia. Registry agencies (*ceride nezareti, defter nazırlığı*) were set up in Istanbul and in the central towns of provinces and districts to analyze census data and record births, deaths, movements into and out of town, and other such matters. These officials also took over from the kadıs the issuance of travel permits, intended to restrict migration (*men'-i mürur, mürur tezkeresi*) into the cities and to improve security in the countryside, where the dispersal of former Janissaries after 1826 had destabilizing effects.[45] One of Selim III's goals had been to improve the system of couriers and way stations (*menzilhane*), a service essential for imperial communications but a source of complaint for centuries. Post coaches replaced couriers between Istanbul and Edirne by 1834 and on numerous routes by the 1840s. The coaches also transported letters and goods for private individuals.[46] The government increased its control over its subjects in some respects and made life easier for them in others.

Mahmud's later reforms dramatized his determination to reassert the sultanate and centralize government. He constantly visited and inspected military installations. Whereas his recent predecessors had scarcely set foot outside Istanbul, he inspected the fortifications as far away as Silistria on the Danube.[47] In 1838, he went the length of abolishing the post of grand vezir (sadr-ı azam), historically the sultan's chief delegate, entrusting the successor post of baş vekil (chief minister) as an additional duty to the interior minister. This was a short-lived measure, reversed soon after Mahmud's death in 1839. How it related to his centralizing goals appears from the fact that Mahmud also divided the deliberative functions of the grand vezir's divan among three councils, convening at the Ministry of War, the Sublime Porte, and Topkapı Palace. The palace council in particular, the Supreme Council of Judicial Ordinances (Meclis-i Vala-yı Ahkâm-ı Adliye), was intended to play a central role in planning future reforms.[48]

Mahmud's later efforts to reconsolidate state and sultanate had to respond, in particular, to the unresolved Ottoman-Egyptian crisis. His revival of Ottoman diplomacy in 1833 formed part of his response. His diplomats advised him, in effect, that European diplomatic support depended on realigning Ottoman domestic policy with European norms. To face the final phase of his struggle with Mehmed Ali, Mahmud particularly needed British support, and that implied adopting the economic and political liberalism of the day. Doing that would be easier if Ottoman and Islamic priorities did not have to be sacrificed totally in the process—a point often overlooked by historians.

Economically, the key innovation was the Anglo-Ottoman Commercial Treaty of 1838, followed by analogous agreements with other states.[49] The 1838 treaty confirmed existing capitulatory privileges, introduced free trade with low import and export duties, and allowed British merchants to trade anywhere in the empire, subject to those duties and low transit tolls. The treaty obligated the Ottomans to abolish all monopolies, and it specified that its terms applied in all Ottoman territories, including Egypt. "Monopolies" referred to both trade monopolies on specific commodities and state enterprises founded by both the Ottoman and Egyptian governments to produce essential goods. With this treaty, free trade officially came to the Ottoman Empire. Many historians have regarded this as a critical turning point in undermining the empire, arguing that Ottoman producers were unable to compete with British factories. In fact, the empire was already undergoing dependent integration into the world economy; the transition to free trade had already begun; and Ottoman production adapted and survived far better than such arguments allowed. British and Ottoman negotiators saw the antimonopoly provision as primarily aimed at

Mehmed Ali, and the specification that the treaty applied also to Egypt shows how they thought it served Ottoman interests.

European liberalism championed freedom not only economically but also politically—indeed in all spheres. The necessary pendant of the free-trade treaty, therefore, was a charter for political reform. This took the form of the Gülhane decree, under discussion before Mahmud II died on 30 June 1839 but promulgated by Abdülmecid on 3 November 1839. The decree has given rise to antithetical interpretations selectively emphasizing its liberal themes at one extreme and its Islamic roots at the other. A close focus on the text proves that it merged several priorities. Perhaps, then, the points most resonant with classical liberalism were emphasized because they aligned with themes from Islamic thought, or even with the drafters' personal interests. The decree incorporates terms and themes from other documents and debates, in which religious functionaries and statesmen associated with the Nakşibendiye, the major religious revival movement of the period (discussed below), were well represented. That fact reinforces the impression of an overall Islamic context, in which other elements appear.[50]

The decree is a fundamental law in the sense that it calls for the adoption of other, new laws to fulfill its promises and prohibit specified abuses. Precisely here appears the most insistently Islamic feature: the decree identifies these new laws as "laws conforming to the sharia" (*kavanin-i şer'iye*). Although a half dozen other adjectives are used once or twice each to refer to these laws, the phrase "laws conforming to the sharia" appears six times.[51] In Ottoman political culture, *kanun* (the singular of *kavanin*) refers to state law, in contrast to Islamic law, the sharia, which exists independently of the authority of any state. Ottoman efforts to establish the conformity of state law to the sharia date back at least to the sixteenth century, and the characterization of state laws as *kavanin-i şer'iye* dates back equally far. The most-repeated phrase in the Gülhane decree asserts this same demand for state law to accord with the sharia. Interpretations of the decree as a Westernizing measure ignore this point.

Specific reforms proposed or abuses denounced in the decree do resonate with Euro-American declarations of rights. The fundamental matters on which new laws are needed are "security of life" (*emniyet-i can*), "security of honor and property" (*mahfuziyet-i ırz ve namus ve mal*), "tax assessment" (*tayin-i vergü*), and "military recruitment and the duration of service" (*asakir-i muktaziyenin suret-i celb ve müddet-i istihdamı*). Alluding to the abolition of monopolies in the 1838 commercial treaty, the decree denounced the kindred evil of tax-farming and promised that henceforth the subjects would be assessed "one appropriate tax" (*bir vergü-yi münasib*) according to their means. The decree also contains provisions about due process of law. Those accused of any crime are to be tried publicly, and no one who has not been convicted under the law is to be "executed or poisoned" (*idam ve tesmim*) publicly or privately. The decree also denounces bribery (*rüşvet*, 64, l. 8) among officials.

Europeans assumed that the decree declared the equality of Muslims and non-Muslims, and most scholars repeat this idea. What the decree says, however, is that among Ottoman subjects, "Muslims and members of other religious communities" (*ehl-i İslâm ve milel-i saire*) shall benefit "from these imperial concessions" without exception. The state's laws and policies could apply equally to Muslim and non-Muslim; the sharia itself obligates the sultan to guarantee the security of all his subjects. In contrast, believer and nonbeliever cannot be equal under the sharia any more than they can be under any other kind of religious law. Noting that its provisions will "completely change the old ways" (*usul-i atikeyi bütün bütün tağyir*), the decree concludes with orders that it be made known throughout the empire and officially communicated to the embassies, followed by a closing prayer. The publicity given the decree in Syria, then occupied by Egypt, did help turn Muslim opinion against Mehmed Ali.[52]

A thorough interpretation of the Gülhane decree has to take account of both its Islamic and its Western references. The wording of the decree offers clues about how to do this. For example, the guarantees of rights evoke liberal themes but are not couched in terms of a rhetoric of individualism. Rather they are couched in terms of equity and justice and the sovereign's desire for his lands to flourish and his subjects to be at peace (*imar-ı memalik ve . . . terfih-i ahali*). The philosophical passages of the decree acknowledge, in terms perhaps transitional between Islamic political philosophy and nationalist thought, the emotional factors that make people "feel warm" (*ısınmak*) about the state or strive (*uğraşmak*) to prosper.[53] The decree identifies military recruitment with protection of the *vatan*, implying that this term had already begun its semantic expansion, from "native locality" to "fatherland." The discussion of tax reform alludes to the "circle of equity," used by Islamic political philosophers to explain the symbiotic relationship between rulers and ruled. Rather than a single ideology, then, the decree evokes themes of statecraft and political philosophy widely shared across differences of culture and period.

At the same time, certain terms signal that the decree also serves particular interests. The guarantees of personal honor repeatedly couple two different words for honor, both *namus* (honor, good name) and *ırz* (honor, usually in the sense of chastity or sexual purity). The clauses on due process of law add that trials are to be public. No one is to be "executed or poisoned," publicly or secretly, without trial. No one's honor (*ırz ve namus*) is to be assaulted by anyone else. The powerful are not to intervene in others' disposition of their property. Perhaps to mask the particular interests served by these provisions, the drafters continue precisely at this point that these concessions apply to all subjects, both "people of Islam and other communities." In fact, the common people, Muslim or non-Muslim, were not those primarily at risk of having their ırz violated and their property confiscated or of being "executed or poisoned" without trial. The sharia obligated the sultan to protect his common subjects.

Those who faced these risks were the members of the ruling class, whose legal status was that of slaves of the sultan. A century and more had passed since many of the sultan's military had literally been recruited as slaves. However, service in the ruling elites, excepting the ulema, still placed officials in the juridical status of slaves of the sultan. The sultan had the power of arbitrary discipline (*siyaset*) over his slaves, including the right to order their execution, and their estates were forfeit to him at death, a circumstance that degraded the women of the family, even if their chastity was not literally violated.[54] The factional rivalries among high officials raised their risks of enduring such fates. A dramatic case of this kind occurred in 1837, when Pertev Paşa, noted both as a statesman and as a prominent member of the Nakşibendi order, was toppled from favor by his factional rivals, sent into exile, and poisoned. Pertev's protégés and household were caught up in his fall. There was at least talk of interrogating his daughter, which would have violated her seclusion, if not her person. Temporarily eclipsed by their patron's fall, Mustafa Reşid Paşa and others associated with the drafting of the Gülhane decree now not only came back politically but also got their new young sultan to change the rules of the political game in their favor.[55] The term *siyaset* was starting to undergo a historic change, from its centuries-old meaning, "arbitrary punishment" of the official elites at the sultan's command, to the more inclusive meaning "politics."

Whatever the Gülhane decree lacked in philosophical consistency, it made up in engaging Ottomans' vital interests. As Mahmud II's reign ended, the Gülhane decree—although seldom so interpreted—set goals for an Islamically grounded advance into modernity.

INTERNATIONAL RELATIONS AND OTTOMAN-EGYPTIAN RIVALRY, 1826–1839

What enabled the civil bureaucrats, specifically Mustafa Reşid and his fellow diplomats, to set in place the commercial treaty and the Gülhane decree was their indispensability as mediators between Ottomans and Europeans in the climactic phase of the struggle with Egypt's Mehmed Ali, once his ambition— frustrated in Greece—turned against Ottoman interests.

Mehmed Ali no sooner appeared to have defeated the Greeks in 1826 than Britain, France, and Russia jointly threatened to intervene on the Greek side if the sultan refused mediation. A British-French fleet confronted the Ottoman and Egyptian navies anchored at Navarino, where an incident started a naval battle (October 1827), which destroyed the entire Ottoman and most of the Egyptian fleet, even though the opposing sides were not officially at war. When Mahmud II resisted concessions, the Russians did go to war (1828–1830), attacking through both the Caucasus and the Balkans. Britain and France evacuated Ibrahim Paşa's Egyptian forces from Greece. By 1830, diplomatic agreements had secured the independence of a small Greek kingdom while preventing Russia from dismantling the rest of the Ottoman Balkans. Meanwhile, the Ottoman-Russian war extended Russia's ethnic cleansing policy across the Caucasus into eastern Anatolia. The policy aimed to push out Muslims as Russian frontiers expanded and to draw in Armenians to create a Christian majority in what later became the Republic of Armenia.[56]

Resenting this outcome in Greece and ever the rival of Husrev Paşa, who was still the top man in Ottoman military affairs, Mehmed Ali ceased behaving like a dutiful Ottoman governor after 1826. Coveting Syria, he asked to be made governor of Damascus as well as of Egypt. Among his strategic motives, he had in mind the needs of his navy of sailing ships. Egypt did not produce essential supplies, especially timber, which could be obtained from northern Syria. While painfully aware of how a rebellious paşa's troops might melt away when ordered to face the sultan's, all the more now that the sultan had new forces, Mehmed Ali prepared to take what he could not get by asking. Invading Syria in November 1831 under his son Ibrahim Paşa, the Egyptians repeatedly beat the Ottomans, advancing into Anatolia, where they captured the grand vezir at Konya in December 1832.

Mahmud II had no choice but to conclude a truce granting Mehmed Ali the governorships of Egypt, Hijaz, and Crete and giving his son Ibrahim Paşa control of Syria. Although Ibrahim urged him to do so, Mehmed Ali did not yet demand independence. He probably still could not imagine himself outside the Ottoman framework. No one was satisfied, however. Mehmed Ali was still only an Ottoman governor, owing annual tribute to Istanbul; his governorships still required annual renewal by the sultan whom he had defeated. Unable to get assistance from Austria, France, or Britain, Mahmud II had concluded an improbable alliance with Russia in 1833. That caused disquiet as far away as London. Mahmud II's accelerating reforms of the 1830s, his reopening of embassies in European capitals (1833), the Ottoman-British commercial treaty (1838), and the Gülhane decree (1839) measured the urgency of competing with Mehmed Ali for European support.

The second and final round of the Syrian crisis started in 1839. Mahmud II was determined to settle scores and thought the Syrian populace might be ready to rebel against Egyptian rule.[57] Mehmed Ali, in arrears in his tribute payments, offered to catch up, but only if Husrev Paşa was dismissed as serasker (minister of war) in Istanbul. Finally, after Mahmud II massed troops in southeastern Anatolia, Mehmed Ali ordered Ibrahim Paşa to attack. At Nizib, on 24 June 1839, Ibrahim routed the incompetently led Ottomans. Mahmud II died six days later, without hearing the news. Amid the confusion, Ottoman fleet commander Ahmed Fevzi Paşa sailed to Alexandria and turned the fleet over to Mehmed Ali, apparently because the latter had misled him with reports that Husrev Paşa intended to place the fleet under Russian command.[58]

Losing its army, navy, and sultan within a few days, the Ottoman Empire reached its lowest point since 1774. Mehmed Ali appeared to be in a position to dictate peace terms. Yet such was not to be. At Mahmud II's funeral, Husrev Paşa appointed himself grand vezir by snatching the imperial seal from the incumbent.[59] Under the new, sixteen-year-old sultan Abdülmecid, the two aged rivals, Husrev and Mehmed Ali, began making demands on one another until the European powers intervened jointly, demanding that the crisis not be settled without their concurrence. That transformed the situation (July 1839). During a year of waiting, neither did Mehmed Ali respond to demands to withdraw from occupied territories and return the fleet, nor did the sultan grant him the independence he sought. Finally, under the Convention of London (July–September 1840), Britain, Austria, Prussia, and Russia jointly issued an ultimatum, offering Mehmed Ali staged options, depending on how quickly he complied. Now backed by France, he did not comply. At that, a joint British-Austrian-Ottoman force defeated the Egyptians and forced them back.

In 1841, Abdülmecid issued a decree naming Mehmed Ali governor of Egypt for life, with hereditary succession for his male descendants. However, he had to reduce his army to eighteen thousand and return the Ottoman fleet. Egypt's obligation of annual tribute payments to Istanbul continued. All Ottoman laws and treaties were binding on Egypt. To the extent that the 1838 commercial treaty and the 1839 Gülhane decree reformed Ottoman domestic law along European lines, in international law the 1840 Convention of London delivered the reward of great power support: these three documents combined symbolically to resite the Ottoman Empire in European public law, domestic and international. The last and biggest warlord, Mehmed Ali, had won often during his career. Now the sultan's men—not Husrev but the young diplomats—had outsmarted him. Forced to choose, the European powers picked Istanbul over Cairo, partly because Ottoman diplomats outmaneuvered Mehmed Ali in aligning Ottoman and European interests.

Much has been written about whether Cairo or Istanbul led in reform during the Mehmed Ali period. Between 1807 and 1826, Mehmed Ali led by default. He achieved centralized control over Egypt much more quickly and thoroughly than Mahmud could have done over his far-flung dominions. However, even Mehmed Ali did not solve his military recruitment problems before 1822, a bare four years before Mahmud's destruction of the Janissaries opened the way for rapid military reform in Istanbul. Mehmed Ali's forces, it also appears, were good only by comparison with those they faced. Even at Nizib, the Egyptians did not win because they had a great army. Two Egyptian battalions went over to the Ottomans on the day of the battle; afterward, victorious Egyptian soldiers joined defeated Ottomans in fleeing the battlefield. What the Egyptians did have was unity of command under Ibrahim Paşa as opposed to the factional conflict among the Ottoman commanders. Mehmed Ali also used well-qualified Europeans as commanders, notably the former Napoleonic officer Colonel Sèves who, as Süleyman Paşa, was second in command after Ibrahim in the 1830s.[60] Mehmed Ali's rootlessness in Egypt and ability to ignore Egyptians' feelings made promoting foreigners possible. The Istanbul government used foreigners as military advisers but resisted allowing them to command. In the service of the leading Islamic sovereign of the age, almost the only way around this resistance was to convert to Islam and enter Ottoman service fully.[61] The Ottoman sultans and their ruling elites lacked neither roots nor legitimate claims to authority. By expressing those claims and coupling them with promises of reform, the Gülhane decree helped turn Syrian opinion against the Egyptian occupation in 1839 and motivate Ottomans in Egyptian service to return to Istanbul. In the long run, especially when Ibrahim died within a few months of his father, Mehmed Ali's descendants and their elites could not show the continuity in leadership and policy that Selim and Mahmud's new elites provided in Istanbul.

THE ECONOMY

The Ottoman economy went through one of its worst periods between 1770 and 1840.[62] Adjusted for inflation, government expenditures may have tripled under Selim and Mahmud. The government could not cope without reorganizing and centralizing its finances. Still the effects of crisis were felt at all levels of the economy, and Mahmud II carried out the most drastic coinage debasements in Ottoman history. As Ottomans tested the limits of their options in economic policy, from state enterprise to free trade, Mehmed Ali's economic policies provided an alternative case study of what Ottoman methods could accomplish in a different environment.

STATE AND ECONOMY

The Ottoman economy operated historically on principles different from those of European capitalism. Economic historians who could not identify those principles interpreted Ottoman economic history in terms of failure to match European performance. Nationalist historians of post-Ottoman successor states also used the Ottomans as scapegoats to explain their countries' backwardness. In contrast, recent studies make it possible to understand the Ottoman economy in its own terms. There was not one economic "rise" or "decline" in late Ottoman history but many of them. Some of them bore the character of "creative destruction," as in the eventual decline of guild-dominated forms of production.[63] Others amounted to "portfolio rearrangement," as investment shifted out of sectors that could not compete into ones that could.

Ottoman practice ascribed to the state extensive powers of command over the economy. In practice, those powers were exercised selectively. Historical Ottoman economic policy has been summed up under three headings: *provisionism, fiscalism,* and *traditionalism.*[64] Provisionism (*iaşe*) amounts to maximizing the supply of goods to prevent scarcity. More concerned with the supply of goods than of money, provisionism encouraged imports and might restrict or prohibit exports. Counterindicated if the focus is on the balance of trade, provisionism makes sense in an environment of scarcity. Earlier Islamic and pre-Islamic rulers used the policy to turn capitals in arid regions into economic centers. Fiscalism, in turn, amounts to maximizing revenue flows into the treasury and, if necessary, cutting expenditures to maintain treasury balances. Not merely an economic practice, traditionalism means taking past practice as normative. As one legal text put it, "the old is that which no one remembers its beginning."[65] Concerned about stability not systematization, Ottoman statesmen looked to the past until the catastrophic acceleration of change shifted the attention of Selim III and his advisers toward rationalization and future-oriented planning.

As the reform era opened, provisionism, fiscalism, and traditionalism lingered in Ottoman economic policy. Domestically, decentralization and the small size of government, particularly in the scribal service that kept financial records, conditioned the implementation of these principles. The empire had not one economy but many regional ones. Even the monetary system was not unified empirewide. With few financial officials, the government could not collect most taxes directly. Inasmuch as customs duties and taxes on trade were comparatively easy to collect by establishing control points in ports and other centers, such duties formed a large part of cash revenue. Like many premodern states, the Ottomans collected customs duties on foreign and domestic trade. The last customs houses were not abolished until 1874 in interior towns, and not until after 1900 in the centers of the domestic coastal trade among Ottoman ports. By adding new taxes or opening new collection points, the government adjusted the internal customs system in response to revenue needs or changes in centers of production and trade.[66]

Externally, provisionism shaped Ottoman policy on international trade, which was governed by "covenants" (*ahidname*) that the Ottomans granted to foreign powers. Europeans called these covenants "capitulations" because they were divided into "headings" (*capitulum* in Latin), not because anyone had surrendered.[67] However, as Europeans sought to promote exports to improve their trade balances, the encouragement that Ottoman provisionism gave to imports did imply an economic advantage for Europeans. As the Ottomans' military fortunes weakened, European powers also pressed to revise the capitulations in their favor. The 1774 Treaty of Küçük Kaynarca was a watershed in that it forced the Ottomans for the first time to grant a foreign power trading privileges unwillingly. The 1838 Ottoman-British treaty marked another milestone in its free-trade provisions. Over time, problems also grew up around customs duties, collected at different rates from Muslims, non-Muslim subjects, and foreigners. Originally favoring Muslims, the terms were gradually changed to favor foreigners. Because diplomatic and consular interpreters were allowed to share in those privileges, a lucrative trade in translators' warrants (*berat*) grew up. Such abuses enabled vast numbers of Ottoman non-Muslims to become subjects of foreign rulers and evade many Ottoman taxes. All these abuses could not be blamed on provisionism, but the capitulations greatly eroded Ottoman economic sovereignty.

By the time that happened, the old practice of tax-farming (*iltizam*) had also evolved into life-term tax-farms (*malikâne*, 1695). The malikâne required from the contractor not only large annual payments out of receipts but also an advance payment (*muaccele*) and chancery fees, new revenues for the treasury. The new system was expected to benefit all parties, not least the taxpayers, by eliminating the incentives that short-term tax-farms gave tax-farmers to ruin the countryside through reckless exploitation. Some malikâne contractors did invest in improving the production processes that they taxed. More typically, their interests were those of tax collectors, not entrepreneurs. The shift to life-term tax-farming implied limited expectations, at best, of future growth in the value of those revenues. Significantly, a study of specific farmed revenues from 1750 to 1800 shows an increase of 178 percent in revenues from foreign trade, compared to an increase of only 14 percent in the revenues from domestic manufactures.[68]

Growth or no growth, the malikane system had the effect of increasing the number of people who invested in state finance. The malikane contractor could sell his contract to others or subcontract it to an agent; a son could also inherit a malikane by paying fees. Members of the taxpaying subject classes also began to invest in malikanes, singly or in groups. A significant feature of Ottoman fiscal practice through the reign of Mahmud II, the malikane system created new problems but also increased the numbers of people with vested interests in the Ottoman system.

In 1775, the treasury devised a new instrument by dividing specific revenues into "shares" (esham), somewhat like government bonds, and selling them to individuals in return for an advance payment (muaccele) equal to several years of the revenue that the "share" would bring to the investor for life. Adopted to help finance the indemnity owed to Russia under the Treaty of Küçük Kaynarca, esham were sold to all Ottoman subjects. Requiring less investment capital than the malikanes, esham remained on the market until the 1860s, having evolved by then into modern government bonds. As of the 1830s, up to ten thousand people held esham.

The interaction between the state's economic powers of command and its economic principles produced especially important consequences in wartime. Just as the government intervened in peacetime to assure the supply of consumer goods to Istanbul and to set prices (narh), it intervened to procure essentials for war at prices below market or even below production costs. Known as "state purchase" (miri mübayaa), this practice amounted to a war tax on critical production sectors. The government might set up purchase monopolies on specific goods. It also created state enterprises to produce essentials like gunpowder and sailcloth (and sometimes luxuries for the court); these too operated as monopolies. Among other consequences of this policy, monopolies provided incentives for smugglers.[69]

Whatever the effects of provisionism and fiscalism under favorable circumstances, applied in wartime, these methods kept war from stimulating production, as it can in a free market. State purchase below market prices, and especially below production costs, created disincentives to produce.[70] Defeat magnified the negative economic consequences. As a result, after trending upward to the 1760s, the Ottoman economy endured unprecedented war-induced disruptions from the 1770s until the 1840s. Internal borrowing through the sale of esham was one response to the crisis. In the 1770s and 1780s, notables and rich merchants were called on to provide interest-free loans to the government and to equip military units at their own expense. Now, too, not only the property of the sultan's official slaves but also that of rich men outside the ruling class was subjected to expropriation (*musadere*).

With no remaining alternative, Mahmud II carried out the severest monetary debasements in Ottoman history.[71] The number of Ottoman silver kuruş required to equal a British pound fell from 19 in 1808 to 104 in 1839. The bad consequences of monetary depreciation are many, and they are obvious as concerns price inflation; but the government also reaped some benefits. It received seigniorage revenue, that is, the profit from producing a nominally larger amount of coinage from the same amount of specie. These revenues could be enhanced by forbidding sale of gold and silver on the market and requiring those metals to be delivered to the mint below market price. For a government with large deficits, debasement also had benefits, including that of lowering the real value of the 400 million kuruş indemnity imposed on the Ottomans after the 1828 Ottoman-Russian war. Contemporaries considered the debasements of 1828–1831 a great success. Such perhaps they were amid the economic crises of 1770–1840.

AGRICULTURE

Far below the lofty heights of state finance, at the grassroots level Ottoman populations were still about 80 percent nonurban, and agriculture and pastoralism dominated the economy. Amid the diversity of the Ottoman lands and peoples, some unifying themes stand out. The Ottoman lands straddled the fortieth degree of North latitude. Ankara sits on it, and most of the world's other most productive agricultural regions are located along it. The precipitation patterns of the empire's Adriatic, Aegean, eastern Mediterranean, and lower Black Sea coastal lands were all of the Mediterranean type, characterized by rainy winters and dry summers. The climate of the interior regions was cooler and wetter in the Balkans, steppelike in Anatolia and parts of Syria and Iraq, and desertic in Arabia and inland North Africa. Wheat-based agriculture, invented in southeastern Anatolia and northern Syria in prehistoric times, remained basic to the agrarian economy and culinary culture of the region.[72] Even the steppelike zones of the empire supported extensive agriculture. Of the great river systems that supported ancient civilizations, the entire course of the Tigris and Euphrates and much of the Nile's course lay within Ottoman frontiers. In zones too arid for agriculture, pastoralists sustained a rich production of sheep, goats, horses, and camels. Except for desert zones that could not be irrigated, however, the Ottoman state was an agrarian empire.

For the most part, the coastal zones belonged to the Mediterranean world of the grain, the grape, and the olive—Braudel's "eternal trinity" of Mediterranean crops.[73] The processed, value-added forms of those crops—flour and pasta, raisins and wine, olive oil and the soap made from it—were among the empire's most distinctive manufactures. The seasonal colors of Mediterranean landscapes—springtime green, summertime yellow-brown accented with the blackish green of the cypresses and the gray-green of the olive trees—constituted the distinctive palette of Mediterranean landscapes. The ancillary crops included products—notably sesame and anise—that further defined the region's culinary culture, adding most of Ottoman territory to the honor roll of Mediterranean lands with anise-flavored strong drink (anís in Spain, pastis in France, ouzo in Greece, rakı in Turkey, arak in the Arab lands).

Variations across space and time diversified the agrarian scene. Local agricultural variations added distinctive products like the hazelnuts of Anatolia's Black Sea coast, the tobacco of Bulgaria or Syria, figs and raisins in the Aegean region, and the ecologically privileged Marmara region's fruits and flowers, which in both size and quality are truly fit for a sultan. From the southern coast of Turkey southward, hot-weather crops took over, including dates and cotton. Over time, fluctuations in climate and in economic incentives greatly altered the agrarian scene, as in the case of Mehmed Ali's introduction of long-staple cotton in Egypt or the rise and decline of silk production in nineteenth-century Lebanon. The crops of Braudel's "eternal trinity" and the local specialties formed a backdrop against which other, often higher-valued crops came and went.[74]

Rich in products, the Ottoman agrarian economy entered the modern era in a depressed state by later standards. Population densities were low enough that empty land was common in many places. In Anatolia, agricultural production could still be increased by extending the area under cultivation as late as the 1950s. In a part of the world where desert, steppe, and arable land adjoined and pastoral nomads always lived, more of the landscape was given over to livestock grazing than would probably have been the case if population densities had been higher. Transhumant stock raising, based on migration between summer and winter pastures, occurred in the Balkans as well as in the Asian provinces. In the Balkans, too, stock raising was the primary occupation of certain nomadic tribes, not to speak of others who took an economic interest in it. Ottoman crop yields were also low by modern standards. Partly because parts of the empire had been subject to cultivation and livestock raising since prehistoric times, environmental degradation was far advanced in many regions. Around some villages in Anatolia, scarcely any plant over a meter high was to be seen.[75]

Land tenure in Ottoman lands was predominantly a matter of small holdings. The Ottoman agrarian ideal, rooted in Byzantine and Roman practice, was that of the *çift-hane,* the small peasant household (*hane*) with the amount of land that one man could cultivate with a yoke (*çift*) of oxen. In traditional Ottoman thinking, the çift-hane was the basic unit of production, reproduction, and taxation. Large estate formation was possible and occurred in some places, often by reclamation of unused, "dead" (*mevat*) land. However, low population densities usually made it difficult to concentrate the labor needed to exploit such estates effectively. In Anatolia around 1840, over 80 percent of the cultivated land was held in farms of 8 hectares or less, which one family could cultivate with its own labor.[76]

If the çift-hane was the Ottomans' ideal unit of agrarian production, their ideal of agrarian land tenure was a system of divided ownership in which the ruler owned the land, peasants owned use rights, and intermediaries had revenue collection rights. Land tenure was regulated by the sharia as modified—and restricted—by Ottoman kanun.[77] The Ottomans recognized various categories of ownership. These included private property (*mülk,* Arabic *milk*), lands held in common, wastelands (*mevat*), property deeded in perpetuity to support a charitable purpose (*waqf*), and state land (*miri*).

Kanun intervened in land tenure most fundamentally by defining virtually all arable land as miri, state-owned. The system of divided ownership protected the peasants' rights to cultivate their miri fields, as long as they paid the "tenth" (*öşür,* Arabic *'ushr*) and any other required taxes and did not leave the land uncultivated for more than three years; and they owned their houses, gardens, vineyards, and orchards outright (*mülk*). Although some Islamic jurists disputed the point, kanun excluded miri land from the sharia's provisions on sale and inheritance. Here, the emphasis in state policy on protecting the family farm as a viable production unit proved significant. Instead of dividing the property into the shares prescribed for different heirs under the sharia, kanun provided that miri land should pass to the son; in the absence of a son, the daughter or widow inherited before remoter male relatives.

The intermediaries, in this period normally tax-farmers, to whom Ottoman practice assigned revenue collection rights added another level to the system of divided ownership. Although tax-farmers as such were only contractors for the state, tax-farmers with local roots might acquire extensive power by combining tax collecting with money-lending or advance purchasing of crops by means of *selem* (Arabic, *salam*) contracts.[78] In that sense, if large plantationlike estates with exploited labor were not common in Ottoman lands, economic dependency networks—virtual plantations—that enriched notables at the peasants' expense were.

A *provincial notable's mansion*, Alaşehir, Anatolia. The caption identifies the
proprietor as a *müsellim* (properly *mütesellim*), a revenue-collector for a provincial
governor-general (vali) or governor (*mutasarrıf*). (From Walsh, *Constantinople*,
2:opp. p. 92, pl. by Thomas Allom.)

The sultan on top, the tax collectors in between, the peasants below—for
good or ill, the system of divided possession worked well enough that peasants
spoke of "selling" or "inheriting" their land. If informed about these transactions at all, conscientious court clerks recorded them with such terms as "transfer" (*intikal*) rather than sale. The Ottoman system of land tenure had not
prevented a market in land from developing. The point demonstrates that the
miri tenure secured peasants' ownership of use rights to their fields. Holding
the fields as state land rather than private property did not in itself disadvantage
peasants. However, poor peasants were at a disadvantage in the land market
compared to those who had capital. Vulnerable as well to drought, disease,
famine, and all the accidents of a premodern agrarian economy, Ottoman peasants had plenty to complain about. Their relations with government agents or
tax collectors were generally strained. Mahmud II's attacks on the warlords and
on brigandage improved rural security, and that stimulated production. By the
mid-1830s, peasant revolts were still common to the point of being expected in
some places; in other places, local rebellions by then had ceased.[79]

MANUFACTURES

The story of Ottoman manufactures under Selim and Mahmud is partly one of guilds and partly one of other types of enterprise, organized by either the state or private initiative.[80]

Although the adoption of free trade later shifted the ground under them, the Ottoman guilds (*esnaf*) reached the high point of their privileges and organizational elaboration in the late 1700s. Ottoman guilds were known for extreme specialization, with different stages in production of the same commodity assigned to different guilds. In a large city like Istanbul, a large guild might also subdivide by neighborhood, apparently to maintain the intimacy of small-scale, face-to-face relations. Relations among guilds were usually weak, although a given city's construction guilds—numbering up to forty—would be under the supervision of a chief architect (*mimar başı, mimar ağa*), and those in other trades would have a weak link to a şeyh (*şeyh-i seb'a, ahi baba*). The kadı supervised relations among guilds and mediated between them and the government. One reason why the guilds needed to be limited in size was that they solved most disputes internally, with no sanctions except warning or appeal to the kadı. Each guild had officers, headed by the *kethüda* (steward) and his assistant, the *yiğitbaşı* ("chief of the young men"). Guilds were often religiously mixed.

Nothing expressed Ottoman solidarism and egalitarianism better than the guilds. With controlled prices (*narh*) on many consumer goods, interest rates of 15 or 20 percent, and serious inflation in this period, their profit margins were supposed to be limited to 10 percent. That limit effectively precluded capital formation through the guilds. Still, the guilds maintained the supply and quality of consumer goods. They also served as solidarity groups to provide mutual aid, sociability, and entertainment for their members.

Along with their egalitarian traits, however, the guilds also had an important part in the proliferation of vested interests. Around 1750, the Istanbul guilds won government approval to create a licensing system for the various crafts and small trades. The number of "slots" (*gedik*) or licenses in each craft became fixed under Mahmud II. Coupled with virtual hereditarization of recruitment, the gedik system marked a trend toward monopolistic privilege for the guilds. Their ties to the state became tighter, too. Janissaries had long since taken up trades and merged with the guilds. By the mid-1700s some tens of thousands of so-called Janissaries, few of them real soldiers, were stationed around the empire.[81] The government took fiscal advantage of this situation by appointing lower-ranking members of the military to paid positions in the private economy, leaving their salaries forfeit to the treasury.[82] Among the posts so used were the guild offices of the steward (*kethüda*) and his assistant (*yiğitbaşı*). The guild had to pay these appointees and probably also one of its members who actually knew how to run the organization; in return, the guild gained a useful official link. The government further expanded its control by providing the physical capital, either directly or indirectly, through investments by malikâne contractors or charitable foundations (*evkaf*), for production facilities that the guilds could not afford to build. The increasing integration of the Janissaries and the guilds did nothing to diminish the guilds' monopolistic tendencies, and that limited their potential to develop modern forms of production. The level of control that major cities' guilds exercised could not be achieved everywhere, however. That fact left openings for innovation.

Efforts to innovate in manufacturing included both state enterprises and private undertakings in new sites. In the 1700s, partly to reduce imports, a number of state enterprises were founded, mostly to produce textiles and munitions for the military.[83] The history of these enterprises became case studies in what could be accomplished under fiscalist and provisionist assumptions. Guildlike traits also appeared in these enterprises. Even something as strategically significant as the powderworks (*baruthane*) would have only fifty or a hundred workers in a workshop. Modern attempts at import-substitution industrialization, including that of the Turkish republic in the 1930s, have always assumed tariff protection for the emergent industries. Ottoman statesmen, thinking in provisionist terms, never considered this option, although in some ways their policies could benefit Ottoman manufactures. Late in the eighteenth century, as foreign demand for Ottoman raw materials grew, provisionist restrictions on olive oil exports enabled Cretan soap works to survive and continue exporting. However, the only state enterprise that appears to have succeeded lastingly was the sailcloth factory (1709), which supplied the navy. Still operating as late as 1826, this became the Ottomans' first vertically integrated textile operation. To support military reform, Mahmud II relied on state enterprises to produces fezes, cloth for uniforms, ordnance, sabers, powder, and muskets.

Efforts to escape both the tax collector and the guilds' restrictions led, meanwhile, to the development of protoindustry in some provincial towns. The government tried to prohibit such efforts, penalizing tax evasion with heavy fines, destroying workshops, even condemning workers to the galleys.[84] However, the growing demand for raw materials exports stimulated their production, and export earnings provided capital. A natural next step was to invest these earnings in processing some of these commodities. Not directed only at the domestic markets, the rural protoindustries expanded with their export potentials. For example, the workshops in and around the Anatolian town of Tokat, still worth a visit to observe their dyeing and printing of cotton textiles, exported as far as Poland and Russia before the 1768 war, after which Russian expansion and protectionism closed that market. Accounting for more of the value of individuals' personal effects than they would today, textiles were so important in the marketplace that in the Arab provinces, a merchant (*tajir*) without further qualification *was* a cloth merchant.[85]

Rural protoindustry developed particularly vigorously in Ottoman Bulgaria.[86] One factor conducive to such initiatives was population density that outstripped the supply of cultivable land. Among low average Ottoman population densities, surpluses could occur locally, especially in hilly or mountainous environments. Peasants often reacted to the spread of warlordism and rural brigandage by retreating into the hills. Some Balkan towns had already become known for their manufactures before 1800, exporting their wares overland to Austria. After Mahmud II's attacks on the warlords and brigands and his destruction of the urban guilds' Janissary allies, the stage was set for the Bulgarian hill towns to expand production vigorously from 1840 through at least the 1870s, and Bulgarian woolens went on to dominate the Ottoman market. The strengthening of Ottoman institutions enabled the economy to flourish; in that sense the modern "renaissance" of the Bulgarians and other Balkan peoples—far from occurring despite Ottoman policy—was facilitated by Ottoman reinvigoration.

MEHMED ALI'S ECONOMIC POLICY

In Egypt, Mehmed Ali's economic policy tied together economic and military history in a test case of what Ottoman methods could accomplish under conditions different from those confronting the Istanbul government. The military competition between Cairo and Istanbul was necessarily an economic competition, which Mehmed Ali approached like the Ottoman that he was. Whatever new ideas he had, his economic policies conformed to Ottoman norms of provisionism and fiscalism—a fact not fully registered in the literature on Egypt in this period. By pushing these policies to the extreme, he subjected himself to their self-defeating consequences. Before that happened, the compactness of the Nile Valley and Delta enabled him to succeed in controlling Egypt's economy with a thoroughness that Mahmud II could only envy.

Mehmed Ali's success in abolishing tax-farming by 1813–1814, something the Ottoman government never managed, indicates the difference in scale between centralizing rule over Egypt, on the one hand, and over the Ottoman Empire, on the other. The methods he used to reach this point were far from new: land survey and aggressive examination of titles, which led to the reclassification of much land claimed for charitable foundations as miri and thus taxable. His export monopolies have been compared to those of other Ottoman warlords. The model for all of them was Ottoman provisionism and fiscalism, particularly the system of government purchase (*miri mübayaa*), which he used to monopolize Egypt's agricultural exports. Mehmed Ali went further than others, "establishing state control of production and internal distribution in addition to the export monopoly."[87] His state purchase monopoly not only paid arbitrary prices for the crops but paid even those prices in promissory notes that the peasants could only redeem at the end of the year, if they held more in notes than they owed in taxes. Particularly to supply uniforms and equipment for his new army, he established some thirty-odd factories and a putting-out system of women spinners. Predictably, these were state enterprises, operated as monopolies, and there were constant problems with late deliveries and defective goods. He has at times naively been credited with an "industrial revolution" in Egypt, as if such a thing were possible with seven or eight steam engines. More realistically, he has been criticized for pioneering a persistent weakness of subsequent Middle Eastern industrialization efforts. This is the reliance on "turnkey" projects, a policy based on the implicit assumption that a government could hire foreign experts to build a plant and turn it over, with the key in the door, for that government to operate, without thought to the infrastructure on which such enterprises depend. In Mehmed Ali's case, the ethnic exclusivism of his regime not only promoted this dependence on foreigners but also degraded, rather than developed, the indigenous Egyptian workforce.

Mehmed Ali's ambition is beyond doubt, and his recognition of Egypt's advantage as a supplier of long-staple cotton to the international market shows his alertness to new opportunities. Yet by the 1820s, his policies showed the vicious cycle effects of an Ottoman-style war economy. The peasantry was subjected to demands for taxes, forced labor, and military service. In a monopoly that combined sale of crops at forced prices and aggressive tax collection, Mehmed Ali's role as Egypt's "sole merchant" deprived the peasantry of both income and incentive. In constant money terms, the price he paid for cotton barely changed from 1822 to 1838. As early as the 1830s, some of his factories were described as scenes of rust and ruin.[88] Although his Ottoman eyeglasses may have kept him from seeing it, Mehmed Ali's problem was that his methods could yield nothing but depressed domestic conditions and dependent integration into the world economy. Unless he could control the world-market price for his exports, his export monopoly could only yield the revenues to support his military and industrial projects by depressing the prices he paid to his own subjects and lowering their purchasing power. Military expansion might give him access to new resources, such as Syrian timber for his navy, but it could not eliminate the vicious cycles from his policy. However well traditional economic policies had worked in the past, their contradictions were likely to become increasingly exposed with tightening integration into a world economy that operated by different rules.

Istanbul policy makers of the 1830s were no different from Mehmed Ali in their economic assumptions. Yet not being in a position to achieve the degree of central control that he did, they could not push their policy preferences as far as he did, and they were better able to seize the risk-fraught opportunity to realign Ottoman policy with Europe's new free-trade liberalism through the 1838 commercial treaty. At least, Mustafa Reşid Paşa and his small band of European-experienced diplomats dared do this so as to undermine Mehmed Ali economically and reassert Istanbul's power to make policy for the whole empire, Egypt included.

OTTOMAN SOCIETY AT THE DAWN OF THE MODERN ERA

The state of Ottoman society and economy around 1800 reveals a great deal about why the turn toward centralization and defensive modernization got off to a slow start. The peoples of the vast empire were prodigal in their diversity. Religion was still the main indicator in their self-identification. Signs of ethnic identification in the Balkans added to the picture of extreme variegation. At the same time, population densities remained very low by modern standards. As a result, the empire historically relied on paradoxically small numbers of men to govern its vast domains. As of 1685, fourteen thousand Janissaries garrisoned thirty-six Arab cities. As of 1770–1790, the Ottoman scribal service still consisted of only fifteen hundred to two thousand men. That is the same branch of service that Mahmud II expanded into his civil service and began appointing to local administrative posts. When Mahmud II's new army faced its first test in the war of 1828–1829, his regulars (*asakir-i mansure*), even supplemented with irregulars and provincial forces, faced Russian forces nominally three times more numerous; and the Ottomans had to fight the Russians in both the Balkans and the Caucasus.[89] The social and demographic challenges confronting Ottoman reformers were complex indeed.

OTTOMAN DEMOGRAPHICS

Reliable population statistics do not exist for this period. Based on records on payment of the *cizye*, the tax required from non-Muslim male subjects, the non-Muslim population of the Ottoman Balkans in 1815 has been estimated at

5.5 million, up from 4 million a century before.[90] The government carried out a census of males in the Balkans and Anatolia in 1831. However, the count was not thorough everywhere; in some districts, the officials did not visit all towns and villages. Doubling figures to account for females, the resulting total of 7.2 million (about 2.6 million in the Balkans and 3.6 in Anatolia) remains low. Early nineteenth-century estimates of total Ottoman population vary between 14 and 23 million, probably underestimating the total by 10–12 million. High-ranging figures from 1844 to 1856 place the total Ottoman population at 35.4 million, of which 15.5 million inhabited the Balkans, 10.7 million Anatolia, 5.4 million the Arab lands of southwest Asia, and 3.8 million Ottoman North Africa (Egypt, Libya, Tunisia). The period 1789–1839 appears to have been one of population growth in Anatolia and especially the Balkans. By 1839, estimated population densities appear to have been about 18 people per square kilometer in Anatolia, more in the Balkans.

Within these numbers, the most salient differences to contemporaries would have been religious. Out of their total of 35.4 million, the figures of 1844–1856 show 21 million (59 percent) Muslim, 13 million (37 percent) Greek Orthodox, 0.9 million Catholic, 0.2 million Jewish, and 0.3 million others; these figures omit Armenian Christians except for those in the Catholic category. The size of the non-Muslim categories had to be taken into account in Ottoman policy, as seen in the Gülhane decree of 1839. Even in the Balkans, however, the Muslim population accounted for about 35 percent of the total in the early nineteenth century, 43 percent after 1878, and 51 percent just before the Balkan Wars (1912–1913). In Anatolia and the Arab lands, Muslims always formed the majority, although non-Muslims formed significant percentages and sometimes local majorities. The gradual increase in the Muslim proportion as Ottoman borders receded made the Ottoman Empire into a predominantly Muslim state, especially after 1878.[91]

A number of demographic patterns shaped the population estimated by these conflicting figures. Population densities were highest in the Balkans and diminished as one progressed southward around the eastern Mediterranean toward Africa. Differences in climate and aridity largely governed both this pattern and its localized exceptions, such as the denser population of Mount Lebanon. By the later 1800s, territorial losses would shift the empire's demographic center toward the southeast. Even though the Middle East of the early 1800s was one of the world's most urbanized regions and had been for millennia, the population was still around 80 percent nonurban. As of the 1830s, among cities, Istanbul had 375,000 residents; Cairo about 260,000; Edirne, Izmir, Aleppo, and possibly Damascus, Baghdad, and Tunis around 100,000 apiece; and Salonica, the major port city in the Ottoman Balkans, perhaps 60,000.[92]

A number of factors constrained population growth. Contemporaries agreed, perhaps wishfully, that non-Muslim birthrates were higher and death rates lower than those of Muslims. Inasmuch as Muslims were liable to military service and non-Muslims were not, reports of Muslim common folk seeking ways to reduce their birthrate come from both Egypt and central Ottoman lands; both Cairo and Istanbul attempted to discourage abortion.[93] Birthrates were high by present-day standards, with Anatolian Muslim women who survived their reproductive years having an average of six children. However, mortality rates were also high and life expectancies short. Half of the children born in Anatolia did not live long enough to have children of their own. Average life expectancy probably did not exceed thirty-five anywhere in Anatolia, although those who reached the age of five would probably survive to forty-five or fifty. Under such conditions, while extended, multigenerational households existed, that ideal was difficult to perpetuate; and many who experienced it at all did so for only part of their lifespan.

Disease, war, and famine played their historical roles in creating this demographic profile. Bubonic plague, endemic since the fourteenth century, recurred across the Asian and European provinces into the mid-nineteenth century. Asiatic cholera entered the Ottoman lands via Russia, first appearing in Iraq in 1821. Malaria, too, was widespread in certain localities. Such diseases caused epidemics that might kill tens of thousands at a time. The annual pilgrimage to Mecca, bringing together thousands from all over the Islamic world, also helped spread disease. Mehmed Ali began to establish quarantines in Alexandria and other ports by 1830; quarantines also protected the pilgrimage by midcentury. Mehmed Ali organized vaccination campaigns against smallpox, exciting peasants' fears that this was a way to mark their children for conscription. However, techniques for inoculation against this disease had been known for centuries across the empire, indeed across Asia. The health that concerned either Mehmed Ali or Mahmud II was not that of the general populace but that of their troops.

War aggravated Ottoman demographic weakness. The empire was at war during nearly half the years between 1800 and 1918.[94] Frequently the wars were fought on Ottoman territory. In Mahmud II's reign, that included the Greek Revolution, the Russian war of 1828–1829, and two wars with Mehmed Ali in the 1830s. Countless men were taken away from their farms to fight, and fields were devastated. Even in peacetime, climatic variations, diseases of animals, and plant pests easily disrupted an agrarian economy of low productivity by modern standards.

THE OTTOMAN SOCIAL FABRIC

The empire's complex populations coexisted in a set of historically evolved relationships that accelerating change and external threats were bound to disrupt. Greek independence and Serbian autonomy signaled the start of a reconfiguration that would ultimately shatter the equilibria and relationships that had held the multinational Islamic empire together. By the end of the empire, the resulting conflicts and tensions became so acute and chronic that from a Turkish point of view, the collapse of the multinational empire and its replacement by a Turkish national state appeared to solve these issues by turning unmanageable internal problems into manageable diplomatic questions. As of 1839, any such resolution was still nearly a century off. Inasmuch as ethnic conflict was only beginning before 1839, an examination of historical Ottoman social norms provides a basis for the assessment of later disruptions in those patterns.

The empire's Islamic character was a fact of paramount salience for Ottoman subjects of all religions. Ottoman ruling institutions were defined and legitimated in preeminently Islamic terms; Islamic law was the basis of Ottoman law; Islamic appeals motivated Ottoman soldiers. Islamic norms and practices were embodied in daily life, and they established uniformities across the empire and the entire Islamic world. The five daily calls to prayer and the temporal rhythms that grew up around them, the religious observances and holidays prescribed in the religious calendar, standards of gender relations and personal ethics, the countless lifeways that conformed to the custom (*sunna*) of the Prophet Muhammad were among the many features that identified Ottoman society as Islamic. Islamic law, as already noted, also accommodated Jews and Christians as "peoples of the book" entitled to live under the protection of the Muslim state. Living and flourishing much of the time under this system, the empire's non-Muslim subjects tended to assimilate Islamic and Ottoman lifeways in many respects. The opposite was also true. For example, non-Muslim customs, saints and shrines became syncretic parts of Muslim popular religion, all the more in that Muslim and non-Muslim often lived in the same neighborhoods, worked in the same guilds, or formed political or commercial alliances across religious lines.[95]

Ideas about the definition of non-Muslim communities evolved significantly during Ottoman times. While to Muslims unbelief in a sense is all one, non-Muslims' differences were also recognized. Evidence from Aleppo suggests that in the seventeenth century Christians were designated generically as one *millet* (*milla* in Arabic), as in *millet-i Nasara*, the "religious community of Christians." The term for sectarian distinctions among Christians was *taife* (*ta'ifa* in

Arabic), "group" or "party," although this distinction was not systematic.[96] In the eighteenth century, as Catholic missionaries began to gain converts, competition among Christian communities intensified. In Istanbul, the patriarchs of both the Greek Orthodox and the Armenian Gregorian churches asserted claims to paramountcy over the other sees of their communions, claims that the Ottoman authorities backed in order to counteract foreign influence. Gradually additional Christian denominations began to gain recognition as millets in their own right. By the 1820s, former members of Eastern churches who had united with Rome competed to have millet status accorded to their new uniate churches, Armenian Catholic, Greek Catholic, and so on. Ultimately, there was not one Christian community (*millet-i Nasara*) but numerous sectarian ones. The proliferation of religious difference paralleled and often crosscut the politicization of ethnic difference, particularly in the Balkans. Even among Muslims, moreover, the meaning of millet began to change from "religious community" to "nation" in the sense of an ethnic group; in the Gülhane decree, for example, the term *millet* appears, but the intended meaning is not entirely clear. Non-Muslim religious communities competed in advancing "historical" claims to privilege, which misled many historians into misidentifying the late Ottoman "millet system" as a "traditional" constituent of Ottoman society. European powers further politicized religious difference by competing to claim protection over specific religious communities, as the Russians did after 1774. Protestant and Catholic missionaries competed, too. Religious difference had always existed in the Islamic world, but the politicization of sectarian difference was as modern as the politicization of ethnicity.

In thinking about Ottoman society as of 1800, classificatory terms like *taife* are revelatory far beyond the realm of interfaith relations. Strongly imprinted on Ottoman social relations were emphases on both egalitarianism and the hierarchical differentiation of groups and categories. However paradoxical that may seem, in a sense the Ottomans' historical deference to custom is enough to explain it. As noted, both equality and hierarchy are rooted in Islam and Islamic law. The Kur'an itself includes an egalitarian discourse in its exhortations to the faithful, male and female. At the same time, law and scripture acknowledge specific status differences—Muslim and non-Muslim, male and female, free and slave—and acknowledge that some are exalted above others. Ideas of patriarchal kinship relations, dating back to remote tribal pasts, reinforced hierarchies of age and gender within community. So did certain voluntary associational forms, of which the most widespread among Ottoman Muslims were the *derviş* orders and the guilds. Especially in Anatolia, these shared much of their histories, organizational forms, and values. They also combined fraternal equality with the hierarchies of apprentice, journeyman, and master in the guilds, or disciple, deputy, and şeyh in the dervish orders.

Egalitarian but not individualistic, Ottoman society constituted a world of communities and collectivities, anticipating the corporatism of the later Turkish republic. In the seventeenth and eighteenth centuries, the proliferation of vested interests had been one of the chief vectors of decentralization, with loss of a sense of common interest as its price. Janissary regiments, factions formed around them, the castelike ulema elite, the restless and episodically moblike medrese students, craft guilds, dervish orders, urban quarters with their religious leaders and congregations (sometimes of different religions, sometimes not), households, the factional networks that articulated elite politics around rival personalities — many social forms expressed the articulation of Ottoman society into particularist interests under the umbrella of the cosmopolitan empire.[97]

At street level, this was a world where rich and poor lived side by side, where the noncompetitive solidarities of the guilds and the piety of the holy set a tone of restraint. At the elite level, contrastingly, proximity to state power and emulation of the imperial household generated an extravagant "grandee mentality" (*ağalık ve efendilik şuuru*).[98] To the extent that those indulging in ostentation were officially slaves of the sultan, appearances were deceiving. Their wealth, like their necks, belonged to their master, who was also legally their heir. The wealth in question constituted a circulating capital that belonged to the state, manifesting the ruler's power and wealth and the advantages of serving him. The rapidity of social mobility, both upward and downward, was another way in which custom reconciled egalitarianism and hierarchy.

SUBJECTIVITY AND SOCIETY

The interest that all theorists of modernity place on individual subjectivity heightens the interest of considering the individual's place in this Ottoman combination of egalitarianism, communalism, and hierarchy. In such an environment, the only "subjects" with much autonomy were likely to be powerful rulers and interest groups. While such titans battled overhead, how did the onset of modernity affect identity formation among ordinary men and women? As fascinating as a panoramic comparison of such changes across all the empire's communities would be, here the chief focus of interest must be on Ottoman Muslims. A brief consideration of them helps define baselines against which to measure later social change.

Most Ottoman Muslims of the early 1800s had few outlets to assert their individuality. Religious norms defined much of what was expected from them. Family hierarchies of gender and age set further limits. Even the eldest siblings were authority figures within their spheres, the big sister (*abla*) and especially the big brother (*ağabey*, colloquially *abi*). Before puberty, boys and girls might be schooled together (or separately) at the neighborhood Kur'an school (*mekteb*). At puberty, girls veiled; and both sexes became subject to the Islamic norms that segregated potentially marriageable males and females. The plain Turkish word for these norms summed things up from the female point of view: *kaçgöç*, roughly meaning "run hide."

After veiling, the most fortunate girls might continue their education at schools that some women ran in their homes to teach girls the Kur'an, music, calligraphy, and embroidery. Girls spent much of their time at home learning weaving—singing songs with many verses to accustom them to the long hours at the loom—as well as sewing and needlework. An adolescent girl's essential goal was to prepare her trousseau (*çeyiz*), largely consisting of embroidered textiles.

Among peasants and pastoralists, both males and females worked from an early age. In the cities and towns, after finishing the Kur'an school, most boys were apprenticed to a trade and spent their lives in the world of craftsmen and small traders. Boys so inclined pursued further religious studies in the medrese. Other educational opportunities included tutors retained by wealthy families, activities of some religious orders, manuscript libraries, and the salons of the learned. Despite the often-cited elite disdain for commerce, guildlike assumptions about occupational life were so prevalent that apprenticeship in adolescence was also the normal way to enter government offices.[99] Not until the foundation of the modern military academies in the late 1700s and the first modern civil schools around 1840 did Ottoman Muslims have modern schools expressly designed to prepare them for other than religious careers.

Marriage occurred by arrangement among the families, for most girls in their later teenage years. In Islamic law, the relationship of husband and wife is "one of complementarity, not equality."[100] Spousal rights and obligations include important safeguards for the woman. For example, before marriage, she has the right to refuse a candidate or appoint her own agent to arrange a marriage for her; if she has been married before, she can choose her own husband. After marriage, the wife retains rights of property ownership, her husband is obligated to support her, and she has legal recourse against a husband who abuses her rights. Islamic law recognizes several forms of divorce. Men have greater freedom in divorce than women, although a woman can initiate one type of divorce (*hul*, Arabic *khul'*) or get an annulment in cases such as abandonment; divorce entails costs and legal requirements under any option. Islamic law also allowed men to have up to four wives at any one time on condition of treating them all equally; it also allowed a man to take any number of consenting slave women as concubines. Although the costs of polygyny and the competition for spouses in a society where all adults were expected to marry made monogamy the norm, having a co-wife remained Muslim Ottoman women's most commonly voiced fear. Often also monogamous, concubinage was perfectly acceptable under Islamic law, which legitimated the children if recognized by their father and automatically freed the mother at the husband's death, if he had not already freed her. The Ottoman dynasty's reproductive practice relied on concubinage for centuries. When the families observed the criteria for making an appropriate match, and when the parties respected sharia law rather than following customary practices that violated it, the durability and compatibility of arranged marriages appears to have been high—as long as the bride and groom expected nothing different. However, no point in Ottoman Muslim society was more vulnerable than marriage to disruption by change in individual self-consciousness.

After marriage, too, many challenges awaited. The state of health care limited life expectancy for all. The continuity of the multigenerational, extended households, for which the fine old houses in Ottoman cities were obviously built, had to be highly unpredictable. As important as children were, the risks of childbirth must have been a great worry. Although information is scarce about reproductive behavior, official sources complain about abortion, reportedly motivated by fear of losing sons to conscription. The risks of childbirth probably affected attitudes more than did future risks of conscription. Male physicians were allowed supervised access into the harems of elite households at least by the 1780s, but only for serious illnesses; only a century later would the imperial harem allow physicians to assist in childbirth. In this period, Ottomans relied on midwives. By one account the prospects of giving birth assisted only by an uneducated crone of a midwife led women to regard childbirth as "a catastrophe." As one wit said: "If her belly comes up to her nose, she's the mother; if her nose comes down to her belly, she's the midwife."[101] Be that as it may, a woman's reproductive, as well as her productive, capacities were the prime determinants of her status in her marital family. Likewise, her good name for moral irreproachability (*iffet ve ismet*) defined her status in the eyes of the world.

While far more could be said about the individual in society, the limited scope of individual self-expression hints at how great the consequences might be if educational opportunities beyond the neighborhood Kur'an school became more widely available. From the 1840s on, the extension of schooling for larger numbers of boys and girls into the adolescent years affected not just the level of their reading and writing skills. As these students continued their education into the years when they began to develop adult personalities, their desires about what they wanted to write and read changed. By the 1860s, outlines of revolutionary sociocultural change would appear, as modern print media emerged to serve their demand.

ISLAMIC AWAKENING

Although the lines for later cultural debates only began to be drawn in this period, the challenges of the times already led some Ottomans to seek greater knowledge of the outside world and others to reexamine the fundamental values of Islam. Before 1839, while the former trend produced significant consequences among the ruling elites, the latter trend generated the greatest Islamic awakening within late Ottoman society. This movement quickly found a broad following in both center and periphery; it still exerts great influence.

Its founder, Shaykh Khalid (Mevlana Halid in Turkish, 1776–1827) emerged out of Ottoman Kurdistan to found a reform movement known as the Khalidiyya-Naqshbandiyya (Halidiye-Nakşibendiye in Turkish). The Khalidiyya had its origins in the Mujaddidiyya, an earlier reform of the Naqshbandi sufi order. Two waves of the Mujaddidiyya had already reached Istanbul, but without producing Khalid's impact.[102] (The color illustrations include a noteworthy work in the form of a calligraphic invocation to the founder of the Naqshbandiyya.)

Born a Kurd near Shahrazur (Iraq), Khalid studied there and in Sulaymaniyya and was initiated into the Qadiri and possibly other orders, the Qadiriyya being predominant in Iraqi Kurdistan at the time.[103] He went to India to study with Shah Ghulam Ali (Shaykh Abdullah al-Dihlawi, d. 1824) of the Mujaddidiyya-Naqshbandiyya, founded by Ahmad Sirhindi (d. 1624), also known as Imam Rabbani and revered as the "renewer" (*mujaddid*) of the second Islamic millennium. Khalid acquired valuable credentials from Shah Ghulam Ali, who both authorized him to teach disciplines like *hadith* and Qur'an commentary and appointed him as deputy (*khalifa*) to spread the Mujaddidiyya in Kurdistan. When he returned to Sulaymaniyya, these credentials enabled Khalid to propagate sufism and hold his own against strict ulema, who disdained many sufi movements but respected learning in hadith and Qur'anic studies. Khalid's return was a disruptive event, especially for the local amir and Qadiri shaykh.

During his remaining years (1811–1827), Khalid faced opposition and moved several times, from Kurdistan to Baghdad, then Damascus. Its location on the pilgrimage route to Mecca made Damascus a strategic site for spreading his order. As he moved, he won followers far and wide; his seventy deputies (*khalifa*) spread his influence to Istanbul, to Chechnya, to Java. His impact as both scholar and mystic won him acclaim as the "renewer" (*mujaddid*) of his century, echoing Sirhindi's honorific. Many who responded to him were bazaar merchants. Among Kurds, he appealed to the younger generation, who had acquired a basic Islamic education and "represented a new emerging class . . . [that] stood above tribal formations."[104] Then and since, propertied elements, both merchants and landowners, supported the Khalidiyya and broadened its social base.

The Khalidiyya-Naqshbandiyya owed its success to many factors, starting with the founder's learning and charisma. Strict observance of the sharia, a cardinal Mujaddidi principle, helped Naqshbandis win support from the ulema, who criticized many other orders' laxity. Khalid's demand for sharia observance by rulers and subjects alike included strict application of the sharia to non-Muslims and dissident Muslims; tracing back to Sirhindi, those points regained urgency in the 1820s, when Christian missionaries were already upsetting intercommunal relations in Khalid's native Kurdistan, and nationalism threatened the empire in Greece and Serbia.[105] The Naqshbandi principle of "solitude within society" (*khalvat dar anjuman*) enjoined social and political engagement, in contrast to some orders' otherworldliness. Early conflicts with Kurdish amirs led Khalid to support the Ottoman state against them. When his fast-growing influence aroused Mahmud II's suspicions, Khalid allayed these suspicions by ordering his followers to pray for the state. Unlike otherworldly sufi orders or anti-Ottoman groups like the Arabian Wahhabiyya, Khalid made his movement a force for religious renewal and political reintegration within the Ottoman Empire as the greatest bastion of Islam.

Central to its appeal was the Khalidiyya's spiritual discipline.[106] To other Naqshbandis' insistence on sharia observance and silent recitation of the order's formulas, the Khalidis added emphases of their own. The practice that most differentiated the Khalidiyya was that of *rabıta*, the disciple's meditative concentration on the mental image of his shaykh. Khalid insisted that his followers meditate on his image alone, and never on his deputies' or successors' images. This requirement maintained the order's centralization — until some shaykhs breached the rule. Among other practices contributing to the order's success, Khalid trained many deputies and sent them elsewhere to propagate the order. There — in contrast to Qadiri practice — the deputy could become a shaykh and send out his own *khalifa*s. This practice facilitated rapid expansion but eventually gave rise to different suborders. Also distinctive was reciting the order's formulas (*dhikr*) not only silently but often individually. Consequently, the Khalidiyya did not require a dervish lodge (*tekke*) to function, although it might use one as a meeting hall.[107] In time, the Khalidiyya had more tekkes in Istanbul than any other order but—paradoxically—could better dispense with them after the Turkish republic ordered tekkes closed (1925).

Historical circumstances also favored the order at times. The establishment of earlier Mujaddidi-Naqshbandis in Istanbul gave it friends in high places; there were also sympathetic Kurdish migrants among Istanbul workers. In the 1820s, the suppression of the Janissaries and the heterodox Bektaşi order benefited the Naqshbandis.[108] With support from leading Mujaddidi officials, Mahmud II demolished some Bektaşi tekkes, turned the others over to Mujaddidi-Naqshbandis, and confiscated Bektaşi endowments for the treasury. Wary of any movement that he did not control, Mahmud also harassed the Khalidis at times, interfering in the succession to Shaykh Khalid and banishing Khalidis from Istanbul. However, Khalidis regained prominence in Istanbul from the late 1830s on, influenced the terms of the Gülhane decree, and made their order virtually synonymous with the Naqshbandiyya in the western Islamic lands. In Ottoman territories, no other Islamic movement of comparable influence emerged until that of Said Nursi, which began its spread in the hostile climate of the early Turkish republic.

CHANGING WORLDVIEWS

The Ottoman elites had a long history of curiosity about the outside world. This was notably true of the scribal service.[109] Exponents of the worldly, belletristic (*adab*) branch of the traditional learned culture, their duties required them to study such subjects as geography, history, and political philosophy. The roles they filled in government also expanded over time. As foreign affairs grew in urgency, they were called on to handle such business. Especially after the Greek Revolution forced the Sublime Porte to stop relying on Greek translators for European languages in 1821, scribes began to learn French and distinguish themselves as diplomats. The worldly adab culture thus expanded its horizons toward the West in a natural progression. A change described later in terms of rupture actually began in a metamorphic way.

The ideas behind the commercial treaty of 1838 and the Gülhane decree of 1839 show the results of this widened world awareness.[110] The ideas circulating in the capitals where Ottoman diplomats served were not all alike, however. Although probably not as clear to them as to Europeans of the day, these differences diversified what Ottoman envoys gained from their experiences. The writings of two ambassadors to Vienna prove the point. Ebu Bekir Ratib Efendi served there in 1791–1792. Sadık Rifat Paşa did so in 1837–1841 and 1842–1843.

They explored European modernity and explained it to their compatriots. They also discovered ideas that engaged their vital interests in European-style modernity and began to set goals that Ottoman and later Turkish statesmen have pursued ever since.

In preparing to launch the New Order, Selim III sent envoys to Berlin and Vienna in 1791–1792. Both envoys were to learn all they could about the countries where they served and report what they had learned. Their parallel reports indicate that both men had the same instructions. They reported on each state's post coach system, economic policy, army, and military supply system. The topics were the same, but each author's approach differed. Ahmed Azmi Efendi wrote a short report later printed in twenty-odd pages. Ratib's work could fill five hundred printed pages. One obvious question is how Ratib produced such a huge manuscript during a five-month embassy (February–July 1792). The answer is a significant story in its own right.[111] Unsurprisingly, signs of haste abound in his work. Still, Ratib advanced important arguments, often through storytelling.

One military institution he visited was the military arsenal where uniforms, weapons, and other essentials were produced and stockpiled. Ratib dwells on the rows of warehouses, the long shelves containing hundreds of thousands of each item with labels at the end of each row, the workshops where workmen produced the goods, and the office where the officials in charge showed him a large book containing measured drawings for each item. Ratib surprised them, he says, by taking an interest in small details and praising their system (*nizam*). In his official visits, Ratib always liked to show how up to date he was by citing facts or books that he could not have known about without coaching, since he clearly knew no European language.

The thrust of such narratives becomes apparent in one of his prefaces to his account of the Austrian military. He couches his argument in terms of military "history." As late as the reign of Mehmed IV (1648–1687), he says, the Ottomans were able to war against five powers at once without allies. About that time, the Austrians began to develop new forces and weapons and to apply the science of engineering to the art of war. Ratib continues that the first rulers to order and regulate (*vaz'-ı nizam-u-kavanin*) their military were the Ottomans. However, later sultans neglected this legacy, until the old forces existed only in name. As late as the second siege of Vienna (1683), the Ottoman forces' discipline astonished the Austrians. The Austrian officers told him, he said, that their systems for recruiting peasants (*reaya*) and training officers were based on Ottoman practice. Elsewhere, Ratib called Austria's current military system its "new order" (Nizam-ı Cedid). When he flaunted his knowledge of military science, he adds, the Austrians asked why the Ottomans, if they knew all this, did not reform their forces. Ratib may have twisted facts, but he did so for a cause. If the Austrians had created their new order by borrowing from the Ottomans, then the Ottomans could create theirs by borrowing back updated forms of what had originally been theirs. Written a year before Selim's New Order was proclaimed in Istanbul and intended to preempt conservative opposition, Ratib's "history" did not record the past; it projected the future.

Undergirding such arguments is the implication that reducing difference between Ottoman and European practice could safeguard Ottoman interests. Also implied is that this reduction of difference applies, not just to this or that European state, but to Europe systemically. Some other diplomatic authors pursued this line of thought. As early as 1763, Ahmed Resmi Efendi in Berlin sketched the basics of balance-of-power diplomacy; he later advocated joining the European diplomatic system. Ottoman intellectuals' propagation of European ideas of public law helps to explain why Selim III responded to Napoleon's invasion of Egypt in 1798 by not only proclaiming a jihad but also denouncing the invasion as contrary to international law and seeking European allies against France.[112]

In 1837, Vienna ambassador Sadık Rifat Paşa expanded such arguments to call for Ottoman admission to the Concert of Europe.[113] For 1837, that was equivalent to Turkey's 1987 application for admission to the European Economic Community. Well versed in Islamic thought, Sadık Rifat deftly showed his compatriots how much Austrian political thought offered them. He emphasized that European statesmen prefer peace and prosperity to war and work to avoid disruptions of international order. European states advance their interests by promoting their subjects' increase in numbers and prosperity. That requires security of life, honor, and property, which depends on enforcement of the essential rights of freedom, the very ones honored among the pure people of Islam. At one stroke, Sadık Rifat preempted conservative Muslim critics by asserting commonality between Islamic and European standards. Rather than the subjects having been created for their rulers, he added, it may be that "the sovereigns of the world have obtained [power by] God's grace solely to watch over the subjects and the progress of the lands." To win the people's hearts, government must respect human rights (*hukuk-i insaniye*). In Islam, everyone recognizes that all depends on the divine will. Humans cannot influence it; yet they have their own sphere of action. While generally respecting their creeds and cults, Europeans follow reason to formulate beneficial policies. Thus Sadık Rifat invoked Islamic theology to justify using reason to achieve a just order.

In these terms, Sadık Rifat sums up the idea of the *Rechtsstaat*, the "law state." This is a Germanic version of the English idea of "rule of law," with the big difference that strong, even authoritarian, government was a fact of life in German-speaking countries. If individuals' rights were going to be protected, that would have to occur, not under the English liberals' "little government," but under authoritarian states. However difficult it may be to maintain a balance between individual rights and an authoritarian state, where the authoritarian state is a given from the start, advocates of human rights cannot ignore it. In developing his arguments about rights, Sadık Rifat discusses Austrian officials' status. Like other Ottoman diplomats, he had discovered how European rights standards served his own interests. Austrian officials had much greater security and, when they fell from office, did not undergo the dire consequences that Ottoman officials' slave status entailed. Sadık Rifat and Mustafa Reşid were colleagues, and it is no accident that the philosophical passages of the Gülhane decree sound like Sadık Rifat.

The Austrian and Ottoman empires also shared another characteristic with critical policy implications. Both states exemplified not a twofold division between the subjects and the state but a threefold one, in which the interests of different ethnic and religious communities required consideration at the intermediary level. By the 1830s, the politicization of religious and ethnic identities was making communal as well as individual rights an issue for both empires. Sadık Rifat used the plural when he wrote of how European rulers sought "to make their lands [and peoples] flourish." This point, too, appears in the Gülhane decree and later policy.

As Sadık Rifat also emphasized, states need order internally and externally. The Ottomans' wars had long since become defensive rather than aggressive; yet they still occasioned great costs. The only remedy was to "enter into the law of nations" as current among the European powers. Since Europe's return to peace in 1815, each European state had become the guarantor of the others' integrity. There are now two types of "governmental law" in Europe: "particular, independent law," and "general, common law."[114] These expressions refer to public law and its two domains, internal and external. The idea that public law includes both internal and international law explains why the 1838 commercial treaty and the 1839 Gülhane decree were prerequisites for the 1840 Convention of London, under which the European powers intervened to settle the Egyptian crisis in Istanbul's favor.

It is vital, Sadık Rifat continued, for the Ottomans to gain admission to this system of law. The difference in religion cannot be an obstacle because multiple cults exist inside the European countries. As the "system of civilization" (*usul-i sivilizasyon*) advances in Ottoman lands, the Ottomans will gain admission to this system of law, and crises will be solved by consultation. In another twenty years, the "gates of war" will be closed for the Ottomans. At the end of the Crimean War, the Treaty of Paris (1856) did admit the Ottoman Empire to the European concert on paper. The European integration that Sadık Rifat prophesied had to proceed by a longer route.

FIFTY YEARS OF CRISIS AND REFORM

The Russian war of 1768 and the French invasion of Egypt in 1798 precipitated the Ottoman Empire into an era of accelerating change and tightening interlinkage between Ottoman and European affairs, trends that reached another menacing climax in the Ottoman-Egyptian crises of the 1830s. Two exceptional Sultans, Selim III and Mahmud II, responded with a new turn toward centralization and defensive modernization.

Ottomans saw the foremost need for reform in military terms yet also quickly discovered, as other states had, that military effectiveness required transforming the entire government. Nor could that occur without transforming Ottoman economy, society, and culture. The acceleration of change and the formulation of reformist policy required a fundamental shift from deferring to custom to rationalizing and planning for the future. Selim's New Order thus signifies a reorientation in Ottoman policy that corresponds to the European Enlightenment's *esprit de système*. Some of his reform measures were imitative; many failed to take root. However, the reformist cause as a totality took firm root because it engaged both the class interests of leading statesmen, who wished to see their conditions of service transformed, and the empire's vital security interests. As this occurred, new forces of economic and social change gathered within the empire, and the advent of the century's most influential Ottoman religious movement guaranteed that attempts at Ottoman revitalization would be guided not only by new approaches to the West but also by Islamic approaches to modernity.

2

THE TANZIMAT

Mahmud II's death in 1839 opened a new period that became known simply as the Tanzimat, "the Reforms." A causative or intensive form from the same Arabic root as the already familiar *nizam*, as in Nizam-ı Cedid (New Order), *tanzimat* implied "giving order" and thus expanding and accelerating the scope and pace of reform. There would not be another sultan as decisive as Selim III or Mahmud II until 1876. Until then, the initiative for reform came not from the palace but from the Sublime Porte (Bab-ı Âli). Europeans applied that term indiscriminately to the entire Ottoman government, but it actually referred to the grand vezir's headquarters, which also included the foreign and interior ministries and several important councils. One of the leading statesmen at the Sublime Porte, Fuad Paşa, expressed the urgency of the times as follows: "Islam was, for centuries, in its environment, a wonderful instrument of progress. Today it is a clock that is behind time and must be set."[1] Fuad was not the last Turk to apply a clock-setting metaphor to the challenge of catching up with modernity.

Crises punctuated this period repeatedly, most gravely during the Ottoman-Egyptian conflict (1839–1841), Crimean War (1854–1856), and Russo-Turkish War (1877–1878). Yet reformist efforts to defend and strengthen the empire also expanded and intensified. As the empire became increasingly engaged in the European modernity of the age of imperialism, old equilibria were unsettled and new forces emerged at all socioeconomic levels—at those of ethnic and religious communities, social classes, kinship networks, and individuals. The rapid-fire bursts of international crisis overlay deep transformations in economic production, individual identity, and class formation, as well as the reconfiguration of politics from personality-centered factionalism to issue-oriented movements and the onset of revolutionary change in Ottoman culture. By 1876, the

The Sublime Porte, the Soğuk Çeşme gate (upper left) and the central
pavilion of the long facade looking toward the Golden Horn (lower right).
(By Abdullah Frères, Library of Congress, Prints and Photographs Division,
Abdülhamid II Collection, 3b29079u and 3b29069u.)

Tanzimat reforms and the reactions they provoked had acted powerfully to further the differentiation of the two great currents of change that emerged from
late Ottoman history.

In the following pages, an examination of political issues, reformist policy,
economic and social change, and the revolutionary cultural significance of the
period—particularly as represented by Namık Kemal (1840–1888)—will illustrate these points. Inasmuch as modern forms of literary production began in
this period and continued after it, literature scholars describe works produced
long after 1876 as Tanzimat literature. This literary continuity is significant but
does not change the fact that shifts in the center of power—from the palace to
the Sublime Porte in 1839 and back to the palace in 1876—define the Tanzimat
in Ottoman political history.

CRISIS AND CONTRACTION

European views of the empire as "the sick man of Europe," a phrase invented
in this period, contrast starkly with the dynamism of the Tanzimat. Accelerating
change created a systemic relationship between disintegration and dynamism,

as crisis provoked reform, and reform raised new demands among both foreign powers and the Ottomans' increasingly self-conscious subject peoples.[2] The danger was worse at some times than others. The Tanzimat period opened and ended with the survival of the empire more threatened than at any other time in the nineteenth century.

Between 24 June and 3 July 1839, the Egyptians defeated the Ottomans at Nizib, Mahmud II died, and the Ottoman grand admiral defected with the fleet to Egypt. Multilateral European intervention turned the situation around over the next year, the Ottoman diplomats who had negotiated for European support became the leading statesmen of the Tanzimat, and Mehmed Ali was left with only the hereditary governorship of Egypt in return for annual tribute payment and continued Ottoman sovereignty. His dreams of empire had failed, but he had consolidated his family's hold on Egypt as an autonomous entity.

As the Egyptian crisis faded, two of the most urgent crises of the early Tanzimat emerged in places that had been under Egyptian rule: Crete and Lebanon. The Egyptians occupied Crete in 1825, and it was only restored to Ottoman control in 1841. The island's population included Christians and Muslims. However, its centuries-old pattern of symbiotic, even mutable religious identities had begun to give way to polarization since the Russian-provoked, anti-Muslim rebellion of 1770.[3] After the Egyptians left, Cretan Christians wanted union with independent Greece, not restored Ottoman rule. Efforts to apply Tanzimat reforms on the island became tangled in a cycle of communal massacres and punitive expeditions, culminating in the great revolt of 1866. Crete remained under Ottoman sovereignty until 1913, but tenuously.

The Lebanese crises of 1841 and 1860 resembled the Cretan situation in their connections to both reversion from Egyptian to Ottoman rule and change in religious identities and international involvements. Yet Lebanon's cultural specifics differed. Both "Lebanon" and "Syria" were geographical expressions that did not match administrative boundaries in the Ottoman Empire. Lebanon forms part of Syria's coastal region. Paralleling Lebanon's coast, from north of Tripoli to south of Beirut, the Lebanon range or Mount Lebanon (Jabal Lubnan), formed one of Lebanon's most distinctive topographical features. Tenuously controlled by the Ottomans in the past, Mount Lebanon had a religiously mixed population. Maronite Christians, a historical Eastern church long united with Rome, were especially numerous in the northern part of the Lebanon range and also lived in the Druze-controlled south. The Druzes, by origin an Islamic splinter sect, were found in the southern part of the Lebanon range and other parts of southwestern Syria. What had defined local sociopolitical order in the past, however, was not religion but the stratification between the common people (*ahali*) and the elite, who were known as *shaykh*s, literally "elders," or as *mukataaji*s, an Ottoman term for revenue collectors. In practical terms, Lebanon was divided not religiously but by a "genealogical geography," in which specific families inherited control of specific districts.[4] Elite families formed alliances with one another and patronage relationships with inferiors across religious lines. The highest-ranking family, the Shihabs, had Christian and Muslim branches. They and other elite families mediated among religions and supported religious institutions with impartiality. The resulting equilibrium could remain stable for a long time, if left alone; it could also unravel fast, if subjected to any shock.

As the Tanzimat opened, new stresses provoked a breakdown. Both Catholic and Protestant missionaries had become active in Lebanon. European writers and travelers also visited the region, identifying it as part of the Holy Land, and constructing polarized images of "tribal" differences that they ascribed to different communities, quite different from indigenous self-understandings. The Egyptian occupation (1831–1840) further unsettled the old equilibrium. Ibrahim Paşa conscripted Christians as well as Muslims. When some Druzes remained loyal to the sultan and revolted, Ibrahim used Maronites against Druzes. Druze and Christian rebels were united against him by the time joint Ottoman-European intervention drove him out of Syria. After that, Lebanon's old equilibrium could not be reestablished. The first serious clash between Maronites and Druzes occurred in 1841. European powers backed different sides, misreading modern conflict as "age-old" antipathy. Paradoxically, just as the Ottomans set out to extend the Gülhane decree's promises to Muslims and non-Muslims impartially, Europeans were starting to intervene on behalf of the Christians.[5] The Ottomans had to defend their sovereignty. In 1842 and 1845, Ottoman attempts to reassert central control while also satisfying European demands led to Ottoman attempts to separate "Christian" and "Druze" districts, north and south, and introduce cumbersome systems of representation for other religious communities into both districts.

As new concepts of communal distinctness worked their way into popular consciousness, a process fostered by missionary education, a peasant movement that began in the north around 1859 added class-based activism to Lebanese politics. In a predominantly Maronite northern district, villagers led by Tanyus Shahin asserted their understanding of the Tanzimat and championed "the interests of the masses" (*maslahat al-jumhur*), demanding equality and abolition of elite privilege.[6] The rebellion spread to the mixed districts of the south, where the rebels went to aid fellow Maronites allegedly in distress in Druze-controlled districts. The conflict expanded into a full-scale communal war that did not express old hatreds but did create new ones. The Druzes emerged victorious in 1860, even killing Muslim notables who had associated with the Christian rebels. The Maronites were totally defeated, and the flight of refugees seeking safe haven "purified" parts of the landscape, leaving places that had flourished with mixed populations desolate without them.

In 1860, rumors of events in Lebanon spread to Damascus, precipitating Muslim violence against Christians. There, too, the causes were deeper, growing out of the differential impacts of reform and socioeconomic change on different communities. The European powers organized a joint diplomatic initiative, and French troops landed in Lebanon. Druze and Christian notables made peace in Lebanon on terms that ignored popular grievances in 1860. The Ottomans announced a new administrative regulation for Lebanon, agreed on with the European powers in 1861. The new regulation ended the partition of 1842 and set up a single administrative district (synonymously either *sancak* or *liva*) of Mount Lebanon under a governor (*mutasarrıf*) who had to be a non-Lebanese Christian assisted by an administrative council including representatives of all religious communities. Bringing relative stability at a price, this system imprinted sectarianism lastingly on Lebanese politics, although old-style elite patron-client relationships survived inside the new sectarianism. In 1860, after the Maronite peasant rebels had spread their revolt into southern Lebanon, the Druzes had defeated them high and low; yet the new system of 1861 awarded victory to the Maronites and their French protectors.[7]

When sectarian violence broke out in Damascus in 1860, the local leadership, largely ulema and merchants, failed to control the situation. Meting out punishments in Damascus afterward, the Ottomans were particularly hard on these notables, banishing many from the city for long periods. A reconstituted local elite emerged to dominate the city's life and its relations with the state for the remainder of Ottoman times. This new stratum of Damascene notables contained fewer religious scholars, many of whom had been alienated by the secularizing Tanzimat reforms, and more landowners, who benefited from developments in the agrarian economy and appreciated the opportunities for office-holding in the expanding Ottoman government.[8]

During the years of crisis in Crete and Lebanon, the empire faced challenges enough elsewhere. In the Balkans, Bulgaria experienced twelve minor insurrections (1835–1876) but flourished economically. In Bosnia, the local landholding elite remained dominant until 1851, delaying introduction of the Tanzimat reforms until then.[9] The most pressing Balkan issue concerned the Romanian principalities of Wallachia and Moldavia, Russian-occupied from 1829 to 1834 and under joint Russian-Ottoman tutelage after that. Romanian nationalists wanted unification. Romania became the only part of the Ottoman Empire caught up in

Ceremony at Topkapı Palace for the religious festivals. Ottoman statesmen assemble in order of precedence to pay their respects to the sultan. Expressing the Islamic legitimation of the sultanate and the unique position of the sultan, this ceremony (*muayede*) was held on the two major Islamic festivals of the year. (Attributed to Kostantin Kapıdağlı, Topkapı Palace Museum.)

Selim III. Kostantin Kapıdağlı, 1803. (Topkapı Palace Museum, Istanbul.)

Mahmud II, old and new in imperial image-making. The scroll of sultans' portraits (left) depicts him as a traditional sultan. The imperial portrait decoration (*tasvir-i hümayun nişanı*) depicts him after the adoption of European-style uniforms; the chain permits the decoration to be worn around the neck. (Both images anonymous, reproductions not to the same scale, Topkapı Palace Museum, Istanbul.)

Mahmud II's New Army before the adoption of the fez, 1826. The soldiers are
wearing new uniforms with a cap (*şubara*). (From the Vinkhuijzen collection of military
uniforms, General Research Division, The New York Public Library, Astor, Lenox
and Tilden Foundations.)

(٧) (٨) (٩) (١٠) (١١) (١٢)

موسيقة نفرى محربه ضابطى بياده ضابطى مكتب حربيآكردى بياده نفرى محربيه سلوع إمه النفرى

SOLDAT MUSICIEN   OFFICIER DE MARINE   OFFICIER D'INFANTERIE   ELÈVE DE L'ECOLE   SOLDAT D'INFANTERIE   SOLDAT D'INFANTERIE

Soldiers in new uniform with the fez. The French caption contains errors. The correct Ottoman gives the sultan's name accurately as Mahmud and states that the picture displays the soldiers after the adoption of trousers and frock coat. (Mahmud Şevket Paşa, *Kıyâfet,* The Rare Books and Manuscripts Library of the Ohio State University Libraries.)

Nakşibendi calligraphic picture in the form of a derviş cap. Calligrapher Mustafa Hilmi used mirror-image calligraphy to make a symmetrical picture of a derviş headdress out of this invocation to the order's founder: *Yâ Hazret-i Şâh Muhammed Bahâeddîn Nakşibendî El-Buhârî kuddise sirruhu'l-âlî,* roughly, "Oh noble sovereign [of mystics], Muhammed Bahaeddin Nakşibendi of Bukhara, may his exalted inmost heart be sanctified." Works like this give an idea why pious Muslims found manuscript culture satisfying and took their time to see advantages in printing. (Date 1249 hicri/1833–1834, 58 × 38 cm; Courtesy of the Klasik Türk Sanatları Vakfı, Üsküdar, Istanbul.)

Ahmed Midhat and Fatma Aliye. She was his literary protégée, and they corresponded, sometimes more than once a day. In 2009, a picture of her was placed on the new 50 Turkish lira banknote; the circular vignette is adapted from this picture. (Ahmed Midhat courtesy of Nigar Sahaf, Asuman Bektaş; Fatma Aliye courtesy of Oya Selen.)

Women of the Constitutional Era. The legend at the top proclaims them "Oriental Beauties" in French and "Ladies of the Constitutional Regime" in Ottoman. The fashionable young women are wearing the *costume moderne*; the veiled woman is wearing the *ancien costume*. (Courtesy of Irvin Schick.)

Muslim refugees fleeing toward Istanbul. Such flights occurred many times before this picture was published in 1912. European interest in them had not always been this sympathetic. (From *Le Petit Journal*, supplément illustré, no. 1149, 24 November 1912, 376, courtesy of Irvin Schick.)

Europe's revolutionary wave of 1848. A revolutionary assembly proclaimed the two principalities' unity and independence. Russian and Ottoman armies intervened jointly to stop that. Cooperation between the two empires could not last long, however, especially after the Ottomans welcomed revolutionary Polish and Hungarian refugees, who later contributed greatly to Ottoman defense and culture.

The war that did not start over Balkan issues began over the Christian holy places but became known as the Crimean War. It erupted over a Catholic-Orthodox dispute about custody of the keys to the Church of the Nativity in Bethlehem.[10] The growing politicization of ethnoreligious difference and European competition to champion different religions among the sultan's subjects turned this question, which could not have produced such crisis in earlier times, into a pretext for war. France reacted as the historic champion of Catholic interests. As the protector of Orthodoxy, Russia issued an ultimatum and announced its intent to occupy the Romanian principalities to protect Orthodox Christians. Britain and France declared war in return for Ottoman promises of further egalitarian reform. Russia then attacked across the Danube.

The war went badly for the Russians in the Balkans, memorably so at their unsuccessful siege of the Silistria fortress on the Danube in 1854.[11] The war expanded to the Crimea and the Caucasus. Invading Anatolia from the east,

Crimean War, British troops camped at Üsküdar, Istanbul,
May 1854. (By James Robertson, courtesy of Bahattin Öztuncay; Öztuncay,
Photographers, 1:132, pl. 115.)

*Ömer Paşa, commander of Ottoman troops in the
Crimea.* Born Michael Lattas of Croatia, he entered Ottoman
service under Mahmud II. (By Roger Fenton, courtesy of
Bahattin Öztuncay; Öztuncay, *Photographers*, 1:134, pl. 116.)

the Russians took Kars. However, they capitulated after the allies captured
Sevastopol in the Crimea and destroyed the Russian Black Sea fleet. The
Crimean War showed what recent advances in industrial production could
do when used for purposes of military destruction. The Ottoman allies' maritime supply lines proved more efficient than the Russian's overland resupply.
The British and French (not yet the Ottomans) were also beginning to adopt
rifled handguns, whereas the Russians still had smoothbore weapons, much
shorter in range and slower in rate of fire. In a foretaste of what future wars
would be like, single battles cost tens of thousands of casualties. Florence
Nightingale's efforts to bring nursing care to the wounded signaled major
improvements in medical practice and enlarged women's roles in wartime.

Telegraph lines reached Istanbul in time to enable war correspondents to report the battles of the Crimean War instantly, while photography produced a new visual record. If the war was a turning point in making the Ottoman Empire immediately present to Europeans, accelerated cultural change among the Ottomans proved the converse equally true.

The war over, the sultan issued the promised reform decree of 1856. A month later, in March 1856, the Treaty of Paris formally declared "the Sublime Porte admitted to participate in the advantages of the public law and system (*concert*) of Europe."[12] Becoming the first non-Western state to conclude a treaty on a footing of formal equality with European powers, the empire thus attained on paper the collective European security guarantee that Ottoman diplomats had advocated for nearly a century. Yet other clauses of the treaty undermined Ottoman sovereignty by neutralizing the Black Sea, internationalizing the Danube, and installing European controls in Romania and Serbia. The Ottoman Empire had emerged from the war without territorial loss and gained nominal admission to the European diplomatic system, but with its sovereignty further diminished. Now, concerted action by European powers, which had helped the Ottomans against Mehmed Ali, was giving way to competition. The collective guarantee of the Ottoman Empire's integrity proved of little value. In the Romanian principalities, where the Treaty of Paris introduced European controls, nationalists exploited great power divisions to work for union, in 1859 electing the same man as prince of both Moldavia and Wallachia. The Ottomans reluctantly recognized unification in 1861. Independence followed in 1878.

Avoided in 1856, territorial losses occurred in the 1870s, a decade of crisis that also included famine in Anatolia (1873–1875) and state bankruptcy (1875–1881). Revolt flared in Herzegovina in 1874, then spread to Bosnia and Montenegro in 1875 and to Bulgaria in 1876. The Ottoman response to the revolt raised inflammatory European outcries about massacres of Christians. Countermassacres flooded Istanbul with Muslim refugees, whose plight Europeans ignored.

In Istanbul, the situation grew volatile when the *softa*s (medrese students) came out, as usual during crises, demanding a change of government. Sultan Abdülaziz gave in; his new ministers deposed him on 29 May 1876 and enthroned Murad V, about whom Ottoman liberals entertained great hopes. Within a week, the deposed Abdülaziz was found dead, probably by suicide, although accusations of assassination persisted. Within three months Murad V, found to be unstable, was deposed and replaced by his brother, Abdülhamid II (1876–1909).[13] His reign would open a new period, but first the Balkan crisis had to be resolved. While Istanbul was in crisis, Balkan revolts had spread.

Ottoman military successes against the rebels roused Europe, and a conference was convened in Istanbul.

As in 1839 and 1856, the Ottomans played the card of domestic reform to cope with international crisis. This time, it worked less well.[14] As the diplomatic conference opened on 23 December 1876, a cannon salute sounded afar. Foreign minister Safvet Paşa announced that the sultan had just granted his subjects a constitution: no need remained for the conference. The Russian ambassador icily demanded to carry on. The fact that the Ottomans now had a constitution, whereas the Russians did not, could not change geopolitical realities. Still, the Ottomans used their constitution as a shield against great power demands. Balkan territory could not be ceded because the constitution guaranteed the empire's integrity; special privileges could not be granted to particular peoples because it guaranteed the equality of all Ottoman subjects; and so on. The same answer greeted each demand at the conference: the government would carry out the reforms promised in the constitution. Stalemated, the conference adjourned in January 1877. Ironically, Abdülhamid used its failure as a pretext to blame grand vezir Midhat Paşa, the leading architect of the constitution, and send him into exile.

Temporarily a constitutional monarchy, the Ottoman Empire elected its first parliament. Convened in March 1877, it functioned until February 1878. Impressing observers by the seriousness of its debates, it symbolized the gains of Tanzimat reformism. During its short life, however, the course of events was determined not by the parliament but by the Balkan crisis. Having defaulted on their foreign debt, the Ottomans could not get European support.[15] Going to work to isolate the Ottomans diplomatically as well, the Russians declared war in April 1877.

In the ensuing Russo-Turkish War, Russia attacked both in the Balkans, aiming for Istanbul, and in the east. Ottoman forces resisted heroically at Kars in the east and at Shipka and Plevna in Bulgaria. Both in rifles and in artillery, the Ottomans had weapons of superior firepower and longer range.[16] Yet the Russians prevailed on all fronts, advancing nearly to Istanbul. The Ottomans signed an armistice on 31 January 1878. With the Russians so near and the city flooded with refugees, panic reigned in Istanbul. Parliamentary criticism of the government and the military grew heated, provoking Abdülhamid to use his constitutional prerogative to dismiss the parliament on 14 February. He never abolished the constitution, but he also did not call new elections. The First Constitutional Regime (Meşrutiyet, 1876–1878) was gone but not forgotten.

Facing the worst military situation since 1839, the government at first had to accept dictated Russian terms at San Stefano (Yeşilköy) in March 1878. These so far exceeded what had been discussed before the war, however, that the other European powers refused to concur. With threats of wider conflict in the air, German chancellor Otto von Bismarck convened a conference in Berlin to examine the entire Eastern Question. Shortly before it opened, Abdülhamid assured himself of British support by assigning Cyprus to British occupation.[17] The Berlin Treaty of July 1878 was less drastic than San Stefano, but still confronted the Ottomans with catastrophic losses. The Berlin treaty recognized the independence of Romania, Serbia, and Montenegro. In Bulgaria, the north was made into an autonomous principality, while the south was constituted as "Eastern Rumelia" under direct political and military control of the sultan but with administrative autonomy. Romania received the coastal Dobruca region; Russia took Bessarabia. Bosnia-Herzegovina remained Ottoman in name but was occupied by Austria-Hungary. In eastern Anatolia, the Russians kept Kars, Ardahan, and Batum but had to return other seized territory. Article 61 incorporated vague references to guarantees for minorities, especially Armenians. As in 1774 and 1829, the treaty required the Ottomans to pay a war indemnity to the Russians, although the amount was less than that demanded at San Stefano.

For Europeans who knew nothing of the Ottoman Empire other than what they called the Eastern Question, it might have seemed logical to dismiss the empire as "the sick man of Europe." Only seeing the empire from inside permits forming a different view.

AN EGYPTIAN POSTSCRIPT

After 1840, Egyptian and Ottoman affairs became more disengaged than theretofore. Yet it is a backward projection of later national viewpoints to write Egypt out of Ottoman history during the Tanzimat. A brief account of developments before the British occupation in 1882 will prove this point. Critical factors in shaping events include Egypt's rulers and its tightening integration into the world economy.

By the time Mehmed Ali died in 1849, old age had made him unable to rule. His son Ibrahim Paşa, who might have been another Mehmed Ali, was confirmed as governor (*vali*) in 1848 but predeceased his father.[18] Grandson Abbas Hilmi I, usually known as Abbas Paşa, became regent, then vali. The period from then until the 1882 British occupation included the governorships of Abbas (1848–1854), Said (1854–1863), and Ismail (1863–1879), as well as the opening years of Tawfiq (1879–1892). These were men of divergent priorities and capabilities; and Egypt's governing elites and institutions, while well developed compared to those of other Ottoman provinces, could not provide the continuity in Cairo that the Ottoman central bureaucracy did during the Tanzimat. Abbas continued Mehmed Ali's post-1841 retrenchment policies; however, the building of the Alexandria-Cairo railway, the first in the empire (and in Africa) began in 1851. Said's rule is remembered for the start of construction on the Suez Canal. He granted the canal concession to Ferdinand de Lesseps in 1854, construction began in 1859, and the canal opened in 1869. Economically and strategically perhaps the most significant public works project of the century in the Middle East, the canal entailed major financial difficulties, which entangled Egyptian and European interests.

Ismail Paşa had a vision of progress and civilization, which he sought to promote through public works, science, and the arts. The boom in demand for Egyptian cotton, caused by the Union blockade of the Southern ports during the U.S. Civil War, initially gave him the means to pursue his dreams. Ismail also wanted further distinctions over other Ottoman governors. He persuaded Istanbul to change the succession principle in Egypt from seniority to primogeniture (1866), grant him the unique, made-up title of khedive (*hıdiv*, Arabic, *khidiw*, 1867), and further enlarge his autonomy (1873). Bribes aside, the cost of these concessions was a near doubling of Egypt's annual tribute payment to the Ottoman government, to 150,000 purses (*kise*, roughly 3.2 million pounds sterling).

The collapse in cotton prices in 1866 quickly undermined Ismail's ability to fulfill his dreams. Foreign borrowing, started under Said in 1860, had continued. Regarding Egypt as a poor credit risk, European lenders demanded increasingly unfavorable terms for new loans. Under Ismail, Egypt's foreign debt rose to nearly 100 million pounds sterling, compared to the Istanbul government's 200 million. In 1875, when Ismail had to sell his 177,000 shares in the Suez Canal Company, the British government, which had let French interests get ahead of it in developing the canal, seized the chance to buy them. Europeans' investments increased their sense of entitlement to intervene in Egypt. As Egypt slid deeper into debt, the 1870s became a critical decade. In 1876, Ismail had to establish first a Caisse de la Dette publique (Public Debt Commission) to administer revenues assigned directly to debt service and then a Franco-British dual control over all of government finance. Soon his cabinet included a British finance minister and a French minister of public works. The fact that the Ottoman government went bankrupt at the same time implies that global economic trends were at work; in Egypt, however, the extent of foreign intervention was greater.

As European eyes fixed increasingly on Egypt, Egyptian eyes looked back warily at both Europeans and Egypt's alien ruling elite. In April 1879, several hundred Egyptians signed a statement of national demands, and Ismail formed a new government excluding the European ministers. Under international pressure, the Ottoman sultan deposed him. Ismail learned of this when he received a telegram from Istanbul addressed to him as the "former khedive" (*hıdiv-i sabik*). As the new khedive, Tawfiq, tried to come to terms with European creditors and carry out reforms, a national movement was taking shape.

Egypt's nationalist movement drew its leadership from elements of an emergent middle class and its broad-based support among the guilds and the urban populace. The bourgeois elements resembled those who transformed Ottoman politics from the 1860s on, except for one important difference. In Egypt, the privileged positions were still monopolized by the Turko-Circassian elite favored by Mehmed Ali. Egypt's middle-class opposition came from native Egyptians who blamed Egypt's travails on the non-Egyptian elite as much as on Europeans. Egypt's oppositional coalition consisted of intellectuals, merchants and rural notables, and especially military officers, whose promotion prospects were blocked by the Turko-Circassian monopoly on high rank. The native Egyptian officers found their leader in Ahmad 'Urabi Bey. In alliance with the notables, the officers forced Tawfiq to form a government with 'Urabi as minister of war and concede real power to the Chamber of Deputies (Majlis al-Nuwwab), which Ismail had set up as a merely consultative body. Egypt's nationalist leaders readily found support among the guilds and the urban workers, who resented the stresses on Egypt's economy and foreign interference in its markets. Making a pretext of Egypt's mounting "disorder," Britain and France sent a joint naval expedition to Alexandria. Soon after, an outbreak of popular violence caused about forty European fatalities. Anxious to prevent the French from gaining preponderance, the British took that as the pretext to bombard Alexandria and invade to "restore order."

Nominally, the Ottoman sultan remained sovereign over Egypt until 1914, and Mehmed Ali's descendants ruled autonomously there as khedives. In reality, the British "agent and consul general" in Cairo became the country's ruler. Squelched in 1882, Egyptian nationalist opposition to foreign rule resurfaced in the 1890s. Significantly, the middle-class elements that supported 'Urabi were analogous to the supporters of new forms of political opposition at the Ottoman center. These were the social strata shaped by the rise of new schools and the modern print media, especially newspapers. Known in Arabic as the "renaissance" (*nahda*), this cultural florescence launched long waves of change—social, cultural, economic, and political—that shaped responses to modernity across the region.[19]

THE REFORMS

Although the scope of the Tanzimat reforms defies brief summary, certain themes stand out: civil bureaucratic hegemony; elite formation; legislation; governmental expansion; changes in intercommunal relations; and transformation of the political process. The drive for centralization and defensive modernization united these themes; the sense of backwardness and the need to catch up underlay everything. The pace of reform seemed to quicken toward the end of the period. If so, a major precipitator may have been Sultan Abdülaziz's European trip of 1867—unique for an Ottoman sovereign—with a large entourage, including several princes and foreign minister Fuad Paşa.[20]

CIVIL BUREAUCRATIC HEGEMONY

What defined the Tanzimat as a period was a change in the locus of power. That happened in fact, not principle. The only source of legal authority that could be used to enact new policies remained the sultan's will. Selim and Mahmud wielded that power personally. In 1839, Abdülmecid came to the throne at age sixteen and had to rely on the ruling elites to cope with the Egyptian crisis. As his reign progressed, he took more of a role. However, he is most remembered for the Westernization of the palace lifestyle. In general, others prepared laws for him to enact. The hegemony of the Sublime Porte consisted of that. The more it grew, the more controversial it became because it could not be legitimated by right.

The same pattern persisted after the accession of Abdülaziz in 1861, although he had a different personality. He showed a will to command but did so erratically. He is credited with a keen interest in the army and navy, which were modernized significantly during his reign. However, palace extravagance ran unchecked, and the empire slid toward bankruptcy. By the late 1860s, his relations with Grand Vezir Fuad Paşa had become quite strained.[21] The death in 1871 of Fuad's colleague Âli Paşa, the last great Tanzimat statesman, ended the de facto civil bureaucratic hegemony of the Tanzimat; and the accession of the next decisive sultan, Abdülhamid II in 1876 opened a new period of rule from the palace.

The fact that those who filled the de facto power gap in 1839 were civil officials, rather than military officers, may seem surprising, given the initially military goals of reform, not to speak of the military's political prominence in earlier and later centuries. However, after the settlement of the Egyptian crisis and despite all efforts of Husrev Paşa and his faction, Ottoman commanders did not regain political dominance before 1908. Reasons for this fact included the greater costs

Fuad, Âli, and Midhat Paşas (left to right). Three of the leading statesmen of the Tanzimat. (All by Abdullah Frères, 1865; courtesy of Bahattin Öztuncay; Öztuncay, *Photographers*, 2:379–81, pls. 373–75.)

and technical difficulties of training modern military elites as opposed to civil officials with a diplomat's facility in French. Another reason was that the empire could no longer protect its interests by its own military strength alone. The men best able to get outside assistance were civil officials, particularly diplomats, of whom a small number therefore dominated the Tanzimat.

The key figure initially was Mustafa Reşid Paşa (1800–1858). His protégés and successors as foreign minister and grand vezir were Mehmed Emin Âli Paşa (1815–1871) and Keçecizade Fuad Paşa (1815–1869), both of whom rose through the foreign ministry.[22] Mustafa Reşid's other prominent associates included Sadık Rifat Paşa (1806–1858) and Ahmed Cevdet Paşa (1822–1895), the latter a religious scholar who transferred from one of the highest religious ranks into the civil service in the 1860s. Many men of religious education served in new civil institutions in this period, but no other changed career at so high a rank. Another outstanding figure of the later Tanzimat was Midhat Paşa (1822–1884), who served largely in provincial administration, then as leading architect of the constitution and grand vezir. These men's swelling ranks of associates and dependents made nepotism and favoritism ongoing issues during the Tanzimat, showing that old patterns of faction-building still operated inside new institutions. The recruitment of non-Muslims to civil office, especially after 1856, added another new factor to bureaucratic networking. At the top, the Tanzimat

statesmen formed a revolving pool of generalists eligible for provincial governorships, ministerial portfolios, and the grand vezirate.

ELITE FORMATION, INTERSERVICE RIVALRY, AND EDUCATIONAL REFORM

During the Tanzimat, efforts at elite formation expanded, spilling over into
educational reforms that benefited the general population; yet the supply of
qualified personnel remained inadequate to meet the reformers' needs. In
place of the roughly two thousand scribes who had been their predecessors
as of 1770–1790, civil officials' ranks expanded to the point of including perhaps thirty-five thousand at a time under Abdülhamid.[23] Much of that growth
occurred during the Tanzimat, as civil officials assumed the leading role in the
new provincial administration. To administer an empire of such size, however,
these were still small numbers, and officials' qualifications varied widely. One
measure of this variation consisted of a gap between civil officials who were
proficient in French, the international language of the day, and those who
were not. Implying different educations and cultural orientations, this skill
opened or shut doors for civil officials.

In the military, comparable disparities resulted from the lack of enough academy graduates to fill all the important commands. The major commanders of
the Crimean War emerged from the provinces, not the academies.[24] Among
military officers, the distinction between "school men" (*mektepli*), who studied
in the new academies, and "regimentals" (*alaylı*), who rose through the ranks
and were not always even literate, created antagonisms for the rest of the empire's
history. Not surprisingly, old forms of factional rivalry persisted, as did their bale-
ful effects on military effectiveness. An efficient command and staff system and
more adequate training programs only emerged later in the century.

In education, the need for new elites induced a top-down approach. Institutions of higher learning were founded first in the form of academies to train
new elites. Preparatory schools for the academies and a general system of modern government schools were added only later. The price of this approach was
that many years passed before the elite academies could perform up to level.
As noted, the founding of elite military schools predated the Tanzimat: military engineering schools for the navy (1773) and the army (1793), the military
medical school (1827), and the Military Academy (Harbiye, 1834). Student
missions were also sent to Europe, and for a time (1857–1864) there was an
Ottoman school in Paris. Systematic efforts to train new types of civil officials
began in 1821 with the Translation Office (Tercüme odası) of the Sublime
Porte, initially more of a school than a bureau. Schools to train civil officials

began to be founded as part of a larger effort to create a network of government schools. The first new schools for civil officials became part of the *rüşdiye* schools in 1839. Upper elementary schools, these were intended to pick up where the Kur'anic mekteb left off and educate students to about age fourteen. Modest as they were, the rüşdiye schools were perhaps comparable in importance to the one-room schoolhouses of the nineteenth-century United States. Middle schools (*idadiye*) began to be founded in 1845, initially to prepare students for the Military Academy. The first lycée (*sultaniye*) opened only in 1868. The most important systematizing measure for the government schools took the form of the public education regulations of 1869 (*maarif-i umumiye nizamnamesi*). New teaching methods (*usul-i cedid*), intended to achieve literacy more quickly and effectively than in the mektebs, were introduced as early as 1847 and came into general use by about 1870, eventually spreading also to Islamic Central Asia. As the new civil schools developed, several became particularly important in training civil officials, the best known being the School of Civil Administration (Mülkiye Mektebi, 1859) and the Galatasaray Lycée (1868), whose French curriculum made it a springboard into diplomatic careers. By the 1870s, the new schools educated far more than the civil and military elites.[25]

Although still small in relation to need, the new schools produced momentous effects, sometimes unintended. If Ottoman sultans wanted new elites to serve them personally, the new ideas these men discovered in school led them to shift their loyalties from the person of the sultan to their own ideal of what the state should be, a fact with major consequences for the Ottoman Empire and Turkish republic up to the present.[26] The schools also produced a new reading public, who provided the market for the emergent print media.

LEGISLATION

If civil officials' de facto hegemony demarcated the period chronologically, the engine driving the Tanzimat was legislation.[27] Much evidence supports understanding the Tanzimat as a movement in legislation. In his essays of the 1830s, Sadık Rifat Paşa elaborated the connection between external and internal public law, between achieving the empire's admission into the European diplomatic system and maintaining a just internal legal order. European demands for internal reform in return for military-diplomatic support in 1839 and 1854 made the same point. Since Selim III's Nizam-ı Cedid, the practical connection between reform and drawing up instructions, regulations, and laws had enforced itself on Ottoman reformers' awareness. There would be no Nizam-ı Cedid without *nizamname*s (regulations, literally "writings about order"). The same was true for the Tanzimat, a term derived from the same Arabic root as *nizam*. The need for instructions and plans became especially clear in cases where a given reform needed to be implemented uniformly throughout the empire.

The peaks marked by the Gülhane decree of 1839, the Reform decree of 1856, and the constitution of 1876 form crests on a wave of legislation that rose and never subsided. When the official volumes of laws and regulations, the *Düstur*, began to be published, this growth became physically measurable; under the same title, the series of legal publications still continues.[28] A systemic relationship also exists among the organic acts of 1839, 1856, and 1876. The Gülhane decree, as noted, was less of a Westernizing measure than has commonly been assumed. It did call for a just order with reforms in taxation, military recruitment, and judicial procedure; and it extended guarantees for life, honor, and property to all subjects, Muslim and non-Muslim. It promised new laws to implement these promises. The flood of new laws and regulations during the Tanzimat shows that the promise did not go unfulfilled. Whereas the wording of the Gülhane decree did not explicitly state the equality of non-Muslims with Muslims, self-interested interpretations of the decree prevailed to that effect.

The Reform decree (Islahat fermanı) of 1856 confirmed the point unambiguously.[29] Practically, the Reform decree has two parts. The second reads like a hasty list of reforms overdue for attention, as in the reference to "doing things like banks" (*banka misillü şeyler yapılıp*). In contrast, the first part is a careful exposition of reforms to be enacted, "as required by the imperial decree read at Gülhane and by my auspicious Tanzimat," for the benefit "without exception, of all my imperial subjects of every religion and sect." The different religious communities were to form assemblies to reorganize their affairs. As a result, non-Muslim communities acquired communal "constitutions" and new quasi-parliamentary bodies by the early 1860s.[30] The decree liberalized the conditions for building and repairing non-Muslim religious buildings. It forbade language or practices that "held some communities lower than others." It proclaimed Ottoman subjects of all religions eligible for official appointment depending on their ability and opened both civil and military schools to all. It extended the obligation of military service to non-Muslims but allowed exemption on payment of a substitution fee (*bedel*), which in practice replaced the cizye, the special tax that the sharia required of non-Muslims. Court cases between parties from different communities were to be heard before mixed courts; cases between coreligionists could still be heard in communal courts.

The Ottoman constitution of 1876 was a logical response not just to the international situation at the time but to a variety of partial organic regulatory acts promulgated as the Tanzimat progressed, in addition to the Gülhane and Reform decrees of 1839 and 1856. In the 1860s, organic statutes defined special administrative regimes for Lebanon and Crete; and the non-Muslim religious communities drew up communal regulations, sometimes referred to as "constitutions." In the Ottoman periphery, Tunisia was under a constitution of its own for a time in the 1860s, and Romania acquired one in 1866. Organic regulation of parts of the imperial system raised demands for organic regulation of the whole.[31] Against this trend, the international crisis of the mid-1870s served more as a precipitator than as a cause for adopting the constitution.

Hastily drawn up between October and December 1876 by a commission including ulema, military officers, and civil officials, the constitution contained compromises and imprecisions. Yet it showed the extent to which ideals such as rule of law, guaranteed rights, and equality had become established in Ottoman thinking. Its articles were grouped in sections pertaining to the empire's territorial integrity, the sultan, and the dynasty; Ottoman subjects' rights and obligations; the ministers of state; the officials; the parliament; the courts; the provinces; and a final miscellaneous section.

The constitution included articles pregnant with future consequences. Article 5 asserted that the imperial personage of the sultan was sacred and unaccountable. Article 7 left his "sacred prerogatives" undefined after first listing vast powers among them. These included appointing and dismissing ministers, conferring ranks and decorations, striking coins in his name, having his name mentioned in the Friday mosque sermon (*hutbe*), contracting treaties, declaring war and peace, carrying out military actions by land and sea, enforcing sharia and kanun, pardoning convicts, and convening and dissolving parliament on condition of holding new elections for the chamber of deputies. The constitution became law only by the sultan's decree; his right to continue legislating by decree was nowhere denied; and his freedom to veto laws passed in parliament, where the ministers retained most of the legislative initiative, was unchecked. Finally, article 113, inserted at Abdülhamid's insistence, acknowledged the sultan's right under martial law to exile anyone on the basis of a police report identifying that person as a danger to the empire's security.[32] Although martial law was not in force at the time, Midhat Paşa went into exile in 1876, an early victim of this provision.

If the reform acts of 1839, 1856, and 1876 formed the crests on a wave of legislation, much of its mass and momentum consisted of new codes. An initial penal code (*ceza kanunnamesi*, 1840), asserting the equality of all subjects before the law without deference to rank, was revised in 1851 and replaced with a code of French origin in 1858. Also French-inspired were the codes of commerce (1850) and maritime commerce (1863). The agrarian code (*arazi kanunnamesi*, 1858), which codified and systematized state ownership over agricultural lands (miri), attempted to protect small peasant cultivators (successfully or not, depending on local conditions), clarify titles, and identify the responsible taxpayers.[33] When Âli Paşa proposed adapting the French civil code as well, the ulema resisted. Instead, a codification of sharia law was undertaken under the direction of Ahmed Cevdet Paşa and published as the *Mecelle* (1870–1877), a work in Turkish, not in the Arabic of Islamic legal treatises. Less conspicuously, thousands more laws, regulations, and instructions swelled the tide of Tanzimat regulations to flood stage and beyond.

To apply the new codes, new courts were created, starting with commercial courts (1840), each presided over by three judges named by the government. In the 1860s, a network of *nizami* courts was set up to try cases under the new codes; an adjective derived from *nizam*, the term *nizami* identified these courts and many other institutions as products of the reforms. The nizami courts were organized in a European-style, three-tiered hierarchy, with courts of first instance, appeals, and cassation, in contrast to the sharia courts, which lacked any formal appeals instance. Members of the ulema often presided in the new courts, serving in panels of judges that also included civil officials and members of the non-Muslim communities.

Generations of scholars have seen in the new codes, often based on foreign models, and in the nizami courts so many steps toward secularization and breaches in the Islamic character of the Ottoman state. Now, some scholars offer alternative interpretations. For example, Abdülhamid's decree promulgating the constitution of 1876 echoed the Gülhane decree's reference to "laws conformable to the sharia" (*kavanin-i şer'iye*) and affirmed the conformity of the constitution to sharia provisions (*ahkâm-ı şer'-i şerif*).[34] The *Mecelle* forms the clearest example of a major component of the new body of law derived from the sharia. The land law of 1858 provides an analogously clear case where traditional Ottoman kanun was codified as part of the new legislation. The major role of ulema as judges in the courts moderated in practice what might otherwise have been starkly secularizing reforms. As the empire progressed gradually toward creating the regulatory apparatus of a "law state" (*hukuk devleti*, a term evoking the German concept of the Rechtsstaat), perhaps the most serious problem was something else. Instead of the tension between Islam and secularism, the greatest problem may have been the gap between the ideal of a "law state" and the authoritarianism that either deified the law without regard to its human consequences, or else used law and regulation instrumentally to extend the reach of a power that placed itself above the law.[35]

EXPANSION OF GOVERNMENT: THE CENTER

During the Tanzimat, many Ottomans thought they saw that kind of abuse of authority in the Sublime Porte. In fact, the practical impact of increasing the volume of legislation in an effort at centralization was to intensify the trends, already noted before 1839, toward expanding government, which intruded increasingly into people's lives, in the center and in the provinces.

The most obvious indicator of central government expansion was the proliferation of new ministries and agencies. The old government agencies had begun to be reorganized along the lines of European ministries in the 1830s. By the 1870s, the process had reached the point where the major branches of government service had headquarters all around Istanbul. In addition to the palace secretariat (*mabeyn*) at the palace, the civil, military, and religious services had their respective headquarters at the Sublime Porte (Bab-ı Âli), Ministry of War (Bab-ı Seraskeri), and central offices of the Religious Establishment (Bab-ı Meşihat). A number of ministries were located elsewhere in the capital: those of finance, charitable foundations (*evkaf*), education, trade and agriculture, customs, and land registry (Defter Emaneti).[36]

Along with this organizational growth of ministries and departments, new councils (*meclis*) proliferated greatly. These have often been interpreted as steps toward the creation of a parliament. In the case of the provincial administrative councils, the inclusion of elected members and representatives of the religious communities supports that interpretation. The proliferation of councils also illustrates another point about the way governmental institutions develop. Creating a board or council often serves as a way to meet a need for which there is not yet a permanent agency, thus expanding the reach of an inadequately staffed bureaucracy. In fact, between 1838 and 1871, the Council on Trade and Agriculture (1838) evolved into a ministry, and the Council of Judicial Ordinances (Divan-ı Ahkâm-ı Adliye) evolved into the Ministry of Justice.

Popular reactions against big government were many. Each stage in the implementation of egalitarianism among religious communities produced reactions, with occasional violence, as in Syria and Lebanon in 1860. Many of the conciliar bodies brought together officials and representatives of the populace to implement policies about which they often disagreed. Taxation was repeatedly reformed. Censuses and surveys of households and their income sources were carried out. The 1843 division of the empire into five military zones with an army based in each created new sites of interaction between the populace and the military. Muslim males from the provinces — Istanbulites were exempt from both conscription and taxation — bore the burden of military service. Regulations of 1869 defined that as four years of active duty, then sixteen years of reserve duty on different levels. About 150,000 men were to be on active service (*nizami*), 60,000 in the active reserve (*ihtiyat*), 96,000 each in the first and second levels of reserves (*redif*), and 300,000 in the home guard (*mustahfız*). New schools offered new educational choices. New courts issued decisions, and new laws affected matters as pervasively important as land tenure. Mailing letters (1840), sending telegrams (1855, even from Baghdad by 1861), and traveling by steamship (about 1850) became possible, wholly or partly by government initiative. The growth of the print media led to controversial attempts to regulate the press. The quarantines set up in 1838 affected not only those who traveled abroad but also Muslim pilgrims. In Istanbul and some other cities, pilot projects introduced such innovations as gas streetlights, new firefighting apparatus, public transport, and regulations on construction. Modern government began to acquire monumental form with the building of headquarters, schools, courts, police stations, and docks. Despite slavery's complex roots in Ottoman society and the lack of indigenous abolitionism, piecemeal steps also occurred (roughly 1847–1890), largely under British pressure, to prohibit the slave trade.[37]

Bosphorus ferry at Beykoz, between Istanbul and the Black Sea on the Anatolian side of the Bosphorus. (By Abdullah Frères, Library of Congress, Prints and Photographs Division, Abdülhamid II Collection, 3b27952u.)

EXPANSION OF GOVERNMENT: THE PROVINCES

Centralization and defensive modernization produced major impacts in the provinces, too. For much of this period, new reforms were introduced gradually or piecemeal, either as pilot projects or in hot spots of crisis such as Lebanon; in many places, local resistance impeded the implementation of the reforms.[38] Not until 1864 were provincial administration regulations (*vilayet nizamnamesi*) issued for general application. Probably reflecting the acute shortage of financial and human resources available to implement reform across the empire, this gradualism long obscured earlier measures, which were energetic and merit recognition.

Following the Gülhane decree, the first goal in the provinces, starting in April 1840, was to eliminate tax-farming and appoint tax collectors (*muhassıl*) instead. These collectors' roles were more extensive than their title implied. Not responsible to the chief administrative officer of the locality, they were supposed to explain the Tanzimat reforms, set up councils, collect taxes, and have their clerks register taxpayers and their property. The councils were to bring together officials and local representatives to discuss tax apportionment and other matters of local interest. The collectors' salaries and expenses were to be provided by the central government. They were expected to raise what they could from the local populace and forward it immediately to Istanbul to cover the expenses of reform. In the long run, replacing a multitude of old exactions with the consolidated tax (*vergü*) announced at Gülhane would produce a significant net tax cut for taxpayers. The local council (*memleket meclisi*, among other names) was to include the kadı, müfti, the collector and his assistants, leaders of the non-Muslim clergy in mixed districts, and four to six elected members, conducting their proceedings according to stated regulations. To deal with problems, inspection missions were sent out across Rumelia and Anatolia in 1840. As of 1841, fifty tax collectors (muhassıl) were serving in ten provinces, from central Anatolia to Bulgaria, Macedonia, and the Aegean islands. The inspection missions sent out in 1840 had heard complaints of every kind, even that of a woman who stated that she was pregnant by the tax collector's assistant.[39]

The new system of direct revenue collection was abandoned as early as 1842, however. Costs for salaries exceeded revenue collections in many places. Instructions mandating that "the most reasonable and prominent" be chosen as candidates made it easy for notables who had oppressed the peasants in the past to dominate the councils and turn the new system to their favor. Orthodox clergy and lay leaders reported to the patriarch in Istanbul that they were ignored or scorned in the councils, and he complained to the Sublime Porte. Tax revolts occurred in a number of places, including Niş and Vidin.[40] Tax-farming made a comeback, with some exceptions, and survived as long as the empire lasted.

Some elements of the abandoned program survived, however. Local councils persisted and multiplied. The surveys of households and income sources necessary to assess the new consolidated tax, launched in 1840, were carried out in revised format in 1845 on such a scale that nearly eighteen thousand registers survive in the Ottoman archives.[41] Replacing many old extraordinary (*örfi*) taxes, that is, taxes other than the sharia-mandated taxes like the tithe (*öşür*) and the tax required of non-Muslims (cizye), the consolidated tax (vergü) survived. For some years longer, it was not farmed out but was collected at the quarter or village level by the headman (muhtar) and the imam or priest. On three occasions, the rate of the combined tax was raised for specific purposes. Dissatisfaction with the tax led to an 1860 reform designed to tax real property and income on a proportional basis. However, this required yet another survey and consequently was implemented only in places where that survey could be carried out.[42]

With the abolition of the muhassıls in 1842, the outlines of the provincial administration system that would be systematized in the regulations of 1864 began to take shape. In 1836, in connection with the introduction of the army reserve (redif), Mahmud II, had changed the titles of the province governors from vali to *müşir*, a title normally associated with the highest military rank. However, this system did not yield acceptable results; and the title of provincial governors was changed back to vali with the beginning of the Tanzimat. In 1842, the hierarchy of administrative districts was revised in regions where the Tanzimat had been introduced, and civil officials began to be appointed to serve as chief administrative officers at all three levels: province (*eyalet*), district (*sancak*), and subdistrict (*kaza*).[43] These had staffs to support them and, at least at the higher administrative levels, councils of the familiar type. In 1845, representatives from all the provinces were invited to Istanbul for a general council. After it dispersed, temporary "development councils" (*imar meclisleri*) were set up in the different provinces. From 1849 on, each province was supposed to have its provincial council (*eyalet meclisi*). As civil officialdom expanded into the provinces to staff the new administrative posts, complaints of abuses from seemingly every district indicated how inadequate the supply of qualified personnel was and how wide a gap opened between reformist ideals and local accomplishments. Separatist movements and foreign intervention expanded such disparities into threats to the empire's unity and survival.

In the early 1860s, as Romania approached independence, Mount Lebanon acquired its special administrative regime, and outbreaks of different kinds occurred from Jidda to Bosnia, the government prepared to revise and generalize its system of provincial administration with laws of 1864 and 1871. Foreigners regarded these laws as triumphs of French influence. Whatever the Ottoman reformers drew from their knowledge of French practice, however, they drew more from the experience accumulated domestically since 1842, not to speak of historical precedents extending back to early Ottoman centuries. Midhat Paşa had conducted a major experiment in administrative improvement since 1861 as governor of Nish. The 1864 law on provincial administration was intended for application in a single, specially created Danube province with Midhat as governor; his appointment in 1869 as governor of Baghdad helped to spread these policies.[44] The law was published with modification in 1867 for application in various provinces, henceforth referred to as *vilayet*. Further revised, the law went into general application in 1871 and remained in effect until 1913. By 1876, that law governed twenty-seven provinces.

The 1871 provincial administration law prescribed a jurisdictional hierarchy in four levels. In descending order, the levels (and their chief administrators) were the *vilayet* (*vali*), the *sancak* or *liva* (*mutasarrıf*), the *kaza* (*kaymakam*), and the *nahiye* (*müdür*). The four levels were one reason why people who did not know much about Ottoman history thought the law imitated the French *département* system. The law assigned the governors a long list of functions and an enlarged staff, many of whom had specialized functions corresponding to those of ministries in Istanbul. Each of the top three levels was to have an administrative council. The councils included both elected members, Muslim and non-Muslim in equal numbers, and official members. In addition, a general council (*meclis-i umumi*) was to bring together representatives of all the province's districts once a year to discuss issues of provincewide interest. The law also included provisions on the nizami courts and on municipal institutions. Special commissions might also be set up for purposes such as refugee settlement. While the evidence indicates that Muslim and non-Muslim council members were becoming more accustomed to working with one another, dissatisfactions with the new system of provincial administration quickly appeared. In the short-lived Ottoman parliament of 1877–1878, a new provincial administration passed the lower house but not the upper.[45]

INTERCOMMUNAL RELATIONS: INTEGRATION OR DISINTEGRATION?

To hold the empire together while modernizing it required promoting unity among its peoples. The Tanzimat reforms included multiple, sometimes contradictory, attempts to do that. The Gülhane decree proclaimed the applicability of its promised reforms to all subjects, Muslim and non-Muslim. The Reform decree of 1856 expanded this into equality across religious lines, while also confirming the non-Muslims' communal privileges. The 1856 decree also proclaimed the goal of strengthening the "heartfelt bonds of patriotism" (*revabıt-ı kalbiye-i vatandaşî*) among all the sultan's subjects.

Simultaneously optimizing individual rights, communal rights, and all-embracing Ottoman patriotism would prove difficult. Yet the struggle to reconcile rights at the individual, group, and all-inclusive levels has confronted modern polities around the world.[46] The Tanzimat reformers faced this problem at a time when identity and difference were becoming politicized in new ways. The concessions to non-Muslims disturbed conservative Muslims, who felt deprived of the superior status that sharia norms assigned to them. Some disorders, as in Syria and Lebanon, expressed such feelings. Be that as it may, the non-Muslim communities set about reorganizing their affairs, and the modernist intelligentsia set about promoting a new, egalitarian concept of Ottomanism (Osmanlılık) to cement unity.

The reorganization of non-Muslim communal affairs responded to several important trends. One was the lengthening list of non-Muslim religious communities seeking official recognition as millets. Another was the corruption and oppression prevalent inside the older millets, Greek and Armenian.[47] At times, both trends interacted. In 1850, Armenian converts to Protestantism, only a few thousand in number, gained recognition as the Protestant millet. Governed by a bishop with lay and religious councils, the Protestants created a model for other communities. The significant role accorded to Protestant lay leaders especially excited envy.

Among the long-established communities, new regulations were adopted for the Greek Orthodox (1860, 1862), Gregorian Armenians (1863), and Jews (1864). Among small Eastern churches, the Assyrians (Süryani) and Chaldeans (Keldani) also gained official recognition. An empire inside the empire, the Orthodox church's heavily Greek hierarchy was vulnerable to nationalism for the same reason that the Ottoman Empire was. This fact resulted in demands for autocephalism (independently headed, national Orthodox churches) in Bulgaria (1870) and Romania (1885).

The non-Muslim religious communities' reorganization had important consequences. Their new statutes—sometimes called millet constitutions—raised Ottoman constitutionalists' expectations. Armenians active in their communal reform also advocated an imperial constitution for the empire; one of them, Krikor Odian, served on the commission that drafted it.[48] Yet while reinforcing solidarity among Ottoman subjects and creating conditions for

each community to flourish were philosophically reconcilable, in the Ottoman Empire of the Tanzimat, the latter could not be done without reinforcing
the separatist tendencies that Ottoman solidarity was intended to overcome.
Inasmuch as the religious differences basic to millet reform seldom exactly
matched the ethnic differences basic to modern nationalism, variable and
unpredictable consequences ensued, as the Greek Orthodox and Armenian
cases illustrated.

Although Greece had long since become independent, the Hellenic Kingdom was tiny compared to the empirewide dispersion of the flocks of the Greek
Orthodox church. The Orthodox hierarchy consequently took a very guarded
position, allowing some lay representation but otherwise limiting reform. In
contrast, although Protestant and Armenian Catholic communities had won
some Armenians, the overlap between ethnicity and religion was much higher
for the Gregorian Armenians. Here, progressive intellectuals proved influential, despite opposition from the financial elite. As a result, the 1863 regulations provided for a community headed by the Armenian patriarch, with
civil and ecclesiastical councils, both subordinate to a general assembly. The
assembly turned into a virtual Armenian parliament, which advanced subversive demands, including autonomy for provinces with Armenian populations.
The Armenian patriarch's role, too, began to reflect the shift from religious to
nationalist emphases. The extent to which the outcome of communal reform in
other millets might differ was well illustrated by Ottoman Jews, to whom ideas
of nationalism or separatism remained foreign.

All the while, the Tanzimat statesmen tried to foster heartfelt patriotism to
hold all Ottoman subjects together. This formed part of Ottoman intellectuals'
larger effort to propagate new political concepts and explain them by redefining
old terms. The word *vatan*, originally used in localized senses, had by the 1790s
begun to be readapted to mean "fatherland," so recapitulating the earlier evolution of the French term *pays* and its counterparts in other languages. For example, the Gülhane decree connected military recruitment with the defense of
the vatan. In 1850, too, the district governor (mutasarrıf) of Jerusalem appealed
to non-Muslims to join Muslims in aiding the poor and old because all were
"brothers in the fatherland" (*ikhwan fi 'l-watan*).[49] Similarly, the Arabic root
from which the term *millet* derived, provided material for the new vocabulary.
The Ottoman usage of the term *millet* to refer to a religious community is amply
illustrated above: *Rum milleti*, the "Orthodox millet," included all who were
Greek Orthodox in religion, including native speakers of Arabic, Bulgarian, or
Romanian, even Turkish, and not just Greek. Yet as political identity gained in
salience compared to religious identity, some Ottomans began to use the term

millet to translate the French *nation*.[50] With time, Ottomans adopted the related terms *milli* to mean "national" and *milliyet* to mean "nationality." The continual adaptation of old terms to express new concepts formed part of the revolutionary transformations occurring in the way meanings were produced and conveyed.

The new "patriotic bond" was to take the form of a redefinition of Ottomanism (Osmanlılık). Historically, the members of the sultan's ruling elite had been the only people referred to as Osmanlı. Equality meant extending that identity to rulers and subjects alike. To consolidate the emotional bond that it identified as "vatandaşî," sharing the same fatherland, the Reform decree of 1856 launched a series of reforms that gradually brought significant numbers of non-Muslims into some branches of the civil administration and into the governmental schools. The results witness tangibly to the seriousness with which the government took this policy.

The reference to "heartfelt patriotism" implicitly recognized the need to infuse the Ottoman ideal with emotional fire. That was a task at which Ottoman officials proved less adept than a new form of Ottoman political opposition that emerged on their flanks. A century earlier, the Ottoman attempt to reconcile individual, communal, and all-inclusive rights and identities might have worked as well as the construction of British nationality did. In its day, it worked no better than Austro-Hungarian attempts to create an "imperial nationalism."[51]

POLITICS TRANSFORMED

Until 1839, Ottoman political participation was still limited—officially—to the Ottoman ruling elites alone. That idea ignored a rich history of negotiation, resistance, and rebellion. Yet to a significant degree, the empire still had administrative institutions but not political ones; and the Ottoman ruling elites and intelligentsia were still virtually identical. With the articulation of policy alternatives still only beginning to assume high relief, such politics as existed still revolved around personalities and factions more than issues.

The reforms of the late 1830s, increasing the security of high office-holding, enabled Mustafa Reşid Paşa, Fuad Paşa, and Âli Paşa to hold on at the top for much longer than would have been possible before. The last two fell out with the first by his later years, but never lost their own ability to work together. Their prolonged tenure would have provoked opposition, even without other factors. In fact, the political game was changing all around them. The flood of new legislation implied policy alternatives, which generated conflict over issues as well as personalities. The manipulation of the sultan's decree power to carry out his officials' will rather than his own clouded the legitimacy of the reforms and exposed the weakness of civil bureaucratic hegemony. The recruitment of non-Muslims into civil office in the name of egalitarianism, and the rapid growth in officials' numbers, posed new challenges to social integration within official ranks. The proliferation of conciliar bodies, bringing together bureaucrats and nonbureaucrats, provided new sites for disagreement and controversy. Gradually, political institutions began to emerge alongside administration ones, most obviously the parliament of 1876–1878. Amid such changes, it was only a question of time until new forces of political opposition emerged, not just among religious minorities or separatist nationalists, but among the Ottoman intelligentsia.

Socioeconomic and cultural changes made sure that this occurred. Selim III had been a major figure in traditional forms of poetical and musical production, not only as a patron but as a poet and composer. In contrast, his successors set standards in the Westernization of tastes, but none of them rated mention as a poet, historically the premier form of literary production.[52] What connected poetry to politics was the essential role that poetry writing played in the old factional politics. Historically every Ottoman intellectual aspired to be a poet. Those who could not excel at it had to find some other way to make a living; employment in a government office was the usual solution. Those who did excel at poetry were often no good at anything else.[53] In either case, the route to material reward was through patronage, of which no one had more to dispense than the sultan. For those not born to privilege, the classic route to form a career-launching connection (intisab) to a great man was to submit proof of one's talent in verse, preferably a eulogy (*kaside*) to the addressee. If that failed, the next-best route to reward was satire, which might elicit a valuable gift from the victim to silence the satirist.

Although these patterns survived into the Tanzimat period, seismic shifts occurred in the context surrounding them. Apparently, the decline of palace patronage for the poetical and musical forms beloved of Selim III struck a major blow to artists devoted to those forms. At the same time, new forms of individual subjectivity and class formation, new media of communication, and new ideas about language and literary genres emerged for writers prepared to address a broad audience. Between roughly 1840 and 1860, Ottoman "print capitalism" emerged—the whole cultural-material complex identified with modern print media, especially the newspapers, and the new bourgeois reading public. The consequences proved nearly revolutionary both in the short term and in the long term of Ottoman and Turkish modernity.

Ahmed Cevdet Paşa thought he saw the origins of what is "known in French as the *Opposition*" in an episode that occurred when a poet-bureaucrat, Hafız Müşfik Efendi, was passed over for promotion by Âli Paşa, who appointed his son-in-law instead. Müşfik turned from praising Âli Paşa to satirizing him. He also took the new step of leaving government service to work for the first privately owned Ottoman-language newspaper, *Ceride-i Havadis*, founded by an Englishman, William Churchill, in 1840. There Müşfik became the nucleus of the group of like-minded intellectuals who brought out the paper.[54] The scope for this kind of endeavor increased with the advent of other privately owned newspapers, especially the first Turkish-owned nonofficial newspaper, Yusuf Agâh's *Tercüman-ı Ahval*, in 1860. Others followed, making the 1860s the founding decade for the Ottoman-language press.

The 1860s also witnessed the formation of the first modern-style opposition movement among Ottoman intellectuals, the Young Ottomans (Yeni Osmanlılar).[55] The connection between them and the rise of nonofficial journalism was close. They acknowledged their debt to Müşfik and his associates. Among the Young Ottomans' founders, at least two—Yusuf Agâh and İbrahim Şinasi—had founded newspapers. The others soon would. These were men of higher social status and greater talent than Hafız Müşfik. Most of them had or could have had patronage relationships with the leading statesmen. What made them different was their fidelity to the new ideas, their persistence in propagating them through the new media, and their willingness to defy their bureaucratic superiors' wrath. Taking to journalism and the new literary genres, they formed a "patriotic alliance" in 1865 to work for constitutional government.

In 1867, the Young Ottomans found a new kind of patron in Mustafa Fazıl Paşa, a descendant of Egypt's Mehmed Ali and the brother of Egyptian khedive Ismail Paşa. Mustafa Fazıl had experienced the frustrations of bureaucratic service in Istanbul. He had experienced even greater frustrations in Egypt, where Ismail had bought Istanbul's consent to change the succession rule to primogeniture, thus excluding Mustafa Fazıl. Still vastly wealthy, he departed for Paris, invited the Young Ottomans to join him, and bankrolled their activities, including the newspapers they published beyond Ottoman censors' reach. The Young Ottomans thus became the first Ottoman intellectuals to choose exile rather than compromise their ideals.

Historians tend to think of the Young Ottomans as something like a political party and emphasize their constitutionalism. In fact, they are more like a cultural movement. They neither achieved power within existing institutions, nor created any effective organization, nor provoked a revolution.[56] Their ideas ranged all across the spectrum of nineteenth-century modernity and its implications for Ottoman society. Compared to the Tanzimat statesmen, they had a more systematic knowledge of both European and Islamic thought. They used this knowledge to critique the Tanzimat and present a new vision to the reading public. Although their political ideas make them heroes of the movement for liberty and constitutionalism, their writings overall identify them as cultural nationalists, as the progenitors of a new Ottoman engagement with modernity. Simplifying their language and adopting new literary forms to appeal to the new audience being created by the new schools, they launched the effort to create a new Ottoman culture that would be modern without sacrificing its identity to Westernization.

The men who became known collectively as Young Ottomans were a heterogeneous group. Among those remembered by name independently of the movement, Ali Suavi, an erratic religious scholar, more nearly resembles Islamic fundamentalists than the other Young Ottomans.[57] İbrahim Şinasi, one of the founders of modern Turkish literature, contributed to the modernization of communications through his role in developing both the print media and a straightforward, journalistic style. The outstanding literary figures of the movement were Ziya and Namık Kemal. Of the two, Ziya was culturally conservative, and Namık Kemal was more the prototype of the politically engaged intellectual. What united the Young Ottomans most obviously was their opposition to the bureaucratic despotism of Fuad Paşa and Âli Paşa. Not realizing that despotism might assume even more menacing forms, they returned to Istanbul after Âli's death (1871) and brought out some of their most influential publications there between 1871 and 1876. Ziya and Namık Kemal both helped draft the constitution. Abdülhamid then made sure that they ended their days in provincial administrative posts.

Examples of Namık Kemal's writings will provide insights below into the wider reaches of his cultural modernism. However, the Young Ottomans' political ideas provide indispensable indications of their significance for Ottoman political development. In contrast to the Tanzimat statesmen, the Young Ottomans engaged more deeply with several traditions of Islamic thought, not just political theory, but also jurisprudence. Their use of Islamic terms to convey pivotal ideas of liberal political theory was not merely a case of recycling old terms to convey new ideas. Rather, adapting the Islamic jurisprudential method of reasoning by analogy (*kıyas*), they attempted to prove that the reforms they advocated were justified in Islamic terms. Namık Kemal used this method to articulate a number of the standard positions of later Islamic modernists. He justified representative government by citing the Kur'anic injunction to "consult about affairs" (*wa shâwirhum fî 'l-amri*). He attempted to legitimate the concepts of responsible government and popular sovereignty in terms of a contractual interpretation of the *biat* (*bay'a* in Arabic, the oath of loyalty originally pledged at the accession of a new caliph). His appeals for law and

justice focused on the sharia, and he violently opposed the legal secularization of the Tanzimat. In his presentation of these ideas, old and new seem
to merge down to the molecular level. In making his case for representative
government, for example, he combines Kur'anic precepts with the argumentation of a European political philosopher. Moreover, he explicitly advocates
assemblies including representatives of the different religious communities, an
Ottoman political necessity unanticipated in the Kur'anic injunction about
consultation.[58]

At the same time that the Young Ottomans advanced a neoconservative critique of the Tanzimat and proposed an Islamic filter against reckless Westernization, their engagement with modernity was unmistakable. They were imbued
with the nineteenth-century belief in progress. In rejecting the complexities
of the old poetical style, they not only addressed new audiences through new
genres and media but also injected into their writing an urgent appeal to the
emotions. They wrote not to display their erudition but to impassion their readers. In addition to elaborating modern political ideas in terms compatible with
Islamic categories, they expanded the vocabulary of Ottoman patriotism. Namık
Kemal elaborated the patriotic imperatives that went with the new meaning
of *vatan* as "fatherland," and of *hürriyet* as political "liberty" and not merely
freedom from slavery.[59] Yet his sense of identity still oscillated among Ottoman
cosmopolitanism, Islamic solidarity, and Turkish self-consciousness in a way
that persisted among Ottoman intellectuals until the collapse of the empire.
Ultimately, the Young Ottomans propagated both constitutionalism and an all-
inclusive Islamic and Ottoman culture of modernity.

ECONOMIC CHANGE

Nothing hindered the success of the Tanzimat reforms more than inadequate
economic resources.[60] Difficulties in government finance worsened progres-
sively. Low agricultural productivity and underdeveloped manufactures contributed to the difficulties. Yet despite such problems and the empire's dependent
position in the world economy, monetary policy, agriculture, trade, and manufactures all registered some gains.

GOVERNMENT FINANCE

Some signs indicate that Tanzimat policy itself contributed to the revenue
shortages. This proposition defies the conventional wisdom about rapacious
taxation in the Ottoman Empire. However, even in the most democratic modern polities, taxation is considered excessive everywhere. In the Tanzimat

reform decrees, the constant emphasis on guaranteeing justice and consolidating the subjects' loyalties, the expectation that consolidating old taxes and replacing tax-farming with direct collection would lower rates, and the failure of the direct collection project cannot have improved revenue receipts at the center in the 1840s. The survival of tax-farming thereafter meant an enduring gap between tax-farmers' collections and the central government's receipts, even if, as has been argued, competition among bidders constrained collection costs to roughly 10 percent of the revenue.[61] Ottoman taxpayers had real grievances over inequitable tax apportionment, the timing of specific exactions, and tax collectors' usurious money-lending practices. Most Ottoman subjects were poor and operated on narrow margins at best. Comparatively, however, tax rates were probably not high. Studies of localities near Izmir (Anatolia) and around Plovdiv (Bulgaria, mid-1840s) conclude that taxation averaged 20–25 percent of income. For Bulgaria, another figure of 20–30 percent of rural income "used other than by the cultivator" also includes rents. Such figures were "not oppressive by European standards of the day." Likewise, taxes in Lebanon after 1861 were "artificially low," based on outdated surveys; yet the region's road network was increased thirtyfold in length in the same period.[62] Whether their subjects thought them rapacious or not, the Tanzimat statesmen perhaps were not hard-nosed enough when it came to matching means and ends.

Ineffective controls on expenditure aggravated this problem. The finance ministry's accounts of annual receipts and expenditures for 1841–1876 record surpluses in only two years (1846 and 1868) and deficits in all other years, ranging from 4.2 million kuruş in 1841 to 505 million kuruş in 1876.[63] Rules for preparing budgets were adopted in 1855 and revised in 1874, and budgets began to be published in 1863. Still, nothing effectively controlled spending, least of all at the palace. In addition to luxuries, Sultan Abdülaziz was so devoted to improving the military that he ordered ships and cannons without consulting his ministers. Young Ottoman critics seized on palace expenditures that exceeded those of the Russian or Austrian empires, the costs of Istanbulites' antiquated exemption from taxation (and military service), and the unfavorable contrasts between French and Ottoman government spending.

A major monetary reform did produce beneficial results, however. This put an end to monetary debasements, which assumed unprecedented proportions between 1770 and 1840.[64] Stimulated partly by a similar Egyptian reform in 1834, the Ottoman government introduced a reformed bimetallic standard in 1844. Silver kuruş and gold lira were both to be legal tender, with 100 kuruş to the lira and the gold-silver ratio set at 1:15.09. All the silver and gold coins minted from then until 1922 adhered to the 1844 standard. Copper coins were also minted in small denominations. Yet the success of monetary reform was not total. The government did not have the resources to withdraw all old coins and had to leave them in circulation. With the decline in the value of silver on the world market, the value of the silver kuruş fell by the early 1880s to 108 to the gold lira. To raise revenue, the government began to issue paper money (*kaime*, 1840–1862). During the Crimean War, the supply of paper money was increased excessively, provoking inflation, and the government had to borrow to retire the paper money. Military crises led to further kaime issues, with comparable results, in the periods 1876–1883 and 1914–1922.

Further changes marked the Ottomans' tightening integration into the world economy. The 1840s were when European-style banks began to be founded in the Ottoman Empire, in addition to the local financiers (*sarraf*), indigenous non-Muslims, largely Armenian, who were sometimes referred to as "Galata bankers" after the district of that name in the European part of Istanbul.[65] The most important of the new banks was the Ottoman Imperial Bank (OIB), founded by a British group in 1856 and expanded into a Franco-British venture in 1863. Inside the empire, it served as a virtual state bank. In 1862, the government relied on OIB loans to retire the paper money.

The Crimean War led the government, which had previously met its credit needs internally, to start contracting foreign loans in 1854. During the war, the Ottomans were able to borrow with support from the British government. Subsequently, they kept borrowing, but the terms deteriorated. The later loans were heavily discounted, and their proceeds were used increasingly for current expenditure, not productive investment. By the late 1860s, new loans were being contracted to service the old ones. The international financial crisis of 1873 brought European overseas lending to a halt at a time when the Ottomans were confronting famine in Anatolia (1873–1875), followed by rebellion and war in the Balkans (1875–1878). The government declared a moratorium on debt service in 1875–1876. The Ottoman foreign debt then stood at 200 million British pounds. This default left the Ottomans without access to European capital markets when it faced war with Russia in 1877–1878. Default stimulated European anti-Ottomanism, thereby also facilitating Russian diplomatic efforts to isolate the Ottomans in preparation for the war.[66]

The debt crisis led to the establishment in 1881 of an international agency, the Public Debt Administration (PDA), to exercise European control over parts of Ottoman government finance and service the foreign debt, the nominal value of which had been negotiated downward by about half. The PDA took control of specific state revenues, using the proceeds first to pay bondholders and turning over any remainder to the Ottoman government. The PDA became one more reason why Ottoman government finances could not be rationalized overall; yet it kept the books balanced in its own sphere, ultimately restoring Ottoman credit to the point that the government could again borrow abroad, and at a fraction of the interest rates paid before 1876. Ultimately, the rhythms of the world economy controlled the timing of Ottoman economic crises: the Cairo and Istanbul governments both went bankrupt in 1875–1876.[67]

AGRICULTURE

Although conditions varied across the Ottoman domains, agricultural growth started from depressed levels and had to be measured against tight constraints. Improved rural security following the reduction in warlordism and brigandage, together with the elimination of monopolies and the state purchase (*miri mübayaa*) system, enabled cultivators to respond to increased demand. Expansion of the cultivated area also increased production, thanks to the widespread availability of vacant land and the influx of Muslim refugees. As a result, while total government revenues nearly tripled between 1848 and 1876, the tithes (*öşür*) collected on agricultural produce nearly quadrupled.[68]

Although exceptional regions existed in different parts of the empire, often accounting for disproportional shares of production in specific crops, Ottoman agriculture in general was characterized by abundant land but scarce labor and capital. The small scale of most agricultural operations thus corresponded not just to the historical state preference. Calculations for various localities as of 1844 suggest that most rural households probably held 25 *dönüm* of land or less, and a vast majority held 60 or less (1 dönüm roughly equals 0.1 hectare).[69] Local development projects of 1844, both around Kastamonu (Anatolia) and in the Danubian delta (Dobruca), assumed that a peasant smallholding of roughly 10 dönüm could be set up with investment of about 1,500 kuruş, divided mostly among land, buildings, and animals, with only a little for tools. The formation of large agricultural estates (*çiftlik*), while not unknown, was hindered by the scarcity of labor, among other factors. Statistically infrequent in most of Anatolia, large çiftliks were more common in Rumelia. Even there, they did not account for much over one-third of the settlements in any province as of 1878; and such estates were small on average—13.8 hectares in Bulgaria. By the 1860s, rising labor costs and diminishing return on investment were causing many çiftlik owners in Bulgaria to sell out, which often meant that land passed from Muslim landlords to Christian peasants.[70] Where large estates existed, many of them still seem to have begun as "virtual" çiftliks consisting not so much of land as of large interests in tax-farming, money-lending, and probably also *selem* contracts for advance purchase of crops. Where money-lending led to the acquisition of ownership through foreclosure, the acquisition of scattered small holdings would have reduced the advantages to the investor. The small average size of individual holdings may, however, conceal how much land some individual investors owned or controlled in multiple locations. An added problem existed in Bulgaria, where former sipahis resisted the abolition of their revenue-collection rights by demanding an additional tithe of one-ninth (*gospodarlık*) after the state tithe. While the land law of 1858 retained the classic, albeit much-violated, principle that land could not be pledged to secure a debt, amendments of the 1860s eliminated this restriction.[71]

The prevalence of small holdings had important consequences.[72] Food crops necessarily accounted for a large part of produce, limiting production of inedible cash crops. So high was the ratio of land to population that only a small proportion of cultivable land was farmed in many places. Extensive forms of pastoralism occupied more of the landscape than would otherwise have been the case. Costs for transport by horse or camel limited the marketability radius for most crops to 75–100 kilometers. For want of roads and navigable waterways in many regions, the only effective alternative would be the railroad, which was only starting to be built in Ottoman lands by the 1870s, mostly in Rumelia. The level of technology remained low, as evidenced by the small proportion recorded for tools in farm inventories. Most Ottoman peasants still plowed with wooden plows rather than metal plowshares, used manure more for fuel than fertilizer, sowed seed broadcast, harvested with a hand sickle, and threshed grain with wooden threshing sleds or flails. Basically consisting of bread and varying little except on special occasions, their diet was inadequate to sustain their labor or disease resistance. Most villages lacked schools. Comparable to those in Russia but far below those in western Europe, such conditions depressed production, limiting the ability of agriculture to stimulate other economic sectors. These conditions did, however, create incentives for peasant households to seek additional income by spending part of their time working for hire on others' land or engaging in productive processes that could in some cases stimulate the rise of rural protoindustry.

While ecological and other factors created a gradation in these conditions across space, from the more verdant Balkans to the hotter and drier zones to the southeast, overall the conditions that depressed production induced complex vicious cycles. For example, underweight draft animals were less able to compensate for the backwardness of the technology or to withstand disease. The same factors that left more of the land surface open for pastoralism increased the scope for conflict between nomads and farmers and rural insecurity in general. This was the Ottoman version of the farmer-ranger problem of the American West.

To the extent that they operated as intended, specific Tanzimat policies stimulated agriculture. Attempts to provide agricultural credit began experimentally in the 1840s and assumed more systematic form with the local funds (*memleket sandıkları*), first introduced in the Danube Province in 1863. The local funds were replaced by the Agricultural Bank (Ziraat Bankası, 1888).[73] In addition to the land law of 1858, an 1859 regulation on deeds (*tapu*) permitted the registration of vacant lands. Such reforms made a difference, but within limits. The amount of credit provided through the credit institutions never exceeded a fraction of the needs, and most of it went to notables rather than poor peasants.

Likewise, the effects of the 1858 land law appear to have varied considerably. In some localities, it was the small cultivators who registered the holdings in their names. In other localities, local notables, tribal shaykhs, or tax-farmers registered large tracts in their names. More research is needed to determine the relative prevalence of these contrasting outcomes. Either way, application of the law over time promoted the government's goal, namely, establishing title and taxing every piece of productive land in the empire. The evidence noted above on the relative size of landholdings suggests that some judgments offered about the land law of 1858 as a stimulus to large estate formation were premature.[74]

TRADE AND MANUFACTURES

The growth of foreign trade became an especially notable feature of the empire's economic growth during the Tanzimat. Between 1840 and 1876, Ottoman exports increased in value from 4.7 million pounds sterling to 20 million. Imports increased from 5.2 million to about 24 million. The negative balance of payments, especially with Britain, was offset in a variety of ways: grain exports to Italy and France, tribute payments from Egypt, and—until the reckoning came due—foreign borrowing.[75] Ottoman exports consisted disproportionately of Balkan agrarian products. Nine commodities accounted for 60 percent of exports from 1850 to 1870: tobacco, cotton, wheat, barley, raisins, figs, silk, opium, and mohair. Europe's industrial revolution stimulated Ottoman exports through long-term growth in demand for raw materials; the U.S. Civil War briefly created an added spike in European demand for cotton. In contrast, Ottoman imports from Europe consisted mostly of industrial products and some colonial goods, such as sugar and spices. As of the 1870s, Britain provided 45 percent of Ottoman imports, followed by France and Austria-Hungary at about 12 percent each.

Foreign commerce, while better documented, gives only a fragmentary idea of the growth of trade in this period. Exports cannot have accounted for more than a fraction—25 percent or less—of agricultural production in most products. Most of the rest either was consumed or exchanged locally or passed into Ottoman domestic trade. About 20 percent of Ottomans were urban, and they certainly created significant demand. Many impressions about Ottoman trade, and about foreigners' and non-Muslims' prominence in it, would change if domestic trade were as well documented as external trade.[76]

Many scholars have believed that the adoption of free trade in 1838 opened the Ottoman market to an influx of British factory goods, which destroyed the Ottoman guilds. By this interpretation, British industrialization meant Ottoman disindustrialization. Recent research, however, has proven this interpretation simplistic. Imports did grow, and certain production processes suffered. But the history of Ottoman manufactures in this period includes dynamic growth stories that conventional accounts have ignored.[77] The destructive phase of the free trade impact occurred before 1870, after which manufactures expanded in many sectors for both domestic and export markets until 1914. Guilds that could not adapt went under, and a government project of the 1860s to reorganize them as industrial cooperatives lasted only a few years. As the rise of rural protoindustry already showed before 1839, the future lay elsewhere.

One of the reasons for underestimating Ottoman manufactures has been foreigners' assumption that big mechanized factories are essential for large-scale industrial production. The Ottoman Empire had comparatively few such factories. The Ottoman state factories collectively did not employ more than five thousand workers by the 1850s. By then, private entrepreneurs had also begun to found factories, such as the silk reeling mills of Bursa or Mount Lebanon.[78] Private capital was central to the increase in Ottoman factories after 1870. Women and girls provided much of the labor force in many such enterprises, depending on the sector.

Probably the larger part of Ottoman manufacturing occurred, however, not in factories but in workshops or domestic settings. When such sites are taken into account, it becomes clear that while some forms of production fell, others rose. Around Arapgir in Anatolia, for example, imported British cotton yarn replaced local hand spinning, freeing the same labor for more profitable work in hand weaving, creating a new industry that occupied several thousand households and lasted for the rest of the century. The impact of increasing imports on the centuries-old textile industry of Bursa was more complex. There, silk weaving and cotton spinning proved unable to compete. Many silk weavers switched to weaving cotton with British yarn. At the same time silk weaving was replaced by silk reeling, and Ottoman raw silk exports soared to meet the demand of European silk weavers.

In the Ottoman Balkans, Bulgaria and Macedonia remained the most productive regions. The Bulgarian upland towns grew strongly between 1840 and 1877, based on internal Ottoman demand. Part of the competition that the urban guilds could not withstand came, not from foreign factories, but from this rural industrial renaissance inside the empire. The leading products were woolen textiles and silk and linen braid (*gaytan*). The narrow peasant looms on which the woolens were woven created the need for braid to decorate the numerous seams in finished garments. Far from being unable to compete, Bulgarian woolens were "so competitive . . . that European goods were largely restricted to the fashion trade."[79] Instead of replacing cottage industries, in this region factories tended to develop only as high-cost production supplements, inasmuch as lack of demand for factory jobs inflated labor costs. Much of the production occurred in winter. In summer, the men of certain Bulgarian towns set out as merchants or tailors for Istanbul, where some settled permanently. In 1863, eight thousand Bulgarian tailors resided in Istanbul. Such operations extended as far as Cairo. Elsewhere in the Ottoman Balkans, cultural and other factors limited the potential for the industrial development seen in Bulgaria. Comparison with independent Serbia, which regressed economically after its independence, shows that the strengthening of Ottoman institutions during the Tanzimat and access to the empire's large internal market stimulated Bulgaria's growth. Bulgaria, too, regressed economically after independence (1878).

Nablus in Palestine offered other examples of how economic facts might differ from abstractions about Ottoman inability to compete with British manufactures. The Nablus region (Jabal Nablus) was famous for its olives. During the Tanzimat, production of the olive-oil soap for which Nablus is still renowned became the most dynamic local industry. Responding to vigorous growth in demand after 1820, Nabulsi merchants invested increasingly in this sector. They took advantage of the Tanzimat reforms to extend their influence in both business and local politics. To be sure, upsets occurred along the way. During the Egyptian occupation of the 1830s, a plot to boil Mehmed Ali's son, Ibrahim Paşa, in a vat of hot soap backfired on the man who cooked up the plan. Money-making opportunities associated with olive oil and soap included making advance-purchase contracts (*salam*) with olive growers, buying and operating soap mills, and selling the much-demanded product to far-flung markets. The salam contracts (*selem* in Turkish) favored the investor, who advanced money early in the year to producers who had to furnish the agreed quantity of oil at the end of the growing season, whatever its market price at the time. Often, this was a way to buy oil for a third of its ultimate value. Anyone with capital to invest in such contracts might potentially also bid on a tax-farm, another way to create economic dependency networks extending from Nablus into the countryside. Under the 1858 land law, this appears to have been one of the regions where peasants' unwillingness to register land in their own names—or to interact with officials at all—played into the hands of urban notables, accelerating an established trend toward forming large holdings.[80]

Even as free trade produced its effects on the Ottoman economy, soap-making became Nablus's dominant industry. The number of factories tripled, and their volume of production quadrupled. This was a capital-intensive business operating over a three-year cycle between the salam contract to buy the oil and the profits from selling the soap. No wonder the factory owners formed an elite powerful enough to confront Ottoman officials over issues such as the taxation of their trade or the auctioning of oil collected as in-kind taxes. Their workers, too, formed a local labor elite. Patron-client ties united owners and workers, among whom a strict hierarchy prevailed. Among the workers, the chief (Arabic *ra'is*) of the cooking team was the boss. Specific jobs were hereditary in certain families to the point that the name of one such family became a generic, dialect term for upstairs worker (*tbeila*). Thus, an ancient form of manufacturing in a small inland city grew and prospered without new technology, markets, or investors.[81] As wine and raisins are to grapes or flour and pasta are to wheat, oil and soap are the most durable and highest-value products made from the olive. In all three cases, the finest products are still produced by artisanal methods.

Bursa silk and Nabulsi soap are two commodities that have a great deal to tell of whether the advent of free trade destroyed Ottoman manufactures. Both still exist in one form or another. Between the Tanzimat and the present, Bursa's premodern silk industry, vertically integrated from feeding the silkworms to spinning and weaving luxury silks, declined to the point that only three kilograms of cocoons were brought to Bursa for sale one year in the late 1990s. Yet the visitor to Bursa at that time found the Koza Hanı (cocoon warehouse) in a restored and flourishing state, with well-stocked shops under every arch. Silks in profusion included neckties and scarves indistinguishable from high-fashion goods in the world's most glamorous shops. The goods were indistinguishable because they actually were the same. Bursa has become a center for the design and printing of silk textiles in an industry that is now horizontally integrated globally, instead of being vertically integrated locally at Bursa. As for the Nabulsi soap factories, since the end of the Ottoman Empire, they have survived changes more drastic than those of the Tanzimat era. Today, the olive oil is imported, mostly from Spain.[82] Yet Nabulsi soap factories are still two-story operations where the soap is cooked downstairs and then carried upstairs and spread on the floor for cooling, cutting, drying, and wrapping.

As much as has changed, the continuities in the soap production process witness to the enduring significance and sophistication of the Mediterranean world's legacy in agriculture, manufactures, and trade.

SOCIAL CHANGE

The outside forces operating on Ottoman society and the state's intrusive initiatives made this a period of transformation at all social levels, for individuals, families, kin groups, social classes, and religious and ethnic communities. It has not been possible to discuss the events and reforms of the period without broaching such topics as Balkan separatism, sectarian politicization, and the non-Muslim religious communities' communal reforms. Against that background, this discussion proceeds selectively, examining change first in the size and composition of the population and then in individual subjectivity and class formation.

POPULATION

As before 1839, the empire's population remains difficult to enumerate. Available estimates suggest a maximum of about 40 million, including semi-independent territories, or 20-odd million for provinces directly ruled from Istanbul.[83]

The high-ranging figures presented in table 2.1 invite comparison with the high estimate of 35 million for 1844–1856. By 1870, some of the territories

Table 2.1. Ottoman population, 1872–1874

Region	Population (in millions)		
	Muslim	Non-Muslim	Total
Ottoman Europe (1872) vilayets:			
under direct rule (1872)	3.833	5.000	8.833
semi-independent (Serbia, Romania, Montenegro)	0.008	5.911	5.919
Subtotal, Europe	3.841	10.011	14.753
Asia (1874)	11.426	2.854	14.280
Africa (including Egypt)	11.308	0.170	11.479
Total	26.576	13.936	40.512

Source: Karpat, *Ottoman Population*, 26, 117.

included in the table no longer belonged to the empire more than tenuously. In the Balkans, that was true of Serbia, Romania, and Montenegro, all lost totally in 1878. Ottoman sovereignty was nearly as loose over Egypt, whose 1860 population was reported at 5.5 million.[84] A more conservative estimate for the Ottoman Balkans in 1870 would imply a total perhaps as low as 5.4 million, compared to the European total of 14.7 million shown above. The disparity is difficult to explain. What is clear is the uncertainty of the figures.

MOVEMENTS AND MIGRATIONS

Whatever the aggregate numbers, the Tanzimat was a time of change and movement for Ottoman populations. Urban growth offers one sign of this. Between 1840 and 1890, urban populations grew from 400,000 to about 900,000 in Istanbul, from 110,000 to 200,000 in Izmir, and from about 10,000 to more than 100,000 in Beirut.[85] As of 1860, Cairo had a population of 300,000, Damascus 100,000, and Baghdad 60,000; the population of those three cities more than doubled by 1914. Economic growth, rural-to-urban migration in search of opportunity, and the benefits of early improvements in public hygiene and infrastructure stimulated urban growth.

Rural populations were in flux, too, and not only because of rebellions and intercommunal disturbances. Each stage of Russian expansion in the Black Sea region and the Caucasus led to expulsions of Muslims, starting with the Crimean and other Tatars after 1783 and continuing with non-Turkish Caucasian Muslims (Circassians, Abkhazians, Daghestanis) in the 1860s. The refugees fled to Ottoman lands, arriving destitute, famished, and sick. Epidemics of smallpox or typhus killed large percentages of the refugees and spread to the populations among whom they settled. The refugee flows numbered in the hundreds of thousands from 1854 on, rising to 400,000 in 1864. The government did what it could to settle refugees, dispersing them from Bulgaria to Jordan. Even though there was vacant land, the refugees—particularly those, like the Circassians, who did not speak the local language—proved difficult to integrate socially. With the Balkan conflicts that culminated in the Russo-Turkish war, Ottoman Muslims also became refugees in huge numbers in the 1870s.

In eastern Anatolia, each stage in Russian expansion into the Caucasus and each Ottoman-Russian war destabilized the equilibria among religious communities, intensifying a trend that culminated tragically in 1915. The Russians not only pushed Muslims out of territory they annexed; they also sought to attract Armenian immigrants into Russian-ruled Caucasian territory. Such migrations followed the Crimean and Russo-Turkish wars, disrupting the old interfaith symbiosis. In eastern Anatolia and the Arab provinces, an added problem was that part of the population consisted of nomadic tribesmen, over whom the Ottoman government had never had much control. In southeastern Anatolia, the tribesmen were usually Kurds and prone to prey on the sedentary agrarian population—both Christian and Muslim—whenever the government could not stop them. In wartime, when the provincial garrisons had to be moved to the front, the government's means for controlling such marauding declined drastically.[86] As the dispersion of the Circassian refugees illustrates, the effects of migration were felt pervasively; yet the Ottoman frontier zones felt them especially.

INDIVIDUAL SUBJECTIVITY AND CLASS FORMATION

Before 1800, most Ottoman subjects still lived lives defined largely by their gender, kinship relations, social status, and religion. Most of them had limited education and limited opportunities for individual expression. By the 1840s, in contrast, new forces were at work, revolutionizing Ottoman society. These were limited neither to invasions and rebellions nor to the state's defensive modernization strategies. Many oddly assorted revolutionary agents also arrived with modernity's vanguard: frockcoats and whalebones, pianos and cameras, novels and newspapers. Such appurtenances of nineteenth-century modernity would not have had the impact they did were it not for the increase in literacy, which depended in turn on expanded educational opportunities. The additional years of schooling, beyond the elementary Kur'an school, extended the period of study into the age range in which adult subjectivity begins to develop, and students' desires about what to write and read expanded accordingly. Here, the most important institutions were probably not the academies designed to train new elites but the lowest level of the new government schools, the rüşdiyes. Providing a few more years of education beyond the Kur'an school, these were the highest schools that most literate Ottoman Muslims attended in this period. These schools began to spread in the same years as the modern print media, especially newspapers (1840–1860). Among Ottoman Muslims, the percentage of the population who benefited from the expanded educational opportunities was still a small but growing minority. The appearance of new Ottoman schools for girls (1859) and women teachers (1870) and the first Ottoman women's magazine (1868) confirm that Muslim women participated in these changes. Documented here as they pertain to readers of Ottoman Turkish, analogous changes occurred among other Ottoman populations, generally earlier among non-Muslims, somewhat later in the Arab lands. Inevitably, one of the greatest challenges to efforts to promote Ottoman unity was this proliferation of alternative literacies.[87]

The advent of a new reading public also made the development of bourgeois subjectivity and class formation into revolutionary developments of the

Tanzimat. From the widening circle of literacy came both the foot soldiers and the charismatic leaders for a long-term cultural revolution that got under way between 1840 and 1860 and has continued ever since. It has abruptly accelerated at climactic moments of change, most notably the Turkish republic's alphabet and language reforms of the 1920s, a peak of intensity in a long-term revolution started during the Tanzimat.

For readers of Ottoman Turkish in the 1870s, the Young Ottomans formed the intellectual vanguard of this sociocultural transformation. However, it was bigger than they; and their contributions to it extended far beyond the political ideas that normally attract historians' attention. The concept of print capitalism, including the emergence of the modern print media and of a modern reading public, captures important parts of this transformation. As palace patronage for old literary genres waned, this reading public created a new demand for all authors who could learn how to address its hopes and feelings. Even more than they demanded constitutionalism, Tanzimat authors responded to that need with an open-ended assessment of the modern world and their place in it.

One of the best exemplars of Young Ottoman modernism was İbrahim Şinasi (1826–1871). He knew the French language and literature unusually well, and he pioneered in publishing newspapers and propagating cultural modernity in Ottoman Turkish. He cooperated with Yusuf Agâh to found the *Tercüman-ı Ahval*, then founded his own *Tasvir-i Efkâr* (both 1860). The very names of the papers—first "Interpreter of Events," then "Portrayal of Ideas"— signify how far their role exceeded merely reporting news. The publication of literary works as serials in newspapers was not new, but Şinasi serialized more serious works. He also became the first Ottoman author to write a European-style play. With one eye on the French comedies of Molière and another on the Turkish popular theater, he wrote a comedy, "A Poet's Marriage" (*Şair Evlenmesi*, 1859).

In Şinasi's play, the would-be poet wishes to marry one of two sisters, not the older one but the taller one. The matchmaker gets confused and produces the wrong sister as bride, and the poet's friend has to bribe the imam to set things right. Although all are treated satirically, the play exploits the misunderstandings between the "modern intellectuals," the poet and his friend, and the neighborhood folk. Given that "poet" was virtually a synonym for "intellectual," the hero stands for all modern Ottomans; and the first modern Ottoman play thus focuses on the question that signaled the emergence of bourgeois self-consciousness in culture after culture, the freedom to choose one's spouse.[88] The subject is the same, then, as in Beaumarchais's *Marriage of Figaro* (1784), still beloved in Mozart's operatic rendition, or in Jane Austen's novels.

Family life in photographs. An Ottoman family with its servant. (Anonymous, 1865; Research Library, The Getty Research Institute, Los Angeles, 96.R.14.)

MUSLIM MIDDLE-CLASS ELEMENTS: INTELLECTUAL SECULARISTS, PROPERTIED CONSERVATIVES

The idea of bourgeois subjectivity implies the impossibility of separating issues of individual self-consciousness from those of class formation. Inasmuch as the Ottoman Empire did not historically have the marked stratification into estates or classes common in Europe, the idea of an Ottoman middle class implies a loose concept of intermediate status. Its difference was clearest in relation to those below: peasants and the urban poor. Because the Ottoman Empire officially had no aristocracy, it is hard to speak of higher social classes, although the dynasty and its top officials were in exalted positions. Historically, religious difference, as well as patron-client relationships among people at different levels in Ottoman society, had made vertical cleavages more significant than horizontal ones.[89] The Tanzimat seems to be a period when a new horizontal stratification was just beginning to overwrite the old, vertical differentiations. At an early stage in the process, it does not follow that all members of an emergent middle class would have seen themselves as such or formed a cohesive group.

One of the most important interpretive questions of late Ottoman social history arises at just this point.

The established interpretation holds that the late Ottoman bourgeoisie, formed out of merchants, officials, and intellectuals, was divided along ethno-religious lines. "Ottoman Muslims developed primarily into the bureaucratic bourgeoisie[,] and Ottoman minorities predominantly into the commercial bourgeoisie." This segmentation led to the "demise of the Empire," as non-Muslims' interests became tied to the outside world, whereas the Muslim bureaucratic intelligentsia fought to defend the state on which their Ottoman identity depended.[90] Although there is evidence for this interpretation, there is much evidence that does not conform to it. Understanding Ottoman social dynamics requires considering the discordant evidence.

One problem with this idea of a bifurcated middle class is that the social groups out of which it is considered to have emerged—merchants, officials, intellectuals—did not have uniform ethnoreligious identities. Modernist intellectuals appeared in more or less all ethnoreligious communities. The officials at least began to recruit non-Muslims after 1856; non-Muslims did not achieve proportional representation in official ranks, but no such goal had been set. The largest issues about the idea of a religiously divided bourgeoisie arise over the merchants. It is true that traditional Ottoman thought patterns—the distinction between large merchants (*tüccar*) and the small tradesmen and craftsmen who worked in the bazaars and belonged to the guilds (*esnaf*)—did not facilitate picturing the commercial bourgeoisie as a coherent social category. However, these very categories, strongly imprinted on Ottoman Muslim thinking about the economy, recognize at least protobourgeois Muslim elements in the market-place. Of the three social groups from whom the religiously divided bourgeoisie was supposed to have formed, then, even the officials were not all Muslims, the intellectuals belonged to all communities, and the merchants were not as solidly non-Muslim as the idea of the bifurcated bourgeoisie asserts.

Recent studies reinforce this point. The evidence on trade and manufacturing indicates that whereas Ottoman non-Muslims competed successfully with foreign merchants to dominate international trade from 1815 through the 1870s, Muslims often dominated interior trade. Certainly in the Arab provinces, partnerships among Muslim and Christian Arabs were known, sometimes involving large amounts of capital. Europeans were more conscious of non-Muslim merchants because they dealt with them directly in port cities and did not pay much attention to their links with the interior.[91] In manufacturing, if the woolens of Bulgaria exemplify non-Muslim enterprise in this period, the olive oil and soap trade of Nablus provide an impressive example of enterprise in a predominantly

Muslim environment. The rootedness of the soap industry in the agrarian economy signifies, as well, that thinking about the Muslim middle strata should not try to segregate landowners from merchants and manufacturers.

Relevant comparisons with other Muslim societies reinforce the argument that the Muslim segment of the Ottoman commercial bourgeoisie has been underestimated. By the end of the 1860s, most Turks lived under the rule of either the Ottoman sultan or the Russian czar. In major centers of the Russian Empire, notably Baku and Kazan, some Turks accumulated large fortunes. Others accumulated modernist cultural capital. In a Russian-ruled, Turkic middle class whose members' assets were cultural in some cases and economic in others, the brains criticized the moneybags but also collaborated with them against the Russians.[92]

Iran also still had much more in common with the Ottoman Empire before World War I than it has had recently. At key moments of crisis and change in Iran from 1890 to 1979, a distinctive alliance of interests played the key role: the modernist intelligentsia, the ulema, and the *bazari* class. This is a heterogeneous coalition, and there also were cleavages within it. Yet different segments of Iran's middle strata worked together at critical moments, and they included Muslims with mercantile interests, the bazaris, who are analogous to the Ottoman merchants (tüccar) and small traders and craftsmen (collectively known as esnaf).[93]

Like the evidence from Ottoman economic history, these comparisons indicate that the argument about ethnoreligious cleavage in the Ottoman bourgeoisie needs revision. The success of the non-Muslim commercial middle class was more visible in some settings. By this period, the Ottoman sense of backwardness was sharpened by comparisons not only with Europe but also with the empire's most prosperous non-Muslims. During the Tanzimat, however, the problem seems to have been not so much the nonexistence of a propertied Muslim middle class as its relative weakness and disunity. Differentials in rates of access to the new education compounded this problem by equipping the modernist intelligentsia to take control of reformist policy and the new print media before their more conservative counterparts. Nonetheless, a recent study of politics and religion rightly emphasizes the emergence in the late nineteenth century of a "new middle class" made up of Turkish Muslim proprietors and merchants.[94]

Tanzimat officials and propertied middle-class elements lacked a sense of community because their interests differed. That became apparent every day in the administrative councils that proliferated across the empire during the Tanzimat. As with the proverbial glass that is either half full or half empty, the new provincial councils either were or were not a significant step toward the

development of representative institutions. They either did help project reformist goals into the provinces or did not because they were subverted by propertied
local notables, who took them over and used them to advance their own ends.
Arguably, the contradictory interpretations are all correct. The officials who
launched the Tanzimat with noble pronouncements about justice and equity
faced rough handling when they had to carry out the negotiations that they had
asked for in the local councils they set up. Their elitist education disequipped
them to cope successfully with propertied interests who lacked an Istanbul
efendi's finesse but had large economic assets, deep roots, and local authority
independent of office. Wherever the land law of 1858 resulted in the registration
of land in large tracts, the central government's own policies consolidated a new
provincial leadership as the official elites' chief local interlocutors. On either
side of their confrontations, personal antipathies and sometimes deceitful, even
criminal, tactics could make things rough indeed. As distinguished a figure as
Ziya Bey (later Paşa), noted as a Young Ottoman intellectual, discovered this
as district governor (mutasarrıf) of Amasya in the early 1860s. The improvements he introduced did not keep two corrupt local figures, who had dominated the countryside for decades before he prosecuted them, from getting him
removed from office and investigated on trumped-up charges. If in other cases,
officials from Istanbul managed to cooperate with local notables or even intimidate them, Ziya was not that lucky at Amasya.[95]

Such clashes of interests have often been analyzed in terms of progress and
secular modernity versus Islamic backwardness. Secularizing nationalists wrote
their opponents out of their historical narrative. The idea that the bourgeoisie had to be created by the state also became part of their ideology.[96] Given
the evidence that the Islamic content of both Tanzimat policy and Young Ottoman thought was greater than such an interpretation allows, a different kind
of interpretation appears to be needed. If the emergent middle-class elements
of Ottoman society were divided, their divisions do not appear to be as simple
as one between non-Muslims and Muslims. Among Ottoman Muslims, a division between the modernist bureaucratic intelligentsia and members of the
propertied classes appears equally salient. Polemics aside, however, the difference is rarely one between progress and backwardness. The soap-makers of
Nablus and their counterparts on the administrative councils of other provinces
scarcely lacked interest in adapting to the modern world. However, their ideas
about how to do this might differ. What clashed in settings like the councils
was not progress and reaction, so much as different approaches to modernity.
One approach generally favored faster change and was championed by central
elites who were already comparatively highly organized; the other was a more

conservative approach identified with propertied interests who were slower to coalesce and much more likely to find their cultural outlet in religious movements, such as the Halidiye-Nakşibendiye, than in the print media. The difficulty these bourgeois elements had in perceiving their common interests became a lasting feature of late Ottoman and modern Turkish history.

NAMIK KEMAL AND CULTURAL NATIONALISM

The key questions of the times—the emergence of a new individual subjectivity, the transformation of class identity, and the collective self-definition and governance of society and polity—all converge in the works of Namık Kemal. Not just a constitutionalist, he was the imaginative architect of an entire culture of modernity. The vistas he opened are not always untroubling. In his work, cultural nationalism does not fail to display a warlike face. He shows himself much more attuned to Muslims' sensibilities than to a cosmopolitan Ottomanism. His vision of the new Ottoman man is far fuller than that of the new woman. Yet he stands as the preeminent Young Ottoman writer, with journalism, poetry, novels, plays, and histories to his credit. No brief discussion can do him justice; yet considering one poem, one novel, and one play may give an idea of his originality. The poem celebrates liberty, the novel explores the abuse of personal liberty, and the play identifies liberty with heroic self-sacrifice for the fatherland.

LOVING LIBERTY

Namık Kemal's *kaside* on liberty is traditional in form but new in content. The Arabic term *kaside* implies purpose, and kasides were usually poems that poets wrote to gain a patron's favor. A kaside has a standardized format, including a prologue, a "take-off" couplet, a section praising the patron, another vaunting the poet's titles to favor, and a final wish or prayer.[97]

Namık Kemal's kaside on liberty uses the stock elements to new effect. Reacting to the reorientation of politics, away from factions grouped around personalities toward movements dedicated to ideas, he writes to praise—not a person—but an idea: liberty. This poem illustrates why he is remembered for redefining the word *hürriyet* to mean political freedom, and not merely the opposite of slavery. In the prologue, he establishes the kaside's symbolic context by identifying greatness and favor not with patronage or office-holding but with withdrawing from government because of the unsound state of affairs. Service to the people is meaningful; service to a tyrant is degrading. The nation's unity of heart is the source of victory (*durur ahkâm-ı nusret ittihâd-ı kalb-i milletde*, 10). The nation must not despair at its backwardness (literally, "slowness," *batâ'et*, 12). As terms for "nation," he uses both *ümmet* and *millet*, two more old terms given new meanings. *Ümmet* originally referred to the community of all Muslims, and *millet* referred to a religious community. Liberty has yet to be mentioned, but the prologue has set the stage.

At the take-off into the main subject, the emotional tone intensifies. It is not the fault of the chained lion that his feet are bound; likewise let fortune be ashamed that people of zeal do not receive their due (*Felekde baht utansın bî-nasîb erbâb-ı himmetden*, 13). The encomium then sings the praises of liberty in relation to those zealous ones, referred to in the first-person plural, who are denied their due without liberty. "We are that noble family of Ottomans" who are red with the blood of martyrdom, who brought forth a world-conquering state out of a tribe, who would never flee the battle for liberty (18). A traditional kaside normally mentions the poet's name toward the end of the encomium, which is followed by the verses of self-praise. Namık Kemal ends this encomium not with his name but with that of liberty (*hürriyet*).

His strategy of praising liberty by stating what "we" Ottomans will do for it in the encomium permits him to retain liberty as the object of praise in the self-referential verses that follow, even as most of the pronouns and verbs shift into the singular. "May I be despised if I turn back on the way of the nation" (20). "Let my hardships be recounted, the least of which is better than the highest office" (21). Adapting an image from the old love poetry, he compares the homeland (*vatan*) to a "disdainful mocker" (*nâzende-i tannâze*, 22), who "does not spare its faithful lovers from the pains of exile. . . . How charming you are, oh countenance of liberty; we became slaves of your love, yet we have been saved from slavery" (27). As shopworn as was the paradox of love's slavery, the love of liberty makes the paradox new. "You are the hope of the future. You are the one who makes the world free from a thousand cares. . . . May God preserve you from every adversity" (29–30), writes the poet, ending with his pious wish.

Namık Kemal's kaside on liberty illustrates why literary scholars compared him to a phoenix arising out of the ashes of the old poetry and why the young Mustafa Kemal, the future Atatürk, recited the poem to other cadets at the Ottoman Military Academy as a call to action.[98]

A DANGEROUS AWAKENING

Creating a modern Ottoman culture required more than transforming old literary forms. Namık Kemal's European exile gave him firsthand knowledge of all the expressions of cultural modernity. Discovering literary forms that existed in European languages but not yet in Ottoman Turkish added to the Ottoman sense of belatedness. The realism cultivated by writers like Gustave Flaubert and the younger Alexandre Dumas was totally different from the fantasy of traditional Ottoman poetry. The fact that European governments still banned many literary works as offenses either to public morals or to crowned heads tightened the connection between literary creativity and political freedom. By the 1870s, the novel, that quintessential expression of bourgeois consciousness, appeared to Namık Kemal as "the greatest gap in our literature."[99] He wrote two such works, starting with *İntibah* (1876). Its full title translates as "Awakening: The Adventures of Ali Bey." The work is experimental, not least in merging elements from both the Ottoman storyteller (*meddah*) tradition and French literary works, particularly *La dame aux camélias* (1848) by Dumas fils, which Namık Kemal may also have seen in operatic form as Giuseppe Verdi's *La traviata* (1852). The same story has been filmed several times as *Camille*, memorably so by Greta Garbo (1937).

It takes a while to see the connections between *Camille* and Ali Bey. Like the heroes of most Ottoman novels, Ali Bey is an official and the son of a wealthy family; and he has lost his father. He is an official because "in our country" that is the only way anyone, especially women like his mother, "can imagine to become great" (32). He is fatherless because in a patriarchal society, that is the only way a young man can have enough personal autonomy for the ill-starred discovery of personal liberty that awaits him. Finally, Ali Bey has to be rich because the Turkish word for "spendthrift" is *mirasyedi*, one who "ate his inheritance."[100]

Ali mourns his father's death, and his mother encourages him to make an outing to Çamlıca on the outskirts of Istanbul. The opening chapters set the mood by portraying the springtime, Çamlıca, and Ali himself. All the book's chapters are headed with a couplet from divan poetry, or at least in that style; and the contrast between the old poetic fantasy and the new prose realism is ever present. "Contrary to what all the divan poets say," if the nightingale is in love, it is not with the rose; "absolutely, it loves freedom" (12–13).

Ali Bey soon becomes fond of his outings to Çamlıca. While he admires the view, his friends make comments or gestures at women who pass by in colorful *feraces* (outer coats) and *yaşmaks* (head scarves). At first Ali is embarrassed. But soon he too gestures at a passing carriage. Its curtains part, and a gesture that he does not understand beckons him. Soon, he is returning to Çamlıca obsessively to watch for that carriage. Finally it stops. A beautiful woman in a filmy, revealing yaşmak steps out, approaches, and begins to speak to him, pretending to reproach him for gesturing to her. One meeting leads to another. Ali soon begins skipping work, going home late, and lying to his mother. Feeling like a man who has opened his eyes for the first time (44), he declares his love to the woman. When he speaks of marriage, she insists he never mention it again. He cannot understand, but their meetings continue. For a time, the effect on him is invigorating. His superiors in the office notice and reward him. Then one day at Çamlıca, he sees another man approach her carriage and talk to her as if he knows her. He overhears someone say: "She must have a new spendthrift on the line" (59). It is not long before he learns from friends that the woman is the prostitute Mehpeyker. "You can get what you want from her for two gold pieces" (65). Any Muslim who grew up with Ottoman-era norms of gender relations should have figured this out the first time the woman spoke to him; but apparently that very fact opened the door to self-delusion in such matters.[101]

Authorial intention is also at work in this encounter. The evidence indicates that Ottoman writers adopted "the novel" and "the drama" not as abstract form but as both form and content. They wanted plays and novels like European ones. They, too, wanted to write "boy-meets-girl stories," even though Islamic norms of gender relations were designed to prevent the encounters from which romantic relationships could spring. Ottoman writers racked their brains over this literary problem arguably more than over any other. Encounters with prostitutes, women from the non-Muslim minorities, or foreign women all appeared in one book or another, not to mention relationships established by fleeting glimpses through a window or by the letter-writing that became thinkable with the advance of women's education.

As a result, novel writing became as subversive socially as agitation for freedom or constitutionalism did politically. This may not have been Ottoman novelists' overt intention. To the contrary, they moralize in unison over their characters' fates. Sharing the new bourgeois self-awareness of their readers, the novelists took the lead in imagining a new Islamic modernity. Where gender relations were concerned, their advocacy of conventional Islamic norms did not stop them from inventing plots characteristically set in motion by incidents that violated or suspended those norms, so implying demands to enlarge the scope of the allowable.[102] Contrived as some of the plots seem, Ottoman novels had eager readers. Women gathered on winter evenings to read pioneer woman novelist Fatma Aliye's works. During Turkey's National Struggle (1919–1922), soldiers at the front gathered during their rare quiet moments to listen to the reading of novels.[103] In *İntibah*, Ali Bey was a fool to fall for Mehpeyker, but Namık Kemal made him do it for a purpose.

Rudely awoken by the truth, Ali swears never to look at her again, but within a week, he returns to confront her. She is ready. Her appearance, all in white, reduces him to speechlessness. "You have finally learned my secrets," she begins, artfully recounting how her poor family sold her honor before she was thirteen. Only Ali can save her. She praises his high character, adding that she knows he will never want to see her again. Overwhelmed, he pleads with her to be his alone (76). She warns him about compromising his honor, but to no avail; and they agree to meet at her house that evening.

Namık Kemal's depiction of their nocturnal tryst at her waterside garden pavilion is luxuriantly erotic. Mehpeyker helps Ali change into a nightshirt of gray moiré silk and a matching fur-lined robe. Then she leads him to a table laid with food and drink. As if troubled by the heat, she loosens her clothing. Ali is about to have his first experience of both passionate kisses and the taste of rakı, the anise-flavored hard spirits. The evening ends as they retire to their private room for "the embrace of union" (*halvethanelerine avdetle hem-ağuş-i visal oldular,* 130).[104]

Soon their meetings consume days as well as nights. Ali's mother, Fatma Hanım, whom he deceives with lies, grows frantic and finally contacts his friends, who break the news that Ali is infatuated with a woman whose name is not fit to mention. The thing for Fatma to do is to buy a beautiful slave girl (*cariye*): an angel to make Ali forget this devil.

At great cost, Fatma Hanım finds a beautiful, golden-haired slave girl, Dilaşub, and waits to see Ali's reaction. He does not respond as expected. Praising the young woman's accomplishments (needlecraft, piano), Fatma gives her son a textbook lesson in the Ottoman rationale for concubinage. It is time he has a family; if he marries a girl from a fine family, he will not see her face before marriage and may not like her afterward. Having two ladies in the house might cause conflict; but a cariye can be trained to please (100).[105] Ali replies rudely, his mother reproaches him for caring more for a whore than for her, and he runs out enraged.

Mehpeyker owes her luxurious lifestyle to an ugly, lecherous, but rich Syrian merchant, Abdullah Efendi. He bears resemblances to real-life "protectors" of Ottoman prostitutes.[106] He likes to keep beautiful women in luxury and let them carry on as they please in return for occasional favors. When he returns to Istanbul unexpectedly, Mehpeyker has to beg Ali, from whom she has never taken money, for three days without a tryst, so that she can find her protector and explain her affair with Ali. The old man can cut off the money if he wants; but as long as the passion lasts, she will not break her liaison. After hard bargaining, Abdullah offers Mehpeyker six months and even increases her money. Then he will want "his share," or his revenge will be terrible. She accepts without demur. She feels lust for Ali Bey, not love. Anything can happen in six months. Thinking all is settled, she returns to her seaside mansion to discover that Ali has returned before she told him to and has spent the night drinking and imagining things. Accusing her of taking up with other men, he hurls a fistful of money in her face and storms out as if never to return (113–14)—a scene straight from Dumas.[107]

Returning to his mother's house, Ali is now ready to appreciate Dilaşub, who is hopelessly in love with him. Fatma Hanım leads Dilaşub to his room that very night (120–23). His new conjugal relationship seems to return Ali's life to order. Mehpeyker writes several times, trying different approaches. Finally, he replies with a brutal rejection (127–28).

Mehpeyker takes her revenge on the innocent Dilaşub. She uses women peddlers (*bohçacı kadınlar*) to go to Ali's house and spy out information that can be twisted into defamatory rumors. Frequenting the neighborhood bath (*hamam*) herself, she observes two moles on Dilaşub's body. With her malevolent "protector's" help, Mehpeyker sets a trap for Ali. At Çamlıca one day, a man approaches him, professes to be a certain woman's lover, and mentions enough details—including the two moles—that Ali recognizes the woman as Dilaşub. Rushing home, he stages a terrible scene, forcing his mother to sell Dilaşub. Planning for that, Mehpeyker has let the slave dealers know that she wants a cariye and will pay a premium. Dilaşub thus falls into the hands of Mehpeyker, who plans to make her a prostitute.

Broken in spirit, Ali sinks into dissipation, loses everything, and lands on the streets working as a petition writer (*arzuhalci*) to earn money for drink.[108] Mehpeyker still wants him; now he is no longer interested. At that discovery, she lures him to a secluded spot to have him murdered, taking the unsuspecting Dilaşub along to witness the crime. However, Dilaşub overhears Mehpeyker and the assassin, warns Ali, and helps him escape. By the time he returns with the police, it is too late. Dilaşub has wrapped herself in Ali's coat, and the assassin has mistaken her for Ali. Surprised by the sound of Ali's voice after he is supposed to have been killed, Mehpeyker emerges from hiding for a final acrimonious exchange, and Ali stabs her.

To whatever extent Dumas's *La dame aux camélias* inspired it, the story of Ali's adventures strays from that model before it reaches its melodramatic end, which recalls the last act of Verdi's *Rigoletto,* based on Victor Hugo's play *Le roi s'amuse.*[109] The biggest difference from Dumas's model is that the title character is not the heroine but the hero. This fact calls attention to Namık Kemal's handling of gender roles. As noted, the spendthrift hero haunts late Ottoman fiction. The frequency of such characters, it has been suggested, signifies not their frequency in real life but rather a motive of social control, a desire to prevent their occurrence. Such characters' downfalls are often associated with superficial Westernization.[110] However, Namık Kemal is subtler than that. Ali Bey cannot blame his downfall on anything European. What ruins him is that his carnal appetites awaken, but his intellect and patriotic zeal do not. In this cautionary tale, the new man who can live up to Namık Kemal's patriotic ideals figures by his absence.

The cultural nationalist elite of Namık Kemal's generation was all male. Yet the new men could not create the new society without new women. Here arise the probable reasons for both the shift in gender of the title character, from Dumas's "lady of the camellias" to Namık Kemal's Ali Bey, and the weakness of the female characters, other than Mehpeyker. Namık Kemal probably could not imagine—his readers certainly could not—a prostitute ennobled by love, worthy to be "pardoned much" because she has "loved much."[111] Consequently he divides the female lead between Mehpeyker, strong but evil, and Dilaşub, virtuous but weak. Namık Kemal's essays champion women's rights and education, but his literary works imply limited ability to imagine women who meet those demands.[112] Biographical evidence reinforces the point. He was married at sixteen; his wife was illiterate and could not share his literary life. Speculating a bit, Ali Bey's temptations in Istanbul might also reflect ones Namık Kemal experienced during his European exile.

DEFENDING THE FATHERLAND

If *İntibah* warns against the dangers of liberty without discipline, Namık Kemal's "Fatherland, or Silistria" (*Vatan yahud Silistre*, 1873) goes to the opposite extreme to depict a hero and heroine ready to defend liberty and fatherland. A paean to warlike nationalism, the play sparked demonstrations when it opened. Sited at one of the empire's major Danubian fortresses, the play appealed to its audiences partly by its implied critique of harsh military discipline. The novelty of the performance added to the excitement. An Armenian theater owner, Güllü Agop, had recently announced that his theater, where both men and women appeared onstage, would perform in Turkish; Namık Kemal himself helped the Armenian actors improve their accents. Probably patterned on patriotic French plays, Namık Kemal's *Vatan* gave the public what it wanted. The government also reacted, exiling Namık Kemal and other Young Ottomans and censoring the theater. The government reacted partly to the fact that the play—intentionally or not—called attention to a fundamental contradictions of egalitarian Ottomanism, namely, that the primary motivator to sacrifice for the empire was Islam. The authorities also disliked the play for another reason. Perhaps because the common noun *murad* (wish) appeared three times in the play, the crowd that cheered the author afterwards chanted: "What is your wish? . . . May God grant our wish!" Sultan Abdülaziz took offense: the heir apparent was named Murad, and he was the focus of constitutionalist hopes.[113]

As the play opens, the heroine, Zekiye, soliloquizes about her grandmother, who educated her, and her long-absent father. She thinks about the man she saw in the street, from whom she has received a letter and with whom she has fallen in love, İslam Bey. He startles her by entering through the window to declare his feelings. The characters' names are significant. She is "Miss Intelligent"; he is "Mr. Islam." As personal names, Zekiye is commonly used; Islam is not. His entrance through the window is also significant. Zekiye protests, and no wonder: İslam Bey's leap through her window makes even shorter work of Islamic gender norms than did the initial encounter with Mehpeyker that started Ali Bey's "adventures."

İslam Bey has come to declare his love and bid farewell before rushing to the front with the volunteers. Zekiye cannot understand. If he loves her, why is he leaving? He rhapsodizes about the fatherland and his duty to fight the enemy. Zekiye responds that she has heard about the fatherland but did not realize it could sunder hearts (21). İslam Bey's motive is love for the fatherland; hers is love for him. About the fatherland, İslam Bey laments: "Most of our men still do not know its meaning; most of our women have not heard its name" (27). He rushes out shouting, "Long live the fatherland!" She collapses. The play is in prose, except for two patriotic songs. However, much of the dialogue is chant-like, with repetitive phrasings. The pervasive feeling of patriotic song and chant must have heightened the play's impact on stage.

Left alone with her feelings, Zekiye hears him outside exhorting the volunteers. "I do not fear ball and bullet. Let those who do, stay beside their women. I will make my body a shield for all my brothers in the fatherland, if possible," he cries, in a censored Ottoman edition. An uncensored, later edition replaces "if possible" (*mümkün olsa*) with a qualifier identifying the compatriots, "who are Muslim" (*Müslüman olan*).[114] The difference shows how even a text as patriotic as this could displease the official sponsors of Ottoman egalitarianism. "Will you swear to God to follow me? . . . Those who love me will always follow me." As the men swear, Zekiye takes his words to heart. She will follow disguised as a male (39–42). European literary models of women disguised to serve as soldiers hover in the background; so do real-life stories from the early phases of Ottoman military reform.

The action shifts to a redoubt at Silistria in the second act. The volunteers are singing a martial song. Colonel Sıdkı warns that the enemy has crossed the Danube and offers the volunteers a chance to withdraw before the battle. They refuse. He spots Zekiye in disguise and is troubled both by her image and what he takes for her childish appearance; she, too, insists on staying. "The one without a moustache insists on staying; the whitebeard insists on staying. . . . May God spare all of them for the fatherland" (58). İslam Bey rushes in, wounded from fighting the invaders. He collapses, and the colonel orders "the child" (Zekiye) to help care for him.

Left alone with another officer, Colonel Sıdkı recounts the story of two officers unjustly court-martialed and punished, and a subplot unfolds. Finally, it
emerges that he is one of those officers. After he had overcome his misfortunes,
he tried to reestablish contact with his family in Manastır and learned that only
his daughter was left, but she had disappeared. As the enemy's assault ends this
colloquy, Sıdkı says: "I cannot get that child out of my mind."

The cannon fire rouses the wounded İslam Bey from unconsciousness as act
3 opens. He extols his volunteers' bravery. Betraying stark realities about social
attitudes, he exclaims: "There was no difference between the lowest peasant
and me. . . . Those wretches whom we do not want to distinguish from oxen
completely disappeared, and in their place a spirit of Ottomanism and heroism
appeared." The very ones who had to be driven before the enemy "with whip
and rod" (*kırbaç değnek*), once the enemy appeared, could not be stopped "with
sword and bayonet" (*kılıçla süngü ile*, 83–84). When he recognizes Zekiye, she
reminds him of what he said before leaving Manastır: "Those who love me will
not leave me" (88). She affirms their hierarchical relationship. "You work for
your fatherland; I, for you" (89).

Just then Sıdkı and other officers rush in with news that the fortress commander has fallen. The situation is desperate. İslam Bey volunteers to infiltrate
the enemy camp and blow up their munitions. Zekiye volunteers to go with
him. They set out as a new attack begins.

Several days later, signs that the enemy is withdrawing begin to appear. Word
arrives that the enemy's munitions have been detonated. İslam Bey enters, and he
and Sıdkı Bey begin to address each other as father and son. Sıdkı asks to see "the
child." Now İslam Bey has to explain that the child is not *mahrem* and cannot
come here (134). Islamic gender norms, which Namık Kemal ignored when he
had İslam Bey climb in through Zekiye's window, are now reinstated, with this
revelation that "the child" is a female and cannot appear unveiled before them
because they are not mahrem, not within forbidden degrees of kinship. İslam Bey
explains that this is a girl from Manastır, that they loved each other at first sight.
Sıdkı exclaims that he had a daughter in Manastır. "Go get her. Maybe I really
will be your father" (136). Hearing her called Zekiye, his daughter's name, Sıdkı
exclaims at his unexpected good fortune (*devlet*), the primary meaning of the term
applied by extension to a dynastic state, like the Sublime Ottoman State (Devlet-i
Aliye-i Osmaniye). In the final recognition scene, family unity is restored, the
hero wins his heroine, and the individual, the family, and the state all triumph
together, as a martial song is sung to cheers of "Long live our Padişah."

Namık Kemal's poem on liberty roused Ottomans to fight for it. His novel
İntibah warned about the dangers of personal liberty without discipline. His

play *Vatan* extols the heroic defense of the fatherland. Other writers would have to go beyond him to imagine full participation for women. Later generations would discover the costs of militaristic nationalism in an empire where Islam did not inspire everyone to fight for an Ottoman future. As stirring as Namık Kemal's works were, they give evidence that the elite males who founded Ottoman cultural modernity still had far to go in discerning how to mobilize all their "others" as defined in terms of gender, class, religion, and ethnicity.

THE SIGNIFICANCE OF THE TANZIMAT

The Tanzimat stands out as a paradoxical but decisive period in Ottoman and Turkish history. On the one hand, the recurrent crises pushed the empire toward the territorial losses that followed the Russo-Turkish War. On the other hand, Ottoman determination to defend the empire made this one of the most dynamic periods of modernizing reform. Those reforms were controversial. Some Turkish conservatives still consider them the start of the degradation of everything Ottoman and Islamic.[115] Defined chronologically by the shift in political initiative from the palace to the Sublime Porte in 1839 and back to the palace in 1876, the period was marked by innovations in elite formation and education, prolific legislation, new governmental interventions in society, and a transformation in the political process that far exceeded anything the leading statesmen could control. The economy, despite its dependent position in the world and the lack of control in state finance, developed appreciably in trade, agriculture, and manufactures, as Bulgaria's woolens, Bursa's silk, and Nablus's olive-oil soap all exemplify. With the old equilibria among the empire's peoples disturbed by accelerating change, social and cultural tensions intensified on many fronts. At the same time, however, the expansion of literacy and the advent of "print capitalism" facilitated the rise of new forms of bourgeois subjectivity and alternative literary cultures for the empire's different peoples. New social collectivities also emerged, not only new senses of ethnic and religious identity, but also new class identities. For Ottoman Muslims, differences in education, interests, and values made it difficult for the elements of the emerging middle strata to perceive common interests between those with cultural and those with economic assets. For the literary intelligentsia, this was hardly the only challenge to overcome in creating a new Ottoman culture and society. They had to expound the essential ideas and mobilize all the others who could participate in this great transformation. So foundational were their cultural innovations that Ottoman works produced long after the Tanzimat ended politically continued to be described as Tanzimat literature.

3

THE REIGN OF ABDÜLHAMID

During Abdülhamid II's reign (1876–1909), the differentiation between the two great currents of change in Ottoman society sharpened, despite continuing commonalities. Politically, this period was distinguished by the sultan's reconcentration of power in his hands. In one of the most decisive reigns in Ottoman history, Abdülhamid wrested power from the bureaucrats who had dominated it since 1839. The contrast between the First Constitutional Period (1876–1878) and the autocracy that followed added drama to the shift in the center of power, until 1908 when the Young Turk Revolution restored constitutional rule.

No Ottoman ruler left a more controversial legacy. A bloodthirsty tyrant to some, to others Abdülhamid was the most legitimate, prestigious Muslim sovereign of his day. Muslims from far beyond Ottoman borders revered him. These contradictory images imply how difficult it was to hold the Ottoman Empire together by his time. They invite reassessment of his reign, which was especially significant for the conservative, Islamically committed forces for change. A consideration of major political issues provides a basis on which to examine economic and social developments as well as their refractions in two neglected literary works of 1890–1891. One is by a man sometimes hailed as the first Ottoman novelist, Ahmed Midhat. The other is by a woman often overlooked as the first female Ottoman novelist, Fatma Aliye. The authors' symbiotic relationship resonates in their novels' titles, his *Müşahedat* (Observations), her *Muhazarat* (Debates), a resemblance worth pursuing into the imaginative realm where the two writers constructed their visions of Ottoman Islamic modernity.

Abdülhamid II as a young man, on the left, at Balmoral Castle, 1867; on the right, in 1876. (Left: by W. and D. Downey of London, courtesy of Bahattin Öztuncay; Öztuncay, *Photographers*, 1:219, pl. 205; right: Abdullah Frères; Research Library, The Getty Research Institute, Los Angeles, 96.R.14, detail.)

THE EMPIRE IN PERIL

After the Russo-Turkish War of 1877–1878, the Ottomans did not experience another such catastrophic defeat until the Balkan Wars of 1912–1913. Yet 1878 left behind dejection and a sense of peril; and crises occurred aplenty. The European powers' policies shifted from the limited support previously given by some to aggressive competition for concessions. By 1908, Abdülhamid had become the proverbial emperor facing crises in every province.

THE CONSEQUENCES OF STATE BANKRUPTCY

At his accession, Abdülhamid faced the aftermath of both military defeat and state bankruptcy. Each made it harder to cope with the other. The Treaty of Berlin deprived the Ottomans of vast provinces and much of their most productive population in 1878; further negotiations gave more territory to Greece in 1881. The treaty saddled the Ottomans with an indemnity to the Russians, supposedly amounting to 350,000 Ottoman gold liras a year for a century (1.10 gold liras equaled 1 British pound). The Ottomans seldom paid the full amount and negotiated away the rest in 1908. Yet the indemnity's impact becomes clear from the fact that the Ottoman budget for 1878–1879 had shrunk to 14.5 million liras, about 60 percent of the prewar total.[1]

The bankruptcy reached resolution officially with establishment in 1881 of the Public Debt Administration, an international agency. It took control of six major revenues to repay bond holders, returning any surplus to the Ottoman government. This arrangement restored a semicolonial kind of order to Ottoman finance, raising the government's international creditworthiness.

If that was the good news about European financial control, the bad news was that it made it impossible to rationalize what remained of state finance or provide for Ottoman developmental needs. The PDA was not the only contributing factor. Abdülhamid matched his drive to centralize with the sharp business sense that other members of the dynasty lacked. As a prince he had managed his finances astutely and made a fortune. As sultan, he expanded the palace treasury and crown estates on a scale never before seen.[2] The consequences of this policy merit further consideration below. At a time when centralization at the palace was stripping civil administrative agencies of power in general, the consequences of having so much of the economy extracted from the purview of the Ministry of Finance by the PDA and palace treasury were vast. No state against which the Ottomans had to defend themselves endured such financial handicaps.

THE CENTER OF CRISIS SHIFTS FROM THE BALKANS TO OTTOMAN AFRICA AND ARABIA

Within the shrunken, post-1878 frontiers, a number of territories were autonomous or had acquired special administrative status because of their sensitivity. Crises emerged from some of these places and others as well. Many factors shaped these crises' outcomes. Not least among the factors was the availability of advanced weaponry. Abdülhamid's reign began at a time when the spread of mid-century advances in arms was still limited enough to favor governments and their armies. By the 1890s, this situation was changing, and situations arose in places like Yemen where Ottoman soldiers faced rebels better armed than they.

After 1878, the main territories in special administrative status were Crete, Lebanon, and eastern Rumelia; the autonomous provinces were Egypt and Tunisia. While Lebanon enjoyed relative quiet under the system introduced in 1861, a Bulgarian nationalist rising resulted in the union of eastern Rumelia with the Bulgarian principality in 1885. In Crete, the kind of administrative reform applied in Lebanon would not work: nationalistic Greeks wanted not improved Ottoman administration but union with Greece. The Ottomans granted Crete special regulations in 1866–1867 and enlarged its autonomy in 1878, later abrogating that concession after a revolt (1889). Another Cretan revolt in 1896–1897 led to an Ottoman-Greek war, ending in military defeat for Greece, which great power interference turned into diplomatic defeat for the Ottomans. The island remained under theoretical Ottoman sovereignty, but with a Greek prince as governor-general.[3]

In North Africa, the Ottomans faced challenges from European imperialism and Islamic protest movements. Abdülhamid responded by bolstering support, as much as his means allowed, in a zone running from Oman to Zanzibar to Morocco.[4] His efforts produced tangible results in Libya. Working through family connections of his Shadhili shaykh, Muhammad Zafir al-Madani, and through the Ottoman governors, Abdülhamid supported the Sanusiyya sufi order as it extended its influence—and his as caliph—into Central Africa. As Italian designs on Libya grew, the Sanusiyya grew in importance for the Ottoman defense of North Africa and the Hijaz.

Flanking Libya, the occupations of Tunis by France (1881) and Egypt by Britain (1882) brought European encroachment to a point of crisis. Tunisia had been ruled since the eighteenth century by the Husaynid dynasty under nominal Ottoman suzerainty. In the mid-1800s, even as the Husaynid *beys* (rulers) emulated the reforms carried out in Cairo and Istanbul, the French occupation of Algeria (1830) and the Ottoman reassertion of control in Libya (1835) changed the world around them. The high costs of reform led Tunisia to bankruptcy and foreign financial control as early as 1868. As France and Italy competed to extend their influence, strengthening ties between Tunis and Istanbul appealed to statesmen in both places. An Ottoman decree of 1871 affirmed Ottoman sovereignty, defined Tunisia's obligations, and made the bey, Muhammad al-Sadik, an Ottoman vezir. The French nonetheless invaded Tunisia in 1881 and established a protectorate, which preserved a semblance of the bey's authority but gave real power to the French resident-general. Literary works imply that Tunisia did not lose its place in Ottoman and Turkish imagination before the mid-1900s; yet colonialism had come to Tunisia.[5]

Just when the approach of the year 1300 in the Islamic religious (*hijri*) calendar, corresponding to 1882–1883 CE, made Muslims look for encouraging signs for the future, Britain's occupation of Egypt followed hard upon France's of Tunisia—certainly not what Muslims wanted.[6] As usual in cases of foreign intervention, from the Napoleonic invasion of 1798 to the present, the fundamental weakness of the policy was that the intervening power's concept of creating or restoring "order" resulted in a state of affairs that could not last if the occupiers left. After the first burst of Egyptian nationalism, led by Ahmad 'Urabi and his associates, failed to prevent the occupation, the British consolidated their control, maintaining an appearance of Ottoman sovereignty until 1914. Egyptian nationalism resurfaced with Mustafa Kamil in the 1890s, around the time that the Young Turk opposition formed against Abdülhamid. Greater freedom of the press in British-ruled Egypt made it a haven for Ottoman opposition intellectuals. This was one of many ways in which Egypt remained a part of the Ottoman cultural world, although power over Egypt belonged to the British, not the Ottoman sultan.

Events in the Sudan, Yemen, and Arabia compounded the challenges from the Ottoman peripheries, calling Abdülhamid's Islamic legitimacy into question as they did. In the Sudan, where the Ottomans had only indirect sovereignty through the Egyptian khedive, a millenarian movement arose in the 1870s around Muhammad Ahmad al-Mahdi (1844–1885). He denounced the corrupt regimes of Cairo and Istanbul and declared a jihad against the Egyptian occupation. The Mahdi defeated Egyptian campaigns against him in 1883 and 1885. The Mahdi's state carried on under his successor (*khalifa*) until the British conquered the Sudan in 1898.[7]

In Yemen, the Ottomans had reestablished a presence on the coast in 1849 and reconquered the highlands in 1872.[8] Yemen was ecologically and religiously diverse. The highlands were home to Shi'is of the Zaydi sect, with a history of rule by their own imams. At the time of the Ottoman reconquest, the imamate had collapsed, the tribes were disunited, and the Ottomans had the advantage in up-to-date weapons, which the imam's partisans acquired only in the 1890s. Until then, the Ottomans controlled the highlands by dividing and ruling, co-opting tribal shaykhs, and conducting punitive expeditions. Yet the Ottomans also gave the tribes a common enemy, thereby setting the stage for a revived imamate to unite them in an anti-Ottoman jihad. Jihad against jihad: for Yemenis, the call to jihad offered a way to unite Zaydi tribes that otherwise fought among themselves; for Ottomans, as in the Sudan, the jihad turned the struggle into one between two Muslim rulers with incompatible Islamic legitimacy claims, the Zaydi Shi'i imam versus the Ottoman sultan-caliph. Compromise became impossible, even though Abdülhamid would compromise with local dignitaries who did not challenge him in religious terms.

In Yemen, the Ottomans applied many techniques later associated with counterinsurgency: policing to secure the countryside, mobile strikes against the imam's partisan bands (*'isabat*), and development projects to win popular support. Ottoman authoritarianism and lack of resources, plus Zaydi gains in military effectiveness, prevented Ottoman success. Imam Yahya's 1905 rebellion turned into a war of attrition. Thanks to the growing Red Sea arms trade, some Yemenis by then had better rifles than the Ottomans. As unequal as the struggle appeared, the costs for Abdülhamid were dire, a fact dramatized in troop revolts motivated largely by grievances over service in Yemen.[9] After 1905, the Ottomans grasped the futility of total war in Yemen. Still, it took the Young Turk regime to negotiate a settlement based on Zaydi autonomy (1911).

Elsewhere in Arabia, the Hijaz was vital because the Ottoman sultans' role as protector or "servitor" of the Two Holy Cities (*khadim al-haramayn al-sharifayn*), Mecca and Medina, gave them their unique title to legitimacy. The Hijaz was one Ottoman province that had to have an exceptional status. The Tanzimat legislation had never been applied there; the modern state schools and nonreligious courts had not been extended there; the populace was exempt from military service and some taxes; non-Muslims were not allowed except in the port of Jidda. The Ottoman governor had to share power with the local ruler, the *sharif* of Mecca. Since before the Ottoman conquest, that office had belonged to a lineage of the Prophet Muhammad's descendants, the Banû Hâshim (Hashemites to Europeans).

Although relations between Mecca and Istanbul had been relatively placid during the Tanzimat, Abdülhamid had reasons for caution. Insecurity persisted along the pilgrimage routes, where bedouin tribes attacked pilgrim caravans unless bought off; epidemics added other dangers for pilgrims. The Suez Canal made the Hijaz more accessible not only to Muslims but also to Europeans. On his own initiative, British consul James Zohrab had already entered into secret discussions with the sharif about making the latter the new caliph. There would be more such schemes. In response, Abdülhamid sent carefully chosen governors and commanders to the Hijaz, who intervened in succession to the sharifate and made infrastructural improvements. Some advisers urged Abdülhamid to eliminate the sharifate and administer the Hijaz like other provinces. Having a subtler understanding of power, he knew that doing so would raise the costs of ruling the Hijaz without guaranteeing bedouin loyalty, which the sharif knew better how to win. A version of the politics of notables would better serve to maintain Abdülhamid's control.

Although the number of pilgrims fluctuated annually, the trend was a strong increase. Abdülhamid's opportunities to enhance his prestige among Muslims by protecting the pilgrimage increased proportionately. As more and more pilgrims from beyond Ottoman frontiers became European colonial subjects, problems concerning pilgrims' safety and health caused diplomatic repercussions. The need to forestall potential European demands to send inspectors inside the perimeter of the Two Holy Cities required increased Ottoman expenditure for quarantines and other improvements, as well as for administrators and garrisons. By the 1880s, Ottoman expenditures exceeded revenues in the Hijaz by more than fifteen to one. No other province so drained the treasury or was so essential to the empire's survival. Partly for this reason, the Two Holy Cities also inspired Abdülhamid's most visionary Islamic-modernist project: the Hijaz railway (1900–1908).

SYSTEMIC THREATS TO OTTOMAN SOVEREIGNTY

If the empire faced localized challenges, it also faced systemic challenges to its sovereignty, as imperialist competition changed in intensity and nature. Global economic change loomed in the background, as expansion, peaking in 1873, gave way to a contraction reaching depression levels in the 1890s.

Once relative confidence had been reestablished in the Istanbul market in 1881, the foreign influx into the empire accelerated.[10] European economic bastions inside the empire included not only the Ottoman Imperial Bank and the Public Debt Administration but also the Régie des tabacs, a company founded in 1884 with European (largely French) capital. All these organizations had many employees and branches. The OIB established ninety-one branches by 1914 in places as far apart as Tripoli (Libya), Kavala (Macedonia), and Basra and Jidda (Iraq). The bank's Istanbul headquarters (1892) formed a target conspicuous enough to make it the site of an Armenian terrorist incident in August 1896 that included taking 140 hostages and threatening to blow up the building. Also headquartered in the same building, the Régie des tabacs was granted a monopoly over purchase and sale of "Turkish" (that is, Ottoman) tobacco, the profits being divided among the PDA, the Régie shareholders, and the Ottoman government. As of 1891, the Régie employed 8,800, mostly to repress smuggling, which the Régie's monopoly made profitable. For its part, in 1886 the PDA had more than 3,000 employees and hundreds of provincial branches to collect taxes. Lest there be any confusion about power relationships, the PDA built its Istanbul headquarters near the Ottoman governmental headquarters, the Sublime Porte, but higher up the same slope and in a taller, finer building. In addition to such institutions as the OIB, PDA, and Régie, a boom in European investment occurred. French interests led, increasing their Ottoman investments from 85 to 511 million francs between 1881 and 1908. While the Ottoman government desired foreign capital and did better than before 1876 in using it for developmental needs, the terms highly favored foreign interests. In railroad building, European rivalries drove the projects as much as did Ottoman needs.

Economic imperialism gained in impact from the fact that Europeans could operate inside the empire with exemption from Ottoman law. With the expansion of the capitulations' commercial terms into free-trade treaties in 1838,

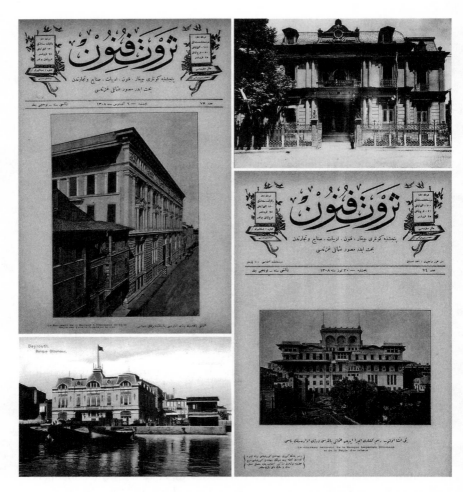

The Ottoman Imperial Bank and the Régie des tabacs. The two magazine covers illustrate the newly opened building of the Ottoman Bank and the Régie des tabacs from the southern side, overlooking the Golden Horn (lower right, neo-Orientalist design) and the northern, street-front side (upper left, neoclassical facade). As viewed from the street side, the right half of the headquarters building housed the Régie, and the left half housed the bank. The branches shown are in Salonica (upper right) and Beirut (lower left). The sign over the entrance to the Salonica branch identifies it in Greek and French, *Othomanike Trapeza Banque Ottomane*. (Courtesy of Edhem Eldem and the Ottoman Bank Archive and Research Center, Istanbul; the magazine covers are from *Servet-i Fünun* [Treasury of sciences] 74 and 75, 30 July and 6 August 1308 [11 and 18 August 1892].)

Ottoman import and export duties came to be set by treaty, depriving the Ottoman government of autonomy to change the rates at will. In 1900, when Abdülhamid attempted to raise import duties from 8 to 11 percent, the European governments raised a hue and cry. They consented to the measure only in 1907 and on condition that the extra 3 percent be used to finance maintenance of order in Macedonia.

Foreign penetration of the empire was as much cultural as economic. Major and minor powers had diplomatic missions in Istanbul and consulates across the empire. Most powers also maintained foreign post offices. Christian missionaries' competition to open schools, dispensaries, and presses peaked in this period. Protestant and Catholic missionaries from Europe and North America vied with one another, Russia backed Orthodox Christian efforts, and the European-based Alliance Israélite Universelle worked to benefit Jews. By the 1890s, foreign schools in the empire numbered four hundred or more.[11] American missionaries opened Robert College in Istanbul (1863, now Bosphorus University) and the American Syrian Protestant College in Beirut (1866, now the American University of Beirut). The Ottoman government countered with efforts to expand the state schools and propagate Sunni Islam.

As beneficent as their work was, missionaries created differences that had not been there before (for example, Protestant and Catholic as well as Gregorian Armenians), politicized differences both new and old (such as that of Maronites and Druzes in Lebanon), and antagonized local authorities, including both the Ottoman government and the traditional Eastern churches.[12] When they ran into difficulty, missionaries routinely sought help from the friendliest, most powerful diplomats (for American missionaries, the British embassy). Not without reason did Ottoman concerns about missionaries grow, not least because they often acted without Ottoman authorization. When Abdülhamid tried in 1901 to shut down unauthorized French institutions, not only did the French send a naval expedition and demand regularization of all their institutions, but the other European powers made parallel demands. Ottomans sometimes suspected missionaries as spies; during World War I, some such suspicions were confirmed.

Such examples support generalizations that others confirm. If some threats to Ottoman sovereignty were localized, others were systemic. As European imperialist methods grew more refined and aggressive, the major powers became more adept—for a time—at dividing the pie in order to prevent conflict among themselves. The balance between local and systemic crises could always shift, however. That happened late in Abdülhamid's reign, as Armenian and Macedonian crises erupted.

THE ARMENIAN CRISIS OF 1894–1896

In eastern Anatolia, different religious communities historically coexisted. This included Muslims, both Sunni and Alevi, and Christians, mostly Armenian, but also Nestorian (Assyrian, *Asuri*), and Syrian Orthodox (*Süryani*). The region's Muslims were ethnically divided, many being Kurds rather than Turks. The settlement of Caucasian and Balkan Muslim refugees complicated the picture. After the Greek Revolution had shaken their faith in Ottoman Greek loyalty, the Ottomans had come to refer to the Armenians as the "loyal millet" (*millet-i sadıka*). Still, conflicts of interest would arise among populations who earned their livings in different ways from the harsh landscapes of eastern Anatolia—urban craftspeople and traders, peasant farmers, pastoral nomads. Those conflicts could set members of different religious or ethnic communities at odds, even when identity politics did not. In particular, the clash of interests between Armenian peasant farmers and Kurdish nomads created chronic tensions, aggravated by Kurdish demands for protection money. Regional politics played out among four actors: the Ottoman government's agents (the governor, his civil administrative staff, and military forces), the Turkish notables of the towns, the nomadic Kurdish tribal beys, and the Armenians.

For much of the nineteenth century, the Ottoman government had struggled to subdue the Kurdish tribes militarily so as to consolidate Istanbul's authority in the region.[13] Article 61 of the Treaty of Berlin made Anatolia's six eastern provinces, where most Ottoman Armenians lived, the object of international scrutiny by calling for British-supervised reforms. The efforts of Britain's Turkophobic prime minister William Gladstone to enforce these demands led to the worst Ottoman-British crisis in years. It emerged that the figures supplied by the Armenian patriarch of Istanbul had inflated the size of the Armenian population of those provinces, as numbers gathered by British consuls later confirmed. Subsequent scholarly analysis of all available evidence indicates that Ottoman official statistics did not err in showing that the Armenians were a minority in all six of these provinces. "From 1878 to 1897 the ethnic-religious ratio of the population in the six provinces remained more or less stable at around 78 percent Muslim and about 17 percent Armenian; only in the district of Van did Armenians represent as much as 41 percent of the population; but Van accounted for only about 10 percent of the total population of the region."[14]

Although most Armenians in these provinces probably would have been content with secure prosperity, others, many of them living elsewhere, organized politically for more radical aims. Inspired by Russian populism, Armenians in the Caucasus began to discuss liberating Ottoman Armenians. The Hnchak (Bell) Party formed in 1887, and the Dashnak (Armenian Revolutionary Federation) Party formed in 1890. They differed in their relative emphasis on socialism (Hnchak) as opposed to nationalism (Dashnak).[15]

Abdülhamid's concerns about securing eastern Anatolia led him to establish a militia, the *Hamidiye alayları* (Hamidian regiments, 1891). Led by tribal beys and patterned on Russia's Cossack regiments, these were supposed to police eastern Anatolia. The regiments recruited some Turks but mostly Kurds. One purpose in forming the regiments was to integrate the Kurds better politically. However, the Hamidiye cavalry raised peasants' and even townspeople's reasons to fear the tribesmen to new heights.[16]

As Hnchak and Dashnak militants worked their way into eastern Anatolia, the stage was set for a triple surge of violence that rent Ottoman-Armenian symbiosis (1894–1896). The first episode occurred at Sasun near Muş (Bitlis province, 1894), when the Armenians forcibly resisted Kurdish nomads' demands for tribute. Hnchak activists had infiltrated and agitated the populace. The governor of Bitlis reported the incident as the rising of "three thousand insurgents." Abdülhamid decided to teach them a lesson and granted full powers to Zeki Paşa, commander of the Ottoman Fourth Army and the Hamidiye regiments. Zeki Paşa defeated the rebels in a pitched battle. News of these events touched off a wave of European Armenophilia and new demands for reforms. As in earlier crises in places such as Lebanon, the proposed reforms included separating the populations along ethnic lines, as if that would not have caused further disruptions for all concerned. Abdülhamid took advantage of differences among the European powers to avoid compliance.

The second phase of the Armenian crisis began when the Hnchak Party organized a demonstration in Istanbul in September 1895 to demand the promised reforms. Several hundred demonstrators planned to march to the Sublime Porte to present a petition. The demonstration was announced as peaceful; however, some Hnchak militants carried weapons, and the government took precautions. After a few clashes, the demonstration degenerated into violence. The *softas* (medrese students) turned out, and for several days Armenians were attacked anywhere in the city. When the European powers protested, Abdülhamid proclaimed reforms. Then towns all over eastern Anatolia broke out in violence at the news of reforms that Muslims perceived as European-imposed and tantamount to Armenian independence. Again, the breakdown of intercommunal symbiosis left devastation behind. Now it was eastern Anatolian Muslims who felt that the sultan had abandoned them and that they would face the fate of their coreligionists in the Balkans or the Russian Empire, a fate that the Muslim refugees in their midst made impossible to ignore.

The third crisis occurred in Istanbul in August 1896. There, the Dashnaks decided to stage terrorist incidents at several sites, notably the Ottoman Imperial Bank headquarters, which they threatened to blow up with all inside.[17] Seizing this fortress of European finance appealed to the perpetrators as a way to pressure Abdülhamid and the great powers for reform in the east. After tense negotiations, the terrorists were allowed to depart for European exile. Saving their own hides, they abandoned forty-five bombs and more than 11,000 kilograms of dynamite at the bank. They also abandoned Istanbul's Armenians to reprisals. Estimates of the fatalities ranged as high as eight thousand, mostly humble folk. The attack on the European-owned OIB also provoked European disapproval. By now, the European powers were exasperated enough with Abdülhamid that they talked of deposing him, but they could not agree enough to follow through.

Foiling a deposition plot at the end of 1896, Abdülhamid emerged strengthened—for a time. European demands for eastern reforms were shelved. The crises of 1894–1896 left the Armenian nationalists weakened and the Armenians of eastern Anatolia diminished by massacres and emigration. Significantly, this was perhaps the first of a series of episodes that led the empire's urban elites to realize that they were no longer exempt from the problems that confronted their country cousins in far provinces.

THE MACEDONIAN CRISIS

Hard upon these Armenian crises, Macedonia sank into a crisis that clouded Abdülhamid's last years. Extending over 10,000 square kilometers, Macedonia covered the Ottoman provinces of Kosovo, Monastir, and Salonica. Its population was exceptionally mixed ethnically, including Turks, Albanians, Greeks, Serbs, Bulgars, Vlachs, and Gypsies. The region had religious diversity to match, including Muslims, Jews, and Christians; among Orthodox Christians, adherents of the Greek patriarchate and those of the Bulgarian exarchate were at odds with one another. Macedonia included both inaccessible interior regions and one of the most cosmopolitan Ottoman port cities, Salonica. The city refracted all of Macedonia's diversity, yet also differed in having a population that was 50–55 percent Jewish.[18] The Ottomans governed Macedonia, but Serbia, Bulgaria, and Greece disputed Ottoman rule; and Macedonian nationalists challenged all those states' claims. In the 1890s, organizations formed to support all these interests. They drew inspiration from the Armenian crisis of 1894–1896, as well as from the Cretan crisis and the 1897 Ottoman-Greek war. It showed that the

Ottomans were still a mighty military foe but that European diplomacy might turn defeat on the battlefield into victory at the conference table. However, if there was ever a place where the idea of an ethnically homogeneous nation-state was illusory, Macedonia was it. For that reason, Italian, French, and Spanish use its name as their term for a mixed fruit salad.

By 1900, Macedonia had become the theater of violent acts by revolutionary committees (*komitacı, çeteci*) of all stripes. Viewed from urban centers like Salonica or Edirne, the countryside did not seem safe at all. Waves of Muslim refugees seemed to flood the roads to Istanbul (see color illustration).[19] To maintain control, Abdülhamid strove to exploit the antagonisms among both the terrorist groups and the outside powers. This approach worked as long as the conflicts in Macedonia remained small in scale.

In 1902, the External Macedonian Revolutionary Organization (EMRO), which favored union with Bulgaria (as contrasted to the Internal Macedonian Revolutionary Organization, IMRO, which favored Macedonian independence), raised an insurrection, which Ottoman forces defeated. Abdülhamid ordered reforms and appointed an inspector general to carry them out, Hüseyin Hilmi Paşa. He likened his task to that of an asylum-keeper. The European powers also presented a plan. Still, the violence intensified.

In April 1903, IMRO rocked Salonica with spectacular attacks. They blew up a French ship in the harbor, the city's gas lines, and the Ottoman Imperial Bank (see the photograph on p. 140, upper right). More explosions followed the next day at the train station, the cafés, and elsewhere. In August, IMRO launched a general insurrection that spread as far as Thrace. Ottoman retaliation turned the April and August events into bloody failures for IMRO. Still, the Ottoman military was hard put to contain the situation, as was Abdülhamid to find a policy that could satisfy Muslims and prevent foreign intervention.

Macedonian crises bedeviled Abdülhamid's later years and continued until the Ottomans lost the region in the Balkan Wars. Not surprisingly, the 1908 revolution was launched from Salonica, Macedonia's "bridgehead of modernity."[20]

THE HAMIDIAN SYSTEM: ACCOMPLISHMENTS AND OPPONENTS

For evaluating Abdülhamid's reign, several aspects of his policies merit consideration: centralization, his Islamic emphases, reformist accomplishments, foreign policy, and the tension between rationalization and autocracy. The results appealed to some of his subjects but not others. From that fact sprang the revolutionary opposition that toppled him.

CENTRALIZATION IN THE PALACE

Although a new turn toward reasserting the sultan's power opened the reform era under Selim III and Mahmud II, the civil officials of the Sublime Porte seized the political initiative during the Tanzimat. As he took control, Abdülhamid needed few words to say how he meant to rule: not like his father, Abdülmecid, but like his grandfather Mahmud II.[21]

The troubled history of Ottoman constitutionalism heightens the drama of the reconcentration of power in the palace. As Abdülhamid's reign began, the 1876 constitution and the short-lived parliament pointed toward an alternative future. In an empire where there had been no institutionalized site for "politics" outside the bureaucracy and the Tanzimat councils, the first parliamentary elections implied a differentiation between politics and administration, a characteristic of modern government. For Abdülhamid and his supporters, however, the empire was not ready for parliamentary governance. By suspending the parliament in 1878 and suppressing constitutionalism, he wrenched the course of change back toward autocracy. Elective local councils would continue, and political debate might develop about municipal affairs in Salonica or Beirut.[22] However, participation in affairs of state would be limited to those in official ranks, and only under tight palace control.

Yet the words and deeds of heroes like Namık Kemal and Midhat Paşa could not be easily forgotten. From 1889 on, constitutionalist opposition reemerged. By Abdülhamid's last years, the Young Turk opposition, as it became known, had grown strong enough to bring about the 1908 revolution. With that, the course of political development shifted again, away from autocracy and back, at least for a time, toward the competitive politics of constitutional monarchy. In sum, the decisiveness of Abdülhamid's shift in the locus of power appears in its contrast not just with the bureaucratic hegemony of the Tanzimat but also with the constitutionalism of both 1876 and 1908.

A highpoint of Ottoman modernity in its way, the palace and palace regime reflected Abdülhamid's personality.[23] Yıldız was unlike his immediate predecessors' ostentatious imitations of European palaces. Yıldız was also unlike the historical Topkapı Palace, made up of courtyards surrounded by galleries with rooms opening off of them and pavilions here and there. Previously an imperial hunting preserve, Yıldız resembled less a palace than an enclosed park. Abdülhamid added an inner enclosure as his Imperial Park (Has Bahçe) and gradually built nearly a hundred structures, ranging from stables to residences for himself, his harem, and visiting royalty. One of his memorable experiences had been traveling to Europe in 1867, where he visited the Exposition Universelle in Paris, among other sights. The resemblance between Yıldız Palace and an exhibition park with buildings in contrasting styles may reflect that experience. However, the enclosure of the compound at Yıldız meant that this palace lacked the visibility of earlier ones. No longer would the imperial household set the style for Ottoman society; rather, the dynasty joined the Ottoman elites in emulating European bourgeois tastes.

Many of the buildings at Yıldız were modern for their time, especially those by Italian architect Raimondo D'Aronco, whom Abdülhamid invited to Istanbul in 1893.[24] D'Aronco's buildings exemplify the latest European styles, especially Art Nouveau. The florilinear forms of Art Nouveau stimulated the Ottomans' calligraphic sensibility, as numerous Istanbul buildings demonstrate. One of D'Aronco's most modernistic buildings was a small one just outside Yıldız Palace in Beşiktaş. This is the tomb of Abdülhamid's spiritual adviser, the Libyan Shadhili shaykh Zafir al-Madani. A modernistic tomb for a Sufi shaykh—that is another futuristic Islamic touch.

Abdülhamid turned Yıldız into the empire's center of power, and the way he did so reflects his personality and priorities. He was a man of unusual fears and phobias. The circumstances of the times aggravated these, and his retainers knew how to take advantage of them. Two depositions in a single year, 1876, had brought him to the throne. Of the two, Abdülaziz had committed suicide—unless he was murdered! Ex-sultan Murad and his immediate family remained Abdülhamid's prisoners at the nearby Çirağan Palace until Murad's death in 1904.[25] Moreover, Abdülhamid lived in an age when assassins felled several ruling figures—Presidents James Garfield (1881) and William McKinley (1901), Tsar Alexander II (1881), Empress Elizabeth of Austria (1898), and Nasiruddin Shah of Iran (1896), among others. More than once (1896, 1905), plots against Abdülhamid were foiled. As the years passed, he secluded himself ever more, minimizing his public appearances to the indispensable Friday noon prayer. He heightened (1898) and reinforced (1905) the palace walls. He stationed troops and police all around those walls on the outside: the headquarters of the military district of Istanbul still abut the walls of Yıldız Palace. He provided mansions for key functionaries like the grand vezir, the *şeyhülislam*, and the minister of war near the palace and required them to reside there. As head of the ulema, the şeyhülislam was the object of particular attention, for this was the man who would have to issue a fetva for a sultan to be deposed. Abdülhamid patronized Sufi shaykhs from far and wide, but he kept his official ulema under tight rein. Likewise, much as he did to modernize the military, he made sure that it was in no position to challenge him.

He built up a palace staff ultimately estimated at twelve thousand, plus fifteen thousand nearby troops. The Grand Chancery (Büyük Mabeyn) formed the political nerve center, with scores of secretaries. Occupying a marble building just inside the main gateway, the chancery secretaries did Abdülhamid's paperwork and controlled access to the imperial presence (*huzur-i hümayun*). Ambassadors and provincial governors corresponded primarily with the Mabeyn and only secondarily, if at all, with the ministries. Foreign policy was conducted from here. An assiduous worker, Abdülhamid was the real minister and micromanager in almost every field. Another institutional mechanism for concentrating power in the palace consisted of permanent commissions set up there under the sultan's presidency, to work on major issues such as refugees, military and financial reform, or the Hijaz railway.[26] Equally important was the Privy Treasury (Hazine-i Hassa), under Abdülhamid a ministerial-size agency that controlled huge interests throughout the empire. But Abdülhamid's ability to concentrate power depended on more than force of character.

AN ISLAMIC REIGN

Abdülhamid inherited vast, legitimate powers de jure. These had deep roots in both Islamic political thought and the Turkic tradition of statecraft. Both traditions extended back into pre-Islamic times and included elements that were not strictly compatible with Islamic belief. Such elements included the Turko-Mongol tradition of legislation on the ruler's authority and the idea of authoritarian kingship. Confronted with realities that had never fully matched Islamic ideals, Islamic thinkers had reconciled themselves to authoritarian rule long before Ottoman times. To most Muslims, Abdülhamid could thus securely invoke Kur'anic precepts such as "Obey God and His Prophet and Those in authority among you" (4.59), a verse embroidered in gold on the regimental banners of the Military Academy.

Earlier sultans had not always exercised their legitimate powers fully; however, nothing had diminished those powers in principle. Even the constitution of 1876 (art. 7) had only listed some of those powers without delimiting them exhaustively. That fact signifies not only the urgency of the moment when the constitution was drafted but also the sacrosanct aura that still surrounded the sultanate for many Ottomans.[27] A strong-willed, capable sultan could take these powers back into his hands.

Equally ready at hand was the idea, reinforced in 1774 with the Treaty of Küçük Kaynarca, that the Ottoman sultan was the caliph of Islam. However much or little earlier sultans had invoked the caliphal title, by the 1800s, when most Muslims lived under European colonial rule, the idea of an independent Muslim ruler who championed Muslims everywhere exerted powerful appeal. As advances in transportation and communication made the Islamic world more perceptible as a whole, Namık Kemal and others began writing about Islamic unity (*ittihad-i İslam*) in the 1870s.[28] Exact in the usages of a pious Muslim sovereign, Abdülhamid was uniquely positioned to appropriate this vision politically. He was well aware that he as caliph had the power to call a jihad and rouse Muslims outside the empire against their colonial masters. He was equally well aware that exercising that power would jeopardize the empire that was his power base. European governments developed inflated worries about pan-Islamism as a threat, and the British in particular did what they could to promote the rival idea of an Arab caliphate. Yet effectively, the caliph was the Ottoman sultan, Abdülhamid.

In addition to his caution in protecting Ottoman interests, Abdülhamid also had limited financial means for pan-Islamic adventuring. Within the empire, he could do a great deal to advance Islamic priorities, all the more when he mobilized the resources of the Privy Treasury for that purpose. He supported prominent religious figures as permanent residents at his court. Examples include Libyan shaykh Zafir al-Madani of the Shadhili order, to which Abdülhamid adhered; the Syrian shaykh Abulhuda al-Sayadi of the Rifa'i order; or Jamaleddin al-Afghani, noted Islamic publicist and unity advocate. Abdülhamid bestowed civil appointments on prominent Muslims from different parts of the empire, as in the case of Izzet Holo (Hawlu) Paşa al-Abid of Damascus.[29] At a time when the treasury could not pay government salaries regularly, Abdülhamid gave his supporters additional stipends from the Privy Treasury, paid regularly in gold. He showered honors and decorations on provincial notables. He sponsored publications in favor of the caliphate. Counteracting the influence of missionaries, he sent Muslim religious teachers to the provinces. While it was far more extensive than this, his building program included providing mosques and schools throughout his dominions.

Beyond Ottoman frontiers, what Abdülhamid could do was limited. He sent Kur'ans and carpets to mosques. Religious teachers were sent to Muslim communities in South Africa and Singapore. His attempts to improve relations with Iran helped win the good will of the leading Shi'i religious scholars of Najaf and Karbala in Ottoman Iraq.[30] Abdülhamid's supreme resource for promoting his Islamic legitimacy was significant for Muslims both inside and outside the empire. His inherited role as the servitor of the Two Holy Cities, Mecca and Medina, made him the patron and protector of the Muslim pilgrims, who came annually from all over the world.

For Abdülhamid, the four prerequisites for the empire's survival were Islam, the dynasty, Istanbul as capital, and the Holy Cities of Mecca and Medina; other prominent Ottomans agreed. What had been essential historically remained so in Ottoman modernity. Among numerous expressions of this realization, none was more momentous than the building of the Hijaz railway in 1900–1908, financed with contributions from Muslims everywhere, and intended to tighten the links between Istanbul and Mecca, to stimulate the regions it traversed economically, and above all to serve the needs of Muslim pilgrims.[31]

MODERNIZING REFORM: DEVELOPMENT AND LOCAL ADMINISTRATION

Some historians have characterized Abdülhamid's reign as a continuation of the Tanzimat. The characterization is apt, as far as it goes. Although it differed radically from the Tanzimat in reasserting palace hegemony, the Hamidian regime continued many of the same reforms. Illustrations of this point appear in provincial administration and in developments in public works, military reform, and education.

One reason for the continuity in such fields as provincial administration is that the Tanzimat statesmen did not fully systematize many of their reforms before the 1860s. In provincial administration, Abdülhamid took over a system that had only lately been fully defined. Under him, the number of provinces (vilayet) varied from twenty-five in 1881 to twenty-nine in 1908. In terms of administrative organization, much of the change probably occurred below the province level and took the form of filling out the lower administrative echelons. The law of 1877 on municipal administration likewise was extended to the provinces in this period. While the administrative presence on the ground was certainly "thicker" by this time than it had been earlier, Ottoman provinces were still much larger than those of most European countries—ranging between 30,000 and 100,000 square kilometers. From that point of view, the increase in the size of provincial administrative staffs was a good thing—in the province of Bursa, from 62 in 1878 to 148 in 1908. With improvements in education, officials' average educational levels also rose. Increasingly, local administrative agencies were headed by graduates of the School of Civil Administration (Mekteb-i Mülkiye), proud professionals.

The rising capacity for administrative performance was expressed in other ways, too. The empire's first modern censuses were conducted in 1881–1893 and 1906–1907.[32] The censuses were only one result of a proposal by one of Abdülhamid's ablest ministers, Küçük ("Little") Said Paşa, to use statistical methods to provide the government with up-to-date information. Similar impulses appear in the increasing publication of official yearbooks, not only for the central government, which had published them annually since 1847, but for individual ministries and provinces.[33]

After the losses of 1878 shifted the empire's center of gravity from the Balkans to Anatolia and the Arab lands, Ottoman statesmen shifted their priorities accordingly. The relative status of the Arab provinces rose. In some cases, organizing local administration required something like internal colonization in order to turn particular localities into secure, integral, flourishing parts of the empire. This was true, for example, in parts of geographical Syria, including what are now Syria, Lebanon, Jordan, and Israel. In the Ottoman districts of 'Ajlun, al-Balqa', al-Karak, and Ma'an, for example, the administrative and socioeconomic foundations for the later state of Jordan were laid in this period. The provincial administration law of 1871 "provided a blueprint for bringing the state to the periphery."[34] The Ottoman land law of 1858 was equally significant, as were such government projects as the telegraph and railway, public building, and refugee resettlement. In order to integrate tribally organized populations more effectively into the state, Abdülhamid founded a special Tribal School (Aşiret Mektebi, 1892), whose graduates went on to special classes in the Military Academy or the School of Civil Administration. The same kind of connection between the organization of local administration and the development (*imar*) of previously underdeveloped territories appears in many other places.

Historical centers also underwent transformation. In Salonica, for example, modern quays were built around 1869; the city walls were demolished to permit expansion (1869–1879); modern boulevards and residential quarters began to be built; and in 1888 this great Aegean port city acquired its rail link to Europe. In this period, many provinces had their "great" governors who rendered particularly significant services in modernization.[35]

Even as Istanbul gained in ability to appoint qualified provincial officials, the politics of notables continued to evolve. The regime relied on local intermediaries, and so did the populace. The notables' positions depended no longer only on their local roots and assets but increasingly on their roles in government service. They might hold either appointive, salaried, bureaucratic offices or part-time, elective memberships on administrative councils.[36] Much as the notables came from the upper tier of the emergent, propertied middle class, their vertical ties to lower strata increased their power, albeit at the risk of factional discord. As distinctive as the notables were of the top of provincial society, so were the leaders and factions that emerged among the workers and the urban poor. Noteworthy examples include the *qabadayat*, who could bring out the crowd for the Damascene notables they supported, and gangs like the *zukurt* and *shumurt*, with which the notables of Iraq's Shi'i shrine cities, Najaf and Karbala, maintained fractious coalitions.[37]

MODERNIZING REFORM: PUBLIC WORKS

Abdülhamid was one of the most prolific builders among all Ottoman sultans. His buildings, in a distinctive range of styles, still leave their stamp on cityscapes from Macedonia to Iraq. The great difference from earlier reigns was that his buildings were less likely to be imperial mosques and palaces than administrative offices, barracks, schools, small mosques, train stations, docks, public markets, and clock towers. If more modest, these buildings were also more numerous and more widely dispersed across the empire. The initiative behind the buildings did not go unnoticed: Salonica Greeks referred to these buildings as *vassilika*, "royal."[38]

Even more significant than the buildings were the improvement in communications and transportation. In addition to road- and bridge-building,

School building under Abdülhamid. Preparatory (*idadi*) schools located (from top right to lower left) in Salonica, Beirut, Baghdad, and Yanya (Ioannina). The Baghdad school was military; the others were civil. (The Baghdad photograph is anonymous, the others are by Sebah and Joaillier, all from the Library of Congress, Prints and Photographs Division, Abdülhamid II Collection, 3b28014u, 3b28172u, 3b27994u, 3b28202u.)

Abdülhamid's reign became the most important period for expanding Otto-man telegraphs and railways. While both had been introduced into the empire in the 1850s, telegraph lines more than doubled in length under Abdülhamid to nearly 50,000 kilometers. Except for some short lines, the railroad reached the empire mostly after 1880, first the Balkans, then Anatolia, and last the Arab provinces. Nothing better illustrates the Ottoman determination to build rail-roads than how the lines were brought into Istanbul. Even the walls and out-buildings of the Topkapı Palace grounds, at the water's edge where the Golden Horn enters the Sea of Marmara, were demolished so that the rail line could be run all the way around the city's Marmara coast and the station could be built at Sirkeci on the Golden Horn. Sultan Abdülaziz expressed his eagerness for railroads in pithy language: "Just get it built; run it over my back, if you want."[39] The fact remains that the Ottoman railway age really began under his successor, Abdülhamid.

MODERNIZING REFORM: EDUCATION

The Tanzimat's most important regulations on education were enacted rather late (1869), and the development of an empirewide system of government schools occurred under Abdülhamid. The 1880s became a major period for the development of public education around the world, the Ottoman Empire included. If a "stormy relationship" between rationalization and the formation of individual subjectivity characterizes modernity, Ottoman schools had to be one of the major storm centers, all the more given the competition from foreign and minority schools.[40]

Expanding on what already existed, the 1869 public education regulations called for a five-tiered hierarchy rising from elementary (*ibtidai*) to upper ele-mentary (*rüşdiye*), middle (*idadi*), lycée (*sultani*), higher professional schools including teachers' colleges for men and women, and a university (*darülfünun*). In addition to lower-level schools, elements of the system that predated 1869 included the military academies, the Franco-Ottoman Galatasaray Lycée (1868), and such professional schools as the colleges for rüsdiye teachers (male, 1848, and female, 1870) and the School of Civil Administration (Mülkiye Mektebi, 1859). Abdülhamid expanded the rüşdiyes considerably, not only in Istanbul but in the provinces. Competition with non-Muslim and foreign schools was a major goal; in Iraq, so was strengthening Sunni Islam as opposed to the Shi'a, which only began to acquire a mass following in Iraq during the nineteenth century.[41]

Under Abdülhamid, the number of upper elementary (rüşdiye) schools increased from 277 in 1879 to 619 around 1908, 74 of them for girls. The number of preparatory (idadi) schools grew from 6 in 1876 to 109 in 1908. By 1908, there were forty thousand students in the rüşdiyes and twenty thousand in the idadis. Aside from the Galatasaray Lycée and the Darüşşafaka (1873, a school for orphans), however, there were as yet no other Ottoman (as opposed to non-Muslim or foreign) lycées. Among the professional schools, that of Civil Administration was upgraded in 1876 into an important institution; new professional schools were founded for law, fine arts, and commerce. From 1890 on, professional schools began to be opened in the provinces: a military school at the site of each of the regional army headquarters; law schools in Salonica, Konya, and Baghdad; a medical school at Damascus.[42] Imposing buildings were built for these. Istanbul University was founded in 1900, one motive being to keep young men from going abroad for higher education (and opposition politics). Despite these gains, it is no wonder that Ottoman statesmen felt threatened by the competition of the foreign and minority schools.

Financing new schools remained an intractable challenge. Grand Vezir Said Paşa found the solution in a surtax added to the tithe (öşür, 1884). To promote Ottoman solidarity, the 1869 regulations explicitly stated that the government schools were to be open to all communities. Still, most non-Muslims continued to attend communal or foreign schools. Far from Ottoman solidarity, those institutions promoted a different goal: "Education is today . . . a flag, and the schoolmaster is a commander who arms minds for the struggle in which everyone sees the future victory of his nation."[43]

MODERNIZING REFORM: THE MILITARY

In the mid-nineteenth century, modern technology revolutionized warfare with the advent of rifled firearms and breech-loading, rifled steel artillery. In its implications for the internal power of states, the military revolution passed through two phases, strengthening the government's control over its populace in the first, and potentially weakening it in the second, as rebellious subjects acquired advanced weaponry. The Ottomans began acquiring the new weapons by the 1860s, but equipping his forces was still a major objective for Abdülhamid. At first, this effort enhanced the state's success in defending itself and securing its provinces. After about 1890, the diffusion of modern weapons eroded this advantage, as events in Yemen, eastern Anatolia, and Macedonia showed. Abdülhamid's success in avoiding foreign wars meant that the Ottomans would not again confront the effects of the firepower revolution externally before the Young Turk period. However, as provincial unrest proliferated after 1890, military modernization became a never-ending struggle.[44]

Ottoman schoolgirls from upper elementary (*rüşdiye*) schools in Istanbul.
From top right to lower left, the schools are those of Eyyüp, Fatih, Molla Gürani, and
Sultan Ahmet. (By Abdullah Frères, Library of Congress, Prints and Photographs
Division, Abdülhamid II Collection, 3b27699u, 3b27692u, 3b27694u, 3b27696u.)

Whatever validity may attach to popular images of Turkish militarism in other periods, between 1826 and 1908, the Ottoman military did not dominate politics. Abdülhamid meant to keep it that way. Having to pick up the pieces from the Russo-Turkish War, he was determined to restore the military's effectiveness while making sure that it could not threaten him. He appealed to Germany for military and financial expertise; thence sprang the special Ottoman relationship with Germany. Internally, essential first steps were to inventory resources and conduct a census as a basis for recruitment. Yet financial shortfalls created insoluble problems for military reform. Throughout Abdülhamid's reign, military expenditures absorbed half the budget and offered no good ways to economize. The only compressible budget item was salaries, and those were paid irregularly, with the result that mutinies over unpaid salaries occurred increasingly after 1888. Naval spending was also limited. The primary security threats were land-based, and Ottoman military policy could not have more than defensive goals.

Adapting military spending to these facts, Abdülhamid provided the navy with torpedoes and mines, which it had lacked, and he equipped the forts of the Dardanelles with Krupp cannons. For the army, the strategic vision was defensive and infantry-based with priority to fortifications and communications by land, particularly the telegraph and railroad. The army, too, was equipped with up-to-date weapons, notably Krupp cannons and Mauser rifles. In the 1880s, Ottoman arms purchases from Germany were large enough— hundreds of cannons at a time, hundreds of thousands of rifles—to worry British intelligence.

Recruitment was a chronic problem, aggravated by its restriction to the provincial Muslim population. Recruiting non-Muslims was debated but not done. Islam was the main motivator to fight for the empire; doubts were raised as to whether Muslim soldiers would obey non-Muslim officers; finally, the treasury needed the tax non-Muslims paid for military exemption. The best that could be done was to rationalize recruitment with a new law (1886) and require refugees to serve. Officer training was strengthened by opening more military preparatory schools, notably in Arab cities. The program of the Military Academy (Mekteb-i Harbiye) in Istanbul was upgraded with assistance from General (later Field Marshal) Colmar von der Goltz, whose long service in the Ottoman Empire (1883–1895, 1908, 1915–1916) embodied Ottoman-German collaboration. Among army officers, this commitment to education raised the percentage of "school men" (*mektepli*, as opposed to "regimentals," *alaylı*) from 10 to 25 percent between 1884 and 1899. The Ottoman army's victory in the Ottoman-Greek war of 1897 testified to the gains of reform in this period, just as its frustrations with provincial guerrillas reflected the spread of advanced weapons beyond government control.

FOREIGN POLICY AND RELATIONS WITH GERMANY

The Ottoman turn toward Germany followed from its victory in the Franco-Prussian War (1870–1871) and Abdülhamid's displeasure at France's adoption of republican government and its occupation of Tunisia. He also needed to break out of the isolation that handicapped the empire in the Russo-Turkish War.[45]

Abdülhamid requested military instructors and financial experts, and Germany sent both. While the Ottoman Empire had a long history of foreign military advisers, this relationship proved more lasting and influential. The German officers still did not command, but they were highly paid and listened to seriously. Ottoman officers were also sent to Germany for training. Increased reliance on German armaments consolidated the relationship, privileging German firms in competing for other concessions. Abdülhamid especially wanted railways in Anatolia. In 1871, Wilhelm von Pressel had presented a plan for a railroad from Istanbul to Baghdad. This plan, or the parts of it that Abdülhamid found militarily significant, resurfaced; and von Pressel was rehired in 1888. A contract was signed with German financiers, and four years later, the first train rolled into Ankara.[46] Kaiser Wilhelm II (r. 1881–1918) visited the Ottoman Empire in 1882.

Kaiser Wilhelm came again in 1898. His reception reveals much about Ottoman-German relations.[47] Occurring two years after the Armenian massacres in eastern Anatolia and an attempt on Abdülhamid's life, the visit implied renewed international respect for the sultan. At Yıldız, new pavilions were built to honor the kaiser and empress. They were showered with gifts, reportedly costing one-tenth of the year's budget. After Istanbul, the imperial couple went to Haifa, Jerusalem, and Damascus, where the kaiser announced that he was "the best friend" of the world's three hundred million Muslims. The implications of the kaiser's visit were many: a chance for Abdülhamid to meet as an equal with a powerful European ruler, a show of support that led him to leave behind old hopes of balance in relations with European powers, international validation for pan-Islamism, and—not least—increased preference for Germany in economic concessions.

The Baghdad railway project combined strategic, political, and economic value. Many questions arose around the project, dividing both Ottoman and European interests. However, after careful diplomacy by German ambassador Marschall von Bieberstein, a preliminary convention was signed (1899) granting an eight-year concession to build a railway to Baghdad. Construction began in 1903. By 1908, only a few segments had been finished. However, refugees had begun settling along them, and irrigated agriculture had expanded around Konya and Adana. Astonishing though it may seem, only in the decade after the railway reached Ankara and Konya (roughly 1895–1905) could Istanbul begin to be supplied with wheat transported overland from Anatolia rather than by ship from the ports of the Black Sea and Marmara basin.[48]

RATIONALITY VERSUS REPRESSION

If the history of modernity is one of tension between rationalization and subjectivization, a modernizing autocrat ought to embody that tension personally and magnify its consequences for his subjects.[49] Abdülhamid did both. Inasmuch as Ottoman reform depended from the start on using the sultan's legislative power to enact new plans and programs, a latent tension between will and reason had existed all along. In the last decisive reign of Ottoman history, Abdülhamid's vigorous centralizing brought that tension into the open more than ever, ultimately guaranteeing that there would not be another reign like his. The tension appears in his instrumental use of rationalizing processes as tools to extend his range of control. In his last years, this tension also appears in worsening repression.

Not paradoxically, the tide of plans, regulations, and laws—already a flood during the Tanzimat—kept rising under Abdülhamid. If the Sublime Porte lost power, it did not lose work to do. Although the most important business was now done at the palace, the Council of Ministers and, just below it, the Council of State (Şura-yı Devlet), still churned out regulatory documents, which made their way to the palace for sanction by imperial decree (*irade*). A 1909 critique of the regime pointed out that the archives of the Sublime Porte contained so many reform decrees that "one would suppose, upon reading them, that Abdülhamid really thought day and night of nothing but ensuring the . . . happiness of the state and its people. Yet, one would also suppose that his orders were not or could not be applied because of the ill will or inability of the authorities at the Porte and in the provinces."[50]

Recent research makes clear that Abdülhamid thought much of the time about implementing policy documents and that his officials achieved "a degree of efficiency for which they are seldom credited."[51] Still, his reign was no ideal rule of law. The 1876 constitution placed the sultan above the law; then he suspended the constitution. Rational planning and regulatory processes were tools for him to use or ignore at will. For example, much of the regulatory apparatus for modern civil and military services was enacted under Abdülhamid. Systematic personnel records on civil officials began to be kept in the late 1870s. Agencies to recommend candidates for appointment evolved, taking the form of the Civil Officials Commission (Memurin-i Mülkiye Komisyonu) by 1896. According to its regulations, nominees were to be proposed by the ministries and forwarded with the candidates' personnel files from the Civil Officials Commission to the palace, where the sultan would chose the appointee. There were exceptions to this procedure; in particular, the sultan made the highest appointments—provincial governors, top officials in Istanbul—spontaneously or on the grand vezir's advice.[52]

Such a system perfectly illustrates how rationalizing and regulating processes, harnessed to the will of the modernizing autocrat, enabled him to extend his range of control in a way that he otherwise could not have. Other techniques served the same end. The sultan who seldom left his palace relied on photography to follow progress in his realm, accumulating a huge collection, from which albums were sent to foreign heads of state in an image-building effort. The telegraph—the first technology of nearly instant communication—extended Abdülhamid's range of control fantastically. The palace became the hub of a network of spies and informers so extensive that countless people felt they were being reported on and had to try to attract favorable attention by reporting on others. Referred to as *jurnal* (from the French *journal*, "daily"), so many such reports were submitted that "cartloads" of them were found at the palace after 1908. All these systems reinforced hypercentralization, making it natural that even the highest officials feared to take any action without "requesting authorization" (*istizan*) from the palace.

The vices of administration did not stop with the repression of initiative. Abdülhamid padded governmental payrolls, implicitly trying to re-create the historical situation where virtually the entire intelligentsia worked for the government and could be subjected to arbitrary discipline as members of the ruler's household. Confirming this inference, the high-handed treatment he meted out to government functionaries seemed at times to reverse the 1830s reforms that ended the vulnerabilities of official slavery. At the same time that he expanded the bureaucracy beyond the needs of the service, the chronic shortage of funds made regular salary payments impossible. The payments that were made were timed to coincide with religious holidays, making them seem like special acts of beneficence. The rest of the time, government employees were subjected to pressures that even the personally scrupulous could not always withstand, the result being systemic corruption and eventually troop revolts over unpaid salaries.[53]

After about 1900, all these problems worsened. The aging sultan restricted his movements ever more, reportedly occupying himself more with spy reports than with policy issues. The influence of favorites grew. Instead of dominating the palace, Abdülhamid was starting to be dominated by it. Censorship, growing severe in the early 1890s, reached absurd extremes. Namık Kemal's writings were deemed harmful and censored from 1892 on. In later editions of Şemseddin Sami's French-Turkish dictionary (1882), politically sensitive definitions vanished, until after 1900 "revolution" was only an astronomical term. Even the most pro-regime editors complained about newspaper censorship, and even the official *Takvim-i Vekayi* was censored. The official publication of laws in the series of volumes known as the *Düstur* lapsed for most of the reign; the laws of this period were published only under the republic. Ironically, the vast legislation of the period was not regularly published in the way required for its enforcement. As spying and denunciation worsened, ever more intellectuals were sent into internal exile. Paradoxically, Abdülhamid thereby helped spread the very ideas that he wanted to repress.[54]

OPPOSITION

Aside from provincial and separatist troubles, Abdülhamid faced Ottoman elite opposition both early and late in his reign. Circumstances enabled him to outmaneuver the Young Ottomans and constitutionalists. After 1889, a new opposition emerged, commonly known as the Young Turks. Abdülhamid coped with them until about 1900. Yet they engineered the 1908 revolution, restored the constitution, and deposed him in 1909.

The question of why organized opposition among Ottoman intellectuals disappeared in the 1880s and reemerged after 1889 is usually answered in terms of Abdülhamid's tyranny, but economic factors may also have contributed. Both the Young Ottomans and later the Young Turks came from official ranks. Both generations of opposition consisted primarily of government employees whose incomes did not fluctuate with market conditions. In contrast, Istanbul prices for major foodstuffs fluctuated roughly in line with world market trends, rising to a peak in 1873, falling into the mid-1890s, then rising again. Their crises of the 1870s kept Ottomans from benefiting from the falling prices until after 1880. Then, Istanbul grain prices also fell below half their 1873 level by the mid-1890s, after which Istanbul prices followed the world trend back upward, rapidly so after 1906. Salary statistics indicate that as those price fluctuations occurred, civil officials' incomes fluctuated only slightly from 1873 to 1908. If salaries remained level but prices peaked in the periods of both the Young Ottomans (1860s–1870s) and Young Turks (post-1889) and fell in between, this evidence implies that government employees' economic distress fueled both generations' opposition activism. In between, in the 1880s, the relative prosperity of those on fixed salaries in a period of falling prices helped sustain relative political calm. Abdülhamid did not have major elite opposition to repress in the 1880s; he did earlier and later.[55]

In terms of the tension in modernity between rationalization and subjectivity, the fatal flaw in Abdülhamid's efforts at elite formation was that the men he trained to serve his will developed stronger loyalties to their new ideas than to their sultan. Seizing the initiative in imagining the future, they assigned sovereignty not to their imperial master but to their own ideal of the state. The first nucleus of the new opposition formed in the Military Medical Academy (1889). Its combination of scientific materialism, military discipline, and enforced religious and political conformism within the confines of a residential college generated extreme radicalizing pressures. An added factor heightened the pressure: all the founders of the Young Turk umbrella organization, the Committee of Union and Progress, came from non-Turkish Muslim communities—Kurds, Circassians, Albanians—that were threatened by non-Muslim separatisms that European powers supported.[56] Opposition quickly spread throughout the Ottoman service academies. At first, this was no more than a student movement. However, the Armenian crises of the 1890s heightened the cadets' sense that the empire was in peril. The authorities began exiling student activists in 1895.

Ottoman exiles grouped increasingly in Europe. In Paris from 1889 on, Ahmed Rıza went into open opposition and became leader of the Ottoman Committee of Union and Progress (CUP). By taking that name, the new opposition joined the international chorus of movements, from as far away as Latin America, which paid tribute to Auguste Comte's positivist philosophy. Significantly, the Ottomans changed Comte's motto from "Order and Progress"—still emblazoned, for example, on the flag of the Brazilian republic (also founded in 1889). For the Ottoman Empire, there could be no order without unity, and the positivist motto required changing accordingly: Union and Progress.[57] To spread their message, Young Turk exiles published newspapers abroad and smuggled them into the empire. They also contacted the European press and other political exiles, including Arabs and Armenians.

Already by 1896, the Young Turks discussed deposing Abdülhamid.[58] A plot was hatched, but the palace got wind of it. Hundreds were arrested, including high-placed collaborators. In 1897, when plotting resumed in the professional schools, nearly ninety cadets were arrested, tried, and given harsh sentences. The dispatch of numerous exiles to Tripoli and Fezzan weakened the movement seriously. Abdülhamid also exploited divisions among his opponents in Europe. One of their greatest weaknesses was that no patron yet financed their endeavors, as Mustafa Fazıl Paşa had done for the Young Ottomans.

Trying to restore the old politics of loyalty and patronage, Abdülhamid alternated between pressuring the exiles and offering them inducements to work for him. In 1897, he sent his chief spy, Ahmed Celaleddin Paşa, to Europe to offer amnesty, reforms, and salaries or stipends. Among those who yielded and returned to Istanbul was Mizancı Murad, editor of the CUP organ *Mizan* and then director of the CUP.[59] The Young Turk newspapers had hardly announced the promises of amnesty and reform before word came that those recently condemned in Istanbul, far from being amnestied, had been exiled. At that, Mizancı Murad looked like a traitor. Still even those who tried to stick to their guns in Europe soon found themselves forced by necessity to accept the sultan's offers. By 1897, hardly anyone was left.

All that changed in 1899, when Abdülhamid's brother-in-law went to Europe with his two sons to join the opposition.[60] Mahmud Celaleddin Paşa had become Abdülhamid's brother-in-law by marrying Seniha Sultan. Mahmud Celaleddin's wealth at last gave the Young Turks financial backing. Abdülhamid vainly offered him 50,000 gold liras to return. Abdülhamid again dispatched his chief spy to Europe, but this time the effort failed. Holding Seniha Sultan hostage at the palace, Abdülhamid worked through his embassies to impugn Mahmud Celaleddin and his sons, Sabahaddin and Lutfullah, as anarchists. Even after the paşa died in 1903, his sons, especially Sabahaddin Bey, remained politically active.

Then twenty-one years old, whereas Ahmed Rıza was forty-one, Sabahaddin symbolized youth and ideological diversity for the Young Turks. He asserted himself as a rival to Ahmed Rıza for leadership and, with his brother, decided to hold a congress of the Ottoman opposition in Paris. An Anglophile, Sabahaddin championed decentralization and free enterprise; a positivist, Ahmed Rıza espoused centralization and the developing trend toward Turkish nationalism. Abdülhamid tried everything to stop the 1902 opposition congress, but the French authorities allowed it to convene in closed session with Sabahaddin presiding. In keeping with his decentralist principles, which implied a federalist approach to holding the empire together, the delegates included Armenians, Greeks, and Albanians, as well as Muslim Ottomans. Disputes broke out, pitting Sabahaddin and the non-Muslims against Ahmed Rıza's supporters.

The congress left the Young Turk opposition split over whether to seek European intervention to support the cause. Favoring European intervention, Sabahaddin wanted to launch a coup with British support. After that failed, he formed the League for Private Initiative and Decentralization (Teşebbüs-i Şahsi ve Adem-i Merkeziyet Cemiyeti) and set about building alliances with other revolutionary organizations and provincial notables. Although this movement added pluralism to the Young Turk movement, Ahmed Rıza and others saw Sabahaddin's ideas as conducive to partition and imperialist domination. They proved more realistic than Sabahaddin in recognizing the need for army officers' support.

All the Young Turks reacted to contemporary European ideas, although their preferences among these ideas differed, as the polarization between Sabahaddin and Ahmed Rıza showed. One prominent difference between the Young Turks and their Young Ottoman predecessors was that while the earlier activists responded to European thought of the Enlightenment and Romantic era, the Young Turk reacted also to the newer social sciences, notably sociology and psychology. However, the biggest ideological difference between the two generations of opposition was that the Young Turks lacked the Young Ottomans' Islamic engagement. The Young Turk thinkers responded instead to the European "scientific materialism" of such writers as Karl Vogt (1817–1895), Jacob Moleschott (1822–1893), and Ludwig Büchner (1824–1899), whose *Kraft und Stoff* (Force and matter) was popular among students in Istanbul's elite service academies.[61] The Young Turks viewed Islam as a means of mass mobilization, but their principles were radically secular.

During the last years of his reign, Abdülhamid managed to keep Istanbul relatively free of overt Young Turk activism. However, discontent was mounting. Satires and caricatures circulated secretly. Criticisms that could not be uttered about imperial politics were diverted into debates about municipal politics or into works of fiction about life in patriarchal households, which modeled the patrimonial sultanate in ways that did not need to be spelled out.[62] Using internal exile to purge his capital of dissenters, Abdülhamid paradoxically helped the Young Turks in the provinces. International events also prepared for revolution. The Japanese victory in the Russo-Japanese War (1904–1905) thrilled Ottomans, calling attention to Japan as a model of constitutionalism and modernity and contradicting European ideas about Asian racial inferiority. In Russia, defeat led to revolution in 1905. Even in Iran, a revolution began in 1906. In 1876, the Ottoman Empire had a constitution, but Russia and Iran did not; after 1905, both Russia and Iran had constitutions, but the Ottomans did not.[63] That was Abdülhamid's fault.

As a revolutionary wave rose in other countries, the Young Turk movement evolved rapidly. In 1906, exiled doctors Nazım and Bahaeddin Şakir brought new organizational skills to the Paris organization. The two doctors turned it into an effective revolutionary organization with an active propaganda effort inside the Ottoman army. A merger followed in 1907 between the Paris organization and the secret Ottoman Freedom Society in Salonica, headed by

Talat Bey. Merging internal and external opposition organizations marked a critical step toward revolution, as did the focus on Macedonia, where Young Turk militancy competed with all the region's nationalist movements. Agitation also mounted in other provinces, as tax revolts occurred in Kastamonu, Trabzon, Erzurum, Diyarbakır, and Van. Fueled by grievances over service in Yemen and unpaid salaries, military revolts became more common. Rising prices fanned unrest, especially among those with fixed incomes. Elitist Young Turk intellectuals, advocates of top-down action so far, took note of this assertiveness among ordinary Turks and began reassessing prospects for success in violent action. Significantly, the Anatolian tax revolts, organized by local notables to protest new taxes and demand a voice in deciding their uses, were the work of the propertied, religiously conservative wing of the emergent Ottoman middle class.[64]

In June 1908, the Young Turks in Macedonia, having learned that the sultan's secret agents planned a preemptive strike against them, seized the initiative and began having Abdülhamid's agents assassinated. News from afar precipitated more drastic action. British king Edward VII and Russian tsar Nicholas II met in Estonia for discussions. Ottomans believed that they were planning to divide the Ottoman Balkans. Ottoman officers and officials convened at Resen to discuss what to do, and on 3 July, local commander Niyazi Bey took to the hills with his men. Now the CUP activists in Macedonia put aside their elitism to work with local Turkish self-defense bands and mobilize the discontented Muslim common folk.

For most of July 1908 Abdülhamid tried unsuccessfully to get a grip on events in Macedonia. However, the CUP strategy was so effective that he could neither foil it nor gain accurate intelligence. Soon insurgents descended on Monastir and staged a dramatic public proclamation of the constitution on 23 July. The scene was repeated in front of large crowds in a dozen other towns. The telegraph, which Abdülhamid had used to use to control the empire, was now turned against him, as telegrams poured into the palace threatening that the Ottoman Third Army would march on Istanbul if the sultan did not yield.

His ministers advised that he had no choice. The next morning, the newspapers of Istanbul, which had not yet been allowed to inform readers about events in Macedonia, startled their readers by announcing the restoration of the constitution. His days of autocracy over, Abdülhamid kept his throne for another year as a constitutional ruler, until an attempted rightist countercoup of April 1909 gave the Young Turks a pretext to depose him and exile him to Salonica.

Trying to steer a course between ethnic revolts and foreign intervention, both of which threatened the empire's survival, the Young Turks proved conservative revolutionaries. They wanted not to destroy the sultanate but to change it. They wanted to restore the 1876 constitution, not because they were liberals, but because they saw it as symbolic of the kind of resurgence that Japan achieved after its 1868 Meiji Restoration. Elitist as well as conservative, they preferred top-down action, until the Anatolian revolts showed them that Turks even more conservative than they would not endure oppression forever. Their secular worldview opened a gulf between them and the conservative middle class, a gulf that they masked by appealing to Islam. For the foreseeable future, however, the vanguard role belonged to the Young Turks.

How much the Young Turks' constitutionalism might differ from the liberal paradigm became apparent from a lesson they drew from other revolutions: that the survival of the parliament depended on an external organization capable of protecting it. The Ottoman parliament of 1876 had been dissolved for want of such a shield; the Russian duma survived an attempt at counterrevolution in 1906 because of the revolutionary secret organizations. The CUP assumed the stance of a secret body, monitoring the constitutional politics from behind the scenes and not seizing control openly until 1913.[65] The same civil and military elites who made the revolution of 1908 governed Turkey until 1950. The guardian role assumed by the CUP, and later by the Turkish high command, became a lasting fact of Turkish politics.

THE ECONOMY

One of the main thrusts of recent studies of late Ottoman economic history has been to refute old arguments about decline and disindustrialization following the advent of free trade. In this period, too, despite the economic strengthening of European global dominance, the Ottomans experienced significant economic development.

STATE FINANCE

In state finance, this period began with debt default (1875–1876) and establishment of the Public Debt Administration in 1881. The 1870s also marked the turning point in the wealthy European countries' monetary policy from bimetallism to the gold standard. The Ottoman economy was not strong enough to follow suit. Under Abdülhamid, the empire stayed on a "limping gold standard," where the value of silver (predominantly the silver *mecidiye* of twenty kuruş) was allowed to slip to the extent that 108 silver kuruş were required to buy 1 gold lira, instead of the previous 100.[66] To maintain silver at this level, the government had to restrict the supply of silver coinage, even though its use predominated for most transactions. Given the global increase in silver supplies, the government could not enforce these rates everywhere. The rates for the silver kuruş in relation to the gold lira increased roughly in proportion to the distance from Istanbul, with figures in the 120s widely quoted, and much higher figures in some places. At the farthest Ottoman peripheries, 1780 Maria Theresa thalers, still minted and exported from Austria, were preferred in Yemen and the Red Sea region.

The Ottoman Imperial Bank retained its primacy as the quasi-state bank and the leader in commercial and investment banking. Although originally a Franco-British venture, it became over 80 percent French-owned by the 1880s. By 1900, European commercial banks competed increasingly in the empire. In Istanbul, some banks — above all, the OIB — built headquarters as monumental as those in European capitals. The government's most important banking initiative consisted of the Agricultural Bank (Ziraat Bankası, 1888), intended to provide low-interest credit to cultivators. While the bank lacked the resources to meet such needs fully, it established more branches than any other financial institution (more than four hundred). It provided an alternative to the usurious rates demanded by rural moneylenders, and it represented an important governmental effort to accumulate capital from domestic savings.

TRANSPORTATION: THE RAILROAD

Although Egypt had acquired its Cairo-Alexandria railroad as early as the 1850s, for the most part the Ottoman railroad age began under Abdülhamid. Mostly after 1890, the empire acquired 7,500 kilometers of track, comparatively very little, yet a transformative stimulus for the regions served. Railway construction raised extremely high demands for capital and technology. The Ottomans had to rely on foreigners for both, the Hijaz railway being the most notable exception. In the Hamidian period, foreign entrepreneurs usually received railroad-building concessions that included kilometric guarantees, that is, governmental guarantees of so much revenue per kilometer of track in operation. This relieved the government of the need to finance construction but left it with an open-ended obligation afterward, while also freeing the concessionaire from the necessity to operate efficiently in order to make money. The Ottoman tendency to place strategic over economic priorities in the choice of routes probably magnified the kilometric guarantees' costs.

The Ottoman rail network developed primarily as an outward extension of European railroads.[67] Salonica was connected by rail to Skopje in 1871 and to Belgrade in 1888. The "Oriental Railway" extended from Istanbul to Edirne to Sofia in the same time frame. In western Anatolia, British commercial interests had

Railroads. Above, a tunnel between Istanbul and Ankara, 1891; below, the branch of the Hijaz railway extending to Haifa, 1905. (1891 photo courtesy of Engin Özendes; Özendes, *Photography*, 157; 1905 photo, Istanbul University Library 90606/4, photo supplied by William Ochsenwald, published by permission of Istanbul University.)

built 1,300 kilometers of lines in the 1860s and 1870s. The main governmental initiative came with the Anatolian railway (1890–1895), connecting Istanbul to Ankara and Konya. The Baghdad railway concession provided for extending the railway from Konya to Basra. If completed, this would have made possible railway travel from Berlin to Basra. However, only 700 kilometers were built by 1914. Elsewhere in the Arab provinces, some short lines were built inward from the Mediterranean coast, mostly by French interests. The major initiative, however, was the Hijaz railway, built for motives both pious and strategic. It was financed by state initiative, which included raising money both inside the empire and abroad by soliciting donations from non-Ottoman Muslims, especially in India. Although the Ottomans still had to rely on foreign suppliers for rolling stock and much of the technological expertise, they were able to increase the proportion of trained Muslim engineers by the time the line entered the Hijaz, necessarily so given non-Muslims' exclusion from the sacred zone around the Holy Cities. Indigenous labor, including Ottoman troops, was mobilized for the project. Once completed, the insecure caravan journey of fifty days from Damascus to Mecca was replaced by a secure train ride of one week. It was too bad for Abdülhamid that the train station in Medina opened on 1 September 1908, after the Young Turk Revolution.

Railroad building conditioned the late Ottoman experience of modernity in manifold ways. To the extent that particular European powers took the initiative in specific regions, railroad building hastened the division of the Ottoman interior into something like spheres of influence. The clearest example is the German "corridor" that would have been created had the Baghdad railway been completed. French interests dominated railroad building in Syria, and the Russians claimed a monopoly on rail construction in northeastern Anatolia. Russian capital to build any such railways was lacking; as a result, the Ottoman Empire entered World War I without a strategic rail connection to its eastern front. Dependence on foreign entrepreneurship and technology also introduced an ethnic, colonial-style division of labor. At the top, Europeans ran the concessionary companies; Ottoman Christians and Europeans filled middle management; the laborers were mostly Ottoman Muslims. The fact that the rail lines tied the Ottoman Empire to Europe gave Ottoman rail workers early contact with European labor activism. As a result, rail strikes occurred already in the 1870s, and railroad unions began to organize around 1908.

The railroads' costs and benefits were both great. The agricultural tithes (öşür) of the provinces traversed had to be pledged to cover the kilometric guarantees. However, the railroads stimulated economic production; and in the long run, as the volume of traffic grew, the amounts needed for kilometric guarantees would decline. By 1910, the Ottoman railways carried some eight million passengers a year and nearly 2 million tons of goods. Railroad building was associated with increases in settlement and in the production and shipment of goods, such as the 400,000 additional tons of Anatolian grain that began to be produced for the Istanbul market after the completion of the Anatolian railway. The railroad, however, was only the most significant of Hamidian public works. This was a major period for the development of new docks and harbors, roads and bridges, trams and gasworks in Ottoman cities—all types of modern infrastructure.[68] Even the caravan trade gained new life with the rise of "feeder" routes to the rail depots.

COMMERCE

Although price trends in Ottoman exports and imports followed those in the world economy, falling from the 1870s into the 1890s and rising again thereafter, additional factors need to be considered to assess the state of commerce. One factor was the post-1878 territorial losses. Despite the empire's overall shrinkage, territorial units of stable size—specific Ottoman ports or provinces—show steady or rising trends in the 1880s and 1890s.[69] More significantly, neither imports nor exports accounted for as much as 20 percent of Ottoman trade. Agricultural products usually accounted for over 90 percent of the exports, with no single commodity predominant, except locally. With time, another noted feature of the merchant community active in external trade was the competitive displacement of foreign merchants by Ottoman non-Muslims, usually operating under consular protection. In many cases, Ottoman Christian or Jewish merchants started as agents of foreign firms, then took over or even established their own European operations.

The fact that 75 percent or more of Ottoman commerce remained internal attests to the importance of domestic trade, dominated by the largely Muslim commercial bourgeoisie, who asserted themselves in the tax revolts of 1905–1907. The railroad greatly stimulated domestic trade. Among many commercially dynamic cities of the period, Beirut saw its population roughly double under Abdülhamid, reaching 150,000 by 1908. The city had a Christian majority from 1860 on, although Sunni Muslims remained the largest single sect. There, Christians achieved the most spectacular commercial successes, thanks to their facility in forming ties with Europe. Yet Muslim merchants succeeded almost as well.[70] Muslims usually traded with the interior; Muslims also invested in land and money lending. To accumulate great wealth, Beirut's Muslim merchants had to acquire at wholesale the goods that they resold in the interior; thus they had to interest themselves in European trade. That remained relatively easy to do in a port city, where merchants had to trade with all comers. Deals between Muslim and non-Muslim merchants helped move goods between Beirut and the interior, and merchants of different religions often did business together.

As the distance from Istanbul grew, the preference for governmental over commercial careers, persistently ascribed to Muslims, seemed less prevalent; and the social standing of merchants became more apparent, whatever their religion. Ottoman development projects further stimulated commerce. That was notably true of regions where the Ottoman administrative network was extended and consolidated in this period. In Transjordan, merchants, including families known from the olive oil and soap business in Nablus (Palestine), tied Transjordan into the regional economy, even as government tied it into the provincial administrative network, and the railroad tied it to the wider world.[71]

AGRICULTURE

The 75 to 85 percent of the population that was still rural experienced appreciable development in this period. Comparably high percentages of Ottoman exports consisted of agrarian products. Over half of tax revenues came from the agrarian economy; yet less than one-tenth of the land was under cultivation. As in the past, the villagers suffered from the weight of taxation, inadequate capital, primitive equipment, the state's incapacity to make significant improvements in the countryside, lack of schools, poor health and diet, and the impact of conscription on Muslims. Not new in the Hamidian period, these handicaps defined a low starting line, from which indisputable progress occurred.[72]

The development of commercial agriculture was the main thrust of change. Previously limited to a few provinces, such as Bursa and Aydın in western Anatolia, commercial agriculture spread to other coastal regions and into the interior with the railroad. Improved transportation was only one contributing factor. Controlling certain agricultural revenues, such as the tithe on raw silk, the Public Debt Administration took a close interest in increasing production. The Régie des tabacs did much the same for tobacco. New state initiatives included founding agricultural schools and model farms and sending agriculture students abroad. The founding of the Agricultural Bank (Ziraat Bankası) in 1888 improved on earlier efforts to provide rural credit.

Not least of the factors stimulating agriculture was Abdülhamid's expansion of the crown estates (*çiftlikat-ı hümayun*), administered through his Privy Treasury. He began massive land purchases in Anatolia and the Arab provinces after the Balkan territorial losses of 1878. His goals were partly strategic, to reinforce the Ottoman hold on these territories. However, the goals were also economic. Some estates were made into model farms. The peasants on them were exempted from military service and certain taxes, and military manpower was also mobilized to work on the estates and on public works projects. Ultimately, Abdülhamid owned 1.25 million hectares in Syria—anecdotal sources say that the crown estates in Aleppo province alone were larger than the entire province of Edirne. The net revenues from the estates were estimated at 1.5 million gold liras per year, not to speak of income from mineral exploitations or the treasury's annual contributions to the civil list, all of which brought the sultan's revenues to 6–10 percent of state revenues.[73]

Grains, as always, dominated Ottoman agricultural production. As of 1908, even in provinces famous for them, other crops accounted for less than one-third of agrarian production: Adana (cotton, 24 percent), Aydın (vineyard and orchard products, 32 percent). Yet export crops drove growth, especially after world market prices turned upward following the bottom of the 1890s. Ottoman cotton producers, who had scaled back after the end of the cotton boom during the U.S. Civil War, saw global demand surge again after 1900. Cotton production doubled in Syria and tripled in Adana's Çukurova plain. Raisins, dried figs, and tobacco also experienced strong growth. The formation of large commercial farms, while limited, became most notable in the areas producing those crops. The Adana region advanced rapidly in large farm formation, in mechanization, and in cotton spinning and weaving. Around Izmir, the large estates were initially developed by foreigners, mostly English, but had largely passed into Greek or Armenian hands by 1900. Greeks and Armenians predominated as large landowners around Adana.

MANUFACTURES

After 1870, Ottoman manufacturing had passed the most difficult phase of adjusting to free trade and began to grow in many sectors.[74] The downward international price trends of 1873–1896 shrank Ottoman cultivators' incomes and ability to purchase imports but created opportunities for manufacturers who could cut costs and wages and produce for local tastes. Importing cost-cutting technologies and benefiting from low wages, Ottoman producers increased their output both for the local market and for export in certain sectors. Expanding export industries included silk reeling and carpet and lace making. Amid these changes, import-substitution industrialization—although not yet a formal government policy—began.

Large factories remained rare. While some state-owned factories continued to operate, mostly producing for the military or the palace, most factories after 1870 were privately owned. In the 1870s, the government at last adopted stimulative policies, such as exempting machinery for use in factories from taxes and allowing entrepreneurs tax exemptions. As the number of factories grew, many of them produced foodstuffs, a sector in which foreign competition was relatively ineffective in local markets. There were factories that produced other types of goods, however, and some of them competed directly with foreign firms. The largest iron foundry in the empire, at Izmir, employed more than two hundred workers. To supply the carpet industry, Ottomans and foreigners founded wool spinning and dyeing factories in western Anatolia. The Régie des tabacs had large cigarette factories, employing workers of both sexes. By 1908, silk reeling mills operated in Mount Lebanon, Adana, Bursa, Istanbul, and Salonica. Despite challenges such as diseases or East Asian competition after the opening of the Suez Canal (1869), the Ottoman silk industry employed some four hundred thousand people around 1900.

Among Ottoman cities, Salonica was probably the most industrialized outside Istanbul. By the 1880s, it had factories producing cigarettes, distilled spirits, soap, bricks, nails, tile, and other goods. In the 1890s, Salonica's raw wool exports declined sharply because of growing demand from its weaving mills. Yarns from cotton spinning mills in or near Salonica were beginning

Silk spinning mill at Bursa. (By Sebah and Joaillier, 1875; Research Library, The Getty Research Institute, Los Angeles, 96.R.14.)

to compete successfully with imports. After 1900, Salonica acquired foundries and machine tool works. Advanced in other respects, the Salonica of the late Hamidian period also became the most advanced of Ottoman cities in working-class consciousness.[75]

In contrast, manufacturing at Adana was not as diversified, but it took advantage of locally produced silk and especially cotton. Adana already had steam-powered silk and cotton mills in the 1880s. By 1912, there were Adana cotton mills with thousands of spindles apiece or hundreds of looms. Nearby Tarsus also had large weaving mills.

Volumes and conditions of production in Ottoman factories are not well documented. Many enterprises did not keep good records. An anecdote about a factory owner who employed a hundred workers and scrawled his accounts on the wall in pencil is not out of character for a commercial bourgeoisie that was as yet much less articulate in writing than its bureaucratic-intellectual counterpart. The labor force included children and women. Many female workers were young and worked for only a few years before marrying. Employing women and children further repressed wages; yet evidence from Salonica indicates that once prices began to rise again after 1896, wages did, too.

Much of the post-1870 expansion in manufacturing still occurred outside factories and depended on work by hand. In the 1890s, nearly all families in Anatolia and probably other regions still owned and used hand looms. While weaving for export was not all done by women, the ubiquity of home looms testifies to the identification of women's work with the textile arts, not to speak of the millennial tradition of carpet-weaving and needlework among Turkic women.[76] In this period, hand workers might use imported thread to weave cloth, or imported cloth to embroider to local taste; and the price declines of 1873–1896 favored these endeavors by lowering the prices of the imports they processed into products with added value. The government favored this expansion of production by eliminating internal duties in this period and making transportation more efficient.

New export industries developed out of hand production. The first of these used imported yarns to produce lace for export, much of it sold as "Irish." With the rise of middle-class lifestyles in Europe and the Americas, demand for hand-knotted carpets soared. Between the 1870s and 1890s, Ottoman carpet exports nearly doubled in value, rising from 17 to 32 million kuruş in value. Carpet production expanded and underwent complex changes, as chemical dyes replaced natural dyes, machine-spun wool began to be used, and much of the weaving was shifted from nomadic tents and village houses to factorylike workshops, where often Greeks or Armenians wove "Turkish" rugs, not that anyone cared. Textile production for the Ottoman domestic market also surged after 1870, and much of it was also done by hand or with simple machines, especially Singer sewing machines, which came into wide use around 1900. As in preceding periods, the scale of production in important provincial centers like Diyarbakır and Aleppo can only be appreciated by comparisons across multiple lines and sectors. Otherwise, the episodic crises of one type of production can paint pictures of decline when overall production was actually increasing.

Earlier economic historians underestimated Ottoman manufacturing by identifying manufacturing too narrowly with mechanization and neglecting the evidence on the larger internal market. Even the growth in imports no longer appears indicative of declining Ottoman production, considering that many imports — thread, cloth, machines — were used to develop new lines of domestic production. Inasmuch as Muslims, as well as non-Muslims, played entrepreneurial roles in expanding internal production, recent scholarship on Ottoman economic history reinforces the argument of this study that two major currents of change interacted to shape Ottoman and Turkish approaches to modernity, and that they were championed by different sectors of the emerging Ottoman bourgeoisie. This thought connects economic to social change.

SOCIETY UNDER ABDÜLHAMID

Society probably changed faster than the economy under Abdülhamid. Numerically, population shrank greatly with the 1878 territorial losses, then stabilized; yet migration transformed its composition. Simultaneously, developments in individual subjectivity, class formation, and social practices transformed the quality of life, particularly for the Muslim middle class.

A POPULATION IN FLUX

The 1878 Treaty of Berlin stripped away Balkan territories with about 4.5 million subjects, mostly Christians, leaving the empire overwhelmingly Muslim and Middle Eastern.[77] Efforts to improve population registration culminated in the first comprehensive Ottoman census (1881–1893), on the basis of which all subjects were to receive identity papers (*nüfus tezkeresi, tezkere-i osmaniye*). The census total for the Ottoman territories in Europe, Anatolia, Iraq, and Syria was roughly 20.5 million. The total in the next census (1906–1907) was 20.9 million. Allowing for the undercounting of women and certain regions suggests an adjusted figure of 25 million for both dates, excluding Arabia and territories such as Egypt, which the Ottomans held only tenuously.

Ottoman demographic dynamism exceeded the numbers' seeming stagnancy. Demographic weakness, especially among Muslims, stood out in comparison with other societies. While Ottoman numbers hovered around 25 million, the Russian Empire's populace was larger and growing (125 million in 1897, 159 million in 1914). Western European populations also grew rapidly, generating emigrant outflows and demands for "places in the sun," which could result in covetous eyes being cast on Ottoman territory. Ottoman population density was low—about seven inhabitants per square kilometer. Especially disturbing to Abdülhamid, his Muslim subjects did not exhibit the same growth rates as the non-Muslims. Muslims were slower to take advantage of modern medicine, more willing to resort to birth control and abortion, and subject to military service in the case of provincial males. In contrast to alarming evidence of Muslim population decline in some places, the non-Muslim communities appeared flourishing, the largest being the Greeks (2.2 million in the 1880s, reportedly 3.8 million in the 1907) and Armenians (about 1.1 million in each census). The small, desolate aspect of Ottoman towns in period photographs helps explain how European Zionists could imagine Palestine as "a land without a people for a people without a land." While that was one of the smaller migratory currents of the period, Zionist settlement began in 1882. Despite efforts to discourage it, by 1908 the Jewish percentage of the population of Palestine had increased from 5 to 10 percent, or 80,000 Jewish residents.[78]

For the empire overall, shifting borders and immigration reinforced the Muslim population dramatically. The Balkan territorial losses raised Muslims' share of the empire's population from 60 percent before 1878 to 72 percent in the 1880s census and 74 percent in 1906–1907. Major Muslim refugee inflows from Mediterranean islands like Crete, the Caucasus, and mostly the Balkans, added roughly 2 million Muslims, nearly one-tenth of Ottoman population.

The refugees' arrival produced major consequences. It encouraged Abdülhamid's Islamic policies. Although not all were ethnically Turkish, refugees made the population both more Turkish-speaking and more Muslim. Those arriving empty-handed received land and helped develop whole regions. Some migrants brought assets, cultural or sometimes even economic. Some joined the secular intelligentsia; others belonged to the same religious movements that appealed to Ottoman Muslims. Migrants thus added to the cultural and economic capital of both sectors of the Muslim protobourgeoisie. Joining Ottoman Muslims at a time when they were pondering the collective identity concepts— Muslim, Ottoman, Turkish, or other—that oscillated before their eyes as the empire's future became more dubious, intellectuals from the Russian Empire added provocatively different points of view to these debates.[79]

Small size of Ottoman towns. Below, Bethlehem, 1857; above, Ankara, 1888. (Both courtesy of Bahattin Öztuncay; Ankara by Guillaume Berggren, Öztuncay, *Photographers*, 1:300, pl. 297; Bethlehem by James Robertson, Öztuncay, *Robertson*, 113, pl. 37.)

As the empire gained 2 million Muslims, it lost about 300,000 emigrants, almost all non-Muslims. The emigrants were predominantly Armenians, Greeks, or Christian Arabs. The usual destination was the Americas, although some Armenians moved into the Russian Empire. Syro-Lebanese emigration to the United States began as a trickle in the late 1880s but exceeded 5,000 a year after 1900 and 20,000 a year after 1910. Lebanese emigration was often temporary, followed by a permanent return to Lebanon. The emigrants blazed individual trails into modernity, often first as peddlers in the Americas and then as social climbers after returning to Lebanon.[80]

INDIVIDUAL SUBJECTIVITY AND CLASS FORMATION

All Ottomans traced their own paths into modernity. Developmental dynamism inside shrinking borders was not the only paradox of the day. Equally striking was the paradox of accelerating modernism under a neotraditional regime of censorship and repression. As Ottomans responded to modernity, old and new rubbed together in ways that produced paradoxes all around. Ottomans spoke as if the entire world was divided into *alafranga* and *alaturka*, from the Italian phrases "alla franca" (Frankish, or European, style) and "alla turca" (Turkish style), with everyone suspended between the two.

In conspicuous cases, modern inventions—printing presses, photographic cameras, steam engines, railroad trains, and steamships—created these paradoxes. However, modernity did not produce only machines. It also spawned "technologies" that were more social or cultural than material. A tourist guidebook of the period (a modern product in itself) made the point when it referred to an "unannounced social revolution" wrought by male physicians and music teachers, whom Ottomans now admitted into their harems.[81]

The paradoxes of this "social revolution" proliferated even under the Hamidian regime. However much the sultan enforced Islamic norms in gender segregation, new transportation technologies such as tramways and ferries made these difficult to maintain, as becomes apparent in the opening scene of a novel discussed below. In Salonica, women frequented the more modern cafés. Paris department stores opened branches in Ottoman cities.[82] Early photographers also awakened desires for pictures of friends and family. Photographs not only challenged Islamic scruples about images of people; they also awakened powerful desires for pictures of absent or lost loved ones and further eroded gender segregation. Many photographs of unveiled Ottoman Muslim women survive from this period, implying that women were neither reluctant to appear before the photographer unveiled nor fearful of losing their respectability if males outside their immediate family saw their picture.

The proliferation of print media similarly offered Ottomans not just new products but a new awareness of the world and new means to achieve a sense of community. Censorship stifled political discussion; but that deflected attention to social and cultural issues, which became alternative sites for debates that could have political implications. The new print media depicted a world in which alternative roles were possible and men and women could socialize in ways that Islamic gender norms precluded. By publishing readers' letters, the magazines further consolidated the new sense of community among a public divided by sex and dispersed in space.

As women's literacy increased, what was true for all was especially so for women. Magazines for female readers appeared as early as 1868 and became another "technology" of change in gender relations. It took time to establish that Muslim women could write for publication and sign their names without losing respectability. The appearance of the first magazine staffed entirely by women (*Şükûfezar*, 1883) and of novelist Fatma Aliye's earliest signed works (early 1890s) indicate when the respectability of women's public "appearance" as writers became established in Istanbul. In the Arab world, it took longer, in Egypt until 1904–1908.[83]

Much of what can be said about the print media as modern "technologies" can be said about the schools, which produced the readership for the new media. Their potential as agents of sociocultural change became clearest in the boarding schools, which extracted their students from their home communities and resited them in a different world of students and teachers. In sociologists' terms, the difference was that of "community" and "society."[84] The typical old environment was a neighborhood (*mahalle*), with its dense reciprocal obligations among residents of all ages and statuses, its sedate pace demarcated by prayer times and religious holidays, its conformist pressures and communal supports, its ethos of custom and piety. There, a boy could play freely in the street, as long as he paid respects to passing elders. The world of the school (*mekteb*) differed, drastically so in the case of the residential military academies, with their drills, inspections, regulations, and hierarchical subordination. Here, a cadet left play behind; now, he marched in formation. Losing neighborhood communalism, cadets from different places gained a new solidarity. They acquired military expertise, scientific ideas, a new sense of self, disdain for the mahalle as backward, and futuristic visions only they could fulfill.

Elite formation was far from the whole story of social change, but it epitomized forces at work throughout Ottoman society. The politicization of ethnoreligious difference, noted in preceding periods, still continued. Large non-Muslim communities remained all across the empire, and their enterprises and cultural

A *neighborhood in Istanbul*. Boys play in the narrow street with overhanging
houses and the neighborhood mosque (*mescid*) in the background. (Photo
attributed to Guillaume Berggren, a Swedish photographer active in Istanbul,
roughly 1870 to 1895, who produced numerous street scenes; Research Library,
The Getty Research Institute, Los Angeles, 96.R.14.)

institutions flourished, sharpening Ottoman Muslims' sense of backwardness.[85]
Muslims, too, experienced wide-ranging social changes. As mining and manufactures developed, Ottoman society acquired an industrial proletariat estimated
at 250,000 (including 70,000 women) by 1908. The rise of a Muslim middle
class produced especially momentous consequences.

MUSLIM MIDDLE-CLASS ELEMENTS

With its two wings, the one endowed primarily with intellectual and the
other with economic assets, the Muslim middle class developed greatly in this
period. Their higher educational levels, command of the print media, and
heroic politics made secularist intellectuals more conspicuous. Non-Muslims'
prominence in particular markets and economic sectors further reduced the
propertied Muslims' visibility.[86] To find them requires taking into account
agrarian enterprise and manufacturing outside of mechanized factories.

The Imperial Military Medical Academy. This display of materialistic science in the military medical school epitomizes the reasons why the differences between the neighborhood communalism and the constraints of school life seem to have been felt even more acutely there than in the other service academies. (By Abdullah Frères, Library of Congress, Prints and Photographs Division, Abdülhamid II Collection, LD-USZ62-77267.)

Abdülhamid's Islamic policies directly addressed these conservative Muslims; yet by 1905–1907, they, too, were in revolt over taxes.

If as yet less likely to speak in print, conservative Muslims had channels for self-expression. Aside from bazaars and marketplaces, these consisted especially of Islamic movements. The point is not that the propertied Muslims' interests were absent from the print media. To the contrary, discussions that appealed to them, about free enterprise, for example, often appeared in print, including in a novel discussed below.[87] Still, the print media were not the primary forum for this sector of society, as they were for the modernist intelligentsia.

In contrast, religious movements stood out as vehicles for conservative Muslim self-expression, particularly the Halidiye-Nakşibendiye. Its roots in

Iraqi Kurdistan and wide geographical reach made the Halidiye an important resource for Abdülhamid in his appeals to Muslim solidarity. The order's following in the Caucasus and Central Asia meant that immigration also reinforced it. Its emphasis on sharia-observance and political activity for Muslim welfare added to its appeal. For Ottoman religious leaders, the Nakşibendis were allies against both lax sufi orders and Islamic radicals, like the Yemeni Zaydis and the Arabian Wahhabis, who both denied the Ottomans' religious legitimacy. Playing a significant integrative role enabled the Nakşibendis to consolidate their strength in the provinces and the capital. In Istanbul, they acquired more meeting halls than any other order. The Gümüşhaneli branch of the Halidiye had its meeting place opposite the grand vezir's offices at the Sublime Porte. Metaphorically, if the Public Debt Administration glared down on the Sublime Porte from up the hill, the Nakşibendis gazed on supportively from their site, closer and only slightly higher on the same slope.[88]

Under Abdülhamid, then, the two currents of change that interacted to shape Ottoman and modern Turkish history differentiated more clearly than theretofore. In the Hamidian social landscape, the settings in which the two currents' supporters formed their networks and expressed themselves also clearly appeared: the institutions and practices of the print world for secularist intellectuals, and those of the religious movements, especially the Halidiye, for conservative Muslims. Alternately competing and converging, these two currents would channel the future course of Ottoman and Turkish history.

MARRIAGE AND THE FAMILY

As social change accelerated, marriage became the most sensitive point where the individual and the collective met in search of modernity. Ottoman literary production in modern genres focused from the beginning on spousal choice, apparently the first question raised by emergent middle-class self-consciousness in every society. By the 1880s, these newly imagined realities corresponded to changes in lived experience, at least for prosperous Istanbul families. One of the most startling measures of the Ottomans' unannounced social revolution emerged from an aspect of life as yet little affected by modern science: reproductive behavior.

For Istanbul's Muslim middle class, the 1885 census data show that household sizes were already small and fertility rates low.[89] The city's population stood at 874,000 in 1885 and about a million in 1900. As of 1907, 46 percent of Istanbul's Muslim households had three or fewer members. Excluding those who lived alone, the mean for family households at the time was 4.7 people. Commonly, such households included only the nuclear family, although relatives often lived nearby and interacted frequently, blurring the distinction between nuclear and extended households. Only 16 percent of Istanbul households were extended in 1907, usually only by including the husband's widowed mother. Only a small percentage of households included more than one couple or live-in servants. Polygyny was also rare: less than 3 percent of Istanbul men were polygynous in either 1885 or 1907. Ottomans—especially high-status families who did not want to "lose" their daughters—idealized grand, multigenerational households in which sons-in-law moved in to join the family. Literary depictions of such households abound; yet in 1907 less than 4 percent of Istanbul households matched the description.

Many factors help explain the small households. For example, Ottoman cities always included large numbers of *bekârs*, literally "bachelors." These men might well have wives and children somewhere but had left home to seek work. In the cities, "bachelors" lived in buildings that doubled as warehouses and hostels. The refugees who flooded into the empire likewise seldom arrived with large families intact. Limited life expectancies meant that even for those who did experience it, life in a multigenerational household was usually temporary. However, the small family size in Istanbul cannot be explained fully without considering changes in fertility and nuptiality.

Together, the decline in fertility and the change in marriage practices caused Istanbul family structures to differ from rural Anatolian patterns and resemble those of Mediterranean population centers farther west. Ottoman literature still dwelt on the evils of early marriage. Possibly that is one reason why it was not typical. Around 1900, the average marriage age for Istanbul Muslims was thirty for men and twenty for women. Expectations about marriage changed in other ways, too, as bourgeois self-consciousness evolved. Marriage began to be seen as less a transaction between families than a search for love and fulfillment, even a matter of personal liberty (*hürriyet-i şahsiye*). Marriage was still far from a matter of individual choice, but the couple's wishes began to matter.

Not only was the age of marriage later than literary sources implied, but fertility rates were already low by the 1880s and fell thereafter. Istanbul Muslim women's mean age at marriage was relatively high and rising over time (19.1 in 1885, 20.5 in 1907), while the mean age for men held high and steady around 30. The later age for men had largely economic explanations: the need to become established in an occupation and the costs of marrying, including the premarital part of the marriage payment to the bride (*mehr-i muaccel*).

Late marriage amounted to a form of fertility control; but Istanbul Muslims also took direct action.[90] Fertility rates in Istanbul had reached levels by 1900 that the rest of the country had still not reached nearly a century later. The age at which Istanbul women bore their last child fell from 33.3 for mothers born between 1851 and 1855 to 28.0 for women born 1911 and 1915. By marrying later and ceasing childbearing earlier, Muslim Istanbulites were reducing their childbearing years at both ends.

The chief means of birth control was withdrawal (*azil*; Arabic *'azl*). Referred to in hadiths (sayings of the Prophet Muhammad) and practiced by early Muslims, this practice was licit for Muslims and did not raise the objections among Muslims that contraception did among Jews and Christians. Islamic legal scholars also permitted abortion during the first 120 days of pregnancy. Writers in the press opposed abortion, and the Ottoman government tried to outlaw it. Little is known about the methods, but the evidence indicates that abortion was common. Istanbul Muslims were heirs as well to lengthy learned and folk traditions, which mention many contraceptive methods. If some of those relied on magic, the range also included barrier methods or pessaries relying on substances—lemon juice, tannin, or soap—that would have been effective spermicides. Douches were also known and used. Breast feeding, while not reliable in preventing pregnancy, was also normally practiced. Contraceptive methods were discussed, not in print, but among women, freely but circumspectly.

The hadith legitimating withdrawal proves that birth control was not new and probably explains why fertility was already low by 1885. Later fertility declines must have been part of the changes swirling around the family with the rise of the new expectations expressed in the print media. Soon, the questioning of marriage practices prompted reconsideration of all familial relationships, although the change was never total: alaturka and alafranga coexisted even in Westernized households.[91] Works of imaginative literature became primary sites for this reconsideration, which began in the imaginative realm and exerted its transformative power from there.

As that occurred, for example, prosperous Ottoman Muslim families ceased to take meals sitting on the floor and eating out of common dishes on a raised tray. Instead they began to sit on chairs around a table set with individual place settings. Instead of the old rule of eating in silence and talking afterward (*evvel taam, bade kelâm*), polite conversation became the mark of good manners. One contemporary described this as a change that was introduced in the boarding schools and spread from there. In this period, the family even ceased to be an *aile*, the good old Ottoman and Arabic word, and became a *familya*, from Italian *famiglia*. That was one alafranga change that was later reversed: *aile* triumphed again by 1945.

While much of the discussion about women focused on educating them to fulfill their household roles in new and better ways, the task of elaborating the image of the desexualized, "serious" woman who could add the honor (*şeref*) of high achievement to that of irreproachable morals (*iffet ve ismet*) was under way.[92] Changes in individual roles heightened the need for changes in familial relationships. The women's magazines, in particular, elaborated ideas of companionate marriage and egalitarian family relations in place of the traditional patriarchal norms. More and more women's magazines were published, among which the longest-running was the "Gazette for Ladies" (*Hanımlara Mahsus Gazete*, 1895–1905). Photographs joined the magazines in recording social change, as families began wanting to see themselves in intimate groupings. Remote, authoritarian fathers did not disappear overnight, but a civilizational shift had begun.

Comparative research is still needed to know how Istanbul Muslims' reproductive behavior compared with that of Istanbul's non-Muslims or Ottomans elsewhere. Available indications show, however, that most Muslims in Salonica had no more than one or two children.[93] In contrast, Bulgarian demographic data indicate that high fertility rates prevailed throughout the century. The Salonica-Bulgaria disparity implies an urban-rural difference comparable to that between Istanbul and Anatolia. In the territories of the future Turkish republic, Istanbul was clearly in the vanguard of change. Of the two wings of the emergent Muslim middle class, although it seems plausible that the conservative, propertied wing would change more slowly than the modernist intelligentsia, Istanbul evidence indicates only slightly higher fertility among the city's Muslim tradesmen than among its bureaucratic elite. While family relations may have changed more slowly for conservative Muslims outside the capital, the evidence on social life suggests that all Ottomans were caught up in the advent of modernity, pursuing many paths toward a changing future. Among the literary evidence, two conservative authors' works support this conclusion.

CONSERVATIVE CULTURAL MODERNITY: AHMED MIDHAT AND FATMA ALIYE

In 1890–1891, Ahmed Midhat (1840–1912) and Fatma Aliye (1862–1936) published two novels with nearly identical titles, his *Müşahedat* and her *Muhazarat*, "Observations" and "Debates."[94] He was the most prolific author of the day. She was just starting to publish, and *Muhazarat* was her first novel. She was both Ahmed Midhat's protégée and the daughter of the great scholar-statesman Ahmed Cevdet Paşa (1822–1895, see color illustration). Both novelists had close ties to Yıldız Palace, as did Cevdet Paşa. Ahmed Midhat's novel has been the object of critical acclaim; Fatma Aliye's has mostly lain forgotten. Some literary scholars insist that there is no connection between the two books. Yet evidence already cited implies the opposite. A complete reading of both works reveals a competitive, reciprocal relationship that yields new insights into conservative approaches to modernity. Moreover, the findings of recent demographic research provide clues to the nature of the connection between the two books.

Earlier literary works have already shown that the advent of modern literary forms brought with it expectations of "boy-meets-girl" plots, despite the fact that even the most Europeanized Muslims still lived under Islamic norms of gender segregation, which had to be suspended somehow in order to imagine romantic relationships. For Ottoman readers, such novels were not mere entertainments. Nor were they reflections of existing reality. Rather, they implied transforming reality. What is most amazing is that conservative writers, who ostensibly upheld Islamic values and patriarchal norms, joined in the social engineering. Their works demonstrate both that modernism was not limited to politics and that Islamic responses to modernity were not produced only by religious movements.

AHMED MIDHAT'S *MÜŞAHEDAT*

As to the "debates" about which these books offer "observations," Ahmed Midhat specifies that his novel displays his view of naturalism. He thought that French naturalist author Émile Zola (1840–1902) misrepresented reality by seeing only degradation. Believing that a novel depicting only the sordid was not natural, Ahmed Midhat wrote about sordid realities but transformed them into a utopian vision of Ottoman modernity. He also experimented with literary technique in *Müşahedat*. He not only wrote as the omniscient author but also included himself among the characters and made the writing and discussion of the novel part of the story. Not only did the novel's subject "actually fall at my feet," he writes, but "I became caught up in the novel as if one of its characters. For an author to mix into a novel like that . . . is something of which Europe has not seen the like" (78–79). However exaggerated the statement, literary scholars appreciate the novel for its experimental technique. His contemporaries more likely identified with the characters and their stories.

In his works, Ahmed Midhat usually solved the boy-meets-girl problem by bringing non-Muslim females together with Muslim males. So he did in *Müşahedat*. The two leading females both have Armenian names (and hybrid family histories). The heroine is the serious-minded Siranuş; her friend is the light-hearted Agavni. The leading males, all Muslim, are the hero, Re'fet; the wealthy, old Egyptian merchant, Seyyid Mehmed Numan; and Ahmed Midhat himself. The plot and subplots unfold from a chance encounter on the ferry between Ahmed Midhat and the Armenian women.

Müşahedat is a novel for entrepreneurs. The hero, Re'fet, is a variation on the antique stereotype of the spendthrift who squanders his inheritance. No intellectual, Re'fet assumes, when Ahmed Midhat introduces himself as a "writer," that this means a public letter-writer (59), a proverbial way for men ruined by drink to end up. Already past the spendthrift stage in this novel, Re'fet is an up-and-coming businessman with the firm of the old patriarch, Seyyid Mehmed Numan. The seyyid has some of the best probusiness lines in the book. Business is the only clean (*helal*) way to make millions, he says, and the best way to overcome "our belatedness, our backwardness" (*teehhüratımız tedenniyatımız*, 134b, 135b). His commercial success makes him the employer or protector of all the main characters, even the two Armenian women. Siranuş and Agavni both enjoy a degree of education and financial independence that young Muslim women could only envy. However, both are orphans, whose roots extend into the sordid depths of Beyoğlu, the "other" Istanbul, infidel and European, the Istanbul of minorities and foreigners. Tracing their roots gives Ahmed Midhat his chance to probe the nether depths. As he does, he moralizes copiously, comparing Christian familial norms negatively with Islamic ones.

The novel revolves around which female will win the hero. Agavni has known Re'fet since his dissolute days, and allusions indicate—without disapproval—that they are living together. The old Egyptian merchant also has a daughter, Feride. So secluded that she is only described by others, she is sickly, ill-favored, and ill-educated, thanks to her father's low expectations for her (220b). Deciding that she loves Re'fet, she acts through intermediaries, dramatizing her unsuitability and the failure of her father's archaic approach to female upbringing. Feride's actions cause Agavni's death. As the merchant's model of patriarchal social order fails, Ahmed Midhat steps in as a new-model patriarch. He helps Siranuş use her talents to support herself as a private teacher of French and music. In contrast to the old seyyid's "senile thinking" (*hikmet-i ma'tuha*, 206a), Ahmed Midhat wants Siranuş to become a "free, independent, hardworking teacher" (*hürr müstakil çalışkan bir muallime*, 211b). As she becomes the desexualized, high-achieving woman who can respectably play a public role, Re'fet takes new interest in her. It is not the love he felt for her dead friend, but one should not marry for love (*sevip varma*, 198a). Having learned that her father was a Tunisian naval officer, Siranuş converts to Islam. She and Re'fet marry and move into his family home, not in infidel Beyoğlu but in Istanbul proper.

Not a religious requirement for a non-Muslim woman's marriage to a Muslim, Siranuş's conversion seems odd in a story full of easy interaction across religious lines. For the book's intended female readers, however, her conversion served a purpose by effacing the primary difference between her and most of them. When Siranuş converts and marries Re'fet, new man and new woman unite—a victory less for Islam than for modernity. What would it take for a Muslim-born woman to accomplish as much?

FATMA ALIYE'S *MUHAZARAT*

For Fatma Aliye, the answer to that question may not be the one that present-day readers would expect. *Muhazarat* does not depict an Ottoman Muslim career woman, although two of her later novels do. Fatma Aliye's objective in *Muhazarat* was more ambitious, namely, to create a heroine strong enough to replace degradation with moral order in the way Ahmed Midhat depicts himself as doing in his novel. Fatma Aliye's heroine is Fazıla, a "virtuous woman" (that being the meaning of her name) who triumphs over adversity to achieve social reintegration, not across religious differences, but across space, by uniting two Muslim households in Istanbul and Beirut. The secret of her triumph is knowledge of a Muslim woman's rights and entitlements. As Ahmed Cevdet Paşa's home-schooled daughter, Fatma Aliye possessed this knowledge prolifically. Whether her display of erudition raised or lowered her readers' self-confidence might be another story.

Fatma Aliye's solution to the novelist's problem of bringing unrelated males and females into proximity reflects her immersion in something that Ahmed Midhat admitted knowing little about: the Ottoman women's world. Perhaps it is an indication of the differences between her and Ahmed Midhat's view of patriarchal family life that Fazıla's encounters with unrelated males begin inside her father's harem in circumstances of moral degradation. Fazıla is the daughter of a privileged family, but she has lost her mother, and her father has remarried. The stepmother has managed to move her paramour into the harem by claiming that he is her "milk brother," a relationship close enough to preclude marriage. In fact, the man is the stepmother's cousin, not her milk brother. Fazıla finds herself living with a "stranger" who ought not even see her. Soon she catches the lovers in the act, entwined (*sarmaş dolaş*) like two vipers (161). Yet Fazıla's subordinate position in the household hierarchies of gender and age prevents her from warning her father. Instead the stepmother schemes to turn father against daughter, thwart Fazıla's intended marriage to a neighbor, and force her to accept a bad marriage in order to get her out of the house. Fazıla learns to love her husband, but he shares none of her interests. Finally, his infidelity turns her love to contempt. Denied refuge in her father's house when she seeks to return to it, she decides on suicide. Wavering between

melodrama and Zolaesque probings into the costs of Ottoman Muslim patriarchy for women and children, the novel indirectly undermines patriarchy while
ostensibly maintaining it. Fatma Aliye answers Ahmed Midhat's moral degradation in infidel Beyoğlu with moral degradation inside a proper-looking Muslim
household.

The story resumes in a rich Beiruti merchant's household. It includes his merchant son Şebib, a daughter, Enise, and her nursemaid, Peyman. The daughter
is strangely distracted, and the nursemaid must find out why. Connections with
the Istanbul story soon emerge. The young man whom Enise has seen passing
in his carriage turns out to be the stricken Mukaddim, once Fazıla's intended,
who has been traveling for his health since her death. The person who arrests
his attention is not Enise but her nursemaid, whom he knows as Fazıla herself.
She arranges a meeting to explain how she had abandoned her plan to commit suicide but ended up sick and destitute. She had herself sold into slavery
to cover the costs of her care. In addition to being a slave, she is still married.
She persuades him to marry Enise, partly on the ground that she as nursemaid
will remain with the bride, and he will see her every day unveiled. Achieving
greater freedom as a slave than she had enjoyed as a lady (327), Fazıla-Peyman
thus begins to reintegrate family relationships through a series of marriages.
Enise's brother Şebib also notices her finer qualities. His growing interest in
Fazıla complicates things because she feels she cannot tell him that she is
married. Then, news from Istanbul propels the story swiftly to its conclusion.
First Fazıla learns that her shiftless husband has been killed in a brawl. Then
Mukaddim learns that Fazıla's father, who still believes she is dead, has learned
how his wife betrayed him and has had a stroke. The news sets off a mad dash
back to Istanbul for a grand reconciliation and a series of marriages that unites
the households. These marriages include that of the model entrepreneur Şebib
and the Ottoman superwoman Fazıla, whose force of character has done for
this novel what Ahmed Midhat's neopatriarchy did for his. Skipping ahead
three years, the concluding scene, depicting the marriage of Fazıla's younger
brother with a daughter of the Beiruti family, shows Fazıla with her and Şebib's
little son, so completing her image as matriarch.

As noted, two of Fatma Aliye's other novels depict heroines who became
career women.[95] Neither of these novels is as substantial as *Muhazarat*, and
neither of their heroines is as powerful as Fazıla. It is as if to say that for Fatma
Aliye, the larger project than careers for women was to imagine a matriarchal
alternative to the patriarchal authority that she found much less benign than
did Ahmed Midhat. If he imagines himself as the new Muslim patriarch in his
novel, Fatma Aliye exposes the sordid underside of patriarchy and imagines a

Muslim superwoman and matriarch in Fazıla. Both writers agree that love is an insufficient basis for marriage. The happiness of the married couple also does not suffice by itself. The ultimate need is for social reintegration, which Ahmed Midhat imagines as reinforcing ties across religious lines in Istanbul and Fatma Aliye imagines as strengthening ties across space between Muslim families in Beirut and Istanbul.

Both novels have other features that merit comparison. Both open with grand scenes that problematize the existing order of gender relations in some way. For Ahmed Midhat, it is a chance encounter on the Bosphorus ferry, where he gets into a conversation with some women about whether the compartment they are sitting in is reserved for women. The problem of maintaining Islamic gender segregation on a public conveyance occupies them in the foreground; in the background, the women's conversation among themselves excites his curiosity about the relationships that become the novel's subject. In Fatma Aliye's novel, the opening scene is the women's party at the bride's house on her wedding day, including the climactic moment when the groom comes to fetch his bride, and the women guests crowd around, staring boldly to catch a glimpse of him and not all bothering even to cover their heads (18). This scene sets the stage for the "debates" implied in the novel's title about the possibilities for women to be "free and autonomous" in anything more than clothing choices.[96]

The most conspicuous difference between the two novels is that Ahmed Midhat is much the more practiced author. He knows how to write more or less in units of thirty-two pages (the size of a "signature" in a printed volume). He can control the pacing of his book. Its second part begins almost exactly at the midpoint in terms of both pagination and the implied chronology of the story. Presumably this mastery of basics freed him to experiment in literary technique.

In contrast, Fatma Aliye displays uncertainties that feminist critics have found predictable in pioneer women writers. She develops parts of her novel at excessive length compared to others. The pace at which events develop starts unbearably slowly, then becomes extremely fast. More isolated from society than Ahmed Midhat, she writes without the same sense of her audience that he had. Still, richly descriptive passages demonstrate her talent; and passages evocative of the psychological novel prove her interest in experimentation. With greater sensitivity to gender issues and greater interest in texts not on canonical lists, more scholars of Turkish literature would find her work worthy of scrutiny.

The neglect of these works probably has several explanations. Within a few years of his novel's publication, the Ottoman-Armenian violence of the mid-1890s surely killed many readers' interest in a novel with an Armenian heroine. Probably the greatest reason why present-day critics have not recognized the impact of Ottoman fiction in reengineering gender relations is, however, that the transformation succeeded. It succeeded so well that contemporary Turks no longer know—perhaps do not want to know—what historical gender relations were like. The fact that authors as conservative as these two participated in imagining alternatives in gender relations suggests yet another reason for the change: the desire for new gender roles and enlarged possibilities for women was not limited to the radical Westernizers who later claimed credit for liberating women. Ottoman works of imaginative literature did not transform society by themselves. However, given the parallels between patriarchal household and patrimonial sultanate, their scrutiny of social relations implied demands for change that could readily expand from the social to the political.

THE LAST DECISIVE SULTAN

Under Abdülhamid II, the empire zigzagged from constitutionalism (1876–1878) to autocracy (1878–1908) and back to constitutionalism (1908). His ability to concentrate power in the palace reflected his force of character, his immense prerogatives, and the shallow roots of constitutionalism. The record of a modernizing autocrat in a multiethnic empire buffeted by separatist nationalism within and European imperialism without was bound to be controversial. The same ruler whom Europeans and domestic opponents vilified was looked up to as caliph and benefactor by Muslims far and wide, and not without reason. He kept the empire out of major wars after 1878. His subjects experienced major improvements in administration, public works, education, and the military. The railway symbolizes the gains in economic development. Ottoman society was transformed by migration, particularly the Muslim refugee influx, and by the impact of modernity on individual self-awareness, marital and family relations, and class formation. The burgeoning print media of the period expanded the imaginative realms for exploring these new realities.

Autocracy turned the modern tension between subjectivizing and rationalizing processes into a cardinal reality of the time for ruler and ruled alike. As the autocrat used all the rationalizing means of modern governance to extend his range of control, his subjects responded by diverting much of their speculation into realms deemed apolitical, such as social commentary and local politics. The only other alternatives were the minorities' separatist nationalism and the Young Turks' antiregime activism. Emerging from the sultan's elite academies, the Young Turks created the coalition of civil and military elites that would rule the empire and later the Turkish republic from 1908 to 1950. Their success suggested that their radical, secularizing approach to change would write the Turks' future history. The Hamidian period was just as significant, however, for the formation of the conservative, propertied wing of the Ottoman Muslim middle class. In the long run, their religiously grounded worldview would turn any apparent triumph of secularism into an ongoing dialectic between alternative approaches to modernity.

4

IMPERIAL DEMISE, NATIONAL STRUGGLE

From the Young Turk Revolution of 1908 through the Turkish National Struggle of 1919–1922, change accelerated catastrophically for the Ottomans. This period is shorter than that addressed by any other chapter in this book. Yet compared to the experiences of the other World War I belligerents, the crisis lasted longer for the Ottomans. Assaults on the empire started hard upon the 1908 revolution, intensified with World War I, then continued immediately with the National Struggle, turning the entire period from 1908 to 1922 into the Ottomans' final crisis.

This prolonged chronology differentiates the Ottoman experience from that of the European belligerents of 1914–1918 but matches experiences in many other parts of the world. The Young Turk Revolution coincided with the global wave of upheaval preceding World War I: the Russo-Japanese War (1904–1905), the Russian Revolution (1905), Iranian Revolution (1906), Mexican Revolution (1910), and Chinese Revolution (1911). After 1918, the Turkish National Struggle coincided with another wave of struggle against imperialism across much of Afro-Eurasia. This included the revolution in Egypt (1919); insurrections in Aden (1919), Iraq (1918–1920), and Syria (1919–1920, 1925–1927), and the anti-Zionist riots in Palestine (1920). Further afield, the list includes Russia's Civil War (1918–1920), India's Amritsar Massacre (1919), and China's May Fourth movement (1919). Turkey's National Struggle differed in that it was fought over the last remnant of an empire that never had been colonized and ended in 1923 by establishing the independence and territorial integrity of the Turkish republic, the new state that became that empire's most direct successor.

Whether deemed short or long, no period manifested more starkly the contrast between the forces destroying the Ottoman polity's multiethnic superstructure and the reformist dynamism that made its heart beat. The empire that Europeans had dismissed as the "sick man of Europe" was finally about to succumb. Inside it, however, the Young Turks generated such dynamism that other languages adopted their name and applied it to radical innovators in any field of endeavor. The simultaneity of dynamism and destruction was not fortuitous. In the most momentous events of the period, the two interacted with tragic synergy. Nationalism displayed both its constructive and its destructive face.

Few periods of Ottoman history are more challenging to assess. In an effort to do so, this chapter will examine the contrast between reformist policy and military crisis, the economic transformations associated with building a "national economy," and the contrast between demographic catastrophe and new social forces. The chapter will also examine the reflections of these changes in Ziya Gökalp's social thought and Halide Edib Adıvar's novels *Sinekli Bakkal* (published in English as *The Clown and His Daughter*) and *Ateşten Gömlek* (Shirt of flame).

These years of crisis also furthered the differentiation and dialectical interaction of the major currents of change that define the course of late Ottoman and Turkish history. Among the official intelligentsia, the military took control of politics in a way not seen since 1826.[1] Often, the momentum they generated swept along others who might not have fully shared their views. For a time after 1908, however, intellectual and political life became more pluralistic than it had ever been before or would be again before the 1960s. Cultural and religious conservatives also benefited from those freedoms. Muslim propertied interests benefited, as well, from the Young Turk regime's economic policies. In the redefinition of collective identities, these years were critical, even catastrophic, for all the empire's inhabitants. Alternative identity concepts that had coexisted — Muslim, Ottoman, Turkish, and their counterparts for other peoples — had to be sorted out. Inside the nascent Turkish republic, the secularizing Turkish nationalists' victory would appear definitive for another generation but face increasing challenges thereafter.

FROM REVOLUTION TO WORLD WAR TO NATIONAL STRUGGLE: POLITICS AND WAR

Scholars debate whether the Ottoman polity really experienced revolution in this period. The term is most commonly applied to the Young Turk Revolution of 1908. Some writers, especially in English, also refer to the National Struggle as a "revolution" or "independence war," the latter term better known as a designation for the American Revolution (1776).[2] If the Ottoman polity underwent revolution in these years, it did so in stages: 1908 established the constitutional form, and 1922 established the national character, of the resulting polity. Preponderant Turkish opinion has always been guarded, however, about applying the term "revolution." Radical as their impact could be, the Young Turks' approach to change was conservative in its dedication to preserving the empire, and their terminology reflected that fact. The most common term for the order introduced in 1908 was İkinci Meşrutiyet (Second Constitutional Government, the first being that of 1876–1878). Similarly, the Turkish name for the events of 1919–1922 was Milli Mücadele, National Struggle; later, the term Kurtuluş Savaşı, Liberation Struggle, also came into use. Among contemporaries of the National Struggle, some used the term *ihtilal*, "revolution," but more preferred *inkılap*, "transformation," the latter being also preferred in the official communications of the period. The early republic both trivialized that term by applying it to each and every reform and exalted it by making "transformism" (*inkılapçılık*) one of the six principles of the official ideology.[3]

THE CONSTITUTIONAL REVOLUTION, REFORM, AND POLITICS

What is known to history as the Young Turk Revolution broke onto the awareness of Ottomans in varying ways in different places.[4] It started in the Ottoman Balkans as an insurrection by officers belonging to the secret organization the Committee of Union and Progress. They precipitated events, took to the hills, and staged gatherings in the towns to demand restoration of the constitution. In Istanbul, although his hand was forced by the news from the Balkans, Abdülhamid II was able to announce the restoration of the constitution as if of his own free will. His censors had kept the Istanbul public in the dark about the Balkan events. Further east and south, the news of revolution was an even greater surprise. Especially in the Arab provinces, supporters of the revolution had to proceed with caution. If this was a revolution, it came on cat's feet, and the issue of gaining international recognition did not even arise.[5]

In general, news of the restoration of the constitution was greeted with joy, and reports from Ottoman cities and towns depicted scenes of celebration and intercommunal fraternization. Souvenir goods were produced for the market, often emblazoned with mottoes such as *hürriyet, müsavat, uhuvvet, adalet*—"liberty, equality, fraternity, and justice." Emigrants from the empire celebrated the revolution as far away as Argentina.[6] After the Hamidian repression, the cornucopia of constitutional freedoms poured forth its profusion. By the time the parliament opened in December, elections had been held, and some ten political parties had formed. By 1910, 353 newspapers and magazines

An Ottoman family reading the newspapers. The newspapers in their
hands are *Hürriyet, İttifak, Karagöz,* and *Tanin,* all launched in 1908. (By
Ali Sami, courtesy of Engin Çizgen [Özendes], *Ali Sami,* 76–77.)

had started publishing. Prominent among them was the newspaper *Tanin*
(Boom, or Buzz), whose editor, Hüseyin Cahit, was a member of the CUP
central committee and somewhat its spokesman. Islamic print culture took off
with the launching of the periodical *Sırat-ı Müstakim* (1908, later *Sebilürreşad*)
and with the publications of such thinkers as Şehbenderzade Ahmed Hilmi
and Said Nursi.[7] More and more, elite women published magazines, formed
feminist associations, and joined women's sections of the Union and Progress
Party. Economically, free enterprise and foreign investment expanded; yet at
the same time, the new freedoms led to widespread labor organization and
action—more than a hundred strikes within six months. A general pardon
enabled political exiles to return in large numbers to a hero's welcome.

Significantly, the CUP leadership did not initially assume the top positions in
Istanbul; but they did intend to serve as guardians of the new regime, and they
ultimately left a legacy that later became all too familiar: single-party rule.[8] For
a time, constitutional politics meant interaction among the palace, the Sublime
Porte, and the parliament. In the parliamentary elections, the two-stage voting
system permitted taxpaying male Ottoman subjects aged twenty-five or older
to vote for secondary electors, who voted for the deputies. Two-stage voting
favored the election of local notables, likely to be more conservative than the
Young Turk intelligentsia but also the kind of men the CUP needed to cultivate

to broaden its base. In this sense, the old pattern of politics as the interaction between central elites and notables from around the empire renewed itself. The opening of the parliament aroused such wide interest that many people came from the provinces to witness it, making lodgings hard to find in Istanbul.

Even this nearly bloodless revolution produced victims and opponents. Starting with Abdülhamid's palace staff and extending into the military and civil official ranks, "reorganizations" (*tensikat*)—actually purges—removed tens of thousands of men from government payrolls. In the military, the purges targeted the "regimentals" (*alaylı*), who had risen through the ranks, as opposed to the "school men" (*mektepli*), academy graduates like the Young Turk officers. Abdülhamid's patronage policy had padded civil and military ranks unsustainably, and culling the payrolls was unavoidable. However, many whose careers were ruined bore little blame for the old regime's faults. For the new regime, the purges made it hard to find suitable appointees for many positions. In Istanbul, a city where government employment was the main source of income, the economic pain made itself widely felt. The once-resplendent Hamidian elites' loss of status and wealth turned them into subjects for the caricaturist's pen.[9]

The new regime also faced active opposition from at least two other quarters.[10] One was Sabahaddin Bey's liberal faction. Now organized as the Ottoman Liberals' Party (Osmanlı Ahrar Fırkası), they contested the December 1908 parliamentary elections but won only one seat. The other opposition in 1908 consisted of conservatives among the lower ulema, medrese students, and dervish orders. A group known as the Muhammadan Union (İttihad-i Muhammedî) emerged in early April 1909 to spearhead the religious opposition, and an armed insurrection in Istanbul ensued. The uprising took the form of a troop mutiny followed by a march on parliament to present demands, including restoration of the sharia. The mob went after CUP leaders, and some twenty were killed.

The situation slipped out of control. The high ulema denounced the insurrection. The Ottoman Liberals' Party tried to limit it to an anti-CUP rebellion. CUP activists went underground and mobilized their base in Macedonia. They dispatched an Action Army (Hareket Ordusu) under Mahmud Şevket Paşa to Istanbul to suppress the revolt. The occasion provided the excuse for Abdülhamid's deposition and the accession of his brother, Mehmed V Reşad (r. 1909–1918). In fact, Abdülhamid behaved circumspectly during the revolt. The active roles in it were more likely played by the liberal opposition, religious conservatives, and purge victims, especially army officers. Except in Damascus, where the Muhammadan Union had a branch, there were few links between the provinces and the rebels in Istanbul, although demonstrations started as far away as Medina and Baghdad once the revolt began. The rebellion did spread to Adana, where conservatives' attacks on CUP representatives expanded into an anti-Armenian pogrom.

The attempted counterrevolution once past, competitive politics and reformist dynamism prevailed from 1909 through 1913. Reform began with amendments to the 1876 constitution, a number of which became law in August 1909.[11] The amendments made the Ottoman Empire a constitutional monarchy. They required the sultan to swear to uphold the constitution, defined his prerogatives more precisely, reduced his role in ministerial appointments to choosing the grand vezir and şeyhülislam and approving the grand vezir's nominees to the other ministries, and abolished the sultan's right to exile individuals arbitrarily (art. 113). The amendments confirmed the ministers' individual and collective responsibility to parliament, the deputies' right to question the ministers, and the legislative initiative of deputies and senators as well as ministers.

The constitutional amendments were only a start. The belief that despotism had fallen opened a new phase in Ottoman legislation. New laws and regulations poured forth, making this a fertile period in the expansion of Ottoman legal culture. Commissions set up in different government agencies examined existing laws and regulations and recommended new measures, many of which became law. Notably, the Provincial Administration Law of 1913 replaced that of 1871 and later became the basic framework for local administration under the Turkish republic.[12] New laws also regulated freedoms and obligations under the constitutional regime. Some laws passed after the 1909 insurrection restricted freedoms announced in 1908, provoking new political opposition. Controversial laws included those on associations, public meetings, the press, strikes, brigandage, and military service, which for the first time became obligatory for non-Muslims as well as Muslims. In addition to purging government payrolls, aggressive efforts were made to cut palace expenditures and recover Abdülhamid's and his family's assets.[13] These measures spelled out the implications of 1908 as a constitutional revolution.

Practical politics changed, too. The years 1909–1913 were ones of mounting tension between the CUP and both the military elite and the parliament. Inasmuch as relatively junior officers wielded great influence in the CUP, the political hierarchy and the chain of military command did not match. Some high-ranking officers, such as Mahmud Şevket Paşa, commander of the Action Army of 1909, thought that officers should stay out of politics. In fact, the revolution showed how much the CUP depended on its military members. Officers on active duty also sat in the parliament, in violation of the constitution. Criticized by its opponents for wielding power without responsibility, the CUP decided in 1908 to form a party. Consisting of the Unionist members of parliament, the party lacked discipline and was not fully trusted by the CUP, whose central committee retained the real power. Opposition to the CUP regrouped after April 1909, and a variety of parties emerged over the next several years, ranging from the Moderate Liberals (Mutedil Hürriyetperveran Fırkası) to the nominally socialist (in fact progressive) Ottoman Socialist Party (Osmanlı Sosyalist Fırkası). As security threats mounted with the Albanian insurrection of 1910 and later crises, so did opposition to the CUP. By 1911, most anti-CUP parties had formed a common front, known by its French name Entente Libérale (Hürriyet ve İtilaf Fırkası). Within three weeks of its formation, this group defeated the CUP candidate in an Istanbul by-election. At that, the CUP mobilized for action, and the 1912 general elections turned into the "big-stick election" (*sopalı seçim*) because of the intimidation employed. CUP deputies packed the new parliament, but it lacked legitimacy and was soon dissolved.

At this point, only the direst international crisis since 1876 saved the CUP's political control, and only at the cost of dictatorial methods that reduced constitutionalism to a sham. The Ottoman defeat in the First Balkan War (1912), discussed below, and the prospect of losing Edirne, once the capital, provoked the CUP leadership to stage a coup at the Sublime Porte, shooting the minister of war, forcing the other ministers to resign, and bringing in Mahmud Şevket Paşa as grand vezir and war minister.[14] As the military threats worsened, he was assassinated (June 1913); and the CUP tightened its grip, taking complete control through 1918.

The CUP regime of 1913–1918 was commonly described as a triumvirate of Enver, Cemal, and Talat Paşas. In fact, they were only three leaders in a larger

Young Turk leaders, from left to right, Enver, Cemal, and Talat Paşas.
(Enver courtesy of Edhem Eldem; Talat and Cemal from Ellison, *Harem.*)

CUP inner circle, which made decisions collectively.[15] Talat Bey (later Paşa) became minister of the interior at age thirty-five. Enver and Cemal Beys (Paşas) became CUP military leaders. Mehmet Cavid emerged as the financial expert. Dr. Bahaeddin Şakir and Dr. Nazım, who reorganized the CUP before 1908, retained large roles. Kara Kemal mobilized guilds and formed cooperatives. Ziya Gökalp developed the ideology.

The CUP was not in a position to impose a consistent party line, but it did develop a far-reaching apparatus of control. Preserving its secrecy, it kept its headquarters at Salonica until 1912. The CUP held an annual general congress, theoretically its highest decision-making organ. In practice, the highest organ of decision was the central committee, which issued directives to the government agencies and the chamber of deputies. In 1913, the CUP added a general assembly to coordinate its activity in parliament and in governing the state. The CUP created a hierarchy of organizations as a show of mass support, and branches were set up to organize women, the ulema, the military, and civilians. A "bandwagon" effect set in, people everywhere wanted to join, and CUP branches proliferated, acting locally with little coordination. The CUP's appeal was blunted by its secrecy and collective decision-making, as well as by the fact that its goal of holding the empire together did not appeal equally to all the empire's peoples. Reinforcing CUP authoritarianism, these problems made the CUP's leaders appreciate the value of a docile sultan whose authority they could manipulate. After 1913, they kept the parliament in suspension much of the time. For policy making, they relied on "temporary laws" (*kanun-ı muvakkat*), confirmed by imperial decree and supposed to be approved later by parliament.

For the CUP, a militarized organization, one of the most important policy fronts was military reform. The reform of the army was again German-assisted. Field Marshal Colmar von der Goltz, who already had long service in the Ottoman Empire (1883–1895), played a leading role in this project. His idea of "the nation in arms" inspired the CUP to dream of a militarized society. Begun in 1910, the military reorganization applied lessons learned from von der Goltz's recent commands in Germany and also from the Russo-Japanese War (1904–1905), which he had followed by corresponding with Ottoman military observer Pertev Bey (later Paşa), who accompanied the Japanese forces. The reorganization brought the Ottoman army in line with contemporary European armies in operational doctrine and ahead of the Europeans in organization.[16] The most radical change consisted of replacing conventional "square" infantry divisions (with two brigades having two regiments each) with a "triangular" division (three infantry regiments), with an artillery regiment of three battalions attached to each "triangular" division. In the trench warfare of World War I, the "triangular" division model proved more effective than the "square" model. The German army began converting its divisions to the Ottoman model in 1915; every major European combatant did likewise by 1918. The reason for Ottoman defeat in the Balkan Wars of 1912–1913 has to be sought elsewhere than in military backwardness. Resumed in 1913–1914, again with German assistance, the Ottomans' military reforms enabled them to achieve notable successes in World War I, even if they could not escape ultimate defeat.

Centralized and militarized, CUP rule raised the level of violence in politics. In addition to the regular military forces, even before 1908, the CUP had "volunteers" (*fedais*), who carried out confidential missions. During the Balkan Wars, these were used to organize temporary government among Turkish-speaking Muslims in zones that the empire ended up losing. This effort became a trial run for the national resistance societies developed later to support the National Struggle of 1919–1922. The "volunteer" officers were formally organized in 1914 as the Special Organization (Teşkilat-ı Mahsusa), which the CUP relied on for secret missions, especially as intercommunal relations approached their final breakdown.[17]

In position to act without accountability, the CUP leadership took the fateful step of entering World War I. Including Enver Paşa (minister of war and acting commanding general), an inner CUP circle concluded the secret agreement that brought the Ottomans into World War I on the German side (2 August 1914). An Ottoman-Bulgarian treaty followed a few days later. The Ottomans wanted a way out of the diplomatic isolation that had hurt them during the Balkan Wars. Within the CUP leadership, different men preferred different choices as to both allies and war or peace. However, overtures to other European powers were rebuffed; France's and Britain's agreements with Russia also posed obstacles. Even in Germany, the chancellor and military opposed allying with the Ottomans; only Wilhelm II's personal intervention sealed the deal.[18] The Ottomans concluded with Germany a basically defensive alliance against Russia, not realizing that German strategy required attacking France across Belgium, an act that would bring Britain into the war as one of the guarantors of Belgian neutrality. The CUP leadership ultimately lost everything by entering the war.

Conservative in many ways, the 1908 revolution turned the Ottoman Empire formally into a constitutional sultanate, establishing the pattern of parliamentary, constitutional government that would remain normative under the republic. At the same time, the CUP's assumed role as guardian of the constitution defined the model of the unelected power center, a role that the military would assume under the republic. The revolution also unleashed an unprecedented outburst of reform and creativity that would have produced even greater results than it did, had not the external environment turned so menacing. As often happens, the regime change gave enemies foreign and domestic excuses to attack, and Ottoman reactions rose to tragic heights.

THE YOUNG TURKS AND NATIONALISM

Like the idea that they carried out a revolution, the entrenched assumption that the Young Turks were Turkish nationalists needs reexamination. Although that label was used in Turkish, it was used in the form Jön Türk, a phonetic transcription of the French Jeune Turc; and European usage was notoriously imprecise in distinguishing between "Ottoman" and "Turkish." Early on, "Young Turk" was a misnomer for a movement that also attracted Arabs, Albanians, Jews, and even Greeks and Armenians. After 1908, the oscillation among alternative identity concepts continued for most Ottomans, until choice became inescapable. Both chronological and geographical factors governed those choices, and questions about the Young Turks and nationalism cannot be answered without noting those factors.[19]

Chronologically, the Balkan Wars created a divide in Young Turk policy on identity issues; geographically, concepts of core and periphery made the difference. In the more optimistic phase before the Balkan Wars, the motto "unity of elements" (*ittihad-ı anasır*) still resounded, implying a cosmopolitan Ottomanism, although with emphasis on the Turks as the empire's ruling people (*millet-i hakime*). In this phase, military conscription was extended to non-Muslims as well as Muslims, and the military substitution tax formerly paid by non-Muslims was abolished. Some policies of the period that provoked accusations about Turkification were more exactly matters of centralization or systematization. Non-Muslims and other non-Turks tended to see Ottomanism as an umbrella identity, more or less significant to the extent that matters of common interest were at stake. For the CUP leadership, Ottomanism was a proactive policy for preventing separatism and promoting commonalities—for example, the learning of Turkish.

The 1909 law on associations prohibited political associations based on differences of nation or "race." The law became a lightning rod for charges of Turkification, but the decisions made under it are revealing. Ethnic or religious organizations perceived as having cultural aims and not promoting separatism were allowed. A Jewish association to promote Zionism and Jewish settlement in Palestine was closed down; a Jewish school that was going to teach about Zionism was allowed to stay open. Analogous decisions were made where the interests of non-Turkish Muslim communities were concerned. A Circassian Unity and Mutual Aid Society was allowed; likewise Kurdish societies were allowed to open schools and carry out other functions that promoted Kurdish advancement. Minority schools were required to teach Turkish, knowledge of which was indispensable for participation in public life; however, those schools were allowed to teach the minority's own language, too. The government was primarily worried about competitors for its subjects' loyalties, including both separatist movements and missionaries, a concern understandable from events before 1908.

The catastrophic Ottoman losses in the Balkans Wars radically changed this situation. The Ottoman losses were not just the military ones: hundreds of thousands of soldiers lost, entire divisions and army corps destroyed or captured. Widespread draft evasion and desertion by Ottoman Bulgarian and Greek soldiers further devalued cosmopolitan Ottomanism.[20] Far worse, the empire abruptly lost 155,000 square kilometers of territory, including some of its oldest, most flourishing provinces, with almost four million inhabitants. Istanbul was flooded with Muslim refugees as it had not been since 1878. Until the Balkan Wars, the population of the Ottoman Balkans was still 51 percent Muslim, including Albanians and others as well as Turks. The Balkans, not Anatolia, were the real homeland of many Turks until then, and Salonica had been the cradle of the revolution. Enver Paşa spoke for many Ottoman Turks when he exclaimed that "after 400 years, to be cast out of Rumelia and to move to Anatolia: this is something that cannot be borne."[21] Borne it had to be.

The consequences for Ottoman identity politics were profound. Facing an insecure future with an increasingly Muslim population and a geography reduced to Anatolia and the Arab provinces, the Ottomans had to rethink Anatolia as their core territory, whence the different policies for Anatolia and the Arab lands. Themes of international modernity in the age of imperialism affected the choices they made. This is true of two ongoing themes of Middle Eastern diplomacy: that of European intervention to restore or create "order" and that of separating religious or ethnic groups, both repeated again and again since Napoleon's 1798 invasion of Egypt and the beginnings of Balkan separatism. Physicians figured among the CUP decision makers and actors in critical events. The surgical metaphors that they applied to ethnic cleansing identify it as a gruesome byproduct of modernity, much as was the machine-age mayhem on the battlefields of the Great War.

In the Arab lands, the Young Turks made decentralizing concessions and emphasized Islamic unity under the sultan-caliph. Efforts to satisfy Arab demands included the expanded authority of local administrative agencies under the 1913 Provincial Administration Law. Other measures permitted the use of Arabic in the courts, government schools, and official correspondence.

In response to complaints about assignment of non-Arabic-speaking officials to Arab provinces, Arabic courses for officials were set up. Before 1908, there had been measures to train officials in languages such as Arabic, Armenian, and Bulgarian; the post-1913 policy on Arabic was not novel but it reinforced a new policy toward the Arab lands.

Studies of Arabs' responses to the CUP regime indicate that they did not identify with any single political trend in this period.[22] Some Arab deputies in the Ottoman parliament supported the CUP's centralizing policies; some supported the liberals' decentralizing policy. The Arab deputies' positions on policy issues of specific interest to Arabs, including Zionist settlement in Palestine or the war with Italy over Libya (1911), did not display a consistent pattern of supporting or opposing the CUP. Arab opponents of the CUP's centralizing policies used charges of Turkification tactically but were not motivated by Arab nationalism or separatism. During World War I, the CUP pursued its Islamist policy toward the Arab provinces, continued trying to co-opt notables, and made concessions to Arab demands. Two Arab secret societies were formed, al-Fatat (Young Arabs) and al-Ahd (the Covenant), but Arab opinion in Syria and Iraq remained largely responsive to Istanbul's initiatives, and dissidence declined or moved to sites beyond Ottoman control, particularly Cairo.

The CUP sent navy minister Cemal Paşa to Damascus as governor of Syria and commander of the Ottoman forces. After his unsuccessful Suez campaign (January–February 1915), Cemal returned to Syria, was granted emergency powers, and staged a reign of terror aimed at presumed opponents of the regime. He had a number of prominent Syrians and Lebanese court-martialed on trumped-up treason charges. Thirty-three were publicly hanged. Cemal ordered many families—two hundred by one source, five thousand by another—deported to Anatolia. At the same time, conscription was taking some three-fourths of the able-bodied men, and natural disasters and famine ravaged the land for three years (1915–1918). The effects on the population were so traumatic that the Ottoman term for military mobilization, *seferberlik*, passed into Syrian Arabic as *safar barlik*, a synonym for "famine."[23] In Syria, the threat of nationalist uprising against the Ottomans was more imaginary than real. However, Cemal Paşa took actions comparable in kind, if not in degree of impact, to those that befell the Armenians in Anatolia at the same time.

The situation in the Hijaz always differed from that in the other Arab provinces, thanks to the sharif of Mecca's semiautonomous status and the sensitivity of everything about the Two Holy Cities.[24] Here the Young Turk Revolution was followed by the dismissal of the two highest Ottoman officials, the governor and the military commander (*muhafiz*) in Medina, and the installation in Mecca of Sharif Husayn ibn Ali in 1908. The official opening of the Hijaz railway's Damascus-Medina link (September 1908) and the prospect (never realized) that the line might be continued to Mecca and Jidda further sensitized the Hijaz. Facing local challenges to his power, Sharif Husayn used his ties with Istanbul and his skill in relations with the bedouin to consolidate his authority and advance members of his family. Trying to master the situation, the CUP consolidated its hold on Medina and relied on the sharif to cope with the bedouin, the Hijazi elites, and Sharif Husayn's Arabian rivals, Abd al-Aziz ibn Saud in Najd and Muhammad Idrisi of Asir. In the Hijaz, tension between the governor and the sharif persisted, given the lack of subordination of one to the other. The outbreak of war in 1914 added international tensions, as the British blockaded the Red Sea ports of the Hijaz. Through his son Abdullah, Sharif Husayn contacted the British in Egypt about possibly allying against the Ottomans. The revolt that Cemal Paşa had feared in Syria emerged out of the Hijaz and became a part of the Palestine campaign of 1917. Couched in Islamic terms and motivated by the sharif's dynastic ambitions, it had nothing to do with the Arab nationalism that later Arab historians read into it.

In contrast to its policy in the Arab lands, the CUP did pursue Turkification in Anatolia from 1913 on, not that doing so contradicted emphasizing Islam and Ottoman identity in its view. The CUP collaborated with Turkist publications and with the Turkish Hearth associations (Türk Ocakları, 1912), which published the nationalist journal *Türk Yurdu* (Turkish homeland) and claimed thirty-five branches and twelve hundred members by 1918.[25] A CUP goal for Anatolia was to form a "national bourgeoisie," a major topic in the economic history of the period, discussed below. Another part of the policy was the resettlement of 435,000 Muslim refugees and migrants after 1913. Many of these refugees were not Turkish, and the preexisting Anatolian populace also included non-Turkish Muslims, such as Circassians, Lazes, Arabs, and, Kurds. One goal of the Turkification policy was therefore to locate or relocate non-Turkish Muslims at sites that would promote cultural assimilation. The fact that Anatolia lacked a clear-cut geographical border in the southeast complicated this task, particularly in the case of the Kurds.[26]

Much more aggressive policies were applied to Anatolia's non-Muslim populations. Before the outbreak of war in 1914, the CUP government negotiated with Greece for a population exchange intended to remove Greeks from Thrace and western Anatolia. Although war broke out before the negotiations were complete, the 1914 planning for an exchange of Ottoman Greeks for Muslims from Macedonia and Epirus shows that the prewar flight of Greeks from those areas was not solely the result of covert operations by CUP agents, although such operations occurred. The Ottomans were not alone in promoting ethnic homogenization; the Greek and Bulgarian governments also negotiated with each other over ethnic homogenization projects before the war.[27] In the east in early 1914, Russian sponsorship of yet another plan, backed by the Armenian Dashnaks, for reforms in the "Armenian" provinces roused CUP suspicions of Russian expansionism.[28] Once the war started, eastern Anatolia became a major combat theater. There, both strategic and security worries combined to erode tolerance for difference. As the Ottoman and Russian empires collided, so did incompatible visions of this region as exclusive national territory for Turks, or for Armenians. More catastrophically than in the instances noted in earlier chapters or in the Syria of 1915–1918, centuries of coexistence collapsed in Anatolia. One side won all, and the other lost all, a grim victory in a desolate landscape. The massacres and deportations of the Armenians and other, smaller Christian communities of eastern Anatolia became a part of the story of the Caucasian front in World War I.

Those events and the question of Young Turk nationalism constitute the two subjects of greatest scholarly controversy about this period. Of all existing interpretations of the Young Turks' positions on nationalism, the concept that their policy differed chronologically, before and after the Balkan Wars, and geographically, with Anatolia as the Turkish core from 1913 onward and the Arab provinces as the periphery, best fits the historical evidence.

IMPERIALISM, IRREDENTISM, AND INTERNAL REBELLION

Just as 1908 opened the way for freer expression of difference inside the empire, the turnover in leadership in Istanbul enticed outside enemies to take what they wanted.[29] In 1908, Austria-Hungary annexed Bosnia-Herzegovina, which it had occupied since 1876; Crete and Greece united, and Bulgaria declared itself independent. The Ottomans could do little, although they did organize an effective boycott of Austrian goods, one sign of a turn toward mass political mobilization. The Albanians revolted in 1910 and became independent in the Balkan Wars, traumatic events for the CUP, some of whose leading members were Albanian. In Yemen, rebellion had broken out in 1905; there the Young Turk regime responded flexibly and concluded peace with the Zaydi imam Yahya (1911), trading local autonomy for loyalty to the empire.

The 1908 revolution did nothing to stop the European powers' search for spheres of influence inside the empire. Britain, France, and Germany had their respective spheres in Iraq, Syria, and Anatolia.[30] Seeking more than influence, in September 1911 Italy demanded Tripolitania (Libya), the last Ottoman province in Africa. War broke out. For the Ottomans, the stakes were high. Arabs everywhere would see the Ottomans' ability to defend Libya as a test of their power to defend other Arab provinces. The war roused pan-Islamic enthusiasm. However, Italian control of the sea interdicted Ottoman intervention in force. Enver Paşa led a group of officers who organized resistance in the Libyan interior, so starting a guerrilla war that lasted for many years. The Italians widened the crisis by bombarding Ottoman coastal sites, including Beirut, and seizing the Dodecanese islands off the southwest coast of Anatolia. The looming prospect of war in the Balkans forced the Ottomans in April 1912 to make peace on Italy's terms.

THE BALKAN WARS, 1912–1913

In the Balkans, signs of anti-Ottoman alignment predated the Italo-Turkish war. By the time it ended, bilateral alliances had been concluded among Serbia, Bulgaria, Montenegro, and Greece. In the midst of an unfinished military reorganization program, the Ottomans struggled to cut their losses in Albania and Libya in time to face the threat. The Balkan states mobilized on 30 September 1912, forcing the Ottomans to do likewise. Then the Balkan states presented an ultimatum demanding reforms in Macedonia that would have undermined Ottoman sovereignty. Diplomatically isolated, the Ottomans were at war by 17 October.

The war quickly turned disastrous. The Bulgarians besieged Edirne and advanced to Çatalca, the last line of defense before Istanbul. In southern Macedonia, the Greeks narrowly beat the Bulgarians to take Salonica (9 November), the Young Turks' launching point.[31] The Serbs installed themselves in northern Macedonia. The Montenegrins besieged Scutari (Albania). The Ottomans agreed to an armistice on 3 December, and negotiations began in London. A proposal to turn over Edirne to the Bulgarians precipitated the CUP's armed coup at the Sublime Porte (23 January 1913) to keep the government from surrendering the besieged city. The London negotiations broke down, and fighting resumed. Despite the new Ottoman government's determination, the result was further losses, including Edirne on 28 March, and finally peace on the Balkan states' terms on 30 May. At that moment, the Ottomans had lost everything in Europe except for Istanbul and a small buffer zone around it.

No sooner was this peace signed than the Balkan states fell out over the spoils. The Second Balkan War pitted Bulgaria against its former allies. The Ottomans did not enter the war but did retake Edirne on 22 July 1913. The Bulgarians had to accept the fait accompli, and Ottoman frontiers in Europe ended up where those of the Turkish republic still remain.

Various lessons were drawn from the Balkan Wars, or might have been. Politically, the CUP leaders drew the lesson that diplomatic isolation was too costly. They would not want to face another war without allies. Unfortunately, when the next war came, they paid an even higher price for their choice of allies than they had paid for their lack of allies in the Balkan Wars. Militarily, the Ottomans' Balkan defeat may have seemed to signal incompetence. Yet at Gallipoli and elsewhere, their enemies paid a terrible price for drawing that conclusion.

In military analysts' terms, the Ottomans had been "defeated in detail" in the First Balkan War.[32] The geography of the war zone created two separate foci—Macedonia and the Istanbul-Edirne region—and a coalition of enemies that could attack either center from more than one direction. Divided and dispersed, Ottoman forces faced unmanageable coordination problems and endured multiple defeats. Their strategic problem was compounded by their inability to back up their German-derived doctrine of aggressive offense with the resources, communications, and intelligence that the Germans had. Despite appearances, the military reforms of the preceding years indicate that the Ottoman defeat was not the result of incapacity. Resumed between wars in 1913–1914, the reforms yielded better results during World War I.

WORLD WAR I

Despite the handicaps created by the empire's sprawling geography and its many weaknesses, the Ottoman army fought to the end of World War I and never mutinied. It suffered huge losses but inflicted the like on its enemies. For most of the war, the Ottomans maintained large fighting forces on four, at times five, fronts, a feat matched by no other belligerent but Great Britain. In 1914, probably few observers thought the Ottomans militarily viable. "However, in November 1918, even after the collapse of Russia, Bulgaria, and Austria-Hungary, the mutinies in the French Army and the German Navy, and after the ejection of the Serbian and Romanian armies from their homelands, the Ottoman Army, although battered beyond recognition, was still on its feet and in the field."[33]

Temporizing in 1914, the Ottomans did not enter the war immediately. However, the unilateral British confiscation on 2 August 1914 of two dreadnoughts commissioned from a British shipyard with money raised by the Ottoman Navy League (Donanma Cemiyeti) inflamed opinion. The Ottoman-German alliance was signed later the same day.[34] The appearance off the Dardanelles on 10 August of two German vessels, the *Goeben* and the *Breslau*, provided a solution, but one that drew the Ottomans into the war. Enver Paşa let the ships into the Sea of Marmara. The Ottomans parried British protests by stating that they had bought the ships. The *Goeben* and the *Breslau* became the *Yavuz* and the *Midilli*; and the commander of the former, Admiral Wilhelm Souchon, became commander of the Ottoman navy.

With the excitement over the ships as background, a few determined men pushed for war. The German alliance did not in itself bring the Ottomans into the fight. In Istanbul, high-placed civilians such as Grand Vezir Said Halim Paşa tried to postpone belligerency. Many army officers still wanted time for reorganization. Yet Enver pushed unwaveringly for war. German ambassador Hans von Wangenheim and Admiral Souchon also played aggressive roles. Enver ordered general mobilization (2 August 1914), which continued into the fall. In October he secured several million pounds in gold from Germany. On 25 October, Enver authorized Souchon to maneuver in the Black Sea and attack the Russian fleet.

The Ottomans entered the fighting on 29 October 1914, when Souchon's Ottoman vessels fired on Russian Black Sea ports.[35] So far from reflecting a clear decision for war in Istanbul, the raids provoked a cabinet crisis. Said Halim and others threatened to resign; reportedly all ministers but Enver expressed opposition, but too late. Russia, France, and Britain all declared war, and the Ottoman sultan-caliph responded by proclaiming jihad against the Triple Entente (2–7 November). The Ottomans were at war.

Entering the war in alliance with Bulgaria as well as Germany forced a quick rethinking of the Balkan strategic orientation that had been necessary until then. Keeping a concentration of forces in Thrace to defend Istanbul, the Ottomans prepared to campaign against the Russians in the Caucasus and the British in Egypt; British-Indian forces invading Iraq opened a third front. The decision to attack on two fronts against more powerful enemies defied the lessons that the most professional Ottoman officers had drawn from experience, reflecting instead Enver Paşa's dangerous mix of comparative military inexperience and grandiose aspirations. He compounded the consequences by leaving Istanbul to command the Caucasian offensive in person.

The Caucasian front. By engaging the Russians on a new front outside Europe, this campaign may have served German interests better than Ottoman ones.[36] How it served Ottoman strategy is unclear, except for the irredentist interest of recovering the corner of Anatolia lost to Russia in 1878. The campaign required advancing into mountainous, arid, cold territory unsuited for offensive warfare. The lack of a railway to the northeast greatly handicapped this campaign, and the Anatolian rail line to the southeast still had gaps.[37] Hostilities began in November 1914. The decisive engagement occurred at Sarıkamış (December–January). The Ottomans sought to envelop the Russians and nearly did; but the Russians brought up reinforcements and enveloped the Ottomans instead with catastrophic losses. Leaving an encouraging message for the troops, Enver left the front and returned to Istanbul. Although the Russians were too exhausted to pursue their advantage, in the wake of the campaign eastern Anatolia fell prey to a typhus epidemic and interethnic violence. Another piece of Enver Paşa's unrealism had been to dispatch an invading force to Tabriz (Iran). This too failed, and the Russians occupied Tabriz and Tehran instead.

Having defeated the Ottomans at Sarıkamış in January, the Russians launched a two-pronged offensive toward Erzurum and Van in May 1915.[38] The Russian offensive dominated the eastern front strategically into 1916, when the Russians took Erzurum, the Ottomans' most highly fortified city in the east, as well as Erzincan and Trabzon. Enver subsequently tried to launch another eastern offensive. Despite some successes, such as the capture of Bitlis and Muş by forces under Mustafa Kemal's command, Enver's counteroffensive ended in failure. After the severe winter of 1916–1917, a lull set in on the eastern Anatolian front. The Ottomans did not realize it at first, but the Russian army began disintegrating in summer 1917 because of the revolution.[39] That unexpected windfall enabled the Ottomans to retake the towns lost to Russia in 1878, then continue into Georgia and Azerbaijan to score fleeting victories (November 1918) after the Istanbul government had accepted an armistice.

The Armenian massacres. While the war with Russia dominated the eastern front strategically, eastern Anatolian demographics created added security worries. Religiously mixed populations on both sides of the front included Muslims living behind Russian lines and Christians behind Ottoman lines. The front lines moved back and forth repeatedly. The local population of the war zone tended to support their coreligionists. Many who did not start out on the "wrong" side of the lines found themselves in that position at some point. Warfare interdicted agriculture for three years (1915, 1916, and 1917). In a region that Ottoman Muslims increasingly thought central to the empire, famine, plague, and war stalked the land. So did ethnic cleansing.

Even if study of the subject were not polarized ideologically, many aspects of the events would be hard to reconstruct.[40] The Ottomans were not wrong in thinking they had a security problem with the local population and that this problem had strategic implications. Armenian volunteers, including Ottoman subjects, fought with the Russians at Sarıkamış. As the Ottomans tried to prepare for the Russian spring offensive, an Armenian revolt inside Ottoman lines materialized at Van (13–14 April 1915), where an Armenian republic was established in May. In a region of rough terrain and poor communications, the main centers of Armenian population lay astride the two routes indispensable for Ottoman operations, those running from Sivas to Erzincan and Erzurum in the north and from Diyarbakır to Bitlis and Van in the south. Further south, the railway passed through Konya, Adana, and Aleppo; and Armenian actions could have interdicted rail transport at some or all of those centers.

Ottoman responses to problems in eastern Anatolia were complicated by events elsewhere. In addition to the Van rebellion and the Russian offensive in the east, in 1915, the British invaded Iraq on 14 April, and the Entente forces landed at Gallipoli on 25 April. Regular Ottoman forces were overcommitted on these fronts, and the Ottoman General Staff had to cope with multiple crises at once from late April until the various fronts stabilized in the fall of 1915.

Amid these crises, Enver ordered several hundred leading Armenians in Istanbul arrested, transported from the city, and executed (23–24 April 1915). He also ordered (24 April) the evacuation of the Armenian population from a region including the six eastern Anatolian provinces and extending southward below Diyarbakır. They were to be relocated further southeast, out of Anatolia. With new Russian offensives launched toward Van and Erzurum in May 1915, the situation quickly deteriorated. Among many factors producing the tragic outcome, it has been argued, one was Enver's propensity for grandiose plans, whose successful implementation hinged on nonexistent capabilities.

By the summer of 1915, large-scale Armenian deportations were under way; smaller Christian communities (Syriac, Chaldean, Nestorian) also became victims. Tragic outcomes were inevitable. Huge numbers—perhaps six hundred thousand—would not survive.[41] Armenian countermassacres of Ottoman Muslims occurred; the number of Muslim victims may have been smaller, and many of them may have suffered in later, retaliatory violence, but that does not stop Turks from justifiably seeing themselves also as victims of intercommunal violence in eastern Anatolia. In 1915, the columns of Armenian deportees included people of all ages and both sexes, except that many of the able-bodied men were killed at the outset. Numerous Armenian girls were taken in by Muslim families; many of them have Turkish grandchildren today. Ostensible responsibility for the deportees was assigned to the interior ministry, which issued instructions for humane treatment, safeguarding refugee property, and the like. With the regular army engaged on different fronts, security fell to the local gendarmes, at best. Bands formed by the Special Organization (Teşkilat-ı Mahsusa) operated in the region, combining Kurdish tribesmen, prisoners released from jail for the purpose, and Balkan and Caucasian Muslim refugees—past victims and now ready perpetrators of ethnic cleansing.[42] The historical clash of interests between sedentary Armenians and nomadic Kurds exposed the deportees to further depredations.

Scholars debate whether the severity and scale of the deportations was decided earlier by the CUP in Istanbul or whether the Special Organization colluded with predatory elements in the region upon the covert decision of a few CUP central committee leaders. Many of the perpetrators thought they were carrying out orders and executing a patriotic duty.[43] By 1916, the Armenian population of eastern Anatolia was essentially gone. The scope of the deportations had expanded to encompass Armenians from western Anatolia and even Thrace; Istanbul's Armenian community survived, minus the communal leaders executed in April 1915. Some Ottoman officials opposed what was occurring and refused to carry out orders; some of them were killed for resisting. Reports from some towns indicate that the Muslim commonfolk were bewildered by what was happening.

Centuries of symbiosis under the banner of a multiethnic Islamic state had ended under the cover of wartime necessity and in the name of nationalist social engineering. Among the many victims from both sides, the most tragic were not the nationalist intellectuals, who had to know the stakes of the all-or-nothing struggle created by their antithetical imaginings of the same ground as "Turkey" or "Armenia." The saddest victims were the masses of ordinary people, who would have been content with secure coexistence and did not understand why they were now supposed to hate their neighbors.[44] Foreign powers had added fuel to the fire by favoring the Armenians, as if oblivious to eastern Anatolia's majority Muslim population and its political integration into the Ottoman state. Within the truncated empire left after the Balkan Wars, World War I created the conditions under which the winner-takes-all struggle, innocently foreshadowed decades earlier in works like Namık Kemal's play *Vatan*—and its counterparts in all nationalist literatures—proceeded to its dire conclusion, a ghastly triumph of modernity.

In the punitive peace imposed on the Ottomans after World War I, one of the initial goals was to punish them collectively for what had happened. Trials were held; some of the accused were convicted; some were executed. To Turks of the period, it seemed that "global humanity had suddenly stamped a bad, black stamp on our foreheads. We were the enemies of civilization who had massacred the Armenians and collaborated with the Germans. . . . We were the people whom humanity must get rid of."[45] Offered in the Turks' defense, the statement's logic—that one ethnic group or another had to be gotten rid of—may reveal more about what had happened than the author intended. The constructive and destructive potentials of nationalism had clashed. Here, the destructive forces had prevailed.

Campaigns against the British. Ottoman entry into World War I brought the status of British-occupied Egypt into question. Since 1882, the British had maintained the appearance that the Ottoman sultan retained sovereignty over Egypt and that Mehmed Ali's heirs remained its autonomous rulers as khedives. Once the Ottomans entered the war on the German side, the British proclaimed their protectorate over Egypt, detached it from the Ottoman Empire, deposed khedive Abbas Hilmi II, and replaced him with his uncle Husayn Kamil as sultan. This made the boundary between Egypt and the Ottoman Arab provinces a potential war front. Hoping to raise a revolt in Egypt, the Ottomans under navy minister and governor of Syria Cemal Paşa daringly attacked across Sinai to take Ismailiyya.[46] They did surprise the British and get across the Suez Canal, but the British repulsed them (February 1915). In Egypt, the British had massed troops from the United Kingdom, India, Australia, and New Zealand for a daring plan of their own.

The Gallipoli Campaign (1915), known to Turks as the Çanakkale campaign, led to the greatest Ottoman victory of the war. Victory in this campaign probably stimulated Turkish national consciousness as greatly as defeat stimulated that of the Australians and New Zealanders, who fought here as British imperial subjects.[47] An Entente victory could have reopened the straits, taken Istanbul, and enabled France and Britain to ship munitions to their Russian ally. But first, the invaders had to get past the Ottoman defenses of the Dardanelles. The Gallipoli peninsula offered many opportunities for naval attack. Its heights also offered opportunities for defense from land.

On 19 February 1915, a British naval attack opened the campaign. Supported by German specialists, the Ottomans had worked feverishly to upgrade their defenses. When a Franco-British fleet attempted to force the straits on 18 March, unconventionally placed mines sank three battleships and damaged others. Concluding that naval power could not force the straits alone, the invaders prepared for an amphibious landing. Having intelligence of this plan, Enver Paşa put German general Liman von Sanders in command of the Ottoman Fifth Army to defend the key terrain. He followed plans prepared by Ottoman staff officers, and Ottoman commanders also distinguished themselves. Sensing the significance of the Entente forces' landing on 25 April 1915 and committing his division to battle without awaiting orders, Mustafa Kemal (the future Atatürk) displayed the heroism that fueled his charismatic legend. The Entente forces were stopped at all their landing sites. They tried repeatedly to break out but by summer 1915 were mired in trench warfare like that on the Western Front. Bulgaria's entry into the war in September 1915 enabled the Central Powers to ship munitions and technicians to the Ottomans. The Entente forces finally withdrew (December 1915–January 1916), abandoning

Mustafa Kemal in the trenches. (From Benoist-Méchin, *Turkey*, 178.)

huge amounts of supplies. They retreated with new respect for the Ottomans and did not attempt another amphibious attack. The Ottomans came away with new self-confidence and proven leaders.

British war plans also targeted Iraq. An Anglo-Indian army occupied Basra and vicinity in 1914.[48] Advancing northward in April 1915, General Charles Townshend's Anglo-Indian force engaged the Ottomans at Kut al-Amara and Selman Pak (Ctesiphon) before being forced back on Kut, where the Ottomans had them under siege by year's end. Townshend did not realize it, but Ottoman forces in Iraq had received significant reinforcements. Enver Paşa also named Field Marshal von der Goltz to take over the command, although he left the daily conduct of operations to the Turkish commander, Halil Paşa [Kut].[49] British forces from Basra tried to relieve the siege, but the Ottomans sustained it, keeping aircraft in operation over Kut. Townshend finally had to capitulate, "the largest mass surrender of Imperial troops between Yorktown in 1783 and Singapore in 1942."[50] The British lost forty thousand men in Iraq. The victories at Gallipoli and Kut made 1916 the most successful year of the war for the Ottomans.

In December 1916, however, a larger British force began to march upriver in Iraq. The Ottomans could not reinforce their forces correspondingly. When Ottoman and British forces again met at Kut al-Amara (February 1917), the British prevailed. Then they took Baghdad in March. The Ottomans still held Mosul in northern Iraq. Enver Paşa responded to this situation by dreaming up a grand plan: the Thunderbolt Army Group (Yıldırım Ordular Grubu) to retake Baghdad and advance into Iran. The project provoked controversy among Ottoman and German officers, but the army was formed in July 1917 under Field Marshal Erich von Falkenhayn. By September, its mission had changed from retaking Baghdad to reinforcing Palestine against the expected British offensive. Mustafa Kemal Paşa was assigned to command one of the armies in the Yıldırım Group, but resigned in disagreement with the strategy.

The Arab revolt and the Palestine campaign. In 1914–1915, Sharif Husayn in the Hijaz acted cautiously.[51] Pressed to support the Ottoman jihad, he remained noncommittal, sensing that the Ottoman's official Islamism encroached on his role as sharif of Mecca. The Hijaz was anything but isolated from the war. Thanks to the Suez Canal, one of the world's most strategic sea lanes passed through the Red Sea. Once the Ottomans joined the Central Powers, the British blockaded the Red Sea ports of the Hijaz. Ottoman ability to defend the region was precarious. Through mid-1915, Sharif Husayn kept up his contacts with the Ottomans. However, he also knew that the Ottomans might try to depose him; and his son, Sharif Faysal, had witnessed Cemal Paşa's repressive acts in Syria.

Sharif Husayn therefore sounded out the British in Egypt about their support for an anti-Ottoman Arab revolt. Between 14 July 1915 and 10 March 1916, he and British high commissioner Sir Henry McMahon exchanged letters, on the basis of which the sharif declared himself independent (5 June 1916) and began the Arab revolt. The letters left major ambiguities unresolved and did not amount to a binding agreement. Still, Husayn chose to seize the initiative while he had the chance. He had no way to know that the British would make contradictory promises to others, at least no way to know until 1917, when the British informed him.[52] The Entente powers' wartime agreements for partitioning the Ottoman Empire became widely known in 1917, when the Bolshevik revolutionaries published them.

The Arab revolt was to be coordinated with the British Palestine campaign of 1917. Launched in 1916, the revolt spread gradually, capturing all the large towns in the Hijaz except the Ottoman base at Medina. In October, Sharif Husayn proclaimed himself king of the Arab lands, a claim not recognized beyond the Hijaz. By July 1917, the rebels had reached Aqaba in present-day Jordan. British subsidies helped Husayn attract many tribesmen to his cause. Beyond Aqaba, the Arab rebels advanced northward in the interior, while British-Egyptian forces advanced along the coast. The Arab rebels entered Damascus on 30 September 1918, and Sharif Faysal briefly became king of Syria (1918–1920); the kingdom of the Hijaz, founded by his father, Sharif Husayn, fell to the Saudis in 1925.

The British took Jerusalem (8 December 1917), then Damascus and Aleppo (October 1918). Major battles were fought along the way. The Battle of Megiddo (or Nablus, as it is known in Turkish, September 1918) was "one of the last great cavalry operations in the history of warfare."[53] Mustafa Kemal distinguished himself as commander of the Ottoman Seventh Army, but other units were routed or destroyed. A month later, Mustafa Kemal was commanding the Yıldırım Army Group, based at Adana, and was preparing to organize the defense of Anatolia.

The Armistice (Mudros, 30 October 1918). Threats to Istanbul finally forced the Ottomans to accept an armistice. Entente forces had landed at Salonica, within striking distance of Istanbul; and most of the forces that could defend the capital had long since been shifted to other fronts. The Entente forces at Salonica concluded an armistice with Bulgaria. Bulgarian withdrawal from the war deprived the Ottomans of their overland link to the Central Powers. After the Ottoman armistice, some further fighting occurred on remote fronts. From Baghdad, the British advanced to take Mosul (8 November). In the Caucasus, Enver's "Army of Islam" briefly took Baku (15 September) and Derbent (8 November). The war was over. The Ottoman army was supposed to demobilized under the armistice, but it "was still in the field" with "approximately one million men still under arms," and it "still retained possession of the Anatolian heartland."[54]

Over the weeks that followed, Entente warships moored off Istanbul. In February 1919, French general Franchet d'Espérey rode into Istanbul on a white horse presented to him by a local Greek—a provocative gesture patterned after Ottoman sultan Mehmed the Conqueror's triumphal entry into his new capital in 1453. Istanbul and the straits were thus occupied in effect before being occupied officially (March 1920–October 1923). Life in the city became very tense. The multinational occupation forces, including Greeks, behaved high-handedly, occupying buildings and houses and inciting the minorities to take advantage of the situation. The Greek patriarchate assumed sovereignty over its community, released Ottoman Greeks from their duties as Ottoman subjects, and called for union with Greece. In hindsight, the wonder is not so much that the Istanbul Greek community later dwindled, from more than two hundred thousand in 1914 to perhaps three thousand by the 1990s, as that it lasted as long as it did.[55] Elsewhere, the French occupied parts of southeastern Anatolia, and the Italians seized the province of Antalya. The Greeks seized points in Ottoman Thrace and invaded western Anatolia in May 1919. The Turkish National Struggle had begun.

Foreign troops occupy Istanbul, above, at Sultan Ahmet square near Aya Sofya; below, outside the gatehouse of the Ottoman Ministry of War, Beyazit. A note on the back of the lower photograph identifies the troops as U.S. sailors. (Both given to the author by Elizabeth Scipio Fisher from the papers of her father, Lynn Scipio.)

WARTIME DIPLOMACY AND POSTWAR PEACE

As that occurred, the Entente powers were deciding how to carry out the plans they had made during the war to carve up the Ottoman Empire. The Ottomans had scarcely entered the war before the Entente began making claims and promises. Ironically, the plans they made had more enduring consequences for the Arab provinces than for the future Turkish republic. Ironically again, although oil was already an interest in Iraq and Iran, Arabia's oil resources remained undiscovered. Consequently, the great powers left Arabia unclaimed, so facilitating the gradual consolidation of the Saudi kingdom. For Iraq, geographical Syria, and Anatolia, the Entente powers made more promises than they could keep. The most important are the Husayn-McMahon correspondence (1915–1916), the Sykes-Picot agreement (1916), and the Balfour Declaration (1917). With Greece's entry into the war in 1917, Greek demands for the Aegean coast of Anatolia added to the list.[56]

The Husayn-McMahon correspondence (14 July 1915–10 March 1916), consisting of ten letters exchanged between Sharif Husayn of Mecca and Sir Henry McMahon, British high commissioner in Egypt, laid the basis for the Arab revolt. Husayn sought British recognition of independence for "the Arab countries" and an Arab caliphate. McMahon expressed a vague willingness to approve the Arab caliphate with reservations about the districts of Mersin and Adana; "portions of Syria lying to the west of the districts of Damascus, Homs, Hama, and Aleppo"; the provinces of Baghdad and Basra; and territories where the French had interests. The exception about parts of Syria lying west of the four cities proved especially contentious. In the letters, the Arabic term used to signify "district" (*wilayah*) was the same as the official Ottoman term for "province" (*vilayet*). The letters applied the term in that sense to Baghdad and Basra, both of which were capitals of Ottoman provinces. In Syria, Aleppo and Damascus were province capitals; Homs and Hama were not; the province Aleppo did extend to the coast and therefore had only water to its west. What the British wished to protect in Syria were France's interests. Later, the question of whether Palestine had been promised to the Arabs became equally acute. Sharif Husayn started his revolt for his own reasons. After the war, his ability to negotiate with the British was gone, and Saudi Arabia quickly absorbed his kingdom, although the British did make two of his sons rulers of mandatory Iraq (Faysal) and Transjordan (Abdullah).

The Sykes-Picot agreement (1916) defined British and French interests. It divided Iraq and geographical Syria (including Lebanon, Palestine, and Jordan) into five zones.[57] There were two zones of direct control: a British zone

encompassing the provinces of Basra and Baghdad, and a French zone including the Syro-Lebanese coast and a vast triangle of what is now Turkey, all the
way up to Sivas. Two spheres of interest divided the interior of Syria and Iraq
between France (northwest) and Britain (southeast). The straight-line border
that still separates Syria from Jordan and Iraq, drawn with a ruler on the map
annexed to the treaty, originally extended all the way across Iraq. Northern Palestine, including the Christian holy places, was to form an international zone. The
agreement refers to an Arab state or states but was neither coordinated with the
Husayn-McMahon correspondence nor revealed to Sharif Husayn until later.

The Balfour Declaration (November 1917) added an ambiguously worded,
public declaration of British support for the Zionist movement: "His Majes-
ty's Government view with favor the establishment in Palestine of a national
home for the Jewish people, and will use their best endeavors to facilitate the
achievement of this object, it being clearly understood that nothing shall be
done which may prejudice the civil and religious rights of existing non-Jewish
communities in Palestine, or the rights and political status enjoyed by Jews in
any other country."

Although commonly misquoted as a British endorsement for the creation
of a Zionist state in Palestine, the declaration makes no such statement. It did
add new complications to those already created by the Husayn-McMahon correspondence and the Sykes-Picot agreement.

Other promises further complicated the postwar peace-making as far as
Anatolia was concerned. When the Italians learned about Sykes-Picot, they
demanded zones of direct and indirect control in southern and western Anatolia (1917); the lack of Russian approval because of the revolution weakened this
claim. Russia's 1915 demands for Istanbul, the straits, and northeastern Anatolia
likewise lapsed with the Bolshevik Revolution. Represented as German allies at
the negotiations of the Russo-German Treaty of Brest-Litovsk (March 1918), the
Ottomans regained the northeastern Anatolian districts (*sancak*) of Kars, Ardahan, and Batum, which Russia had taken in 1878; Turkey later ceded Batum
(1921), but its recovery of Kars and Ardahan remains one lasting effect of the
Brest-Litovsk Treaty.[58]

The Treaty of Sèvres (August 1920) resulted from negotiations in which
Sykes-Picot trumped Husayn-McMahon, and Balfour trumped everything
else where Palestine was concerned. The treaty amounted to the comprehensive death warrant for the Ottoman Empire. The treaty disposed of every territory that had belonged to empire and at least one—Morocco—that never
had belonged to it. Sèvres referred to the mandate that the League of Nations
had awarded to France for Syria (including Lebanon), as well as to the two

mandates awarded to Britain for Iraq and Palestine (initially including Trans-jordan). After jawboning over the mandates, France had traded other claims (Mosul, Palestine) for direct control throughout Syria, with no zone of indirect control. The treaty affirmed Britain's protectorate over Egypt and annexation of Cyprus. The treaty recognized the Hijaz as an independent kingdom.

As if assuming that the Turkish people were as dead as the empire, Sèvres gave away most of the future Turkish republic. The Armenians were to have an independent state in northeastern Anatolia. The Kurds were entitled to autonomy or independence in southeastern Anatolia. The straits and Istanbul were to be internationalized. Greece was to have Izmir and western Anatolia. Another agreement recognized spheres of influence for Italy in southwestern Anatolia and for France in the southeast. By default, part of central Anatolia and the Black Sea coast remained to the Turks. But the treaty was never rati-fied. Greece had already occupied Izmir in May 1919, launching the Turkish National Struggle.

The long shadow cast by the Treaty of Sèvres confuses historians in two major ways. Inasmuch as the Treaty of Lausanne (1923), in recognizing the Turkish republic, negated Sèvres clauses pertaining to Anatolia, Turkish historians dis-miss the treaty as a "dead letter." In Turkey, charges of a "Sèvres mentality" still greet any alleged derogation to Turkey's national sovereignty.[59] However, the treaty's provisions on the Arab lands embodied the Entente powers' final provi-sions for the partition of the Ottoman provinces, and Lausanne did not overturn any of those provisions. In that sense, the Sèvres treaty's impact on the Arab lands still continues. Therefore, two errors circulate about the treaty. Turkish historians err in thinking that Sèvres had no lasting effects. Some other histo-rians err in failing to recognize that the Turks, uniquely among the defeated belligerents of World War I, forced a renegotiation of the punitive peace terms dictated at Sèvres.[60] Yet Lausanne overturned Sèvres only as concerns the Turk-ish republic, not as concerns the other territories covered by the treaty.

THE NATIONAL STRUGGLE, 1919–1922

Turkey's National Struggle consisted of two simultaneous struggles. One was the political struggle to create a united nationalist movement. The other was the military struggle. This focused on recovering western Anatolia from the Greeks, although there was also fighting in the east. Astonishingly, a people who had lost lives at four times the rate of the French and Germans in the Great War now produced a charismatic leader for this struggle. This fact has greatly affected the way the history of these events has been written. However, the story is not that of one man alone, and it did not begin with him.

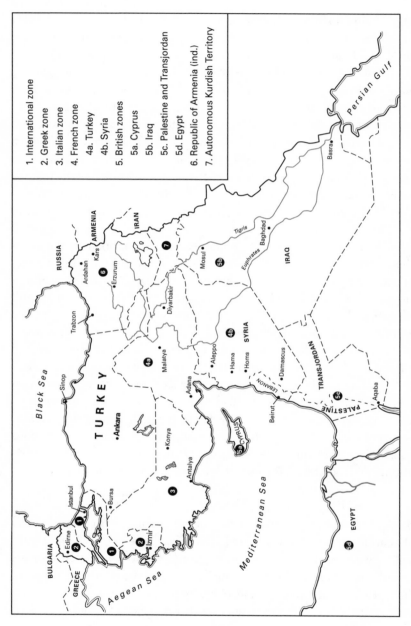

1. International zone
2. Greek zone
3. Italian zone
4. French zone
4a. Turkey
4b. Syria
5. British zones
5a. Cyprus
5b. Iraq
5c. Palestine and Transjordan
5d. Egypt
6. Republic of Armenia (ind.)
7. Autonomous Kurdish Territory

Provisions of the Treaty of Sèvres, 1920. The Treaty of Lausanne (1923) nullified the provisions pertaining to the Republic of Turkey; elsewhere the Sèvres treaty took effect.

Immediately after the 1918 armistice, the top CUP leaders and those most implicated in the Armenian massacres resigned and left Istanbul to evade prosecution.[61] However, CUP men still filled the parliament, military, and bureaucracy. The CUP leadership had worked during the war to create stay-behind organizations that could provide the basis for a national resistance in Turkish-inhabited areas. Characteristically, Enver Paşa thought that only the first phase of the struggle had ended in 1918. His pan-Turkism would take him to a quixotic death leading Central Asian Turkic guerrillas against the Bolsheviks in Central Asia (1922). During the war, he and Talat Paşa had ordered the Special Organization to store arms around Anatolia. Reorganized after the armistice as the General Revolutionary Organization of the Islamic World (Umum Alem-i İslam İhtilal Teşkilatı), this organization sent emissaries into the countryside to mobilize guerrillas, many of whom already formed bands that had participated in intercommunal violence during the war. In 1918, the CUP leaders created Karakol (The Guard), to provide postwar security for Unionist leaders and to strengthen resistance capabilities in Anatolia and the Caucasus. To prepare a popular base for defense of threatened areas, the CUP organized local Defense of National Rights Societies (Müdafaa-i Hukuk Cemiyetleri), each intended to demonstrate the Turkishness of its locality and its entitlement to the "secure sovereignty" that Wilson's twelfth point demanded for the "Turkish portion" of the empire. The rights societies soon formed an extensive network. They held twenty-eight congresses by 1920, usually packed with CUP men, but religious leaders, notables, landowners, and merchants also participated. Of the latter two groups, many had profited from government contracts during the war. Many, too, had acquired "abandoned property" (*emval-i metruke*) whose Greek and Armenian owners had been driven off or killed. Once again, the interests of conservative Muslim property owners and those of the military-bureaucratic intelligentsia converged.

The Greek invasion cemented this alliance and a national mass mobilization extending far beyond it. In the military phase of the national struggle, western Anatolia was not the only place where the Turks had to fight for self-determination. The rights societies were also not all they had to commit to the struggle. Bands of irregulars, made up of Turks and Muslim refugees, were still in the field. Some use would have to be made of them for a time. The irregulars lacked discipline, however; and for complex political reasons, the Caucasian refugees' adhesion to the nationalist cause could not be taken for granted.[62] The Ottoman army was still standing, strongest in the east, but demobilization was supposedly under way. This is the point at which the National Struggle acquired its charismatic leader.

On 19 May 1919, Mustafa Kemal Paşa, the most successful Ottoman commander of World War I, arrived at the Black Sea port of Samsun. The Istanbul
government had sent him with the ostensible mission of demobilizing military
forces in the east but a covert mission to do the opposite.[63] Working to unify
the national resistance, he sent out a circular proclaiming the national danger and calling for a congress in Sivas. In July, when the Istanbul government
tried to recall him, he resigned from the Ottoman army rather than obey. His
authority was restored and enhanced, however, when Kâzım Karabekir, the top
military commander in the east, acknowledged Mustafa Kemal as his superior,
an example followed by most of the army. Also in July, a regional congress
in Erzurum adopted a ten-point nationalist statement. Before adjourning, the
congress elected a standing committee (*heyet-i temsiliye*) with Mustafa Kemal
as president. Convening in September, the Sivas congress, crowded with officials and officers but with representatives from only fifteen cities, showed that
Mustafa Kemal's ability to mobilize the local notables was still limited.[64] Nonetheless, the Sivas congress defined itself as a combined meeting of the rights
societies of Anatolia and Thrace, adopted the Erzurum platform, and again
elected a standing committee with Mustafa Kemal as president. Throughout
this period, he used the telegraph to cut Istanbul's communications with the
provinces and expand his authority. Moving to Ankara in December, the standing committee evolved into the nucleus of a national government. Chosen as
a central Anatolian site with a rail line to Istanbul and good communications,
Ankara now began its evolution from provincial to national capital.

For the time being, two rival governments existed. The last Ottoman parliamentary elections occurred in 1919. Throughout Anatolia, the rights societies
controlled the elections, and the elected deputies traveled to Ankara to consult
Mustafa Kemal before heading to Istanbul. In January 1920, the parliament
adopted the National Pact (Misak-i Milli), affirming the integrity and complete
independence of the "territories inhabited by Ottoman Muslims" and applying
the name "Turkey" to these lands for the first time in official usage.[65] When the
Entente officially occupied Istanbul (16 March 1920) and began arresting prominent Turks, including deputies, and exiling them to Malta, Mustafa Kemal
invited those who could to come to Ankara. There deputies from Istanbul and
representatives of local rights societies combined to form the Grand National
Assembly (Türkiye Büyük Millet Meclisi, 23 April 1920), the name by which the
Turkish parliament is still known. The assembly both elected Mustafa Kemal
as its president and chose a protocabinet of ministers. He launched the official newspaper *Hakimiyet-i Milliye* (National sovereignty). Relations between
Ankara and Istanbul sank into open enmity.

Critical events in the military phase of the national struggle occurred at the same time. By summer 1920, the Greeks had seized control all over western Anatolia and Thrace and would have entered Istanbul had not Entente forces already been there. In the west, the nationalist regular army was still relatively weak and had to rely on irregulars. In the east, the army was stronger and ready to take the field to defend territory that the Sèvres treaty had promised to Armenia. At the same time, Ankara was trying to negotiate an agreement with the Bolsheviks. Several months of alternately negotiating and fighting in the east ended with the Armenian republic's defeat by Kâzım Karabekir's army (December 1920; the Bolsheviks toppled the Armenian government soon after). A Turkish-Russian friendship treaty followed in March 1921. The treaty brought the Turks gold and military supplies at the cost of abandoning claims to Batum. Now the nationalists could concentrate their regular army in the west.[66]

The regular army, led by İsmet Paşa (1884–1973), won its first significant victory in the west when it defeated the Greeks at the First Battle of İnönü (10 January 1921), in memory of which İsmet later took İnönü as his surname. Now that the nationalists had won victories in east and west, the war-weary Entente powers began to reconsider the costs of claiming what the Treaty of Sèvres had promised them. The British tried unsuccessfully to broker Greek-Turkish negotiations early in 1921. In March France and Italy offered concessions, which Ankara rejected. In Anatolia, the Greeks resumed their offensive, again were defeated at İnönü (7 April 1921), but took Eskişehir in the summer. At that, the assembly voted full powers to Mustafa Kemal for three months, he took personal command, and the government mobilized for a final offensive. The crucial battle occurred on the Sakarya River (August–September 1921). The Turks forced the Greeks to withdraw but were too exhausted to pursue them.

After the Sakarya battle, the war front stabilized for nearly a year, but the political front shifted in the nationalists' favor. The French abandoned claims to the Adana region in October. Distancing themselves from the Greeks, the Entente powers declared neutrality. On 26 August 1922, Mustafa Kemal attacked, surprising and routing the Greeks, capturing their commander and much of their army. The Turkish army entered Izmir on 9 September. On 13 September, a fire broke out in the Armenian quarter, and most of the city burned. Boats covered the sea, as far as the horizon, as more than two hundred thousand people tried to escape.[67]

Mustafa Kemal's military success won him the title Halaskar Gazi, Deliverer and Defender of the Faith. Still, military victory was not the same as political victory. Mustafa Kemal faced opposition from "left" and "right."[68] The political spectrum included everything from a communist party, led by Mustafa Suphi until he was opportunely murdered (1921), to an eastern, conservative group promoting the "preservation of sacred institutions" (Muhafaza-ı Mukaddesat Cemiyeti). The still-active CUP held its last congress in Istanbul in 1923. In the assembly, the status of the sultan-caliph and Mustafa Kemal's aspirations for control were key issues.

To master this political landscape, Mustafa Kemal deployed the tactical skills that distinguished him on the battlefield.[69] He got the assembly to pass the Fundamental Organization Law (Teşkilat-ı Esasiye Kanunu, 1921). Sometimes regarded as the republic's first constitution, this law affirmed popular sovereignty while concentrating all power in the assembly. He organized his supporters in the national assembly into the Defense of Rights Group (May 1921); most others grouped together as the "second" Defense of Rights Group or "Second Group."[70] In December, he announced his intention to convert the Defense of Rights societies into the People's Party (Halk Fırkası). In the spring of 1923, he dissolved the assembly and held new elections, in which he approved all candidates. When the new assembly met, the Defense of Rights Group, the whole assembly by then, reconstituted itself as the People's Party and the successor to the Association for the Defense of the National Rights of Anatolia and Rumelia (August 1923). The resistance became the party, and it became Mustafa Kemal's.

The domestic political struggle went hand in hand with the international struggle to renegotiate the peace.[71] When the Entente powers invited both the Istanbul and the Ankara governments to send delegations to negotiate, the assembly in Ankara voted to abolish the sultanate (1 November 1922). The last sultan left on a British battleship, and his cousin Abdülmecid succeeded as caliph only. İsmet [İnönü] was chosen to head the Turkish delegation to Lausanne.

The Lausanne treaty negotiations were difficult but highly successful.[72] The Turks inflexibly opposed any concession of sovereignty, and the Entente powers' negotiating positions were weakened by the fact that their home publics would no longer support war over such issues. Finally, the treaty was concluded and signed on 24 July 1923. With few exceptions, the Turks achieved the goals stated in the National Pact, although the boundaries prescribed in the treaty were criticized for excluding western Thrace, the Aegean islands (except for Imbros and Tenedos), and Hatay (Alexandretta). The treaty officially abolished the capitulations. It canceled the war debt to the Central Powers and apportioned the Ottoman public debt (142 million British pounds as of 1914) among Turkey and the independent Ottoman successor states, Turkey's first payment

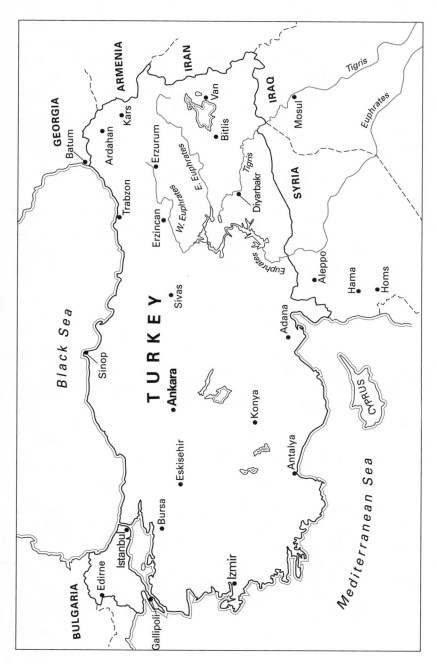

GEORGIA

ARMENIA

IRAN

IRAQ

Tigris

Euphrates

Batum

Ardahan

Kars

Van

Bitlis

Mosul

Erzurum

E. Euphrates

Tigris

SYRIA

Diyarbakr

Trabzon

Erzincan

W. Euphrates

Euphrates

Aleppo

Hama

Homs

Black Sea

Sivas

Sinop

T U R K E Y

•Ankara

Konya

Adana

CYPRUS

Eskisehir

Antalya

Mediterranean Sea

Bursa

Istanbul

Izmir

BULGARIA

Edirne

Gallipoli

The Republic of Turkey, showing post-Soviet borders in the Caucasus.

on the debt was postponed until 1929, and the Public Debt Administration was closed. Although the treaty froze import tariffs until 1929, Turkey would then regain tariff autonomy. An international commission, permanently chaired by Turkey, would supervise passage through the straits, and non–Black Sea naval powers were allowed limited passage. The treaty provided, as well, for a population exchange: one million Greeks (more exactly Greek Orthodox Christians) from Anatolia for four hundred thousand Muslims from Greece.[73]

Through the only negotiated peace of World War I, Turkey had won international recognition as an independent nation. The assembly then voted to proclaim Turkey a republic (29 October 1923) and abolish the caliphate (3 March 1924). The Treaty of Lausanne had nullified the Treaty of Sèvres, but only as it applied to the Turkish republic, not to the many other, mostly Arab territories covered by the 1920 treaty. The costs of the Turkish victory included not only those of the National Struggle but also the heavy human costs, to both countries, of the 1923 Greco-Turkish population exchange. That and the 1915 destruction of the Ottoman Armenian communities nearly completed the Islamization of Anatolia.

THE ECONOMY

The Turkey of 1923 was a ravaged land. Over the preceding century, national independence and the spatial separation of formerly coexistent communities had repeatedly left the newly independent populations economically depressed. The Turks at last experienced what other peoples had experienced when they broke from the Ottoman Empire.[74] Yet these years were not ones of disaster alone. Positive gains from the "national economy" policy and the home front experience are as much a part of period's history as the demographic disasters.

FROM LIBERALISM TO "NATIONAL ECONOMY"

English-style liberal ideas had found a readier audience among Ottomans in politics than in economics. Parliamentary government and guaranteed rights served Ottoman interests; free trade and rugged individualism served others' interests. After 1908, liberal and "national" economics competed for the last time, until the "national" triumphed after the Balkan Wars.

During its final heyday, Ottoman economic liberalism had influential advocates. Prince Sabahaddin and his followers championed individual initiative and decentralization. Prominent Unionists and the Istanbul Chamber of Commerce supported free trade. CUP finance minister Mehmed Cavid Bey promoted liberalism in his journal, *Ulum-ı İktisadiye ve İctimaiye Mecmuası* (Journal of economic and social sciences, 1908–1910). He believed in foreign investment and comparative advantage, arguing that "today and tomorrow, we are an agrarian country."[75] Although such views were common in nonindustrial countries, when he defended his views in parliament, even deputies from minority communities challenged him, demanding renegotiation of the empire's unequal trade treaties and pointing out German and Swiss protective tariffs.

The Balkan Wars and the January 1913 CUP coup marked the end of the liberal economics in Young Turk policy. The loss of Salonica, home to both the CUP and a multiethnic commercial bourgeoisie, reinforced this trend. As the CUP relocated to Istanbul, its leadership became increasingly Muslim. In Istanbul, the CUP leaders found both the largely non-Muslim Chamber of Commerce and the largely Muslim guilds, and the guilds increasingly influenced the CUP. As the "national economy" policy triumphed, it had destructive implications for minorities but creative ones for the Turkish managerial-technocratic elite. That elite's rise, one of the greatest themes of the twentieth century, is inexplicable without noting its Ottoman roots. The "national economy" policy contributed to the consolidation of a Turkish-Muslim propertied middle class and created another convergence between its interests and those of the official intelligentsia.

Influential intellectuals also advocated the neomercantilist "national economy" philosophy, whose European roots extended back to Friedrich List and beyond.[76] CUP ideologue Ziya Gökalp and Tekin Alp (Ottoman Jewish intellectual Moise Kohen's pen name) helped popularize Listian ideas. A former Russian revolutionary and speculator active in Turkey, Parvus (Israel Alexander Helphand) also promoted "national" economics. The collapse of international trade upon the outbreak of war in 1914 left no alternative.

Adopting interventionist, "war socialist" policies for the same reasons as the other belligerents, the Ottomans also took advantage of the wartime rupture in international relations to repudiate some of the most-resented infringements of their sovereignty. They repudiated the capitulations and adopted protective tariffs (September 1914).[77] Although those changes would not be accepted internationally until 1923 at Lausanne, wartime conditions enabled the Ottomans for the first time to revise their tariffs at will and enforce Ottoman law and taxation on foreign corporations, such as insurance companies that had cheated local policyholders. In 1916, the government established an export control board. It also required the use of Turkish in business correspondence, thus indirectly forcing foreign companies to employ more Turks. To supply this demand, vocational schools and courses were opened, including classes for women.

"National" economics would be impossible without domestic capital formation. The question was how to do this.[78] During the war, the Ottoman government seized many foreign firms. Inasmuch as many basic public works—railways, harbors—had been built and operated by foreign firms, some such "nationalizations" had strategic significance. The geography of the empire made coastal shipping very important. Much of that had been under Greek flag; in 1916, the use of Ottoman ships was required. Foreign investments from allied or neutral countries still had to be treated with care. One approach to this was a 1917 measure requiring partnerships between foreign and local investors. Projects that were proposed included ones as visionary as a suspension bridge across the Bosphorus, a dream not fulfilled until the 1970s.

"National economics" called attention to the hybrid Ottoman Imperial Bank.[79] It was the closest thing to an Ottoman state bank and bank of issue, yet was responsible to foreign directors and kept much of its capital in France. Deciding not to challenge the OIB, the CUP encouraged formation of new banks. The Pious Foundations Bank (Evkaf Bankası, 1914) sold shares only to Muslims and had the Ministry of Evkaf as a major shareholder. The National Credit Bank (İtibar-ı Milli Bankası, 1917) sold shares only to Ottoman subjects; the government granted it tax exemptions and other privileges, intending it to become the state bank in future. The expectation that it would draw private savings into the capital market further expressed the project's "national" goals. Acting locally, merchants and landowners formed "national" banks, of which some, like the Konya National Economy Bank (Konya Milli İktisat Bankası), also founded companies for other business purposes.

"National" economic development required new developments in company formation and commercial law.[80] Trying to create a conducive environment for company formation, the CUP passed an antistrike law after the wave of strikes following the 1908 revolution and set up a commission to draft a new commerce law, the first part of which went before parliament in 1910. Still, the limited possibilities of capital formation among Muslims forced resort to nonmarket mechanisms. The state had to act in favor of certain interests, and that led to drawing distinctions "between 'the national' and 'the other.'"[81] Fought not with a remote enemy like Russia but with peoples who had been Ottoman subjects a few decades before, and many of whose members still lived inside the Ottoman Empire, the Balkan Wars prompted aggressive action. Ottoman Greeks' contributions to support Greece in the Balkan Wars, including a donated battleship that interdicted the Ottoman fleets' access to the Aegean, came in substantial part from profits earned from Turkish Muslim customers. In reaction, the 1913–1914 boycott of Greek merchants was regarded as the real start of the "national economy" policy.

By 1918, Turkish Muslim manufacturers and merchants possessed a weight in the economy that they had lacked in 1914. This was the result of forceful efforts both to eliminate competition and to benefit Muslims' interests. Company formation accelerated with time, and the proportion founded by Turkish Muslims grew even faster. By 1918, there were 129 Ottoman joint stock companies, of which only 9 predated 1908.[82] Some new companies were highly profitable. The attitudinal change accompanying this development was momentous. In the press, many writers argued in favor of careers in business. Turks no longer looked down on commerce, especially not after government salaries fell below subsistence levels because of war inflation.

The same pressures and European example stimulated formation of cooperatives, another route to capital accumulation.[83] In contrast to the liberals' individual enterprise, cooperatives appealed to the Ottoman communal spirit and found support in Ziya Gökalp's sociology. In many places, even the small neighborhood grocer was not Turkish. Consequently, nationalist motives added to the demand for consumer cooperatives. In the agrarian sector, forming credit cooperatives offered a way out of relying on the Agricultural Bank (Ziraat Bankası), known for its limited capital and dealings with large landowners. By 1918, some consumer cooperatives in Istanbul had thousands of members. Government agencies formed cooperatives for officials, and cooperatives appeared in provincial towns. Around Izmir, with CUP leadership, producers of export crops such as figs and raisins organized cooperatives in order to confront powerful exporters' syndicates with a single seller; some such cooperatives evolved into joint stock companies and fostered other enterprises. The cooperative movement advanced the "national economy" cause by organizing export markets in favor of producers, shifting commerce from non-Muslim to Muslim hands, and offering consumers some shield against price inflation.

In 1914, as the Ottoman Empire entered a war whose costs to the state were later estimated at nearly 400 million Ottoman liras, the "national economy" policy had to adapt to wartime conditions. War created catastrophe for Ottomans in general, but it also created a hothouse for the development of the national bourgeoisie, whose party the CUP more and more became.[84]

THE OTTOMAN HOME FRONT AND THE WAR ECONOMY

For better or worse, the home front experience was one more way in which the Ottomans experienced the modernity of their day. After 1914, the Ottoman home front replicated the Euro-American experience in many ways and exceeded it in some.[85] For Europe as a whole, the war provoked lasting economic loss. Globally, Europe's shares of both production and trade were lower in 1923 than in 1913. The war's economic effects on Europe grew worse from west to east. Between 1914 and 1918, the cost-of-living index rose by a factor of two or three in western Europe, twelve in Austria-Hungary, and eighteen in the Ottoman Empire. Moreover, war for the Ottomans went on almost continuously from 1912 to 1922. In the Turkish republic, per capita income did not regain 1914 levels until 1930; real wages did not return to 1914 levels until 1950.

The economic ordeals on the home front did as much to destroy the Ottoman order as the military ones on the war front. The fate of the monetary system provided a leading indicator of the disruption. On paper, the 1916 monetary law eliminated the "limping gold standard" by abandoning bimetallism in favor of gold.[86] In fact, the government had already started issuing paper money (*kaime*) in 1915. Ostensibly backed by gold or, later, German treasury bonds, its fate was to be no better than that of earlier issues. Seven issues of paper money roughly quadrupled the amount of money in circulation, and the kaime lost 96 percent of its value by war's end. Ottomans had no experience to prepare them for the inflation and scarcity that ensued. The outbreak of war caused panic in the Istanbul market and disrupted government finance, leading to postponement of debt payments, suspension of banknote redemptions in gold, special war taxes (*tekalif-i harbiye*), requisitions, and a 50 percent cut in official salaries, later partly reversed. When the downward inflationary spiral forced the Ottomans to float an internal loan in 1918, they used all current tactics to motivate subscribers: electric signs, posters by known artists, press campaigns, public speaking tours, publicity films, appeals inserted into cigarette packs, films, and promotional songs, including a "Loan March" (İstikraz Marşı). Raising 18 million lira, the loan campaign succeeded. Used to retire large amounts of paper money, the loan improved the monetary situation; still, one more issue of paper money followed before war's end.

Government's expanded role in the economy, dubbed "war socialism" in Europe, became understood here as "war statism," a precursor for the statist economic policy (*devlet iktisadiyatı, devletçilik*) adopted by the Turkish republic in the 1930s.[87] As the problem of provisioning slipped out of control, especially for Istanbul, a leading example of war statism became the founding of supply agencies, eventually including three "national" joint stock companies to supply bread and other goods and a National Economy Bank (Milli İktisat Bankası). Istanbul CUP deputy Kara Kemal, controlling the city's guilds, played a key role in these developments. The sequence from government intervention, to company formation, to "privatization" of the company by selling shares set a precedent followed under the republic. Efforts to solve supply problems by creating agencies continued, leading to one final effort to solve provisioning problems by creating a Ministry of Provisioning (İaşe Nezareti, July 1918) with Kara Kemal as minister.[88] Even after the war ended and the Dardanelles were reopened to navigation, the Istanbul cost-of-living index peaked at the end of 1918, then hovered around 1917 levels through 1920.

As efforts to solve supply problems failed, the human consequences mounted. Those on fixed salaries fell into poverty; for officials, salary cuts made this distress real already in 1914.[89] Those who ruled the empire joined those in need of help. By 1918, an Istanbul porter (*hammal*) made as much as some generals; and two hundred thousand Istanbulites depended on public soup kitchens (*aşhaneler*). The best that could be said in Istanbul was that not many people died of hunger. Rationing, price fixing, and other methods helped achieve equity in distribution of supplies.

The war produced both its "war poor" and its "war rich." While facilitating profiteering among its supporters, the CUP government made an example of others in May 1917.[90] After a raid on a warehouse that was a center of profiteering, more than two hundred merchants were arrested and tried. A Commission to Prevent Profiteering (Men-i İhtikar Komisyonu) was formed. A new law transferred prosecution of profiteers to the military courts. The commission was not highly successful, and those penalized tended to be disproportionately non-Muslims. The CUP's simultaneous attempts to crack down on profiteering and promote "national economics" were inherently contradictory. A 1917 effort to pass a war profits tax, of the sort imposed by other belligerents, did not make it through the parliament until 1919, after the war and after the CUP government fell.

The Ottoman home front experience also emulated that of the other belligerents in its effects on women.[91] Women had always worked in agriculture; now they had to take over for conscripted males. Agricultural production dropped by more than half in many crops and did not recover before 1918, or even 1923 in some regions. In urban workforces, non-Muslim women had some positions before the war; Muslim women had a few occupational roles, mostly not highly respectable. With the war, Muslim women, too, moved into the workforce in all areas. The Islamic Society to Promote the Employment of Ottoman Women (Osmanlı Kadınları Çalıştırma Cemiyet-i İslamiyesi) was founded in 1916. Women volunteered for the army and served in work battalions in rear areas. Government offices employed women for the first time. In Istanbul, a Women Merchants' Bazaar (Kadın Tüccarlar Pazarı) was opened. Paradoxically, the government also introduced its first pronatalist population policy during the war.

Women were not the only ones mobilized to boost agricultural production. Some military units made up of either non-Muslim soldiers or women

Turkish women support the war effort, making munitions.
(From Benoist-Méchin, *Turkey,* 179.)

volunteers were assigned to fieldwork. Incentives were provided to encourage men beyond military age, including retirees, to go into agriculture. Prisoners of war were assigned to landowners who lacked workers. The labor shortage heightened incentives to import farm machinery from Germany and Austria-Hungary. Measures to benefit smallholders included forming a Peasants' Association (Çiftçiler Derneği), distributing seed, and increasing credit through the Agricultural Bank. As a result, the area under cultivation increased, but not back to prewar levels. Except where fields became battlefields, farmers benefited from the war through improved prices and orientation to wider markets.

Research is still needed to broaden the study of the Ottoman home front in World War I beyond the focus on Anatolia, mostly on Istanbul, that characterizes the works studied here. Well before war ended, the Ottoman authorities had to face the fact that their policy of relocating or deporting different populations in the countryside had disrupted agriculture and trade, distorted prices, and magnified food shortages.[92] Syria and Lebanon, too, suffered agricultural famine conditions during the war, partly brought on by locusts and other natural calamities. Wealthy Syrian or Lebanese families enriched themselves through grain speculations that played on the distress of the poor, then tried to enhance their standing as notables by providing meager assistance. The wartime loss of export markets deepened the crisis, such that most of Lebanon's mulberry trees were cut down and used for firewood during the war. Cemal Paşa's governorship worsened the tensions. Syrian men died at the front, and their wives and children starved at home, seemingly without the benefits that "national economics" brought to Anatolia. Extensive campaigning in Iraq and reports of commercial disruption and disease imply that conditions there cannot have been a great deal better.[93]

SOCIETY

Imperial collapse produced catastrophic social consequences for all Ottoman subjects, but far worse for some than others. For non-Muslims, despite false hopes raised by events like the occupation of Istanbul or the Greek invasion of Anatolia, the storm clouds had no silver linings, unless they could fulfill their dreams elsewhere. In some of the territories the Ottomans lost, Muslims also faced uncertain futures. Anatolian Muslims endured demographic catastrophe, too; yet for them the storm clouds had silver linings. In addition to benefiting from "national economics," they gained from the Young Turks' wartime reformism and the victory in the National Struggle. The period also proved a fertile one in social thought, as Ziya Gökalp illustrates.

WAR AND DEMOGRAPHIC CATASTROPHE

The Ottoman Empire of 1914, as compared with that of 1800, had about half the geographical area and roughly the same number of inhabitants, about 26 million. The comparison between the two dates implies that population densities had doubled. The Muslim percentage of the total had increased as that occurred.[94] The 1914 population then suffered catastrophic losses. During World War I, 2.85 million men were mobilized, 800,000 were killed or died of disease, and 250,000 were captured, mostly by the Russians or British. Military losses were only part of a much larger picture. For Anatolia, the losses of 1914–1923 have been calculated at 20 percent lost to death, another 10 percent to emigration, and up to half the survivors displaced as refugees. For greater Syria, the mortality of 1914–1918 has been placed at 18 percent. The rate is similar; the relative weight of causes probably differed. Compared to Anatolia, Syrian mortality seems to have been caused more by famine, and the famine more by natural causes; however, famine could not occur without undermining social relations, even if intercommunal conflict did not become a primary cause of death, as in Anatolia. Orphans became so numerous in Syria and Lebanon that the number of orphanages rose from virtually none before 1914, when relatives cared for orphans, to twenty by 1918. Mortality of 18 to 20 percent across a zone as large as Anatolia and Syria compares starkly with French and German wartime population losses of less than 5 percent each.

The Anatolian zones hardest hit by fighting were in the east and west.[95] Eastern Anatolia endured the cumulative effects of the Armenian deportations and massacres, the shifting of the battle lines, the constant losses of Muslims or non-Muslims who were trapped on the wrong side of the front or died in flight, and the insecurity of the period between the Russian collapse and Turkish victory in the National Struggle. In western Anatolia, apart from the prewar pressures to promote Greek emigration, the major demographic losses coincided with the Greek occupation (1919–1922) and its elimination. So great were the losses that the Turkish Republic's 1927 census found rates of widowhood exceeding 30 percent in nearly every west Anatolian province. Comparable data were not available for most of the east; however overall death rates there were higher than in the west. At rates exceeding 25, even 35 percent, Muslim mortality around Erzurum, Bitlis, and Van exceeded anything experienced since the Black Death of the 1340s.

In a land where Muslims, Christians, and Jews had coexisted since ancient times, the combined effect of war, ethnic cleansing, and the Turkish-Greek population exchanges was to reduce the non-Muslim communities outside Istanbul to vestigial remnants. The all-or-nothing struggle unleashed by competing nationalisms and foreign powers' interventions in the name of first imperialism and then self-determination left even the victors decimated.

REFORM AND CONSTRUCTIVE SOCIAL CHANGES

Amid the carnage, positive gains occurred in social life. Positively stimulated by Young Turk reformism, earlier trends toward change in individual subjectivity, gender relations, family life, and class formation intensified, even in the face of war. Reluctant as they were about political revolution, the survivors among the men and women shaped by the search for "a new Ottoman type" must have felt that they had lived through revolutionary change.[96]

In addition to the wave of reforms launched in 1908, major social reforms also occurred in the 1914–1918 period.[97] Under the CUP dictatorship, Ottoman reformism turned radical and thereby controversial for conservative Muslims. Islam was a frequent target for "progressive" reforms. In 1916, the medreses were reorganized; new schools were founded for kadıs (Medreset ül-Kuzat), preachers (Medreset ül-Vaizin), and vakıf administrators. The duties of muftis and procedures for issuing fetvas were regulated, and muftis were required to consider all schools of Islamic law in issuing fetvas. The şeyhülislam was removed from the cabinet; and control of the religious courts, schools, and charitable foundations was taken out of ulema hands and reassigned to the ministries of justice, education, and foundations (*evkaf*), respectively. Although family law remained the most sensitive bastion of the sharia, a German-derived inheritance law (1913) was followed by a law regulating religious court procedure (1917) and a family law (1917). The radicalism of the family law appears in its blending of provisions from the four schools of Sunni jurisprudence, in its granting Muslim women a partial right of divorce, and especially in its including provisions for non-Muslims as well as Muslims. The state thereby claimed authority to legislate in matters of personal status across lines of religious difference. The requirement that marriages had to be performed by government magistrates in order to be legally valid continued under the republic, although religious ceremonies could also be performed.

The urgency of reform in education can be gauged from an announcement that education minister Emrullah Efendi published in the newspapers in 1910: "Only those knowing how to read and write will be given teacher's licenses."[98] The gap between financial means and reformist ends was so great that it shaped the entire debate on education. Nonetheless, initiatives of the period included declaring elementary education for girls compulsory in 1913, opening a women's university (İnas Darülfünunu) in 1915, and merging it with Istanbul University in 1920. This was a period of rising standards and growing professionalization in many fields, as witnessed by the proliferation of vocational schools including ones for women, as well as of professional societies and journals for civil officials, teachers, and many other occupational groups.

Women's status animated many social debates. Women's activism and official reformism would have kept them in the spotlight, even without wartime demands. Although even relatively Westernized Muslims were still not accustomed to socialize in mixed company, the CUP elite encouraged women to appear in public with their husbands. Ottoman women expanded their feminist initiatives. Women's publications proliferated, and the women's press became more autonomous and better established. Women's societies grew in numbers and range of activities, supporting causes such as the Ottoman navy or defense in general. Women increasingly assumed public roles, and not only in the workforce. While the first women orators of 1912 probably addressed all-female audiences, after the 1918 armistice and occupation of Istanbul, women gave truly public, impassioned speeches at huge protest meetings.[99] Vast numbers of women participated in the National Struggle, some in uniform. By 1918, Muslim women of all classes had begun to appear in public in Istanbul in European dress with their heads uncovered. By the early 1920s, Turkish women demanded the vote.

For the Ottomans even more than in postwar Europe, there was no going back to the ways of 1914. Too much had been destroyed, and the National Struggle had already started. The imperatives of national defense and the common economic interests built up through "national economics" ensured that this was true not just for the secularizing intelligentsia but for the propertied Muslim middle class, the only propertied bourgeoisie left in postwar Turkey. In a war-ravaged society, where most peasants were still uneducated and politically inarticulate and where many of the disadvantaged were rootless refugees ready to obey those who sheltered them, the social bases had been laid for the experiment in nation building that was just beginning in 1923.[100]

ZIYA GÖKALP: SOCIOLOGY AND IDEOLOGY

Ideologue, sociologist, even poet, Ziya Gökalp (1876–1924) left an enduring legacy as one of the most influential and systematic modern Turkish thinkers. He served the CUP as a central committee member, but his early death prevented his serving the Turkish republic for long. That fact may have deprived him of recognition as the republic's official ideologue. Or else, early death may have perpetuated his influence by turning him into a symbol, who could not criticize later admirers' uses of his ideas. Gökalp produced the worldview that framed a long series of ideologies and philosophies. CUP Unionism (1908–1918), early republican Kemalism through 1950, its continuations among the political

Ziya Gökalp, ideologue and pioneer sociologist.
(Collection of the author.)

and military elites, even the Nationalist Action Party's ultranationalism–all are variations on his thought. One reason for Gökalp's enduring impact must be that he formulated appealing answers to the two key questions of nationalist politics: How should the nation be governed, and who make up the nation?

Gökalp was Turkey's first sociologist. For him, ideology and sociology went together: sociology was a science not only of society but also for society, a science that should serve to solve society's problems.[101] Gökalp's thought combined original insights with inspirations from contemporary European thinkers. Above all, French sociologist Émile Durkheim (1858–1916) inspired Gökalp to become Turkey's founding sociologist. Until Gökalp discovered Durkheim around 1910, nineteenth-century liberalism remained the most advanced European political ideology widely current among Ottomans, despite its mismatch with the Ottomans' economic needs and communalistic values. At a time when European thinkers also questioned liberalism, Gökalp found a new alternative in Durkheim's solidaristic corporatism. Gökalp then also created a "synthesis of Turkism, Islamism, and Modernism," which became "the only plausible, comprehensive cognitive map for Turkey's passage from . . . empire into . . . nation-state."[102]

To the Young Turks, who promoted constitutionalism as their symbol of modernity, Gökalp offered corporatism as an alternative to both liberal individualism and Marxist class conflict. Corporatism called for a society in which "all the agents of the same industry" would be "united and organized into a single body," which Durkheim termed a "corporation" in the sense of an occupational group.[103] These "corporations" would unite all who worked in a given sector irrespective of class and form intermediary groups between the individual and the state. As a way to promote labor-management cooperation rather than class conflict, corporatism was anti-Marxist. While compatible with capitalism economically, corporatism was antiliberal in providing an alternative to the individualism that made Ottomans uneasy. In time, corporatism developed two variants, solidaristic and fascistic. Solidaristic corporatism, advocated by Durkheim and Gökalp, is democratic; here the occupational groups serve as organs of civil society and protect the individual from the state. In the fascistic version, the occupational "corporations" become organs of state control. Solidarism is compatible with a functioning parliamentary system in which the delegates represent occupational groups, rather than other types of constituencies. Gökalp prescribed a "confederation of corporations" with a "general assembly."[104] Fascism would control any parliament from above.

Gökalp's social solidarism (*ictimai tesanütçülük*) suited his environment very well. It could fit within the framework of Young Turk constitutionalism. It meshed with the communalism of Turkish society. His thought expressed the Young Turks' and later the Kemalists' ambivalence about revolution. For Gökalp, the Turks had experienced *inkılap*, meaning not revolution but "accelerated evolutionary change" or "transformation."[105] He saw the members of society as reacting to transformism (*inkılapçılık*) either as "transformists" or as "traditionalists," an insight evocative of the two currents of change emphasized in this study. The ideological principles later known as the "six arrows" (*altı ok*) of republicanism—nationalism, republicanism, laicism, statism, populism, and "transformism"—have their origins in Gökalp. For him, unlike the later republican elite, *halkçılık* meant not only "populism" but also "democracy." Nationality for Gökalp is based on ties of culture, not blood or race; he also condemned social Darwinism and made a case for peace and cooperation among nations. These and other facets of his thought confirm the pluralistic nature of Gökalp's corporatism and the nonchauvinistic nature of his nationalism. His later emulators did not equate populism (*halkçılık*) with democracy at all; yet his benign example may help explain how Turkey managed succeeding decades without the self-inflicted catastrophes endured by Germany, Italy, and Japan.

The insights Gökalp derived from Durkheimian sociology gave him new answers not only to the essential nationalist question of governance but also to that of identity. He published his best-known ideas on that question, first as a series of articles (1912–1914), later as a book on "Becoming Turkish, Islamic, and Modern" (*Türkleşmek, İslamlaşmak, Muasırlaşmak*, 1918).[106] He also published a later work elaborating on the "Principles of Turkism" (*Türkçülüğün Esasları*, 1923). Nonetheless his reflections on Turkishness, Islam, and modernity still resonate for their more inclusive perspective on the Turks' place in the world.

At a time when many Ottomans were unsure how to combine or choose among competing collective identity concepts, Gökalp drew on his sociological theory to show how his readers could be at once Turkish, Islamic, and modern. Gökalp, like Durkheim, saw modernity as characterized by increasing structural and functional differentiation, occurring at both the cultural (national) and civilizational (international) levels. For Gökalp, Turkism, Islamism, and modernism were the three ideals that the Turks needed to define their identity, and the processes of differentiation operating on the levels of culture and civilization defined the planes on which they must do so. On the national level, different peoples were creating their own cultures by division of labor; the Turks were belated in being the last Ottoman people to do so. On the civilizational level, international orders defined in terms of religion were being displaced by the new internationalism of modern science.

If nationalism was redefining cultures, and modern science was replacing religion as the hegemonic ideal defining civilization, where did religion fit in? Unlike the radical Ottoman secularists' "scientific materialism," Gökalp's sociology, like Durkheim's, assumed religion as an enduring reality. For Gökalp, if civilization was no longer defined by religion, then its significance lay primarily on the level of culture, which was the level of the nation. Religion also still formed international bonds among coreligionists, as Islam did for the Islamic community (*ümmet*); yet religion was no longer the defining principle of modern international civilization. Gökalp's vision of modernity was secular and scientific in that while he saw religion as vital to national culture and transnational fellowship, he saw modernity as being defined overall not by religion but by science. The fact that this book was not a tightly integrated treatise but a collection of articles enabled him to expand his argumentation in different directions, enlarging on global solidarity among Muslims in one article, on cultural solidarity among Turkic peoples in another, on promoting Turkish ethnic pride across urban-rural and class lines in another. References to contemporary events, particularly the Balkan Wars, again differentiate the work from abstract theory. Ottomanism has been harmful; to the extent that it still has relevance, Turkism supports rather than contradicts it. Both Arabs and Turks have their place as peoples within the Ottoman state and Islamic fellowship (*ümmet*); other peoples are not mentioned. The essential task for the Turkish people is this: "We Turks must work to create a 'Turkish-Islamic' culture equipped with the reason and science of modern civilization."[107] Islam and Turkishness go together on the national, cultural level; and the universality of modern science opens the international, civilizational level to all.

Amounting to state control of religion, later republican laicism owes more to scientific materialism and French anticlericalism than to Gökalp's sociology. Still, Gökalp deserves his place in history for at least two major contributions. His corporatism helped make it possible for parliamentary, constitutional government to endure in a society that was not highly democratic in the liberal, individualistic sense. His answer to the urgent collective identity questions of the day reconciled Turkish and Islamic identity with full participation in global scientific modernity. His three reference points—Turkishness, Islam, and modernity—still orient Turkish identity politics.

HALIDE EDIB: CULTURE, GENDER, AND MODERNITY

Among writers, none contributed more to reimagining the Turks' place in the world than Halide Edib [Adıvar] (1882–1964).[108] She particularly embodies the potentials of this period for women. Her education at the American Girls

College in Istanbul was of the kind offered at the time in top-quality U.S. girls' schools. Compared with Fatma Aliye's less systematic reading in French literature a generation earlier, Halide Edib's education may explain not only her ability to write for publication in both Turkish and English but also the ongoing readership for her work. Halide Edib wrote one of the best-loved of all Turkish novels, first in English as *The Clown and His Daughter* and then in Turkish as *Sinekli Bakkal*. When male authors were writing great war novels about World War I in other countries, Halide Edib also wrote Turkey's great war novel about the National Struggle, *Ateşten Gömlek* (Shirt of flame).

If earlier writers struggled to create believable heroines and solve the problems that Islamic gender norms posed to their playing leading roles, Halide Edib solved these problems with unprecedented proficiency. When she wrote *Ateşten Gömlek*, set in 1921–1922, she could speak about Turkey's National Struggle on the basis of her own experiences as Corporal Halide Edib. *Ateşten Gömlek* made its heroine a victim of the 1919 occupation of Izmir and the embodiment of the struggle to retake it. *The Clown and His Daughter* (or *Sinekli Bakkal*) returns to the eve of the Young Turk Revolution to depict a girl named Rabia.

THE CLOWN AND HIS DAUGHTER

In the unpromising surroundings of Sinekli Bakkal (literally, "The Fly-Plagued Grocery," the name of the neighborhood where the action occurs), Rabia's empowerment depends on all the circumstances that could invert the normal hierarchies of age and gender.[109] Rabia's grandfather is the neighborhood's dour imam, whose daughter has married badly. Her husband, Tevfik, although heir to the neighborhood grocery shop, is at heart an actor. What is worse, he plays female roles. When Rabia is still quite small, Tevfik's impersonations land him in exile. After that, Rabia's life with her unloving mother and grandfather has but one compensation. Her good voice and memory give the grandfather the idea of training her as a hafız (Qur'an reciter), practically the only prestigious traditional public role for Muslim women. As Rabia's fame spreads, the neighborhood's wealthiest residents, Minister of Security Selim Paşa and his wife take an interest in her education. Rabia finds herself studying music with Vehbi Efendi, an elderly Mevlevi dervish, and Peregrini, a former monk turned music master. The two men embody East-West cultural choices, but their philosophical natures make the choices complementary.

After her father's return from exile, Rabia moves in with him and runs the grocery shop. Another marginal male, the dwarf Rakim, also a performer, shares in the household and Tevfik's theatricals. Addressing her father by his given name, Rabia assumes mastery of this bizarre household, while continuing her musical studies and public performances in Istanbul's greatest mosques. When her age requires it, she adopts the poor working women's outer dress: a loose black cape, white head cloth, and black veil, always thrown back by working women. Rabia is approaching the age when she must restrict her contacts with non-kin males of marriageable age. As a non-Muslim, Peregrini could not marry a Muslim woman. Still, the thought of no longer seeing him troubles her especially.

The tensions of impending revolution swirl around the characters. Selim Paşa and his wife are the neighborhood's benefactors. Yet their son is a Young Turk conspirator. Rabia's father, Tevfik, in female disguise, has been caught carrying documents for him. Both men are exiled to Damascus; if Selim Paşa were not the minister of security, their fates might have been worse. Those left behind worry about Rabia, none more than Peregrini. When he confides in the old dervish, Vehbi Efendi says that Peregrini should marry her. However to do so, he would have to convert, not something to do lightly. As Rabia's musical opportunities expand, she begins performing the much-loved Turkish "Ode on the Prophet's Nativity" (*Mevlud-i Şerif*), introducing a new modulation into her rendition. The change of tonality expresses her feelings for Peregrini. After much soul-searching, he proposes. She accepts on condition that he convert and they remain in Istanbul. He converts, taking the name Osman, and they marry.

When she realizes she is pregnant, they refurbish and move into her late grandfather's house. Complications of her pregnancy force her to undergo examination by two paragons of "German" medical science from the Imperial Medical School. They report that her alternatives are abortion or caesarean section. Osman fears for her life, but Rabia will hear nothing of abortion. Rabia's condition becomes steadily more perilous, but she undergoes the operation in late winter and becomes the mother of a son. The 1908 revolution occurs the following July. Among many amnestied exiles, Rabia's father, Tevfik, returns home to learn he has a grandson.

Ahmed Midhat brought non-Muslim women together with Muslim men in his novels, but Halide Edib found an irreproachably authentic way to do the opposite. Once again, the hero's and heroine's happiness does not suffice without the greater social good; and their son's difficult birth foreshadows the advent of the revolutionary utopia of freedom and modernity.

SHIRT OF FLAME

In writing Turkey's most memorable war novel, *Ateşten Gömlek* (Shirt of flame), Halide Edib again foregrounded her heroine. Today's readers may find the story melodramatic. Early readers probably read this story as their own.

The story opens in November 1921 in Istanbul with scenes from the life of Peyami, an unheroic young man whose name is not even revealed until other, bolder characters have been introduced. Peyami is the son of an Istanbul society lady. He is a foreign ministry official. His personality "smells of yellow paper" (1), and he furtively envies the veterans he knows (14). Still unmarried at thirty-six, he has evaded all his mother's efforts to find a bride, including her attempt to marry him to a somewhat "provincial" (*vilayetli*) cousin from Izmir, Ayşe.

By the end of the novel, Peyami is a changed man. Most of the novel consists of flashbacks. At last a veteran who has lost both legs, he lies in a military hospital in Ankara. He remembers the past and rereads letters and diary entries from November 1921 through April 1922 as he awaits an operation to remove a bullet from his skull. His prognosis is bleak.

The narrative chronology of the novel extends back to 1919 and the Greek invasion of Izmir. Its effects make themselves felt immediately, even in Peyami's circle. His "provincial" cousin Ayşe has by then married someone else and had a son. Now, the Greeks have killed both the husband and the son.

Halide Edib [Adıvar]. On the left, a stylish portrait inscribed to Grace Ellison, December 1913. On the right: Halide Edib speaking at the 1919 Sultan Ahmet protest meeting attended by the leading characters of her novel *Ateşten Gömlek.* The banner attached to the rostrum proclaims Wilson's twelfth point: "The Turkish portion of the present Ottoman Empire should be assured a secure sovereignty." (Left, Ellison, *Harem;* right, photographer unknown, a widely published photograph of the period.)

Ayşe arrives in Istanbul just in time for the huge Sultan Ahmet protest meeting
(6 June 1919). All in black and with her arm in a sling, she goes to the meeting
with her brother Cemal and cousin Peyami. Together they brave the streets of
Beyoğlu, where the local Christians, confident of British and French support,
show open contempt for Turks (26). After her return to Peyami's mother's salon
in the chic neighborhood of Şişli, Ayşe's strength of character so impresses the
young soldiers that they kneel and dedicate their swords to her. İhsan Bey, the
most heroic, leads the others in swearing not to resheath their swords until they
recapture Izmir (40).

Throughout the rest of the book, Ayşe embodies the wounded nation that
must be rescued. All the men are in love with her, just as they are with the
cause that she embodies. They worship her (71). They kiss her hand, a gesture
of respect that Ottoman etiquette reserved for elders or superiors of either sex.
All the characters in the book are wearing their own shirts of flame, a much-
repeated phrase; the heroic İhsan's has been ignited by Ayşe's eyes.[110] But the
cause comes first. In contrast to Namık Kemal's *Vatan* (1873), in which the hero
loves the fatherland and the heroine loves him, here Ayşe personifies the fatherland, all the men love her, and it is she who sees only the national ideal.

The Entente occupation of Istanbul has created a topsy-turvy world. Enemy
battleships anchor in the Bosphorus; colonial troops wander the streets (51);
machine guns aim downward from the balconies of minarets (58); non-Muslim
children make fun of Ottoman uniforms (60); the sultan-caliph behaves like the
"caliph of the English" (67). The arbitrary home searches and evictions force Ayşe
into hiding. Falling sick with typhus, Peyami awakens to discover the city occupied (53–55). He reestablishes contact with Ayşe and another friend; they flee the
city to join the National Struggle. From now on, Ayşe is a nurse (73), and the men
are soldiers. Peyami receives his weapons training in the field and proves himself
on his first important mission to transport munitions forward to the front.

Inasmuch as Turks divided on whether they had experienced revolution
(*ihtilal*) or reformist transformation (*inkılap*), part of the excitement of *Ateşten
Gömlek* comes from Halide Edib's insistent use of the term *ihtilal*. However,
ihtilal means not only "revolution"; secondarily, it also means "disorder" or "dis-
turbance." The role of undisciplined irregulars in the National Struggle means
that not all instances of *ihtilal* actually support the nationalist cause. Debates
among the characters in the novel oscillate between the opposing meanings of
the term, emphasizing the need for discipline.[111]

Danger is everywhere, and not only from the advancing Greeks. The linger-
ing prestige of the sultan-caliph among Anatolian Turks creates a danger of
counterrevolution (*mukabil ihtilal*, 79). The bourgeois elitism of the leading

characters, the political unreliability ascribed both to the Istanbul regime and the peasantry, and the confused statements of some of the characters (91–92) reveal how far the Turkish nation still is from possessing a cohesive identity. Especially revealing are the subplots revolving around Kezban, an ignorant peasant girl, and Mehmed Çavuş. Kezban cannot understand why Ayşe will not let her nurse the wounded; later, she turns up at the front disguised as a man (114). Mehmed Çavuş (Sergeant Mehmed) is a veteran of the pre-1908 Balkan guerrilla fighting (*ihtilal* in its secondary meaning) and an embodiment of the irregulars, whom the disciplined army turns against, once it gains strength (111, 120). Demonstrating his lack of discipline and national consciousness, Mehmed Çavuş becomes infatuated with Kezban. He also defects to a counter-revolutionary band claiming to be part of the "caliphal army" (*hilafet ordusu*). Although the rebels briefly capture both İhsan and Peyami, the sergeant pays with his life after the rebellion is suppressed (128). The question of whether both regular disciplined forces and irregulars can work together for the cause preoccupies the characters as the First Battle of İnönü occurs (131–33).

Letters from Ayşe at the Eskişehir military hospital to the narrator, Peyami, keep him informed of the streams of "dust-colored" (*hâkî*, 135) men carried into her military hospital on stretchers. At different times, the wounded include some of those who had dedicated their swords to her, even İhsan. These men are in love with Ayşe; she cares only about Izmir (137). As preparations begin for the Battle of Sakarya, demands for a Greek-speaking photographer bring Peyami to the front again. As the scene passes in front of him "like a cinema film" (*bir sinema şeridi gibi*, 153) and planes pass overhead, he sets his intention on getting wounded (156). He encounters İhsan again, and they talk at length about their love for Ayşe. In dramatic scenes at the hospital when she was nursing İhsan, she promised at one point to marry him after they reentered Izmir (168). However, as they race toward the climactic battles, jealousies and tensions intervene. Eventually she tells İhsan that they can only be "travelers on the same road" (187). As even Peyami comes under heavy fire for the first time (197), İhsan and Ayşe are both killed in action. They are buried side by side, as if they were married (205–8). Peyami dreams that he will be the first to prove himself worthy of Ayşe's love by raising the Turkish flag on the docks of Izmir. Then the story leaps forward to December 1922, when he lies mutilated in the military hospital, awaiting the final, fatal operation to remove the bullet from his brain.

Among Ottomans survivors, a girl who was like Rabia before 1908 could have grown into a young woman like Ayşe in 1919, or like Halide Edib, who lived to tell their tale.

A FORT AND A FRONTIER, AN END
AND A BEGINNING

Today, visitors to Edirne, climbing to the top of a large mound, find themselves peering down into the courtyard of massive brick fortifications covered with even more massive earthworks, obviously the result of a huge commitment in resources and planning. In the distance appear the fences marking Turkey's borders with Greece and Bulgaria.[112] Two incompatible geopolitical projects stand in mute contradiction: one defending the capital of a multiethnic empire against armies from as far away as Russia; the other dividing the empire into homogeneous nation-states. The forts last saw action during the siege of Edirne in the Balkan Wars. The nation-building projects that made everything 100 percent Turkish on this side of the fence and everything 100 percent Greek or Bulgarian on the other side began earlier but concluded a decade after that siege.

The fort reduced to a historical monument, the border fence glinting in the sunlight—these are arresting images from the Ottomans' final crisis. It eliminated the imperial superstructure, leaving in its wake a plethora of nations or future nations, among which the Turkish republic stands as the empire's most direct heir. The Young Turks' reforms and policy initiatives made their name an international byword for dynamism. They gave Ottomans their first experience of contested elections. Further reforms, aiming at secularizing and consolidating sovereignty, anticipated policies of the 1920s. An undemocratic, militarizing trend also appeared in the maintenance of an unelective power center as guarantor of the constitution, in the culture of political violence, and in the dictatorship of 1913–1918. Externally, the 1908 revolution offered the Ottomans' enemies pretexts to attack, and those attacks propelled the empire toward its end. The Ottoman military scored notable successes during World War I, enduring beyond defeat to provide the basis for victory in the National Struggle. Internally, as the competition among collective identity concepts approached final, forced choices, the territorial losses of the Balkan Wars changed perspectives, starkly differentiating outcomes in the Arab lands and Anatolia, which Ottoman Muslims now had to rethink as their homeland. Intercommunal violence and ethnic cleansing wrote the most tragic pages of late Ottoman history.

The victors in the Great War imposed a peace that dismembered the empire; yet the Turks became the only one of the peoples defeated in 1918 who forced a renegotiation of the peace terms, at least as pertained to the Turkish republic. Despite the devastation, the war years also imparted positive stimuli to socio-economic development through the "national economy" policy, aspects of the home front experience, bourgeois class formation, and expanded women's roles. The National Struggle brought forth the leadership and institutions for a new nation. In literature, Halide Edib exemplified the creativity of this period and its significance for women. In social thought, Ziya Gökalp's corporatism offered a blueprint for a constitutional government adapted to Turkish societal norms. His reflections on Turkishness, Islam, and modernity defined the reference points in relation to which radicals and conservatives charted their course into their post-Ottoman future.

5

THE EARLY REPUBLIC

Founded amid devastation, by 1939 the Turkish republic arguably became the second most successful independent developing nation outside Europe and North America, outstripped only by Japan. Turkey under Atatürk produced evolutionary change in institutions and elites, substituted a secular national republic for the Islamic empire, reformed society extensively, and wrought a cultural climacteric in its alphabet and language reforms. These measures severed the imperial past from the national future, lastingly politicizing language and culture. Founded in stark conditions, the republic displayed developmental shortfalls: a single-party regime, top-down "populist" mass mobilization, external economic dependency severed with little growth to show. Arguably, even the laws emancipating women were required by Turkey's war-battered demographics. The republic did have visionary leaders, who responded to the depression by inventing the statist economic policy—protectionist import substitution, central planning, state initiative in key sectors—that set the standard for developing countries until the 1980s. Also politically beneficial, this policy probably saved Turkey from the 1930s regime crises seen in other, comparable developing countries.

The republican elites' official laicism and elitist "populism" illustrate their determination to force-march the Turkish people upward and onward toward their vision of modernity. Any who resisted were dealt with harshly and excluded from the teleological national narrative. That did not stop the most influential religious thinker in more than a century from defying this secularizing teleology at just this time. Said Nursi (1873–1960) had his own vision of modernity. A leading literary figure, Ahmet Hamdi Tanpınar (1901–1962) also showed a capability for irony and self-reflection that distanced him from early republican convention. He probed the intersections of old and new in his futurist fantasy about a

"Chronometric Institute," *Saatleri Ayarlama Enstitüsü*—just what Turkey needed to get it up to speed.

POLITICS, DOMESTIC AND INTERNATIONAL, 1923–1950

From the late eighteenth to the early twenty-first century, the 1920s and 1930s were the only period when global interconnectedness loosened rather than tightened. The Turkish republic benefited markedly from this conjuncture. In sharp contrast to the late empire, the early republic was relatively free of foreign threats until menaced by fascist expansionism and the approach of World War II. Even the Ottomans' greatest enemy became an ally for a time with the Turkish-Russian friendship treaties of 1921 and 1925, the last alliance with Russia having been the perilous one of 1833–1839.[1] Internally, the Turkish republic resembled almost all the world's nations in not fully exemplifying the one-to-one correspondence between state and people implied by the term *nation-state*. Most of the ethnic conflicts that had bedeviled the Ottoman Empire had been turned from domestic into foreign policy issues, however, and most of those no longer posed serious threats. Although there were foreign policy issues to deal with, the early republic could concentrate on domestic policy in a way that the empire could not. World War II reversed priorities, but until 1939 attention could be focused internally.

TURKEY UNDER MUSTAFA KEMAL, 1923–1938

With victory in the political and military phases of the National Struggle, the task of creating the Turkish nation began. As demands for the unison-voiced mass mobilization required for victory in the National Struggle persisted, opposition emerged but found little accommodation.

Mustafa Kemal proved as successful in politics as in war. The steps from abolishing the sultanate (1922) to declaring the republic (1923) and abolishing the caliphate (1924) were carefully prepared. So were the steps that turned the Defense of National Rights societies into the People's Party and the Grand National Assembly into the national parliament. Its members all belonged to the party, and they elected the president and the ministers (*vekil*).[2] The assembly elected Mustafa Kemal president, declared Ankara the capital, and approved a new constitution (1924), replacing that of 1876 as amended in 1909 and again in 1921 by the Law on Fundamental Organization (Teşkilat-ı Esasiye). The assembly passed a high treason law in 1920 and amended it in 1923 to proscribe efforts to restore the sultanate. What legitimated the new regime was its victory in the

Gazi Mustafa Kemal, President of the Republic, 1927,
signed in Arabic script, "Gazi M. Kemal." He did not add
the surname Atatürk until 1935. The photograph shows him
in his prime and gives an idea of his intensity and charisma.
(From Gazi Mustafa Kemal, *Nutuk,* 1927, frontispiece,
photographer unidentified.)

National Struggle and its claim to represent the entire nation without distinctions of groups or classes.

Opposition to Mustafa Kemal's leadership, active throughout the National Struggle, met determined resistance. The Treaty of Lausanne provided for a general amnesty, but the government reserved the right to exclude 150 individuals. Forced into exile, some of these formed an external opposition. Internally, the Ankara regime faced ongoing criticism from the Istanbul press. In 1921, the Defense of National Rights societies divided into a First Group (Birinci Grup) led by Mustafa Kemal and a Second Group (İkinci Grup) under collective leadership. In 1924, this kind of opposition led to the idea of creating a separate party. Led by Rauf [Orbay], thirty-two deputies, including leaders of the National Struggle, created the Progressive Republican Party (Terakkiperver Cumhuriyet Fırkası). This choice of name prompted the People's Party to change its name to the Republican People's Party (RPP, Cumhuriyet Halk Fırkası). The opposition party defined a liberal, democratic program and favored economic decentralization and direct (rather than indirect) elections.[3] However, with the Kurdish rebellion of 1925, the party was closed on the pretext that it provoked religious opposition. This episode may be compared with the fate of another opposition party formed in 1930.

For Kurds, the transition from cosmopolitan Islamic empire to secular Turkish nation-state politicized old, familiar differences, as had happened many times before. The destruction of eastern Anatolia's Armenians made Kurds more conscious of their numbers; and the abolition of the caliphate created a fork in the road, as the Ankara regime turned away from Islam toward nationalism. Previously, the Iraqi Kurdish origins of Mevlana Halid, founder of the most influential late Ottoman Islamic movement, the Halidiye-Nakşibendiye, helped reinforce religious solidarities that bridged ethnic differences; conservative Muslims' religious solidarity still bridges Turkish-Kurdish difference in Turkey. Under the new republic, all that was jeopardized by a Kurdish revolt that strengthened Ankara's hand to attack religion in general. Divided by tribe, sect (Sunni and Alevi), and language (Zaza and Kurmanca), Turkish Kurds of the 1920s found themselves also divided by new national boundaries that crossed their tribal lands. About one-fifth of Turkey's population was Kurdish. The Sèvres treaty included provisions for the Kurds. The Lausanne treaty did not mention them by name, although it specified that "no restrictions shall be imposed on the free use by any Turkish national of any language in private intercourse, in commerce, religion, in the press, or in publications of any kind or at public meetings." Furthermore, "adequate facilities shall be given to Turkish nationals of non-Turkish speech for the oral use of their own language before the courts."[4]

Having begun to organize before 1914, Kurdish activists formed a Freedom (Azadi) Society in 1923. At its 1924 congress, one of the leaders who attracted attention was a Nakşibendi, Şeyh Said of Palu. The Nakşibendi and Kadiri sufi orders were the only organizations that united Kurds across tribal lines. In reaction to the Turkish republic's abolition of the caliphate and its restrictions on the use of Kurdish, a rebellion erupted, planned by the Freedom Party and led by Şeyh Said of Palu (1925). Not all Kurds joined the revolt: the Alevi Kurds, historical victims of Sunni discrimination, favored the secular republic. The

Alevi Kurdish Lolan and Khormek tribes, in particular, fought the rebels more effectively than the government's forces did. Many Kurdish landlords also knew Mustafa Kemal from his 1916 campaigns in the region and preferred working with him to thoughts of Kurdish nationalism or foreign intervention. The bonds of common interest between official power holders and economically empowered provincial notables could also span the Turkish-Kurdish difference.

The Ankara government responded vigorously to the revolt. It proscribed political use of religion as treason. It declared martial law in the east and passed a law for the maintenance of order (*takrir-i sükûn*), authorizing the government to ban organizations or publications that undermined law and order. Two independence tribunals (*istiklal mahkemesi*) were set up, one for the southeast and one for the rest of Turkey. The Şeyh Said revolt was repressed; many Kurds were executed; and more than twenty thousand were forced to migrate to western Turkey. In the east, Kurdish guerrilla resistance continued. Of eighteen revolts in Turkey between 1924 and 1938, all but two were eastern, Kurdish revolts, mostly localized, although the Mount Ararat (1929–1930) and Dersim revolts (1937) were serious.[5]

The law for the maintenance of order tightened the regime's control nationally. Major Istanbul newspapers and periodicals were closed.[6] Journalists were hauled before the independence tribunal. The trials also provided the pretext to abolish the Progressive Republican Party.

After the Şeyh Said revolt, the law for the maintenance of order and the independence tribunals served as tools for a generalized purge of opposition, actual and potential.[7] What precipitated the purge was a foiled plot to assassinate Mustafa Kemal in Izmir (June 1926). The leading plotter, Ziya Hurşit, was a former assembly member and secretary of the Defense of National Rights group. Reconvened in Izmir and later Ankara, the independence tribunal rounded up members of the recently abolished opposition party and the CUP, including assembly members, and staged show trials, in which the CUP's past policies and opposition to Mustafa Kemal eclipsed the conspiracy as issues. The tribunal handed down nineteen death sentences, including ones against defendants whose participation in the assassination plot remained unproven. Those condemned included CUP finance expert Mehmet Cavid Bey. The crackdown following the plot had turned into a purge of prominent National Struggle veterans who had questioned Mustafa Kemal's leadership. He officially closed this period with a thirty-six-hour oration at the 1927 RPP Party Congress. Ostensibly a history of the period 1919–1927, the speech justified the purge. Officially published in English, French, German, and Turkish, the speech shaped historical writing on the early republic for two generations, without critical inquiry into the text. Mustafa Kemal understood the power of "history" not just to record the past but also to produce the future.[8]

Mustafa Kemal undertook radical, Westernizing reforms even as he eliminated opposition. Like a modern enlightened despot, he moved Turkey closer to the West culturally while moving it further from Western democratic practice.[9] Like the CUP leadership of 1913–1918, he preferred strengthening the state rather than the constitution or the electoral system. The abolition of the caliphate on 3 March 1924 was followed quickly by secularizing measures that abolished or closed the office of Şeyhülislam (the mufti at the head of the Ottoman religious hierarchy), the Ministry of Religious Affairs and Pious Foundations (Şeriye ve Evkaf Vekaleti), the sharia courts, and the medreses. Training of imams and preachers was entrusted to special high schools and a new faculty of divinity (*ilahiyat*) at Istanbul University, all under the Ministry of Education. A new Directorate of Religious Affairs (Diyanet İşleri) was created and placed under the prime minister. A new directorate-general for pious foundations was established. In 1925, the dervish brotherhoods were banned. In 1928, Turkey amended its constitution to eliminate the clause designating Islam the state religion. Pious Muslims had to cope as best they could. Kurdish Nakşibendis rebelled in 1925; with time, other Nakşibendis sought jobs in the Directorate of Religious Affairs, colonizing it from within.

The scope of Westernizing reforms quickly widened. The international clock was adopted in 1925 instead of *alaturka* time, by which the day began at sunset; and the international calendar replaced the Ottomans' religious (*hicri*) and solar (*mali, rumi*) calendars. In 1925, men were ordered to wear Western-style hats rather than the fez; for women, veiling was discouraged but not officially banned. This was the start of a "dress revolution" (*kıyafet inkılabı*) as controversial as the one launched when Mahmud II introduced the fez (1829). By 1926–1927, one background factor in Turkey's attacks on Islamic practices was the Soviet regime's "attack" (*hujum*) against the same targets in the Central Asian republics.[10] Turkey adopted the metric system (1931), changed the call to prayer from Arabic to Turkish (1932), and moved the weekly day off from work from Friday to Sunday (1935).

In addition to dismantling the official bastions of Islam in the Ottoman polity, the purpose of the laicizing reforms was, not to separate religion and state, but to bring religion under state control. One effect of these reforms was to eliminate institutional dualisms that had complicated life under the empire, which had had both secular and religious courts, schools, calendars, and so on. The name of the Unification of Instruction (Tevhid-i Tedrisat) law and the use of the same term to refer to the unification of the courts under the Ministry of Justice demonstrated the reformers' aggressiveness in reappropriating the old order's terms and symbols for the new. To Muslims, *tevhid* refers first and foremost to God's unity and to the believer's affirmation of it. It was a materialist assault to apply the same term to an antireligious reform. The dress reform, while minimizing differences between Turks and Europeans, invaded believers' lives just as aggressively. Speaking in Kastamonu in 1925, Mustafa Kemal did not hesitate to single out one man in the crowd that had turned out to hear him.[11] He said he saw a man in the crowd who "has a fez on his head, a green turban on the fez, a smock on his back, and on top of that a jacket like the one I am wearing. . . . Would a civilized man put on this preposterous garb and go out to hold himself up to universal ridicule?"

That man's personal story is another of the early republic's suppressed narratives. No wonder those who did not share the reformers' mindset came out in widespread opposition, especially to the hat reform. The independence tribunals repressed their resistance with a reign of "political-judicial terror," denying prisoners legal counsel and overstepping the terms of the penal code. By the time the two tribunals were closed in 1927, more than seven thousand people had been arrested, and 660 death sentences had been handed down.[12] The law for the maintenance of order remained in force until 1929.

As the reforms moved beyond dismantling official Islam into wider-ranging sociocultural transformations, other measures addressed issues of law and civil status.[13] Following the closing of the sharia courts in 1924, legal reform resumed with the 1926 adoption of legal codes borrowed and translated from various continental European countries, civil (Swiss), penal (Italian), and commercial (Italian and German). The Swiss civil code prescribed ostensibly equal rights for men and women. Women got the vote in municipal (1930) and national (1934) elections. Two 1934 laws made family names mandatory for all and abolished traditional titles of address, such as *efendi* and *bey* for men or *hanım* for women (notwithstanding which Turks still address one another with "bey" and "hanım" following the given name). The surname law took effect in 1935, and Mustafa Kemal selected the surname Atatürk, "Father Turk."

The laicizing reforms opened the way for revolutionary change in national culture. Latin letters and European-style numbers were adopted in place of the Arabic script (1928). In addition to the Westernizing implications of this decision, the modified Latin alphabet that was adopted was much more phonetic for Turkish than the Arabic script had been. As it happens, all the Soviet Turkic republics had also adopted the Latin script by 1928.[14] National societies were founded for the study of both Turkish history (1931) and the Turkish language (1932). The Language Society amplified the script change into an ongoing effort to eliminate Arabic and Persian elements from Turkish.

The alphabet reform took getting used to. Above the smiling
shopkeeper, the old-script signs announce the "Students' Bazar." The
new-script sign turns it into the "New Students' Bazar." The old signs
are calligraphic and correct; the new one is neither. (Maynard Owen
Williams, *National Geographic* 55 (1929): 94; National Geographic
Image Collection.)

With state initiatives expanding in cultural affairs, the Turkish Hearth associations (Türk Ocakları) attracted attention. Founded in 1912, they grew to 217
branches and thirty thousand members by 1925. In the 1930s, their independence
from state control made them suspect. They were merged with the Republican
People's Party and replaced by People's Houses (Halkevleri), which performed

Hicret!..

The alphabet reform in cartoons. Hicret, "emigration," is the title. The old, worn
out Arabic letters limp into the past. (Cemal Nadir [Güler], by permission of his
daughter, Gönül Tunaman, from the archives of the Museum of Caricature and
Humor [*Karikatür ve Mizah*], Istanbul.)

similar but state-controlled functions; in 1939, People's Rooms (Halkodaları)
were added in the villages. Emphasizing the arts and adult education, the
People's Houses—nearly five hundred of them by the time of their closure in
1950—brought republican modernity to provincial towns.[15] Bozkurt Güvenç
describes what they meant to his town in 1936: "I remember the first talkie that I
saw in the People's House of our small town (probably Hugo's *Les misérables*), the
play that we staged (Faruk Nafiz Çamlıbel's *Akın*, "The Raid"), the jazz concerts
by the military band, the people's library, the Republic Day Ball, the Friday night
dances, and the pingpong table without a ball. The sputtering diesel generator of
the People's House also provided electric light outside the school. The People's
House was the school for both the adults and the children. We first saw contemporary Western civilization in the People's House together with our parents and
teachers, and I think we caught on faster than they did."[16] Patriotic pageants also
reenacted nationalist understandings of "history." A later chapter will present an
account of a school play from a novel by Adalet Ağaoğlu (b. 1929). More ironic,
her account also acknowledges the impact of such events on young minds.

In the 1930s, the cultural reforms expanded into speculations about Turkish
identity that lacked strong factual moorings but were comparable to nationalist
theorizings elsewhere at the time and to later ethnic pride movements. As the
Turkish Language Society resurrected words from old dialects and coined new
ones, the language filled with new words. Although many of them did not last,
many did, and the language changed profoundly. An obscure Viennese scholar,
Hermann Kvergič, had a theory that all languages derived, through Turkish, from
an ancient Central Asian tongue. Despite scholarly skepticism, Atatürk liked

this "Sun Language Theory" and promoted it officially. The Turkish Historical Society propounded a matching "Turkish Historical Thesis," also approved by Mustafa Kemal, which held that the Turks had originated in Central Asia and expanded from there to found the great civilizations. This meant that ancient Near Eastern peoples, the Sumerians and Hittites, had been proto-Turks. As archaeological discoveries expanded knowledge of the millennia before the Turks' eleventh-century migration into Anatolia, and as linguists and historians studied the Turks' Central Asian origins, the theorizing about language and history reprocessed everything into a "national" form suitable for a teleological canon leading up to the Turkish republic, whose founding Mustafa Kemal had expounded in his 1927 speech. Although some excesses of the 1930s did not last, language and history remained politicized. The subjugation of history to state power meant that Turkish schools still teach history "in total isolation from the scientific standards and values of the rest of the world."[17]

While some of the early republican reforms were more significant than others, together they signified a radical transformation for Turkey. A laic nationalist state had replaced a multiethnic Islamic polity. An all-out push for secular modernity had replaced Ottoman gradualism. Many reforms—changes in alphabets, units of measure, clothing, clocks, and calendars—reduced differences between Turkey and Europe, facilitating interaction between the two. Despite the "Jacobinism" of the methods and some of the goals of Mustafa Kemal and his associates, they clearly stopped short of social revolution, in the sense of the class upheaval associated with the French Jacobins of the 1790s. The most divisive Ottoman social differences had been ones of ethnicity, not class; and the empire's collapse had converted most of the ethnic conflicts from domestic into foreign policy issues. Inside the new republic, the vigor with which the government crushed Kurdish revolt and resistance to Westernizing reforms left no doubt as to its determination. In culture, the Kemalists did aim at revolution, both by excluding religion from public life and by making the Ottoman cultural heritage inaccessible to future generations through disruptive change in the alphabet and language. In the long run, secular Turks would find it difficult to tame Islam or replace it with nationalism and secularism as alternative belief systems. However, the secular reformers' efforts to shape citizens and to infuse conviction into slogans such as "How happy the one who says 'I am Turkish'" (*Ne mutlu Türküm diyene*) lastingly imprinted the consciousness of Turks, both secular and religious. The early republican reformers understood that the transition to modernity required both macrosocietal rationalization and individual subjectivization; but they, too, tried to subordinate the latter to the former in order to produce their idea of model citizens.

Although the wilder fantasies about the Sun Language Theory were abandoned by the late 1940s, language reform developed a self-propelling dynamic that lasted decades longer and only recently has shown signs of a vague stabilization. For this reason, a recent study characterizes the Turkish language reform as "a catastrophic success." What was most "catastrophic" was a paradox seldom noted in Turkey: failure to stabilize the literary language interferes with the cultural nationalist goal of endowing the Turks with a great—and accessible—literary heritage. Atatürk's own speeches have had to be translated into "contemporary" Turkish more than once. Turkish literary works newer than that, including the novel discussed at the end of this chapter, are in a language that many high school students could not read with ease today. The most radical thing about the early republic's alphabet and language reforms was that on the rapid-fire scale of short-term events, they defined the critical turning points in a revolution in semiotics that began with the rise of the modern print media in 1840–1860 and has not ended yet.

To the extent that the republican reforms were the work of a modern "enlightened despot," what made it possible to carry them out was that the president of the republic wielded essentially dictatorial powers.[18] Under the 1924 constitution, all power resided in the Grand National Assembly as representative of the sovereign people. Parliamentary elections were held at four-year intervals, but the president chose all candidates. After the 1924 experience with an opposition party, the RPP tightened discipline in the assembly so much that free discussion occurred only in closed party meetings, after which the assembly deputies had to vote for the party policy. Under the RPP's 1927 regulations, the president served without term as party chairman and defined the party's ideology and policy. In the assembly, debate diminished, many laws were passed without debate, and votes became a formality.

State and party became increasingly integrated.[19] In 1936, the state took control of all private radio stations, creating a state monopoly of electronic media that lasted until the 1990s. Also in 1936, the interior minister became the secretary general of the party, and the provincial governors became the party heads in their provinces. The party had branches at all the levels of provincial administration, down to the village. One price of the single party's power monopoly was the decline, especially in the east, in numbers of urban party organizations, which fell from fifty-seven in 1927 to forty-nine in 1935. The RPP's municipal offices in the eastern provinces closed after the Şeyh Said rebellion and did not reopen until the 1940s. The party-state monolith was not exempt from favoritism, abuses of patronage, and financial corruption, abuses criticized by writers of the period. Even joining the party, easy at first, became harder. At the lowest levels of the hierarchy, the membership reflected the social makeup of the local-ity. At the higher levels, the membership was dominated by members of the two wings of the bourgeoisie, both propertied (local notables and merchants) and bureaucratic-intellectual (officials, teachers, physicians, lawyers). The politics of notables lived on in the party's strange alliances with provincial notables, whose interests and power bases did not correspond to RPP ideology. The state-party monolith added to the discomfort of the times by closing other, independent organizations—the Turkish Hearths, the Masonic lodges, and teachers' and women's organizations. The prominent journal *Kadro* was also shut down.

Known as Kemalism (Kemalizm) or Atatürkism (Atatürkçülük), the offi-cial ideology evolved gradually. Never a tight theory, it consisted of general principles. In the long run, that fact helped maintain its viability. The essen-tial principles were defined in the 1931 party program as the "six arrows" (*altı ok*): republicanism, laicism, nationalism, populism, statism, and reformism.[20] Among the six principles, the tension between "laicism" and "populism" was particularly significant. Laicism was something that a large proportion of the populace did not want. Had populism truly prevailed in Turkey, laicism would have had to change. However, the republic's populism was of a top-down kind, elitist and collectivist rather than individualist and libertarian.

Even the party-state monopoly of politics in the 1930s could not suppress all opposition and had to find ways to deal with it. Some resistance was passive, as when citizens stayed home from the polls. Some resistance was active. In 1930, Mustafa Kemal decided to allow another experiment in opposition party for-mation.[21] Headed by his old associate Fethi Okyar, the Free Republican Party (Serbest Cumhuriyet Fırkası) aroused popular enthusiasm. Its relative success in winning votes in the 1930 municipal elections awakened the party leaders' ambitions of assuming power and forming a government. When Atatürk showed that he was not ready for such a change, Okyar himself shut down his new party. Three other small parties briefly existed in the 1930s. The RPP's top-down com-munications and intolerance of an opposition press made it difficult for party leaders to assess public opinion. Consequently, Atatürk made frequent inspec-tion tours—perhaps more to be seen more than to see. In another effort, in 1931, when the RPP's central administration was reorganized in thirteen bureaus, the second was made responsible for petitions and requests. As if to confirm the point that a modern "enlightened despot" had replaced the Ottoman sultans, petitioning resumed its Ottoman era role as one of the people's main channels for communicating with their rulers.

Sometimes, however, the people expressed their opposition violently. Aside from the repeated Kurdish revolts in the east, Turkey's Aegean coast also witnessed violence in 1930 at Menemen, near Izmir.[22] A small group of religious militants led by Derviş Mehmed, who claimed to be the *mehdi* ("rightly guided one," who will appear as the world nears its end), announced the restoration of the sharia and gruesomely murdered a lieutenant and two policemen who turned out against them. The government responded by declaring martial law in the vicinity and embarking on a witch hunt against suspects likely and unlikely, from the Free Republican Party to the Nakşibendi religious order. The preeminent Nakşibendi Şeyh Esad, aged eighty-four, with no plausible connection to an incident so unlike his order, died in prison. Of those charged in the case, thirty-four were hanged; forty-one received prison sentences. Blaming one of the most serious-minded religious orders for the acts of village millenarians was typical of an official attitude that equated the most learned religiosity with reaction and superstition, intending to replace the lot of them with scientific materialism and modern nationalism.

The rigidities that set in as the leadership aged in power did not preclude significant policy innovations. Announced in the 1931 party program and fully implemented with the first five-year plan in 1933, the statist economic policy (*devletçilik*) not only constituted the republic's first significant innovation in economic policy. It also made a significant show of leadership in response to the 1929 depression. Fuller analysis of the policy belongs in the discussion of economic history, below. However, statism also had political significance, which comparison with other developing countries reveals. At a time when nationalist leaders of similar mentality were failing to respond to the world economic crisis and being overthrown, replaced by dictators as in Brazil and Argentina, or militarists as in Japan, statism may have saved Turkey from succumbing to a serious regime crisis. The quality of Turkey's post-1918 leadership proved itself again in the 1930s, even if single-party rule otherwise had much to its discredit.

As in economics, cultural initiatives of the 1930s also displayed significant creativity, some of which provided alternative, nonpolitical channels for participating in national modernity. This creativity assumed material form in architecture, especially in Ankara's transformation from country town to national capital. "Republican Ankara in the 1930s was one of the earliest manifestations of the historical alliance of modernism with nation building and state power."[23] The Ottoman revivalist "national" style of the 1920s had already endowed Ankara and other cities with distinguished buildings. With the 1929 depression and the consolidation of single-party control, however, came a rejection of neo-Ottomanism and a "new architecture" using the unadorned "cubic" forms of European modernism to express Turkey's transformation. Ankara's urban fabric was lastingly shaped by such grand projects as the complex including the Grand National Assembly and the ministries (Bakanlıklar), as well as by the Garden

Suburb (Bahçelievler). As European intellectuals fled the Nazis in the 1930s, Turkey welcomed them to build up its universities and professions. Architecture benefited particularly from the central European influx, although there was no shortage of Turkish talent. The modern buildings literally created the space for new man and—iconically—new woman to engage in all the activities of national modernity. In time, its foreign inspiration raised questions about the suitability of architectural modernism for national self-expression. A search for a "national" style that had progressed from Ottoman revivalism in the 1920s to cubic internationalism in the 1930s then rediscovered vernacular and folk traditions to create a "national architecture" (*milli mimari*) in the 1940s. Every stage of republican politics produced a shift in architecture.

Sports and physical culture became another realm of participation. Here, public policy competed with popular preference. With international trends such as social Darwinism and eugenics in the background and fascist and communist youth movements in the foreground, the government worked steadily to expand its control over the citizens' physical development so as to prepare them

Physical culture for modern Turkish girls. Both modern and respectable, the girls are wearing baggy bloomers and leggings. Government policy preferred such group activities to competitive sports such as soccer. (Collection of the author.)

for national defense and economic productivity. Through World War II, state efforts to intervene in this field progressed steadily. Addressing the Union of Turkish Sports Clubs (Türkiye İdman Cemiyetleri) in 1926, Mustafa Kemal told them: "I want robust and resolute children" (*gürbüz ve yavuz evlatlar isterim*). The statement sounds fiercer in Turkish than in translation.[24] By 1940, a Physical Education Obligation (Beden Terbiyesi Mükellefiyeti) had been imposed on Turks between the ages of twelve and forty-five. Yet several factors impeded the state's efforts to impose its plans on its citizens' bodies, starting with lack of resources. Sports also proved to be one field where popular enthusiasm did not yield to state control. Given the mania for soccer (*futbol*) in Turkey, it may seem surprising that early republican policy opposed it, not always consistently, on the ground that futbol was elitist, competitive, and obsessed with scores and records. Officials preferred physical training performed noncompetitively by masses of people, along with sports of direct military relevance. The formation of Turkey's professional futbol leagues in 1951 turned the page on official sports policies, but they helped shape the Turkish experience of national life through the early 1940s.

As the 1930s wore on, political tension developed at the top, particularly between Mustafa Kemal and İsmet İnönü (prime minister, 1925–1937).[25] Mustafa Kemal withdrew from daily politics in his later years, focusing on specific projects, and devoting much of his energy to all-night dinner discussions. He still had indisputable authority, but his acts became uncoordinated with those of his cabinet. İnönü had years of experience in playing Number Two to Mustafa Kemal's Number One. Yet in 1937, even he had to resign. Undermined by a lifetime of drinking, Atatürk's health declined rapidly, and he died, on 10 November 1938, of cirrhosis of the liver. Despite his recent resignation, İnönü remained the obvious successor, and the assembly elected him president the next day.

Before considering how Turkey's situation changed after Atatürk's death, it is essential to reflect on his impact. His dominance in life and his mythic aura after death complicate this task. Clearly, he was extraordinary. After the crises of 1908–1923 had inflicted graver demographic losses than those suffered by any other of the Great War's belligerents, it was almost miraculous for the Turkish people to produce a visionary, charismatic leader. In contrast to CUP leaders like Enver, Atatürk proved able to set attainable goals. In contrast to Hitler, Mussolini, and Stalin—civilians who always appeared in uniform—he was a victorious marshal who set aside his uniform when he assumed the presidency, donning it only occasionally when attending maneuvers. Without doubt, the true foundation of his power was, not the ballot box or the constitution, but his prestige as the nation's savior warrior (*halaskâr gazi*). His concept of the republic was plebiscitary and in that sense dictatorial. Yet he also defined the "golden rule" that soldiers who intended to enter politics should resign from the military. Under him, the military budget was restricted in favor of civilian priorities. Turkey in the 1930s was less democratic than the Young Turk regime before 1913. Yet Turkey never abandoned the forms of parliamentary, electoral government. Aspirationally if not actually, Turkey was a Western-style republic. It never veered to the extremes exemplified by Germany, Italy, Japan, or the Soviet Union. The comparison with Japan is particularly illuminating: while more developed economically, Japan abandoned its democratizing trend of the 1920s for militarism and foreign aggression in the 1930s, bringing ruin on itself in World War II, whereas Turkey steered an entirely different course. Whatever was dictatorial about the Atatürk presidency, he did not elaborate his "six arrows" ideology into a totalitarian form, and he rejected fascist-style militarism and expansionism. To this day, one of his most universally accepted maxims is "peace at home and peace abroad" (*yurtta sulh, cihanda sulh*). Among world leaders of the 1930s, the only one for whom he expressed warm feelings was Franklin Roosevelt. Although aspects of Atatürk's private life were controversial, the ultimate measure of his stature is that among all the strongman leaders of the 1930s, he is unique in the world in still being revered by the majority of his countrymen.[26]

FOREIGN POLICY, 1923–1950

Compared to Ottoman times, one of the early republic's greatest differences was the lowered urgency of foreign policy issues, at least until the approach of World War II. During Atatürk's presidency, therefore, it usually makes sense to consider first internal developments and then foreign policy. During İnönü's presidency (1938–1950), the order of priority reverses. As a result, this chapter considers foreign policy next, and then internal politics under İnönü.

During the National Struggle, when the Turkish nationalists were struggling to fend off the Greeks and nullify the Treaty of Sèvres, they sought international support, which at the time could come only from the Bolsheviks.[27] The result was the Turkish-Soviet Friendship Treaty of 1921 (revised 1925) and aid in money, arms, and ammunition. Although it was natural for Turks to be interested in Turks living under Bolshevik rule, Mustafa Kemal and his associates resolutely avoided pan-Turkist adventures; they also made sure that efforts to spread communism in Turkey went nowhere. After Lausanne in 1923, Turkey's main foreign policy complaint through 1926 concerned the status of Mosul. Britain occupied the province as holder of the League of Nations mandate over Iraq; Turkey contested the claim on the ground that Britain had occupied

Mosul after the Mudros (1918) armistice was signed. The matter ended up before the League of Nations and the International Court of Justice. Britain's claims were upheld, but Turkey got 10 percent of the province's oil revenues for twenty-five years. After that, Turkey sought friendlier relations with western Europe without sacrificing relations with the USSR. Turkey joined the League of Nations in 1932. As the Balkans increasingly became the focus of national security concerns, Turkey concluded a friendship treaty with Greece in 1930

Sabiha Gökçen, Turkey's first female military pilot,
1938. (Library of Congress, Prints and Photographs Division,
LC-USZ62–93241.)

and in 1934 joined the Balkan Pact, which also included Greece, Romania, and Yugoslavia. Sabiha Gökçen, Mustafa Kemal's adopted daughter, who was trained as a military pilot, made a solo flight tour of the Balkan capitals, showing off Turkish women's accomplishments and modernity, to celebrate this event.[28] Turkey tried to extend the same kind of security arrangements eastward with the Saadabad Pact (1937), which also included Iraq, Iran, and Afghanistan.

As war approached in the late 1930s, three security objectives stood out for Turkey: removing the Lausanne Treaty's demilitarization of the straits, modernizing the armed forces, and allying defensively with Britain and France while maintaining relations with the USSR.[29] Convergent British and Turkish priorities facilitated a new straits agreement at Montreux in 1936. Under it, Turkey regained the right to remilitarize the straits, the international control commission that had existed until then was eliminated, and complete freedom of commercial navigation was guaranteed.

Benito Mussolini's Mediterranean ambitions raised the need for Turkish military preparedness. The army's budget share had dwindled from 40 percent in 1926 to 23 percent in 1932–1933. It was raised to 44 percent in 1938, but Turkish resources alone could not meet all needs. Military financing for Turkey was becoming a competitive issue between Britain and Germany when İnönü became president.

As president, İnönü controlled Turkish diplomacy. His goal was a defensive alliance with Britain and France, with the Turkish-Soviet relationship integrated into it. Vivid memories of 1914–1918 ruled out allying with Germany. However, hopes for a pact with London were delayed by British reluctance until Germany invaded Czechoslovakia in March 1939. Agreeing with France required settling differences over Alexandretta (Hatay), a partially Turkish-inhabited region. France's 1921 mandate over Syria had included this region, and France had begun negotiating in 1936 for Syrian independence. In 1938–1939, France collaborated with Turkey in a sequence of events through which the local assembly in Hatay first declared independence and then Turkey incorporated it as a southern appendage along the eastern Mediterranean coast. The Turkish-British-French treaty was signed on 19 October 1939, including provisions that would exempt Turkey from going to war under certain circumstances. However, the Nazi-Soviet nonaggression pact of 23 August 1939 killed hopes of bringing the USSR into the arrangement.[30]

Turkey remained neutral de facto until the last phase of World War II, a fact suggesting that this was the intention all along. Yet if so, Turkey's British, French, and Soviet policies through 1939 become inexplicable. The transition from alliance-seeking to skillfully maintained neutrality probably has its explanation in Turkish statesmen's long memories and their reactions to rapidly unfolding events.[31]

The guiding star of Turkish policy was protecting Turkish interests, and the neutrality policy evolved accordingly. Initially allied with Britain and France (1939), Turkey cited a treaty provision exempting it from compliance if war with the USSR would result, adding that France's withdrawal from the war relieved Turkey of its treaty obligations. Turkey moved toward fuller neutrality with its nonaggression pact with Germany (1941). Turkish chromite, needed for steel-making, served as a bargaining chip coveted by both sides. In 1943, Turkey tilted toward the Allies, offering to enter the war, but only as part of a major—and unlikely—offensive in the Balkans. Turkey moved decidedly away from neutrality only quite late. It stopped exporting chromite to Germany in April 1944, severed relations with Germany that August, and entered the war on the Allied side in February 1945 in time to join the founding members of the United Nations. As the German threat waned, the Soviet threat waxed. In March 1945, the Soviets proposed purely bilateral Soviet-Turkish discussions about the straits and denounced the 1925 treaty. Soviet moves to dominate southeastern Europe magnified the security threat.

The postwar years of İnönü's presidency (1945–1950) reoriented Turkish policy decisively westward. Soviet demands for bases on the straits and for the eastern provinces of Kars and Ardahan (Russian-ruled, 1878–1918) provided motivation, as did Soviet troop buildups in Bulgaria, Soviet attempts to seize control of Iranian Azerbaijan, and the Greek civil war between royalists and communists. Turkey needed a counterweight; but Britain was no longer able, and the United States was unwilling until President Harry Truman became convinced of Soviet intent to invade Turkey.

In March 1947, he stated what became known as the Truman doctrine, justifying aid to Turkey and Greece in terms of a choice between two ways of life, one based on the will of the majority, and the other based on the forcibly imposed will of a minority.[32] This policy encouraged the Turks, as well as the Greek anticommunists. In 1948, Turkey began receiving Marshall Plan aid. By the time the North Atlantic Treaty Organization was formed in April 1949, Turkey was determined to join. The outbreak of the Korean War in 1950 demonstrated that the Cold War was a global one, thereby increasing Western interest in including Turkey and Greece in NATO. Turkey quickly announced that it would send troops to Korea and formally requested to join NATO. By this time, İnönü's presidency had ended, and the sequel therefore belongs to the next chapter.

TURKEY UNDER İNÖNÜ, 1938–1950

İnönü's presidency ended with his party's defeat in the 1950 elections by the new Democrat Party, which brought the era of single-party rule to an end. Some observers and scholars have facilely concluded that this, too, was a change driven by foreign policy and hopes of consolidating Western goodwill. As at earlier turning points in Ottoman and Turkish history, however, the change proves at least as deeply rooted in Turkey's domestic history as in its foreign relations.

İnönü differed from Atatürk in personality but had worked with him for decades and favored similar policies. However, World War II created new demands, which affected domestic policy profoundly. The domestic history of the war years was dominated by the fact that Turkey had to mobilize militarily for defense, even if it did not become a belligerent. Proclaimed by the RPP as the "National Chief" (Milli Şef, Atatürk's death having made him the "Eternal Chief," Ebedi Şef), İnönü reinforced state power. He reversed the 1936 fusion of party and state, but he controlled both.[33] The National Defense Law (Milli Korunma Kanunu, 1940) gave the government extraconstitutional powers, which martial law reinforced. With revisions, the law remained in effect until 1961. The law gave the government extensive control over production, supply, and labor, including powers to seize enterprises and force peasants to work at nominal wages on public works and in coal mines. Turkey's military forces were increased to over one million men, mostly peasants; large numbers of draft animals were also conscripted.

Atop the wartime economic stresses, some policy choices aggravated public unease. The worst was the Capital Levy (Varlık Vergisi, 1942). Announced as a wealth tax, it was applied so that 70 percent of the proceeds came from Istanbul, 65 percent of them from non-Muslims. It was clear that "the purpose was to crush the minorities, intimidate political enemies, and protect cronies. The tax assessed on a man by a commission operating in secret could be five or ten times his assets, but there was no recourse or appeal. A man liquidated all his assets at derisory prices, paid what he could, and went into debt for the rest; as a debtor, he joined the throng headed for [the labor camp at] Aşkale near Erzurum," set up for those who could not pay the tax.[34] In 1942, Prime Minister Refik Saydam also demanded that Jews be dismissed from the state news agency and from hotels and restaurants. The press was given free rein for negative stereotyping of the country's non-Muslims, despite the fact that these small minorities no longer played any political role.

By the end of the war, much of the Muslim majority was also alienated. The war's impact on different strata of society illustrates why the demand for a change of regime prevailed by 1950. The vast majority of the populace, the peasantry, suffered most during the war. The burdens of military mobilization, requisition of animals, and forced labor caused major hardship and were inequitably distributed, inasmuch as landowners with over 40 dönüm (about 4 hectares) were exempted. The Soil Products Tax (Toprak Mahsulleri Vergisi, 1944–1946), conceived as a way to recapture war profits, also became a burden on producers too small to produce for the market. By 1945, RPP leaders feared with reason that radical ideologies might spread among the masses after the war. Partly to forestall this, the government launched a much-publicized land distribution program. At the same time, even though 99.75 percent of farms consisted of 500 dönüm (about 50 hectares) or less, the government used the occasion to promote the idea that large landowners were to blame for deteriorating rural conditions. This tactic backfired. When the assembly debated the land reform, Adnan Menderes, a landowner from the Aydın region near Izmir, challenged the government, starting the process that created Turkey's first successful opposition party. Through 1950, in regions where there were large landholdings, the RPP retained the loyalties of eastern landowners but not western ones, even though the latter had historically supported the RPP.

The impact of war alienated urbanites, too. Like large landowners, some urban merchants and manufacturers made much money during the war and wanted political as well as economic power. They criticized government economic policy, from statism to the more recent wartime measures. In short, while World War II in some ways offered the Turkish bourgeoisie opportunities for enrichment comparable to those of World War I, the political consequences worked out in opposite directions: support for the National Struggle in 1919, alienation from the single-party regime after 1939. The situation of urban wage earners also deteriorated during the war. As military demands drained resources, the government responded with inflationary policies coupled with wage and price restraints. City dwellers suffering from these problems saw others enriched through nepotism, hoarding, and speculation. People in high office, including Prime Minister Saydam, had profited in this way.

By 1945 the RPP, which had lacked organic links with the people, was losing support; and the coalition of elites, both bureaucratic-intellectual and mercantile-agrarian, that had once supported the single-party regime was losing its cohesion. The press was also growing more assertive.[35] Whatever the transition to multiparty politics owed to international factors then, as at other critical moments, both internal and external causes were at work.

Turkey's return to multiparty politics began with attacks on the government in the assembly debate on the draft Law to Transfer Land to the Peasants (Çiftçiyi

Topraklandırma Kanunu).[36] RPP discipline sufficed to pass the law unanimously. However, four deputies—Adnan Menderes, former prime minister Celâl Bayar, Refik Koraltan, and cultural historian Fuat Köprülü—submitted their "Memorandum of the Four" (*Dörtlü Takrir*, June 1945) demanding democracy and full implementation of the constitution. The assembly rejected the memorandum without punitive action against the four. In September, the RPP expelled Menderes, Köprülü, and Koraltan for articles they had published. On 1 November, İnönü announced that the next general elections would be free and direct, so ending the two-stage system of voting practiced since the Tanzimat.

Turkey permanently entered its era of multiparty politics when the Democrat Party registered officially in January 1946. Another, small party, the National Development (Milli Kalkınma) Party was founded first, but the Democrat Party was the one that made history. Among "the four," Celâl Bayar played a critical role in easing the Democrat Party into existence. A former Young Turk, he had İnönü's trust and could be counted on not to diminish republican laicism.

The popular enthusiasm for the new party came as a shock to the RPP.[37] Hiding its iron fist inside a velvet glove, it enacted liberalizing measures and appealed to peasants by abolishing the Soil Products Tax and to workers by creating a labor insurance system; it also advanced the elections by twelve months, to July 1946, trying to catch the Democrats unprepared. Even so, the Democrats managed to win 62 out of 465 assembly seats, despite massive RPP vote fraud. Sharing basic Kemalist commitments to nationalism and laicism, the two parties strove to outmaneuver each other by stealing platform planks and by taking advantage of the Cold War atmosphere to accuse opponents of communism. In Turkish political culture, the difference between opposition to the government in power and to the state itself seemed to many people, then and since, altogether too fine a distinction. For want of an established concept of loyal opposition, RPP hardliners, including Prime Minister Recep Peker, wanted to crack down on the Democrats. After negotiating with both sides, President İnönü intervened with his "Twelfth of July Declaration" to legitimate opposition and call for impartiality on the part of state agencies. As the May 1950 election approached, contention focused on changing the electoral law to guarantee fair and direct, rather than two-stage, elections.

In May 1950, a fair, direct election was held, with over 80 percent voter participation. The Democrats won 53 percent of the vote; the RPP got 40 percent. The electoral law gave the Democrats 408 seats in the assembly and the Republicans 69.[38] The Democrat Party carried the western, developed part of Turkey; the RPP carried only eastern provinces, where local notables functioned as RPP power brokers. A military coup could probably have been arranged. Sensing the course of history, İnönü accepted the return to multiparty politics (last experienced 1908–1913) and went into opposition. The elite that had governed Turkey since 1908 had split; the propertied elements, which had benefited from decades of effort at bourgeois class formation, had succeeded the bureaucratic intelligentsia, which had ruled since 1908. İnönü's defeat was Turkey's victory.

İsmet İnönü and his family, 1940. Between the president (right) and his wife, Mevhibe (left), are their children; younger son Ömer (left), daughter Özden (center), and elder son Erdal (right). (Photograph by Margaret Bourke-White, Time & Life Pictures/Getty Images.)

Like Atatürk, İsmet İnönü (1884–1973) left a complex legacy; and his longevity gave him decades more to influence Turkish politics. Assessments of İnönü differ in ways that are significant for the interpretation of this period. To one critic, İnönü was "one of the most Machiavellian *Realpolitik* figures in Turkish history." After the record İnönü compiled as "the infamous 'National Chief' of the single-party era known for his hard-liner political attitudes," he sensed the course of history and "did not resist" the transition to multiparty politics.[39] In another interpretation, İnönü sought to control the transition, establish a tame opposition, and exclude the entire left and objectionable segments of the right; but the surge of support for the Democrats got out of control.[40] A more favorable interpretation sees in the İnönü presidency neither a "complete suppression of dissent" nor a "truly open, representative democracy," but rather "a path to multi-party politics, a truncated form of democracy, the promise of which has yet to be fulfilled."[41] Another scholar goes further, arguing that after "the national revolution of Atatürk, the democratic revolution of İnönü" was Turkey's second revolution. Ending the single-party regime, far from a cynical response to postwar conditions, fulfilled a goal İnönü had held ever since becoming president in 1938.[42]

Such divergent interpretations point anew to the preeminence of constitutions and parliaments as symbols of a political modernity inspired only partly by European liberalism. Much of the inspiration was authoritarian, corporatist, and defensive of state power. One of the most democratic things about İnönü was that he retained his focus on the symbols of parliamentary, constitutional government throughout his life.

THE ECONOMY AND STATISM

Early republican economic history divides into two phases. The first (1923–1929) was a time of reconstruction and openness to foreign trade and investment. Responding to the global depression, the second (1929–1950) introduced the innovative policy model of statism (*devletçilik*). Wartime and postwar conditions introduced variations. In economic policy, however, no change as momentous as the advent of statism occurred before the turn toward privatization in the 1980s.[43] The historical significance of statism has to be appreciated in both national and global perspectives.

ECONOMIC RECONSTRUCTION, 1923–1929

In the 1920s, the republic did not deviate markedly from the Young Turk "national economy" policy.[44] The Lausanne treaty did restrict options in two important respects. Turkey would not regain autonomy to set tariffs until

1929. Then it would also have to begin repaying its share of the Ottoman debt. At Lausanne, no one foresaw how economic conditions would change in 1929.

The Izmir Economic Congress (1923) indicated key themes for that decade. It brought the Ankara power elite together with businessmen from Istanbul and Izmir, major economic centers isolated from Ankara during the National Struggle. Its debates adapted the "national economy" concept to the new republic. As for the interests of workers and peasants, the congress took matters forcefully in hand by organizing the representation of cultivators, merchants, manufacturers, and workers on a corporatist basis. Each group voted as a block, and big capitalists and landowners headed the organizations representing workers and peasants.[45]

Notable examples illustrate the workings of "national economics" in this period. The trade agreement accompanying the Lausanne treaty froze tariffs, prohibited different rates on imported and domestic products, and allowed exceptions only for goods where the state established monopolies to generate revenue. To strengthen Turkish capitalists, the government established monopolies over many goods and services, from matches to spirits, explosives, petroleum, and port management, and then conceded the monopolies to privileged firms. Taking politically influential figures as partners or shareholders, the firms usually earned inflated profits.

The İş Bankası (1924) epitomized the alliance between political and financial capital. Its name translated the French term *banque d'affaires*, or commercial bank; and the pejorative French term *affairiste* passed into Turkish as *aferist* to refer to the influence peddlers and deal makers, mostly veterans of the National Struggle, surrounding what amounted to a politicians' bank. As Mustafa Kemal stated, foreign capital was also welcome on condition of respecting Turkish law and not seeking the legal privileges that had turned the Ottoman Empire into a virtual semicolony. In the 1920s, foreign capital usually entered the country via partnerships, in which the foreign partner provided the capital and the Turkish partner provided influence. The excesses of the period fill the pages of many books.[46]

Despite shortfalls, the 1920s produced significant developments. One was the elimination of foreign control over essential transportation infrastructure. A railroad concession had been granted to U.S. capitalists in 1922, but this Chester project came to nothing because of investors' disagreements.[47] In 1924, the Turkish government decided to eliminate foreign capital from the railways. It nationalized major railways, as well as the port adjoining the Haydarpaşa rail station, the head of the Istanbul-Ankara railway. The railways thus became the new republic's first major state enterprise. Turkish coastal navigation was nationalized. Management of the ports was taken over and let out on contract to Turkish firms. Given Turkey's lengthy coastline and bad roads, coastal navigation was critical for the movement of passengers, goods, and mail, as well as for national security. Nationalization of railways and shipping together implied better national economic integration. In 1925, another Ottoman relic, the Régie des tabacs, was bought out and nationalized. The Law for the Encouragement of Industry (Teşvik-i Sanayi Kanunu, 1927) provided tax exemptions and other inducements for industrial enterprises. A Bank of Industry and Mines (Sanayi ve Maadin Bankası, 1925) was founded to promote those sectors.

The most important measure affecting agriculture was the abolition of the tithes (*aşar*, 1925), a measure that probably helped protect small peasant landholdings, even though the tithes were replaced by other taxes.[48] Tax-farming (*iltizam*) was also abolished; that was indisputably a step toward modernity and an easy victory for the new regime's self-proclaimed populism. As 1929 approached, government prepared new tariffs to apply, even though leading importers opposed raising duties. The government also had to get ready to pay its first installment of 15 million liras (about 10 percent of export earnings) on the Ottoman debt. While the government tried to prepare, importers accelerated imports before the new tariff took effect. The combined result was a 1929 monetary crisis in Turkey, even before the global crisis hit.

Through 1929, Turkey remained an exporter of raw materials and an importer of manufactures, including consumer goods. Open to foreign trade and investment, it was far from a liberal economy, for state intervention in the economy was already extensive. Nonetheless, the return of peace in 1923 appears to have resulted in real improvements for all sectors, particularly agriculture.

STATISM

With the collapse of international trade and the global rise of high tariffs after 1929, Turkey, too, went protectionist. For the few independent developing countries in the world at the time, mostly in Latin America, the collapse of the trade in imported manufactures created sudden incentives to learn how to manufacture previously imported goods. Economists call this import-substitution industrialization (ISI). The same was true for Turkey. The difference was that Turkey went beyond ISI to create an overall economic policy, to which it gave the name statism (*devletçilik*).

Ottoman and Turkish economic policy had alternated between relative openness to the outside world and relative closure since at least the 1830s, and state enterprise and elements of a command economy had figured in Ottoman

"*On the road of transformation.*" Zeki Faik İzer's *İnkılap yolunda* (1933) expresses Turkey's modern transformation by adapting the composition of Eugène Delacroix's *Liberty Leading the People* (1830). Now, is it Liberty or Nationalism who leads the people? She looks over her shoulder to Mustafa Kemal for guidance. On the right, the republic's soldiers overwhelm white-bearded reactionaries. On the left, a child holds up a book entitled "Turkish Language and History" (*Türk Dili ve Tarihi*), and Mr. and Mrs. Young Turkey look up for leadership. Behind them, a woman rips off her veil with a look of fierce determination. (By permission of the artist's son Sadi Faik İzer and granddaughter Ayşegül İzer; from the collection of the Istanbul Painting and Sculpture Museum, Mimar Sinan Fine Arts University.)

The Bosphorus Bridge, opened 1973. A second bridge opened in 1988, farther up the Bosphorus. (Courtesy of the Turkish Highways Department.)

Poster announcing the May Day, 1977, demonstration at Taksim Square, Istanbul. Issued by the Confederation of Revolutionary Workers' Unions (Devrimci İşçi Sendikaları Konfederasyonu, DİSK), the poster bears the slogan "unity, struggle, solidarity" (*birlik, mücadele, dayanışma*). For scenes of the demonstration and its violent end, see the illustration on p. 319. (Collection of the International Institute of Social History, Amsterdam.)

1 mayıs
1977
taksim
DİSK
birlik
mücadele
dayanışma

New styles in music, Orhan Gencebay. "Love I didn't create," proclaims the album title (1980). He did not invent it. He does lament it. (Courtesy of Kervan Müzik.)

Prime Minister Recep Tayyip Erdoğan meets with the public. The right-of-center prime minister stands just left of center in this photograph. (Courtesy of the Office of the Prime Minister, Ankara.)

Opposite page (bottom): *Alevi ceremony at Karacaahmet, Istanbul.* Alevi men and women perform the *semah* dance during an assembly (*cem*) at the Karacaahmet meeting house (*cemevi*), 3 December 2006. The pictures on the wall proclaim their loyalties to Atatürk and to the holy figures of Alevi tradition. The Alevis' deep roots in Turkish culture have fascinated Turkish nationalists. At the same time their nonconformity to the sharia and their mixed-gender ceremonies have subjected them to persecution by Sunni Muslims. (Murad Sezer, AP/Wide World Images.)

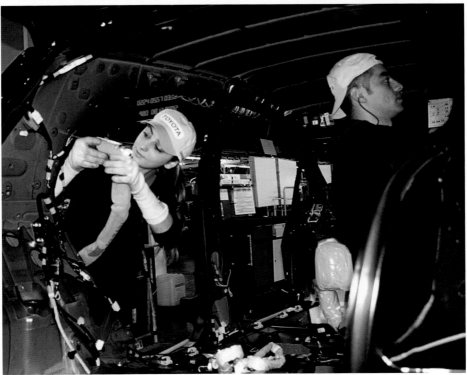

Turkish women today, heads uncovered. Scenes from the workplace and the world of spectator sports, in work clothes and in casual Western dress. (Courtesy of *Zaman* newspaper.)

Turkish women today, heads covered. Television producer Seyhan Sara (seated) in the studio with her assistant and taking a break (second from the left) with her friends. (Courtesy of Seyhan Sara.)

Secularist demonstration in Izmir, 2007. (Burak Kara, Getty Images.)

economic policy centuries before that. Except during World War I, "national economics" had coexisted with openness to foreign trade and investment from 1908 through 1929. In 1929, however, the collapse of world trade created economic difficulties of new magnitude, and the Turkish government either had to respond effectively or pay the price of failure.

Under these circumstances, one of the early republic's greatest achievements was to elaborate "statism"—import substitution, protectionism, public sector expansion, and central planning—into a systematic model.[49] The goals of "national" economic development and bourgeois class formation had not changed. However, in a way unprecedented in more than a century, global economic integration had loosened rather than tightened, and that created the opportunity to pursue "national economics" under conditions of virtual autarky. Although conditions and policies varied after 1939, the themes of 1930s statism resonated for a half century, exposing both its positive and its negative potentials.

The biggest failure of Turkish economic policy in the 1920s was that industrialization had not advanced beyond Ottoman levels. As a result, although Turkey was part of the original home region of wheat-based agriculture, Turkish millers could not compete with imported flour. When the 1929 depression depressed prices of raw materials more than those of manufactures and caused tariffs to rise globally, the costs of import dependency increased unbearably. The only way to cope was to substitute domestic manufactures for imports. For Turkey, that meant starting with the "three whites": flour, sugar, and cloth. Promoting sugar production from beets became so emblematic of the republic's commitment to popular welfare that "the new crop and the new nation-state" became lastingly linked symbolically.[50]

Statism, in the sense of a mixed economy in which private enterprise prevailed overall but the state intervened, was inscribed into the Republican People's Party program in 1931. Full implementation of statist policy began in 1932. Several important developments prepared the way. Contributors to the influential journal *Kadro* (1932–1935) discussed the key ideas.[51] The creation of Turkey's Central Bank (1930) at last ended the Ottoman Imperial Bank's role as central bank by default, and special legislation brought foreign exchange under government control. The Sümerbank (1932) and the Etibank—named after the Sumerians and the Hittites in a nod to the Turkish Historical Thesis—were founded as state enterprises and holding companies. Laws were passed to limit imports and promote exports in 1931. Much of foreign investment was nationalized. The government remained willing to receive loans or credits from other governments. As in other countries, the depression prompted growing use of clearing agreements and barter in international trade; the growth of Turkish-German clearing trade was particularly significant.[52] Manufactures and mining registered high growth rates for 1929–1932, partly as a result of tariff reform and import reductions.

Under statism, the state became a major investor and producer. Not only did it control domestic markets and support agricultural commodity prices. It also began transferring the state monopolies, mostly run by private contractors in the 1920s, back to the public sector. Rail and shipping lines, nationalized in the 1920s, were turned into state monopolies. As the state expanded its investor role, it founded state economic enterprises (SEEs) as a way to realize strategic economic objectives. A five-year industrial plan was also placed into effect. Work on the plan began in 1932.[53] It was widely debated in Turkey, and foreign models and experts were consulted. Given the apparent success of the first Soviet five-year plan (1928), Soviet experience aroused particular interest. Turkey's plan called for restricting imports and investing 45 million Turkish liras in industry (1934–1938). A second plan was launched in 1938, but many of its industrial projects could not be realized until 1945–1948. The industries targeted for development included not only light consumer goods (textiles, glass, and paper) but also the commanding heights of heavy industry (chemicals, iron, and steel). The Karabük Steel Mill (in operation by 1939) symbolized the planners' hopes.

Although economists debate its merits, statism made a difference.[54] Under the plan, growth in gross domestic product (GDP) averaged 7 percent a year through 1938. Public investment doubled in real terms from the late 1920s through 1938 and began to shift from transportation toward industry, education, health, and agriculture. Much of the growth was still in agriculture. While that may seem to contradict the plan's goals, the large state enterprises created under the plan employed only a small percentage of industrial workers; and the labor force in industry and mining (561,000 in 1938) was still small compared to that in agriculture. A significant factor in promoting agricultural growth was Turkey's surplus of land in relation to labor. At the same time that it was promoting import-substitution industrialization, the government was still granting uncultivated public land to the landless.

World War II and the post-1946 return toward global integration changed Turkey's economic situation.[55] During the wartime military mobilization, agricultural output dropped by an estimated 42 percent; manufacturing dropped by 50 percent. Wartime policies that reduced producers' incentives worsened conditions. The National Defense Law (Milli Korunma Kanunu, 1940) enabled the government to intervene in the economy to ration goods and to control prices and labor. New agencies for trade and provisioning were set up and empowered to purchase agricultural products at below-market prices. Tantamount to a revival of the old Ottoman *miri mübayaa* system of state purchasing, this policy predictably led to black marketing, hoarding, and corruption. Wartime taxes introduced to offset profiteering and inflation—the 1942 Capital Levy (Varlık Vergisi), the 1944 Soil Products Tax (Toprak Mahsulleri Vergisi)—discriminated against non-Muslims, left propertied Muslims feeling as if they might be next, and angered the agrarian population high and low. Turkey emerged from the war with a foreign currency surplus on the order of 250 million dollars, but that was spent by 1948; meanwhile, production had fallen, and prices had increased by a factor of four to five.

The return of peace opened a period of exceptional economic growth for the world economy (1945–1973). The years 1945–1950 were part of the transition to that period. Internally, groups dissatisfied with the RPP's wartime economic policies pressed for change. Many Turks, especially urban entrepreneurs, attacked statism. Externally, post-1945 conditions completely reversed the interwar trend toward loosened international ties. Responding to new incentives to seek integration with the West, Turkey joined the Bretton Woods agreement (1945), adjusted the value of the Turkish lira to the U.S. dollar (1946), began to receive aid under the Marshall Plan, and joined both the World Bank and the International Monetary Fund (1947). Now, greater attention had to be paid to U.S. experts, who had no intention of backing a command economy and advocated dismantling state enterprises, including the Karabük Steel Mill. The regime began to move toward greater emphasis on private enterprise and agriculture, which rapid "tractorization" was transforming. The government still carried out planning exercises in 1946 and 1947, but changing international conditions invalidated both plans.[56] The RPP offered a new concept of statism, reserving railroads, utilities, mining, and heavy industry, especially militarily significant industries, for the public sector but proposing that other public enterprises be privatized—one policy goal destined for a long history of nonfulfillment. Even as the global environment changed, the distinctive themes of the statist experiment thus did not lose their resonance in Turkey.

The economic record of the early republic (1923–1950), although mixed, included developments significant for the future. The national bourgeoisie that the Young Turks strove to promote was now the only one. These years formed another important period in the evolution of both the bureaucratic intelligentsia and the propertied elements, from whom the modern Turkish entrepreneurial-technocratic elite gradually emerged. In policy, no innovation proved more significant than the invention of statism. In the wake of the 1929 depression, this responded to the needs of a developing country somewhat as the U.S. New Deal addressed those of a developed capitalist economy. Leaving most of the economy in private hands but asserting state leadership in planning and key sectors, the policy reorganized the environment for Turkish entrepreneurs and landowners, workers and peasants. Starting with Mexico in 1933, other developing countries adopted such policies, not necessarily by imitating Turkey but by responding to the same needs and models. In the 1930s, to judge from relevant comparisons, such as the Latin American nations and Japan, governments that could not formulate effective policy responses to the depression sank into regime crises and authoritarianism. The significance of Turkish statism, then, was more than economic. Later, experience would reveal the limits inherent in the statist, protectionist, import-substitution model. However, after the post-1945 decolonization, developing countries around the world followed versions of this policy until the 1980s turn toward privatization. After 1945, statism still had advocates in Turkey; and an enhanced version of statism prevailed again between 1962 and 1977. Statism imprinted Turkish economic policy from 1930 to 1980, somewhat as free trade imprinted that of late Ottoman times or as "national economics" imprinted Young Turk policy. After a century of worries about backwardness, Turkey in the 1930s became a vanguard country in economic policy innovation.[57]

TURKISH SOCIETY AND POPULISM

Turkey's 1923 population had gained in ethnoreligious homogeneity but was battered demographically. As the republic implemented its concept of populism, it became apparent how great a struggle would be needed to weld these battered fragments into a nation. The Turkish nation in 1923 was no Sleeping Beauty waiting to be awoken by a Prince or Poet's kiss. To adapt the pithy formulation of a leading expert, the Turkish nation did not even exist, so how could it be asleep? If it could not be asleep, how could it be awoken?[58] In terms of the scholarly debate about whether nations create states or the other way around, here a modernist intelligentsia gained control of the state and then wielded state power to shape the nation to its specifications, rejecting or repressing whatever did not fit its model. To a great extent, the political actors were men from a middle class that was still in consolidation. For them, women's emancipation and the remolding of peasants into citizens were still works in progress. Against the backdrop of the Turkish population's slow demographic recovery, the elites set about those projects with an elitist "state feminism" and a paradoxical "populism."

DEMOGRAPHIC RECOVERY

The Turkish population grew again after 1923, although growth slowed from 1939 on. Taking off from its growth in this period, Turkey later experienced its full share of the Third World's twentieth-century population explosion. Yet before 1950, Turkey was still considered underpopulated.[59]

The population within Turkey's 1923 boundaries declined from 16.3 million in 1914 to 13.6 million by 1927, the date of the republic's first census. Turkey's 1923 population has been estimated at 13 million.[60] Its composition in terms of age and sex was highly abnormal, and the most ravaged parts of the age pyramid were those of the active adults needed for economic recovery. In the estimated 1923 data, the number of males per 100 females was only 88 in the fifteen-to-forty-four age bracket and a mere 76 in the forty-five-to-sixty-four bracket. In many provinces, rates of widowhood exceeding 30 percent of the adult female population testify grimly to Turkey's losses, as well as to its need for women's socioeconomic participation. Outside Istanbul, Turkey's non-Muslim populations had almost disappeared.

Much of the war-related population loss had occurred in the cities. Istanbul had lost 39 percent of its 1914 population, falling to 691,000. The larger cities in general—from Istanbul to Izmir, Edirne, Bursa, and Sivas—had dropped below 1880s levels. Although the urban population of the central Anatolian towns had fallen by only around 10 percent, in the former war zones of eastern and western Anatolia, aggregate urban population losses exceeded 40 percent.

Nor was the quality of life good. The 1927 census showed literacy at 11 percent. In 1924, the number of schools at all levels was five thousand, with 12,400 teachers, and 359,000 pupils, of which only 3,000 were in postsecondary education. The number of students who received university diplomas in 1950 was still only 3,061.[61] The Turkey of 1924 had only about a thousand doctors and fewer than ten thousand hospital beds. Ignorance, poverty, and poor health limited prospects for the republic's citizens, whose life expectancies averaged only 38 years in 1945–1950.

Population growth rose as high as 2.1 percent per year (1928–1935), then fell as low as 1.1 percent (1941–45) before returning to nearly 2.2 percent (1946–1950), after which Turkey's population explosion took off. The populace remained overwhelmingly rural, and the depression created incentives—in Turkey as elsewhere—to stay on the land in an effort to ensure subsistence. The percentage of the working population employed in agriculture declined only slightly from 80.9 in 1927 to 77.7 in 1950; industrial employment rose from 8.9 percent in 1927 to 11.7 in 1935 but then dropped and did not regain the 1935 level until the 1960s. The effort to form a Turkish business class produced limited results in the 1920s and then accelerated under statism. It stimulated both the public and the private sector, of which the latter attracted talent from trade, the public enterprises, and the bureaucracy.[62]

Cross-border migration during the empire-republic transition consisted more of emigration than immigration. For Turkey, a more homogeneous population was the most benign result of these movements. Turkey's 1927 population was 99 percent Muslim. Its native languages were reported as 86 percent Turkish and 9 percent Kurdish, not counting those who were bilingual (and others who concealed their knowledge of Kurdish). The Kurds constituted Turkey's only sizable ethnic minority but got no accommodation as such from the early republic. Many were deported to other parts of Turkey after the rebellions of the 1920s and 1930s, and many others migrated in search of opportunity. The government tried to force Kurds to assimilate and let the eastern provinces languish as the country's most backward.[63] After 1923, border changes did not again factor in demographic change except for the annexation of Hatay (1939), which added 208,000 new citizens. Turkey did, however, receive about 1.2 million immigrants through 1935. Some 400,000 of these were Muslims from Greece, exchanged under the Lausanne treaty against Greek Orthodox Christians from Turkey. Other immigrants into Turkey after 1923 were mostly Balkan Muslims, including ethnic Turks and Bosnians.

The steps toward forming a new business elite, while dramatically successful by the 1980s, did not change the fact that pre-1950 Turkey was rural and underdeveloped. The ruling elite that proclaimed Turkey a classless society was very small and privileged. To understand social change under their rule, it is instructive to consider how they assessed the condition of society and what they chose to do about it. Their attitudes toward women and peasants prove illustrative. This leaves the question of grassroots social changes that did not spring from state policy; the most significant such development forms the subject for a separate consideration of religion and social change.

WOMEN UNDER STATE FEMINISM

Although the Ottoman women's movement had a fifty-year history by then, the early republic gets credit for inscribing women's emancipation into the law. In a way that reappears in their policy toward peasants and all their "others," however, Turkey's elite male politicians assumed that they knew what women needed without having to ask.[64]

What later women's historians label the "state feminism" of this period did not come from only one person; yet Mustafa Kemal's example is germane to understanding the climate of the times. He resembled nationalist leaders of his generation in other developing countries in combining patriarchal authoritarianism in private life with strategic motivation to mobilize women for nation building. In his personal life, he did differ from many other developing countries' leaders in not trying to found a dynasty. Only briefly married, he had no biological children but adopted a number of orphans or took them under his protection, giving them different surnames and preparing them for different careers, so taking an original approach to being the father of his country. A civics manual, *Medeni Bilgiler,* was published, ostensibly by Atatürk's adopted daughter, Afet İnan; in fact, he dictated it to her. Embodying state feminism, she also produced a later book on *The Emancipation of the Turkish Woman.*[65]

In the 1920s, women's emancipation became a major policy front with the dress reforms and the civil code, which outlawed polygyny. No more egalitarian than its Swiss model, the new code still designated the husband as the family head. Women's enfranchisement in the 1930s put Turkey in advance even of France and Switzerland, which did not give women the vote until 1944 and 1960, respectively. The single party's control of the electoral process enabled Turkey to have higher percentages of women elected to the Grand National Assembly (3.7–4.5 percent from 1935 through 1946) than ever since.[66] Women of the period responded with enthusiasm, eager to play new roles in the construction of society as teachers, civil servants, architects, physicians, and assembly members. New forms of sociability acted out the changes in gender relations, for example ballroom dancing and beauty contests, although it sometimes took high-pressured methods to get the dancers or contestants to perform; foreign visitors, too, might unexpectedly be called on to join in the dancing.[67] Expectations that Turkish women would continue to meet conventional standards of respectability and perform all customary domestic duties while playing their new public roles did not make life any simpler.

Women's efforts to take the initiative were not well received. When women proposed to form a Republican Women's Party in 1923, the demand was denied.[68] In 1935, when the Turkish Women's Federation hosted an international feminist congress in Turkey, despite the opportunity to showcase Turkish women's enfranchisement, the government was displeased at positions the congress adopted on peace and disarmament and closed the federation. It would be left for later Turkish feminists to assert their initiative and critique the early republic's "state feminism."

"State feminism" affected middle-class urban women most directly. One sign of differential rates of change for women in different settings comes from the evidence on fertility. In the 1930s and 1940s, when Istanbulites were "barely replacing themselves," families in provincial towns and cities were having four children, and rural families were still having seven on average. However, World War I and the National Struggle had already changed peasant women's lives. Satı Çırpan, a heroine of the National Struggle, became head (*muhtar*) of her village and was elected to the Grand National Assembly. Girls in the country-side who went to school, especially the few who continued past elementary school, experienced all the patriotic lessons and ceremonies that conditioned them to be dutiful daughters of Atatürk. The still-limited radio broadcasts of the 1930s helped to spread similar messages to all within hearing.[69] Reform in gender relations was not felt equally across the nation, but it was not entirely limited to the urban middle class, either.

POPULISM AND NATION BUILDING

In republican social engineering, "populism" offered as powerful an ideolog-ical tool as "laicism" did. The challenge confronting "populism" was, however, that Turkish nation building, in any sense that would encompass the entire population, was still an aspiration. The nationalist elites were the ones with ideas about the people, practically speaking, the peasantry. The latter as yet lacked the communications skills and class solidarity to counter elite statements and policies effectively. After 1945, when the common people learned to speak for themselves, the results would astonish the elites.

Under the early republic, the elites commanded the rostrum, and what they had to say is also astonishing. An elite "populist" movement had already existed under the Young Turks.[70] For a time, a Peasantist Society (Köycüler Cemiyeti, 1918) operated in parts of Anatolia, delivering services and possibly mobilizing Turks for the National Struggle. Then, the depression created new urgency about populism. Policy responses included the People's Houses. Intellectuals also spoke out, notably Yakup Kadri Karaosmanoğlu in his novel *Yaban* (The stranger, 1932).

Yakup Kadri (1889–1974) was not an obvious choice to be the common people's spokesman. A descendant of the Karaosmanoğlu notables who domi-nated the Manisa and Aydın regions near Izmir for two centuries, he received much of his secondary education in a French school, and *Yaban* abounds with allusions to European literature, ancient and modern. Perhaps not by chance, his depiction of peasants, ostensibly about Turkey, lacks none of the filth and brutishness in Guy de Maupassant's (1850–1893) portrayal of French peasants. Luckily for Yakup Kadri, Turkey experienced a national struggle rather than a social revolution; and his class origins—which might have gotten him executed right away in Jacobin France or Bolshevik Russia—did not stop him from answering Ankara's call in 1921. In 1921, he, Halide Edib, and others served on a commission to investigate Greek atrocities in western Anatolia.[71] With his French literary readings in the background, that experience provided the inspiration for *Yaban*.

He opens his novel by stating that the commission found the manuscript lying amid the ruins, scorched and torn. The "stranger" (*yaban*) of the title is a former officer, Ahmet Celal, who lost his right arm in World War I and finds himself "retired" at age thirty-two (85).[72] One of his former enlisted men, Mehmet Ali, has invited Ahmet Celal to his village. The Istanbulite is unprepared for the villagers, as they are for him. To them, he is "some kind of stranger" (*yabanın biri*), even though he stays in the village through several changes of season, tries to help villagers with their problems, and rents a field to cultivate.

Chronologically, the novel unfolds on two time scales. On the fast-paced scale of daily events, successive episodes introduce different characters and new aspects of rustic degradation—the greedy landlord who swindles his neighbor out of her land; his young son, who sexually exploits the village's blind girl; the adulterous Cennet, who makes a fool of her husband and gets away with it; and more. These episodes, in particular, recall de Maupassant. The longer-term time scale of months and years is marked by the agricultural cycle of the seasons and the ebb and flow of the National Struggle, announced by the distant thunder of artillery, planes overhead, ox carts transporting munitions, and files of refugees (94, 115–17, 145–47). The peasants want to think only about the agricultural cycle, despite Ahmet Celal's warnings. But the war overtakes them. The time when they should flee comes when they can think only of the harvest (167–69). Greek troops march through the village twice, first advancing, then retreating. As they retreat, they destroy the village in the orgy of rape and mayhem that ends the book.

The unfolding of events enables the author-narrator to develop several themes. Far from national solidarity, a yawning gulf separates the hero from the villagers. This is partly because the hero never learns to talk the talk of crops and seasons. For him, the peasants have nothing positive to their credit. They are presocial, like beings from the Old Stone Age (90), or the time of Noah (87) or of the Hittites (48). The National Struggle means nothing to them except their fears of being called to the colors (44, 70). They will not even admit to being Turks; they are "Islam" (173). They are so ignorant that they think "Avrupa" is a queen who is trying to help the sultan in Istanbul (58, 141). The only person they revere is Şeyh Yusuf, a rustic holy man who comes to dispense blessings and receive gifts. Yakup Kadri's hero has even less tolerance for holy men than for the rest of the villagers (63–65, 141).

In the village, disease and deformity are so common that the villagers scarcely notice Ahmet Celal's empty sleeve; they certainly do not think he sacrificed his arm for them. Cleanliness and sanitation are totally lacking. Ahmet Celal's opinions join sexism with classism. The women are completely unattractive. He understands how birds and cats copulate, but "I cannot imagine how the people of this village have sex. Do they look each other in the eye, like us? Do they touch hands?" (51–52). The cultural gap between an educated Istanbulite and an Anatolian villager is greater than that between "an English Londoner and a Punjabi Indian" (53).

Modernity and subjectivity—this would not be much of a novel without romance. Could love bridge the unbridgeable? Ahmet Celal does catch sight of one village girl who has charms the others lack. He goes out of his way to see her, finding that he often runs into İsmail, the younger brother of his former subaltern, Mehmet Ali. They are both interested in the same girl, Emine. She chooses the village boy. To her, Ahmet Celal is "a stranger in the land" (*elin yabanı*); and the village has almost no young men left (98–101, 121–25). But marrying İsmail does not make her happy. On the horrendous final night, as the Greeks herd the villagers together, separate males from females, and start selecting females to rape, Ahmet Celal tries to save Emine. They run for it, but both are hit by bullets. At dawn, they are lying in the village cemetery. She is too weak to go farther. He leaves with her the notebooks in which he has been recording his experiences. Bleeding, he struggles on toward the endless horizon.

Where is populism in this? So far, this is truly a stranger's view, a discourse of control and avoidance, as demobilizing as it is mobilizing. The author does express compassion for the child born in the village, "the child of the two stepmothers," one being the birth "mother who beats [him]," the other being "the motherland that beats [him] every day" (55). The author credits the villagers with a tough realism that "dominates all other feelings" (72). The nation's "only strength is these villages, these nests of sickness, poverty, and despair" (94). There is no doubt about the villagers' degradation. But whose fault is this? With that question, the novel makes its point for the elite populists in Ankara.[73]

The reason for this, Turkish intellectual, is again you! What have you done for this ruined country and [its] wretched people? . . .

Anatolia's people have a spirit; you have not influenced it. They have a head; you have not enlightened it. They have a body; you have not nourished it. There is a land on which they live! You have not worked it. You have abandoned them to bestial feelings, ignorance, poverty, and famine. They have grown up like weeds between the hard earth and the empty sky. Now you have come here with the sickle for the harvest. What have you sown that you should now reap? These nettles, these dry thorns? Naturally, they will stick in your feet. See, you are bleeding all over, and you contort your face with pain. You clench your fists from rage. What causes you this pain is your own doing, your own doing.

The acclaim for *Yaban* upon its publication proves that Yakup Kadri's views were not out of line for the time. Literary works with a sympathetic view of the peasantry soon appeared. Sabahattin Ali (1905–1948) became famous for novels and short stories that attributed dignity and honesty to villagers and criticized urban intellectuals for their contempt.[74] Orhan Kemal (1914–1970) wrote about men who found village women quite attractive and had no trouble making love to them, as a novel discussed in the next chapter demonstrates. Yakup Kadri outlived both these men. As the republic moved toward its most populistic policy experiment, thinking like his did a lot to guide it.

EDUCATION AND THE VILLAGE INSTITUTES

A basic reason for the gulf between the intellectuals and the villagers was illiteracy. Not accidentally, then, the early republic's truest experiment in populism was designed to spread literacy in the villages. In the region of the world where writing had been invented thousands of years earlier, the Turkish republic finally faced the challenge of democratizing literacy. That was a vast project to undertake in the wake of the 1929 depression and on the eve of a population explosion unprecedented in human history.[75] The impact of rapid population growth would not become fully apparent before the 1960s. The stark conditions of the early republic were, however, the ones under which Turkey paid the start-up costs of its transition to mass literacy.

Among notable milestones in this transition, the unification of school systems in 1924 and the introduction of coeducation at all levels in 1927 added efficiencies to Turkish education. The alphabet change in 1928 and the language reform and adult education programs of the 1930s did likewise. The 1933 university reform and the windfall opportunity from 1933 on to employ highly qualified refugees from Nazi Europe transformed higher education and the professions.[76] The number of universities increased from one in 1900 to three in 1946. Between 1924 and 1950 total enrollment in elementary schools advanced from 300,000 to 1.5 million. Literacy rose from 11 percent (1927) to 33 percent (1950), with a wide gap between 46 percent literacy for males and only 19 percent for females.[77]

Most illiterates were in Turkey's forty-two thousand villages; and the hardest problem was to bring literacy to them at bearable cost. Extensive debates and pilot projects culminated in the founding of the first Village Institutes (Köy Enstitüleri, 1940).[78] Ultimately twenty-one in number, the institutes emphasized learning by doing. The curriculum combined academic, agricultural, and technical subjects. The institutes would train villagers to return to their villages as teachers and community leaders, spreading new skills and improving rural life. A central goal was to elicit enthusiasm and volunteerism for the exertions that the program required. The local villagers were expected to provide land for their institute at low prices and work twenty days a year for it. The students were expected to provide labor for making improvements, cultivating crops, and tending animals. The institutes were expected to promote nationalism and Kemalism and to Turkify the peasants. Institute programs included creative efforts to appeal to young people. Reciprocal visits among institutes and group trips to other parts of the country broadened students' national awareness. Students taught their regional folk dances to visitors. Thanks to the institutes, Turkey's regional folk dances began to be danced by people from other regions and become national for the first time. The institutes trained some seventeen thousand students. Among graduates who went on to noteworthy careers were authors who wrote real village novels.

The Village Institutes ran into criticism, both locally and nationally, including accusations of communism, which ricocheted all about in 1950s Turkey. Products of the single-party period, the institutes probably could not long have survived it. By 1954, they had been merged with conventional primary teachers' colleges. Even had they survived, rapid population growth and even faster urbanization would have transformed the problem they were designed to solve. Turkey's truest experiment in populism made a difference but fell victim to the fears it aroused.[79] A measure of the early republican leaders' commitment to nation building in the countryside, the institutes had also trained new men and women who would become the established elites' future competitors for power in a Turkey where political mobilization was no longer limited to the middle class.

RELIGIOUS REVIVAL AND SOCIAL CHANGE: SAID NURSI

Nothing puts top-down policies of laicism and populism into perspective better than the fact that one of the three most influential religious revival movements of the past two centuries emerged under the early republic.

Comparable in influence to the Halidiye-Nakşibendiye, this movement also emerged from the peripheries to challenge the center. Given the difference between the cultural climates of their respective periods, this time the official response was much more hostile. Still, Said Nursi (1873–1960) offered a vision of Islamic modernity and critiqued the official vision in ways that attracted a wide following and created lasting reverberations. An overview of Nursi's life, his message, and his media for propagating it illustrate how he challenged the secular state, even as it tried to exclude him from its construction of national modernity.[80]

A LIFE IN THREE PHASES

Nursi described his life in three periods. Through 1923, he was the "old Said." From then until 1950, he was the "new Said." From 1950 until his death in 1960, he was the "third Said."

The "old" period takes him from birth to the founding of the republic. He was born in the village of Nurs near Bitlis. Like his fellow Kurd Mevlana Halid,

Bediüzzaman Said Nursi, 1918, the most influential religious leader under the early Turkish republic. (Courtesy of Yeni Asya Neşriyat.)

Said entered a world where encroaching modernity had destabilized old equilibria. Said tried to gain a religious education in the medreses of the region. He proved himself to be both an intellectual prodigy and a rebel against the established curriculum. He also rebelled in other ways. He carried weapons and dressed like a Kurdish mountaineer rather than a religious scholar. Such eccentricities never left him: he refused to wear the gown and turban of a religious scholar under the empire, when that was normal; he later refused to wear anything else under the republic, which restricted religious garb. The young Said's talents attracted attention, including that of several governors. Taken into their households, Said continued his religious studies, began to learn Western subjects, acquired a wider world awareness through reading the print media, and served the governors, one of whom relied on him to mediate tribal disputes.

In Van, the title *Bediüzzaman*, "the wonder of the age," became widely applied to him. One scholar had previously called Said that for his religious knowledge; in Van, he was considered a "wonder" for his knowledge of the modern world.[81] Said not only learned quickly but also reacted vividly to his discoveries. Upon reading a newspaper account of a speech in which the British colonial secretary denounced the Kur'an, Said went into a rage, roaring that he would prove to the world that the Kur'an was an "inextinguishable sun" of inspiration. Dissatisfied with the state of education, he proposed to found an eastern Anatolian university, Medreset üz-Zehra, to teach Western sciences as well as Islamic religious studies in a new curriculum. Attracting the attention of Sultan Abdülhamid's courtiers, Said went to Istanbul in 1907. He had an audience with Abdülhamid and presented a petition containing proposals for reform, including the university modeled on al-Azhar. At his audience, he appeared in mountaineer clothing, spoke his idiosyncratic Turkish, and upbraided the sultan for timidity as leader of the Muslims. Characteristically, Abdülhamid offered both the carrot and the stick. He first sent Said to an asylum to have his sanity tested and then tried to neutralize him by offering him a salaried position.

The "old Said" period was one of political involvement. His religiously grounded belief in constitutionalism remained with him even after he withdrew from politics.[82] Turning down Abdülhamid's job offer, Said supported the 1908 revolution only to find himself in court after the failed 1909 countercoup, tarred by membership in the Muhammadan Union (İttihad-ı Muhammedi). Vindicating himself, he accompanied Sultan Mehmed Reşad on a Balkan tour and obtained a promise of funding for his university at Van; then the Balkan Wars killed that prospect. During World War I, Said both fought and engaged in religious polemics. The Russians captured him and held him as a war prisoner in Siberia until he escaped in 1917. Returning to Istanbul, he was appointed to an Islamic academy (Dar ül-Hikmet il-İslamiye). He had gone from war captivity to a potentially comfortable professional life.

Starting in Siberia, however, a spiritual crisis began to turn him into the "new Said." He was getting older, and politics and Western "philosophical sciences" had not given him satisfaction. He could find this contentment only by returning to religious studies. He came to believe that Ahmad Sirhindi was transmitting him a message from the beyond: "Unify your *kıble*," essentially, "face in only one direction to pray." He must find a single master, and that could only be the Kur'an.[83] Said supported the National Struggle and visited Ankara in 1923, where Mustafa Kemal offered him an assembly seat. The religious indifference of most assembly members disappointed Said, however. Leaving the "old Said" behind, he declined the offer and retired to a cave near Van to study the Kur'an.

The "new Said" (1923–1950) became the most influential religious figure in Ottoman and Turkish culture since Mevlana Halid. Leave politics though he might wish to do, politics would not leave him alone. When Şeyh Said of Palu led his revolt in 1925, Said Nursi refused to join.[84] Throughout his life, he opposed nationalism and insisted that Turks and Kurds were brothers. After the revolt, he nonetheless was one of the Kurds forced to move to western Anatolia. At Barla near Isparta, he began writing his major works, known collectively as the *Risale-i Nur* (Treatise of light), largely dating from 1925 to 1944. Thereafter, he spent most of his life in forced residence at different places. His followers, "the students of light" (*talebe-i nur*), reproduced and circulated his writings, and his influence grew. Official suspicions that he was trying to found a religious brotherhood, which had been forbidden, or to undermine the republic resulted in repeated trials on the same charges. Said defended himself against the brotherhood charge with the observation that many people who did not belong to orders had gone to heaven but that none who lacked faith had done so. When he was again on trial with many followers in 1943, a commission of experts was appointed to examine his writings. Their finding that his writings dealt only with religion and did not constitute the ideology of a secret brotherhood resulted in his acquittal. Said's own views of the commission will merit further comment. All the while, Said lived a life of extreme asceticism and devotion that established his charisma as the religious leader of the age.

The end of single-party rule in 1950 opened a new period. The Democrat Party was somewhat friendlier toward religion. This did not mean an end to Said's troubles, but it created enough of a change to start a new phase of his life. The "third Said" still abstained from politics but encouraged his followers to participate. Until 1956, circulation of the *Risale-i Nur* could still be prosecuted because it existed only in Arabic script. A follower, Tahsin Tola, then obtained permission to publish Said's works in Latin letters; Tola also edited a biography. Said's third period proved brief. He died in 1960 and was buried at Urfa, but not for long. His remains were taken away on a military plane and reburied at a secret location near Isparta. The same government that had imprisoned and tried him in life feared him enough to make sure that his tomb could not become a place of visitation and prayer for his followers, who grew in numbers after his death, dividing into several branches as they grew.

SAID NURSI: MESSAGE AND MEDIA

To understand Said Nursi's appeal requires considering both his message and his means of projecting it, which combined the traditional with the innovative and modern.

If the tension between rationalization and subjectivization characterizes modernity, Said Nursi understood the significance of this tension for pious Muslims alienated by republican laicism.[85] In this sense, his methods constituted a modern response to modernity itself. Republican education blamed the ulema, on whom the people had depended, for the decline of the empire but also tacitly assumed that the good citizen was an ethical, conscientious Muslim. The republic proposed new civil rituals—civil weddings, civic holidays, visits to Atatürk's tomb and other ways to honor him. Most of these did ultimately become meaningful to Turks. However, it is also true that the civil rituals did not replace religious ones and could not answer the needs of major life transitions as well as the religious rituals. Not only secularists, but many religious Turks, too, felt that the sufi brotherhoods had outlived their usefulness or needed reform. With the 1925 closure of the dervish meeting halls as an added deterrent, all the more reason, then, for Said not to found a new order. He did not need a brotherhood to tap the riches of Islamic mystical thought, which asserted God's omnipresence in the universe as well as his omnipotence over it. Better, then, to have an imam rather than a şeyh, a religious teacher and congregational leader rather than a master of otherworldly mysteries. Better to have someone who could guide individuals and society toward spiritual fulfillment amid the distractions of modern times. Likewise, followers struggling to lead good lives under stressful conditions responded gratefully to Said's reassurances that as long as they fulfilled their basic religious obligations and abstained from major sins, then even their daily work would count as worship.

The need to adopt a new kind of organization and method of spreading the message turned Said Nursi and his followers into prominent pioneers of Islamic "print capitalism." As in the case of the Westernizing intelligentsia a century earlier (1840–1860), the term applies not restrictively to print shops and book-stores alone. Suggestively and symbolically, the term refers rather to the whole social-economic-cultural complex encompassing authors and audiences, new media, new styles and genres, the socioeconomic organizations required to pro-duce and circulate the new cultural content, and the new social interactions that grow up around the new media. Said Nursi had participated personally in the explosion of publication after the 1908 revolution and was obviously not the only force at work in creating new Islamic media. Yet he is a particularly good example of a still-unrecognized fact of Turkish history, namely, that the attack on the sufi brotherhoods coincided chronologically with the florescence of an Islamic counterpart to the nineteenth-century Westernist print culture. The brotherhood model had still worked in Mevlana Halid's day; but now, with that model under attack, different methods of organizing and communicating established their functionality for religious thinkers. The nineteenth-century print culture had never been entirely secular, but that is not the point. The point is rather that religious activists went through their transition from an oral to a text-based movement in the early twentieth century, producing their own parallel universe of print media.

During Said's lifetime, his movement accomplished the entire transition from manuscript to print. He wanted his followers to see charisma not in his person but in his writings. The renewer (*müceddid*) of the previous century had been Mevlana Halid; the renewer of this century was not Said Nursi but his "Treatise of Light" (*Risale-i Nur*). It ultimately included 130 parts, many of them grouped under names such as "The Flashes" (*Lem'alar*) or "The Rays" (*Şualar*). The students of Nur met in reading groups, called *dershane* (the common term for "classroom"). A person became a *Nurcu* ("Nur-ist," follower of the Nur movement) by joining a group of *talebe-i nur* ("students of Nur"), who met to study the *Risale-i Nur*. Initially, the group that formed around Said included no women, but women's groups later formed.[86] Reading groups proliferated, until anytime after 1950 major cities in Turkey had hundreds apiece, appealing to different segments of society. However, Said's early followers had been largely rural, and so were their systems for propagating his message.

Through the mid-1920s, Said's writings seem to have been printed without particular difficulty.[87] Thereafter, as the *Risale-i Nur* took shape, things became difficult. He was in internal exile, and his refusal to give up the script of the Kur'an made it illegal to print and circulate his works after the alphabet reform. Said's treatises had to be copied by hand and circulated secretly. By the mid-1930s, some villages around Isparta, near Said's first place of exile in western Anatolia, had become centers for manuscript reproduction, so much that his treatises became a factor in propagating rural literacy in the old script, among women as well as men. Ultimately the number of handwritten copies of the various parts of the treatises allegedly amounted to six hundred thousand. If that was remotely true, it would imply that one of the largest manuscript-copying projects in history occurred in the twentieth century. Duplicating machines were the first modern device that permitted mass reproduction of the texts. The interest that women and children took in his works convinced Said that his ideas would live on after him. His interest in the young led Said to have some of his writings typed in Latin letters in 1942–1943; some of his works were also printed photographically at that time. By 1946–1947, some of his writings were being reproduced in Latin letters for the young, while the hand copying of most of them continued with the explicit motive of preserving the Arabic script. With these techniques of text production, the problems of proofreading and correcting copies were endless, taking much of Nursi's own time. In 1956, a court decision finally confirmed that the treatises did not violate the law, so opening the way for printing the entire collection of treatises in the new letters. This increased the number of readers into the hundreds of thousands and started the process of moving publication and distribution of the treatises closer to the mainstream of the Turkish media.

The message was what made the media appeal to their audience. Assessments of his writings have run to irreconcilable extremes. The *Risale-i Nur* has been described as "helter-skelter, relatively unsystematic" in structure.[88] Conversely, it has been described as possessing a "unity and complexity," without an understanding of which the significance of Said's thought cannot be understood.[89] Once he had "unified his *kıble*" and made the Kur'an his only master, Said used Kur'anic exegesis to address his contemporaries' problems. The basis for the "helter-skelter" assessment lies largely in the associations Said made to establish parallels between Kur'anic passages and contemporary needs. The foremost problem of his religiously committed contemporaries was the laicist assault on religion, which had its intellectual roots in nineteenth-century European "scientific materialism." Said's unifying goal was to provide a Kur'anic answer to the materialist challenge.

Perhaps it was an irony of "backwardness" that this "scientific materialism" had not confronted the same kind of philosophical critique among the Ottomans that it had faced in late nineteenth-century Europe. Instead, scientific materialism had endured and become enshrined in Kemalism and the republican vision of modernity. That fact left it to Said Nursi to critique scientific materialism in Islamic terms. Several signs make clear that Said saw European philosophers, particularly the scientific materialists, as his targets. When he was on trial in 1943 and a commission of religion experts was convened to examine his writings, he not only challenged the competence of the religion experts but demanded that philosophers be brought from Europe to examine his works.[90] Likewise, in the part of Said's treatises known as the "Flashes of Light" (*Lem'alar*), the twenty-third essay is entitled "Treatise on Nature" (*Tabiat Risalesi*). Presenting his treatise as a theriac (*tiryak*) for the kind of error (*dalalet*) that comes from atheistic science, he summarizes the arguments offered by the materialists to explain the order of nature and compares them with the argument that God created nature. He concludes that the materialists confuse natural law with the creator.

With this observation, Said made essentially the same point as one of the most telling European attacks on the scientific materialists, namely, that they professed to rely only on sense perceptions while positing the universality of natural law, which is not verifiable by sensory perception. Scientific attacks on the Kur'an he answered by arguing the inability of natural science to speak about metaphysics. Unlike Islamic modernists who tried to reconcile faith and reason, Said criticized materialists as naive. For Said, there were three ways to acquire Islamic knowledge: the Kur'an, the Prophet, and the "Grand Book of the Universe," a phrase expressing his debt to Islamic mystical thought. Within this universe, just as God "makes the sun and the moon attend to [their] duties," the manifestations of his omnipotence also include "a magical emanation of true planning, administering, regulating, purifying and assigning duties."[91] Said Nursi's message is that the Master of the universe is the Master of modernity.

GETTING TURKEY ON TIME: AHMET HAMDI TANPINAR

Tanpınar (1901–1962) wrote some of the best-loved novels about the early republican period. Living through that period and publishing novels from the late 1940s onward, he wrote with an ironic detachment that Kemalist ideologues lacked. Culturally conservative but not overtly religious, he wrote of a world in which the old refuses to die and the new has a hard time a-borning. Ironic and witty, he challenges his readers to reflect on the paradoxical interactions of old and new, time and identity, modernity and subjectivity. Only occasionally, he offers programmatic statements:[92]

> Our greatest problem is this: where and how are we linked to the past; all of us are children of a crisis of consciousness and identity; more acutely than Hamlet all of us live in a crisis of "to be or not to be." . . .
>
> The best is to leave our memories to choose for themselves the hour when they will speak within us. Only at such moments of awakening does the voice

of past times become a discovery, a lesson, in short something added to our times. What we should do is to submit ourselves to the wind of today, new, productive, and vital. It will bring us to an industrious and happy world where the beautiful and the good, consciousness and dreaming will go hand in hand.

Part of the fascination of Tanpınar's novel about the "Chronometric Institute" (*Saatleri Ayarlama Enstitüsü*) is that it depicts a Turkish Everyman, Hayri İrdal, as he struggles "to be or not to be."

THE CHRONOMETRIC INSTITUTE:
BACKWARDNESS AND CATCHING UP

Although published in 1961, the novel is all about the 1930s. The imagined chronology of the hero's life starts before World War I but does not include World War II. The book does not mention the 1929 depression. Yet the idea of a bureaucratic agency created to synchronize all the watches and clocks in Turkey "modernizes" the Ottoman and Turkish desire to overcome backwardness by adapting it to the era of statist developmental solutions.

To site the book for an English-speaking audience requires noting that Turkish uses the word *saat* rather as German uses *Uhr* to mean "hour," "time of day," "watch," and "clock." English not only uses different words to express those meanings, but also derives many compounds about time from the Greek roots "horo-" and "chrono-." Turkish conveys those meanings with derivatives of *saat*. Tanpınar's Saatleri Ayarlama Enstitüsü could be either the Chronometric Institute or, less fluently, the Clock-Setting Institute.[93] Some of the projects associated with the institute in the book challenge translators considerably. The Saatleme Bankası forces the translator to choose between the Horologization Bank or (a wild guess) the Clock Promotion Bank. Often, it is unclear whether the intended meaning is "watch" or "clock." Anyone discussing this book in English faces something of the befuddlement endured by Turkish Everyman Hayri İrdal in making his way in the modern world.

PARADOXES OF OLD AND NEW: HAYRI İRDAL'S ROOTS

Tanpınar sets the scene by depicting Hayri's antiheroic qualities and his roots in late Ottoman society, with all its cultural diversity and communalism. Any reader expecting an autobiographical novel will find Tanpınar's opening sentence perfectly hysterical: "Those who know me know I do not care a great deal for reading and writing." The statement applies only too well to Hayri. Struggling to write his memoirs, he is overwhelmed by his own insignificance (14). However, the only person who could write the institute's history better than he, former director Halit Ayarcı, is no longer alive. Before he met Halit Ayarcı, Hayri's life was no life. So colorless was Hayri that when his boss, Cemal Bey, gave him an old suit of clothes, the latter's one weakness, his love for his wife, Selma, rubbed off on Hayri. Later, when Halit Ayarcı, his boss at the institute, gave Hayri a suit, some of the latter's boldness and creativity rubbed off on him (20).

Hayri was born into a family that had fallen on hard times. People talked about freedom, but its only meaning for him was a child's freedom (25). His life began only when his uncle gave him a watch. The family already had several clocks. "Everyone knows that our old way of life was governed by the clock. As I later learned from Timekeeper (*Muvakkit*) Nuri Efendi, European watchmakers' biggest customers were the Muslims and among them our own people, who were the most pious. The five daily prayers, the meals after sundown and before dawn during Ramazan, every form of worship was by the clock. The clock was the surest way to find God, and as such it regulated old-timers' lives."[94] All mosques had a timekeeper (*muvakkit*). Passersby were never too rushed to pull out their watch and set it, reciting the *besmele* and praying that the time measured would be blessed for them and theirs.

Most notable of the clocks in Hayri's childhood home was a tall clock that his father often talked of selling but never did. Known as Mübarek ("blessed"), alternatively as Menhus ("inauspicious"), the clock was a mixed blessing. A prosperous ancestor once made a vow to build a mosque and began accumulating goods for it. Toppled from office before fulfilling his vow, he left his impoverished descendants with a house full of mosque furnishings, including Mübarek. For young Hayri, a poor student held back in school, life began with the gift of a watch. Soon Hayri was spending more time with Timekeeper Nuri than in school (32), becoming his apprentice.

An epitome of all the values popularly associated with Ottoman guilds, Timekeeper Nuri was more like a "clock doctor" (34) and a philosopher. Based on Nuri Efendi, Hayri later wrote a book about a mythical Ahmet Zamanî Efendi (*zamanî* being an adjective from *zaman*, time), thus providing the Chronometric Institute with a history extending back to the seventeenth century. A mythical sufi saint as a precursor for an Ottoman guildsman and a modern technical agency—Tanpınar was a man of profound insights into the linkages within Ottoman and Turkish society.

Young Hayri's contacts with Nuri Efendi's customers, who came from the poor and picturesque Vefa neighborhood and its vicinity, widened the boy's social roots. (39) The most notable customer was Abdüsselâm Bey, an old gentleman of Tunisian origins. At its height, his mansion, housing thirty-seven relatives and dependents from all over the empire, symbolized Ottoman imperial integration. As the empire fell apart, Abdüsselâm Bey's household did, too. Another of Nuri Efendi's customers, Seyit Lûtfullah, was once a minor religious functionary known for strict sharia observance but had become an eccentric of drug-enhanced delusions. As Abdüsselâm Bey's fortune dwindled, he pinned his hopes either on Seyit Lûtfullah's dreams of magically discovering treasure or on the attempts of another neighbor, Greek pharmacist Aristidi Efendi, to produce gold in his secret laboratory. Aristidi met his end in an explosion in his laboratory one night in 1912. Seyit Lûtfullah disappeared after he proclaimed in mosque one day that he was the *mehdi,* only to be ruled insane and sent into exile, from which he sent word that he was turning over both his imaginary beloved Aselban and his magical treasure to Hayri (73). In later years, Hayri sometimes thought he lived his life through these people; in contrast, he had strained relations with his son (54). In 1912, Nuri Efendi died, leaving Hayri half trained in watchmaking and unable to find another master to train him. The boy wanted nothing else, having learned much from Nuri.

The most astonishing character was Hayri's father's sister. Father and sister were complete opposites. He was healthy but poor. She was sickly and mean-spirited but was a rich man's widow, living in sanctimonious retirement with a half-crazed servant woman. The fact that she had no other heir poisoned relations between her and Hayri's father. Finally one day the servant woman brought word that Hayri's aunt had died. His father made arrangements for the funeral. Then, instead of accompanying the body to the cemetery, he went to her mansion to make sure that nothing happened to her property. At the cemetery, just as she was about to be lowered into the grave, the aunt came to, sat up in the coffin, and demanded to be taken home. There she found her brother stuffing his pockets with her jewelry, gold pieces, and securities, while Hayri was busy taking apart the dining room clock (65). Her return from the dead brought about a "revolution or transformation" (*ihtilâl veya inkılâp,* 68): no more hypochondria or penny-pinching. Instead, she lived lavishly, remarried, and traveled to Vienna. Embodying Tanpınar's theme of the old that refuses to die, "Shroud-Ripper Zarife" (*Kefenyırtan Zarife,* 272) figures prominently throughout the book. Lacking her dynamism, Hayri drifts. Only with the outbreak of World War I do his feet "touch ground for the first time" (75).

THE TURKISH EVERYMAN BEFORE
THE CLOCK-SETTING INSTITUTE

The story continues with Hayri's demobilization at the end of World War I. Like Tanpınar's diversion of the politically charged terms "revolution or transformation" (*ihtilâl veya inkılâp*) to characterize Aunt Zarife's return from the dead, it seems characteristic of his novels to bypass the violence of World War I and the National Struggle. Hayri's troubles are not over, however. His life becomes one of degradation until, at rock bottom, a paradoxical encounter starts him back toward social reintegration. In terms alternately absurdist and comedic, Hayri's ups and downs take him through alternative models of Turkish communalism, from Ottoman to republican.

Returning from the war, Hayri finds himself taken into Abdüsselâm Bey's household, married to his ward, Emine, and enrolled in telegraphy school. Soon, Hayri and his bride are the only ones left with Abdüsselâm Bey. Their first daughter is born shortly before the old man's death. He assumes the right to name the child, forgetfully naming her Zehra after his mother rather than Zahide after Hayri's mother (88). The old man dies, leaving many wills and debts, and the young couple become embroiled in heirs' and creditors' conflicts. Court cases soon become the talk of the neighborhood. One evening, when an acquaintance takes Hayri out drinking and plies him with questions about Abdüsselâm Bey's debts, Hayri drunkenly remembers Seyit Lûtfullah's imaginary treasure, including his Şerbetçibaşı diamond. He mentions it, thinking only to test his questioner's gullibility. Fantasy gets taken for fact, and another trial begins. At first a witness, Hayri soon becomes the accused in a surrealistic proceeding resembling trials in period films, not to mention historical trials in Turkey and other countries in the 1920s and 1930s. Hayri ends up sentenced to psychiatric incarceration (98).

At the Judicial Medicine facility (Adlî Tıp), Hayri finds himself in the care of Dr. Ramiz, newly returned from Vienna. The doctor also has a problem. Believing that psychoanalysis provides "the sole means to reform the entire world," he is angry because Turkey does not offer him "a fulcrum on which to change the axis of the entire country with this miraculous lever" (100). Hayri's misfortune is to be Dr. Ramiz's first patient. The maladjusted doctor needs Hayri more than he needs the doctor. The doctor appalls Hayri by telling him that his psychoanalysis will take several years (106). He decides that Hayri has a "father complex" and has never reached maturity because he endlessly seeks an alternative father for himself. "Great and small, are we not all struggling with this? What is this love of ours for the Hittites, the Phrygians, and I don't know what all other peoples? Anything but a father complex?" (113). Dr. Ramiz wants to use dream analysis, but Hayri's dreams dissatisfy him and he decides that he must use his own new "directed dream" method (*dirije rüya*, 116). Meanwhile, Hayri repairs the watches of the director and others at the asylum, and the director becomes fascinated with the Şerbetçibaşı diamond (107). Soon the doctor is giving Hayri a short course on psychoanalysis and is rediscovering dream manuals and other riches of Ottoman culture from Hayri. They become "like two colleagues," and the doctor informs the judge that Hayri has recovered and should be freed (119–20). The night after he learns of this, Hayri finally manages to have the kind of dream Dr. Ramiz wants him to.

Hayri's dream begins in Aristidi Efendi's laboratory. Suddenly, the alembic, which is also a mirror, is enveloped in strange-colored lights and vapors, amid which Hayri sees the face of his wife, Emine. Her hair already half-aflame, she cries, "Save me!" Horrified and begging for the experiment to stop, Hayri tries to move, but something—Seyit Lûtfullah with hooklike hands—restrains him. The face looking at him through the glass fades until nothing is left but two eyes wide with fear. "All this is because of you" (120–22).

Released from psychiatric incarceration, Hayri returns to his family and finds a job in the post office. Reentering society, he progresses through three different social circles. First, Dr. Ramiz introduces him to a coffeehouse near the Vefa quarter, where the patrons have already heard Dr. Ramiz praise Hayri as a man of extraordinary qualities. The clientele comes from every walk of life. They become intimates within twenty-four hours and keep no secrets from one another. A microcosm of Istanbul male society, the patrons are divided into three groups: the *Nizamıâlemciler* ("world-orderers"), the *Esafili Şark* ("the wretched of the East") and the *Şiş taifesi* (literally, "skewer team"), completely unrefined and numerous enough to have their own underclass, the *Yarım Şiş* ("half skewer," 128–29).[95] Hayri is initially admitted to the "world-orderers" but is later demoted to the "wretched" after misfortune strikes. Hayri also has to have a new name in the coffeehouse. In view of his supposed psychosis, the obvious choice is Öksüz, "Orphan." Hayri is fascinated by the eccentrics at the coffeehouse, including a Swiss "orientalist," down on his luck, who tries to make his living as an architect and designs buildings by piling up matchboxes (136). Sinking into the coffeehouse world, Hayri awakes with a start when his wife, Emine, falls ill and dies, fulfilling his dream at the mental institution. With Emine's death, "the worst that could happen had happened," leaving Hayri again "free."

As in childhood, the idiosyncratic meaning attached to "freedom" accentuates the mismatch between Hayri's subjective state and the utopic ideal of Turkish society. Hayri sinks into dissipation, neglecting his children until his son Ahmet's illness forces him to pull himself together. About the same time, Dr. Ramiz founds a Psychoanalysis Society and makes Hayri its first director. At one of his lectures to the society, Dr. Ramiz introduces Hayri as his first analysis patient in Turkey. That is how he attracts the attention of his second wife, Pakize (143).

After the coffeehouse, Hayri joins two societies, the Psychoanalysis Society and the Spiritism Society. Both have mixed-gender memberships, but neither absorbs him as fully as the coffeehouse had. Instead, his second wife, Pakize, and a new employer, Cemal Bey, assume larger roles in his life. The trend from communalism toward individuation, the mixed-sex membership of the new societies, and many narrative details show Hayri caught in his own transition from tradition to modernity.

When they marry, Pakize does not yet have thyroid trouble and has not yet become nervous and ill-tempered (145). Pakize's passion is the cinema. She is Jeanette MacDonald or Rosalind Russell. Hayri is Charles Boyer, Clark Gable, or William Powell. Or—taking out his old reserve officer uniform—they are Napoleon and Josephine (147–48). Only after Pakize's parents die and her two sisters—"orphans" at the ages of thirty-five and twenty-eight—move in does she find something new to think about, much to the detriment of Hayri's young children and his finances.

As for the Spiritism Society, it is jollier than the Psychoanalysis Society, largely because of its many women members. This is where he meets Cemal Bey, the least likely person to be a spiritist, were it not for Cemal's infatuation with a female member, Nevzat Hanım. Discovering Hayri at the society, Cemal Bey treats him condescendingly. Hayri puts up with it because he is infatuated with Cemal's wife, Selma. Hayri soon finds himself working for Cemal Bey. The romantic infatuations include a number of the society's other members and end badly in one of the novel's later bits of cinematic modernism. The Spiritism Society may have been "modern" in expanding mixed-gender socializing into extramarital affairs. Otherwise, Hayri did not take long to see that this was Seyit Lûtfullah's fantasy world all over again (168).

Hayri's job at Cemal Bey's Miscellaneous Trades Bank (Türlü Meslekler Bankası, 19–20, 168) brings him a salary raise and signs of rising status. However, Cemal's behavior toward him worsens. Something is making Cemal hard to satisfy. About the same time, ladies from the Spiritism Society find pretexts to visit Hayri at home and ask leading questions about Cemal. Hayri's wife, Pakize, and her two sisters are so impressed by the ladies that they must dress like them; and a polite comment by one visitor convinces the youngest sister that she must enter that year's beauty contest. In another sendup of Kemalist modernism, Tanpınar depicts the ruinously costly "dress revolution" at Hayri's house (*evimizdeki kıyafet inkılâbı*) as each visiting lady sets a new standard of chic (171). Meanwhile, the tensions around Cemal Bey multiply, and he abruptly fires Hayri. At home, Hayri cannot even get his wife and her sisters, who worry only about the beauty contest, to understand what has happened.

HAYRI İRDAL AND THE CHRONOMETRIC INSTITUTE

Hayri hits bottom again; then Dr. Ramiz introduces him to an old classmate, Halit Ayarcı (180). His surname indicates his future role in the book, its relevant meaning here being "setter," from the same word *ayar* as in the title of the Clock-Setting Institute (Saatleri Ayarlama Enstitüsü). Halit Ayarcı has complained about his watch. Exaggeratedly praising Hayri's watchmaking skills, Dr. Ramiz urges his friend to let Hayri look at the watch. Hayri recognizes it as a fine piece that simply needs demagnetization (182–83). Hayri's fortunes are about to turn upward.

Halit Ayarcı proposes that the three of them go out for the evening. As they drive along, Hayri remarks offhandedly that the public clocks they pass all give different times. As the three men enjoy an evening of drink in a restaurant on the Bosphorus, Hayri discovers that fate has turned him into a gentleman (*beyefendi*, 199). When Hayri starts to recount his worries about his family, Halit Ayarcı cuts him off: Hayri has no experience of people and life. What matters is newness (213). Hayri's problem is that he is an idealist and an old type of man (*eski adamsınız*); he does not see reality. From now on, they will work together. Hayri concludes that all his life he has looked through the wrong end of the telescope. Halit Ayarcı has shown him which end to look into (214–15).

Thanks to Halit Ayarcı, Hayri becomes one of the first employees of the Chronometric Institute. The launching of the institute satirizes early republican affairism and nepotism. For example, the mayor's visit leads to talk of a new building, new departments, and the necessity to hire only applicants with "complete references," half of them from their own relatives and friends and half from people in high places (230). Even as the institute makes Hayri important, he has trouble understanding. Halit Ayarcı challenges him: "Why don't you believe? . . . The Chronometric Institute above all needs to be believed in" (236–37).

The institute expands into a futurist fantasy, complete with watch-setting stations on the streets, staffed by young women to set gentlemen's watches and handsome young men to set ladies' watches, in return for a small fee and a receipt (240). The institute's personnel policy soon makes it a regroupment site for all the people Hayri has known in other social settings, including "shroud-ripper" Aunt Zarife. A visit by a big shot leads to a discussion of the grandiose things the institute could do with more funding, and Hayri finds himself maneuvered by Halit Ayarcı into promising to publish his "life's work," a book on the great seventeenth-century Ottoman clockmaker Ahmet Zamanî Efendi. Hayri has never heard of Ahmet Zamanî; but Halit Ayarcı offers a hint by telling the visitor that Hayri's old master, Timekeeper Nuri Efendi, was from the same

Istanbul by Night. When Hayri İrdal and his companions set out by
car for the evening of carousing on the Bosphorus that turned Hayri into a
gentleman, the scene as they left the old city and crossed the Galata Bridge
might have looked like this. In the background appears the Yeni Valide
Mosque at Eminönü, with lights suspended between the minarets for one of
the religious festivals. (Photograph by Ara Güler, 1956; Magnum.)

school. Worrying about this book, Hayri feels like a criminal caught in the act (253). Yet—when he considers how things have changed for his wife, daughter, and sisters-in-law—he realizes that the institute has saved his life (259).

While Hayri frets over his book, the institute grows so prominent that the press begins to criticize it. Hayri finds himself alternately vilified and praised as "our unrecognized Voltaire" and "the Faust of the East." When he complains about the exaggerations, Halit Ayarcı retorts: "Is it my fault if you resemble Voltaire or Faust? . . . Is it easy to catch up with a civilization and all its history in fifty years? You bet some exaggeration will come into play! . . . Sit down, write your book, look for ways to improve our institute!" (263). When Hayri protests that Ahmed Zamanî never existed, Halit Ayarcı answers that "history serves the needs of the day" (*tarih, günün emrindedir*, 270). So it did in 1930s Turkey.

Of all the articles, none tops that by the journalist who interviewed Hayri's wife, Pakize. As if she has not mistreated him for years, she turns him into something out of the movies. They have loved each other since childhood; it is pure misfortune they married others. As soon as they were free, they wed. They have made great sacrifices for his success. She does not complain; she knows what it means to be a great man's wife. Hayri has all the marks of distinction. His one weakness is that he frequently falls in love. She understands. At his level, women will not leave him alone. She sacrificed offers from Hollywood and from a Swiss watch manufacturer to marry him. He has endured great injustice from his relatives but has forgiven them (265–66). Pakize even throws in that he sleeps naked on top of the covers; when he asks where she got that idea, she says that she meant to say he slept in a hammock but slipped up and said "naked" (*çıplak* instead of *hamak*, 277). As for unjust relatives, that can only mean one person. Shroud-ripper Zarife storms into the office to vent her outrage. Halit Ayarcı charms her by responding that they would have come to her had she not come to them. They are going to found a Clock Lovers Society (Saat Sevenler Cemiyeti), and she must direct it. The aunt donates land for a new building and cooperative, and she and Pakize become fast friends.

Aunt Zarife's reappearance signals that Hayri's social world is reknitting. Expanding her role, she hosts a cocktail party for the Clock Lovers Society. As the ladies hear her tell it, Hayri is the one who came back from the dead. During World War I, news came that he was dead. Even though she did not believe it, she held memorials for him; then he came back safe and sound (282). Now she praises him and his father. Instead of raking up past unpleasantness, she embellishes the past (283). Apparently, historical mythmaking is as useful for individuals and families as it is for nations. Halit Ayarcı arrives at the party and announces that the institute will found a Clock Promotion Bank

(Saatleme Bankası) and a personnel cooperative; that is how Hayri learns that he, as always, is to produce both sets of plans. Hayri has become a success; but what did this all add up to?

With the enthusiastic response to the publication of his *Life and Works of Şeyh Ahmet Zamanî*, the institute's success reaches a new high. Few people knew before that a Turk made world-class discoveries in reckoning time two hundred years ago. When Hayri confides his fears of being found out, Halit Ayarcı upbraids him: "You think there is such a thing as a lie. . . . For today, Ahmet Zamanî cannot be a lie; on the contrary, he is truth itself. . . . Ahmet Zamanî is a need of our times. He satisfied this need at the end of the seventeenth century, that's all. . . . You have accelerated our movement by transporting it into the past. Moreover, you have shown that our forebears were always reformist (*inkılâpçı*) and modern. No person can live in anger with the past" (285–87).

Except for a few scholars who dare to say no such person ever lived, the book is well received. The most disruptive criticism comes from Cemal Bey. A born liar and jealous of Hayri's involvement with his now-former wife, Selma, Cemal publishes an article asserting that Ahmet Zamanî is fictitious and that the advances Hayri credits to him were made by an equally fictitious Fennî Efendi. Fighting falsehood with falsehood, Cemal succeeds in creating doubts, and interest in the book falls. Advised by Halit Ayarcı that something astonishing is needed to divert the public, Hayri despairs. Then inspiration strikes.

The Chronometric Institute should impose fines on owners of timepieces that are ahead or behind. The penalty for being behind should be higher, of course. For repeat offenders, instead of increased fines, there should be discounts. The system will have premiums, a lottery, and subscription booklets. Halit Ayarcı conducts a Hollywood-style campaign to launch the system. Following on this public relations coup, the institute, by now known simply by its Turkish initials as S. A. E., adds staff, opens new departments including a Ping-Pong Room, and hires an unemployed orchestra conductor to keep time for the typists.

By now, the institute's fame has spread abroad. Aunt Zarife must host a reception for foreign dignitaries. After the party has lasted nearly until dawn, Halit Ayarcı approaches to introduce Hayri to the great van Humbert. Hayri learns that he invited van Humbert (it was done in his name without his knowing it). As van Humbert begins to ask minute questions about Ahmet Zamanî, Hayri tries to divert him by giving him champagne and getting him to dance with the ladies.

As the party builds to its conclusion, Hayri and Halit Ayarcı get into a deep conversation. When Hayri complains, Halit Ayarcı describes him as incurably unhappy. What matters is not knowledge but action. Hayri cannot turn back. Despite his self-doubt, he has a lovely wife, a mistress he is crazy about, a devoted son and daughter, plus fame and a sphere of action that he loves. Hayri tries to protest. He wants truth. Halit Ayarcı counters that Hayri made him love life. The first time they met in the coffeehouse, Hayri's despondency made Halit Ayarcı love life more. "You are my best mirror" (328–39). He would not want to change Hayri completely, because then one of them would not be needed. Just then, the approach of Hayri's family with van Humbert interrupts them, but "it was clear that we had broken each other's hearts" (329).

As the institute's high point and downfall approach, Hayri İrdal and Halit Ayarcı's mirrorlike characters react to those events in contrasting ways, from which one of the novel's most important messages emerges. By now, the institute has become such a success that Clock Lover Societies have formed in more than thirty countries. With money from fines, the institute plans to build both a new building for itself and then Clock Houses for its personnel. The project begins with a competition for a modern design that conforms to the institute's name inside and out. Despite many proposals, two competition rounds fail to produce satisfactory plans. Halit Ayarcı is frantic. Turkey will soon host the international congress, and he wants the new building by then. If the architects cannot design it, Hayri must.

After unsuccessful attempts to develop a design based on his pocket watch, Hayri realizes that he could base it on Mübarek, his heirloom tall clock. A long, rectangular plan would be easier than a circular one. Hayri and his son Ahmet work happily together to produce a futuristic concept. For Hayri, the most important thing he gets out of the project is being together with his son again. When Hayri presents his son's amateurish drawings and his matchbox mockup, Halit Ayarcı delightedly calls a press conference. Some hail the project; others denounce Hayri as a charlatan. Real architects dislike the plan. Still, Hayri is elected an honorary member of the International Society of Architects.

For the next project, the Clock Houses, no sooner does Halit Ayarcı select Hayri as architect than protests erupt from the very people who hailed his institute design. Halit Ayarcı cannot understand how people who approved the one cannot approve the other. For once, it is Hayri who explains things to him; but the controversy over the houses trains on. Meetings with the future residents reach the point where Halit Ayarcı cannot make himself heard. His magic is gone. By the time the International Clock Congress opens in the new building, he is no longer his old self. He is not even there the day of the incident that ends the institute.

When the foreign delegation comes, only Hayri is present. He is enthusiastic, but nothing impresses them. At the end of the tour, the delegation leader picks up the phone, dials "0135," and asks what time it is. "With such a convenience, what need is there for this organization?" (353). Hayri has been asking Halit Ayarcı such questions since the first day. He tries to answer but lacks his boss' conviction. Three days later, the institute's abolition is announced. Halit Ayarcı expresses no regret. His three hundred employees lack such detachment but are relieved to learn that all will have jobs in the "permanent liquidation commission." Hayri never sees his boss again. Then the fatal automobile accident occurs.

During the controversy about the Clock Houses, the lesson Hayri İrdal draws for Halit Ayarcı is this: "They like innovation as long as it does not upset them personally. . . . But they prefer to be safe and sound in their own lives."[96] It was one thing to experiment with the institute building, but let them have their houses as they wish. In a 1930s world, a chronometric institute was perhaps the most advanced possible agency for modernizing a developing country. In imagining how such an organization might have worked in Turkey, Tanpınar has even found a way for Turkish Everyman Hayri İrdal to best his elitist counterpart. Perhaps no writer of this period was more sensitive than Tanpınar to his fellow Turks' questions about how "to be or not to be" amid the past, present, and future.

THE EARLY REPUBLIC IN RETROSPECT

The elites of the period included real-life Halit Ayarcıs who saw no need for sensitivity to their fellow citizens' subjective needs and were sure of their plans for getting Turkey on time. Success legitimated high-pressured leadership during the National Struggle and empowered the republican leadership in a way that went beyond ballots and constitutions. As historical perspective deepened, scholars looking back on this period identified its contradictions. As sociologist Şerif Mardin recalls, "My earliest conceptual frame for the study of society was simple: it consisted of a suspicion that the official Kemalist ideology propagated by my Turkish schoolteachers disguised an authoritarianism that contradicted their ubiquitous libertarian discourse." In the formulation of feminist political scientist Yeşim Arat, "Feminist criticisms of Kemalist discourse attempt to free liberalism, democracy, and secularism from a polity that has long repressed those qualities in the name of those very qualities themselves."[97]

Although such contradictions long survived the end of the single-party period, time has provided perspective for its reassessment. Most notably, the Kemalist reforms lastingly reshaped Turkey, even if controversy continues about religion and gender issues in particular. In foreign relations, the lessons that Turkish statesmen drew from World War I proved enduringly beneficial. The statist policy of the 1930s stands out as a globally significant response to the 1929 depression. Despite the elitist bias of social policy, the republic did enact women's emancipation into law, and the Village Institutes did produce tangible results in mobilizing villagers into national life and expanding literacy. Kemalist ideology, although prematurely triumphal in its laicism, did work itself deeply enough into Turkish consciences to make itself a lasting part of the country's ideological mix. Even the Atatürk personality cult has shown a durability that makes it a subject of fascination to scholars.[98]

The other side of the history of this period, of course, includes all the Hayri İrdals, all who were publicly shamed for their dress or beliefs, all who were silenced by the nationalist elites' unison-voiced national mobilization project. The list is long, including the remaining non-Muslim minorities, the Kurds, and religiously committed Muslims, both Sunni and Alevi. Some of the excluded groups were marginal, others not so. One of the most influential Islamic renewal movements of the past two centuries, that of Said Nursi, spread in the face of official hostility in this period. In later decades, as in other developing countries, those who controlled the official narrative, the upholders of the Atatürk legacy, have faced challenges to recognize that these excluded elements also made history, that maintaining national unity and equality requires accommodating difference.

In the long run, as the enduring, broad-based veneration of him suggests, perhaps the greatest achievement of Atatürk and his associates was that many of those excluded from the early republican national narrative came to value his legacy in its essentials. As of 1938 or 1950, however, that sort of accommodation between the official makers of history and its rejects remained a project for the future.

6

TURKEY'S WIDENING POLITICAL SPECTRUM

Under both Democrat Party rule (1950–1960) and the Second Republic (1961–1980), Turkey continued its transition to multiparty politics. As the scope of political mobilization broadened, the rise of extremist movements led to political polarization and the military interventions of 1960, 1971, and 1980. Neutral during World War II and subsequently threatened by the USSR, Turkey confirmed its Western orientation, joining NATO in 1952, fighting in the Korean War, applying for membership in the European Economic Community in 1959, and becoming an associate member in 1963. As Turkey—in common with all developing countries—experienced its share of the twentieth century's unprecedented population explosion, rapid demographic growth, faster urbanization, labor migration to Europe, and 1960s youth activism transformed society. Despite a new push for planned development, the exhaustion of statist import substitution and the 1973 oil shock added economic to political stress. As the early republic's unitary nationalist mobilization faltered and social change accelerated, it was not clear whether the greatest challenges to Kemalism would come from right or left. Leftist movements proliferated in the 1960s. Ultranationalists outdid them in the 1970s. Islamic activists competed for influence, as exemplified by the emergence of the National Salvation Party and the growth of Islamist print media. By the late 1960s, the scope of political mobilization had expanded for the first time to encompass the entire population. As that happened, political and social differentiation advanced, and the ability of any single trend to tell the story of the times diminished. Amid the cacophony, the underclasses found their voices. Perhaps no literary work illustrates this more memorably than Orhan Kemal's *Bereketli Topraklar Üzerinde* (On these bounteous lands).

POLITICS

As the Turkish republic moved beyond single-party rule, the political spectrum widened and new tendencies emerged, including extremist movements not committed to operating within constitutional limits. Chronologically, the period 1950–1980 divides into the decade of Democrat rule (1950–1960) and the Second Republic (1961–1980); but three military interventions (1960, 1971, and 1980) also punctuated this period. The formulation of alternative political visions still seemed to favor secularist ideologies, leftist in the 1960s and rightist in the 1970s; yet religious conservatives also made their voices heard. The course of domestic political development was profoundly conditioned by international relations, as well as by sociodemographic, economic, and cultural transformations going on inside Turkey.

THE DEMOCRAT DECADE

Under Prime Minister Adnan Menderes (1889–1961), the Democrat Party (DP) ruled throughout the 1950s, successfully through mid-decade, less and less so thereafter. Assuming office, it confronted a bureaucracy that had been tightly integrated with the Republican People's Party, İnönü as a larger-than-life-sized opposition leader, and a military high command of uncertain loyalty.[1] The DP leadership outmaneuvered the military by retiring many high officers. Over the next several months, strong DP showings in local elections further consolidated the new regime. Before coming to power, the DP had vigorously demanded repeal of antidemocratic laws. In power, it at first gave the impression that it would repeal them. By 1951, however, the DP was already backtracking and using such laws to harass the opposition. Deciding in 1951 to confiscate the real estate that the RPP had acquired during the single-party years and transfer it to the treasury, the DP government held the law in reserve as a threat and did not act on it until 1953, an unjustifiable act in implementation of a justifiable decision. If İnönü had aimed for a tame multiparty democracy, with nothing to his left and little to his right, the Democrats went further, launching a "white terror" and arresting "communists" on grand scale.

To conservatives, the DP made some concessions, once again allowing the call to prayer (*ezan*) in Arabic (1950) and replacing the linguistically modernized 1945 text of the constitution with the original text. Yet the DP was not going to breach republican laicism. As the Cold War developed, the DP acted on its pro-Western orientation most dramatically in foreign policy. The DP attempted to match its diplomatic orientation with liberal economic policy by encouraging foreign investment, although the laws passed for this purpose produced limited effects.

Prime Minister Adnan Menderes (right) with President Celâl Bayar,
Istanbul, 1954. (Popperfoto/Getty Images.)

It liberalized foreign trade and founded a Turkish Industrial Development Bank
(Türkiye Sınai Kalkınma Bankası) to loan state funds to private entrepreneurs.
With a major push in road building, public works also contributed greatly to fos-
tering the commercial middle class. Agriculture benefited from the distribution
of unused state lands. The credit provided through the Agricultural Bank (Ziraat
Bankası) was greatly increased. Mechanization—specifically "tractorization"—
expanded rapidly; the Orhan Kemal novel discussed below imaginatively depicts
some of the consequences. By the time of the 1954 general elections, some intellectuals were beginning to be uneasy about the drift of DP policy. However, the
economic trend was still favorable, the general public was complacent, and the
DP won the elections by a larger margin than in 1950, ending up with 503 seats
in the assembly, compared to only 31 for the RPP.[2]

Drunk with success after the 1954 elections, the DP leadership dug its own
grave. With a hold on the Grand National Assembly that left no effective opposition, the Democrats generated opposition within their own ranks, and party
leaders reacted in increasingly undemocratic fashion. The electoral law was
changed to erect additional obstacles to opposition politics, for example, by
forbidding both political propaganda over the radio and candidacy for office by
politicians who had changed party (defected from the Democrats) within the
past six months. Further laws eroded the job security of officials, judges, and
university faculty members. Opposition journalists were prosecuted, and RPP

meetings were disrupted or forbidden. The economic situation deteriorated, and inflation and goods scarcities appeared.

In 1955, when the British invited Turkey and Greece to negotiate about the future of Cyprus, the DP government sought to promote a demonstration to display its popular backing. However, after an Istanbul newspaper published a report that the house in Salonica that was thought to be Atatürk's birthplace had been bombed, the event degenerated into a rampage against the Greeks of Istanbul and Izmir (6 September 1955), with destruction of property on a scale that did not appear accidental.[3] The old tactic of using a foreign enemy to unite opinion at home had backfired, and the government declared martial law in both cities. Public opinion, which the Democrats had hoped to focus on Cyprus, focused on them instead. Most of the remaining Turkish Greeks emigrated, along with other minorities. Recriminations divided the DP leaders. By November, Menderes's cabinet had fallen, but he had persuaded the deputies to give him a vote of confidence. Discontented DP deputies left the party to form the Freedom (Hürriyet) Party in December. The remaining DP deputies had to submit to an increasingly dictatorial and paranoiac leader.

Forming a new government, Menderes again announced a liberal-sounding program to answer his critics' demands; yet no such policies would be carried out with him as prime minister. Reenergized, the RPP attacked Menderes persistently. The DP reacted with an all-out attack, including freewheeling allegations about communism and sedition. İnönü responded prophetically: "Turning back democracy is not something just any fellow can pull off (*herhangi babayiğidin harcı değildir*). Whoever tries this . . . , the world will become his prison; and he will thrust himself, his colleagues, and his organization into a nightmare." Menderes charged ahead, dismissing officials and judges, prosecuting journalists, passing menacingly vague laws to forbid publications or meetings "based on special motives" (*maksad-ı mahsusa müstenit*), and using the laws against opposition leaders.[4] By 1957, Menderes had united the opposition against him. Even DP founder Fuat Köprülü resigned and joined the opposition. With elections coming in 1958, the DP resorted to the tactics used against it in 1946, advancing the elections by a year and passing a new electoral law expressly to obstruct the opposition. In the 1957 election, even though the DP vote declined somewhat, the rules in force still translated that into 424 assembly seats for the DP, 178 for the RPP, and 8 for two small parties.

Menderes formed his fifth cabinet and resumed his antidemocratic policies. However, the economic situation worsened until Menderes had to impose severe austerity measures in 1958, restoring Turkey's credit but alienating even his supporters. Officials and military officers found their salaries eroded by inflation. Industrialists complained of inconsistent economic policies. At the same time, Iraq's 1958 revolution and the use of a military base in Turkey for the 1958 U.S. intervention in Lebanon also destabilized the DP government's foreign policy and raised its revolution phobia to new heights.

As the RPP took the lead more and more in organizing the opposition, the roles of a decade earlier were reversed. Now, the RPP was the vanguard of democracy, while the DP played at single-party rule, reckless of the consequences. Menderes experienced one final surge in popularity when he miraculously survived a plane crash that killed many of his entourage on a trip to England in 1959. That did not help for long. İnönü launched an opposition "grand offensive"; his appearances frequently sparked incidents, at least once endangering his personal safety. In May 1959, there was even fighting between DP and RPP deputies in the assembly. In April 1960, the DP decided the time had come for a parliamentary commission, endowed with dictatorial powers, to investigate the RPP, whose representatives—including party chairman İnönü—were barred from the assembly by vote of the Democrat deputies. Street demonstrations began in Istanbul and Ankara and continued until 27 May 1960, when the military staged a coup. The greatest damage done by the DP "was that it almost forcibly brought the army into politics, permanently injuring the tradition of civilian rule meticulously preserved since Atatürk."[5]

FOREIGN RELATIONS UNDER THE DEMOCRATS

In foreign policy, Turkey's pro-Western reorientation continued during the 1950s.[6] The Menderes government committed Turkish troops to the U.N. force in the Korean War so as to demonstrate Turkey's commitment to the Western alliance. The founding of NATO in 1949 prompted Turkey's application for membership the next year. As an "unsinkable aircraft carrier" adjoining the Soviet Union, Turkey was strategically valuable to NATO. Turkey's admission to NATO membership in 1952 consolidated Turkey's pro-Western alignment, producing significant consequences. Large numbers of U.S. and NATO bases and other facilities were located in Turkey. Between 1948 and 1964, U.S. military aid to Turkey totaled nearly $2.5 billion, aside from perhaps another $1.5 billion in Western economic aid. The Turkey of the 1950s could not have experienced growth in both its economy and its military without such investment.

Over time, the military concentration of the investment, and the overseas experience that Turkish officers gained through NATO assignments, created gaps in different elites' understanding of modernity. With their history of elitism going back to Ottoman times and their new NATO experience, by the 1960s

Turkish military officers tended to be better informed about the world than most other elites, a difference that quite likely had a bearing on the frequency of military interventions in politics.[7] Be that as it may, the Turkey of the 1950s fulfilled its NATO obligations to the letter and also supported related efforts to create both a Turkish-Greek-Yugoslav Balkan Defense Pact and a Middle Eastern alliance (the Baghdad Pact, 1955) combining Turkey, Iraq, Iran, Pakistan, and Britain. The Balkan pact was undone by Marshal Tito's reconciliation with the USSR and his leadership in the nonalignment movement; the Baghdad Pact provoked negative reactions across the Arab world and was wrecked by the Iraqi revolution of 1958. Its remains were reorganized as CENTO (the Central Treaty Organization, 1959).

The most sensitive foreign policy issue, that of Cyprus, emerged in 1954, when Greece began to press for an end to British rule and the island's union with Greece. How quickly the issue heated up for the Turkish public became apparent with the 1955 anti-Greek violence in Istanbul. Negotiations about the future of the island, as well as violence between its Greek and Turkish residents, continued for the rest of the decade. In 1960, Cyprus was proclaimed independent with a constitution that mandated a power-sharing arrangement between Cypriot Greeks and Turks and a treaty that made Britain, Greece, and Turkey guarantors of the unity and independence of the island. Independence marked more the beginning than the end of international complications over Cyprus.

THE SECOND REPUBLIC, 1960–1980

The 1960 military coup set a precedent for armed intervention whenever the civilian politicians had made too great a mess of things. It also set the precedent that military rule should be temporary and that power should be returned to civilians after corrective measures had been taken. In their self-understanding, the officers should save the nation when it was in peril, but they should not sink into the bog of politics.[8] As the size and political activation of the Turkish population grew, economic growth buoyed Turkey as it lived through its share of the global agitation of the late 1960s. After the military intervention of 1971–1973, the broadening of the political spectrum continued and became even more complex under the harsher economic conditions created for oil-importing countries by the huge increases in the price of petroleum in 1973 and 1979. The political and economic deterioration culminated in the military intervention of 1980–1982, which ended the Second Republic. Amid the chaos, the economic crisis also precipitated the most profound reorientation in economic policy since the early 1930s.

The 1960 coup was the work of a small group of officers, whose seizure of power came as a fait accompli to the rest of the military hierarchy as well as to civilian politicians and the public. The coup-makers set themselves up as the National Unity Committee (Milli Birlik Komitesi). Once they had seized power and amended the constitution to justify their position, pressures for a return to civilian rule began building from within and without. The committee members were divided over how soon this should occur. A minority of fourteen, led by Alparslan Türkeş (1917–1997), a leading figure in ultranationalist politics for half a century, favored prolonged military rule and authoritarian reforms from the top. The majority favored a quicker turnover and was more sensitive to the harm military rule could do to the army itself. The committee's intervention had violated the chain of command. It quickly retired five thousand officers to secure its own flank; but that did not end the problems about the chain of command. Among the committee members were lower-ranking officers who made decisions affecting superiors who were not on the committee. Civilian politicians also divided over how fast the committee should relinquish power, with İnönü calling for a quick turnover. The only way the committee could deal with its internal divisions was for one faction to remove the other. The majority faction did this in November, ousting the fourteen and dispatching them to postings outside Turkey. Plans were then made for a constituent assembly along corporatist lines, including representatives of the surviving political parties (the DP having been outlawed), as well as of major sectors of society, veterans, teachers, merchants, youth, and so on. The constituent assembly met in 1961, examining drafts prepared by academics. A popular referendum approved the final version in July 1961.

The 1961 constitution was a great advance over that of 1924 in guaranteeing the rights of citizens and separating the executive, legislative, and judicial powers in government.[9] Nearly a third of the document addressed rights and their safeguards. The provisions on government provided for a bicameral legislature, including a new Senate in addition to the Grand National Assembly. To differentiate the executive more clearly from the legislature, the president was to be elected henceforth for a single seven-year term. The presidents would thus be free of worry about reelection, and the seven-year term would not coincide with the four-year term of the assembly members. The president was to chair the National Security Council (Milli Güvenlik Kurulu), which would include the prime minister and the military chiefs. Autonomy was guaranteed to the universities and the Turkish Radio and Television Authority. The provisions on the judiciary created a Constitutional Court to rule on the constitutionality of laws, guaranteed the independency of the judiciary, and gave it oversight over all actions of government. To systematize economic policy, an autonomous state agency, the State Planning Organization (Devlet Planlama Teşkilatı) was created and charged with preparing five-year plans. Compared to that of 1924, the 1961 constitution created a liberal framework, with the notable exception of the political role assigned to the military in the National Security Council. In 1961, no one foresaw either the proliferation of new political forces, including ones not loyal to the constitution, or the severe stresses generated by the demographic surge of the 1960s and the economic crises of the 1970s. Those stresses overloaded the new constitutional order and provoked two more military interventions.

As the constitution was being prepared, political parties were allowed to resume their activity. The Democrat Party had been banned but still retained its majority among voters. Two new parties were formed to replace the old one; of these, the Democrats' successor, the Justice Party (JP, Adalet Partisi), became a major party. The return to civilian rule was complicated by tensions within the military about whether officers who had supported the coup would be subjected to reprisals and by the trials of Menderes and other Democrat leaders. The trials ended with fifteen death sentences and many prison sentences. Despite appeals, three of the death sentences were carried out: those of Adnan Menderes, his foreign minister, Fatin Rüştü Zorlu, and his finance minister, Hasan Polatkan. The elections a month later showed that the abolished party's supporters still formed the largest block of voters. Even though the Democrats' successors controlled more seats in the new parliament, a recently formed pressure group, the Armed Forces Union (Silahlı Kuvvetler Birliği), threatened another takeover. İnönü defused that threat through negotiations. He emerged as the prime minister; the former chair of the Committee of National Unity, Cemal Gürsel, became the new president; and the cabinet was a JP-RPP coalition.

This was the republic's first coalition government; it was not the last. The JP-RPP coalition was a forced alliance. Not wanting a coalition that excluded the two major parties, the military supplied the force. However, the two parties had a long history of enmity. They disagreed as well over the legitimacy of the 1961 constitution, the origins of which the JP politicians, as the Democrats' heirs, did not consider legal.[10] As the spectrum of Turkish politics continued to widen, many problems might have been avoided, if the two large, centrist parties had been able to work together. Their inability to do so led each of them to form coalitions with smaller, more extreme parties, so polarizing politics. Between 1961 and the 1965 general elections, Turkey had four governments, all coalitions. As the only politician who could negotiate with the military, İnönü became the prime minister in three of them. The urgent economic problems left over from the Democrat regime could not be addressed, far less could the new constitution's promises of economic planning and a welfare state. As tensions mounted over Cyprus, international issues became equally acute. Nonetheless, by the time İnönü resigned as prime minister for the last time in February 1965, and largely thanks to him, the transition to civilian politics was becoming consolidated. The Justice Party emerged from the October 1965 general elections with an absolute majority (240 assembly seats, compared to 134 for the RPP).

A JP era was about to succeed the Democrat decade of the 1950s. Over the next thirty-five years, JP chairman Süleyman Demirel (b. 1924) became one of the most durable figures of Turkish politics, serving as prime minister seven times (compared to İnönü's total of ten) before ending as president of the republic (1993–2000). Under the JP, the period 1965–1971 maintained multiparty politics in Turkey, although conditions destabilized rapidly from 1968 on through the military intervention of 12 March 1971. In these years, the liberal provisions of the constitution combined with demographic growth and Turkey's long-term trend toward political mobilization to produce a sudden proliferation of new political movements, both right and left. Numbers of these were antisystem parties or movements, operating partly or entirely outside the electoral, parliamentary system and not considering themselves bound by the constitution.

Leftist movements were not the only ones, but they were the first and most vigorous in the 1960s. The influence of Marxist thought, which became widely available in Turkey for the first time in the freer climate created by the 1961 constitution, played a critical part in this flowering on the left. Much as constitutionalism and scientific materialism had provided a common intellectual currency for late Ottoman bureaucratic intellectuals, Marxism became the common currency for the 1960s' enlarged cohorts of students and intellectuals. Very likely, too, collectivism and "democratic centralism" made Marxism and its derivatives appealing to Turks of the '68 generation for much the same cultural reasons that Turks of Ziya Gökalp's generation had found corporatism and Durkheimian solidarism more appealing than classical liberalism.[11] The early 1960s witnessed the emergence of non-Marxist socialist movements as well as a Marxist Workers Party of Turkey (WPT). Dominating the left from 1965 to 1968, the WPT operated within the system and had elected deputies in the assembly. On the non-Marxist left, one influential trend emerged around journals published by Doğan Avcıoğlu, first *Yön* (Direction) and then *Devrim* (Revolution), a "left Kemalism" that blended Marxism with Kemalism. Seeking a new role for itself, the RPP also adopted a "left of center" stance in 1966, at the price of splitting the party. Becoming secretary general of the RPP in 1966, Bülent Ecevit (1925–2006) embodied this trend toward turning the RPP into a social democratic party. At the other extreme, the ultranationalist right began to organize. In 1965, Alparslan Türkeş took over the leadership of a small party, which he transformed in 1969 into the Nationalist Action Party (NAP, Milliyetçi Hareket Partisi). The name of the party can also be translated as Nationalist Movement Party, and it may reflect Türkeş's interest in Francisco Franco's Movimiento Nacional in Spain.[12] However, with a majority in the assembly and carefully cultivated relations with the military, the JP majority government under Demirel gave Turkey a fairly smooth-running multiparty democracy from 1965 to 1968.

In the late 1960s, the global wave of disturbances swept through Turkey, too, with the excitement concentrated in the upsurge of leftist radicalism. Historians of the Turkish left have argued that Turkey differed from other countries in that the excitement of 1968 was concentrated in leftist politics and did not diversify across the full spectrum of the Euro-American counterculture, including the sexual revolution, the U.S. civil rights movement, the hippies, pacifists, environmentalists, feminists, and so on.[13] In a global comparative perspective, however, it may be more accurate to argue that the conflicts of the 1960s commonly began in confrontations of pro- and antiestablishment alignments. The antiestablishment wave typically crested and crashed at the same time, roughly 1968, provoking both a backlash from the forces of order and a fragmentation on the left into the politics of identity and difference. Even in the highly developed Western countries, one of the lessons from the aftermath of 1968 was that it should be possible to be equal and different at the same time. In the Turkey of the late 1960s, the only hippies were foreign ones, who began to appear at just that time. That did not stop Turkey from living through its own version of the 1960s' global pattern and its aftermath. Granted, the differentiation among the antiestablishment forces did not become fully apparent in some cases—such as the new feminism or environmentalism—before the 1980s. In Turkey, assimilating the lesson that people who differ in gender, ethnicity, sect, and personal preference can still be equal citizens remains a work in progress, even yet.

In Turkey, the leftist upsurge resulted in a destabilizing spiral that ended in the military intervention of 1971. After the economic and demographic growth of the 1960s, particular segments of the population became highly volatile, workers and students in particular. Provocative world events fanned the flames: the Palestinian liberation struggle, the U.S. expansion of the Vietnam War

(1965), the Chinese Cultural Revolution (1966), and Ché Guevara's activities in Bolivia (1967). In 1968, the global tempo accelerated with the Tet Offensive in Vietnam (February), the French student uprising (May), and the Soviet invasion of Czechoslovakia (August). The Turkish left reacted passionately. Competition among its factions intensified. The upshot was defeat for the WPT and its strategy of operating by legal means. The party tried to broaden its appeal by championing the causes of the Kurds and the Alevi religious minority, but that did less for the WPT than it did for the turn toward identity politics.[14] As the radicals gained ascendancy on the left, militant actions began in June and July as students seized Istanbul University, workers occupied a tire factory, and young leftists attacked sailors of the U.S. Sixth Fleet in Istanbul. The antisystem left gained traction but lost unity. The Federation of the Revolutionary Youth of Turkey, known as Dev-Genç (a contraction of its Turkish name), split in 1969–1970, as Maoist and Guevarist factions broke off. Deciding that the time had come for armed action, several factions took to the hills.

Leftists were not alone in becoming increasingly organized and militant in the late 1960s. Rightist students grouped around the National Turkish Student Union (Milli Türk Talebe Birliği) and began to form Hearths of Ideals (Ülkü Ocakları) and "commando" training camps in 1968. Once appropriated, the terms *ideal* and *idealist* (*ülkü, ülkücü*) acquired a bad name as virtual ultranationalist trademarks. The ultranationalists maintained their unity far better than the leftist radicals; but they were not the only force on the far right. Beginning with a mass prayer meeting in May 1968, Islamic political assertiveness found a political outlet in the newspaper *Bugün* and a leader in Necmettin Erbakan, who founded the National Order (Milli Nizam) Party in 1970. This was the first version of the Islamist party that was abolished and restarted successively as the National Salvation (Milli Selamet, 1972–1980), Prosperity (Refah, 1983–1998), Virtue (Fazilet, 1998–2001), and Felicity (Saadet, 2001–) parties; in the background, a broader National Outlook (Milli Görüş) movement provided continuity all the while. In 2001, the religious Right divided, with the "traditionalists" carrying on as the Felicity (Saadet) party and the "innovators" forming a new kind of center-rightist party, Justice and Development (Adalet ve Kalkınma).[15]

As movements and tendencies proliferated in the late 1960s, the democratic order defined by the 1961 constitution came under increasing strain from interests that were not all loyal to it. The major parties had their criticisms of the constitution, too, although they differed in what they criticized. From 1968 on, the policy of the Demirel government changed in response to the increasing disorder. Embarking on a struggle against the left, it gave a free reign to the extralegal right, condoning the commando camps and turning the state security forces loose. The riot police raided student housing in Istanbul, causing the first death of a political victim since 1961.

By the time of the 1969 general elections, Turkey was becoming ungovernable. Despite the decline in the JP vote to 46.5 percent in 1969 and subsequent crises, Demirel hung on as prime minister. But the economy was deteriorating, and politics was sinking into violence, particularly from the left. Strategies for revolution were discussed almost openly, and guerrilla movements were forming: Deniz Gezmiş's People's Liberation Army of Turkey (Türkiye Halk Kurtuluş Ordusu) and Mahir Çayan's People's Liberation Party-Front of Turkey (Türkiye Halk Kurtuluş Partisi-Cephesi). Early 1971 witnessed Turkey's first politically motivated bank robbery, the abduction of U.S. military personnel, and the indefinite closure of Istanbul University. Elements of the radical left believed that revolution might come through a power seizure by a "radical junta." The hopes they placed in their allies in the military proved naive.

When the military high command acted, on 12 March 1971, it suppressed its left-leaning subordinates and issued an ultimatum demanding the formation of a strong government that could end anarchy and carry out reforms "in a Kemalist spirit"; otherwise, the army would "exercise its constitutional duty" and take power directly.[16] A new government was formed with Nihat Erim as prime minister; from the conservative wing of the RPP, he won İnönü's acquiescence to the change of government. Erim formed a technocratic government, which produced a program for economic reform. With radical political violence continuing, the National Security Council proclaimed martial law in eleven provinces and pursued a rigorous "counter-guerrilla" campaign against leftist elements. When militants kidnapped Israel's Istanbul consul general, Ephraim Elrom, in May 1971, the entire population of the city was confined to its houses for fifteen hours to facilitate the search for the perpetrators.[17] After the 1971 coup, this and other actions against leftists resulted in some five thousand arrests and many allegations of torture.

Prison is the best university, it is often said. By the time many of the leftists rounded up in 1971 were freed, Maoism had gained ground among them.[18] Meanwhile, the Erim government enacted constitutional amendments limiting civil liberties and press freedom; ending autonomy of the universities, radio, and television; expanding the powers of the National Security Council; curtailing those of the constitutional court; and introducing State Security Courts (not abolished until 1976). The only party to oppose these changes was the RPP, in which Bülent Ecevit's opposition to these measures enabled him to supplant İnönü as party leader in 1972.

The military intervention of 1971–1973 differed from that of 1960 in being a "coup by memorandum," in which the military did not take power directly but told the civilian politicians what to do. Among the reasons for this reserve was the spectacle of Greece, under military misrule since 1967. Controlling events by memoranda was not a workable solution for the long run, however, and that fact enabled the civilian politicians gradually to reassert themselves. Free elections resumed in October 1973. Ecevit's RPP emerged as the largest party with 33.5 percent of the vote, compared to 29.5 percent for the JP.

From 1973 through 1980, no party had an absolute majority. The six governments of those years were all coalitions, inherently unstable.[19] Even though Turkey's 1974 invasion of Cyprus (discussed below) made Ecevit a hero, Demirel succeeded him as prime minister and formed a Nationalist Front (Milliyetçi Cephe) government in 1975, including Erbakan's National Salvation (NSP) and Türkeş's Nationalist Action (NAP) parties. The JP's hold on power depended on the small parties, which gave them disproportional influence. In 1975, the NAP had only three deputies in the assembly but two ministers in the cabinet. In an effort to increase their influence while they had the chance, the ministers from the small parties treated their ministries as fiefdoms, dismissing or demoting civil servants to replace them with party loyalists. In the 1977 elections, the RPP got 41.4 percent of the vote, the most it ever got in a free election,

Prime Minister Bülent Ecevit welcomes Justice Party head Süleyman Demirel, February 1974. (Anatolia Agency.)

and the JP got 36.9 percent. Again, first Ecevit and then Demirel failed to form viable coalitions. Ecevit finally put together a cabinet of RPP and independent ministers (January 1978–October 1979). Distrusted by the military and savagely attacked by Demirel, this government was distracted by its members' attempts to purge the ministries colonized by the ministers of the preceding government. Demirel returned to power in November 1979 with a minority government of the JP and independents.

By 1980, politics had become so paralyzed that the assembly could not elect a new president of the republic after 115 votes. For years, the most puzzling political question had continued to be why the two, large centrist parties, JP and RPP, could not form a coalition, which would have had a large majority in the assembly had they done so. The parties' past histories, their leaders' rivalries, and each party's hopes of achieving a majority in the next elections probably explain why this did not happen. In fact, the reasons for the Second Republic's demise extend far beyond the formal politics of elections and parties.

In terms of the socioeconomic context of Turkish politics, the biggest contrast between the 1960s and the 1970s was that social stress, which economic growth had mitigated in the 1960s, was compounded by a global economic downturn in the 1970s. In terms of the "non-system" political forces active at opposite extremes of the right-left spectrum, the biggest difference between the 1960s and the 1970s was that the left, which had dominated the 1960s, was more than counterbalanced in the 1970s by the right, particularly the violence unleashed by Türkeş's ultranationalist paramilitary.[20] The left of the 1970s was divided between independent, Maoist, and pro-Soviet groups, all with subdivisions. The left showed its strengths and weaknesses most memorably at a huge demonstration at Taksim Square in Istanbul on May Day, 1977. Called by the Revolutionary Workers' Unions (Devrimci İşçi Sendikaları Konfederasyonu, DİSK), the demonstration brought out perhaps half a million people representing different, competing tendencies. As a Maoist group attempted to force its way into the square, some of them fired into the air. From the surrounding rooftops, more shots answered, causing a stampede and thirty-four deaths. For the next three years, the divided left was locked in a violent struggle with the far right, which was united, numerous, and supported by elements in government, as the advantageous placement of the rooftop gunners of May Day implied.

Turkish ultranationalists had difficulties uniting in earlier periods, but the rise of the Nationalist Action Party opened a new phase. The leadership principle and firm hierarchical subordination figured prominently among the movement's fascistic traits. In the elections of the 1970s, even though it received small percentages of the vote, the coalition politics of the period gave the NAP

May Day, 1977, Taksim Square, Istanbul. At top, the huge crowd, including many women, assembles in the square in front of the Atatürk Culture Center (background), with a broad banner on its facade depicting a worker with outstretched arms and the date "1 Mayıs." After gunfire from surrounding rooftops broke up the demonstration, one of the dead lies on the ground, with her arms similarly outstretched. (Both photos from the Collection of the International Institute of Social History, Amsterdam; top photo labeled *DİSK Foto Film Merkezi*, Photo and Film Center of the Confederation of Revolutionary Workers Unions.)

disproportional representation in the cabinets of 1975 and 1977, opening the way for the "bureaucratic feudalism" that resulted in the colonization of major government agencies, including the ministries of commerce and education and the State Statistical Institute, with party supporters.

The NAP's influence was magnified by its usefulness to the Justice Party as a strike force against the left, in other words by the NAP's strength in the streets. That depended in the first instance on the young militants, the "gray wolves" (*bozkurt*) and the organizations of "idealists" (*ülkücü*) in the universities and schools. The military regime of 1971–1973 had shut down the NAP's commando camps of the 1960s, but the gray wolves' training with firearms resumed after 1973, at first secretly. Demirel condoned NAP violence, and no legal proceedings were ever undertaken against the party, despite growing concern among some elements of the JP.[21] Championing corporatism and opposing class-based politics, the NAP also created "idealist associations" for workers, policemen, officials, teachers, tradespeople and artisans, peasants, financiers and economists, journalists, and so on, all strictly controlled by Türkeş. Active in the Turkish diaspora, the party had 129 associations in Europe by 1978, mostly in Germany. NAP fund-raising was also international, with much of the party's money and property registered in Türkeş's name. NAP foundations and companies, extortion by party militants, even alleged ties with the "Turkish mafia," added to the party's resources, as did an official newspaper, *Hergün,* and other sponsored publications.

In the late 1970s, the government's ability to maintain law and order dwindled.[22] The death toll from political violence rose from 231 in 1977 to 2,812 in the twelve months before the military intervened again in September 1980. This is to say nothing of the numbers of people who were injured or kidnapped, the loss of property, or the fear that confined people to their homes after dark. Ultimately, the violence did not remain confined between militants of left and right; ethnic, religious, and other differences also became engaged. The Alevi religious minority, historically persecuted by the Ottoman government and Sunnis in general, tended politically to support secularists and the left, which exposed them particularly to violence from the right, as evidenced in the massacres at Kahramanmaraş in 1978 (at least 109 dead and 170 seriously injured) and Çorum in 1980 (30 dead and a mass Alevi exodus).

In regions of the country where significant cleavages existed among the local population, rival militias staked their turf, claimed their "liberated zones," even took control of local government; and the populace had no choice but to accept their protection. In one zone in central Anatolia (the provinces of Çorum, Yozgat, Niğde, Nevşehir, and Ordu), the critical cleavage was between Sunni and Alevi. Forming another, highly explosive zone, the provinces of Sivas, Maraş, Malatya, Elazığ, Erzincan, Tunceli, and Bingöl divided along both religious (Sunni and Alevi) and ethnic (Turkish and Kurdish) lines, with religious difference determining affiliation more than linguistic. In a third zone made up of the provinces of Kars and Erzurum, the politically significant cleavages were primarily linguistic (Kurdish-Turkish) and secondarily between tribespeople (mountaineers) and migrants (sedentary). The fourth zone (the provinces of Diyarbakır, Urfa, and Mardin), was nearly homogeneous ethnically and religiously, but its Kurmanca-speaking, Sunni Kurds were divided along lines of both tribe and party: the Kurdistan Workers' Party (Kurdish acronym PKK, Partiya Karkerên Kurdistan) versus the National Liberators of Kurdistan (Turkish acronym KUK, Kürdistan Ulusal Kurtuluşçuları).[23] Led by Abdullah Öcalan and advocating a mix of Marxism-Leninism and nationalism, the PKK was also blamed for more than two hundred murders between 1978 and 1980. The local conflicts from these regional hot spots spread into shantytowns of Istanbul and Ankara, where migrants commonly settled together with others of the same origin, and into diaspora communities in Europe.

Huge amounts of arms later confiscated from militant groups led to speculations about a Soviet role in destabilizing Turkey. However, internal strains inside Turkey sufficed to explain the downward spiral. Much of the blame goes to governments that failed in their primary task of maintaining law and order. After the Kahramanmaraş massacre, the declaration of martial law (in effect, 1979–1980) proved the civilian government's failure in this task. Even under martial law, the violence continued until the coup of 1980, then suddenly stopped, quite likely because those most affected by it were willing to see the army replace the militias as their protectors. The one remarkable initiative amid this record of failure was the change in economic policy signified by the appointment of Turgut Özal as undersecretary for planning in 1979, a change that opened a new economic era in 1980.

The rise in political violence again drew the military into the thick of politics.[24] On 12 September 1980, when the army intervened for the third time since 1960, the general public received the news with relief. The leaders of the major political parties were rounded up. Political activity in public was forbidden. A cabinet was soon formed under retired admiral Bülend Ulusu. Turgut Özal was kept on as deputy prime minister responsible for economic affairs to implement his economic policy reforms. This military coup was much better prepared than its precursors. The initiative came from the high command, and there was no mismatch between the hierarchies of military rank and political power. Martial law put an end to the political violence. NAP leader Türkeş was arrested with two hundred party members; he was accused of murdering six hundred people and fomenting civil war. Although terrorist charges would not stick against NSP leader Erbakan, he was also arrested and charged with violating constitutional provisions that mandated laicism and forbade calling for an Islamic state. As for political reconstruction, it proceeded so gradually that the return to civilian rule did not occur until 1983. By then, the military regime would be blamed for many excesses of its own. However, the Second Republic was over as of 12 September 1980, and Turkey was beginning to move beyond the political turbulence of the 1960s and 1970s.

FOREIGN RELATIONS, 1960–1980

Although foreign policy had almost been crowded off the screen during the domestic turbulence of the late 1960s or the late 1970s, several issues of the period produced important consequences. Cyprus remained an acute issue, prompting far-reaching questioning of Turkey's 1945 pro-Western policy orientation. Although Cyprus had become independent in 1960 as a bicommunal state under Turkish, Greek, and British guaranty, Greek Cypriots wanted union with Greece. Under Cypriot president Archbishop Makarios, the Greek Cypriots abandoned the constitutional power-sharing in 1963 and excluded Turkish Cypriots from government. Massacres of Turkish Cypriots soon started. In 1964, Turkey retaliated by canceling the residence permits of Greek citizens living in Turkey. As nine thousand Greeks left Turkey, the country's historical Greek population suffered its last sizable emigration. Prime Minister İnönü gave diplomatic warning that Turkey might intervene in Cyprus to enforce the treaties if nothing was done. He prepared to do so in June 1964, only to receive a letter from U.S. president Lyndon Johnson.[25] The letter warned, among other things, that weapons supplied by the United States could not be used for purposes it had not approved, and that if the Soviet Union were to use this as an occasion to intervene in Turkey, NATO could not be relied on to respond. Interpreted in Turkey as disrespectful to an elder statesman, the letter caused deep disillusionment with the post-1945 pro-Western foreign policy. Turkey began looking for ways to diversify its international ties, started developing its own arms industry, and established its new Aegean Army Corps outside the NATO framework. Turks discussed whether they should even remain in NATO, but the defensive value of such an alliance and the Western aid to Turkey kept this discussion from leading to a break.

In 1974, Cyprus again seized the headlines.[26] The ultrarightist military junta that had ruled Greece since 1967 appeared to be plotting a coup to unite Cyprus with Greece and get rid of Archbishop Makarios. Massacres of Turkish Cypriots again made the news, and now Turks had television to cover them. The coup in Cyprus occurred in July 1974, but Makarios escaped and continued his fight against the coup and the junta from abroad. In Turkey, Prime Minister Ecevit, governing in an uneasy coalition, made diplomatic overtures to Britain and the United States with thoughts of a combined British-Turkish intervention. However, the British favored diplomatic over military action, and the United States was preoccupied with the Watergate scandal and Secretary of State Henry Kissinger's Arab-Israeli peace-making efforts. Of the treaty guarantors of Cypriot independence, only Turkey was prepared to act. It did so, invading Cyprus on 20 July 1974. In Greece, the junta decided to declare war but was unprepared, collapsed, and was replaced by a civilian government. Meanwhile in Cyprus, a UN ceasefire took effect on 22 July. Up to this point, Turkish actions were soundly based in international law. The problem was that Turkish Cypriots living outside the northern zone occupied by the Turkish forces were still surrounded by the Greek Cypriot national guard. In August, Turkish forces began a second advance, which effectively partitioned the island, causing a massive flight of Turkish Cypriots to its north and Greek Cypriots to its south. Turkey had the military superiority in Cyprus but, having exceeded its treaty role as guarantor, could not convert this into diplomatic recognition. Thereafter, as Greece and Turkey persisted in failing to compromise, the Cyprus problem became internationalized, with UN mediation continuing for decades. In Cyprus, the north declared its independence in 1983 but was recognized only by Turkey, whereas the south remained internationally recognized as the Republic of Cyprus. The Cyprus issue also continued to poison Turkey's relations with the United States and Europe.

Relations with Europe constituted Turkey's other foreign policy topic of note.[27] The European Economic Community was founded in 1957, and Turkey and Greece both applied for membership in 1959. For Turkey, this was a natural extension of the desire, dating back at least to the late eighteenth century, for admission to the European alliance system. Turkey became an associate member of the EEC in 1963 under an agreement providing for a process with preliminary, transitional, and full-membership stages. By the time the additional protocol for the transitional stage was up for approval in 1970, the process was beginning to be controversial in both Turkey and Europe, but the protocol was approved in 1971. Later in the 1970s, opposition from both Islamists and supporters of statist economic policy became more vocal. Practical policy issues also impeded economic integration: conflicts over Turkish manufactured exports' access to European markets, the numbers of Turkish workers already in Europe, the volume of their remittances to Turkey, restrictions of the movement of additional Turkish workers to Europe. Stalled when the 1980 coup occurred, negotiations over these issues resumed only in 1986. In 1979, the Soviet invasion of Afghanistan and the Iranian revolution resensitized Europeans to the need to protect democracy in Turkey; yet the 1980 coup set back action on these intentions for several years.

While most other international issues that arose under Turkey's Second Republic were less momentous, one other left lasting scars: the rise in anti-Turkish terrorism in the 1970s.[28] Between 1973 and 1983, a string of terrorist attacks targeted Turkish diplomats, airline offices, and other targets, including one American professor of Ottoman history. ASALA (the Armenian Secret Army for the Liberation of Armenia), founded in Beirut in 1975, continued these attacks until 1986, ultimately killing thirty-one Turkish diplomats and members of diplomats' families. ASALA moved its offices to Cyprus in the 1980s, where the Greek Cypriot republic became a center of anti-Turkish activities.

POLITICAL RETROSPECT, 1950–1980

To sum up the political developments of the years between 1950 and 1980, Turkey experienced political mobilization on unprecedented scale. The Democrat decade of the 1950s widened the scope of competitive party politics and helped to bridge the gap between the cities and the countryside, where the Democrats' following was largely based. In the 1960s, cross-class political mobilization began to occur as urban youth identified for the first time with the problems of workers and peasants, not that many of the common people shared the young radicals' enthusiasm for revolution. Between the 1971 coup and the amnesty of 1974, bloody repression and harsh imprisonment gave the '68 radicals plenty of time to reflect on the disparity between their own subjectivity and the modern state's effort to turn them into dutiful citizens; the ultrarightists who wrought so much violence in the 1970s were put to the same school after 1980. The broadening of the political spectrum inside Turkey, and the headlines about Cyprus and integration with Europe, would continue to shape Turkish politics long into the future. Meanwhile, the economic, social, and cultural roots and ramifications of these political transformations ran throughout the history of this period.

THE ECONOMY

The world economy experienced unprecedented growth from 1945 to 1973. Then, several factors, particularly the increases in oil prices by factors of 4 in 1973–1974 and 2.5 in 1979, reversed this trend, throwing the world into recession. As a populous, developing country dependent on oil imports, Turkey felt the shift of trend acutely. Turkey responded in 1979 with its first truly fundamental shift in economic policy since the adoption of statism in the 1930s. As chronological perspective deepens, future economic historians may therefore look back on the entire period 1933–1979 as a unit. Between those years, economic responses to changing conditions nonetheless differentiated subperiods. In the years discussed in this chapter, these include agriculture-led growth (1947–1962), state planning and import substitution (1963–1977), and the crisis (1977–1979) that prompted adoption of the export-led growth strategy.[29]

AGRICULTURE LEADS GROWTH, 1947–1962

Through 1950, despite all attempts to stimulate business and industry, the Turkish economy remained predominantly agrarian. The agricultural share of total employment held steady above 80 percent, and the agricultural share of gross domestic product oscillated between roughly 35 and 55 percent from year to year without showing any consistent downward trend.[30] After 1950, both these conditions began to change. However, when the agrarian-rooted Democrats came to power in 1950, the potential still existed for agriculture-led growth; and that is what prevailed until the early 1960s.

Between 1947 and 1953, agricultural production more than doubled. The driving factors in this growth were the distribution of state lands and communal pastures, policies that primarily benefited peasant smallholders, and the use of Marshall Plan aid to promote mechanization, specifically "tractorization," a policy benefiting large landowners. The number of tractors in Turkey jumped from fewer than ten thousand in 1946 to forty-two thousand by 1960, and their impact was felt in social, economic, and cultural life, as notably reflected in literary works of the period. The Menderes administration also used U.S. aid to extend the road network. Between 1950 and 1980, roads of all kinds increased in length more than two-and-a-half times (from 89,000 to 233,000 kilometers). Better roads brought some fruits of modernity to the village. More than that, they brought villagers to the city. In the 1960s, rural-to-urban migration transformed Turkish cities and spilled over into the labor migration to Europe and, subsequently, into a global diaspora.[31]

Agriculture boomed until 1953, and the Democrat government pursued its policies in a spirit of economic liberalism. As conditions deteriorated after 1953, the government used inflationary policies to protect its agrarian base, introducing price supports for wheat and expanding the money supply. The resulting inflation and goods shortages created hardships, particularly for urban

Tractors become widespread in Anatolia. Faces wreathed in smiles,
everybody turns out for a ride, 1957. The tractor was made by Koç Holding
in partnership with Minneapolis Moline. (Collection of the author.)

populations and people on fixed incomes. That included officials and military
officers, whose mounting resentments contributed directly to the 1960 coup.
As tension mounted, the Democrats sacrificed economic as well as political
liberalism, adopting interventionist policies and finally accepting a devaluation
(1958) and stabilization program backed by the International Monetary Fund
and the Organization for Economic Cooperation and Development.

The way Turks later looked back on the 1950s was not governed solely by
the short-term successes or failures of economic policy. For those with roots
in the countryside, the Menderes government was the first that understood
them. The Democrat party was the first in modern Turkey to attempt a populist, redistributive economic policy. Competitive party politics required members of the Grand National Assembly to behave more as representatives of their
districts. The Democrats' accelerated road building helped to bring city and
countryside closer together. Not only in kilometers did the new roads shorten
the distance between the countryside and Ankara or Istanbul.

STATE PLANNING AND IMPORT SUBSTITUTION, 1963–1977

The Democrat government had been criticized for lacking a long-term
approach to economic policy; consequently, a broad consensus favored establishing the State Planning Organization (SPO, Devlet Planlama Teşkilatı, 1960).
Using methods and models more rigorous than those of the 1930s, the SPO again

promoted central planning, import-substitution industrialization in a protected domestic market, and expanding the state sector by founding state economic enterprises. Private business and industry depended on the SPO for credit, import privileges, tax exemptions, and foreign exchange. The SPO left agriculture largely to its own devices. The renewed push for import substitution again enlarged the role for state enterprises. Unlike the 1930s, however, when SEEs had led in efforts at industrialization, private firms, mostly large family-owned holding companies with diverse interests in manufacturing, distribution, banking, and services, had grown strong enough by the 1960s to lead in many sectors. The rise of the family-owned holding companies marked an important phase in the development of the modern Turkish managerial and technocratic class, one of the most significant changes in Turkish society in the twentieth century.

In developing economies, ISI characteristically goes through a first, "easy" phase, when the protected domestic market still provides adequate demand for local manufacturers of consumer goods, many of which could not yet compete in an unprotected domestic market, let alone foreign export markets. In this stage, Turkey was still able to obtain adequate foreign exchange through its traditional agricultural exports and remittances from Turkish workers, of whom more than a million migrated to Europe between 1961 and 1975. As a result, Turkish GNP per person grew at an annual average rate of 4.3 percent from 1963 through 1977, remaining at an annual average of 3.5 percent even under crisis conditions in 1978–1979. Between 1960 and 1979, while the share of national income derived from agriculture fell from 38 percent to 21 percent, the share derived from industry rose from 16 percent to 21 percent, and the contribution of the service sector rose from 43 to 49 percent.[32]

The domestic-oriented development policy had important consequences, many of them positive. Urbanization and competitive, multiparty politics enabled urban industrial groups to gain power at the expense of the state elites, so opening a new phase in the long-term evolution from "national bourgeoisie" to modern managerial-technocratic elite. Import-substitution industrialization required businesspeople to have close relationships with the state but left large opportunities for those who managed those relationships successfully. Large firms like the Koç and Sabancı groups had already expanded significantly in the 1950s. In the early 1960s, Vehbi Koç led in reorganizing his companies under a holding company, patterned on Siemens in his case. Although Turkish businesses were previously required to join an all-inclusive Union of Chambers and Exchanges, the founding of the influential Turkish Industrialists' and Businessmen's Association (Türk Sanayici ve İşadamları Derneği, TÜSİAD, 1971) marked another milestone in their collective development.

Reinforcing the consolidation of the business elite, the engineering profession also developed greatly at this time.[33]

In this period, much larger percentages of the population—workers, civil servants, elements of the rural population—acquired access to the benefits of modern technology and to a wider range of goods, including consumer durables. Real wages nearly doubled, as domestic demand for workers grew and labor emigration to western Europe lowered demand for jobs inside Turkey. The 1961 constitution strengthened labor unions and their ability to bargain. Not having to compete in export markets, manufacturers also benefited up to a point from the stimulus that higher wages imparted to demand for their own products.

Turkey's economic development passed momentous milestones in these years. Having imported all its automobiles before, Turkey finally began mass-producing autos in 1966, thus passing the turning point toward widespread automobile ownership, with traffic congestion and accident rates to match. The number of cars per thousand people soared from below four in 1970, to ten in 1977, twenty in 1988, thirty in 1991, and sixty by 2000.[34] To put it another way, Turkey's car "population" grew even faster than its human population, from 0.4 million cars in 1975 to 4.4 million in 2000. To celebrate the launch of the first Turkish auto, the Anadol, people wrote poems, comparing it to a gazelle or praising it as the "rose of the roadways" (*yolların gülü*). The opening of Istanbul's first Bosphorus Bridge in 1973, see color illustration) again measured

Personal automobile ownership comes to Turkey. A young couple poses proudly with their Anadol, 1970s. (Collection of the author.)

technological achievement and the democratization of access to its benefits, as did the second Bosphorus bridge in 1988.[35]

Despite these triumphs, the "easy" phase of ISI inevitably gives way to a "hard" phase in proportion as domestic demand is satisfied. Even had not global economic conditions deteriorated after 1973, Turkish manufacturers would have faced this problem by then. They had virtually ignored exports. By the early 1970s, Turkish industrialists had enough experience to begin competing in export markets. Turkey's political interest in closer integration with Europe also pointed in the direction of harmonizing economic policy with the European Economic Community, which would require moving toward the free market.[36] However, the policy incentives to support such a shift were lacking. Many vested interests had built up around protectionist import substitution and the state enterprises. That is to say nothing of the tradition, going back into Ottoman times, of making money by proximity to power and by investing in state finance. The weak coalition governments of the 1970s could not cope effectively with this problem. Turkey failed to readjust its economic orientation after the first jump in oil prices in 1973–1974, and the 1970s turned into a period of crisis, economically as well as politically.

CRISIS AND TRANSITION, 1977–1979

Facing mounting crisis, Turkey's coalition governments continued expansionary policies. External debt ballooned as a result from 9 percent of GNP in 1977 to 24 percent in 1980.[37] Confronted with its worst balance-of-payments crisis since 1945, the government expanded the money supply. Inflation surged, reaching 90 percent in 1979. That year's 250 percent increase in the price of oil worsened the situation, all the more as energy shortages led to frequent power cuts, which further hurt production. Turkey really needed a strong government to change the established policies.

Surprisingly, the needed policy change, the most significant since 1933, was inaugurated in January 1980. The government of the day, a minority government under Demirel, probably could not have enacted such a decisive policy change on its own. However, a major foreign exchange crisis and several years of strained relations with the International Monetary Fund and other foreign creditors provided the impetus for unexpectedly decisive action. Turgut Özal, former head of the State Planning Organization, was brought in to oversee the reforms, which were intended not only to respond to the inflation and foreign exchange problems but also to end statism and protectionism and shift the country toward free-market economics and export-led growth. The Demirel government could not generate the political support to make these policies succeed. However, the military government that took power on 12 September 1980 enforced the policies and kept Özal as deputy prime minister responsible for the economy. A finance technocrat thus far, Özal became a politician of historic importance in Turkey after 1980.

ECONOMIC GROWTH AND HUMAN DEVELOPMENT

Most of this thirty-year period coincided with the historic growth phase in the world economy (1945–1973), and the effects of this global trend showed in Turkey. Between 1950 and 1980, while the population slightly more than doubled from 21 million to 45 million, GNP quintupled, growing from 39 to 206 billion Turkish liras (stated at 1968 prices).[38] GDP per person increased more slowly, but still rose by nearly 250 percent. Compared to western Europe and the United States, Turkey did not gain in GDP per person over those years but remained stable at 24–25 percent of the developed countries' average. Compared to developing countries, however, Turkey's GDP per person was nearly twice as high in 1950, at 188 percent of the developing countries' average; and the gap widened by 1980 to 219 percent.[39]

As a broader-based indicator of quality of life, the human development index (HDI) is a composite statistic that aggregates GDP per person, life expectancy, and education (adult literacy and years of schooling) to produce a score ranging in value from zero to one. Turkey increased its HDI score from 0.382 in 1950 to 0.592 in 1975, compared to 0.707 and 0.848 for western Europe. Western Europe started much higher, but Turkey improved proportionately more. Such statistical indicators back up the observation that economic growth buoyed Turkey through the 1960s and continued in some respects even as the global trend turned downward after 1973. The demographic components of the HDI also call attention to the social context of economic change.

SOCIETY

Twentieth-century Turkey swung from one demographic extreme to the other, from the battered profile of the 1920s to the Third World population explosion. The population surge in the developing countries between the 1930s and the 1980s was unprecedented in human history, and Turkey fully participated in it. Such numerical growth also could not fail to change the quality of life profoundly. In 1982, sociologist Mübeccel Kıray described what had happened as "the most profound, irreversible transformation in Anatolia since the Neolithic period."[40] The intersection of social and political change produced the tumult of the 1960s and the increasing differentiation of causes and movements that grew out of it.

POPULATION EXPLOSION AND SUPERURBANIZATION

In Turkey, as in other developing countries, the population boom began in the 1930s but became a major policy concern only by the 1960s. The population of the Turkish republic (or the same territories before 1923), shrank during World War I, rose from 13 million in 1923 to 21 million in 1950, then more than doubled to 45 million in 1980.[41] Average annual population growth rates, after hovering below 2 percent in the late 1930s and faltering during the war years, rose swiftly thereafter. Population growth peaked at 2.8 percent for 1956–1961, plateaued around 2.4 percent from 1964 through 1975, and began to trend downward only after that. Between 1950 and 1980, the growth rates for the under-twenty-five age cohort peaked between 1955 and 1970. These figures alone might not explain the late 1960s, but several factors magnified their significance.

One was urbanization. The urban percentage of Turkey's population rose from 25 in 1950, to 32 in 1960, 39 in 1970, and 44 percent in 1980.[42] The rural percentage of the population, steady under the early republic near 80, fell in this period, passing below 50 percent in the mid-1980s. The proportion of the labor force employed in agriculture dropped analogously, from 84 percent in 1950 to 51 percent in 1980. Atop rapid population growth, these trends could only mean that Turkey's urban population grew much faster than the rest. The *superurbanization* that has transformed Ankara and Istanbul almost beyond recognition set in, transforming Turkey's provincial capitals as well. Between 1950 and 1980, while Turkey's total population slightly more than doubled, its urban population quadrupled from 5 to 20 million.

The country had come to town, and Turkish cities would never be the same. In this period, Istanbul was conquered a second time. In 1453, the Ottomans conquered the city. Five hundred years later, the Turks conquered it, that is, Turks from rural Anatolia. A manageable city of 1.2 million that still retained significant minority communities in 1950, Istanbul mushroomed by 1980 into a congested supermetropolis of 4.7 million, about 98 percent Muslim. Between 1950 and 1980, Ankara's population grew from 800,000 to 2.9 million. Rural-to-urban migration became even more rapid than the nation's overall population growth and magnified the latter's effects in several ways. The overloaded urban transportation systems, including not only buses but also the *dolmuş* (shared taxis) so familiar before the wide spread of private automobile ownership, illustrated this fact unmistakably.

Starting in the 1950s, the inability of the cities to absorb the influx also led to the growth of vast shantytowns. The Third World population explosion made shantytowns a global phenomenon, to which different languages gave their own colorful names. In Turkish, the shanty towns became known as *gecekondu*, literally, "put up at night." The term comes from a legal loophole that protects occupants of houses put up between dusk and dawn from being forced to move without legal process.[43] The Ottoman tradition of state ownership of land, which protected the former migrants' smallholdings in the village, now protected them again in the sense that much of the vacant land on which the shantytowns went up belonged to the state. That meant that gecekondu dwellers who were astute enough to manipulate the political process could protect their interests by creating patronage relationships with powerful politicians. Shantytown settlers often started by building a mosque and a school, then putting their houses in between. Any politician had to think twice before demolishing a mosque and a school.

What politicians saw in the gecekondus was not illegal occupation and building code violations, but votes. The tendency of migrants from the countryside to rejoin their fellows in the urban shantytowns created large blocks of shantytown dwellers with shared ties of geographical origin, sect, or ethnicity, as well as group leaders who could negotiate with politicians and deliver votes. A pattern well known in provincial politics reappeared. Favors rendered, such as extending urban utilities into the shantytowns, won votes in ways that might not make sense in terms of party ideology. Businesspeople and industrialists saw something different in the shantytowns: an increase in the urban labor supply and a restraint on wages. That inclined employers to condone gecekondus, even when built on privately owned land. The growth of the shantytowns also affected the development of urban transportation, as the dolmuş routes expanded with the new settlements.[44] Leftist militants of this period placed high hopes on the gecekondus and created "liberated zones" in some of them. However, the fact that shantytown dwellers, certainly the early ones, occupied their own houses and most of all wanted secure title to their dwellings made them generally conservative and fairly inert to left or right radicalism. With time, the originally primitive conditions of the settlements improved. By 1970, land was becoming a commodity in the gecekondus, too; and apartment buildings were replacing single-family houses. Yet the decisive steps toward legalization of title were taken only in the mid-1980s.

LABOR EMIGRATION

In the 1960s, much the same forces that brought the country to town inside Turkey also pushed Turks to migrate to western Europe as industrial workers.[45] Turkish and European needs had to converge to make that happen. In the divided Germany of the Cold War, the building of the Berlin Wall in 1961 sealed the East-West border and cut off the East German worker flight that had supplied the West German labor market. Needing workers, the Federal Republic of

Germany concluded labor recruitment agreements with eight Mediterranean countries, including Turkey (1961). The number of Turkish workers in Germany expanded from 6,700 in 1961 to some 600,000 in 1973. Nearby countries, from France to Sweden, also made labor agreements with Turkey. Turks had migrated internally in search of work for centuries. Specific parts of the country were known as sources of, or destinations for, workers; and they followed well-worn routes, often on a seasonal or short-term basis. Population growth and economic change now expanded this kind of migration, adding new, international routes.

As Turks began to venture as far as Germany, the expectation that their migration was temporary persisted. Germany and Switzerland shared that expectation, referring to the migrants as "guest workers" (*Gastarbeiter*). France differed as a former colonial power with long experience with non-European populations. In France, Turkish workers, like North Africans, were classed as *immigrés*. However termed, Turkish migrants commonly expected to return after making some money. They were also vulnerable to recessions, which struck first in 1966 and then more drastically in 1973–1974. Some 400,000 Turkish workers did return to Turkey in the 1970s. Yet even the end of the 1945–1973 boom in the world economy did not reduce the number of Turks in Europe. Even as some workers returned in the 1970s, other workers' family members took advantage of a right of family reunion under German law to enter the country.

As a result, Germany's Turkish community grew and acquired a more normal demographic profile in terms of age and sex ratios. Demographic normalization did not stop the Turkish communities in Europe, especially in the early phases, from responding to all the causes and movements of the times in Turkey. After 1980, as Germany and other industrial countries began to outsource much of their manufacturing and Turkish labor emigration became a thing of the past, Turkish communities remained as large minorities and began to focus as much or more on adapting to their new homelands as on participating in all the politics and causes of their old one. For children and grandchildren of the migrants of the 1960s, complex identity issues emerged out of the situation of still being a "foreigner" in Germany but also standing out as "Germanish" (*almancı*) on return visits to Turkey. With this, new forms of hybridity contributed to the post-1960s proliferation of difference among Turks.

1968: FROM NATIONAL UNITY, TO PROSYSTEM AND ANTISYSTEM, TO IDENTITY AND DIFFERENCE

The most revolutionary thing about social change in this period was that modern processes of class formation and individual subjectivation expanded in scope to mobilize all of Turkish society. Over the previous century, those processes had made history by forming the Turkish bourgeoisie and the beginnings of an industrial proletariat. Having expanded during the National Struggle and under the early republic, the impact of those processes now became all-encompassing. The numerical growth of the population contributed to this fact. As human densities and interactions increased with the numbers, so did changes in the quality of life.

At the critical flashpoint of change in this period, 1968, Turkey lived through its own version of the social upheavals that produced major political and cultural consequences around the world, especially in the developing countries. Politically, the result was a transition from the national unity demanded by the early republic, to the pro- and antiestablishment confrontations symbolized by "1968," to the multiply divided politics of identity and difference that emerged afterward. To speak in this way of 1968 is to speak symbolically of changes that may have peaked in a single year but lasted longer. Many Turks will understand this point, including a prominent novelist who refers retrospectively to the young militants of this period as "the sixty-eights."[46]

The processes of social mobilization that reached critical mass in the late 1960s operated in multiple dimensions. Economic growth stimulated the expansion of the industrial labor force, and the 1961 constitution allowed freedom for labor organization. As a result, organized labor grew in the 1960s from 250,000 to 2 million. Unemployment in the cities and underemployment in the countryside remained very high, however; and even labor emigration to Germany did not solve the problem. Official unemployment figures rose from 600,000 (1967) to 1.5 million (1977). The job market could absorb only about 40 percent of new job seekers each year; many high school and university graduates also could not find jobs. As the idea of the welfare state gained currency, Turkey had started a system of social insurance for workers (*işçi sigortaları*) in 1945; but fewer than one in thirty workers was covered by it in its early phases.[47]

In education, between 1950 and 1980 Turkey faced the ironic consequences of the fact that it had finally begun to achieve mass literacy, but only in the midst of a population boom unprecedented in human history. Recipients of high-school (*lise*) diplomas increased from fewer than 6,000 in 1950 to 30,000 in 1968, and 138,000 in 1980. The number of universities grew from three (1946) to eight (1967) and nineteen (1978).[48] Yet throughout this period, the number of university places satisfied only a fraction of the demand: 60,000 places for 360,000 aspirants in 1977. Even so, the number of those awarded diplomas from institutions of higher learning rose from roughly 3,000 in 1950 to 14,000 in 1968 and 71,000 in 1980. Under those circumstances, as in other developing countries, the expansion of education proved more successful in quantitative than in qualitative terms. Pressures on the educational system and resource shortages resulted in serious shortfalls in the quality of education at all levels. However, diploma recipients were more worried about the fact that so many of them could not find jobs.

The conspicuous gender gap in literacy rates provides another lead into the problems of the educational system. Although Turkish males achieved majority literacy in the early 1950s, Turkish females did not do so until about 1980. The population as a whole achieved majority literacy in the late 1960s, precisely when the radicalization of students and workers peaked. The 1961 constitution had allowed for university autonomy, as well as for labor organization. Given these facts, plus the high rates of unemployment and economic frustration among workers and students and the news pouring in from around the world, the stage was set for the violent political mobilization of the 1960s and 1970s. Turkey's terrorists of the 1970s were characteristically young males aged between fifteen and twenty-five.[49] The inability of the two major political parties to control politics resulted as much as anything else from the rising human flood and the proliferation of issues and differences that came with it.

For females, the consequences of the gender gap in literacy were linked to the regional inequalities that impeded Turkey's development. On balance, birthrates were highest, literacy rates lowest, and the gender gap in literacy widest in southeastern Turkey. There, linguistic difference between the populace (mostly Kurdish) and the Turkish schools compounded religiously grounded concerns that attending coeducational, secular schools would compromise the female "sinlessness and chaste behavior" (*ismet ve iffet*) on which family honor depended.[50] The many illiterate Kurdish girls who stayed out of school and married early perpetuated both high birthrates and ignorance of Turkish among Kurds. Many villages simply lacked schools. For students who did go to school, prevailing problems started with ignorance of the language of instruction (Turkish only) and extended to include inadequate resources and facilities, high student-teacher ratios, and emphasis on rote learning rather than critical thought, on theory rather than application.

As greatly as such human-development indicators as life expectancy improved in this period, then, Turkish achievement in education lagged not only behind highly developed economies but also behind levels in some comparable developing countries. Qualitative shortfalls in education also had a lasting economic price. Turkey had reached the point where its economic growth would require, not just "significant increases in the technology and knowledge component of the economy," but also "a better educated labor force," not just elite education but mass education.[51]

The trend toward mass literacy was accompanied by important developments in the media.[52] In the print media, not only did the freedoms of the 1961 constitution open the way for Marxist thought to become widely available; this was also an important period in the development of Islamist print culture, as discussed below. The effects of these developments in the print media reverberated throughout the politics of the day.

The electronic media developed even more significantly. Transistor radios became commonplace in the countryside in the 1960s. As for television, some Turks remember U.S. astronauts' 1969 moon landing as the first notable event they saw on television.[53] Status symbols at first, black-and-white televisions became widespread in the 1970s, even in rural coffeehouses, exciting imaginations and raising expectations. New patterns of sociability developed, as the first owners of television sets suddenly discovered how many long-lost relatives and friends they had, a phenomenon especially significant for women, who did not frequent the men's world of the coffeehouse. If urbanization drove social mobilization in the 1950s, "the transistor radio in the 1960s, and the black and white TV sets in the 1970s[,] were the added influences" that accelerated social change.[54] The new media diminished the isolation of rural from urban lifestyles, brought dramatic events like the Cyprus invasion of 1974 into Turks' homes, and excited new consumerist demands.

Turkey's vibrant musical culture also produced a new popular style in the late 1960s to express the hopes and frustrations of the newly urbanizing gecekondu dwellers. Known—originally derisively—as *Arabesk*, this hybrid genre mixed Turkish, Western, and Arab elements. Given the politicization of culture in Turkey, the spontaneity and autonomy of Arabesk made it controversial as a matter of both taste and politics. Banned from state radio and television for not conforming to approved musical norms, it nonetheless made itself heard everywhere by the mid-1970s, thanks to the spread of audiocassettes and cassette players. To urban sophisticates, this was "dolmuş-driver music" (*dolmuşçu müziği*) because it blared from the minibuses running to and from the gecekondus. Only after 1980 did Arabesk begin to gain an element of political respectability, even becoming an accessory of efforts to woo voters.

Just as social change had given rise to new forms of subjectivity among the Ottoman protobourgeoisie of a century earlier, mass social mobilization gave rise to new forms and expressions of subjectivity in all levels of society in this period. Significantly, writers about both the leftist and the rightist radicals have emphasized the significance of those movements for the participants' subjective development. For leftist radicals who ended up in prison after the 1971 coup, "political self-criticism was combined with personal tragedies."

As the realization of their tactical errors and ideological shallowness set in, there was "an inevitable mystic-moralistic quality in these very human inner conflicts, inevitable because of the subjectivity imposed by prison conditions and the inadequacy of their socialist *culture*." Nonetheless, those who did not abandon their leftist convictions "launched into action again after prison in the midst of an utter confusion of ideas."[55] On the right, the ultranationalist gray wolves and idealists were "frequently socioeconomically and psychologically deprived youngsters, many of whom had migrated from villages to cities, and had been faced with culture shock and maladjustment. They sought to realize their aspirations and resolve their identity problems through the authority of a leader, group solidarity, and scapegoating of 'internal enemies.'"[56] After the 1980 coup, many ultranationalists had time for self-reflection in prison, something leftists had already experienced after 1971. Among Turks of humble origins, far larger numbers lived through the changes of these decades by becoming the human raw material of economic development, getting caught up in movements of internal or external worker migration, having to cope with gecekondu life, and gaining exposure to the more prosperous and Westernized sectors of society through watching television or by working for prosperous families as maids, drivers, or gardeners. A major reason for the popularity of Arabesk music was that it sang the song of those who lived those experiences. From Orhan Gencebay in the 1960s to İbrahim Tatlıses in the 1980s, the most popular Arabesk singers hailed sequentially from the parts of Turkey that were then sending the most migrants to Istanbul.[57] The cover of one of Orhan Gencebay's well-known albums appears among the color illustrations for this period.

Putting social and political history together makes it possible to understand the multifaceted turning point of the late 1960s. The legacy of the National Struggle and early republic had been a unison-voiced national mobilization with no tolerance for difference. After 1945, demands for change and greater pluralism grew too strong to suppress. As the semblance of unity faltered, bipolar confrontations of broad, pro- and antiestablishment fronts ensued. Between 1946 and 1950, the Democrat Party had played something of this role in opposition to the Republican People's Party. Later, as the political spectrum widened, the conflict between antisystem and prosystem forces grew sharper in the 1960s and 1970s. In Turkey and globally, as the demographic surge and youth activism raised levels of conflict in the late 1960s, that kind of broad-front antisystem coalition fragmented, and a new, more highly differentiated politics of identity and difference began to emerge. Globally, the axes of difference multiplied to include race, ethnicity, religion, gender, class, social disadvantage, and issues of personal preference. In Turkey, race was not a pertinent category, but all the others were. Among the antisystem oppositional forces, the ultranationalist right did a better job than the left of maintaining its unity, only to be eclipsed later by religious conservatives, starting with the National Salvation Party. By comparison, the left was much more prone to ideological factionalism; later, the Soviet collapse drove another nail into its coffin. The divisions that emerged within the broad-front alignments sowed conflict between Turks and Kurds, Sunnis and Alevis, religious practitioners and secularists, men and women, workers and employers. In Turkey as in other countries, that happened in complex ways. Most Turks' positions in society were defined in terms of more than one of those pairs. Not all such differences became politically salient in Turkey before 1980. In that or other specifics, Turkey's experiences may have differed from those of some other countries; but in the aggregate, Turkey was not behind in crossing over into the age of identity politics after the late 1960s.[58]

The proliferation of identity and difference raises questions, obviously, about the central thesis of this book. Its remaining chapters will have opportunities to consider whether the proliferation of difference has brought an end to the age when the two great currents of the last two centuries—the radical, secularist and the conservative, Islamically committed approaches to modernity—interacted dialectically to shape the course of Turkish history. Potentially, that could happen; if it did, the result for Turkey might be an age of pluralism and greater democratization. However, the main lines of Turkey's post-1980 political history suggest that the proliferation of difference has occurred on a landscape still shaped at the deeper, tectonic level by secularist and religious forces. Evidence to support this interpretation comes not only from the historical record but also from the realm of imaginative literature as represented in a novel to be discussed in the concluding chapter, Orhan Pamuk's *Kar* (Snow).

ISLAMIC PRINT CULTURE

Of all phenomena associated with the media in midcentury, the elaboration of Islamic "print capitalism" was among the most significant. In the long run, Islamic thinkers and media were destined to exert greater influence than those of the left or the ultranationalist right. The radical ideas that animated—and divided—the left had little hold on most Turks. The Turkish identity championed by the rightists did mean a lot, but not necessarily in their fascistic, pan-Turkist version. For most Turks, Islam had more to do with defining their identity here and now than did ideas about remote Central Asian origins. Islam also answered the great existential questions of life and eternity and defined the moral universals in terms of which Turkish migrants might hope to find their way in Turkish cities and diasporic communities abroad.

As noted in earlier chapters, although their origins extend further back, the Islamic print media differentiated and developed fully only after about 1908. Said Nursi and the Nur movement lived through all phases of the Islamists' transition from manuscript to print culture between the 1930s and 1950s. However, they were not that culture's only pioneers.

Amid the explosive growth in publishing early in the Young Turk period, one of the best-known Islamic periodicals appeared under the title *Sırat-ı Müstakim* (September 1908). It changed its name to *Sebilürreşad* in 1912 and continued publishing until closed down under the law for the maintenance of order in 1925. Significantly, it resumed in 1948 and continued publishing until 1965. Its publisher in both periods, Eşref Edib Fergan, opposed specific secularizing reforms of the republic. Yet he positioned his journal "as 'a symbol of religious freedom'" intended to "provide a religious, rather than ethnic understanding of Turkish national identity" and committed to building "a future based on republican institutions."[59] Sometimes interpreted as reactionary, the journal published articles that sought rather to give an Islamic understanding to modern concepts such as nation and democracy. It also defended religion, for example, by arguing that if religion is to be separate from politics, then just "as religion does not interfere in politics, politics must not interfere in religion." For Eşref Edib, secularism was a matter of governmental style in a country where the people were Muslims.[60] Much as the newspapers of the 1860s and later had done for the intelligentsia of that period, *Sebilürreşad* set the example for a journal addressed to religious-minded readers of this period.

If *Sebilürreşad* defined a model for an Islamist periodical, Necip Fazıl Kısakürek (1904–1983) defined a model for the professional Islamist man of letters, as distinct from the professional man of religion. Published in 1975, his memoirs state that his life passed through three phases: those of the "Young Poet" (through 1934), the "Mystic Poet" (1934–1943), and the "Former Poet" (after 1943).[61] The three periods recall Said Nursi's, but his names for them identify major differences between the religious thinker-leader and the literary man. The Young Poet came from a distinguished family, studied in the best schools, went to study philosophy at the Sorbonne (1924–1925), but wasted his money gambling and was sent home. Or so he later wrote. To judge from his life and works, he may have owed more than he wished to admit to French writers and their growing self-definition as *intellectuals*, who were not only thinkers but also committed activists. Much as corporatism and Durkheim's solidarism impressed Turkish social thinkers like Ziya Gökalp, the rightist Catholic literary figures of the period seem to have inspired Necip Fazıl to strive to make a comparable, nationalist-religious impact on Turkey. This is particularly true of Charles Maurras (1868–1952), known not only as a journalist and author but also as the leader of the rightist, Catholic Action Française.[62] It is probably not accidental that the term *aksiyon* began to be used in Turkish with an extended semantic range much more like that of the French term *action* than of its English counterpart.

Just as Maurras was conventional neither as Catholic nor as monarchist, Necip Fazıl took an idiosyncratic approach to Islam and Turkish nationalism. Before he ever went to France, he won fame as a poet (1924).[63] Introspective and lyrical, his poems dwelt on feelings of fear and loneliness, expressing his and his readers' heightening subjectivity in an uncertain world. Returning to Turkey, the Young Poet worked in banks and taught in schools, writing on the side. He also drank and gambled. Already he was critical—intemperately so—of prevailing cultural and political trends and a proponent of literature that combined ideas with action.

Necip Fazıl's encounter with the influential sufi Abdülhakim Arvasi precipitated the crisis that turned the Young Poet turned into the Mystic Poet (1934), who wrote thenceforth under the influence of his spiritual master. The Mystic Poet turned into the Former Poet in 1943, when Necip Fazıl abandoned other work to live solely by the pen. In 1943, he founded *Büyük Doğu* (The great East), a periodical that he published with interruptions for thirty-nine years. He formed a political association by the same name in 1949. Touring the country to give speeches before large crowds, he endured frequent prosecutions on far-fetched charges, including that of defaming Turkish identity (*Türklüğe hakaret*), and imprisonments for his writings and actions. In addition to publishing *Büyük Doğu*, the Former Poet maintained a prodigious literary output, much of it consisting of prose works with such titles as *Büyük Doğu'ya Doğru* (Toward the Great East, 1959), *İdeolocya Örgüsü* (The weave of ideology, 1968), and *İman ve Aksiyon* (Faith and activism, 1964). He envisaged his "Great East" as a utopia in which the material achievements of the West would be grafted onto the spiritual roots of the East. His "ideological weave" amounts to an authoritarian, Islamic-nationalist pastiche that would have turned Turkey into a paradise somewhat like Franco's Spain, although his demand that minorities be "cleansed" resembles Hitler, not Franco.[64] It also does not live up to Islamic norms of intercommunal relations.

Like him or not, everything about Necip Fazıl marks him as a new kind of literary figure and a new phenomenon in Turkish "print capitalism." Just as two publishing firms are still devoted to publishing Said Nursi's works, the Great East (Büyük Doğu) publishing firm, originally set up under Necip Fazıl's son Mehmet in 1973, is still dedicated to publishing his writings. Significantly, the title of Necip Fazıl's memoirs, *Bâbıâli*, does not refer to the historical Sublime Porte, the headquarters of the Ottoman grand vezir. Rather, the title refers metaphorically and broadly to the established print media, still centered at that time in the part of Istanbul adjoining the Sublime Porte. Necip Fazıl attacked the conventional print media for supporting all the wrongs that Westernizing politicians had committed since 1839, for having undermined the foundations of Turkish-Islamic society, for sensationalism and low standards.[65] Whatever the merits of such opinions, Necip Fazıl certainly understood the explosive potential of culture for the transformation of society and polity, and he self-consciously embodied the opposition between the older, secular press and the newer Islamic media.

TALKING BACK TO THE ELITES: ORHAN KEMAL

As Turkey lived through unprecedented social transformations, the common people found their voices and talked back to the elites who used to speak for them. As that occurred, writers of imaginative literature again surpassed scholars in conveying what it was like to live through tumultuous times. No writer dramatized the plight of ordinary Turks caught up in the move from village to city better than Orhan Kemal (1914–1970). He himself endured many of those experiences. Among more than twenty novels, his best loved is *Bereketli Toprak-lar Üzerinde* (On these bounteous lands, 1954). The bounteous lands are those of the Çukurova, the steamy cotton-growing delta around Adana, and the story is that of migrant workers who poured in from Anatolia, even Syria (Urumdan, Şamdan), to seek seasonal work: "God has no pity on them; neither have his servants. These are the people whom God forgot. Prophets have brought them books full of patience, resignation, contentment . . . , which do not help at all and never will."[66]

In a way reminiscent of "slice-of-life" novels produced in other countries in this period, Orhan Kemal plunges his readers immediately into the world of illiterate villagers. His characters tell their own story in their own language. Orhan Kemal himself was a native of the Adana region. Adana was big enough to dazzle villagers with its size and bustle, its shops filled with goods, and its "Holivut" neighborhood (Hollywood, 387). However, it was also a provincial city. In Adana, the few rode by in either a horse-drawn *kerusa* (*fayton* elsewhere in Turkey, 337) or a *tomofil* (*otomobil*, *oto*, 388), while the many walked to work at a *kerhane* (*kârhane* in standard Turkish, "factory") or took their chances on a farm outside the city, manning a threshing machine, *patoz* (*batöz* in standard Turkish, from the French *batteuse*, 31, 212, 370). The local workforce encompassed Turkey's ethnic diversity, including Albanian, Laz, and Kurdish workers. Some of them also had experience across the Syrian border, and their distinctive accents add to the range of the colloquial language.

The characters betray their lack of education in many ways, starting with their lack of marketable skills. One of the leading characters does not even know until he takes work in a cotton gin that he is supposed to have a surname (69). Aside from the nicknames used for many characters, some others are known only relationally. One of the leading characters is identified as İflâhsızın Yusuf, a combination implying that this particular Yusuf was the son or descendant of someone who had been either "incurable" or "incorrigible." Other relationally named characters are Idiot's daughter, Aptal kızı (179), and Hidayet's son, Hidayet oğlu (326). Idiot's daughter plays the temptress without ever revealing her right name. In contrast, Hidayet oğlu gains in importance at the end of the book and finally becomes known as Mıstık, short for Mustafa (326). A murderer who proves to be one of the more compassionate characters in the book, he attempts a pious exclamation at the book's tragic conclusion. What comes out of his mouth is *rahmânirracim* ("the merciful, the stoned," the latter being an epithet applied to Satan, 391). Presumably what he meant was *rahmânirrahim* ("the merciful, the compassionate," two of the names of God). That is as pious as anyone gets in this book.

At the same time that they display their lack of education, the characters also display their immersion in the oral folk culture and its moral universe. Their speech is filled with proverbs. It is even more filled with rhyme, alliteration, and repetitive rhythmic patterns, which make their statements sound like proverbs whether they are or not. Getting together excitedly to have a smoke and discuss another man's wife's infidelity, one of the main characters exclaims to another "Yak hele yak da dinle bak," something like "Light up, look here, listen to me" (141). The proverbial sayings define the morals of the story. The three main characters set out to seek their fortune, *anca beraber, kanca beraber*, essentially "one for all and all for one" (142). The most-repeated phrase in the book is a moral aphorism: *ya ver canını insan için, ya da etme kalabalık dünyamıza*, "either give your soul for humankind or do not crowd the world."[67] The characters do not always live up to these morals, but those with a moral compass fare best in the end.

All the characters are rooted in the folk culture, but they have begun to move beyond it. Heard at both the beginning and end of the book, a folk song ending with the line *doğurmaz olaydı analarımız*, "better if our mothers had not borne us" (13, 398), foreshadows the later emergence of Arabesk, the musical culture whose hybridity matches that of the singers of this folk song after their move to the cities. By the end of the book one of the three main characters is trying to learn how to read. Some of the skilled workers in the book are literate. Just before the tragic climax, a comic vignette relieves the tension by characterizing the mechanic responsible for maintaining the threshing machine. A Beethoven admirer, he spends the off-season reading everything he can find about Beethoven and dreaming of owning a piano. The mechanic swears at the thresher all summer and sobs over Beethoven's deafness all winter (368).

The book begins as the story of three villagers from the Sivas region who set out together by train to seek work in Adana. They have heard that a man from somewhere near Sivas now owns a factory in Adana, and they are confident that their "fellow countryman" (*hemşeri*) will give them work. All three are illiterate and childishly naive, not least in their expectations about their "fellow countryman." However, they differ in ways that have significant consequences. Köse Hasan already has a wife and daughter in the village but lacks the physical strength to endure what awaits him. İflâhsızın Yusuf is the only one who has ever left the village before. He has been as far as Sivas, where he worked briefly in the railway workshop. His other resource is his uncle (*emmi*) in the village, whose wise sayings he quotes at tedious length. Yusuf knows the importance of "being himself" and not succumbing to the wiles of city people, especially women, who are "the devil in clothes" (142, 145). In Adana, Yusuf is the one who manages to single himself and his two friends out from the other job-seekers thronging the gates of the cotton mill by leaping in front of the owner's car and getting him to stop long enough to hear their claims to *hemşerilik*, the bonds of common geographical origin (51–52). The book's unforgettable hero is Pehlivan Ali. The nickname *pehlivan* implies that he is a "champion," specifically a "wrestler," and he has the physical strength to prove it. He is also an extrovert with the most appealing personality of the three. Other characters at times make jokes about his intelligence: "a stupid horse is an ambler; a stupid man is a wrestler."[68] People often call Ali a "bear" (*ayı*), in short, a "lummox." Whatever wrestling he might ever have done in his village, Ali never gets to wrestle in Adana. Aside from occasional banter and horseplay, the only interest the other men take in Ali's physical strength is to exploit it on the job. Women notice Ali, for sure. His simple honesty makes him a winning personality.

Although migrant labor around Adana is mostly a man's game, women and children also get caught up in the flows of migrants toward the city. Gender inequity, social uprootedness, and exploitative working conditions take their grim toll. The cotton gin where the three friends first find work is part of a vertically integrated mill that transforms the "white gold" (*beyaz altın*) of Çukurova's bountiful lands from raw bolls into thread or cloth. The mill employs both males and females, starting as young as eleven or twelve, and their work brings them together in ways that conform less to idealized gender norms than to the popular saying *eli işte, gözü oynaşta*, "his hand is on his work, his eye is on his playmate"—or "her hand . . . , her eye. . . ."[69]

> Most of these girls would be pregnant before their breasts filled out. They would give birth, become mothers, get pregnant again, again give birth, over and over. In the end, they would either become unrecognizably ugly, or be abandoned by their husbands . . . and passed from hand to hand, or wind up enduring the abuse of someone old enough to be their father.
>
> Among these women, some ended up in brothels. Even those who did not would hoe in who-knows-what cotton field, reduced to skin and bones, and go to an early death from malaria or sunstroke.

This passage is one of several early ones that foretell later events. Clearly the degraded conditions do not stop the male and female characters from taking an interest in one another.

The consequences can be memorable, never more so than in the passionate story of the leading man and woman, Pehlivan Ali and Fatma. By the time they meet, Ali has moved on from the cotton mill to a construction site where Fatma is the most attractive of several women who live in shacks on the site. To Ali she is "everything a woman ought to be." Paying her the workers' supreme compliment, he describes her as "a tough broad" (*zorlu avrat*)—a phrase much used in this book. Fatma lives with a man named Ömer Zorlu, who abducted her from her village and is not legally married to her.[70] In a book where surnames are never mentioned for most characters, Ömer's surname may be significant, for he is *zorlu* in a different sense than she. She has "powerful" (*zorlu*) femininity; what has him "in difficulty" (*zorlu*) is his addiction to gambling. While all the other men's eyes are on his Fatma, his mind's eye is on whether his "black" (*arap*)—his luck personified—is smiling on him. Ömer's constant need for money makes him depend for loans on the very men who crown him with the cuckold's horns.

As the "champion" (*pehlivan*) on the construction site, whose masculinity best matches Fatma's femininity, Ali literally moves in with the couple, ostensibly as a boarder (144). No match for Ali physically, the supervisors at the construction site excel him in money and power. Not only do they shake down the male workers for a cut of their salaries and run rackets on the side in gambling and hashish, but they take sexual advantage at will of the women on the site. Consequently, on the night when Ali first takes Fatma physically, he is the second of three men with whom she has sex in a single night. The first is the Laz labor boss (*taşeron*), who has generously loaned Ömer Zorlu money to gamble, scheming to have Fatma delivered to him while her husband is thus occupied.

The second is Ali. The third is Ömer, who returns from his gambling, impressed by the labor boss's generosity and exultant that his "black" has smiled on him at last. As always, Fatma wants some of the money.[71]

Ali and Fatma soon run away together and reappear on a farm, where he works in the fields and Fatma is kept near the house, supposedly to help with the cooking but actually to be more accessible to the supervisors. They make an issue of the fact that Ali and Fatma are not married, tempt Ali into having sex with Idiot's daughter to create jealousy, and soon separate him and Fatma. By the time Fatma realizes what has happened to her, she has been passed from man to man, put out into the fields to work in the sun, and taken sick with malaria.

Long before that happens, the fates of the three leading males who set out from Sivas together have diverged. Köse Hasan's tale is the briefest and saddest. Weakest of the three, he is put to work in the cotton gin in the department that washes the dirty cotton bolls to prepare them for ginning. The workers there do nothing but carry wet cotton for twelve hours. Constantly wet, they quickly sicken and get pneumonia. Within a couple of weeks, Hasan begins to miss days because of sickness; the foreman hires someone else to replace him. Hasan's condition deteriorates rapidly. When Yusuf and Ali get a chance to go work at the construction site on what they think will be better terms, they abandon their comrade to the landlord of the former stable where they have been lodging. They later learn that the landlord has been murdered and Hasan has died a wretched death in the hospital.

Yusuf's tale illustrates an entirely different potential of labor migration. At the construction site, when Ali takes up with Fatma, the disapproving Yusuf forms a new association with a Laz mason, Kılıç Usta. A father of five from a region whose men historically have to migrate to work in order to support their families, this master craftsman (*usta*) sets out annually with his tools and spends most of the year away from home. He is demanding but willing to teach his craft to others. Although Orhan Kemal does not make the point explicitly, the usta's combination of skilled craftsmanship and ethical standards carries on a tradition centuries old, going back to the craft guilds and sufi orders of Ottoman times and, earlier, to the *ahi* brotherhoods, which had fused qualities later found in the guilds and brotherhoods. The image of Yusuf's wise uncle in the village recedes as Kılıç Usta becomes his new authority figure. The day comes when Kılıç Usta tells Yusuf that he, too, is now a master (*usta*). Yusuf rushes to tell Ali the news, only to find Ali gathering up his bedroll to go move in with Fatma and Ömer Zorlu. Even Yusuf finds Fatma a "tough broad" (*zorlu avrat*, 150). But he also listens to Kılıç Usta's firm ethical voice. Kılıç is one of those who repeats the aphorism "either give your soul for humankind or do not crowd the world." Informed about Ali and Fatma, the usta reacts with an aphorism about sexual propriety: "I've wandered far from home for twenty-five years. . . . Not once have I unfastened my waistband for anything forbidden."[72] As master masons, both Yusuf and Kılıç move on to other jobs, and Yusuf reappears only at the end of the book.

Ali's story fills the second half of the novel. He and Fatma have run away together and found work on a farm, not foreseeing how the other men there will separate and exploit them. The time has come to harvest the wheat. Everything now centers on the big yellow threshing machine (*patoz*), standing in the middle of the field and powered by a belt attached to a tractor standing in front of the thresher. The whole combination looks like an enormous insect. Twenty sheaf-carriers (*desteci*) run toward the machine, one after another, with sheaves as thick as their bodies. On the machine itself, the two "seat-men" (*koltukçu*) perform the most difficult jobs. One hoists the sheaves to the other, who feeds them into the mouth of the thresher. Inside it, blades rotating at twelve hundred revolutions per minute thresh the grain, releasing the grain into sacks in one direction and the ground-up straw in another. The work begins before sunup and ends after dark. The heat is unbearable. The powdered straw is so irritating that the two men on the thresher have to wear goggles and bind their faces and necks with rags.

Ali finds himself assigned along with Hidayet oğlu to be one of the carriers, endlessly running sheaves to the machine. The men working the machine are Halo Şamdin and Zeynel, two Kurds. Foul-mouthed and barely articulate in Turkish, Şamdin and Zeynel have long experience in their dangerous jobs. But they also complain about the wretched food, twenty-hour workdays, and thirty-five-man crew on a machine that requires forty-five workers (277). They try to raise class consciousness among the workers—not a promising endeavor. In a past labor dispute, one of them had set fire to someone's harvest (246). Knowing this, the threshing supervisors do not take long to get the idea of replacing the two Kurds with Ali and his new companion, Hidayet oğlu. The Kurds reciprocate the supervisors' scorn. They reproach the foreman for selling his daughters to brothels (*kerhane*, the same word as for a factory) in Adana (269). Zeynel also threatens one of the supervisors with a knife (272–78).

For the workers on the farm, the labor market is no abstraction in economic theory. Rather, it is a specific place, the "worker bazaar" (*ırgat pazarı*) in Adana. At the end of their five-and-a-half-day workweek, they have to make their way there on foot, ill-shod, famished, and exhausted, to wait for their pay and hope to be rehired for the next week. Night falls before they get there, and the workers have to stop for the night in a cemetery. Ali thinks about Fatma and hopes to find her in the city. Unbeknown to him, she is sitting only a few steps away from him in the darkness, her head already throbbing from malaria. A man finds her, but he is not Ali. Offering her a couple of atabrine pills for her malaria, he leads her away and takes sexual advantage of her (302–5). The next day in the labor market, the landowners or their labor bosses first hire the workers for the coming week and only then distribute the wages for the past week, after deducting for gambling debts and for the tea and hashish (*esrar*) they sell on the side. While this is going on, some of the supervisors from the farm get together with the "little ağa," the younger of the two brothers who own the farm, and plan to replace Şamdin and Zeynel, as well as the mechanic who maintains the threshing machine. The new "seat-men" (*koltukçu*) on the machine are to be Ali and Hidayet oğlu, who only after this point begins to be called by his personal name or nickname, Mıstık (326). Ali and Mıstık spend a night on the town. Visiting the "tough broads" of Adana's brothels, they seek out the daughters of the foreman from the farm. Ali picks the one in the red dress; and by the time they part, they are infatuated with each other. The next day, the threshing crew for the next week is loaded onto a truck and driven back to the farm.

Work resumes at two in the morning. The foreman, whom Mıstık now jokingly refers to as their father-in-law, awakens Ali and Mıstık first, hands them their goggles and face rags, and gives them cursory instructions while the other workers are being woken up. As the work picks up, they are bothered by the heat, the necessity to maintain an unceasing rhythm for long hours, and the itching from the powdered straw thrown out by the thresher. A few days pass, and the "little ağa" drives up in his shiny car. He is impressed and predicts that the threshing will be finished that week. Getting excited, the "little ağa" begins to cheer the workers on, and the foreman joins in. Atop the machine, Ali also gets caught up in the rhythm. However, the dust and sweat reach the point where he cannot open his eyes, and he becomes dazed. The work has continued a good half hour beyond the workers' break time. Suddenly there is a horrible noise, the thresher shudders, and everything stops. Mıstık pulls off his goggles and gapes in horror at Ali's body over the mouth of the machine. The workers lift him down and discover that he has lost a leg. The workers plead with the "little ağa" to put Ali in his car and drive him to the hospital. The ağa panics. He does not want blood in his car. He runs to his car, pulls a pistol, and threatens to shoot if the workers get near. They watch in horror as he drives away. Ali is left lying beside the thresher. There is nothing they can do but cover him with a sack while he bleeds to death and they wait for the gendarmes to return with the ağa.

That night in the darkness, two men creep out of a ditch at the far end of the field. One of them advances toward the threshing machine and smells a strange smell that he does not understand until he lifts the corner of the sack and sees a body. Detecting the sound of motor vehicles approaching from a distance, he realizes that there has been an accident and the authorities are coming to investigate. Quickly, he slinks over to the heaps of harvested grain and sets them on fire, sending yellow-orange flames skyward. Zeynel sets the fire, and the other man in the ditch is Şamdin; they were dismissed so that Ali and Mıstık could take their places on the thresher. Moving off into the darkness, Zeynel and Şamdin watch from a distance as the other workers, who have been sleeping on the ground, wake up. As the workers frantically try to move Ali's body and the threshing machine away from the fire, the "little ağa" arrives with the gendarmes, accuses them of arson, and demands that they all be jailed or shot on the spot.

Of the three friends who had boarded the train in Sivas at the start of the season, now none is left but Yusuf. Proud of himself and of the portable gas cookstove he has bought for his wife, he is even starting to think about moving to the city (386). His mood changes when he runs into Mıstık at the Adana train station and learns what has happened to Ali. Now he must return to the village alone and break the news to both Hasan's wife and daughter and Ali's mother. Back in the village, as he does that, a voice nearby breaks out in the folk song Ali used to sing: "Better if our mothers had not borne us."

So ends a story of human degradation. More memorably, it is also a story of human dignity within the constraints of poverty, economic underdevelopment, and accelerating social change.

THREE TURBULENT DECADES

Between 1950 and 1980, Turks lived through a political mobilization so powerful that it threatened the integrative capacity of republican institutions. Replacing the early republic's unison-voiced national mobilization, a wave of pro- and antisystem confrontations crested in the late 1960s, then began to shatter, leading through the violence of the late 1970s to the finer divisions of post-1980 identity politics. As antisystem forces proliferated, the military punctuated the political chronology with three coups. Internationally, despite tensions over issues like Cyprus, Turkey's pro-Western foreign policy continued and gained strength through this period. Against the backdrop of the Cold War, the infusion of U.S. aid into Turkey and the internationalization of military officers' horizons through NATO service tended to create a differential between military and civilian elites, so intensifying the militarizing trend. All the while, rapid socioeconomic change destabilized politics. Economically, these decades coincided with an unprecedented growth phase in the world economy (1945–1973) followed by the global downturn of the 1970s. Nonetheless, inflation-adjusted GDP per capita rose in this period. In the 1950s, this occurred largely through the extension and mechanization of agriculture. Later, business and manufacturing contributed more significantly to the growth, until the import-substitution policy passed its "easy" stage and the crises of the 1970s set in. Still, quality-of-life indicators also showed significant gains. The per capita growth in real incomes is all the more remarkable given the population explosion that replaced Turkey's demographic deficits of the 1920s with surging growth, superurbanization, and the political turbulence that boiled over in the late 1960s. The consequences of the population explosion were further magnified by the advent of mass literacy, increased ease of travel, and new communications media. Gone were the days when elitist intellectuals could speak for the common people. Now they spoke for themselves in literature and in song. Still only beginning when Orhan Kemal published his story of Pehlivan Ali and his friends, these social and cultural changes would transform city and country alike in the decades that followed.

7

TURKEY AND THE WORLD

In recent decades, Turkey and other nations have formed parts of a world increasingly disordered by the tension between globalizing and localizing forces, the latter closely identified with identity politics. While globalization has sometimes misleadingly been equated with the worldwide spread of a single set of ideas and practices originating in the West, globalization can be fully understood only by acknowledging *all* the networks that gird the world together. However far back in time earlier stages of global interconnectedness extend, the acceleration of technological change reached a point of critical mass in the late twentieth century. Especially with the proliferation of instantaneous electronic communications, differences of space and time seemed to collapse. The global and the local could be experienced everywhere at once, and the interactive-conflictive, protagonist-antagonist friction between them created the symbiotic relationship between globalization and identity politics that distinguishes the contemporary condition. In the midst of these changes, what had been the building blocks of modernity—including nation-states, alliance systems, and international organizations—remained powerful actors. Yet they no longer defined global order. Instead they were caught up in countercurrents of globalism and localism.

For Turkey, these changes have created acute stress in some respects but opened wide new vistas in others. Politically, the guardians of republican laicism have had difficulty adapting to the proliferation of difference inside Turkey. Externally, the tightening of global interlinkages—even with European Union accession hopes shining on the horizon—has shaken assumptions about national sovereignty, formed in the 1920s and 1930s, when global interrelatedness was loosening rather than tightening. At key moments, modernist, Islamically committed "conservative democrats" have appealed to voters more effectively than secularist nationalists, a success at least partly attributable to the better fit between religious universalism and globalization. What has been true in politics has also been true in economics, as Turkey abandoned the autarkist assumptions of protectionist import-substitution and launched an export-led growth strategy that transformed its place in the world economy. Turkish society in the same period has benefited from the abatement of explosive population growth but has had to struggle with its proliferation of difference. Not just a social matter, identity issues affect all of life, particularly politics. In Turkish-Kurdish relations, identity politics has generated serious violence. Yet once the political mobilization of Turkish society became complete in the 1960s, all identity issues became political. As Turkey's place in the world changed, it also experienced its third great religious awakening of the past two centuries. Led by Fethullah Gülen, this has evolved from a local to a national and global movement. As this occurred, the intimate connection between modernity and subjectivity generated Islamist as well as secularist explorations of subjectivity. Some of the most memorable literary explorations of modern subjectivity from this period nonetheless are found in secularist writer Adalet Ağaoğlu's trilogy, *Dar Zamanlar* (Hard times).

POLITICS UNDER THE THIRD REPUBLIC

After three years of military rule (1980–1983), a new constitution and elections opened Turkey's Third Republic. Turkey experienced decisive political leadership in the 1980s under Turgut Özal and after 2002 under Recep Tayyip Erdoğan. In the 1990s, ineffective leadership exposed Turkey's political fissures. Identity politics challenged old assumptions about national unity, especially in the Kurdish insurrection. The end of the Cold War and accelerating global interlinkage altered external relations. Yet the emergence of five post-Soviet Turkic successor republics and the prospects of EU accession created excitement about the future.

MILITARY RULE AND CONSTITUTIONAL CHANGE, 1980–1983

If 1960s Turkey had benefited from a liberal constitution but suffered from the rise of illiberal political movements at the extremes of the political spectrum, the military set out to change all that in 1980.[1] They voided the 1961 constitution, suspended the Grand National Assembly, and replaced it with the National Security Assembly (NSA, Milli Güvenlik Konseyi). General Kenan Evren chaired it and took over as head of state. The new cabinet included generals and civilian technocrats. Recognizing the challenges of managing the economy and reassuring the business elite, the military commanders ceded the economy to civilian ministers. The military government's first priority was to crack down on "terror organizations" and the political violence of the precoup period. Relying on martial law, excessive force, swift trials, and harsh sentences, the crackdown produced unforgettable consequences. Within a year, more than forty-three thousand people had been arrested, over seven hundred thousand weapons had been confiscated, and 167 mass trials were proceeding against "terrorist" organizations, some of which had done nothing worse than exercise their rights under the 1961 constitution. The martial law commanders suspended newspapers. Under the new Higher Education Law, they restricted university autonomy and dismissed many faculty members, often for little or no cause. They purged teachers' ranks and revised curricula throughout the nation's schools. Collaborating with conservative intellectuals, they propounded a "Turkish-Islamic synthesis," a new stage in the political manipulation of "history," more indicative of the future they wanted to create than of the nation's past. Preparing cautiously for the return to civilian rule, the military government convened a consultative assembly to draft a new constitution, approved by popular referendum in 1982. Military rule ended, and civilian rule resumed with the 1983 elections.

The return to civilian rule was highly controlled. Containing measures meant to prevent disorders like those before 1980, both the constitution and the

The 1980 coup. Tanks and troops in the streets of Ankara after the coup led by General Kenan Evren. (Hulton Archive/Getty Images.)

electoral law resembled those of some other developing countries that have had difficulty in achieving political stability under the stress of rapid change. The new constitution expanded the president's powers, even though the prime minister remained the head of the government. Elected by the assembly for a seven-year term as head of state, the president had the power to appoint the prime minister, all members of the constitutional court, and other high officials; to return draft legislation to the assembly (but not veto it); to call general elections early in certain circumstances; to rule by decree under a state of emergency (although the decrees were subject to parliamentary approval); to appoint the chief of staff; and to chair the National Security Council (NSC, Milli Güvenlik Kurulu).[2] Concern about these powers at the time was magnified by the fact that General Evren stayed on as president until 1989. Twenty years later, it was the military's turn to worry about the powers of a civilian president not to their liking.

Expanded presidential powers were not the only constitutional changes. The senate, introduced in 1961, was abolished as unneeded, and Turkey returned to a unicameral system with its Grand National Assembly. Article 118 on the National Security Council provided that its decisions on major security issues had to be "considered with priority" by the Council of Ministers (*öncelikle dikkate alınır*).[3] That empowered the NSC to dictate policy to the cabinet without responsibility to the assembly or the electorate. Many Turks criticized this arrangement as an army regime in camouflage; such criticisms proved justified at times. Another salient feature of the 1982 constitution was that its guarantees of rights were accompanied by clauses designed to prevent abuse of those rights. For example, article 28 guaranteed freedom of the press but prohibited publications in "any language prohibited by law" (Kurdish), as well as publications that threatened state security, tended to incite crime or rebellion, or committed various other vaguely defined offenses. A fictional court case in a novel discussed later in this chapter illustrates what could spring from this provision. Trade unions likewise were allowed to exist but not to support or be supported by political parties (article 52).

Other laws enacted under military rule similarly restricted democratization. The 1983 electoral law required parties to win at least 10 percent of the vote nationally in order to hold assembly seats.[4] The point was to prevent splinter parties from any longer playing decisive roles in coalitions. However, many voters ended up without representatives in the assembly. In an extreme case, the 2002 election left 45 percent of voters (and seven parties) with no representation in the assembly because none of those parties reached the 10 percent threshold.[5] Two 1983 laws on unions also tightened the prohibition of political action by labor.

The 1983 elections occurred, then, under new conditions. The old parties had been abolished; many old politicians were banned. The military allowed only three new parties to participate. Voters showed their feelings by giving a majority to the one party at all independent of the military, Turgut Özal's Motherland (Anavatan, ANAP) Party.[6] The 1983 election was the first followed on television by significant numbers of Turks. Demonstrating his expertise on the economic issues that preoccupied voters, Özal was effective on television.

The military regime of 1980 left a mixed legacy, and analyses of the 1982 constitution have varied. What some regard as a relatively democratic charter that remedies defects of the 1961 constitution appears to others as a missed chance to create a constitution enjoying wide consensus, a weakening of Turkey's parliamentary system of government, a dangerous expansion of the president's and the NSC's powers, and a serious restrictions of rights.[7] Average Turks were relieved that the pre-1980 political violence was over and the economy was improving; yet they paid a heavy price in mass arrests, trials, and rights violations by the military. The ban on the old politicians and parties also did not last. What Turkey really needed was something the military could not provide: political leaders with vision. Finally, the "regimented and solidarist view of society" that the military sought to enforce left no room for identity politics.[8]

TURKEY UNDER ÖZAL

Prime minister (1983–1989) then president (1989–1993), Turgut Özal showed that he had vision. Embodying the combination of economic liberalism and Islamic values that bested overtly Islamist parties in gaining voter support, he reoriented Turkish politics more significantly than anyone since Atatürk. Economically, he replaced the inward-oriented, import-substitution policy pioneered in the 1930s with an export-led growth strategy, so adjusting to the global trend toward privatization.

Özal's other, less-known innovations are no less significant. In 1984, responding to the problems of hyperurbanization, Greater City Municipalities (Büyükşehir Belediyeleri) were created for Istanbul, Ankara, and Izmir. A dual-tiered system including both metropolitan (*büyük şehir*) and district municipalities, the system was designed to provide better services and new outlets for political participation. Despite problems, remarkable improvements resulted, including a spectacular cleanup of the waterfront along Istanbul's Golden Horn. Public interest in municipal politics grew, particularly when Turkey's two largest municipalities elected mayors from the Islamist Refah Party in 1994, Melih Gökçek in Ankara and Recep Tayyip Erdoğan in Istanbul, setting off alarms among secularists. The rise of the Refah Party, owing as much to grassroots

Turgut Özal brought a new vision of policy and a new
style to Turkish politics. (Courtesy of the Office of the
Prime Minister, Ankara.)

organization and effective urban services as to religion, did not keep large numbers of voters from voting for other parties in 1999. In any event, as the number
of greater municipalities grew to fifteen, urban governance began to catch up
with growth, and big-city mayorships became springboards to national office.[9]
Erdoğan went on to become prime minister by 2002.

Education also changed significantly under Özal. Private universities began
to be founded, starting with Bilkent (1984). Academically enriched high schools
known as Anatolian lycées grew greatly in numbers. Combining science and
mathematics with foreign languages, they provided large numbers of Turks
from nonelite backgrounds for the first time with foreign-language education.
The high schools for training mosque functionaries, the *imam-hatip* (prayer
leader–preacher) schools, also expanded in number; and many girls enrolled
in them. Girls could not become mosque functionaries. However, conservative
families' greater willingness to enroll their daughters in religious schools gave

many more girls access to secondary education. Graduates of both sexes also went on to the university. Most imam-hatip graduates who went on for higher education did so in secular subjects.[10]

Özal also enlarged cultural freedoms. He made the pilgrimage to Mecca while prime minister, and he publicly acknowledged that he was a Nakşibendi. He allowed greater cultural freedom to the Kurds, and the 1983 law banning use of the Kurdish language in public or private was repealed in 1991 when he was president. In 1987, Turkey applied for membership in the European Economic Community (since 1992 the European Union). Under Özal, individuals were allowed to appeal to the European Commission on Human Rights, and EU conventions on human rights and the prevention of torture were officially ratified. Adherence to EU norms began to figure, as it continues to, as a way to enlarge space for religious conservatives and minorities who were not comfortable with the early republic's laic model of citizenship without difference.[11]

Özal not only reoriented the economy but demonstrated truly broad vision.[12] The vision would not have worked politically had it not appealed to many voters. With Özal, the religiously committed, business-oriented, Anatolian-rooted but now increasingly urbanized sector of society finally came to power. After decades as the targets of state policy, they became policy makers. Significantly for the future of Turkish democracy, the party that won a parliamentary majority for this segment of society in 1983, Özal's Motherland Party, was not overtly Islamist. By origins, it was a center-right coalition, including elements from the precoup Republican People's, Justice, Nationalist Action, and National Salvation parties. Özal was a pragmatist, and the party took an eclectic approach to the many questions about Turkey's place in the modern world.

POLITICAL ZIGZAGS, 1993–2002

By the time Özal died in 1993, political instability was rising. His Motherland Party was already losing cohesion and support when he engineered his election as president in 1989. Many reasons have been cited for the erratic shifts of the 1990s. The military government ban on party politics in 1981 had unsettled voter loyalties. Along with the collapse of socialism in eastern Europe, infighting and lack of new ideas virtually killed the left half of Turkey's political spectrum. The Kurdish insurgency, starting in 1984, continued for years with huge costs. The 1987 liberalization that allowed many old politicians and parties, or replacement parties, to resume activity did not add new alternatives. Economic crises compounded political instability. Yet compared to the preceding and following decades, the root cause of 1990s voter zigzags among parties was the leading politicians' lack of any vision beyond short-term deal-making.[13]

Throughout the 1990s, Turkish voters' shifting choices led to coalition governments, which by nature could not rule as decisively as a single-party government. The 1991 election produced a coalition with Süleyman Demirel (True Path Party, a remake of the Justice Party) as prime minister and Erdal İnönü (Social Democrat Populist Party, İsmet İnönü's son) as his deputy. When the assembly elected Demirel to succeed Özal as president in 1993, Turkey acquired its first woman prime minister, Tansu Çiller, also of the True Path (Doğru Yol) Party. Many Turks were happy to have a woman prime minister, but not so happy that it was she. Çiller has been criticized for mismanaging the economic crisis, her "negative impact on Turkish democracy," and personal enrichment while in office.[14]

Building on its success in bringing out voters, the Islamist Prosperity Party (Refah, a remake of the earlier National Salvation Party, Milli Selamet) springboarded from its 1994 municipal victories to outperform any party in the 1995 general elections (21.4 percent of the vote, 28.7 percent of the assembly seats). To prevent Refah from coming to power, months of effort went into trying to form a coalition between the two secular parties with the most assembly seats, Motherland and True Path; but the antipathies of their respective leaders, Mesut Yılmaz and Tansu Çiller, thwarted that effort. Finally formed in June 1996, the next government combined Prosperity and True Path in a startling power-rotation deal. Prosperity leader Necmettin Erbakan, now becoming Turkey's first Islamist prime minister, and Çiller, who had already served as its first woman prime minister, were each to serve as prime minister for two years in rotation. What sealed the deal was Erbakan's agreement to stop demanding that the National Assembly investigate Çiller for corruption.

Çiller never got to succeed Erbakan. His inflammatory rhetoric and idiosyncratic, Islamic-themed policy ventures alienated interests as far apart as the military high command and the leader of the branch of the Nakşibendiye with which he had once been affiliated.[15] Visiting Libya in 1996 over the opposition of his own foreign ministry, Erbakan got humiliating lectures from Libyan leader Muammar Qaddafi about Turkey's policies toward the West and the Kurds; Turkish voters resented that. On 31 January 1997, Sincan, a municipality on the outskirts of Ankara controlled by Erbakan's Refah Party, organized a meeting to show support for Iran and the Palestinian movement Hamas. The next day, tanks rolled into Sincan. On 28 February 1997, in what has been called a fourth, "postmodern," coup, the NSC presented the government with eighteen "decisions" for enforcing laicism. Article 118 of the constitution requires the government to "consider with priority" all such decisions. In May, the chief state prosecutor asked the Constitutional Court to shut down Erbakan's party.

By June, as assembly members deserted Çiller's party, Erbakan had no choice but to resign, and a new coalition government took over with Mesut Yılmaz (Motherland Party) as prime minister. From then until the 2002 election, the governments represented the military more than the electorate. Meanwhile, the high court closed the Prosperity (Refah) Party in January 1998 and banned Erbakan from politics for five years. His followers reorganized as the Virtue Party (Fazilet, 1998–2001), but a struggle between "traditionalists" (*gelenekçiler*) and "innovators" (*yenilikçiler*) divided them.

Politics zigzagged again in 1999. Bülent Ecevit, who had last served as prime minister in 1978–1979 and now headed the Democratic Left (Demokratik Sol, DSP) Party, succeeded Yılmaz as prime minister of a minority government in January. Foreign and domestic politics intersected to magical effect in February when Ecevit announced on television that the authorities had captured Kurdish insurgency leader Abdullah Öcalan in Kenya and brought him back for trial in Turkey. After twenty years out of power, accidental good timing made Ecevit the man of the hour. Resurgent national pride persisted through the April general election, from which Ecevit's DSP emerged as the largest (22.2 percent of the vote, 24.7 percent of the assembly seats). As prime minister, he headed a new coalition that also included the Motherland and Nationalist Action (Milliyetçi Hareket) parties. Ironically, the party that Ecevit had headed during his premierships of the 1970s, Atatürk's Republican People's Party, won only 8.7 percent of the votes in 1999, therefore getting no assembly seats at all.

For two more years, things only got worse. In August 1999, an earthquake shook Izmit near Istanbul, leaving more than ten thousand dead, half a million homeless, and vast economic damage. Neither the government nor the army responded adequately; after Erbakan's recent fall, the Islamists were also too disorganized to exploit this failure, as the secularists feared they would. Now, the kind of nationalist pride that had swept the government into office looked foolish, especially when Minister of Health Osman Durmuş of the chauvinistic Nationalist Action Party declared that Turkey did not need foreign help to cope with the disaster. The effective help did come from foreigners and domestic nongovernmental groups, like the volunteer AKUT search-and-rescue team, which was also one of the first non-Greek groups to respond to the earthquake that struck Athens a month later.[16] By 2001, Turkey's economic crises had become drastic. Ecevit responded by bringing in Kemal Derviş from the World Bank to take over as minister for the economy. Derviş restored confidence within a year. By then, Ecevit's health was declining, and his Nationalist Action Party coalition partners overplayed their hand. They called for early elections, expecting to come out stronger.

Instead, the 2002 elections ended the zigzags of the 1990s, turned out all parties to the 1999 coalition, and left only two parties and some independents in the National Assembly. The Republican People's Party came back with 19.4 percent of the vote and 32.4 percent of the seats. The big winners, however, were a new party organized only fifteen months earlier when Erbakan's followers split. The "traditionalists" had joined the Felicity (Saadet) Party, and the "innovators" formed the Justice and Development (Adalet ve Kalkınma, AK) Party. In the 2002 elections, the AK Party won 34.3 percent of the vote and 66 percent of the seats. Now, Turkey had a single-party government for the first time since the Motherland Party lost its majority in 1991.[17]

TURKEY UNDER THE JUSTICE AND DEVELOPMENT PARTY

The Justice and Development Party won decisive majorities in 2002 and again in 2007. Its Turkish name, Adalet ve Kalkınma, yields the Turkish acronym AK, which matches the common word *ak*, "white" or "bright" and by extension "pure" and "uncorrupt." Organizationally a descendant of Erbakan's Islamist parties, in vision, quality of leadership, and breadth of support the AK Party more nearly recalls Özal's Motherland Party of the 1980s. In some respects, the AK Party even fills the place that a more effective social democratic party might fill.[18]

Several factors helped the party win a majority in national elections within fifteen months of its founding. It presented itself not as an Islamic party but as a "conservative democratic" (*muhafazakar demokrat*) party. It displayed greater seriousness than its main competitor, the Republican People's Party, about cleaning up corruption. The priority it gave to economic policy and its probusiness stance recalled not Erbakan but Özal. In matters of religion and family values, the party is conservative; but it takes accommodative positions toward those who do not share its views. It combines this conservatism with emphases on socioeconomic justice, democracy, individual rights, and EU integration; on those points the AK Party resembles European social democrats. While diehard laicists have persisted in seeing it as a threat to laicism, as of the elections of 2007, the AK Party signified the "transformation of Turkish political Islam . . . into a moderate conservative democratic party" and a "significant step toward bridging the . . . cleavage between secularists and Islamists, thus contributing to the consolidation of democracy in Turkey."[19]

One way to understand the AK Party is by considering its leader, Recep Tayyip Erdoğan.[20] From a working-class Istanbul family, he made his way through the imam-hatip high school to the university. Graduating from the university made him a member of the elite, but he never forgot his origins, as the color illustration of him meeting with voters suggests. He states metaphorically that there are "black Turks" and "white Turks," and he is one of the black ones, an allusion to the partial correspondence between skin tone and social class in Turkey. As an adult, he belonged to a Nakşibendi group, Istanbul's İskenderpaşa congregation, led by the charismatic Şeyh Mehmet Zahit Kotku (d. 1980). Many influential figures have come from this group. Erdoğan won the mayorship of greater Istanbul in 1994 for the Refah Party, and his success in that office helped him become a national figure.[21] However, some of his actions provoked controversy, and his reactions to those experiences redirected his career. At the time, he was known to imply that democracy was only a means to an end, thus agitating the secularists' worst fears. Sharing the Turkish fondness for poetry, he delivered a speech in the southeastern town of Siirt in which he quoted a poem that landed him in court in 1998. The poem is a famous one by Ziya Gökalp, depicting an imaginary battle between a pre-Ottoman sultan and a Byzantine emperor. The sultan proclaims, "The minarets are our bayonets, the domes are our helmets, the mosques are our barracks, and the believers are our soldiers." Although the poem was written by a hero of Turkish nationalism and was included in schoolbooks, Erdoğan's recitation of these lines in a political speech resulted in his trial and imprisonment for inciting hatred on the basis of religion and seeking to establish an Islamic state. After serving ten months in prison in 1998, he continued to be attacked in the media and to face legal charges in court. Becoming a leader among the "innovators" who founded the AK Party, he elaborated his stance as a Muslim committed to democracy.

His changing relations with Erbakan illustrate how Erdoğan changed. They clashed over party matters as early as 1978. In the 1980s and 1990s, Erdoğan worked to enlarge women's roles in the party, criticized Erbakan's autocratic style, emphasized expertise over piety, and introduced up-to-date communications systems. As mayor of greater Istanbul, he presided over improvements in services that even his political opponents appreciated. In a speech after leaving prison, he said he had left behind "conducting politics with religious symbols" but would "show everybody how believers should act in politics." When the Justice and Development (AK) Party was founded in 2001, women, all with heads uncovered, made up nearly half the group that filed the papers with the Ministry of the Interior. The name of the new party was chosen to signal its commitment to justice and equity, as well as to religious values. The party accepted laicism as a governing principle for the state, although not necessarily for the individual, recognizing that a religiously neutral government could guarantee freedom of conscience, from which AK Party supporters would benefit. Erdoğan's recent conviction still barred him from the 2002 election. A caretaker prime minister, Abdullah Gül, took office. In 2003, after Erdoğan's ban was lifted, he won election to the National Assembly in a by-election in Siirt, site of the speech that had landed him in jail, and took over as prime minister. The party won a majority again in 2007, Erdoğan remained prime minister, and Gül was elected president of the republic.

The party's differences from Erbakan's positions match voter preferences. Surveys show that the issues most on Turkish voters' minds in 2002 were unemployment, the economy, and inflation, not religion.[22] Almost all of those surveyed believed in God, but the proportion who went to mosque once a week (23 percent) was lower than that of those who never or rarely went (30 percent). Equally high proportions believed that women university students should be free to cover their heads (78 percent) but opposed a sharia-based state in Turkey (75 percent). It is no wonder that the political scientists who study the AK Party seldom share the fear, voiced by some secularists, that it will turn Turkey into an "Islamic republic."

Assuming power in 2002, the AK Party stabilized the economy and reduced inflation. It accelerated EU integration, carrying out enough reforms that EU accession negotiations could begin in October 2005. The reforms ranged from greater cultural freedom for Kurds to changes in the NSC. The AK Party's ability to produce what EU commissioner Günter Verheugen optimistically called "the second revolution after the establishment of the Republic" is something that the party's electoral success alone cannot explain, given the extent to which the Turkish political system vests powers in unelected bodies. Rather, the AK Party's impact results from its advance beyond the rigidities of both Erbakan-style Islamism and Kemalist state laicism.[23]

Ostensibly mainstream but not without radical Islamist links, Erbakan's Refah Party had seen laicism as the crux of all problems, denounced all the Westernizing reforms since the Tanzimat, and opposed EU integration. In contrast, the AK Party appealed to conservatives proud of Ottoman and republican achievements, ready to support a secular state that guaranteed their rights, and cognizant of European integration more as an opportunity than as a threat. The AK Party's success in using the integration process to leverage democratizing reforms favorable to religious interests has left opposition parties looking defensive, as they demand that the EU make exceptions for Turkey on the accession criteria. The AK Party's future success will depend not only on whether it can hold together its support base, remedy domestic problems, and maintain its accommodative positions on sensitive issues, but also on whether EU integration succeeds.

The AK Party's successes in 2002 and 2007 reflect the thoroughgoing political mobilization of the populace and the interaction between identity politics and globalization, with EU integration as its brightest prospect. The same factors have combined to challenge the early republican assumptions about state-controlled, laicist-nationalist development and the institutions that drew power from those assumptions. This chronological survey of Turkish politics from 1980 until 2007 has raised several topics that merit further comment: political corruption and public cynicism, the Kurdish issue, foreign policy in general, and the EU in particular.

POLITICAL CORRUPTION, VOTER CYNICISM

By the late 1990s, Turkey had entered an impasse of "political instability, clientelism, corruption and a drastic loss of societal trust." "A radical reconstruction of Turkish politics" was needed if the country was "to deal effectively with both economic problems and cultural transformations."[24] The corruption spilled out spectacularly in 1996 at the town of Susurluk when a truck crashed into a car in which four bodies were found, those of a member of the National Assembly, Istanbul's former deputy police chief, a mafia figure known for his role in the gray wolves in the 1970s, and a prostitute with false identity papers. Press reports alleged that the trunk of the wrecked car was full of types of weapons used in assassinations, that the car was part of a convoy, and that the other vehicles fled the scene. Of those in the car, only the National Assembly member survived. He was hospitalized for months, during which his memory of events changed. The assembly member, Sedat Bucak, was both a member of the True Path Party, then part of the government, and the chief of a pro-government Kurdish tribe in the southeast, from which hundreds of relatives came to visit him in the hospital. The Turkish public was riveted by revelations that confirmed its worst suspicions. Blaming the government for dragging its feet in investigating, civic associations asked the public to turn off their lights each night at 9 p.m. for one minute to protest. The campaign shows the growth of the voluntary forms of civil society in Turkey. Yet the cynicism that the Susurluk incident evoked was a widely, deeply rooted problem that did not redound only against the government.

A systemic relationship exists between political corruption and public cynicism in Turkey. The public demands "favoritism, cronyism, and free riding."[25] The pattern implies Turkish society's participation in a wider, Mediterranean pattern in which individuals lack a sense of moral obligation to social entities beyond the family; and this lack of a sense of the common good makes it rational to exploit the public realm for private gain.[26] The pattern has both cross-cultural parallels and deep roots in the patriarchal family structures and patrimonial rulership of Ottoman times.

Such expectations create distinctive problems in governance. One such pattern appears when rival families in a given locality support different national parties, disregarding mismatches between their interests and the parties' platforms. Scholars have found such rivalries in the party preferences of rival clans in the Black Sea region near Trabzon, as well as in the pro-Turkish or pro-PKK alignments of Kurdish clans. In fact, some Kurdish landowners' ability to deliver their tribespeople's votes by the thousand guarantees national politicians' fidelity less to their platforms than to the landowners' wishes.[27] The more politics becomes a matter of favoritism and free riding, the more it becomes impossible for governments to balance investment, consumption, and debt. The broadening political mobilization of the populace has led to major increases in demands for public spending. As business and industry developed, new patronage networks and clienteles grew up to share the benefits. The growth in demand for state services, a global trend, merged with a historical Turkish concept of the Father State or Mother State (Devlet Baba, Devlet Ana). The "mother-fatherland" (*anavatan*, compare French *mère patrie*) had to be bountiful mother and powerful patron in one.

Such expectations generated an "image of the state as an 'omnipotent hegemon,' controlling every social process and suffocating any freedom of social, economic, or cultural action, yet possessing vast resources to deliver" to those it favored. Turkish commentators often conclude that the state stifles the development of civil society; however, survey data indicate that the grassroots initiatives needed to develop a dynamic civil society occur in Turkey at much lower levels than in Europe or the United States. As of the 1990s, fewer than 15 percent of Turks had ever signed a petition, and only 5–6 percent had ever participated in a legal demonstration, let alone anything radical.[28] The debility of civil society has as much to do with societal passivity as with state suppression.

A seeming paradox illustrates the point. Turks revere the state as Father State and Mother State; yet the state does not treat its citizens well and sometimes deploys high levels of violence against them. In contrast, Anglo-American polities, whose citizens historically idealized "little government," have to treat those citizens much better. If civil society were more vigorous in Turkey, the Turkish side of the seeming paradox would diminish: less revering the state, less abusing its power. In Turkey, the debility of civil society also does nothing to discourage individuals from exploiting the public realm for personal or familial benefit. The pattern reinforces the importance of primordial solidarities based on kinship, religious brotherhood, common place of origin, and the like, networks that extend into the Turkish diaspora as well.

Confronting such groups and their demands, political parties have to promise more before an election than they can deliver afterward. Governments pass laws; indeed Turks idealize the "law state" (*hukuk devleti*, a concept recalling the Germanic *Rechtsstaat*). Yet the laws do not produce rule of law. Budgetary discipline is undermined; economic crisis and political unrest ensue. Governments find it an intractable problem to keep the benefits flowing as long as they remain in power. Efficient tax collection becomes impossible. As of 2003, out of a Turkish population of 70 million with 41.5 million eligible voters, only 6 to 7 million paid income tax. Turkish consumers paid the value added tax, which is included in the price of goods. Yet the indication of a huge gap between those who expect services from the state and those willing to comply with its tax laws persists. If questioned about the matter, tax evaders might answer that if they did pay their taxes, the money would disappear into the pockets of politicians and their cronies. The financial and other crises of the 1990s provided evidence to confirm such cynicism.

Coming to power in 2002, the AK Party took unprecedented action by strengthening the laws and prosecuting businesspeople and politicians suspected of corruption. The momentum in favor of EU integration reinforces efforts to achieve democratization and rule of law. The success of these efforts remains to be seen.[29]

IDENTITY POLITICS: THE KURDS

Before 1980, ideology rather than identity seemed to drive politics; yet even then, left-right ideology often masked other conflicts.[30] Politics has since shifted openly toward identity issues defined along all Turkey's axes of difference—ethnicity, religion, gender, and personal preference or disadvantage. All these differences have political implications, but not all of them generated the conflict that ethnicity did in the Kurdish case, turning Turkish-Kurdish relations into the hottest identity issue of this period.

The Kurds' politicization entered a new phase after the 1960s. They, too, were caught up in the move to the cities, including Izmir, Ankara, and Istanbul. Kurdish identity began to lose its regional concentration. Yet the Kurdish birthrate remained high, and urbanization did not reverse Kurdish population growth in the east. Worry about the rising Kurdish proportion of the population complicated Turkish reactions to Kurdish issues. In 2007, Turkey's Kurdish population was estimated at 11.5 million, nearly 16 percent of the total, 73 million.[31]

Turkish Kurds' positions on identity issues span a wide spectrum, from high acculturation to the opposite extreme. Turkish nation-building has integrated citizens of many ethnicities, including non-Turks from Bosnians to Chechens.

All the republic's constitutions (1924, 1961, and 1983) have defined citizenship in civic rather than ethnic terms.[32] Many elite Kurds opted to work within the system, and many prominent figures in public life were, or were alleged to be, of Kurdish origin. Turkish-Kurdish intermarriage was common, especially among pious Muslims, who value religious over ethnic identity.

For Kurdish activists, however, urbanization and politicization went together, given the landlords' (*ağas'*) hold on the east. Urban Kurds escaped the landlords but confronted discrimination and official claims that Kurds were not ethnically distinct. Their experiences perfectly illustrate the emergence of identity politics from the fragmentation of a broader antiestablishment coalition. The late 1960s witnessed the first urban-based Kurdish defiance of state authority. Turkish leftists' propensity to ignore Kurds until "after the revolution" motivated Kurds to form underground parties in the 1970s. Kurdish militancy endangered the Turkish nation in a way that other assertions of difference did not as a result of the Kurds' concentration in a border region. Activism spread into the countryside, alarms about separatism sounded, and state security forces began operations. Still, in 1983 few anticipated that Kurdish insurgency would become Turkey's greatest internal security challenge.[33]

The PKK shattered the silence in 1984 by attacking Turkish forces in Kurdish areas. PKK is the Kurdish acronym for Partiya Karkerên Kurdistan, the Kurdistan Workers' Party, led by Abdullah "Apo" Öcalan. Like many urban Kurds, he spoke Turkish but not Kurdish. A veteran of Turkey's leftist movements, Öcalan broke away and returned to southeastern Turkey in 1975 to build a following. Motivations included desires to combine Kurdish nationalism with class war and to recover an identity and language whose loss Kurds blamed on the Turkish state. The PKK's enemies included not only the state but also many Kurds. Many ordinary Kurds, while perhaps admiring the PKK for its daring, were more interested in supporting their families than in waging guerrilla warfare. PKK radicalism had particularly little appeal to pious Kurdish Sunnis. Historically identified with the Kadiri or Nakşibendi orders, they shared more with the Turkish right than the Kurdish left. The PKK's obvious Kurdish enemies were the landlords, whom the PKK attacked by exploiting clan rivalries. Öcalan's 1979 attempt to assassinate a landlord and assembly member from the Bucak clan started a blood-feud and confirmed the clan's alliance with Ankara, whence another Bucak's starring role in the 1996 Susurluk scandal.

Before the 1980 coup, Öcalan and others had already taken refuge in Syria. After the Turkish military crushed domestic Kurdish and leftist movements, the PKK reemerged in 1984 to challenge it.[34] Syria and Lebanon's Syrian-controlled Biqa' Valley remained major PKK centers; the PKK also had bases in northern

Iraq. Resuming operations in Turkey, the PKK selectively targeted landlords, whose hold over rural Kurds and monopolization of political power were increasingly resented. Assassinating landlords who collaborated with the government showed that the government could not always protect its supporters, and so did ambushes of security forces. Still, PKK violence and radicalism made many Kurds ambivalent. Ankara soon found a way to exploit those doubts.

In 1985, Ankara created "village guards," somewhat like the old Hamidiye regiments. Clans opposing the PKK supported the guards, and poor Kurds liked the stipends of about $230 per month. By the 1990s, more than thirty thousand had enlisted. Powerful landlords enrolled their clansmen, collected their pay, and used the money to maintain their authority by providing largesse to their retainers. The guards were soon mired in abuses; yet the government kept pressuring tribes to join. Caught between the PKK and the guards, more Kurds migrated to the cities.

As the PKK strengthened its network in the southeast, the government stepped up its efforts, with counterproductive results.[35] It prohibited the use of Kurdish or expressions of Kurdish culture. A governor-general was appointed for eight Kurdish provinces, and a state of emergency was proclaimed (1987). By the early 1990s, two hundred thousand troops were stationed in the region. The governor-general had the power to evacuate villages and deport the population. By 1994, 750,000 deportees were homeless. Despite efforts to police the border, the conflict also complicated Turkey's relations with Syria, Iraq, and Iran. As the conflict went through its most acute phase, the PKK initially overplayed its hand in attacking village guards and landlord families but gradually shifted its strategy more against the Turkish security forces.

Voices were raised in favor of constructive efforts to defuse the situation. Kurdish political parties formed and got several members elected to Turkey's Grand National Assembly. However, prospects for electoral politics to resolve the conflict were wrecked by provocative incidents, such as taking the parliamentary oath in Kurdish, which inflamed Turkish opinion. In 1993, President Özal, describing himself as the Turkish son of a Kurdish mother, wrote a letter to Prime Minister Süleyman Demirel warning that a "social earthquake could cut one part of Turkey [off] from the rest."[36] Yet Demirel backed the military approach. PKK operations showed that the military could not guarantee stability in the region. Yet the government had the advantage militarily in the southeast and internationally in its ability to pressure Syria and Iraq.

The government also adopted a regional development policy, known by the Turkish acronym GAP (Güneydoğu Anadolu Projesi, Southeast Anatolia Project). The project was based on a series of hydroelectric dams to harness the potential primarily of the Euphrates (both the Tigris and the Euphrates rise in eastern Anatolia). Although much of the project's significance was economic, it had general relevance to attempts to solve southeastern problems. Yet excitement over the project left serious questions unanswered about how it would benefit a region where 8 percent of the families owned over half the land and the majority of the people were illiterate and too unskilled for new economic pursuits.[37]

By 1994, the PKK had a coherent Kurdish national movement; further success depended on being able to negotiate with the Turkish government. The PKK episodically offered ceasefires, but the Turkish military remained committed to a military solution. By 1999, more than three thousand villages had been evacuated, sometimes brutally.[38] Emptying the villages caused hothouse population growth in the southeastern cities. By 1996, Diyarbakır's population had nearly tripled within five years, to 1.3 million. Kurds flocked to cities as far away as Istanbul. The state used "special teams" (*özel tim*) for targeted assassinations of suspected enemies. One sign of the state's growing military advantage was the lifting, in 1997–1998, of the state of emergency in four out of ten eastern provinces. In 1998, Turkey threatened war against Syria to get it to stop supporting the PKK. Forced out of Syria, Öcalan searched for asylum, ending up in Nairobi, Kenya, where Turkish special forces captured him. Brought to Turkey, he was tried for treason and sentenced to death, although legal appeals and Turkey's EU accession hopes reduced the sentence effectively to life in prison. Offering only an apologetic defense at trial, Öcalan called from prison for PKK militancy to cease.

These events left the PKK leadership in crisis. Yet the Turkish triumph was not without its perils. The Kurdish conflict was only the most glaring case of the rigidity with which the guardians of Kemalism reacted to the rise of identity politics. Turkey's prospects of EU integration were immeasurably complicated by human rights complaints growing out of the Kurdish conflict. Some Turkish analysts interpreted EU criticisms of Turkey's Kurdish policy as an attack on the nation's unity. Yet among the major institutions of Turkish civil society, both the Turkish Union of Chambers of Commerce and Exchanges (TOBB, 1995) and the Turkish Industrialists' and Businessmen's Association (TÜSİAD, 1997) published reports demanding social and cultural openness; TÜSİAD also called for the end of the NSC in its present form.[39]

The most destabilizing consequence of the military approach to the Kurdish problem was that policies designed to solve a regional problem helped make it a national and international one. All this might not have happened, had not the Turkish National Struggle tied Turkish understandings of unity so narrowly to territorial unity. As of 1992, while "70 percent of Kurds insisted they did not want an independent state, no fewer than 89 percent of Turks were convinced that they did."[40] Most Kurds were more interested in rights and freedoms inside Turkey than in separatism; yet most Turks saw only Kurdish separatists.

In 2007, the continued operations mounted by an estimated three thousand PKK guerrillas from Iraq against targets in Turkey led the Erdoğan government to seek authorization from the National Assembly for possible operations in northern Iraq.[41] Following the 2003 U.S. invasion of Iraq, Iraqi Kurdish autonomy had been confirmed, and that region had come to seem like the one part of Iraq where the original U.S. objectives were reached. After a five-year ceasefire following Öcalan's trial, the PKK resumed violent actions, reasserting its importance in the regional equation. The 2007 threat of military operations against PKK bases in Iraqi Kurdistan perhaps resembled the 1998 threat of war with Syria in being more a political than a military maneuver. Located in mountainous terrain among sympathetic Iraqi Kurds, the PKK bases in Iraq would be difficult to eliminate by military means. By this time, too, twenty Turkish Kurds were serving as elected members of Turkey's Grand National Assembly. As an Iraqi Kurdish leader commented, "When you have the door to the [Turkish] Parliament open, why are you going to the caves?" In identity politics, assimilation and ethnic mobilization are not mutually exclusive.[42] The future of relations between Turks and Kurds might be one of conflict; yet increasing intermarriage and the rising prominence of Turkey's Kurds in politics and business point to constructive possibilities for reconciling different identities with equal citizenship.

FOREIGN RELATIONS

The end of the Cold War (1989–1991) marked a historic turning point, opening exciting vistas in relations with the new Turkic republics of Central Asia. Regional issues persisted, however, particularly over Cyprus. Turkey's relations with the European Union also grew, eclipsing other issues in importance.

The period opened with new regional tensions created in 1979 by the Iranian revolution and the Soviet invasion of Afghanistan. Turkey criticized the invasion and took in several thousand refugees (ethnic Kyrgyz) from Afghanistan.[43] Relations with Iran were complicated by the Islamic regime's hostility to Kemalism. Yet economic interests prevailed, and Iran became a major Turkish export market. During the Iran-Iraq War, both Iran and Iraq depended on Turkey economically. Turkey's profits outweighed the strategic costs after Iraq began to provide bases for the PKK. By the late 1980s, as Turkey began to build dams on the Euphrates for its Southeast Anatolia Project, water issues increasingly complicated relations with Syria and Iraq, both dependent on the river's downstream flow. Still resentful of losing Hatay (Alexandretta) to Turkey in 1939, Syria tried to gain leverage by supporting the PKK. That attempt backfired when Turkey threatened war against Syria in 1998.

Following Iraq's 1990 occupation of Kuwait, when the U.S.-led UN coalition invaded Iraq in 1991, Turkey under President Özal turned in an exemplary performance as a NATO member, probably in the interest of reaffirming Turkey's post–Cold War strategic relevance. Supporting the economic blockade of Iraq meant stopping Turkish exports, transshipment of European goods via Turkey to Iraq, and oil pipeline deliveries from northern Iraq to Turkey's Mediterranean coast. Countless Turkish businesses were ruined as a result.

Özal's pro-U.S. policy, which included allowing the use of military bases in Turkey for operations against Iraq, was not popular. Its costs were aggravated after the Iraqi Kurds revolted, with U.S. encouragement, against Saddam Husayn. Once his regime recovered from the war and cracked down, Iraqi Kurds tried to flee into Iran and Turkey. Turkish forces stopped them from entering, and Özal proposed creating a security zone in northern Iraq, where the Iraqi air force was forbidden to fly; the UN provided relief, and a multinational force provided security. After Iraq's Saddam Husayn regime was toppled in 2003, Kurdish autonomy continued in northern Iraq, as did Turkish concerns about the Iraqi Turkmens, some of whom lived in the Kurdish zone.

Turkey's relations with Israel, strengthened in the 1990s, hindered close relations with the Arab countries while helping consolidate Turkey's claims to U.S. support. However, by also maintaining correct relations with the Palestinian authorities, Turkey avoided provoking the Arab states into combined action against its interests. After the 2007 election, Prime Minister Erdoğan also voiced more open criticism of Israel's treatment of the Palestinians.

Turkey's relations with its Balkan neighbors centered on Greco-Turkish issues pertaining to the Aegean and Cyprus. In 1989, however, Bulgaria's tottering communist regime decided to expel its Turkish minority. More than three hundred thousand refugees fled to Turkey.[44] The crisis ended with the collapse of Bulgarian communism (November 1989), conditions for Bulgarian Turks improved, and some returned to Bulgaria.

Greco-Turkish relations remained deadlocked until 1999. The principal issues were the treatment of the Greek and Turkish minorities in the two countries, sovereignty over the Aegean, and Cyprus.[45] The Turkish minority in Greece was bigger than the Greek minority in Turkey; however, the latter also raised issues concerning the Greek Orthodox patriarchate in Istanbul, and Turkey's EU accession hopes sensitized such issues. Tensions rose over the Aegean in

1987, when Greece proposed to explore for oil in waters claimed by Turkey, and Turkey also sent out its own survey vessel. Such incidents continued, raising complex legal questions about continental shelf rights and territorial waters in the Aegean, where many islands under Greek sovereignty are close to the Turkish mainland.

Just before Turkey's return to civilian rule in 1983, Turkish Cypriots proclaimed their sovereignty as the Turkish Republic of Northern Cyprus (TRNC). However, no country but Turkey recognized the TRNC. The Greek Cypriot government's 1990 application for full membership in the European Community (since 1992, the EU) confronted Turkey with an added irritant, all the more in 1995 after Greece linked its approval of Turkey's customs union with the EU to Cypriot accession, with or without a solution to the island's division. Diplomatic efforts did not regain momentum until 1999, from the sympathies aroused when earthquakes struck both Turkey and Greece. As the two countries moved beyond nationalist antagonism toward a new appreciation of cultural commonalities, Cypriots remained divided. In anticipation of the island's EU accession in 2004, UN secretary-general Kofi Annan proposed a confederation of two Cypriot states under a common federal government. In a referendum held in April 2004, 65 percent of Turkish Cypriots approved, but 75 percent of Greek Cypriots rejected the plan. Instead of a reunited Cyprus, only the Greek-ruled Republic of Cyprus, the island's southern part, entered the EU in May 2004.

Although it failed to end headaches over Cyprus, the end of the Cold War produced exceptionally benign consequences for Turkey. At a stroke, the colossus that had been the Turks' greatest enemy for three centuries collapsed, and five independent republics with predominantly Turkic populations emerged: Azerbaijan, Turkmenistan, Uzbekistan, Kazakhstan, and Kyrgyzstan.[46] It was not only Turkey's ultranationalists who felt the excitement. Even visitors to Turkey could feel the thrill as official missions went back and forth, collaborative ventures were discussed, streets and squares were renamed, and the evening news reported the weather from Berlin to Bishkek. In Ankara and other capitals, debates began about whether other Muslim countries or Islamic radicalism would gain influence in the newly independent states. Turkish officials hoped to capitalize on cultural affinities with Central Asian Turks, and Turkey's allies shared those hopes. Some of the highest hopes proved self-frustrating. After seventy years of the Soviet "big brother," Central Asia's Turks were not keen on having a new "big brother" (*ağabey*, colloquially *abi*, an affectionate but also authoritarian image in the Turkish hierarchies of age and gender). Turkey had limited resources to put into grand projects. Its efforts to promote linguistic reform underestimated the extent to which the Soviet policy of differentiating the Central Asian Turkic languages had taken root; indeed, it corresponded to the wishes of many pre-1917 Central Asian intellectuals. The Turkish of Turkey has mutual intelligibility with Azeri and Turkmen but far less with the other Turkic languages.

The excitement felt in Turkey at the new possibilities for fraternal relations with the other republics was not always reciprocated at the other end. Official reactions varied among republics, from cordial with Azerbaijan and Turkmenistan to openly hostile with Uzbekistan, which had its own ideas about regional preeminence, not to mention an influential minority of Tajiks (Central Asian Iranians). Turkey's most successful official efforts were in cultural exchange, particularly the ambitious program launched in 1992 to bring ten thousand students from other Turkic countries to study at Turkish universities. Small numbers from Turkey also studied in Central Asia. The Turkish government founded a number of schools in Central Asia and collaborated with the governments there to cofound Ahmed Yesevi University in Kazakhstan and Manas University in Kyrgyzstan. In the long run, the most effective bridge-building between Turkey and the Central Asian republics was carried out by private interests, especially the followers of Fethullah Gülen, now Turkey's most influential religious leader.

TURKEY AND THE EUROPEAN UNION

With time, Turkey's prospects of EU accession overshadowed other political issues foreign and domestic.[47] Although expert opinion commonly interprets this as a continuation of the Westward orientation defined under Atatürk and consolidated when Turkey joined NATO in 1952, deeper historical perspective shows that Turkey's hopes about the EU are the latest flowering of Ottoman statesmen's desire, already in the late 1700s, to gain admission to the European state system. In recent decades, new issues have complicated Turkey's prospects. The EU has evolved beyond a common market into a far-reaching harmonization of economic, political, and social policy. A country's eligibility for membership is a matter of meeting not just economic conditions but also the Copenhagen criteria, established in 1993.[48] These are defined in terms of *politics* (democracy, rule of law, human rights, protection of minorities), *economics* (a market economy able to withstand the economic forces within the EU), and the country's *capacity* to take on all membership obligations. The candidate country has to conform to the totality of EU law and policy, known as the *acquis communautaire*. As EU membership grew, the *EU's absorptive capacity* became an additional criterion, which will be especially significant for

Turkey. Not only did changes in circumstances and leaders alternately start and stop Turkey's candidacy for accession. The goal posts of EU membership have also moved ever further off as the acquis communautaire grew, reaching 97,000 pages of laws and treaties by the early 2000s. If one goal of Atatürk's reforms was to eliminate differences between Turkey and Europe, EU accession redefined this challenge in ever-more exacting terms.

Stagnant in 1980, Turkey's relations with Europe remained so until 1987, when Prime Minister Özal formally applied for full membership, linking his liberalizing economic reforms to that goal.[49] The response cited points on which Turkey fell short of European standards and recommended a customs union. The collapse of communism also changed thinking about EU expansion in ways that caught Turks by surprise.

The communist collapse not only inspired many Turks to seek closer relations with the Turkic peoples formerly under communist rule; it also required EU leaders to think anew about eastern Europeans, who now freely expressed their desire to "return to Europe." One cost of Turkey's nationalistic history curriculum seems to be that few Turks know European history well enough to understand why Europeans might think that countries such as Poland and Romania are unquestionably European and admissible to the EU before Turkey, despite its earlier application for membership. The EU leadership, for its part, understood eastern Europeans' cultural affinities well enough; what was not so clear in Brussels was whether the EU could stand the costs of absorbing the eastern European countries and providing subsidies to bring them up to European standards. The EU reforms of the 1990s were consequently designed not only to introduce major innovations such as the euro but also to control the eastern European countries' accession, which did not occur until 2004–2007. The same reforms subsequently complicated Turkey's accession prospects, too.

During the 1990s, as Turkey's domestic politics zigzagged, its EU membership prospects also rose and fell. Turkey's chances seemed to improve, up to the achievement of the customs union in 1996. Then prospects declined, as the accession of the eastern European countries approached. EU agencies criticized Turkey's human rights record. With identity politics on the rise in Europe, too, immigration and the presence of foreigners became hot European issues, and European conservatives questioned whether Turkey should ever join the EU. Turkey's population and its level of economic development raised worries about the free movement of labor from Turkey to Europe and the costs of implementing EU policies in Turkey. Erbakan's brief premiership in 1996–1997 and his talk of the EU as a "Christian club" did not pacify European doubts. Not only were east European countries placed on the "fast track" to membership; so was Cyprus. Turkey was left out. The "European Strategy for Turkey" adopted at the EU's Luxembourg summit in 1997 did not sugarcoat this trend.

Turkey's 1999 earthquakes and European generosity in sending aid seemed to improve the outlook and reinforce the view that Turkey could not be left out indefinitely. By then, the 1996 customs union was proving a net benefit to the Turkish economy. Tangible evidence of Turkey's improving accession prospects came in 1999 at the Helsinki summit, when Turkey was officially recognized as a membership candidate, subject to meeting specific conditions before talks could begin. Until then, most Turks saw EU membership as a yes-or-no question and knew little about what membership required. That soon changed, as the EU Council adopted the Accession Partnership (2001, amended in 2003 and 2006).[50] Turkey drew up its plan to meet EU terms. The EU Council found that Turkey sufficiently met the political criteria to open negotiations (December 2004), which started when the council adopted a Negotiating Framework for Turkey (October 2005), and a chapter-by-chapter examination of EU legislation began. Turkey's prospects seemed to turn down again in December 2006, when negotiations were suspended on eight policy chapters, including Cyprus. From the terms of the framework, it can be deduced that negotiations, if successful, will take at least a decade. Outcomes short of full membership may result, but "it must be ensured that Turkey is fully anchored in the European structures through the strongest possible bond."[51] Turkey's progress in the negotiations will be measured in terms of the Copenhagen criteria, relations with its neighbors, settlement of border disputes, and a comprehensive Cyprus settlement.

The outcome of the negotiations is impossible to predict, but their occurrence in itself constitutes the ultimate test of Turkey's engagement with European modernity. The acquis communautaire sets standards in environmental policy (adhesion to the 1997 Kyoto convention on climate change) and penal law (abolition of the death penalty) that a country as highly developed as the United States could not have met, as of 2008, without significant reform. The comparison underscores the ambitiousness of Turkey's quest to join the EU. Moreover, the AK Party leadership has stated that the EU's criteria are Turkey's criteria. That implies intending to meet those criteria with membership or without it, an aspiration that can be taken seriously given the way it serves the party's objectives in engineering reforms favorable to its interests in Turkey.[52]

As much as the success of Turkey's bid for membership depends on what happens in Europe, it also depends on Turkish leaders' ability to maintain consensus on the value of EU membership. A great deal is at stake. In European perspective, after most of the formerly communist European countries were admitted in 2004 and 2007, Turkey was the largest remaining candidate. The only other active candidates were Croatia and the Former Yugoslav Republic of Macedonia, in addition to which Albania and the remaining Yugoslav successor states were regarded as potential future candidates. In Turkish perspective, both Ottoman aspirations to admission to the European state system and republican aspirations to Westernization now have chances of fulfillment in ways that earlier generations scarcely could have imagined.

EXPORT-LED GROWTH, GLOBALIZATION

Turkey's post-1980 economic history began with the shift from import substitution to export-led growth, continued through the crises of the 1990s, and turned toward stability and harmonization with EU standards after 2001. Turkey's record does not rank it among the high-growth NICs (newly industrializing countries), yet is remarkable in many ways. Between 1980 and 2005, Turkish GDP per person nearly doubled, from $4,020 to $7,500.[53] Over the same span, industrial output advanced at an average of 5.8 percent. Agricultural output grew only by an average of 1.2 percent. Yet for the whole twentieth century, agricultural output grew faster than population, and Turkey remains mostly self-sufficient in food. These benchmarks invite examination of Turkey's economic performance and its implications for human development.

THE TRANSITION TO EXPORT-LED GROWTH

The economic policies that Özal introduced in 1980 aimed to improve the balance of payments, reduce inflation, and shift the economy toward the free market and export-led growth. Depreciation of the lira, liberalization of trade and payments, elimination of many government subsidies, supports for exports and foreign investment, and repression of wages were also included. After Özal became prime minister in 1983, further liberalization aimed to open up enterprises created during the import-substitution period to competition. The response of the private sector was mixed.[54] The privatization lists were drawn up arbitrarily and frequently revised. Groups close to government received favors, and the import-substitution industries lobbied for protection. The limited success of privatization remained a drag on the effectiveness of the policy shift. However, support from the International Monetary Fund, World Bank, and international banks facilitated rescheduling debt, attracting investment, and reducing foreign exchange constraints. Merchandise exports nearly tripled in a decade to reach 8.6 percent of GDP in 1990, ranking Turkey first among all nations in export growth for the decade. Manufactures—primarily textiles, clothing, iron, and steel—accounted for 80 percent of the increase.

Özal's policies had their shortfalls. They did not elicit the high levels of private investment, domestic or foreign, that long-term growth required. The foreign debt kept growing, quintupling to $50 billion during the 1980s. Wage repression worsened income inequality. Real wages in agriculture declined by 34 percent to 1987. Özal was criticized for governing by personal decisions, to the detriment of rule of law. For that reason, the increased corruption of the 1990s forms a part of his legacy. As opposition criticism of Özal mounted, the government sought to maintain its popularity by increasing wages and public salaries, nearly doubling real wages from 1987 to 1990. Facing large public-sector deficits, Özal eliminated obstacles to international capital flows in 1989, seeking capital to finance Turkey's deficit.

In the absence of overall economic stability and adequate financial regulation, vulnerability to external shocks and capital flight made the 1990s the most unstable economic period since 1945. Many policies worsened the public-sector deficits: cheap credit for business, lowered retirement ages and increased benefits, high agricultural price supports, and the costly war against the PKK (1984–1999). Mounting debt, high interest rates, monetary instability, and annual inflation rates above 50 percent from 1994 through 2001 resulted. GDP per person continued to rise, albeit more slowly than in the 1980s, but the income distribution became more unequal. Economic crises recurred in 1991, 1994, 1998, and 2000–2001.

STABILIZATION, GLOBALIZATION

Turkey's EU customs union in 1996, perhaps the economic bright spot of the decade, symbolized the linkages between Turkey's economic stability and its integration into the world economy. Negotiations with the IMF led to a stabilization program in 1999. Inadequately designed to correct the financial problems, the plan failed and the 2001 crisis followed, with massive capital flight and drastic depreciation. The government then invited Kemal Derviş of the World Bank to take over as minister for the economy. With IMF support, he introduced structural reforms. After the AK Party came to power in 2002, it maintained fiscal discipline; the low interest rates of the early 2000s also helped.

The economy recovered remarkably. Real GDP declined by 9.5 percent in 2001 but grew by 35 percent over the next four years. For the first time in forty years, the inflation rate declined as low as 8 percent. Foreign investment began returning to Turkey by 2005. Even progress in privatizing state enterprises improved. Unemployment stood above 13 percent through 2005, but debt, after exceeding GDP in 2001, fell to less than 70 percent of it by 2005.

One of the greatest changes in twentieth-century Turkey was the formation of a modern business class. With precursors in the Ottoman mercantile and landowning Muslim proto-bourgeoisie and in the "national bourgeoisie" promoted by the Young Turks, increasingly this evolved into a technocratic and managerial elite. One of its most notable manifestations consisted of the rise of the "Anatolian tigers" (*Anadolu kaplanları*), manufacturing firms in provincial cities across Turkey. In contrast to the industrialists of Istanbul or Ankara, these provincial entrepreneurs were more likely to mobilize capital through family or religious networks. They benefited from local craft traditions and nonunionized workforces and did not depend on state support or foreign investment. Soon accounting for sizable percentages of Turkey's exports, their interests differed from those of the big-city industrialists. There were also cultural differences, reminiscent of the Ottoman Muslim mercantile protobourgeoisie. Much of the old business elite was Westernized and secularized. In contrast, the Anatolian tigers were more likely to draw inspiration from religious movements and support political parties sympathetic to their values.

As the propertied, entrepreneurial wing of the Turkish middle class grew and differentiated internally, the difference assumed organized form in rival professional associations, known by the Turkish acronyms TÜSİAD and MÜSİAD. The two formed against a backdrop that includes chambers of commerce and analogous organizations, going back to late Ottoman times. TÜSİAD, the Turkish Industrialists and Businessmen's Association (Türk Sanayici ve İşadamları Derneği, founded 1971) included many of Turkey's largest and best-known firms, mostly in big cities. Its history has been shaped by the political and economic realities of its times; it has also performed significant, sometimes controversial public services through the reports that it publishes on topics like education.[55] Formed in 1990, MÜSİAD, the Independent Industrialists and Businessmen's Association (Müstakil Sanayici ve İşadamları Derneği) constituted one of the organizational expressions of Islamic revival and allied politically with the Refah Party. MÜSİAD also issued publications, including a manifesto characterizing the Muslim businessman as *Homo islamicus*, compared to TÜSİAD's secular *Homo economicus*.[56] Though the differences between two groups might seem predictable, their responses to AK Party policies could be surprising. TÜSİAD was more satisfied with the government's overall economic performance than was MÜSİAD. Both groups favored EU integration and the democratizing reforms it required. However, many large TÜSİAD firms were already highly integrated with the EU, with or without membership; and the smaller MÜSİAD firms had different needs in matters such as credit and monetary discipline.[57]

AGRICULTURE AND GAP

After the 1960s, Turkey's ability to feed its people depended on more intensive agriculture. Thanks to the Ottoman preference for small landholdings, they still prevailed except in the southeast and in regions reclaimed for agriculture in modern times. Since the 1950s, politicians courted rural voters by supporting agriculture, furthering the rural population's incorporation into the national market.

Among all such policies, the Southeast Anatolia Project, usually known by the Turkish acronym GAP (Güneydoğu Anadolu Projesi), stands out.[58] The economic impact of the oil price increases of the 1970s inspired Turkey to unify a dozen different projects into GAP in 1976. The concept takes advantage of the fact that although Turkey must import oil and gas, it has surplus water resources. Two of the most important rivers of the Middle East, the Tigris and the Euphrates, rise in eastern Turkey and possess great potential for irrigation and electrical generation. The original plan envisioned a complex of dams on the Euphrates to irrigate 1.6 million hectares. This was later expanded into one of the world's most ambitious regional development projects in order to develop one of Turkey's most backward regions. A great engineering achievement, the project became a source of national pride. The strategic relevance of GAP to the Kurdish-Turkish conflict was obvious. The project generated vast enthusiasm in Turkey with little critical discussion, except as related to the large number of archaeological sites that would be flooded before they could be excavated. The controversies seen in other countries over the socioeconomic and ecological effects of vast hydroelectric projects did not seem to emerge. For much of its history, GAP was carried out with a top-down approach and a lack of understanding between planners and intended beneficiaries. Only gradually, as the military conflict in the region wound down, could the project be turned from an infrastructural project into one of social development, eventually with increased scope for private as well as state initiative. At this point, GAP connects economic development with larger questions of human development and the regional disparities that complicate its assessment in Turkey.

HUMAN DEVELOPMENT

The human development index, introduced in chapter 6, is a statistic that combines information about GDP per person, life expectancy, and education into an indicator of quality of life, ranging in value between 0 and 1. Turkey improved in terms of the HDI from 0.612 in 1980 to 0.751 in 2002.[59] Over the same interval, western Europe's HDI rose from 0.849 to 0.935, higher levels but a proportionately smaller advance. Comparing Turkey's performance on the different components of HDI with that of other developing countries produces a mixed picture. Turkish life expectancy at birth increased from sixty-two years in 1980 to seventy years (sixty-eight for men, seventy-three for women) in 2004, gains comparable to those in other countries with similar incomes. The poverty rate was lower than in other comparable countries. Turkey's literacy rate rose from 69 percent in 1980 to 89 in 2005; however, the 2005 figure concealed a wide gender gap between 95 percent literacy for men and 82 percent for women. Assessments of education that take account not only of literacy but also of years of schooling and school enrollment rates show that Turkey has lagged behind other developing countries with similar GDP.

Inside Turkey, differences of gender, class, and region opened wide gaps in quality of life, and the widest gender gaps tended to be found in the lowest-performing regions. Regional inequalities in Turkey display a marked east-west polarization.[60] That was true of incomes throughout the twentieth century. Private sector industrialization also concentrated in the west, at least until the Anatolian tigers' rise. Commercialized agriculture displayed the same pattern, except in coastal areas. Provision of infrastructure and services, especially education and health, has been worse in the east. Around the year 2000, the average HDI of Turkey's ten most developed provinces in the northwest and west was 0.825, comparable to that of Slovakia, a formerly communist east European country that had become a candidate for EU integration. However, the average HDI of Turkey's ten poorest provinces in the mostly Kurdish southeast, at 0.600, corresponded to that of Morocco or India. Among the factors that go into calculating the HDI, women's life expectancy exceeded that of men. However, in the southeast as of 2000, women's primary and secondary school enrollment rates and their adult literacy rates tended to range from 40 to 60 percent of the rates for men in the same provinces. Women's earned incomes, too, were distinctly lower than those of men in the eastern provinces. In contrast, in the Izmir-Istanbul region, all the component statistics of the HDI were much higher; and women lagged men in literacy, school enrollment, and earning potential to a much smaller degree. In Istanbul, women's estimated earned income actually exceeded men's as of 2000.

Since 1980, many innovations have improved life quality in Turkey in ways that the HDI does not measure, usually with similar inequalities in access. In addition to the state radio and television, privately owned television channels and radio stations proliferated in the 1990s. The proliferation of alternative print and electronic media greatly diversified the outlets for self-expression. Fax transmission, personal computers, electronic mail, and Internet access further transformed communications from the mid-1980s on. The advent of cellular telephones in the mid-1990s meant that Turkey's hopelessly inadequate land-line telephone system could finally be bypassed. Growing urban congestion meant that even those who had conventional telephones spent less time near them and more time stranded in traffic, with cell phones in hand. By 2000, cell phone usage was extremely widespread. By 2008, 24 percent of Turkish households had Internet access as well, although with wide male-female and urban-rural gaps in computer and Internet usage.[61] Like the HDI statistics, such disparities reinforce the point that Turkey's future development depends on reducing inequalities among genders, sectors, and regions.

SOCIETY

After 1980, Turkish society moved beyond the midcentury population explosion. As it did, the proliferation of identity and difference accelerated. Among many examples, the struggles of women for empowerment and of Alevis for acceptance illustrate this point.

DEMOGRAPHIC CHANGE

Turkey's population grew from forty-five million in 1980 to seventy-two million as of 2004.[62] After 1980, Turkey moved beyond the population explosion, but not beyond all its effects. The growth rate, as high as 2.8 percent in 1961, trended downward thereafter with fluctuations in the late 1970s and early 1980s. By 2000, the growth rate stood as low as 1.7 percent. Yet the downward trend in growth had not continued long enough to slow, let alone reverse, the increase in national population. Official statistics do not project the rate of population growth to fall to zero until 2050, by which time Turkey's population would stabilize around ninety-six million. Long-term demographic projections are not noted for their accuracy; however, the demographic facts underlying these projections have significance here and now.

One positive effect of the current stage in Turkey's demographic transition consists of the growth in the economically productive parts of the age pyramid. Since 1985, the majority of the population has also been urban. As the rural-to-urban balance tipped, demographic trends stimulated economic development in the sense that the age dependency ratio fell from highs above 80 before 1980 to 55 in 2000.[63] Moreover, as the birthrate fell, most of the drop in the dependency ratio occurred among the young; the dependent elderly population has thus far not grown as a proportion of the total. The fact that the fourteen-to-sixty-four age bracket also includes the reproductive phase of the life span largely explains why the decline in the birthrate has not yet slowed population growth. With a median age of 24.8 in 2000, Turks were still far from experiencing the age-related problems then burdening many other societies; they were also still far from a population of stable size.

Demographic change since 1980 has produced benign outcomes in other respects, too. The number of high-school (*lise*) diploma recipients rose from 137,000 in 1980 to 380,000 in 2005; the proportion of girls among high-school diploma recipients rose from 36 to 48 percent during the same years. Recipients of diplomas from institutions of higher learning rose more rapidly, from 71,000 in 1980 to 347,000 in 2005; women's share of diploma recipients rose even faster in higher than in secondary education, from 23 to 44 percent over the same quarter century. The number of universities rose from 27 in 1982 to 115 (85 public and 30 private) in 2006.[64] The number of workers in industry and mining grew from 2 million in 1980 to 3.3 million in 2000; parts of the service sector grew even faster. Among improvements in health care, the number of people per physician fell from 1,631 in 1980 to 725 in 2003. Deaths of babies under one year of age fell from 32,000 in 1980 to 11,000 in 2004.

The changes in Turkey's cities have also been profound and not of unmixed benefit. The pace of hyperurbanization hardly slowed. Istanbul's 1980 population of 4.7 million was 2.5 times its 1960 population; after another twenty years, the city's estimated 2000 population of 11.3 million was 2.4 times the 1980 population. The 1999 earthquake in the adjoining Marmara region may at last have slowed migration to Istanbul.[65] Ankara's population increased from 2.9 million in 1980 to 4 million in 2000; its growth rate stood above 4 percent in 1970 and still around 2 percent in 1990. Provincial cities also grew rapidly. Estimates for 2004–2006 place the population of Izmir at 3 million, Bursa at 1.9 million, Konya and Adana at 1.5 million, Antalya and Mersin at 1.1 million, and another dozen or more cities at 500,000 to 1 million.[66]

IDENTITY AND DIFFERENCE AMID GLOBALIZATION

After 1980, technological innovation accelerated change and effectively shrank distance until differences of space and time virtually vanished, making the global and the local simultaneously perceptible everywhere. Individual subjectivity flowered in new ways, as Turks became more resistant to top-down efforts to turn them into dutiful citizens and more assertive in taking hold of citizenship as a way to respond to authority. Growing sensitivities about individual and minority rights furthered the shift from unitary, conformist nationalism and stimulated debate about the meaning of Turkish identity. If Kurdish-Turkish relations generated greater conflict, the Alevi and women's movements also illustrate the salience of identity issues.

The Alevis. Alternately persecuted as heterodox Muslims and ignored under the empire, the Alevis survived under the republic as isolated rural communities.[67] The fact that men and women participated together in their rituals, which included music, song, and dance, made Alevis easy targets for accusations of sexual license and heresy; the color illustration of an Alevi ceremony provides a check on such ideas. The Bektaşi order, with which the Janissary infantry historically identified, shared the same beliefs but was organized as a sufi brotherhood. Suppressed with the Janissaries in 1826, the Bektaşis went underground a century before the general suppression of the sufi orders in 1925. The rural Alevis maintained their invisibility for centuries until caught up in urbanization and labor emigration.

Rural Alevis were historically organized in communities led by spiritual "elders" (*dede*) from charismatic lineages known as "hearths" (*ocak*). Migration to cities and diaspora communities profoundly changed things for Alevis. The old communities and the charismatic authority of the elders, all tracing their lineage to the Prophet Muhammad, proved practically impossible to maintain in the urban setting. New types of communal associations emerged, and a new elite began to compete for leadership, although the dedes eventually regained prestige from the eclipse of leftism and the growing interest in Alevi identity. Amid the general rise in identity politics, the Alevis finally began to write and talk about themselves publicly.

Highly controversial, estimates of the size of the Alevi community range between 15 and 30 percent of the population of Turkey; Kurds may account for one-third of the total Alevi population.[68] Despite the fact that Alevi identity is not confined to ethnic Turks alone, the Alevis hold a large place in the Turkish imagination. The religious poems (*deyiş, deme, nefes*) that they sing in their services (*cem*) have been adopted by Turks in general, who lump them together with secular folksongs (*türkü*) and regard the lot as "folk poetry," an authentically Turkish form of self-expression from the long centuries when Ottoman divan poetry was overloaded with Arabic and Persian and nearly incomprehensible. The Alevis' hymns have thus been appropriated by Turks in general. Nationalists have also interpreted the Alevi cult as a survival of pre-Islamic "shamanism" and in that sense as preeminently Turkish. Yet the Alevis' practices have made them the targets of bloody attacks by bigoted Sunnis, from Kahramanmaraş (1978) and Çorum (1980) to Sivas (1993) and the Alevi neighborhood of Gaziosmanpaşa in Istanbul (1995).[69]

By the 1980s, the Alevis' numbers and public visibility were making them politically significant. Memories of persecution under the empire made them early, willing supporters of republican secularism. Their support was not always well rewarded, however. In effect, the religion that Turkish laicists do not practice, but which they created a government agency to control, is Sunni Islam. As a result, republican secularism has not stopped government agencies from driving highways through Alevi shrines or building mosques in Alevi villages on a scale that the Ottoman government might have envied. The state-controlled religion lessons in the schools also equate Islam with Sunnism. Still, the Alevis vote secularist. Ironically, Turkish secularists' ability to hold their own politically partly depends on a religious minority's votes. The 21 percent of the vote that Republican People's Party got in 2007 included many Alevi votes, especially those of educated Alevis.[70] The positions taken by Erbakan-style Islamist parties ruled out Alevi support for them. The AK Party has not done much better. Only since the 2007 election has the AK Party had any Alevi assembly members, and there are only three of them.

Women. The early republic taught that Atatürk had liberated Turkish women. A generation later, those who contested that idea joined the left. Not until after 1980 did Turkish women speak for themselves autonomously.[71] The new feminists then identified those still willing to rely on state initiative as "Kemalist feminists."

Several themes characterize the new Turkish feminism. Perhaps most basic is the growth of women's organizations from about 10 (1973–1982) to more than 350 (2004). The network includes organizations in provincial cities. It also includes shelters for battered women and 70 organizations opposing violence against women; such organizations also emerged in the southeast, where so-called honor killings were a major concern. International pressure and the EU's emphasis on equal rights drew Turkish feminists into international organizations such as the European Women's Lobby, which elected Turkish feminist Selma Acuner to its executive committee. With activism and organization went new frankness in talking publicly about taboo subjects, such as female sexuality and sexual violence.

Relations with the state formed another theme for Turkish feminists. In 1980, when the government created a Directorate for Women's Status and Problems, most feminists opposed it as a cooptation mechanism. However, in a way reminiscent of the Nakşibendis' colonization of the Directorate of

Religious Affairs, feminists took positions in the new organization; and many women recognized the need to cooperate with, as well as contest, the state in order to change policy. The new feminists found a focus for autonomous action in a 1986 petition campaign for implementation of the Convention for the Elimination of All Types of Discrimination Against Women (CEDAW), which Turkey had signed. Attacking the nationalist doctrine that republican legislation guaranteed women equal rights, feminists criticized Turkey's Civil and Penal Codes. In 2001, the civil code was revised to remove the designation of the husband as the family head and better protect women's property rights in case of divorce. Until 2005, however, the penal code still classed sexual crimes against women as offenses against public morality and order, not as crimes against specific victims; the code also recognized extenuating circumstances in honor killings. After the civil code, women organized to revise the penal code. In 2005, Prime Minister Erdoğan made a last-minute effort to criminalize adultery through the code, but international and domestic pressure forced him to back down. The revised code passed with most of the amendments women sought. By then, women made up about a third of Turkey's professionals in law, medicine, and academia but held fewer seats in the National Assembly than when women first got the vote in the 1930s. Women began demanding larger representation in elected office, although the results have not yet been large.

Gender issues in Turkey have intersected significantly with ethnic and religious issues. Kurdish feminists not only opposed state policy and Kurdish patriarchy but also had their doubts about Turkish feminism. In 1989, Turkish and Kurdish feminists split over the use of Kurdish, for example. Nonetheless, Turkish and Kurdish feminists' common interests led them again to cooperate against domestic violence.

At the same time, young women's willingness to adopt the Islamic dress and lifestyle, even the idea of Islamic feminism, destabilized entrenched convictions that laicism was a prerequisite for women's emancipation. Gradually, religious women began to make the point that they, too, sought to make their way in the modern world, combining their personal values with the opportunities and rights that the republic offered them. Our color illustrations of young Turkish women today, with heads both covered and uncovered, show examples of how both participate in contemporary modernity. Moreover, at a time when the female membership of most other parties was negligible, women of the Refah Party set new standards in promoting women's voting and political participation. Secular and religious feminists' common struggle to assert their agency against the state again created common interests.

Like their laicist sisters, Islamist feminists sought to use Turkey's ties to Europe to their advantage. In 1998, when Turkey began to enforce the head-scarf ban in the universities, they appealed to the European Court of Human Rights. The court upheld the decision of Turkey's Constitutional Court that in Turkey, laicism guaranteed democratic values and the citizens' legal equality. The legal reasoning and the underlying concept of equality are the same ones that ban Islamic headscarves or other open displays of religious difference from the public schools in France. Ten years later, things had changed enough inside Turkey that the AK Party government passed a law to permit women wearing Islamic headcoverings to attend public universi-ties. Secularist forces mounted a full-scale counterattack against the party. In response, the Constitutional Court restored the headscarf ban, upheld the legality of the AK Party by a narrow vote, but placed restrictions on it in certain respects.

Depending on how it is worn, then, the same square of silk can put women on opposite sides of one of Turkey's keenest conflicts. The scarf that a secular woman might wear as a European-style accessory, if tied or pinned around the face according to Islamic criteria of modesty, becomes a battle flag in a culture war. This situation speaks volumes about gender and religion, about social and cultural change, and about the rise of a new Islamic subjectivity to rival the secular subjectivity explored in earlier chapters.

ISLAM AND GLOBALIZATION: FETHULLAH GÜLEN

Of the three Ottoman and Turkish religious movements that exerted the greatest influence since 1800, the newest achieved prominence after 1983 under Fethullah Gülen's leadership.[72] Although outsiders sometimes call its members Fethullahçı (Fethullah followers), they do not call themselves that. Inasmuch as this is the largest of several successors to Said Nursi's Nur movement, some scholars call it a neo-Nur movement. Reading Nursi's *Risale-i Nur* (Treatise of light), along with the Kur'an and other religious texts, is basic to the Gülen movement. Gülen, too, is a prolific author but has been more influential as a preacher. There is also continuity between Nursi's and Gülen's movements in that each has adapted to new challenges. Conditions of the early republican period—the outlawing of the sufi brotherhoods, the emergence of Islamic print media—helped shape Nursi's movement. Gülen's movement has adapted to ongoing changes in Turkey and the world as it has expanded from local to national, international, and global scale.

GÜLEN'S CAREER

Fethullah Gülen was born in 1938 near Erzurum, site of the major Ottoman fortress defending Anatolia's northeastern frontier.[73] His family had deep roots around Ahlat on the shores of Lake Van. Near Ahlat lies Malazgird, site of the battle in 1071 that opened Anatolia to the influx of Turkish Muslims from the east; further south lies Bitlis, Said Nursi's natal region. The inhabitants of Erzurum are known for nationalism and piety. Gülen has displayed both qualities: a Turkish nationalism suffused with Ottoman nostalgia and an Islamic response to the era of globalization. He was the son of an imam, and he first learned to read the Kur'an from his mother. He was most influenced in his early education by a sufi şeyh, Muhammed Lütfi, known as "Alvarlı Efe." The boy discovered Said Nursi's writings in the 1950s when the people of his village began reading them. The only religious career available at the time being that of a preacher, he chose that calling, assuming a position in Edirne in 1958.

Fethullah Gülen, the most influential Turkish
religious leader of his time. (Courtesy of Tughra
Books, Somerset, New Jersey.)

He was transferred to the Kestanepazarı mosque in Izmir in 1966 and founded his movement there. Never married, he became noted for his ascetic lifestyle, as well as his moving preaching.

Compared to Nursi, Gülen has produced his impact less through writing than through practice: his preaching, activism, and innovative leadership. In addition to his works in print, Gülen's ideas have circulated electronically via audio- and videocassettes, compact discs, and the Internet.[74] Different scholars have sought to sum up the key concepts of his teachings. Hakan Yavuz has written of Gülen's "pious activism," emphasizing service, zeal, and sincerity (*hizmet*, *himmet*, and *ihlas*); the term *aksiyon*, familiar from Necip Fazıl Kısakürek, reappears in the Gülen movement, even as the name of a periodical. Bayram Balcı has written of Gülen's emphasis on love (*sevgi*), mercy (*merhamet*), tolerance (*hoşgörü*), and dialogue (*diyalog*) with non-Muslims as well as other Muslims. Many of these terms have more extended or more specific meanings in Gülen's thought. He has the religious learning required to explain the Kur'an and the *Risale-i Nur* to his followers. He also has wide knowledge of modern thought, which enables him to explain Islamic ideas in modern terms, as Nursi sought to do. Like Nursi, Gülen defined a new model of leadership. His followers call him *hocaefendi* (roughly "master teacher"), in contrast both to the ulema, experts in Islamic religious studies, and to şeyhs, masters of sufi brotherhoods.

As much as the stages of Gülen's career have corresponded to the phases of Turkey's development since the 1960s, they have also reflected his positive orientation toward the state, possibly a legacy of his origins near Erzurum. The historical record suggests that a Turkish religious leader's chances of gathering a mass following without having trouble with the state are slight. Still, Gülen has been noted for his positive statements about the state, even the army. Although nationalism and Islam do not combine well in general, one being particularist and the other universalist, the nationalist strains in Gülen's thought invoke Ottoman as well as Turkish themes. His movement has directed its expansion toward the formerly Ottoman Balkans and Turkic Central Asia. Some Turkish Islamists have criticized him for not expanding into the Arab lands, most of which shared the Ottoman past. Perhaps, in this sense, Gülen again expresses the significance of Ziya Gökalp's reference points: Turkishness, Islam, and modernity.

The cultural and economic changes of the Özal decade facilitated the movement's expansion from local to national, then international. Özal created a relatively favorable climate; still, Gülen did not escape troubles with the authorities, which had started on a small scale in his Edirne days. Ultimately, even his endorsement of the 1997 military crackdown that toppled Erbakan's coalition government did not prevent an attack on him in 1999 as a "reactionary" and an indictment against him as an enemy of laicism in 2000. That attack forced him into exile in North America. His movement's media launched an unprecedented counterattack to defend him. He had sought to redefine laicism so as to create more freedom for religious movements, and he and his schools had challenged the secularists' monopoly on the definition of modernity. His exile paradoxically completed the globalization of his movement. Henceforth, his supporters were physically present in Turkey and many other lands; electronically, he was present everywhere.

THE MOVEMENT

Gülen's movement has evolved in stages. From 1970 to 1983 he worked locally to build a movement based on his pulpit in Izmir, the local Kur'an school, the Nur movement's reading groups (*dershane*), summer camps that brought male university students together for religious education and outdoor activities, and "houses of light" (*ışık evleri*). Those were communal apartments that the movements' supporters made available to provide housing and a motivational environment for same-sex groups of university students.[75] In 1979, the movement began to publish its monthly, *Sızıntı*, which combined editorials by Abdülfettah Şahin, Gülen's pseudonym, with articles about modern science. Gülen's movement is a network united by common beliefs. There is no formal procedure for joining other than service (hizmet) to those beliefs. There are no formal ranks, other than proximity to Gülen and length of service, which entitle one to be known as an "older brother" (*ağabey*, colloquially *abi*) or "older sister" (*abla*).

Between 1983 and 1997, new possibilities opened. The law on charitable foundations (*vakıf*) had been revised in 1967, and the 1980s economic climate made it easier to take advantage of the law. Foundations created by Gülen's supporters contributed to the spread and decentralization of the movement. Spreading across Turkey, it acquired supporters in all walks of life. His supporters' activities concentrated in three areas: media, business, and education.[76] The end of the state monopoly on broadcasting prompted them to launch media ventures. They bought the newspaper *Zaman* (Time) in 1986 and made it into a large-circulation newspaper. In addition to the monthly *Sızıntı*, they launched other periodicals: *Aksiyon* (a weekly), *Yeni Ümit* (theological), *Ekoloji* (environmental), *The Fountain* (religious, in English). The movement branched out into the electronic media with *Samanyolu* TV (Milky Way) and Burç FM (Tower or Zodiacal constellation). The media ventures led to the formation of the Turkish Journalists and Writers Foundation (Türkiye Gazeteciler ve Yazarlar

Vakfı, 1994), which worked to develop communications between the movement and outsiders.

As businesses, the media ventures could not have started without supporters able to mobilize capital. In this period, Turkey's major religious movements, including the Nakşibendis and the Nurcus as well as Gülen's followers, stimulated economic growth by persuading conservative families, who distrusted banks and kept their money in gold, to put their resources to economically productive uses. The rise of the Anatolian tiger firms owes much to religiously endorsed capital mobilization. The businesses that supported Gülen were organizationally independent, owned by supporters, not by the movement. Gülen himself owned little; his supporters, however, controlled an impressive array of firms, associations, and foundations. Among these is the Turkish Teachers Foundation (Türkiye Öğretmenler Vakfı). As the movement's capabilities grew, its efforts to house university students expanded from houses of light to dormitories. The Akyazılı Foundation for Secondary and Higher Education (Akyazılı Orta ve Yüksek Eğitim Vakfı) owned hundreds of dormitories by the 1990s. Gülen's supporters set up "The Light" Insurance (*Işık* Sigorta) in 1995. The Ülker firm, noted for chocolate and biscuits, predated the Gülen movement but became identified with it. Gülen supporters set up Asia Finance (Asya Finans), a bank formed after the Soviet collapse to promote investment in Central Asia. The movement also has its own business association, İş Hayatı Dayanışma Derneği (İŞHAD, Association for Solidarity in Business Life).

After 1983, Gülen's supporters took advantage of the new possibility to found private educational institutions. In addition to dormitories, they opened dershanes, in this case not Nurcu-style reading circles, but the literal "classrooms" of private cram schools to prepare students for the national university placement exams. Gülen supporters founded private lycées. In 1995, they founded Istanbul's Fatih University. By shaping the students' personhood (*kişilik*) and identity (*kimlik*), the goal is to shape a golden generation (*altın nesil*) of Turks who can be producers, not consumers, of modernity.

Gülen's movement responded adeptly to the opportunities created by the collapse of socialism.[77] The newspaper *Zaman* launched editions in the Central Asian capitals in 1992. Turkish businesses, often run or staffed by Gülen's supporters, extended their operations into the Central Asian republics. Turkish businesspeople struggling to adapt to Central Asia formed business associations, often full of Gülen's followers; and the different republics worked with the associations to attract investment. These ventures helped lay the base for the movement's greatest success in Central Asia, its schools. Estimates of the number of private high schools supported by the movement soon ranged as high as 400. Figures of 1996–1997 indicated 148 Gülen movement schools outside Turkey, 84 of them being in the five post-Soviet Turkic republics and serving over seventeen thousand students. A decade later, Gülen supporters spoke of over 1,000 schools in more than a hundred countries, figures suggesting the movement's full globalization by then.

The movement's schools are almost always single-sex schools, and few are for girls. Enrollment is not, however, limited to Muslims. Gülen's supporters have founded an institution of higher learning in each capital of the Central Asian Turkic republics. Supported by businesses in the region, the movement's schools have also benefited from collaboration with the governments of both Turkey and, to varying degrees, the Central Asian republics. Those governments have their own aspirations to control religion; consequently, the schools have to refrain from religious advocacy. The schools are in demand, however, both because of the teachers' dedication and because of the state of the region's post-Soviet government schools.

Although most Gülen schools are in the Ottoman-Balkan and Turko-Islamic zones, the growing numbers founded elsewhere express the movement's globalization. For example, Gülen followers have founded schools in Pakistan, which are in demand as alternatives to schools run by religious activists lacking scientific qualifications. The movement purportedly had six million members worldwide by 2007, enough to found schools in Australia and conduct retreats in the United States. In exile since 1999, Gülen's response to globalization has emphasized tolerance and dialogue. He has met with non-Muslim religious leaders, and his followers have developed new forms of outreach. Notably, the Turkish Journalists and Writers Foundation organized a series of meetings, known as the Abant Platforms, in which members and nonmembers meet to discuss topics such as religion and the state (1999) or Islam, secularism, and democracy (2004).[78]

Neither did patriotism exempt him from prosecution, nor have Gülen and his movement lacked critics. The movement competed with other religious movements and had deep differences with Erbakan's political parties. Even sympathetic analysts pointed out that the schools did not promote critical thinking and that strong support for the Turkish state was not always the way to promote democracy. As concerns gender relations, although Gülen took the position — controversial to his followers — that women's covering their heads was not fundamental to Islam, his movement was criticized for maintaining gender segregation, lacking women in high positions, and providing fewer schools for girls than boys.[79]

Such observations cannot diminish Fethullah Gülen's eminence as founder of the third great awakening of the past two centuries among Muslims of the

Ottoman and Turkish cultural world. Just as the earlier movements of Mevlana Halid and Said Nursi responded to changing times, Gülen responded to change inside Turkey and globally. In the world at large, Islamic movements that responded antagonistically to the tightening of global interlinkage attracted greater notice. The difference is that while violent Islamic radicals use all contemporary means of networking to lash out against global modernity, Gülen's movement uses the same global interlinkages to offer a constructive engagement of Islam with modernity.

ADALET AĞAOĞLU: TIME, SUBJECTIVITY, CONSCIOUSNESS

If Gülen epitomizes Turkey's religious creativity, Adalet Ağaoğlu (b. 1929) exemplifies its literary vigor in the secularist vein. To Turks who lived through the military coups, her novels speak powerfully, particularly her *Dar Zamanlar* (Hard times) trilogy.[80] It begins with *Ölmeye Yatmak* (Lying down to die, written 1968–1971), continues with *Bir Düğün Gecesi* (An evening wedding, 1974–1978), and concludes with *Hayır . . .* (No . . . , 1984–1987). The characters belong to two generations. Heroine Aysel Dereli, her siblings and schoolmates, are children of the early republic. The younger generation are "the sixty-eights," as they come to be called in *Hayır. . . .* The novels owe their grip on Turkish readers to several facts. They express the anguish of the coups of 1971 and 1980. Rising above the passions of the times, they pursue great existential questions of time, subjectivity, and consciousness. They are experimental in technique, too, and that experimentation is integrated into the existential questioning.

The title *Dar Zamanlar*, "Hard times," invites attention to time as a focal issue.[81] The characters struggle with the lack of time and the difficulties of their times, and none of the novels pursues a single, linear chronology. In *Ölmeye Yatmak*, Aysel lies down to die at 7:22 a.m. and abandons her apparent attempt at suicide at 8:49 a.m.; during those eighty-seven minutes, fragments of her and her associates' lives as well as of early republican history unfold. In *Bir Düğün Gecesi*, the chronological focus is the three or four hours of the evening wedding on 26 November 1972; however, the participants relive their pasts at the wedding. In *Hayır . . .* , the least linear of the novels, section headings implying a span of slightly over a day—"Morning," "Toward Evening," "Night," "Daybreak," "The Moment"—align with a plot about an evening award ceremony at which the honoree, Aysel Dereli, fails to appear; but every event or thought in the book recurs from beginning to end, and nothing comes up only once. Such issues of narrative time are the first of many questions about time and

perceptions of time, all of which direct attention to subjectivity and consciousness as the author's ultimate concerns.

ÖLMEYE YATMAK (LYING DOWN TO DIE)

Aysel's eighty-seven minutes in the hotel room launch the trilogy and its existential questionings. After walking all night through Ankara, she goes there to
die, not realizing that she will have to struggle with death (3). Her body and
mind show just how alive they are. Trying to lie still as if in a coffin, she frets
about forgetting to hang the "Do Not Disturb" sign on the door (55). Examining
her toes, she thinks about her pedicurist and how she advertises her importance
to her by talking about typing, books, and professional engagements (157–58,
229). It never becomes perfectly clear whether "lying down to die" is literally
an attempt at suicide or a deathlike exhaustion brought on by the stresses of
her times (274). She has an episode of vomiting, which might mean that pills
had made her sick without killing her. Yet the book does not mention pills, and
Aysel finds a different meaning in the episode. Cravings for pickled watermelon
rind (37) make her realize that she has missed her period. She has not slept with
her husband, Ömer, lately (57) but did spend one night with her student Engin,
and her vomiting might mean that she is carrying his baby (92–93). Later, won-
dering what time it is and why she does not seem to be dying, she places a call to
Aydın, who has pursued her ever since they were elementary schoolmates (230).
When she finally reaches him, he says he always wanted to sleep with her. She
says she knows, and they agree for him to join her (311). The book ends as she
dresses, turns over the "Do Not Disturb" sign, goes down in the elevator, pays
her bill, and leaves without waiting for him (316–17).

The great and small facts of female existence are not all that separates Aysel
from death. From the hotel room, her mind conjures up the entire book,
including not only her memories but also letters, other characters' diary entries,
newspaper items, and several grand scenes.

Scarcely has Aysel lain down to die before she is back on stage for the school
play in the country town where she was one of eight in the first class, which
graduated the year Atatürk died. Teacher Dündar, a comically earnest republican true believer, is staging the town's first school play (*müsamere*) for the
parents and local officials (6–20). Amid all the mishaps with costumes, curtains,
and cues, the boys and girls on stage are to perform patriotic numbers and
model modernity by dancing in mixed couples. The reluctant boys and girls are
supposed to touch each other for the first time (14–15). In a scene about flowers
and insects, Aysel appears as a butterfly; but the public prosecutor's daughter
Sevil (a rose) breaks off one of her wings, and the local chief official's son Aydın

(a bee) embarrasses her by grabbing her around the waist and buzzing in her ear. The teacher proudly proclaims that their town has produced its "first soldiers for our nation's army of enlightenment" (*ülkemizin aydınlar ordusuna ilk erlerimiz,* 14).

The school's republican message of citizenship and equality, including gender equality, remains with Aysel ever after, sustaining her at points and jangling with her experiences at others. In the audience at the play, not everyone is convinced. Seated in the front row, the local officials raise such a cloud of cigarette smoke that the rest of the audience can barely see. The officials sit men and women together and are the only ones in modern dress (9–10). Behind them, the men and women of the town find themselves together in a public place for the first time. If this is what being civilized (*medenî*) means, at least it is not their fault (15). Neither of Aysel's parents attends. The play really disillusions her father, Salim Efendi, a shopkeeper formerly proud of his role in the National Struggle (15, 18).

Aysel will be one of the lucky few who continues her education. At times, the image hovering over the school play, that of the nation's great, undying father (*Ulu Ata, Ölmez Ata*), will shield her from the patriarchal demands of people like her "little father" (*babacığım*), Salim Efendi, and her older brother İlhan. This is especially true of republican laicism. When "country" (*memleketli*) relatives show up at the wedding in the second novel in Islamic attire, they are asked to remove their head coverings or else stand back; later, they leave muttering disgustedly (*BDG,* 178, 286). That is as far as Islam intrudes into the entire trilogy. Yet secular modernity is not securely established in gender relations, either.[82] Aysel's personal problem will be that people like her own "little father" do not understand the desexualized high-achiever role supposedly defined for her by her "great father," Atatürk. Among those who know the idea, the men will show that their view of her is anything but desexualized. As an exchange student in France, she meets a young Frenchman who seems able to appreciate her mind. Why are the young men of her country not like Alain? The man she marries, Ömer Uzel, is an exception, but six years at Oxford gave him that "English coolheadedness" (*ÖY,* 296).

Near the end of her stay in the hotel, at a moment when she did not expect to awaken again at all, Aysel awakens from a terrifying dream (271–75). It is time for the examination for her promotion to professor. She has devised the surefire formula for Turkey's development, and it is time to present her thesis. She is in a long hall with a row of old men at the far end behind a table. Approaching with mounting anticipation, she sees Atatürk sitting in the middle with a yellow face; to either side of him sit six old men with green faces. By the time she reaches them, she has regressed to age ten, and everything goes wrong. She is wearing snakeskin heels, one of which breaks, and a fox fur, which comes to life and bites her on the chin. Running about frantically, she searches for her thesis; but she finds all the wrong things, even an Edith Piaf record. Atatürk begins chanting: "Where's your thesis? Show us your thesis!" She must have written her formula for Turkey's development on a scrap of paper and put it in the pocket of her school apron. Restraining her fox fur with one hand, she rummages her pockets with the other. As she does, the books in the hands of the old men turn into plates. The men bang on the table with knives and forks and yell, "Bring us your thesis!" She does not realize that what she puts before them is not her thesis (*tez*) but a pot (*tencere*) of dolmas. Humiliated, she wants to explain to Atatürk that this is not her thesis. But the one who was Atatürk has turned into a hunter, and he is aiming his rifle at her fox fur. She tries to cry out: "It's not a live fox. It's a fur for the school play (*müsamere kürkü*)." But she cannot utter a sound. Had she been about to expire and come to out of an instinctual resistance against death?

Another nightmare at the end of the book bridges the gap between Aysel's conditioning as a daughter of the republic and her existential concerns as a woman. She is in a large, crowded space like the courtyard of Topkapı Palace (313–15). From there, she enters a hall full of young people all in gray-green outfits, seated in rows. She is accompanied by people who helped her reach this day. It seems they are supposed to perform some great duty—press a button to start a train or launch a ship. All eyes are on Aysel. She is the one whom the great duty awaits. Suddenly random distractions break out, starting with an old schoolmate, parading like a bride. After several disruptions, Aysel realizes that she has forgotten about the task for which she came. At that, she finds herself riding a donkey in a prison corridor with barred cells on each side. Five or six benign-looking men await at the far end. A man who looks like a general advances, comes to attention, and announces, "You may begin." She affirms, "Let's begin." At that, the benign-looking men quickly undress. "It turns out that my duty is to lie with them." She awakes screaming, takes a sleeping pill for the first time ever, and decides not to tell her husband.

Living through the student turmoil of the 1960s as a midcareer faculty member, Aysel becomes personally involved with a student, Engin. Once, she goes to his room and goes to bed with him (39, 195–99). She had the nightmare recounted at the end of the book that night. On another occasion, the two of them spent the entire night talking and enjoying leftist songs and poems at her apartment. That night, "even I nearly believed in the revolution" (158). The thought of all the other things she could have done with those ten hours of her "always inadequate time" (*hep dar gelen zaman*) expands a single sentence into a catalogue longer than a page (159–60), but what were those things by comparison? At one point in the conversation, Aysel says to Engin: "The highest stage of socialism is to make the human being (*insan*) a person (*kişi*)" (161). Leaping up, Engin retorts: "That's individualism! How can you reconcile a socialist philosophy with individualism?" Despite her enthusiasm to bridge the gulf, Aysel has shown her distance from the student ideologues. Repeated references show that her goal is to find fulfillment as a person and be recognized by others not just as a woman, a citizen, or a sociologist but as a human being.[83] This refrain runs throughout the trilogy.

BIR DÜĞÜN GECESI (AN EVENING WEDDING)

Aysel refuses to attend the wedding on the night of 26 November 1972 but is all the more on the minds of those who do. Ironically, she is the one who ends the night in police custody, something not likely to have happened had she gone to a wedding celebrated under armed guard in a time of martial law. Her refusal to attend arises from the interference between politics and family. The novel owes its power to the author's insight into just such interactions among individual subjectivity, familial relations, and national politics.

Occurring during the military intervention of 1971–1973, the marriage is a shabby alliance of money and militarism. The bride, Ayşen, is the daughter of Aysel's estranged older brother İlhan and his wife, Müjgân. After dabbling in ultranationalist politics as a youngster, İlhan has made his way into circles where money rules. He and his wife are consolidating their success, at least to outward appearances, by marrying their daughter to Ercan, the son of Major General Hayrettin Özkan and his wife, Nuriye (Nuriş to her friends). Many of the wedding guests are "postrevolutionary" survivors of the upheavals of the 1960s, unable to forget that they are now "outside" while others are "inside" the prisons. At least in her aspirations, the survivors include the bride, Ayşen. The survivors include absent Aunt Aysel and an aunt and uncle who do attend. That aunt is Aysel's sister Tezel, a talented artist who has never gotten over her "revolutionary" experiences. The uncle is Aysel's husband, Ömer, an economist admired by the student radicals. In the opening scenes of the book's twelve numbered chapters, Ömer generally speaks as narrator. No one voice dominates the book: the twelve numbered chapters include sections with titles indicating which character is speaking, and many voices are heard. Second in importance only to Ömer as a commentator on the wedding is Aysel's sister Tezel, the artist.

No reader of this book will ever forget Tezel's drunken, all-night bus trip from Istanbul to Ankara to attend the wedding (20–31, 33–54). Born in 1945, she is fifteen years younger than Aysel, and brother İlhan is older than both sisters. The prettiest and most accomplished of the family (15), Tezel has drowned disillusionment in drink. Older brother İlhan, the bride's father, sends her a plane ticket with the wedding invitation, but she cashes it in and spends the money. She gets drunk at the bar of the Park Hotel in Istanbul and buys herself a bottle for the road before boarding the bus. Then, in long monologues, she pours out her bitterness about everything from her ex-in-laws to the military to people who play at revolution. Crossing the Bosphorus Bridge, she sees the lights of her ex-husband, Oktay. Giving birth to their son, Kerem, was "one of my biggest mistakes."[84] Her mother-in-law expected her to stay home nursing that baby when her friends expected her to be in Taksim Square yelling, "America go home!" (*Amerika defol!* 39). However, the day comes when a young couple shows up at her exhibition, criticizes her for not painting oppressed workers, and threatens to deface her paintings (41). Now, the woman who did not have time to nurse her baby reacts like a mother to save her paintings. Going taut, she swears at the couple as she never has before. One of them slaps her; the other spits in her face. Drink cannot erase that memory (65, 88). At the wedding, Tezel repeatedly cries, "If we aren't going to commit suicide, let's at least drink!" (*İntihar etmeyeceksek içelim bari!* 5, 6, 14, 267, 297). She stands at the sidelines, following her own advice and commenting ironically while Ömer keeps her company and brings her drinks. Just when the actual wedding is about to occur, Ömer mentions a former student who was a revolutionary. "Revolution!" (*Devrim!*) Tezel shouts and flings her glass at the wall (186). The groom's mother nearly faints, mistaking the shattering glass for a gunshot, not without reason.

The qualities that make Ömer different from other Turkish men have not been noticed by his wife, Aysel, alone. "Big brother Ömer" (*Ömer abi*) is "a god in the heavens" to the university students (242). Niece Ayşen, who was one of the students, especially wants her aunt and uncle to come to her wedding. When Aysel refuses because of being at daggers drawn with brother İlhan (128–29), Ayşen begs "big brother Ömer" to come (172, 261). Going to the wedding with his drunken sister-in-law, Tezel, he quickly realizes that he is going to need whatever refinements he retains from his father's ambassadorships and his Oxford days (7). Ayşen's mother, Müjgân, also wants Ömer there to watch Tezel's behavior and make a showing for the bride's side (10, 12). When time comes for the actual wedding and cake cutting, even Ayşen's father, İlhan, looks for Ömer and Tezel to join the group at the family table (179, 274).

Ömer, man of science that he is, also has things on his mind. At a wedding, almost everyone "rakes over the old accounts of other marriages" (*eski nikâh*

"America go home!" (defol). At this Revolutionary Youth (Devgenç)
demonstration in Istanbul, March 1970, the banner bears the defiant
message *defol,* roughly "get out," "get lost." (Courtesy of Fahri Aral,
Bilgi University, Istanbul, with additional thanks to Nur Bilge Criss
and Barin Kayaoğlu.)

defterlerini kurcalar, 93). He learned about Engin when Aysel began receiving
letters from him in prison (91–94). Was that when he sank in his own esteem,
from the thought that she had spent time alone with someone she did not care
much about? The way she told him proved her integrity. In time, Ömer also got
to respect Engin, one of the few students who had taught him things. Engin's

letters from prison were among the few bright rays in those dark days. Now, at the wedding, Ömer gets a furtive pleasure from knowing that a twenty-year-old girl is infatuated with him. He gazes at Ayşen while trying not to be obvious (57), sensing that she is also thinking about him. He tries to size up the young man—is his name Ercan or Ertan?—who "will soon be her husband on paper" (81–82). Ayşen has told Ömer that she admires him, in fact more than admires him (167). As the wedding is about to start, she gives him an imploring look (172). He's over forty-five now; it is up to him not to look ridiculous (173). Later, when Tezel asks him what he is thinking about, Ömer tells her he is writing a bad novel and wonders if he should tell her about Ayşen (185). The exchange of vows leaves him with the feeling that they have sacrificed a lamb together and are praying over it (189).

The interaction between individual subjectivity, familial relations, and national politics emerges above all from the plights of the wedding's younger participants. While there are several guests whose personal stories illustrate this theme, the inner turmoil of the bride, Ayşen, revealed only after the night is mostly over, eclipses all others. Like many of her contemporaries, she has found herself caught at a vulnerable stage of life between her parents' and her contemporaries' expectations. At the university, she wants nothing more than to fit in. The fact that the student radicals idolize Uncle Ömer helps her somewhat in her struggle for acceptance. Ömer is the only one who ever asks her what she thinks (245). But the students know about her parents' wealth, especially after her mother waits for her outside one afternoon in her big car and yells at Ayşen to hurry so they will not be late to the fashion show (229). At the university, Ayşen is so desperate for acceptance that she is the first to volunteer to set fire to the American's car. When she finally manages to get arrested with her friend Gül, she is happier in jail than at home; but her parents get her out, while Gül stays in (236–37).

The day comes when the radical students demand that Ömer step down from the lectern, and the most antagonistic revolutionary woman, Zehra, taunts Ayşen about her aunt's close relations with one of her students (248). Soon, Ayşen thinks, they will be talking about her grandmother. She can no longer tell the difference between the students and her parents (249). It is a revelation for Ayşen, but no solution to her problem, to discover that Zehra's militancy also hides personal griefs. The other radicals reproach Zehra: just because her rich father abandoned her mother for a singer does not mean that every relationship between a man and a woman is dirty (249). Zehra breaks down and never forgives the one who revealed this. Meanwhile, it is not as if Ayşen revered her parents. Her voice, always wavering around the students, never wavers when she fights with them. When she returns home from the university in anguish after her friends are arrested, her mother asks her to make martinis for the women with whom she is playing cards and will not hear what is on the girl's mind. In explosive scenes, she tells her father that he is her worst enemy and her mother that she is ashamed of her (189, 230).

When the radicals debate how to smash the system, Ayşen wonders whether people learn their hatred of the system from books or from loveless homes (240). She thinks that if she did not have to be ashamed of her parents, fear her companions, and suppress her feelings, maybe that would smash the system (244). Her mother constantly pushes her to go out with Ercan, who is inexplicably in love with her. Usually she refuses. But gradually, her mother, Ercan, and his brother Hakan say things that make her realize she will be freer if she marries than she is now (218, 251, 252). Brother Hakan is jealous, perhaps because he also loves Ayşen. He is absent but has threatened to shoot Ercan at the wedding (181). That is why their mother nearly faints, mistaking every pop of a flash-bulb for a shot. Dancing with her new husband, Ayşen thinks that she could never have believed her wedding would be so ugly or that her feelings for Ömer would increase instead of decrease (215).

By the time Ömer and Tezel leave the wedding, making their way past the plainclothesmen inside and the soldiers outside, a call home has informed them that Aysel has a visitor, Sevil, long ago a classmate in the town where Sevil's father was the public prosecutor and now a self-proclaimed "urban guerrilla" in need of money and a place to stay (270–71). The two old schoolmates are enjoying themselves together; Ömer and Tezel should come join them. Then another call informs them that Aysel and Ömer's apartment has been raided on the charge that they were harboring an anarchist, and Aysel has been taken in for interrogation (293). As they disappear into the night to look for Aysel, Ömer and Tezel hear a shot ring out behind them.

HAYIR . . . (NO . . .)

In *Hayır* . . . even more than in the earlier novels, the present and the past, the near and the far, the actual and the contingent converge to cloud what happens and invite reflection on the consciousness that grounds all these perceptions. Aysel again takes center stage. The context implies that the action occurs under the military government of 1980–1983, and internal references combine to suggest 1982 as the year.[85] With time's passage, "the sixty-eights" have taken shape retrospectively as a group (36, 89, 102, 117, 142, 184). Time has not been kind to them. The geographic scope of Aysel's experience has expanded to include Europe. She has achieved prestige and won honors. But she, too, has endured losses and encountered obstacles. Famous lines from

Dylan Thomas, repeated in English and translated into Turkish, portend the novel's mysterious ending:[86]

> Do not go gentle into that good night.
>   Rage, rage against the dying of the light.

Ostensibly the novel recounts the day—22 December of an unstated year—when Aysel is to receive an award at an evening ceremony from the Independent National Culture Association (Özerk Milli Kültür Kurumu, truly an oxymoronic name). As Aysel awakens that morning "with pleasant feelings" and "clear thoughts" (5), her consciousness churns out a fantasy about the ceremony (6–11). A sensation in her left ankle reminds her that since the break, it swells if she has to stand on it very long. The mysterious, twenty-year-old Yenins, watches her from the shore: a given day, hour, moment, the seashore, a boat that beckons her. Catching her cane on the taxi door as she gets out and stumbling badly, she makes her way with bystanders' help into the ceremony. After the greetings and a photograph in which her handbag looks like plastic, she imagines giving an acceptance speech the exact opposite of what they expect. She has a hard time finding words to express her resentment of this new honor. The history of our army of enlightenment (*irfan ordumuz*) is like the unwritten history of our common soldiers. Our nation has abused its thinkers. Then (to the selection committee), it is shameful that they waited until a foreign organization gave her an award to decide to honor her. It is as if they are weighing her with a borrowed scale. Then come the committee chairman's canned speech and the press conference. Answering questions as the flashbulbs pop, she tells them that she is doing a study of *Intellectuals' Suicides and the Resistance of the Future*, which will also include heroes of novels who commit suicide. She wants to understand why they choose endless freedom. It seems to her that as the level of consciousness rises, the number of those who question existence, who resist attacks on their personhood, and who choose endless freedom will increase. The reporters find this vista disquieting. She finally has to break off because her dental work has come loose and she cannot talk anymore. Her writer friend (*yazar dostu*) tries to engage her in small talk and is puzzled when she says something about keeping Yenins waiting. Aysel comes to from her morning reverie, a thematic prelude to the novel, noting that her dental plate is fine, and her ankle does not hurt. As she prepares for her day, she mentally writes letters—contradictory versions of the same letters—to different people.

Whether present facts or future worries, the aches and pains point to the losses that Aysel and others have experienced. Many of the losses emerge from the undignified later histories of "the sixty-eights." Sevil, the "urban guerrilla" whose unexpected visit landed Aysel in jail at the end of the preceding novel, despite being the daughter of a public prosecutor, has a history of shoplifting. The night she called on Aysel, she had just been caught stealing eyeshadow. Screaming that she was a communist and that fascists were accusing her falsely, she got away long enough to get to Aysel's apartment. That is Sevil the urban guerrilla (168–69). The selection committee that chooses Aysel for the award from the Independent National Culture Association turns out to be a rogues' gallery from the past (94–95). Its members include Ercan Özkan, now Ayşen's ex-husband and a cultural consultant to an Arab bank. The committee also includes a faculty member in business administration, Dr. Zehra Sezer—could she be the same as Ömer's radical student who yelled at him to join the guerrillas in the hills? Better still, the committee chair, Dr. İhsan Türközü, is the former dean of the faculty who forced Aysel to resign for entering into "personal relations with her students" (104). She answered at the time with a principled defense that this charge had already been disposed of before the coup, that it concerned only one student (Engin), and that any allegation that she had allowed her private life to bias her teaching was baseless (104–5). Aysel's liaison with Engin had become known at the university because a jealous young man, Cemal, informed on them. He also turns up again. He has taken "political asylum" in Europe, has gone insane, and ends up an inmate in an asylum where Engin works as a keeper (108–10, 129–35, 153–54, 173, 177, 179–80).

Aysel has lost the men in her life. Her niece Ayşen, who has been divorced for a long time and has had many adventures of the heart, invites Aysel to meet and announces that she is going to have a baby by Ömer, Aysel's husband (53–71). This leads to awkward exchanges between Aysel and Ömer, an argument in which Engin is mentioned, acceptance of the fact that the baby has to have its father's name on its identity papers, and Ömer's marriage with Ayşen, obviously after an unmentioned divorce from Aysel. Going to Denmark to receive an award from the International Social Anthropology Institute gives Aysel a chance to discover the sun that never sets, make new contacts, and again see Engin, who now works there. Engin is still "incapable of living a day better than those of the sixty-eights" (184). But his and Aysel's meeting does not rekindle any old flame for either of them (117, 128). For good measure, Petra has taken up with Engin and is now carrying his baby, and Engin asks Aysel whether he should marry Petra. However, Petra has no way to know what it means to be a political refugee and can never share body and brain with him as Aysel did in 1968 (138, 142). Aysel is left to fill her need for a significant other with the image of Yenins, who seems to metamorphose from a real person in Denmark (41) into a mythical presence, and her "writer friend" (*yazar dostu*), also referred to at one point as her "platonic (*platoncu*) writer friend" (61). Aysel and her writer friend seem like ego and alter ego. About an artist's attempted suicide (190, 234), the writer's novel-in-progress, *Fragments of Broken Time*, likewise becomes a fictional parallel to Aysel's study of intellectuals' suicides.

Aysel also has been tried for defaming the state and government and inciting the people to rebellion (44–50). One June morning two years before the time of this novel, she finds herself in court to hear the prosecutor charge her with writing the following:

> Once upon a time, there was a country. . . . Yes . . . it is necessary to begin like a fairy tale. How else to relate a place and time where the law has been abandoned.
>
> It is a fact that there had been another military coup in this country, that thousands of people have been imprisoned under martial law, that penalties in excess of the law have been imposed without charges being brought, that some have undergone torture, that others have disappeared . . . , that some have gone mad under torture or killed themselves.
>
> All these things happened on charges of changing, amending, or replacing the constitution. Yet all these things occurred because you changed the constitution. You made things that were not illegal before illegal by laws that you imposed. . . .
>
> All people of this nation!
>
> . . . I call you to say "No!" to all orders of this lying government.
>
> Prof. Dr. Aysel Dereli

Farcically yet clinically, the trial problematizes both justice and authorship. She wants it recorded that she wrote the document three years ago, before the coup, and that it is only a handwritten draft. As for inciting others, she wrote this in anger and only for herself. Just then it was alleged that her well-known study of *The Use of Free Spaces by Individuals and Societies* was not her work but that she had published a report belonging to the sociology department, from which she had been dismissed, as if she wrote it. She sued her accusers and won, but the newspapers kept playing up the plagiarism charge rather than her court victory. She wrote her thoughts about the suspension of the constitution believing that no one would believe her because of the court case, feeling that the best she could do was a resistance that started and stopped within herself. She starts to point out that what fills up the free spaces in people's lives is militarism, but the judge admonishes her. Now she stands accused because of an uncirculated, handwritten draft. Her house was raided like many others, her books and papers were scrambled together, and three years later she stands in court. Even private life has been abolished. The trial is adjourned to a later date. Word of acquittal comes months later.

After Aysel fails to appear at the evening award ceremony that she has spent the day imagining, the last part of the book turns into a search for her and for the meaning of her disappearance. First her writer friend goes to her apartment to look for her (187–200). Stumbling up the stairs and fumbling again for the timed light switch at each landing, he imagines myriad scenarios, mostly about finding Aysel dead by suicide, alternatively about her coming to the door to welcome him and discuss his work on *Fragments of Broken Time*, a title applicable to the writer's imaginings on the stairs. Aysel's colleague Dr. Üner also leaves the ceremony to look for her. The two men's thoughts and memories turn the search for Aysel into philosophical questions about the differences between social scientific research and literary production (209), "organic time and consciousness time" (213), "outer time" and "inner time" (219). Repeatedly they notice the sentences, all in capitals, on the paper in her typewriter:[87]

IN EVERY SITUATION, TO PRESERVE OUR FREE PERSONHOOD DEPENDS ON UTTERING AND APPLYING THESE WORDS: NO TO REPETITION.

NO TO SAMENESS. . . .

Then she had rolled down and typed again, condensing the statement to end with ". . . DEPENDS ON ONE FINAL WORD: NO."

By 11 that night, Dr. Üner has arrived with Alev, and they have joined the writer in a discussion over coffee and cognac about Aysel. As the writer had earlier (229, 239), Dr. Üner notices that Aysel had repeatedly written on a paper: "Yenins." He exclaims: "Mustn't that mean freedom or New Person (*Yeni İnsan*)." At that epiphany, he throws himself out the window, into the "endless freedom" that has been talked about throughout the book.

Yenins's metamorphosis from someone Aysel met in Denmark into a personification of ideal subjectivity, the New Person (*Yeni İnsan*), renews Ağaoğlu's focus on fulfillment as a person (*insan, kişi*). Now the emphasis shifts implicitly from what happened to Aysel to what remains if Aysel is gone (240–42). At dawn, Aysel's writer friend sees a boat on the sea in the fog with a woman in it, Aysel. He sees only the woman. In the boat, Aysel hears the call. Yenins beckons her on. "You have passed the boundary. You have emerged from repetition and sameness." She answers: "I must try to see the New Person's face. Your true face." The writer knows Aysel will never be seen again on these shores. The final pages (243–45) examine the philosophical implications of Aysel's disappearance, tying together the novels' existential questions. "Fragments of broken, slippery time can be lined up side by side, piled up, set at different distances." As they are, they change places. Time and space change back and forth, one into the other. The calendar's time is sequential; the brain's time disrupts that sequence. What grounds these perceptions is what cries "No!" to sameness, repression, and the dimming of the light: the consciousness (*bilinç*) that makes one a person.

Aysel is gone; her quest for personhood remains. The effects of the military coups on Turkish society and culture linger. In bringing her heroine's story to a close, Adalet Ağaoğlu has reflected on death and loss with a profundity rarely if ever exceeded in Turkish secular culture. Ağaoğlu devoted another novel to the effects of the 1980 coup, effects that other Turkish artists are exploring even still.[88] Much as the newer works have added, Adalet Ağaoğlu's "Hard Times" trilogy continues to inspire through both its creativity and its ardor in the quest for human dignity and personal fulfillment, indispensable prerequisites for a humane and just society.

THREE DECADES IN RETROSPECT

Ağaoğlu's fictional heroine Aysel faced prosecution in 1982 for much the same reasons that Fethullah Gülen did in 2000. As Turkish modernity entered the era of globalization and identity politics, both religious and secular Turks shared corresponding concerns with issues of subjectivity and identity and risked comparable difficulties with the governmental authorities, who were hard pressed to adapt to a changing global environment. The context for reflections on subjectivity and consciousness was defined in these years by the struggle for political order and integration, the proliferation of identity issues, the most significant reorientation in economic policy since the 1930s, the tapering off of the midcentury population explosion, and the globalization of the Turkish diaspora. Turkey had, it seemed, turned the corner on the turmoil of the 1960s and 1970s. New challenges emerged, but the benign consequences of the end of the Cold War, epitomized by the emergence of five new Turkic republics and by hopes of EU integration, lent conviction to the idea that the gathering momentum of globalization—in the broad sense that encompasses all forms of global interlinkage—offered attractive future possibilities.

CONCLUSION: REFLECTING ON THE PRESENT AND THE PAST

A panoramic perspective on political, economic, social, and cultural history unfolding across two centuries has revealed a developmental dynamic quite different from the linear, secularizing trend presented by the works of the 1960s that launched the modern historical study of Ottoman and Turkish modernity. The added perspective of succeeding decades makes it possible instead to perceive a dialectical interaction between two great currents of change. Since the 1960s, a new competition between forces of globalization and localization has also arisen to compete with, perhaps eventually to override, this dialectic. Concluding this book creates the opportunity to consider this possibility while reflecting on the dominant pattern of the past two centuries and the factors that governed its unfolding over time. Again, a novelist's reflections on Turkish society add depth and nuance to this consideration.

ORHAN PAMUK'S *SNOW*: KARS AS A MICROCOSM OF CONTEMPORARY TURKEY

Nobel Prize–winning novelist Orhan Pamuk's novel *Kar* (Snow), written between 1999 and 2001, challenges its readers with profound reflections on the tensions between individual aspirations and societal constraints, between fantasy and reality in the eastern Anatolian city of Kars. Marginalized by its poverty and its frontier location, the Kars of the novel is further cut off from the world by a three-day snowstorm. The isolated city turns into a theater where all Turkey's sociopolitical forces and pressures converge in a "revolution onstage."[1] To understand how that happened requires starting with the protagonist Ka and the reality-fantasy world of the city and its inhabitants.

Ka is not heroic, but he is a respected poet. Made from the initial letters of his real name, Kerim Alakuşoğlu (11), which he never liked, "Ka" has become his pen name. Ka's life has not been happy. He has spent twelve years in exile in Germany for political ideas he no longer believes in (296). In Germany his poetical inspiration has dried up. When he returns to Istanbul for his mother's funeral, an old friend, now a journalist for the newspaper *Cumhuriyet*, offers Ka a chance to go to Kars for an assignment that none of the regular reporters wants, to cover the municipal elections and a mysterious epidemic of suicide by young girls. All it takes to persuade Ka, who has never been married, is the added information that the beautiful İpek, whom he remembers from the university, is in

Kars. Street scene with snow and ice, February 2009.
(Hüseyin Demirci, Anatolia Agency.)

Kars, has separated from her husband, and lives with her sister at their father's hotel, the Snow Palace (*Karpalas*, 14). Reaching Kars by bus just ahead of the snowstorm, Ka checks into the same hotel.

Ka's inner life quickly rekindles. He falls in love with İpek, and his poetical inspiration returns. During his three days in Kars, nineteen poems come to him like revelations, so suddenly that he has trouble writing them down before he forgets words or lines. By contrast, the poor novelist Orhan has to work, "like a clerk" (415), morning and night, to get his writing done. In ways recalling novels discussed in earlier chapters, Ka is clearly the author's alter ego, the author also becomes a character in the novel, and the "real" book is not the one before us but one we only read about, in this case, Ka's poetry manuscript, which he intends to publish with the title *Kar*, "Snow" (257). It disappears when Ka is mysteriously murdered on the streets of Frankfurt four years after his return from Kars. When the author goes to Frankfurt to bring back Ka's effects, all he can find is the notebooks in which Ka wrote about his poems. Paradoxically, the only poem that may have survived is the one that Ka never managed to write down. He did, however, recite it onstage the night of the "theater revolution," which was televised. That poem may have survived in the video archives of Kars television. Before he died, Ka asked the author to go to Kars and transcribe it.

When the author goes there, he not only falls in love with İpek. Studying the videos, he also concludes that the poem contains proof of Ka's responsibility for the death of a rival in Kars. Ka's later assassination in Frankfurt must have been an act of revenge, and his lost poetical manuscript must now be in his assassins' hands. If recovered and completed, the poetical manuscript, with each poem assigned to a point on a starlike snowflake diagram, would exemplify the ideal order totally absent in Kars. Opposing radii of the six-branched star are labeled "logic," "memory," and "fantasy." One poem, "I, Ka," is situated at the center, where all six radii meet (261, 429). The poetical star thus perfectly exemplifies Ka's artistic subjectivity. The fact that İpek's family name is Yıldız ("star") symbolically unites Ka's lost love with his lost poetical masterpiece. As if to reinforce the point, İpek's sister, Kadife, is interested in astrology. Her talk about İpek's and Ka's compatibility as two Geminis inspires one of his poems, "The Companionship of the Stars" (*Yıldızların Arkadaşlığı*, 117–19, 219).

In Pamuk's Kars, fact and fantasy collide. The city has multiple histories. It was Russian-ruled for forty years after 1878; briefly it was occupied by British and Armenians; it was even its own independent republic (366). The city's buildings bear mute witness to Russians and Armenians long gone. The editor of the local newspaper, the *Serhat Şehir Gazetesi* (Frontier city gazette), makes a regular practice of publishing the news before it happens, and he claims a high record for accuracy (16, 29, 309, 335–36). His headlines heighten the air of unreality. However, he has to publish what his subscribers want; most of his subscriptions come from government offices; the agents of the state make things happen in Kars (301–2); and it is no wonder that the headlines published in advance prove true, as Ka learns to his cost.

Kars is a small enough city that everyone knows everything (112). The army, the police, and the national intelligence (MİT, Milli İstihbarat Teşkilatı) also have the city "bugged" with wiretaps, informants, and hidden microphones. In such an environment, conspiracy theories proliferate, particularly ones attributing everything to the state (79, 162, 226). On the lighter side, another narrative that holds the city together is a Mexican soap opera, *Marianna*. The heroine's televised struggles against adversity unite all Kars — all Turkey — in an electronic "imagined community" (87, 238–39, 242). When Ka is called in for interrogation at one point, some members of the "special team" watch *Marianna* while others rough him up. He wonders if he will get back to the hotel to watch the end of the show with İpek and her father and sister (355–56).

The idea of a present-day epidemic of suicide among Turkish girls and women who wear the Islamic headscarf is in itself a narrative with no basis in fact, whether at Kars or elsewhere in Turkey.[2] In the novel, however, this theme becomes another source of Kars's narrative fecundity. Ka's "journalistic" efforts to gather information about the "suicide girls" generate multiple narratives. The explanations offered for their actions — unhappiness at school, at home, in love — are as contested as their bodies. Their suicidal acts are paradoxically undramatic (19–22, 121–25); however suicide becomes a way for the girls to take charge of their own bodies and for girls who have been falsely accused and threatened to defend their innocence and purity (125).

The male Islamists' ardor is no less intense. In the scene where Ka and İpek get to know each other over tea, a masculine narrative about headscarf girls emerges at a nearby table, as a deranged young militant reproaches the director of a school who has had to deny such girls admission to class, pulls a pistol, and shoots him (41–42, 43–51). Among the students of the religious high school, two especially seem like something out of myth. So inseparable that their behavior sometimes rouses suspicion, they choose to be known as Necip and Fazıl, so sharing the names of the Islamist-nationalist writer Necip Fazıl Kısakürek, whose works they read devotedly. Necip aspires to be a poet, and Ka thinks of him as a younger alter ego. Both boys are in love from afar with their idea of exemplary Islamist girls. Fazıl loves Teslime, or did; she is one of the suicide girls. Necip loves Hicran, his idealized image of İpek's sister, Kadife (83–89). Necip is working on an Islamic science fiction novel and reads his plot summary to Ka. It is about two Islamist students of the future, Necip and Fazıl, who both love Hicran. They realize that one of them is going to die, that the other will marry Hicran, but the spirit of the dead friend will return. Necip is writing an alternate version of Pamuk's novel (104–11, 137).

One of Pamuk's subtlest ways of reflecting on life in Turkey is in elaborating competing narratives and ideologies and probing the difficulties that arise in applying those ideas in daily life. Not only do the narratives and beliefs clash, but the language in which they are expounded differs markedly enough to sound like distinctive voices, as the tirade of the school director's assassin (43–51) and Necip and Fazıl's earnest questionings illustrate.

All the ideologies, from Marxist to Islamist, and all the politically salient identities found elsewhere in Turkey plus more — Azeris, Circassians, and other, small groups of transborder migrants — jostle together in Kars. In Kars as generally in Turkey, Ka observes, everyone wants to belong to a *cemaat* (literally congregation), and anyone like Ka who thinks like an individual is alien and suspect. In Turkey, Ka notes, believing in God is not a matter of an individual's encounter with the Creator; primarily, belief is a matter of belonging to a group (64). Sometimes, group affiliations change with time. The later histories of some of the leftist militants of earlier decades vary astonishingly; for example, Muhtar, İpek's estranged husband, has returned to Islam and become the Refah Party candidate for mayor (61–62, 162). By the book's last pages, some of the Islamists lose their ardor, too. Relations among groups are particularly contentious. At a key moment in the drama, representatives of all the political forces meet secretly to draft a joint communiqué for Ka to have published in Europe, but their disagreements and their fears that they are being spied on nearly derail the meeting. In fact, a lamp in the form of a fish with a bulb in its mouth has a "state microphone" (*devlet mikrofonu*) hidden in its eye (268), and one of the socialists is an informer (269).

The leading Islamist is the charismatic and elusive Kurd Lacivert ("deep blue"), so called because "the blue of his eyes approached that deep blue that will never be seen in a Turk" (75). The subject of a legend highly embroidered by the media (72–74), Lacivert is narrative profusion on two feet. That seems to be one source of his mystique. In successive meetings with Ka, Lacivert recounts the story of Rüstem and Suhrab from Firdawsi's *Shahname*, a story about mistaken identity and a battle to the death between father and son (79–82); he dictates his address to the West for Ka to have published after his return to Germany (226–27); after being arrested, he reads to Ka the life story that the police demanded he write, winding off with a veiled warning to Ka in the form of a story about the 1969 Gillo Pontecorvo film *Quiemada* (321–23).

İpek's sister, Kadife, is Lacivert's mistress and the leader of the headscarf girls. Her life makes another complicated story. She has gone from leading a secular life and making fun of the so-called turban girls to covering her head initially as a one-day gesture of solidarity, then keeping it covered because of the criticism she encountered for having taken the matter lightly (115–16). The students at the religious high school revere her under the name Hicran, but most of the stories they tell about her are not true, she says. Whether the Islamist men like it or not, gender identity inflects Kadife's narrative. At a meeting with Ka and Lacivert, she speaks up, saying that if the coup had not occurred, maybe she would have "uncovered her head and become like everyone else at last" (234). To Lacivert's protestations she answers that most of the educated women like her do not cover their heads. The only woman at the secret political meeting to draft the joint communiqué for publication in Germany, she announces that she also has something to say to the German paper. "A young woman who adopted the headscarf like a flag because of her beliefs . . . , uncovered her head in front of everybody because of the revulsion that overcame her " (281–82). Fazıl cuts her off, threatening to commit suicide, if she persists. Kadife's personal story is headed for a dramatic climax, literally so because it occurs on stage on the final night of the "theater revolution."

Compared to the literary works discussed in earlier chapters, one of the newest features of this novel is its questioning of art's power to reshape society and artists' competence to solve society's problems. This questioning pervades Ka's unheroic trajectory and the two evening performances of Kars's "theater revolution." Getting off the bus in Kars, Ka finds Sunay Zaim, a famous actor in the leftist theater of the 1970s, and his actress wife, Funda Eser (13). Ka wonders what they are doing there. In fact, Sunay's travails in touring the provinces and in competing for top roles nationally add memorably to the book's narrative profusion and motivate him to assume his greatest role in Kars (188–97). Hegel, he says, was "the first to grasp that history and the theater are made of the same materials" (198). History might not have given Sunay quite such a great role had he not found in Kars an old school chum, Osman Nuri Çolak, now a colonel in the army, commanding officer by default because all his superiors are out of town for different reasons when the snowstorm cuts Kars off from the world (195–96).

The military, the police, the intelligence, and the "special team" of Z. Demirkol, a sinister former communist turned government agent, all provide supporting cast for a memorable night at the theater, broadcast live by Kars Television. Onstage, Sunay Zaim and his troupe mount a "play within a play" in the form of a variety show culminating in an updated playlet from the 1930s.

The variety show includes even Ka's recitation of a new poem. He learns that he is to perform from the previous day's newspaper; at that point, he has not produced a poem in years. On the way into the theater, he encounters Necip, who tells him about a horrifying vision he has when he tries to imagine what the world would be like if God did not exist, a vision like a dark street with blank walls on either side, at the end a single, leafless tree that alternately glows red with an infernal light, goes dark, and glows red again (144). The vision inspires Ka, enabling him to recite "The Place Where God Does Not Exist" in front of the camera. The way the evening ends keeps him from writing down the poem.

The climax of the evening consists of the playlet *Vatan yahut Türban* (Fatherland or headscarf). While the title of the piece harks back to Namık Kemal's *Vatan yahut Silistre* (Fatherland or Silistria, 1873), the play itself started as a didactic 1930s piece against veiling entitled *Vatan yahut Çarşaf*, the term *çarşaf* referring to the full-length women's outer garment still worn at that time. Not much about the play has been updated except the title. In the play, a woman comes on stage in a black *çarşaf*, proclaims her emancipation, unveils, and is rescued by soldiers from reactionaries who want to stop her (147–52). Restaged in a time when the headscarf (referred to by its detractors as *türban*) had become the banner of Islamist women, not the *çarşaf*, the play sends mixed messages, which for different reasons disturb both the officials seated in the front and the religious students in the back of the hall. No longer young, Funda Eser plays the heroine. She has spent her career using her sexuality to excite male audiences, and her movements do not look much like those of a "heroine of enlightenment" (153). By the time the soldiers come to her rescue, the audience is highly agitated. As the soldiers onstage turn their guns toward the audience, more soldiers enter from the rear, passing down the aisles to the stage. The soldiers begin firing. When people in the audience begin falling, most spectators think it is part of the play. Not until the third volley does realization spread that the shots are real. Sunay Zaim, on stage with a pistol, announces, "This is not a play; a revolution (*ihtilal*) is beginning"; and the soldiers start rounding up the religious students (160). One of those who runs out through the audience with a pistol is Z. Demirkol, head of the "special team" (162).

Ka no longer cares about anything but poetry and taking İpek to Frankfurt with him, but the course of events rapidly entangles and compromises him. Called in by the police to identify militants, he recognizes no one but Necip, whose body he discovers at the morgue among those shot in the theater (185–86). Now behaving more like a military commander than an actor, Sunay Zaim and his wife, Funda, pressure Ka to help them by wearing a wire to track down Lacivert, whom they know to be Kadife's lover (205). Ka refuses. Not long afterward, Kadife summons him to a secret meeting with Lacivert, who wants to give him a message about the coup to publish in the West (220–36). Ka parts ways with the truth by leading Lacivert to believe that he knows a German journalist, who will publish a story about the coup for them. As they discuss how to couch a declaration from an Islamist to a progressive German paper, Ka comes up with the idea of bringing together representatives of all different tendencies to draft a joint communiqué. In addition to fabricating his connections with the German press, Ka thus makes himself responsible for the chaotic political meeting and its tragic consequences for its leading participants. Lacivert tells Ka that he is not sure Ka is not some kind of agent, even if Ka does not know it. "Like all good people, you do your harm without knowing it. But now that I have told you this, you can no longer be considered innocent" (236). As plans begin to take shape for the secret political meeting, Ka concludes that everyone in Kars talks on two levels. In his case, trying to persuade Kadife and her father, Turgut, to go to the political meeting masks his desire to take İpek to his room for rapturous lovemaking, his first in four years (241–49, 262–65).

Ka learns about his further descent into the maelstrom from a newspaper headline denouncing him as "A Godless Man in Kars" (293). İpek is at last prepared to go to Germany with him (306), but Ka is soon summoned before Sunay Zaim, who informs him that Lacivert has been captured. For years, the actor has wanted to stage Thomas Kyd's *Spanish Tragedy*, a tale of revenge with a play within the play. He has changed and simplified the play so that "our people" can understand it, and he wants Kadife to play in it. As Sunay later hints during the play (403), the nature of the role intended for her implies that Kadife's statements at the secret meeting were indeed overheard by intelligence. With Funda playing her wicked rival, Kadife is to come onstage with her head covered, repudiate nonsensical customs, and unveil in front of everyone. If she plays her part, Lacivert will be released.

Ka must play his part offstage by talking Kadife and Lacivert into cooperating. When he tries to get out of this, Sunay points out the newspaper article denouncing Ka, forcing him to comply in return for protection. Persuading the two by promising more than he can deliver, Ka makes himself the guarantor of an arrangement whereby Kadife is to go onstage only after receiving word from Lacivert that he is free and in a safe hiding place and will be able to leave Kars safely (324). Conscious that he has told lies and that Kadife may be hurt as a result (331), Ka reports back to Sunay Zaim. As preparations for the second performance of the "theater revolution" intensify, events become more chaotic. Sunay Zaim has serious heart trouble and is conscious that once the snow ends and the roads are cleared, Ankara will demand an accounting for what has happened in Kars. Summoning Ka to his hiding place, Lacivert tries through Ka to tell Kadife not to participate after all (349). On his way back from the meeting, Z. Demirkol's special team picks up Ka and takes him in for some rough treatment. The physical blows are not as bad as the psychological manipulation. Z. Demirkol tells Ka that İpek was once Lacivert's mistress, adding convincing details from transcripts of their conversations (356–58).

Jealousy now intrudes into Ka's dreams of achieving personal happiness far away. In a tearful meeting at the hotel, İpek tries to convince Ka that it is all over between her and Lacivert and that she wants to go to Frankfurt with Ka (363). Tension mounts relentlessly. The television announces that evening's live broadcast of the dramatic action, which will "rescue Kars from the religious prejudices that have held its people back from modernity and gender equality" (366). Admission will be free, security will be in place, and the students have promised to remain orderly. By now, her whole family wants Kadife not to go on stage, but no one can stop her. As curtain time approaches, dramatic news arrives. Word comes from Ka that he has been taken into military custody and, willing or not, will be put on the evening train to Erzurum; İpek will be picked up to join him onboard (388). The next message is that Lacivert has been killed (390). At that, İpek refuses to leave with Ka; she must go to the theater to tell Kadife.

At the theater, Sunay Zaim has changed the name of the play at the last minute to *The Tragedy in Kars*. The play depicts an unexplained blood feud in a backward town, with additions and improvisations (392–406). Gradually, the action focuses on Sunay Zaim and Kadife. After all the earlier narrative eloquence of the novel, their improvised dialogue is startlingly clumsy. Yet it focuses on the tense issues of suicide and unveiling. "Women commit suicide to win," says Kadife, "men when they see no more hope of winning" (399). At that, Sunay pulls out his revolver and asks, "When you see that I am totally defeated, will you shoot me with this?" The intermission between the second and third acts gives İpek a chance to tell Kadife that Lacivert has been killed, that she is not going to Germany with Ka, and that she thinks Ka gave away Lacivert's hiding place (400). Kadife goes back on stage for the third act, and the lame improvisation between her and Sunay resumes until both agree that "it is time to end this play." Sunay again pulls out his revolver and makes flourishes to convince the audience that it is not loaded. Kadife is to uncover her hair and then shoot him. The revelation of Kadife's long, beautiful hair brings an anguished look to her face but mesmerizes the audience. Sunay hands her the pistol, she fires it, and he falls convincingly to the floor. Four more quick shots, no death monologue but blood on the stage, and Kadife exclaims: "I must have killed him" (405). "Good job," yells one of the religious students from the back of the hall. Sunay Zaim has made sure that he will not be there when, a few hours later, the roads open, and the troops roll into town to repress Kars's little "military coup."

By the time the author arrives four years later, Kadife has gotten out of prison, married Fazıl, and had a child by him. Now Fazıl is trying to write the science fiction novel begun by his dead friend Necip, but his religious ardor has cooled. After studying the videos of the theater revolution and touring the city with Fazıl, the author finds his proof that Ka betrayed Lacivert. Necip's horrifying vision of the place where God does not exist, which Ka worked into this poem, is a sight visible from the window of the religious high-school dormitory where Fazıl and Necip had stayed as students, a tree at the end of an alley, lit up in red on and off during the night by the light of a sign in the next street. After the theater revolution, Z. Demirkol's "special team" used the same dormitory as its headquarters. Ka sited this poem on the "memory" branch of his star, and he could not have remembered this place unless he went there his last night in Kars, between leaving the theater and boarding the train. If he went to Demirkol, Ka's jealous betrayal must have caused Lacivert's death.

Pamuk's intricately constructed novel *Kar* offers its readers an imaginative reflection on the clashes between religion and secularism, between the competing claims of identity politics, between individual subjectivity and societal constraint, between life and art, narrative and experience. The proliferation of identity and difference now clearly competes with the dialectic between religion and laicism to organize the field of political conflict; yet that dialectic still defines the opposing sides in the "theater revolution." This book goes further than those discussed in earlier chapters in probing political violence, particularly that of state agencies. In a way uncharacteristic of earlier periods, this novel implies that artists and intellectuals, too, are compromised in societal problems and are not seers who can solve all those problems from on high. Where do the city's conflicts lead, and how might they end? Are there perhaps clues in the deradicalization of the leftists of earlier decades or that of the Islamist former students as the author finds them four years after Ka's visit? A vignette near the end of the book has the author, Fazıl, and two policemen, one of them the secret agent who had followed Ka, walking down the snowy street together (425). Compared to four years earlier, as Fazıl informs the author, Kars is poorer and shabbier but little changed except for the proliferation of dish antennas (426–27). Vernacularizing globalization at the expense of identity politics, people seem less interested in the issues that divided them four years earlier and more interested in staying home to watch movies from all over the world for free.

TWO CENTURIES IN RETROSPECT

Any such appearance could prove misleading, however, given the propensity of Turkey's national politics to produce dramas in real life. The Susurluk scandal, discussed in chapter 7, illustrated this point in 1996. After the 2007 election, the Turkish public's attention was again riveted by discovery of a cache of weapons and suspicious documents in the home of a retired ultranationalist military officer. In July 2008, eighty-six people from different walks of life, including two retired generals, were arrested; charges were also brought later against many others. A lengthy indictment charged them with forming a conspiratorial organization, known as Ergenekon, named after a legendary place associated with Turkish origin myths, and plotting a coup against the ruling Justice and Development Party. At the same time, a court case against the party, resulting from Prime Minister Erdoğan's reference in a speech made in Spain to the headscarf issue, narrowly missed closing the party and did place certain restrictions on it. In the wake of these events, a less conciliatory tone began to come into party statements and government policy; eventually, some observers accused the ruling party of turning the Ergenekon prosecution into an assault on secularism. Like the Susurluk scandal, the Ergenekon case seemed to expose the unelected power centers of Turkey's "deep state" and their capacity to disrupt democratic politics. Some of the more optimistic interpretations of the 2007 cases, both Ergenekon and the attempt to shut down the Justice and Development Party, came from the left. As an Ankara law professor put it, both the conspiracy indictment and the case against the ruling party were about "whether you support a law state and better democracy in Turkey."[3] Amid the many differences of identity politics, the sharpest polarizations are still those over issues of religion and secularism. If the allegations about the Ergenekon conspiracy are well founded, Pamuk deserves credit for intuiting a "revolution on stage" not unlike one that the conspirators apparently wanted to carry out on the streets of Ankara. Once again, a writer of imaginative literature has shown far deeper insight into Turkish society than most of his academic colleagues in history and the social sciences.

Orhan Pamuk's imaginative evocation of present-day Turkish realities as refracted in a frontier city richly complements the panorama in the foregoing chapters of the historical developments from which those realities emerged. The historical perspective on political, economic, social, and cultural history

since the late 1700s has suggested that the course of late Ottoman and modern
Turkish history has been determined by successive generations' choices over
identity issues, both ethnolinguistic and religious, and by their responses to the
challenges of modernity. From the critical vantage point of 1918, Ziya Gökalp
had the profound insight to identify the Turks' three essential reference points
as Turkishness, Islam, and modernity and to offer a way to unite all three. The
challenges of modernity included both its threats, which gave the later empire its
dually imperial character as a multiethnic empire menaced by both nationalism
and imperialism, and its attractions, which stimulated both radicals and conservatives to develop alternative visions of modern futures for themselves. While
analogous observations could be made, with variations, about all the empire's
peoples, the focus of this study has been on those who thought of themselves as
Ottomans and Turks. For them, all the late Ottoman uncertainties about geography and demography fixed their loyalties on the state and their own ideals of
what it should be in the future. This fixation linked the history of the late empire
directly to that of the republic, also perpetuating the awe of the state and state
power that so deeply imprints Turkish political culture.

The choices made by Ottomans and Turks among the reference points, ethnolinguistic and religious, in relation to which they charted their course into
modernity generated two major currents of change, one radical in the sense
of favoring rapid change and Westernization, the other Islamically grounded
and more conservative. The dialectical interaction between the two shaped late
Ottoman history, the transition from empire to republic, and the history of the
republic. Since the tumultuous 1960s, a more finely divided identity politics
has created a new diversity of interests and choices. These may transform the
dynamics of Turkish history in future. Yet as in Pamuk's novel, the secular-
religious difference represented by the two historical currents still defines the
underlying tectonics and fault lines of Turkish politics.

Channeled in their flow by Islam, nationalism, and modernity, the secularist and Islamist currents of change differentiated gradually in the nineteenth
century, sharpened from the paradoxes of late Ottoman dynamism and disintegration, clashed as the secular republic succeeded the Islamic empire, and
moved uneasily toward symbiosis after the 1960s. The gradualness with which
the two currents assembled and differentiated results from the fact that both
are complex sociocultural formations. The opposition between them has generally become clearest in times of crisis, in moments of forced choices. Such
historical turning points have made the contradictions between the two currents more conspicuous than their convergences. The Young Turks' ardor for
scientific materialism illustrates that point, as does the militant laicism of the

early republican leadership and of its heirs today in the military and some of the civilian elites. Conversely, some religious conservatives' blanket condemnation of all the changes since the Tanzimat is equally unaccommodating. Turkish culture is highly politicized; intellectuals tend to state their positions in confrontational terms; and few have yet joined Pamuk in questioning the elites' omnicompetence to cure society's ills. Compromise is more often understood as betraying one's principles than as splitting differences to reach agreement. Still, the Turkish polity probably could not have survived as a coherent entity if the two trends had only clashed and never achieved moments of synthesis. In fact, the convergences have been many. Like Namık Kemal and Ahmed Hamdi Tanpınar, all but the most doctrinaire individuals have commonly participated in both of the great currents of change, unless forced to take sides.

The course of events likewise created convergences. Despite such notable exceptions as 1914, Ottoman and Turkish diplomatic history is full of astute choices about relations with the outside world. Although the diplomatic establishment throughout its history has been one of the Westernizers' bastions, examples from the Gülhane decree of 1839 and the Egyptian crisis of 1839–1841 to present-day debates over EU accession indicate that cultural conservatives also contributed to or endorsed these prudent choices at significant moments. Domestic history, too, includes significant convergences of interest. The land law of 1858 served the interests of both the office-holding and the property-holding wings of the proto-bourgeoisie. The sociocultural transformations of the Tanzimat and Hamidian periods created desires for change in gender relations, desires shared even by conservatives, to judge from the novels of Ahmed Midhat and Fatma Aliye. The Anatolian tax revolts of 1905–1907 helped bring on the 1908 revolution and convinced the Young Turk leadership that conservative propertied Turks also had revolutionary potential. After 1908, the Young Turks' "national economy" policy, aiming to form a Turkish bourgeoisie, privileged common ethnicity over ideological uniformity. At another major convergence, the victorious National Struggle of 1919–1922 and the foundation of the republic created a wave of gratitude that enabled republican leaders to enact reforms for which most of the populace was unready. In retrospect, the formation and political activation of an Ottoman or Turkish Muslim bourgeoisie, ultimately including a modern managerial-technical elite, became the most momentous social transformation of the century leading up to 1960, just as the political activation of the entire population became the most momentous social development thereafter. The fact that the Turkish middle class assembled out of both secular and religious elements and still displays the TÜSİAD-MÜSİAD dualism between the more secular big business interests and the more religious Anatolian tigers suggests how intertwined the histories of the two currents of change can be. That Atatürk is the only strongman leader of the 1930s still revered by most of his own people points to another convergence, proving that Turks of divergent cultural orientations share pride in the changes over which he presided. Secular Turks have shown greater reluctance to recognize the contributions of the religious; still, Turgut Özal's and Recep Tayyip Erdoğan's success in "mainstreaming" religious Turks hints at a lessening of such rigidity.

Even as they interacted in their clashes and convergences, the two major currents of change diverged in their chronologies. The origins of what became the Westernizing, secularizing current lay in Selim III and Mahmud II's efforts to form new military and civil elites to serve their programs of defensive modernization. This current began to exceed the bounds of state control with the rise of the modern Ottoman-language print media (1840–1860). Simultaneous with the first efforts to create a new system of government schools extending beyond the elite service academies, those years became the takeoff point for Ottoman print capitalism, soon followed by the new form of political opposition and ideological creativity embodied in the Young Ottoman movement. These developments also contributed critically to the constitutional movement of the 1870s. The Islamic emphases in Young Ottoman thought illustrate that the new print culture was far from all-out secularism; however, it was the site for the propagation of knowledge about the outside world and for expression of a new Ottoman bourgeois self-consciousness. Ironically for Abdülhamid, the spread of scientific materialism in the elite service academies during his reign more nearly sites the point at which militant secularism gained ground as the most advanced ideology with any following. In 1908, the Young Turk Revolution brought this elite to power, which it retained, with rotation in the top leadership, until 1950. In nonelective institutions such as the military, certain ministries, and the judiciary, like-minded people control important power bastions to this day. By 1950, too, republican schools, cultural programs, and media had propagated secularism to the extent that it became and remains a lasting belief system for important elements of the populace, as the color illustration of a secularist demonstration in Izmir in 2007 demonstrates.

In contrast, the historical chronology of the conservative current of change has been punctuated primarily by the emergence, relatively sudden in each case, of three major movements of religious renewal, each of which added lastingly to the religious landscape of the country. The series began with Mevlana Halid (1776–1827) and the Halidiye-Nakşibendiye and continued with Said Nursi (1873–1960), Fethullah Gülen (b. 1938), and the movements they launched. The earlier movements have remained active and adapted to changing circumstances, up to the present. Religious interests wielded variable, sometimes considerable, influence in Ottoman politics at times, as a reexamination of the Gülhane decree and the 1876 constitution indicates. In proportion as radical intellectuals began to inject militantly secularist ideas into the nineteenth-century print culture, cultural conservatives needed to create a parallel universe of print media for themselves. Particularly after 1908, this happened with the rise of Islamic journals such as *Sebilürreşad* (originally *Sırat-ı Müstakim*), Necip Fazıl Kısakürek's quixotic creation of a model for the Islamist man of letters, and the gradual transition from manuscript to print reproduction of Said Nursi's treatises. Ahmed Hamdi Tanpınar's works show that there were also cultural conservatives who did not express themselves in an overtly religious idiom. Religious interests faced an extremely hostile climate during the early republic, as Said Nursi's travails notably illustrate. During his lifetime, although some Kurdish Nakşibendis rebelled, other Nakşibendis made the best of things by taking jobs in the new Directorate of Religious Affairs and colonizing it from within. By the 1980s, the conservative current of cultural change was regaining access to the political center at the same time that it was generating new forms of economic enterprise, electronic as well as print media, and new schools. The careers of Turgut Özal and Recep Tayyip Erdoğan show that religious conservatives' greatest political successes have come, not with narrowly religious movements, but with center-rightist parties able to appeal to business interests as well as "values voters."

Although the radicalism of the secularists and the conservatism of the Islamists suggest that their respective currents of change may have flowed at different rates of speed, such was not the case. The history of both currents includes processes of change that occurred at different rates of speed. Common as it is to identify the 1928 alphabet reform and the language reform as Turkey's cultural revolution, those were only the sharpest accelerations of change in a longer curve that began with the rise of the modern print media and continued long after 1928. Contrastingly, although cultural conservatives might have preferred gradual change, disruptive change was sometimes forced on them, as with the closing of the religious brotherhoods in 1925. Sometimes, too, they generated disruptive change. The rise of all three of the most influential religious movements occurred in relatively short time spans. The most active phase of Mevlana Halid's career occurred between 1811 and 1827. Said Nursi produced most of his treatises between 1925 and 1944. Fethullah Gülen's movement assumed more than local importance only from 1983 on.

To explain the differences in the chronologies of the two currents of change requires recognizing that external as well as internal factors governed their dialectical interaction. As the reconfiguration of the world into nation-states advanced, the elites who committed the multiethnic, Islamic empire to modernizing reform, while preferring to preserve the empire that gave them a grander stage to play on, eventually had to adapt to the trend of the times. If the secular-nationalist synthesis was less inclusive than the Ottoman-Islamic one, unitary mass mobilization was vital for success in the National Struggle. Two generations later, maintaining unison was not so urgent. By then, too, surging demographic growth and new ideas were making it impossible to maintain Kemalist unanimity. As demands for diversity and pluralism rose, Turkey moved in step with a gathering trend, which subjected all nation-states to opposing pulls of globalizing and localizing forces. With the global upsurge of identity politics, the high salience of Islam among the markers of Turkish identity increasingly problematized republican laicism. Islamically committed statesmen not only recaptured power. They also excelled the secular nationalists both in recognizing the value of a religiously neutral government as a guarantor of pluralism and in espousing the reforms required to advance Turkey's EU candidacy. As they did, they built on a desire for integration into the European system that Ottoman diplomats had articulated more than two centuries earlier.

In recent decades, as the issues symbolized by Islam, nationalism, and modernity have continued to shape their national experience, the people of Turkey have grown increasingly assertive about their diversity of identities and interests. This assertiveness has raised one of the most distinctive features of modernity to a new level of significance. Modernity affected society at all levels, from the most inclusive to the individual level. As a result, one of its most characteristic features has been the tension between its macrosocietal and its individual impacts, a tension commonly experienced, certainly in Turkey, in the form of discords between the state's demands and the citizens' expectations. Modern schools, armies, tax collectors, courts, and prisons, modern ideologues and politicians, all have attempted to impose set ideas of what the nation should be collectively and what its citizens should be individually. At the same time, new schooling, new media, and new ideas have raised individual expectations and desires whose fulfillment requires much more than being a model citizen. At the start of a new century, even as the grand issues surrounding ethnolinguistic and religious identity and modernity still set the terms of existential debate, the rise of a new, more finely differentiated identity politics implies new possibilities to moderate the modern tension between rationalization and subjectivization, reduce the arbitrariness and violence of political life, and build a pluralistic and humane society where difference and equality can coexist.

One of the great, potential gains of such a transformation might also be to free history from the politicization that suppressed dissident narratives and produced the "Turkish Historical Thesis" of the 1930s, the Turkish-Islamic synthesis of the early 1980s, indeed all the "official theses" (*resmi tezler*). Such doctrines disequip students and citizens to understand the world, their place in it, and the tragedies as well as the triumphs of their past. For nationalists of earlier generations, mobilizing the human and material resources of the present and the cultural resources of the past was essential to survive in the present and create the future. In the twenty-first century, perhaps new generations of readers will rediscover how Ahmet Hamdi Tanpınar defined "our greatest problem." As he wrote, "More acutely than Hamlet all of us live in a crisis of 'to be or not to be.'" All are "children of a crisis of consciousness and identity." The greatest problem, as Tanpınar saw it, is "where and how are we linked to the past."[4] By recovering suppressed narratives, by seeking to arrive at more inclusive, open-minded, and factually grounded understandings of the past, perhaps the Rabias, Ayşes, Hayri İrdals, Pehlivan Alis, Aysel Derelis, and Kas of the future can arrive at those "moments of awakening" when "the voice of past times becomes a discovery, a lesson, in short something added to our times."

They cannot do this by themselves, however. The past of a nation or of an empire cannot simply be remembered. "Impossible to remember as it truly was, [history] is vulnerable to being remembered as it wasn't. Against *this* challenge, memory itself is helpless. 'Only the historian, with the austere passion for fact, proof, evidence, which are central to his vocation, can effectively stand guard.'"[5] The writers of imaginative literature have excelled the scholars in illuminating their own times. May their creativity inspire historians to rigorous discipline in pursuit of proof and evidence as they strive to discover lessons from the past, lessons that can enlighten all the children of Tanpınar's "crisis of consciousness and identity" as well as others around the world who seek to understand Ottoman and Turkish history.

ABBREVIATIONS USED IN THE NOTES AND BIBLIOGRAPHY

EHMENA   Charles Issawi, *An Economic History of the Middle East and North Africa* (New York: Columbia University Press, 1982)

EI₁, EI₂   *Encyclopedia of Islam*, 1st ed. (Leiden: Brill, 1913–1938), 2nd ed. (Leiden: Brill, 1954–), online at www.encislam.brill.nl

ESHOE   Halil İnalcık and Donald Quataert, eds., *An Economic History of the Ottoman Empire, 1300–1914* (Cambridge: Cambridge University Press, 1994)

HEO   Robert Mantran, ed., *Histoire de l'Empire ottoman* (Paris: Fayard, 1989)

HOEMT   Stanford J. Shaw and Ezel Kural Shaw, *History of the Ottoman Empire and Modern Turkey*, Vol. 2: *Reform, Revolution, and Republic: The Rise of Modern Turkey, 1808–1975* (Cambridge: Cambridge University Press, 1977)

İA   *İslâm Ansiklopedisi*, 13 vols. (Istanbul: Milli Eğitim, 1940–1988)

IJMES   *International Journal of Middle East Studies*

ITD   Zafer Toprak, *İttihat-Terakki ve Devletçilik* (Istanbul: Türkiye Ekonomik ve Toplumsal Tarih Vakfı, 1995)

LOE   Suraiya N. Faroqhi, ed., *The Cambridge History of Turkey*, Vol. 3: *The Later Ottoman Empire, 1603–1839* (Cambridge: Cambridge University Press, 2006)

MENA   J. C. Hurewitz, ed., *The Middle East and North Africa in World Politics: A Documentary Record*, 2 vols. (New Haven: Yale University Press, 1975–1979)

MIMB   Zafer Toprak, *Milli İktisat—Milli Burjuvazi, Türkiye'de Ekonomi ve Toplum (1908–1950)* (Istanbul: Türkiye Ekonomik ve Toplumsal Tarihi Vakfı, 1995)

MÜSİAD   Müstakil Sanayici ve İşadamları Derneği

SAE   Ahmet Hamdi Tanpınar, *Saatleri Ayarlama Enstitüsü* (1961; reprint, Istanbul: Yapı Kredi Yayınları, 2004)

T. C.   Türkiye Cumhuriyeti ("Turkish republic," official usage)

TIM   Ziya Gökalp, *Türkleşmek, İslâmlaşmak, Muasırlaşmak* [1918], ed. Kemal Bek (Istanbul: Bordo Siyah, 2004)

TMW   Reşat Kasaba, ed., *The Cambridge History of Turkey*, Vol. 4: *Turkey in the Modern World* (Cambridge: Cambridge University Press, 2008)

TÜİK   T. C. Başbakanlık Türkiye İstatistik Kurumu, Ankara (State Statistical Institute)

TÜSİAD   Türk Sanayici ve İşadamları Derneği

Notes

INTRODUCTION

1. Karpat, *Politics*; Lewis, *Emergence*; Mardin, *Genesis*; Davison, *Reform*; Robinson, *Republic*; Berkes, *Development*.
2. Levy, "Military"; Shaw, *Old and New*; Quataert, *Social*; McCarthy, *Muslims and Minorities*; Findley, *Bureaucratic*.
3. Citino, "Modernization," 579–97.
4. Bozdoğan and Kasaba, eds., *Rethinking*, 5–6.
5. I am indebted to the anonymous reviewer who suggested that as the title for this book.
6. Said, *Culture*, 329.
7. Ağaoğlu, *Hayır . . .* , 235.
8. Ahmed, *Women*, 64–65.
9. Masters, *Christians and Jews*.
10. Anderson, *Imagined*.
11. Anderson, *Imagined*, 34–35.
12. Schick, "Matbuat Kapitalizmi," 58–63; Reed, *Gutenberg*.
13. Chatterjee, *Nation*, 6.
14. Duara, *Rescuing*.
15. Jusdanis, *Necessary Nation*, 8, 18–19, 22, 34.
16. Jusdanis, *Necessary Nation*, 41.
17. Therborn, *Modernity*, xi, 4–5.
18. For example, Touraine, *Modernity*, 201–351 ("Birth of the Subject"); Taylor, *Self*; Giddens, *Self-Identity*; Sayer, *Capitalism*, 56–91 ("Power and the Subject"); and Delanty, *Modernity*.
19. Touraine, *Modernity*, 39.
20. Vahdat, *God and Juggernaut*, 2.
21. Vahdat, *God and Juggernaut*, 73.
22. Vahdat, *God and Juggernaut*, 22.
23. Jusdanis, *Necessary Nation*, 34.

24. Özyürek, *Nostalgia*, 18–19.
25. Gökalp, *TIM*; Parla, *Thought*; Parla and Davison, *Ideology*.
26. Abu-Manneh, *Studies on Islam*; Foley, "Khalid."
27. Karpat, *Politicization*, esp. 89–116.
28. Mardin, *Religion*; Vahide, *Islam*.
29. Yavuz, *Islamic Identity*.

1. THE RETURN TOWARD CENTRALIZATION

1. Aksan, *Wars*, 129–60.
2. Başbakanlık Osmanlı Arşivi (Istanbul), A.DVN. DVE (1), dos. 9, docs. 42 and 44, two registry copies of the Ottoman text of the Treaty of Küçük Kaynarca; Archivio di Stato (Venezia), Dispacci di Costantinopoli, filza 216, 109a–118b, Italian text of the treaty, following dispatch from Ambassador Polo Renier, 3 November 1774; Aksan, *Statesman*, 163–69; Hurewitz, *MENA*, 1:92–101; Druzhinina, *Mir*, 351–54; Ortaylı, *Uzun*, 139–40; Bostan, *Denizcilik*, 285–360.
3. In the Ottoman and Venetian archival copies of the treaty and in Druzhinina's Russian text, cited above, the wordings for the caliphal title are: *imam ül-mü'minin ve halifet ül-muvahhidin* (translation as quoted in the text), *supremo califo maometano*, and *verkhovnogo kalifa magometanskogo zakona* ("supreme caliph of the Mahometan law").
4. In the Ottoman and Italian archival copies of the treaty and in Druzhinina's Russian text, cited above, the terms referring to this church were: *kenisa-yı avam olub Rusograka kenisası tabiriyle tesmiye* ("a public church known as the Russo-Greek church"), *chiesa . . . publica Russo-greca chiamata* ("public church called Russo-Greek"), and *publichnuiu grekorossiiskogo ispovedaniia tserkov* ("public church of the Greek-Russian confession"); thanks to David Hoffmann and Miroljub Ruzic for assistance with the Russian references.
5. Aksan, *Wars*, 160–70; Aksan, *Statesman*, 170–84; Faroqhi, *LOE*, 292–97 (Eldem, "Capitulations").
6. Şanizade, *Tarih*, 2:99–100; Cevdet, *Tarih*, 10:19, 11:273.
7. Cole, *Napoleon*, 24, 53–56, 93–105; Hathaway, *Households*, 17–31; Hathaway, *Arab Lands*, chs. 5, 10.
8. Aksan, *Wars*, 229–37; Shaw, *Old and New*, 257–62; Jelavich, *Balkans*, 118–19.
9. Cole, *Napoleon*, 30–34, 75, 79–81, 101–10, 134–42, 146–48, 159–60, 166–67, 173–80, 187–98, 200, 219, 227–29; al-Boustany, *Journals*, 9:60, 87, 122, 125, 129, 141, 161, 178, 199–221.
10. Al-Jabarti, *Napoleon*, trans. Moreh, 3–15, 67–71, 83–84, 106–11.
11. Brown, *International*, the pioneering analysis of this pattern.
12. Hodgson, *Venture*, 64–69, 91–93.
13. Faroqhi, *LOE*, 135–56 (Khoury, "Provincial Power-Holders"), 157–85 (Adanır, "Balkans and Anatolia"), 186–206 (Masters, "Arab Provinces"); Aksan, *Wars*, 215–24; Hathaway, *Arab Lands*, ch. 5; Meeker, *Nation*.
14. Meeker, *Nation*, esp. 24–26, 170–72.
15. Faroqhi, *LOE*, 143 (Khoury, "Provincial Power Holders"), 197–202 (Masters, "Arab Provinces").

16. Meeker, Nation, xx–xxi, 24–39, 147–52, 176–81, 185–50, 240–47.

17. Beydilli, Mühendishâne, 23–94; Sabev, Müteferrika; Mantran, ed. HEO, 422–24 (Mantran, "Débuts de la Question d'Orient"); Levy, "Military," 6–26.

18. Aksan, Wars, 193–95; Beydilli, Mühendishâne; Shaw, Old and New, 86–166; Levy, "Military," 27–44.

19. Aksan, Wars, 184–85, 195–97.

20. Güran, Tarım, 15–42.

21. Çadırcı, Anadolu, 18–19, 25–36, 81–82, 113–16.

22. Findley, Bureaucratic, 120–25, 126–32.

23. Cevdet, Tarih, 6:221; Karal, Selim, 43–44.

24. Galip, Beauty, xviii–xix; Holbrook, Shores, 108–12.

25. Aksan, Wars, 241–52; Shaw, Old and New, 378–83.

26. Cevdet, Tarih, 8:357–59.

27. Mantran, HEO, 436–39 (Mantran, "Débuts"); Levy, "Military," 48–56; Cevdet, Tarih, 9:278–83.

28. Cevdet, Tarih, 9:278–283, including twenty-five signature blocks, each beginning with an Arabic phrase identifying the signer as al-muta'ahhid bi-ma fihi (one who is obligated by or maintains the contents) or other equivalent phrase containing the term muta'ahhid; Kili and Şeref Gözübüyük, Anayasa, 3–7, text without the signature lines; Aksan, Wars, 261–65; Shaw and Shaw, HOEMT, 2–3.

29. Mantran, HEO, 440–41 ("Débuts"); Aksan, Wars, 282–85; Palairet, Balkan, 85–88; Ortaylı, Uzun, 47–69.

30. Khoury, Mosul, 167, 170, 173–74; Aksan, Wars, 191 (Canikli Ali Paşa of Trabzon); Litvak, Scholars, 135–49; Levy, "Military," 89–92.

31. Jelavich, Balkans, 204–29; Aksan, Wars, 285–88; Fleming, Muslim Bonaparte.

32. Findley, Civil, 70–80; Bouquet, Les pachas, 32–37; Aksan, Wars, 238, 306–7; Levy, "Military," 185, 226–41, 314, 382, 460–79, 543; Fahmy, Men, 56–57, 66, 79–81, 272–73, 285–305.

33. Levy, "Military," 89–121.

34. Fahmy, Men, 1–37, 52.

35. Fahmy, Men, 76–111.

36. Fahmy, Men, 89–111, 226–63; Tucker, Women, 132–46.

37. Aksan, Wars, 288–99.

38. Levy, "Military," 122–71; Cevdet, Tarih, 12:158; Aksan, Wars, 313–28.

39. Faroqhi, Bektaschi, 107–27; Alkan, "Hacı Bektaş."

40. Heinzelmann, Militärpflicht, 47–114; Moreau, Militaire, 23–24, 52–58; Şimşek, "Recruitment," 30–40, 56–79; Erdem, "Recruitment," 189–206; Yaramış and Güneş, eds., Askerî.

41. Aksan, Wars, 334–36, 380–83; Shaw and Shaw, HOEMT, 2:43; Levy, "Military," 242–358, 375–76, 545–89, 595–600, 617–41; Moreau, Militaire, 60–72.

42. Findley, Civil, 22–26; Findley, Bureaucratic, 146–47; Lutfi, Tarih, 5:132–33, 180–81.

43. Mantran, HEO, 455–56 (Mantran, "Débuts").

44. Çadırcı, Anadolu, 15–23, 38–40.

45. Çadırcı, Anadolu, 38–39, 44–50, 63–72; Behar, Neighborhood, 79, 96–97, 120–29.

46. Çadırcı, *Anadolu*, 73–78.

47. Levy, "Military," 457–60.

48. Seyitdanlıoğlu, *Meclis-i Vâlâ*, 35–39.

49. Issawi, *EHMENA*, 19; İnalcık and Quataert, *ESHOE*, 764, 825–26 (Quataert, "Age of Reforms"); İnalcık, art. "Imtiyazat," *EI2*, www.encislam.brill.nl.

50. Abu-Manneh, *Studies*, 73–97 ("The Islamic Roots of the Gülhane Rescript").

51. Lutfi, *Tarih*, 6:61–65. If one numbers the lines on these pages from top to bottom, the decree refers to *kavanin-i şer'iye* on p. 61, ll. 5, 9, 14; p. 63, ll. 9, 27; and p. 64, l. 3. In other references to the laws that will be required to implement the decree, they are referred to twice as "necessary" (*muktaziye*, p. 61, l. 24; p. 63, l. 22) and once each as "high" (*münife*, p. 61, l. 12), "new" (*cedide*, p. 61, l. 23), "compulsory" (*icabiye*, p. 62, l. 25), "regulatory" (*nizamiye*, p. 63, ll. 6–7), and "established" (*müessese*, p. 64, l. 15).

52. Abu-Manneh, *Studies*, 93–96 ("Islamic Roots").

53. Lutfi, *Tarih*, 6:62. Strikingly, the philosophical argumentation is concentrated in one part of the decree, mostly on p. 62 in Lutfi. Of the decree's thirteen references to "laws" (*kavanin-i şer'iye* and variants), only one appears on p. 62. The use of plain Turkish verbs (*ısınmak, uğraşmak*) in the philosophical passages and the absence of references to law suggest that the philosophical part of the decree may have had a different author. The philosophical content resembles the thinking of Mustafa Reşid's associate, Sadık Rifat, discussed below, although the literary style of his published works is more elaborate.

54. Faroqhi, *LOE*, 253–54 (Zilfi, "Muslim Women").

55. Findley, *Civil*, 25–26, 30, 32, 51, 63, 69–80.

56. Aksan, *Wars*, 299, 343–44; McCarthy, *Death*, 31–35; Swietochowski, *Azerbaijan*, 1–12.

57. Fahmy, *Men*, 273–75, 288–89; Levy, "Military," 642–49; Hurewitz, *MENA*, 1:252–53.

58. Fahmy, *Men*, 288, n. 32.

59. Fahmy, *Men*, 288–305; Hurewitz, *MENA*, 1:268, 271–78; İnalcık, "Husrev Paşa," *İA*, 5:614–16.

60. Fahmy, *Men*, 80, 269–75; Levy, "Military," 385–92, 608–17.

61. Aksan, *Wars*, 427–29 (Ömer Paşa, born Michael Lattas of Croatia); Nazır, *Mülteciler*, 81–87, 186–90 (examples among post-1848 Hungarian and Polish refugees).

62. Pamuk, *Monetary*, 170–71.

63. Palairet, *Balkan*, 54–55; Faroqhi, *LOE*, 356–75 (Faroqhi, "Declines and Revivals").

64. Genç, *Ekonomi*, 43–96; İnalcık and Quataert, *EHSOE*, 44–54 (İnalcık, "Economic Mind"); Faroqhi, *LOE*, 307–8 (Eldem, "Capitulations").

65. Genç, *Ekonomi*, 49, 92, "kadim olan odur ki onun evvelini kimse hatırlamaz."

66. Genç, *Ekonomi*, 196–202.

67. İnalcık and Quataert, *ESHOE*, 188–204 (İnalcık, "International Trade"); Faroqhi, *LOE*, 292–97 (Eldem, "Capitulations"); İnalcık, art. "Imtiyâzât." *EI2*, www.encislam. brill.nl.

68. Genç, *Ekonomi*, 126, 229; Tabakoğlu, *Maliye*, 129–35.

69. Doumani, *Palestine*, 102.

70. Genç, *Ekonomi*, 211–25, 235.

71. Pamuk, *Monetary*, 188–204.
72. Times of London, *Atlas*, xxviii–xxix and pl. 5; Hütteroth and Höhfeld, *Türkei*, 230–31.
73. Doumani, *Palestine*, 33, citing Fernand Braudel.
74. Tabak, *Waning*.
75. Palairet, *Balkan*, 59, 60–61, 64–65, 93–94, 98–103, 106–8, 143–44; Faroqhi, *LOE*, 376–90 (Faroqhi, "Rural Life"); İnan, *Öykü*, 2:19–20, treelessness near Eskişehir in Anatolia; İnalcık and Quataert, *ESHOE*, 853 (Quataert, "Agriculture"), lack of trees in Anatolia and Arab provinces.
76. İnalcık and Quataert, *ESHOE*, 864 (Quataert, "Agriculture").
77. Cuno, *Peasants*, 64–84, Faroqhi, *LOE*, 381–83 (Faroqhi, "Rural Life"); İnalcık and Quataert, *ESHOE*, 854–56, 861–85 (Quataert, "Agriculture"); Hathaway, *Arab Lands*, ch. 8.
78. Doumani, *Palestine*, 135–49.
79. Palairet, *Balkan*, 158 (twelve peasant revolts in Bulgaria, 1835–1876), 162; Çadırcı, *Anadolu*, 26–29, 30–32, 35–36, 82–85; Meeker, *Nation*, 245 (no more rebellions in the province of Trabzon after 1834).
80. Genç, *Ekonomi*, 293–307; İnalcık and Quataert, *ESHOE*, 890–98 (Quataert, "Manufacturing"); Faroqhi, *LOE*, 336–55 (Faroqhi, "Guildsmen").
81. İnalcık and Quataert, *ESHOE*, 699–702, 704–7 (McGowan, "Merchants and Craftsmen"); Faroqhi, *LOE*, 346–47, 352–54 (Faroqhi, "Guildsmen").
82. Genç, *Ekonomi*, 229–32.
83. Genç, *Ekonomi*, 237–64; Levy, "Military," 518–36.
84. Genç, *Ekonomi*, 232–34.
85. Doumani, *Palestine*, 57–61.
86. Palairet, *Balkan*, 54–57, 66–81, 157–63.
87. Cuno, *Peasants*, 104, 136–37; Doumani, *Palestine*, 97–102; Fahmy, *Men*, 10–11, 129, 185–88, 291–95; Zahlan, *Science*, 18–20; Zahlan, "Impact," 31–58.
88. Cuno, *Peasants*, 136–37; Fahmy, *Men*, 293.
89. Mantran, *HEO*, 353 (Raymond, "Provinces arabes"); Findley, *Civil*, 22; Aksan, *Wars*, 345–46.
90. Palairet, *Balkan*, 6, 20; İnalcık and Quataert, *ESHOE*, 646–55 (McGowan, "Population"); Karpat, *Population*, 18–24, 109–16.
91. Karpat, *Population*, 45–77; McCarthy, *Death*, esp. 135–36; İnalcık and Quataert, *ESHOE*, 647–50 (McGowan, "Population").
92. İnalcık and Quataert, *ESHOE*, 652–55 (McGowan, "Population"), 781 (Quataert, "Population"); Palairet, *Balkan*, 25–33; Raymond, *Villes*, 62–66; Issawi, *EHMENA*, 100–103.
93. Fahmy, *Men*, 260–62; Cuno, *Peasants*, 72–76, 124, 176; Levy, "Military," 595–600; Lutfi, *Tarih*, 5:135–36; İnalcık and Quataert, *ESHOE*, 790 (Quataert, "Age of Reforms").
94. İnalcık and Quataert, *ESHOE*, 787–90 (Quataert, "Age of Reforms"); Aksan, *Wars*, 352–56.
95. Masters, *Christians and Jews*, 33, 126–29; Hathaway, *Arab Lands*, chs. 7, 9.
96. Masters, *Christians and Jews*, 61–65, 98–111.

97. Ülgener, *Ahlâk*, 17, 202; Meeker, *Nation*, 24–25, 172 (Janissary factions); Çadırcı, *Anadolu*, 40, 97–98 (medrese students); Anastassiadou, *Salonique*, 74–75 (urban quarters, religiously mixed or not).

98. Ülgener, *Ahlâk*, 45, 68, 96, 171, 177.

99. Findley, "Ratib," 41–80; Findley, "Writer," 23–57.

100. Tucker, *Law*, esp. 179–86; Faroqhi, *LOE*, 238–55 (Zilfi, "Women"); Hathaway, *Arab Lands*, ch. 9.

101. Ali Rıza Bey, *İstanbul Hayatı*, 1, "Karnı burnunda olursa gebedir, burnu karnında olursa ebedir"; both this work (pp. 1–11) and Abdülaziz, *Âdet*, 1:2–32, contain information about childbirth. On physicians' access to harems, d'Ohsson, *Tableau*, 2:200, 3:286; Georgeon, *Abdulhamid*, 144.

102. Abu-Manneh, *Studies*, 41, 61–63. In Turkish, Khalid becomes Halid, Khalidiyya-Naqshbandiyya becomes Halidiye-Nakşibendiye, and so on. The context of this book favors Turkish usage; however, the frequency of religious terms and Iraqi and Syrian references favors Arabic usage in this section.

103. Foley, "Khalid," 86; cf. Abu-Manneh, "New Look," 282.

104. Abu-Manneh, "New Look," 279–314 (quotation, 293).

105. Ulutaş, "Naqshbandiyya"; Abu-Manneh, "New Look," 288–93; Bruinessen, *Agha*, 24–25, 228–31.

106. Lifchez, ed., *Dervish*, 209–27 (Algar, "Devotional"); Abu-Manneh, *Studies*, 31–40.

107. Bruinessen, *Agha*, 224–28; Lifchez, *Dervish*, 222–24 (Algar, "Devotional").

108. Abu-Manneh, *Studies*, 43–51, 66–71; Abu-Manneh, "New Look," 303–4; Lifchez, *Dervish*, 211–12 (Algar, "Devotional"); Foley, "Khalid," 209ff.; Alkan, "Hacı Bektaş."

109. Berkes, *Development*, 23–85; Findley, *Bureaucratic*, 118–19, 130–32.

110. Findley, "État," 39–50; Findley, "Siyasal," 1195–202.

111. Findley, "Ratib," 41–80; Findley, "Writer," 23–57.

112. Cole, *Napoleon*, 156–57; Aksan, *Statesman*, 70–71, 84, 199–205.

113. Mardin, *Genesis*, 201 and ch. 6; Findley, "État," 39–50; Findley, "Siyasal," 1195–202.

114. Findley, "État," 49; Findley, "Siyasal," 1201: Sadık Rifat's term for "governmental law" is *hukuk-i hükumet*. In going on to name the two categories, he appears to have repeated the word *hükumet* (government) where he meant *hukuk* (law): "particular, independent government" (*hükumet-i müstakille-i hususiye*) and "general, common government" (*hükumet-i müştereke-i umumiye*). My translation amends these designations to refer to two types of *law*.

2. THE TANZIMAT

1. Davison, *Reform*, 90.

2. Mantran, *HEO*, 500–522 (Dumont, "La période des *Tanzîmât*").

3. Greene, *Shared*, 201–9; Kostopoulou, "Crete."

4. Makdisi, *Sectarianism*, 28–37; Fawaz, *Beirut*, 41–42, 48–60.

5. Makdisi, *Sectarianism*, 11.

6. Makdisi, *Sectarianism*, 96–145 (quoted expression on 105).

7. Makdisi, *Sectarianism*, 146–65; Hurewitz, *MENA*, 1:344–49.

8. Khoury, *Notables*, 8–52.
9. Palairet, *Balkan*, 129–35, 157–65; Aksan, *Wars*, 425–31; Ortaylı, *Uzun*, 146, 192–93; Nazır, *Mülteciler*.
10. Mantran, *HEO*, 505–9 (Dumont, "Tanzîmât").
11. Aksan, *Wars*, 449–77.
12. Hurewitz, *MENA*, 1:319–22, art. 7.
13. Georgeon, *Abdulhamid*, 48–53.
14. Mantran, *HEO*, 515–22 (Dumont, "Tanzîmât"); Jelavich, *Balkans*, 352–61.
15. Pamuk, *Monetary*, 217; Georgeon, *Abdulhamid*, 71–78; Rumpf, *Rechtsstaatsprinzip*, 45–48.
16. Georgeon, *Abdulhamid*, 71–89; Grant, "Sword," 16.
17. Hurewitz, *MENA*, 1:411–14; Georgeon, *Abdulhamid*, 101–6.
18. Holt and Steppat, art. "Misr," parts 7c and 7d, in *EI2*, www.encislam.brill.nl; Hurewitz, *MENA*, 1:391–94; Cole, *'Urabi*; Owen, *World Economy*, 122–35.
19. Cole, *'Urabi*, 110–32; Hanssen, *Beirut*, 5–8, 163–89, 213–35.
20. Georgeon, *Abdulhamid*, 31–35.
21. Findley, *Bureaucratic*, 163–67.
22. Bouquet, *Les pachas*, esp. 21–31; Shaw and Shaw, *HOEMT*, 2:61–71; Ortaylı, *Uzun*, 179–93.The name *Âli* should not be confused with the more common *Ali*. Two different forms from the same Arabic root, both are common adjectives that also serve as proper names and have overlapping meanings of "high, tall, sublime, exalted, excellent." However, *Ali* is a personal name (*isim*) given to boys in honor of the Prophet Muhammad's son-in-law. In contrast, *Âli* is an acquired name (*mahlas*), either assumed as a pen name or conferred by someone else, such as a teacher, in recognition of talent or accomplishment. The grand vezir in question was Mehmed Emin Âli Paşa. Mehmed Emin is his personal name, Âli his mahlas.
23. Findley, *Civil*, 22–23, 131–210, 212–18; Bouquet, *Les pachas*, esp. xxvii.
24. Aksan, *Wars*, 378, 408–10; Ortaylı, *Uzun*, 97–102, 145–52; Mantran, *HEO*, 478–81 (Dumont, "Tanzîmât").
25. Ergin, *Maarif*, 2:264–676; Akyüz, *Eğitim*, 137–93; Somel, *Education*; Findley, *Civil*, 131–73.
26. Göçek, *Bourgeoisie*, 45–46.
27. Kramers, art. "Tanzimat," *EI1*, 8:656; Young, *Corps*, 1:xii; Ortaylı, *Uzun*, 179–80.
28. Saraçoğlu, "Vidin," 83–84 (ch. 2.2), 310 (bibliography): legal volumes (*Düstur*) were published in 1863, 1866, and sequentially after 1872.
29. Kili and Gözübüyük, *Anayasa*, 14–18.
30. Mantran, *HEO*, 497–500 (Dumont, "Tanzîmât").
31. Davison, *Reform*, 114–35; Jelavich, *Balkans*, 295–97; Findley, *Bureaucratic*, 224–27.
32. Devereux, *First*, 60–79; Davison, *Reform*, 358–408; Georgeon, *Abdulhamid*, 68–71.
33. İnalcık and Quataert, *ESHOE*, 856–61 (Quataert, "Age of Reforms"); Ortaylı, *Uzun*, 137; Çadırcı, *Anadolu*, 283.
34. Kili and Gözübüyük, *Anayasa*, 29–30.
35. Ortaylı, *Uzun*, 76–80; Findley, *Bureaucratic*, 163–65.
36. Findley, *Bureaucratic*, 167–90; Çakır, *Maliye*, 35–76; Çadırcı, *Anadolu*, 185–90.

37. Toledano, *Abolition*, 10–11, 32–37, 81–111; Toledano, *Suppression*; Toledano, *Silent*; Çadırcı, *Anadolu*, 254–72, 360–71; Çakır, *Maliye*, 24–33; Aksan, *Wars*, 408–14, 477–80; Ortaylı, *Uzun*, 115–32; Mantran, *HEO*, 481–83 (Dumont, "Tanzîmât"); Shaw and Shaw, *HOEMT*, 2:91–95; Kayalı, *Arabs*, 32 (telegraph reached Baghdad by 1861).

38. Aksan, *Wars*, 416–22, 427–31.

39. Çakır, *Maliye*, 41–47, 101–30, 285–300; Çadırcı, *Anadolu*, 208–18.

40. İnalcık, *Tanzimat*; Uzun, *Tanzimat*.

41. Kütükoğlu, "Temettü," 395–417; Kayoko and Aydın, eds., *Temettuat*.

42. Çakır, *Maliye*, 50–56, 130–40; Çadırcı, *Anadolu*, 212–18, 343–48.

43. Çadırcı, *Anadolu*, 22–23, 199–202, 208–48.

44. Litvak, *Scholars*, 157–60; Marufoğlu, *Irak*, 95.

45. Çadırcı, *Anadolu*, 249–78; Bingöl, *Yargı*; Findley, "Evolution," 3–29; Davison, *Reform*, 136–71; Anastassiadou, *Salonique*, 137–40.

46. Jusdanis, *Necessary Nation*, 19: "nationalist thought . . . added the prerogative of collective difference to the already established list of individual freedoms."

47. Davison, *Reform*, 118.

48. Davison, *Reform*, 120–35; Devereux, *First*, 259; Adanır and Bonwetsch, eds., *Osmanismus*, 153–64 (Safrastyan, "Die armenischen Liberalen").

49. Lutfi, *Tarih*, 6:62; Doumani, *Palestine*, 176.

50. Mardin, *Genesis*, 189 (Sadık Rifat Paşa), 273–74 (İbrahim Şinasi), 327–29 (Namık Kemal); Özön, *İbret*, esp. 104, 107.

51. Ortaylı, *Uzun*, 90.

52. Banarlı, *Edebiyat*, 2:748–49, 770–71, on Selim III; no index entry for any subsequent sultan; Georgeon, *Abdulhamid*, 34, 142; Aracı, *Donizetti Paşa*.

53. İnal, *Şairler*. This biographical encyclopedia, about late Ottoman "poets" according to its title, is actually the most extensive biographical source on late Ottoman bureaucrats, most of whom wrote poems only incidentally.

54. İnal, *Şairler*, 1018–20; Mardin, *Genesis*, 124–27, 257–59.

55. Mardin, *Genesis*, 10–56; Findley, *Bureaucratic*, 212–18.

56. Findley, "Advent," 153–55.

57. Mardin, *Genesis*, 360–84; Çelik, *Ali Suavi*.

58. Namık Kemal, *Makalat*, 165–75 ("Wa-Shawirhum fi'l-Amri"); Mardin, *Genesis*, 287–323; Findley, "Advent," 149–50; Çakır, *Maliye*, 177–215; Özön, *İbret*.

59. Mardin, *Genesis*, 284, 319–20, 326–32.

60. Ortaylı, *Uzun*, 178.

61. Palairet, *Balkan*, 47.

62. Güran, *Tarım*, 174, 207; Palairet, *Balkan*, 48; Khater, *Home*, 20–21; Hanssen, *Beirut*, 142.

63. Çakır, *Maliye*, 24–33, 55–76; Çadırcı, *Anadolu*, 254–72, 360–71; Aksan, *Wars*, 408–14, 477–80; Ortaylı, *Uzun*, 115–32; Mantran, *HEO*, 481–83 (Dumont, "Tanzîmât"); Shaw and Shaw, *HOEMT*, 2:91–95.

64. Pamuk, *Monetary*, 188–230.

65. Pamuk, *Monetary*, 200–204, 211–24; Hulkiender, *Zarifi*; Eldem, *Bank*; Autheman, *Bank*.

66. Mantran, *HEO*, 518–19 (Dumont, "Tanzîmât").

67. Findley, art. "Maliye," *EI2*, 6:288.

68. Güran, *Tarım*, 58.

69. Güran, *Tarım*, 54–59, 63–73, 83–84, 112–27; İnalcık and Quataert, *ESHOE*, 864–65 (Quataert, "Age of Reforms").

70. Palairet, *Balkan*, 43–44, 46; Güran, *Tarım*, 56, 96, 123.

71. Doumani, *Palestine*, 135–49; Güran, *Tarım*, 131–44; Palairet, *Balkan*, 43; Rogan, *Frontiers*, 109.

72. Güran, *Tarım*, 63–127.

73. Güran, *Tarım*, 148–59.

74. İnalcık and Quataert, *ESHOE*, 856–61 (Quataert, "Age of Reforms"); Rogan, *Frontiers*, 82–94; Bruinessen, *Agha*, 182–85; Reilly, *Hama*, 93–134; Litvak, *Scholars*, 159; Marufoğlu, *Irak*, 85–103.

75. Pamuk, *Monetary*, 220; Palairet, *Balkan*, 42–43; Mantran, *HEO*, 493–97 (Dumont, "Tanzîmât").

76. İnalcık and Quataert, *ESHOE*, 834–41 (Quataert, "Age of Reforms").

77. İnalcık and Quataert, *ESHOE*, 888–933 (Quataert, "Age of Reforms"); Quataert, *Manufacturing*; Palairet, *Balkan*, 50–57, 66–84, 139–42, 157–69.

78. Khater, *Inventing*, 26–31; Quataert, *Manufacturing*, 116–33.

79. Palairet, *Balkan*, 72–76 (quotation on 72), 80.

80. Doumani, *Palestine*, 159–64, 208.

81. Doumani, *Palestine*, 182–232; Rogan, *Frontiers*, 28–29, 37.

82. Doumani, *Palestine*, 179.

83. İnalcık and Quataert, *ESHOE*, 779 (Quataert, "Population").

84. Issawi, *EHMENA*, 94–95; Palairet, *Balkan*, 20, table 1.9.

85. Mantran, *HEO*, 487 (Dumont, "Tanzîmât"); Fawaz, *Beirut*, 2, 28–60; Issawi, *EHMENA*, 101.

86. McCarthy, *Death*, 23–58.

87. Çakır, *Kadın*, 22–25; Cole, *'Urabi*, 110–32; Hanssen, *Beirut*, 162–89, 213–35; Hanioğlu, *Brief History*, 94–103.

88. Mardin, *Genesis*, 252–75; Ebüzziya, *Şinasi*, 350–51; Şinasi, *Wedding*; Şinasi, *Şair*; Banarlı, *Edebiyat*, 858–68, 1003.

89. Makdisi, *Sectarianism*, shaykhs and ahali in Lebanon; Khoury, "Quarters," 507–40 (*qabaday* and *zgriti*); Litvak, *Scholars*, 10, 119–26, 135–44 (the notables and the "gangs"—*Zukurd* and *Shumurt*—of Najaf and Karbala). Both *zgriti* and *zukurd* appear to derive from the Turkish *züğürt* (poor, destitute). Qabaday (Arabic plural, *qabadayat*) derives from Turkish *kaba*, "rough, crude," plus *dayı*, "maternal uncle."

90. Göçek, *Bourgeoisie*, 3, 45, 138.

91. İnalcık and Quataert, *ESHOE*, 837–41 (Quataert, "The Age of Reforms"); Masters, *Christians and Jews*, 141–45; Fawaz, *Beirut*, 85–120.

92. Khalid, *Politics*; Kırımlı, *Crimean Tatars*; Swietochowski, *Azerbaijan*, 25–67.

93. Keddie, *Iran*, 58–72, 123–31, 214–39; Abrahamian, *Iran*, 73–74, 81–85, 267–80, 501–29.

94. Karpat, *Politicization*, 390.

95. Akyüz, *Ziya*; Ortaylı, *Uzun*, 86; Çadırcı, *Anadolu*, 254–72, 324–30; Doumani, *Palestine*, 165–81, 216–32; Khoury, *Urban Notables*, 17, 23; Litvak, *Scholars*, 159, 161–64; Kayalı, *Arabs*, 35; Meeker, *Nation*, 11, 29–39, 210–13, ayans as created or shaped by the state.

96. Parla, *Thought*, 109–10, identifying this "myth of 'a bourgeoisie created by the state'" with the Committee of Union and Progress and Kemalist nationalism, but not with Ziya Gökalp.

97. The terms for the five sections of a kaside are *nesib, gürizgâh, medhiye, fahriye,* and *dua.* Andrews, *Introduction*, 146–59; Göçgün, *Namık Kemâl*, 7–10 (numbers in parentheses in the text are the numbers of the couplets in the kaside).

98. Tanpınar, *Tarih*, 595; Atay, *Çankaya*, 31.

99. Tanpınar, *Tarih*, 331; Namık Kemal, *İntibah* [1993], 9; Namık Kemal, *İntibah* [1875]. Page references inserted in the text in parentheses refer to the 1993 edition unless otherwise indicated.

100. Parla, *Babalar*, 51–77, 87–99; And, *Culture*, 112, noting that spendthrift sons were also stock characters in professional storyteller (*meddah*) narratives.

101. Abdülaziz, *Âdet*, 341–42 (prostitutes), 390–94 (dancing boys).

102. Here I disagree with Parla, *Babalar*, esp. 23–50, about the coherence or hegemonic role of an Islamic epistemology in controlling innovation. On the prevalence of boy-meets-girl plots, a letter from novelist and journalist Ahmed Midhat to the first female Ottoman novelist, Fatma Aliye, is indicative: "As everyone knows, in a novel, it is essential to have a hero. The hero also has a heroine. . . . In the first chapter, they get to know each other."(Atatürk Kitaplığı, Istanbul, Fatma Aliye Papers, 14/217, from Ahmed Midhat, 11 Kanun-ı evvel 1309/23 December 1893: "malumdur ki bir romanda bir «hero» [*héro*] bulunmak esasdir. O heronun bir de heroini [*héroïne*] bulunur. . . . Bab yahut kısm-ı evvelde «hero ve heroinin kesb-i muarefeleri»").

103. Banarlı, *Edebiyat*, 2:1210 (Reşat Nuri Güntekin's childhood memories of his mother's friends gathering on winter evenings to read novels, including Fatma Aliye's *Udi*); Halide Edib, *Ateşten Gömlek*, 152 (near the front, off-duty drivers gather to listen to readings from translated novels by Xavier de Montepin; Halide Edib "quotes"— parodies—the inflated language of the translations, in contrast to her direct style).

104. Namık Kemal, *İntibah* [1875?], 130.

105. This is one of many literary examples illustrative of Ottoman attitudes toward elite forms of slavery: Toledano, *Abolition*, 112–34; Parlatır, *Kölelik*.

106. Abdülaziz, *Âdet*, 336.

107. Compare the end of act 4, scene 7, in Alexandre Dumas Fils, *La dame aux camélias* (Borgerhoff, ed., *Plays*, 410) and Giuseppe Verdi's *La Traviata*, act 2, where Alfredo throws money at Violetta.

108. Abdülaziz, *Âdet*, 337, public letter-writing as a role in which men ruined by drink ended up.

109. Okay, "İntibah," 133–36.

110. Mardin, "Super Westernization," 403–46; Findley, *Civil*, 174–79, 187–95; Parla, *Babalar*, 129–53.

111. Borgerhoff, *Plays*, 415, from the closing words in *La dame aux camélias*.
112. [Namık] Kemal, *Müntahabat*, 90–98, "Terbiye-i Nisvan Hakkında bir Layihadir ki . . . ,"
originally published in *Tasvir-i Efkar*, no. 457, 4 Şevval 1283/February 1867; Özön,
İbret, 95–99, "Maarif," originally published 4 July 1872; Ulutaş, "Namık Kemal."
113. Namık Kemal, *Vatan* [1889], 13, 109, 151 (references to *murad*), unless otherwise
specified, page references are to this edition); Namık Kemal, *Vatan* [1993]; Mardin,
Genesis, 67, 331; Tanpınar, *Tarih*, 339, 362–65; And, *Tanzimat*, 102–4, 113–52; Banarlı,
Edebiyat, 1003–4; Davison, *Reform*, 298–301.
114. Namık Kemal, *Vatan* [1889], 36: "Mümkün olsa bütün vatan kardeşlerime şu zayıf
vücudümü siper edeceğim"; Namık Kemal, *Vatan* [1993], 26: "Müslüman olan bütün
vatan kardeşlerime."
115. Çınar, "Transformation," 474.

3. THE REIGN OF ABDÜLHAMID

1. Pamuk, *Capitalism*, 209; Georgeon, *Abdulhamid*, 119; Mantran, *HEO*, 523–25 (Georgeon, "Le dernier sursaut"); Jelavich, *Balkans*, 352–61.
2. Georgeon, *Abdulhamid*, 29–31, 165–69.
3. Georgeon, *Abdulhamid*, 232, 335–38, 413; Kostopoulou, "Crete."
4. Karpat, *Politicization*, 258–75.
5. Brown, *Tunisia*; Abun-Nasr, *Maghrib*, 272–97. Compare Ahmed Midhat, *Müşahedat*, 292–94 (heroine Siranuş, born of an Armenian mother, learns that father was a Tunisian naval officer of Turkish heritage); Tanpınar, *Saatleri Ayarlama Enstitüsü*, 39–42 (Abdüsselâm Bey, an Istanbul gentleman of Tunisian background, whose large household formed a microcosm of the empire, until both disintegrated together).
6. Karpat, *Politicization*, 217.
7. Hourani, *Arab Peoples*, 284; Anscombe, *Gulf*; Cleveland, *Middle East*, 102, 117–18; Georgeon, *Abdulhamid*, 229–31.
8. Wilhite, "Yemen"; Dresch, *Tribes*, 219–24.
9. Georgeon, *Abdulhamid*, 191, 395.
10. Georgeon, *Abdulhamid*, 234–39; Pamuk, *Capitalism*, 53–54; Eldem, *Bank*, 233–40, 290–91; Autheman, *Bank*, 45–47, 160–63, 180–86, 233–36.
11. Fortna, *Classroom*, 77–78; Somel, *Education*; Rodrigue, *Alliance*.
12. Rogan, *Frontiers*, 122–59, 182–83, 200–201, 218, 244; Hanssen, *Beirut*, 180–87; Georgeon, *Abdulhamid*, 235–36, 357–61; Bruinessen, *Agha*, 229–33; Fawaz, *Beirut*, 112–20.
13. Bruinessen, *Agha*, 175–89.
14. Karpat, *Politicization*, 211.
15. Suny, *Ararat*, 24, 77–78, 94–100.
16. Bruinessen, *Agha*, 185–89; Georgeon, *Abdulhamid*, 268; Özbek, "Policing," 47–67.
17. Eldem, *Bank*, 233–39.
18. Georgeon, *Abdulhamid*, 280–81, 366–73; Anastassiadou, *Salonique*, 58–62, 387–410; Mazower, *Salonica*, esp. 252–54; Veinstein, ed., *Salonique*, esp. 65.
19. Aydemir, *Adam*, 9–22.

20. Veinstein, ed., *Salonique*, 157.
21. Findley, *Bureaucratic*, 221.
22. Georgeon and Dumont, eds., *Sociabilités*, 123–44 (Yerolympos, "Conscience citadine"); Hanssen, *Beirut.*
23. Georgeon, *Abdulhamid*, 33–34, 127–46, 481 (map).
24. *Raimondo D'Aronco in Turchia*, 30–32.
25. Personal communication from Edhem Eldem, 25 July 2002.
26. Findley, *Bureaucratic*, 227–39, 265–66.
27. Findley, *Turks*, 31–32, 47–48, 123–26, 167, 230–32; Deringil, *Domains.*
28. Karpat, *Politicization*, 121, 176–82, 241–75; Georgeon, *Abdulhamid*, 192–212.
29. Keddie, *Al-Afghani*, 373–423; Khoury, *Urban*, 37–39; Rogan, *Frontiers*, 150–59; Georgeon, *Abdulhamid*, 272; Karpat, *Politicization*, 199–203.
30. Karpat, *Politicization*, 275; Litvak, *Scholars*, 165–69.
31. Georgeon, *Abdulhamid*, 203–7, 225, 361–66; Karpat, *Politicization*, 241–57, 336; Ochsenwald, *Arabia*, 153–227; Ochsenwald, *Hijaz Railroad.*
32. Karpat, *Population*, 33–35, 122–69.
33. Findley, *Bureaucratic*, 198, 273, 285–87.
34. Rogan, *Frontiers*, 48.
35. Anastassiadou, *Salonique*, 136–200; Veinstein, ed., *Salonique*, 158–76 (Yerolympos and Colonas, "Un urbanisme cosmopolite"); Georgeon, *Abdulhamid*, 170–91, 267–70.
36. Khoury, *Urban*, 26–52; Litvak, *Scholars*, 160–69, 177–78.
37. Khoury, "Quarters"; Litvak, *Scholars*, 135–44, 158, 161–63, 184, 221, n. 28; Meeker, *Nation*; Reilly, *Hama*. On the terms used for the gangs and their leaders, see chapter 2, n. 89.
38. Veinstein, ed., *Salonique*, 34 (Moutsopoulos, "Une ville entre deux siècles"); Anastassiadou, *Salonique*, 136–57.
39. Ortaylı, *Uzun*, 120 ("tek yapılsın da isterse sırtımdan geçsin"); İnalcık and Quataert, *ESHOE*, 804–15 (Quataert, "Transportation"); Shaw and Shaw, *HOEMT*, 2:120–21, 226–27.
40. Fortna, *Classroom*, 47–48, 99–129.
41. Nakash, *Shi'is*, 25–48; Fortna, *Classroom*, 62–66.
42. Akyüz, *Eğitim*, 146, 201; Rafeq, *Al-Jami'a*, 9–38.
43. Anastassiadou, *Salonique*, 402 (quoting a French consular report); Findley, *Civil*, 132–43; Georgeon, *Abdulhamid*, 250–53, 388.
44. Wilhite, "Yemen," 16–21; Georgeon, *Abdulhamid*, 228–29, 246–50; Karpat, *Politicization*, 171–72, 192–93, 221–22, 264.
45. Karpat, *Politicization*, 264.
46. İnalcık and Quataert, *ESHOE*, 806 (Quataert, "Transportation"); Georgeon, *Abdulhamid*, 227–29.
47. Georgeon, *Abdulhamid*, 132, 342–49, 481.
48. Findley, *Civil*, 365–66; Georgeon, *Abdulhamid*, 364–65; İnalcık and Quataert, *ESHOE*, 808, 815 (Quataert, "Transportation"). The German ambassador of this period was not a military officer; Marschall was his family name: Baron Adolf Marschall von Bieberstein.

49. Touraine, *Modernity*, 39.

50. Osman Nuri, *Abdülhamid*, 2:591–92.

51. Rogan, *Frontiers*, 84.

52. Bouquet, *Les pachas*, 47–105; Findley, *Bureaucratic*, 233–35, 267–68, 274–76; Findley, *Civil*, 281–92.

53. Findley, *Civil*, 250–51.

54. Findley, *Bureaucratic*, 232, 285, 411; Georgeon, *Abdulhamid*, 257, 265.

55. Findley, *Civil*, 311–33, 343–69; Pamuk, "Prices," 451–68; Pamuk, *İstanbul*, 3–18.

56. Hanioğlu, *Brief History*, 145; Georgeon, *Abdulhamid*, 296–97, 303–4.

57. Hanioğlu, *Opposition*, 71–74, 203–5; on Latin American positivism, see Hale, *Transformation*; Woodward, ed., *Positivism*.

58. Georgeon, *Abdulhamid*, 339–42; Hanioğlu, *Opposition*, 71–101.

59. Saraçoğlu, *Mizancı*.

60. Georgeon, *Abdulhamid*, 380–84; Hanioğlu, *Opposition*, 142–216.

61. Özdalga, ed., *Late*, 28–116 (Hanioğlu, "Blueprints for a Future Society"); Hanioğlu, *Brief History*, 138–40; Poyraz, "Science."

62. Duben and Behar, *Households*, 194–238.

63. Sohrabi, "Global," 45–79.

64. Karpat, *Politicization*, 352; Sohrabi, "Global," 62–64; Georgeon, *Abdulhamid*, 393–402; Hanioğlu, *Brief History*, 147–49, 159.

65. Sohrabi, "Global," 50, 56–59.

66. Pamuk, *Monetary*, 205–22.

67. İnalcık and Quataert, *ESHOE*, 804–15 (Quataert, "Transportation," railroad map, 805); Georgeon, *Abdulhamid*, 361–66; Ochsenwald, *Hijaz Railroad*.

68. Dumont and Georgeon, eds., *Villes*.

69. İnalcık and Quataert, *ESHOE*, 824–41 (Quataert, "Commerce"); Owen, *World Economy*, 151, 176–77, 182, 241, 246–47, 250, 260, 275; Fawaz, *Beirut*, 85–120.

70. Fawaz, *Beirut*, 31, 48–50, 95–97, 118; Hanssen, *Beirut*.

71. Rogan, *Frontiers*, 95–12; Marufoğlu, *Irak*, 210–23.

72. Mantran, *HEO*, 547–50 (Georgeon, "Dernier sursaut"); İnalcık and Quataert, *ESHOE*, 843–83 (Quataert, "Agriculture"); Güran, *Tarım*, 63–159; Owen, *World Economy*, 200–209; Shaw and Shaw, *HOEMT*, 2:230–34.

73. Georgeon, *Abdulhamid*, 164–69; Özbek, *Sosyal Devlet*, 127–31; Ali Rıza, *İstanbul Hayatı*, 344.

74. İnalcık and Quataert, eds., *ESHOE*, 888–933 (Quataert, "Manufacturing"); Quataert, *Manufacturing*; Quataert, *Miners*; Quataert, *Social*.

75. Veinstein, ed., *Salonique*, 177–94 (Quataert, "Premières fumées d'usine"); Quataert, *Manufacturing*, 107–33; Anastassiadou, *Salonique*, 195–200, 338–41.

76. Findley, *Turks*, 25–26, 57, 96–99, 135–36, 235–37; Quataert, *Manufacturing*, 134–60.

77. Karpat, *Population*, 28–35, 122–151; Georgeon, *Abdulhamid*, 313–27.

78. Elon, *Israelis*, 33, 195; Mandel, *Arabs and Zionism*; Georgeon, *Abdulhamid*, 318–20.

79. Karpat, *Population*, 65–77; Karpat, *Politicization*, 341–45; Georgeon, *Akçura*; Anastassiadou, *Salonique*, 388 (identity concepts also oscillated for Macedonia's Christians).

80. Khater, *Inventing*, 48–70; Hyland, "Mahjar," ch. 1.

81. Georgeon, *Abdulhamid*, 325, "une sournoise révolution sociale."
82. Anastassiadou, *Salonique*, 190, 192–95; Hanssen, *Beirut*, 252–55.
83. Çakır, *Kadın*, 22–26; Baron, *Awakening*, 43–50; Frierson, "Unimagined Communities."
84. Mardin, "Religion and Secularism," in Hourani, Khoury, and Wilson, eds., *Modern Middle East*, 347–74; Fortna, *Classroom*, 155–63.
85. Georgeon, *Abdulhamid*, 320–24; Uşaklıgil, *Kırk Yıl*, 81–84; Fortna, *Classroom*, 67–68; Eldem, *Bank*, 275–304; Hanssen, *Beirut*.
86. Anastassiadou, *Salonique*, 361, 364.
87. Fortna, *Classroom*, 79–83 (from a memorandum on education by Mehmed Kâmil Paşa: "It is necessary to inculculate the benefits of increasing our national wealth as of old by producing in our own country better products"); Çakır, *Kadın*, 26 ("the king's highway of free enterprise," literally of "labor and work," *şâh-râh-ı sa'y-ü-amel*, citing *Şükûfezar*, no. 1, 1301/1883–1884); Findley, "Say-ü-Amel," 23–29 (Ahmed Midhat's book on free enterprise).
88. Eyice, "Gümüşhaneli," 500 (map showing relative positions of the Gümüşhaneli tekke at Fatma Sultan, the Sublime Porte, and the Public Debt's "Çiftesaraylar" site); Ulutaş, "Naqshbandiyya"; Karpat, *Politicization*, 89–116, 408–22; Bruinessen, *Agha*, 205–64.
89. Duben and Behar, *Households*, 14–15, 50, 63, 70, 92, 126–31, 143–49. They date the Istanbul data from the first Hamidian census (1881–1893) to 1885. They explain the reasons for limiting their research to the Muslims of the city on p. 8.
90. Duben and Behar, *Households*, 159–93.
91. Dumont, "Said Bey," in Hourani, Khoury, and Wilson, eds., *Modern Middle East*, 271–87; Duben and Behar, *Households*, 194–238.
92. Karakaya-Stump, "Debating," 155–81; Duben and Behar, *Households*, 194–248; Çakır, *Kadın*; Frierson, "Unimagined Communities."
93. Anastassiadou, *Salonique*, 248–53; Todorova, *Demographic*, 55, 62–65, 80–81.
94. Midhat, *Müşahedat* [1890]; Fatma Aliye, *Muhazarat*. In the following discussion, page numbers in parentheses refer to whichever novel is discussed at that point. See also Moran, *Eleştirel*, 53–65; Finn, *Novel*, 13–14; Evin, *Novel*, 90, 95–96; Parlatır, *Kölelik*, esp. 156–63; Demir, *Zaman*; Findley, "Occidentalist," 15–49.
95. Findley, "Fatma Aliye," 153–76.
96. References to Ottoman ladies' freedom in mixing European and Ottoman clothing initiate recurrent questions about women's possibilities of being free and autonomous (*hürr ve muhtar*): Fatma Aliye, *Muhazarat*, 32–33, 92, 327, 353, 396–97, 422, 429, 440, 443–44.

4. IMPERIAL DEMISE, NATIONAL STRUGGLE

1. Kasaba, ed., *TMW*, 81–82, 109–10 (Hanioğlu, "Second Constitutional Period").
2. For example, Shaw and Shaw, *HOEMT*, 340 ("war of independence"); Robinson, *Republic*, 65 ("The Ataturk Revolution"); Dodd, *Politics*, 20 ("Revolution and Republic"); Zürcher, *Turkey*, 133 ("The Struggle for Independence," title of ch. 9); cf. Sohrabi, "Global," 49.

3. For example, Adıvar, *Gömlek*, 84, 90–91, 98, 99, 101, 104, 109, 121–23 (*ihtilal*); Karaosmanoğlu, *Panorama*, 43, 44, 45, 53, 56, 62, 65, 108, 109, 111–14, 118, 121–22, 125, 148, 150, 175, 211, 215, 218, 222, 277, 301, 337, 350, 366, 484, 487, 494–96, 500, 551–53, 555–57, 572 (*inkılap*); Ağaoğlu, *İhtilal*. One social scientist who focused on the semantic issues surrounding *inkılap* is Parla, *Thought*, 82–84, discussed below. On the impact of this semantic confusion on Leftist thought, see Schick and Tonak, eds., *Transition*, 151 (Samim, "The Left").

4. Zürcher, *Turkey*, 93–103; Göçek, "Meaning"; Mantran, ed., *HOE*, 584–88 (Dumont and Georgeon, "La mort d'un empire"); Kayalı, *Arabs*, 52–80; Toprak, *MIMB*, 1–9; Sohrabi, "Global," 67–72; Çakır, *Kadın*, 22–78; Ahmad, *Young Turks*.

5. Kasaba, ed., *TMW*, 67 (Hanioğlu, "Second").

6. Personal communication from Steven Hyland, 2 February 2008, citing *La Nación* (Buenos Aires), 8 September 1908, 7 ("La constitución otomana—manifestación patriótica") and 9 September 1908, 6 ("La constitución otomana—la demostración de anoche"). In Latin America, "los Turcos" were mostly Syro-Lebanese, whatever their religion; Kayali, *Arabs*, 56; Brummett, *Image*; Göçek, "Meaning."

7. Poyraz, "Science," ch. 5; Bein, "Ahmed Hilmi," 607–25; Vahide, *Islam*, 50–173; Mardin, *Religion*.

8. Kasaba, *TMW*, 66 (Hanioğlu, "Second"); Göçek, "Meaning."

9. Brummett, *Image*, 60–61, 194–96, 255–57; Toprak, *Cihan Harbi*, cover design of impoverished bureaucrat in tattered uniform, adapted from a 1918 caricature by Sedat Semavi; Findley, *Bureaucratic*, 294–98; Kayalı, *Arabs*, 56–60.

10. Kayalı, *Arabs*, 72–74; Georgeon, *Abdulhamid*, 403–25.

11. Kili and Gözübüyük, *Anayasa*, 74–78; Rumpf, *Rechtsstaatsprinzip*, 49–51; Özçelik, *Meşrutiyet*.

12. Findley, *Bureaucratic*, 294–300, 310–13.

13. Boratav, *İktisat*, 21.

14. Zürcher, *Turkey*, 106–10; Mantran, *HEO*, 606–11 (Dumont and Georgeon, "Mort d'empire"); Hale, *Military*, 41–45; Göçek, "Meaning," 28.

15. Kasaba, *TMW*, 74–83 (Hanioğlu, "Second"); Zürcher, *Turkey*, 106–10.

16. Erickson, *Defeat*, 25; Erickson, *Effectiveness*.

17. Göçek, "Meaning," 24, 29–37; Stoddard, "Teşkilât-ı Mahsusa."

18. Kasaba, *TMW*, 91 (Hanioğlu, "Second"); Karpat, "Entry," 687–733; Erickson, *Ordered*, 11–12, 25–27; Toprak, *MIMB*; Aksakal, *War*; Mantran, *HEO*, 586–92 (Dumont and Georgeon, "Mort d'empire").

19. Ülker, "Turkification," 613–36.

20. Göçek and Bloxham, "Armenian," 23.

21. Quoted in Akçam, *Empire to Republic*, 95.

22. Kayalı, *Arabs*, 51, 81–115, 174–205; Visser, *Basra*, 40–47; Anscombe, *Gulf*.

23. Thompson, *Colonial*, 19–23.

24. Kayalı, *Arabs*, 140–73, 181–84; Ochsenwald, *Hijaz Railroad*; Teitelbaum, *Arabia*; Dawisha, *Arab Nationalism*, 34–35.

25. Hanioğlu, *Brief History*, 187–88; Üstel, *Türk Ocakları*, 43, 92.

26. McDowall, *Kurds*, 102–9.

27. Akçam, *Empire to Republic*, 144–49; cf. Dragostinova, "Motherlands," 152 and 188, n. 34.

28. Davison, *Essays*, 180–205; Bloxham and Göçek, "Armenian"; this was one of the infringements of Ottoman sovereignty that the CUP annulled unilaterally after entering the war.

29. Kasaba, *TMW*, 84–96 (Hanioğlu, "Second"); Clayer, *Nationalisme albanais*; Gawrych, *Crescent*; Shaw and Shaw, *HOEMT*, 287–98; Mantran, *HOE*, 580–81, 600–611; Çetinkaya, *Boykot*; Sönmez, *Arnavut*; Blumi, *Rethinking*; Wilhite, "Yemen," 421–50.

30. Erickson, *Defeat*, 72–74, 349–51; Mango, *Atatürk*, 101–11.

31. Erickson, *Defeat*; Veinstein, ed., *Salonique*, 247–53 (Lory, "1912, Les Hellènes entrent dans la ville"); Mantran, *HEO*, 604–11 (Dumont and Georgeon, "Mort d'empire"); Zürcher, *Turkey*, 106–9.

32. Erickson, *Defeat*, xvii, 1–35, 48–67, 138–46; Hale, *Military*, 41–45.

33. Erickson, *Defeat*, 344; Erickson, *Ordered*, xvi, 213–16.

34. J. C. Hurewitz, ed., *MENA*, 2:1–2, 15–16, 73–74; Sancar, *Denizcilik*, 286–92; Beşikçi, "Navy League," 100–115; Langensiepen and Güleryüz, *Steam Navy*, 27–59, 83–85, 102–5, 132, 141–42, 151; Langensiepen, Nottelmann, and Krüsmann, *Halbmond*; Fromkin, *Peace*, 54–61.

35. Mantran, *HEO*, 618–23 (Dumont and Georgeon, "Mort d'empire"); Zürcher, *Turkey*, 110–21; Erickson, *Ordered*, 15–47; Langensiepen and Güleryüz, *Steam Navy*, 44–45.

36. Erickson, *Ordered*, 51–65.

37. Aydemir, *Adam*, 71–76, to join his unit on the eastern front, he had to walk from Ulukışla near Adana.

38. Erickson, *Ordered*, 95–109, 120–37, 160–61, 179–93; Allen and Muratoff, *Caucasian*, 293–310; Mango, *Atatürk*, 161–64.

39. Aydemir, *Adam*, 111–14, the day the Russian soldiers came across the lines bringing bread and salt.

40. This topic is the academic equivalent of a battlefield where, long after the guns fell silent, anyone who ventures onto the field risks stepping on hidden land mines. Ottoman specialists' interpretations differ to the point of irreconcilability, and any attempt at summary remains subject to revision. Accounts considered here include Shaw and Shaw, *HOEMT*, 214–17; McCarthy, *Muslims and Minorities*, 47–88, 121–30; McCarthy, *Death*, 179–253; Erickson, *Ordered*, 93–104; Zürcher, *Turkey*, 114–17; Quataert, *Ottoman Empire*, 186–88; Akşin, *Turkey*, 109–10; Akçam, *Empire to Republic*; Göçek, "Turkish Historiography," 337–67; Bloxham and Göçek, "Armenian"; McCarthy, Arslan, Taşkıran, and Turan, *Van*.

41. McCarthy, *Muslims and Minorities*, 101–6, 130. Turkish official historiography claims smaller numbers of Armenian fatalities, on the order of 400,000, whereas Armenian historiography claims numbers on the order of 800,000 to 1.5 million; see Bloxham and Göçek, "Armenian."

42. Erickson, *Ordered*, 99–100; Akçam, *Empire to Republic*, 158–66; Göçek, "Meaning," 33ff.

43. Göçek, "Meaning," 33–37; Akçam, *Empire to Republic*, 158–79.

44. Hirschon, *Heirs*, 30; Quataert, *Ottoman Empire*, 174.

45. Adıvar, *Gömlek*, 15: "insaniyetin ortadan kaldırması lazım gelen insanlar bizdik."

46. Erickson, *Ordered*, 68–72; Kayalı, *Arabs*, 185–90.

47. Erickson, *Ordered*, 76–95; Erickson, *Effectiveness*; Langensiepen and Güleryüz, *Steam Navy*, 29–32; Mantran, *HOE*, 622–23 (Dumont and Georgeon, "Mort d'empire"); Mango, *Atatürk*, 140–56; Fewster, Başarın, and Başarın, *Gallipoli*.

48. Erickson, *Ordered*, 110–15, 149–53, 164–72; İhsanoğlu and Kaçar, *Çağını Yakalayan*, 524–54 (İhsanoğlu, "Osmanlı Havacılığına Genel Bir Bakış").

49. As mentioned in the Note on Usage, a law requiring Turks to adopt surnames went into effect in 1935. In referring to Turks whose active lives spanned that date, it is common practice to give the surname in brackets when referring to dates before 1935.

50. Erickson, *Ordered*, 119–20, 137–49, 151 (quotation, surrender date 29 April 1916).

51. Kayalı, *Arabs*, 183–92; Teitelbaum, *Arabia*.

52. Teitelbaum, *Arabia*, 116–25.

53. Erickson, *Ordered*, 199.

54. Erickson, *Ordered*, 179–93, 203–4 (quoted passage, 204); Hurewitz, *MENA*, 2:128–30; McDowall, *Kurds*, 109, 115–21.

55. Alexandris, *Greek Minority*, 52–76; Shaw, *Empire to Republic*, 1:147–56; Erickson, *Ordered*, 204; Mantran, *HEO*, 637–39 (Dumont and Georgeon, "Mort d'empire"); Atay, *Çankaya*, 132; Criss, *İstanbul*.

56. For the diplomatic documents discussed below, through the Treaty of Sèvres, see Hurewitz, *MENA*, 2:16–24, 46–56, 60–64, 94–96, 101–6, 128–30, 219–28. See also Mango, *Atatürk*, 197, 270, 281; Tibawi, *Anglo-Arab*, 64–100 and endpaper maps; Vasiliev, *Arabia*, 250; Smith, *Palestine*, 59–64; and McDowall, *Kurds*, 115–47.

57. Smith, *Palestine*, 66, map 3.1.

58. Possibly the only lasting effect of that treaty: Hurewitz, *MENA*, 2:113–18, 250–53; Davison, *Essays*, 215–16; Kasaba, *TMW*, 119, 127, 131, 136 (Kayalı, "Struggle"); McDowall, *Kurds*, 107.

59. Kasaba, ed., *TMW*, 130–31 (Kayalı, "Struggle").

60. As prominent a European historian as E. J. Hobsbawm has mistaken this point. Hobsbawm, *Nationalism*, 134: "In spite of various shortlived attempts to redraw the frontiers of the succession states of the Austrian and Turkish empires, they are still more or less where they ended up after World War I, at least south and west of the Soviet borders." Compare Hurewitz, *MENA*, 2:326, terming Lausanne "the only negotiated peace of World War I."

61. Kasaba, *TMW*, 119–32 (Kayalı, "Struggle"); Zürcher, *Turkey*, 134–36, 153–54, 158; Zürcher, *Unionist*, 68–105; Tunçay, *Tek-Parti Yönetimi*, 26–67; Tanör, *Kongre*; Hale, *Military*, 59–65; Göçek, "Meaning of 1908."

62. Gingeras, "Caucasian," 89–108; Atay, *Çankaya*, 231–68.

63. Zürcher, *Turkey*, 138–39, 147–52; Mango, *Atatürk*, 220–52; Zürcher, *Unionist*, 106–17.

64. Tekeli and İlkin, *Cumhuriyetin Harcı*, 1:187–98 ("Bölgesel Kurtuluş Savaşı'ndan Ulusal Kurtuluş Savaşı'na").

65. Mango, *Atatürk*, 269; Shaw, *National Liberation*, 2:803; Kasaba, ed., *TMW*, 129 (Kayalı, "Struggle").

66. Zürcher, *Turkey*, 152–56; Mantran, *HEO*, 643–47 (Dumont and Georgeon, "Mort d'empire"); Mango, *Atatürk*, 310; Hurewitz, *MENA*, 2:250–53.

67. Mango, *Atatürk*, 345–47.

68. Kasaba, *TMW*, 132–36 (Kayalı, "Struggle"); Schick and Tonak, eds., *Transition*, 149–51 (Samim, "The Left"); Tunçay, *Sol Akımlar*, 1:98–103.

69. Zürcher, *Turkey*, 156–65; Zürcher, *Unionist*, 118–37; Kasaba, *TMW*, 134–39 (Kayalı, "Struggle"); Kili and Gözübüyük, *Anayasa*, 91–93.

70. Demirel, *Muhalefet*; Frey, *Political Elite*, 306–23, 376–77.

71. Hale, *Foreign Policy*, 52–56; Hurewitz, *MENA*, 2:325–37; Kasaba, *TMW*, 141–43 (Kayalı, "Struggle").

72. Davison, *Essays*, 224–32; Kasaba, *TMW*, 142–43 (Kayalı, "Struggle").

73. Shorter, "Independence," 425; other sources give slightly different figures; Yıldırım, *Exchange*; Yıldırım, *Göç*; Hirschon, *Crossing*.

74. Palairet, *Balkan*, 111–12, 141, 163, 168, 171, on Balkan independence as associated with economic contraction rather than expansion; cf. Makdisi, *Sectarianism*, 63–69 (Lebanon in the 1840s), 139 (depression left in wake of Maronite-Druze segregation following Lebanese conflict in 1860).

75. Toprak, *MIMB*, 2–5, 23–36 (quotation from Cavid Bey, 32); Boratav, *İktisat*, 11–27.

76. Here, "national economy" in quotation marks refers to this school of economic thought; without quotation marks, the phrase refers to the economy of this or that nation. Karaömerlioğlu, "Parvus," 145–65; Parla, *Thought*, 107–16; Toprak, *MIMB*, 65–66.

77. Elmacı, *Kapitulasyonlar*; Ahmad, "Capitulations," 1–20; Toprak, *MIMB*, 37–38, 44–63.

78. Toprak, *MIMB*, 64–78.

79. Toprak, *ITD*, 51–87; Eldem, *Bank*, 305–64.

80. Toprak, *MIMB*, 79–106; Boratav, *İktisat*, 23–24; Akyıldız, *Anka*.

81. Toprak, *MIMB*, 106–11 (quoted passage, 107).

82. Toprak, *MIMB*, 111–24; Ökçün, *Sanayi*.

83. Toprak, *MIMB*, 125–44.

84. Toprak, *ITD*, 159.

85. Toprak, *ITD*, 3, 159–68; Shaw, *World War I*, vol. 1.

86. Pamuk, *Monetary*, 222–24; Toprak, *MIMB*, 46–50; Toprak, *ITD*, 6–50; Köroğlu, *Ottoman Propaganda*.

87. Toprak, *ITD*, 88–112, 121, 148–58; Toprak, *Cihan Harbi*, 151–78.

88. Tekeli and İlkin, *Cumhuriyetin Harcı*, 2:1–44 ("Osmanlı İmparatorluğu'nun Birinci Dünya Savaşı'ndaki Ekonomik Düzenlemeleri İçinde İaşe Nezareti ve Kara Kemal Bey'in Yeri").

89. Boratav, *İktisat*, 24–27.

90. Toprak, *ITD*, 113–30; Toprak, *Cihan Harbi*, 160–78; Boratav, *İktisat*, 18–20.

91. Toprak, *ITD*, 131–58; Çakır, *Kadın*; Karakışla, *Women*.

92. Shaw, *National Liberation*, 1:236–45; Thompson, *Colonial*, 15–38.

93. Majd, *Iraq*, 372–408.

94. İnalcık and Quataert, *ESHOE*, 777 (Quataert, "Age of Reforms"); Karpat, *Population*; McCarthy, *Muslims and Minorities*, 117–44; Thompson, *Colonial*, 19–30; Yanıkdağ, "Sons."

95. McCarthy, *Death*, 255–332.

96. Adıvar, *Gömlek*, 11, "yeni bir Osmanlı enmûzeci."

97. Kasaba, *TMW*, 104 (Hanioğlu, "Second"); Zürcher, *Turkey*, 121–23; Shaw and Shaw, *HOEMT*, 305–10; Berkes, *Development*, 411–28.

98. Akyüz, *Eğitim*, 237, 245.

99. Çakır, *Kadın*, 43–78; Özdalga, *Late*, 135–61 (Frierson, "Women in Late Ottoman Intellectual History"); Adıvar, *Gömlek*, 23–24, 213–15, 216–19; Criss, *İstanbul*, 44–47; Shaw, *National Liberation*, 1:289–92, 3:1070–74.

100. McCarthy, *Death*, 337–38.

101. Parla, *Thought*, 7–8, 52–56. Except as otherwise indicated, the sources for this discussion are Parla, *Thought*, and Davison, *Secularism and Revivalism*, 90–133.

102. Parla, *Thought*, 21–22; cf. Shissler, *Between*, 64–81.

103. Parla, *Thought*, 42–50. In French, trade guilds were historically referred to as *corporations de métier*.

104. Parla, *Thought*, 62–64.

105. Parla, *Thought*, 82–84, 110.

106. Gökalp, *TIM*; Davison, *Secularism and Revivalism*, 90–133; cf. Jusdanis, *Necessary Nation*, 44–70, culture and civilization, culture and nationalism.

107. Gökalp, *TIM*, 54: "Biz Türkler, çağdaş uygarlığın akıl ve bilimiyle donanmış olduğumuz halde bir 'Türk-İslâm' kültürü yaratmaya çalışmalıyız" (in this modernized version).

108. Halide Edib [Adıvar], *Clown*; Adıvar, *Sinekli Bakkal*; Adıvar, *Gömlek*; Enginün, *Halide Edib*, 18–68; Kasaba, *TMW*, 481–82 (Göknar, "The Novel in Turkish: Narrative Tradition to Nobel Prize").

109. Adıvar, *Clown*; Adıvar, *Sinekli Bakkal*.

110. Adıvar, *Gömlek*, 18, 48, 52, 64, 66, 175, 176, 190, 209, 210 (references to the "shirt of flame" theme).

111. Adıvar, *Gömlek*, 111, 121, 131, 134; cf. Gingeras, "Caucasian," 89–108.

112. My thanks to Mine Enginün for verifying my recollections about seeing both borders from the Edirne fortresses; personal communications of 2007–2008 (I was there in 1998).

5. THE EARLY REPUBLIC

1. Hale, *Foreign Policy*, 71; Hurewitz, *MENA*, 2:250–53, 368–70.

2. Zürcher, *Unionist*, 137–41; Zürcher, *Turkey*, 166–75; Uyar, *Tek Parti*, 58–78; Kili and Gözübüyük, *Anayasa*, 109–33; Rumpf, *Rechtsstaatsprinzip*, 52–65.

3. Tunçay, *Tek-Parti Yönetimi*, 99–109, 146–49; Uyar, *Tek Parti*, 99–165; Yeşil, *Terakkiperver*.

4. Hurewitz, *MENA*, 2:330 (art. 39, paras. 4–5); Zürcher, *Turkey*, 169–72; Bruinessen, *Agha*, 270–99; Heper, *Kurds*, 147–55, 158–60; Natali, *Kurds*, 70–91; McDowall, *Kurds*, 137–47, 184–211.

5. Kasaba, ed., *TMW*, 338–42 (Bozarslan, "Kurds and the Turkish State"); Tunçay, *Tek-Parti Yönetimi*, 127–49; Aybars, *Mahkemeler*; Bruinessen, *Kurdish*.

6. Yalman, *Gördüklerim*, 2:991–1009; Tunçay, *Tek-Parti Yönetimi*, 146–47; Uyar, *Tek Parti*, 117–18.

7. Zürcher, *Unionist*, 142–67.

8. Duara, *Rescuing*, 147–48, 235; Parla, *Nutuk*; [Atatürk], *Nutuk*; [Atatürk], *Speech*.

9. Tunçay, *Tek-Parti Yönetimi*, 68–86, 127–83, 331; Zürcher, *Turkey*, 172–75; Zürcher, *Unionist*, 142–67; Schick and Tonak, eds., *Transition*, 223 (Toprak, "Religious Right"); Ulutaş, "Religion."

10. Kamp, *New Woman*, 189; Northrop, *Veiled*.

11. Lewis, *Emergence*, 264.

12. Tunçay, *Tek-Parti Yönetimi*, 166–71.

13. Tunçay, *Tek-Parti Yönetimi*, 149–83, 225–40, 295–99; Schick and Tonak, eds., *Transition*, 223 (Toprak, "Religious Right"); Miller, "Fikh"; Mango, *Atatürk*, 498–99; Atay, *Çankaya*, 567–68.

14. Khalid, "Backwardness," 241, 246.

15. Bozdoğan, *Modernism*, 93–95, 242–55; Üstel, *Türk Ocakları*, 180, 359–61; Kara-ömerlioğlu, "Cult," 65–111; Karaömerlioğlu, *Orada*, 51–85.

16. Güvenç, *Türk Kimliği*, 38; Meeker, *Nation*, 372–78; Alexander, *Personal*, 28–29.

17. Müge Göçek: "Nationalism" (quotation on p. 180); Behar, *İktidar*; Aytürk, "Linguists," 1–25; Aytürk, "Episode," 275–93; Laut, *Ursprache*, 95–135; Lewis, *Turkish*, 57–74; Copeaux, *Espaces*.

18. Zürcher, *Turkey*, 176–85; Tunçay, *Tek-Parti Yönetimi*, 175–79, 283–95, 304–22; Uyar, *Tek Parti*, 67–97, 231–68; Atay, *Çankaya*, 378.

19. Koçak, "Kaynaşma," 74–79; Bozdoğan and Kasaba, eds., *Rethinking*, 221, 226 (Özbek, "Arabesk"); Kocabaşoğlu, *Radyo*; Meeker, *Nation*, 3–39, 285–317.

20. In Turkish, *cumhuriyetçilik, laiklik, milliyetçilik, halkçılık, devletçilik, inkılapçılık*; Parla, *Söylev*; Parla, *İdeoloji*; Parla, *Thought*, 77, 82–85; Kili, *Kemalism*; Tunçay, *Tek-Parti Yönetimi*, 208–218, 312; Karaömerlioğlu, *Orada*, 21–49.

21. Tekeli and İlkin, *İktisat*, 2:154–86; Tunçay, *Tek-Parti Yönetimi*, 245–82, 319; Uyar, *Tek Parti*, 115–38; Koçak, *Serbest Cumhuriyet Fırkası*; Akın, "Petitioning," 435–57.

22. Tunçay, *Tek-Parti Yönetimi*, 127–28, 293–95; Mango, *Atatürk*, 476–77; Bozarslan, "Mahdisme," 297–320.

23. Bozdoğan, *Modernism*, 5 (quotation), 72, 72, 155, 163–66, 163–66, 255–71.

24. The usual connotations of "yavuz" are closer to "fierce"; Akın, "Sports," 44, 66, 85, 146, 203; Akın, *Gürbüz*.

25. Zürcher, *Turkey*, 182–86; Heper, *İnönü*; Mango, *Atatürk*, 492–511; VanderLippe, *İnönü*, 23–33.

26. I owe the international comparison to James Bartholomew; Atay, *Çankaya*, 521–22 (Roosevelt); Kalaycıoğlu, *Dynamics*, 86; Hale, *Foreign Policy*, 64–65; Parla, *Nutuk*, 62–68, 70–71, 77–82, 90–97, 136–38; Volkan and Itzkowitz, *Atatürk*.

27. Hale, *Foreign Policy*, 44–63; Barlas, *Diplomacy*.

28. Personal communication from Sabiha Gökçen, Ankara, 1994; Altınay, *Myth*, 33–58; Bozdoğan, *Modernism*, 126, 130.

29. Hale, *Foreign Policy*, 63–78; Hale, *Military*, 81–87; VanderLippe, *İnönü*, 37–75.

30. Hurewitz, *MENA*, 2:548–52; Hale, *Foreign Policy*, 69–70.

31. Hale, *Foreign Policy*, 79–108; Deringil, *Neutrality*; Güçlü, *Menemencioğlu*. Leading Foreign Ministry official Numan Menemencioğlu reportedly needed few words to state his position on neutrality: *harp varsa, biz yokuz*, roughly, "If there's a war,

we're not in it" (personal communications from his niece, Nermin Menemencioğlu Streater, London, 1960s–1970s).

32. Kuniholm, *Origins*, 413; Hale, *Foreign Policy*, 109–21; VanderLippe, *İnönü*, 151–65.

33. VanderLippe, *İnönü*, 37–39, 47–53, 81–86; Karaömerlioğlu, "Return," 89–107.

34. Yalman, *Gördüklerim*, 2:1251 (quotation); Aktar, *Varlık*.

35. Uyar, *Tek Parti*, 207–23.

36. Zürcher, *Turkey*, 209–18; VanderLippe, *İnönü*, 97–136; Eroğul, *Demokrat*, 9–21.

37. VanderLippe, *İnönü*, 137–51; Eroğul, *Demokrat*, 22–39; Zürcher, *Turkey*, 219–28.

38. Eroğul, *Demokrat*, 45; Zürcher, *Turkey*, 221; VanderLippe, *Politics*, 189–209; Heper, *İnönü*, 193; Schick and Tonak, eds., *Transition*, 102–6 (Eroğul, "Establishment of Multiparty Rule").

39. Karaömerlioğlu, "Return," 90.

40. Schick and Tonak, eds., *Transition*, 105, 109 (Eroğul, "Establishment").

41. VanderLippe, *İnönü*, 5.

42. Heper, *İnönü*, 128–63, 181–93, 212–13, 254–58 (quoted passage, 254).

43. Hansen, *Turkey*, 312, 319; Boratav, *İktisat*, 28, 45, 63, 73; Owen and Pamuk, *Middle East*, 10–29.

44. Hansen, *Turkey*, 312–18; Boratav, *İktisat*, 28–44; Tekeli and İlkin, *İktisat*, 2:33–74.

45. Boratav, *İktisat*, 33–34; Tezel, *İktisadi Tarih*, 130–33.

46. Atay, *Çankaya*, 449–60; Tezel, *İktisadi Tarih*, 203–5.

47. Tekeli and İlkin, *Cumhuriyet*, 3:233–70 (İlkin, "Chester Demiryolu"); Can, *Chester*.

48. Reşat Kasaba, ed., *TMW*, 276 (Pamuk, "Economic Change in Twentieth Century Turkey"); Hansen, *Turkey*, 315–16; Boratav, *İktisat*, 40–42; Tezel, *İktisadi Tarih*, 318–22; Karaömerlioğlu, "Return," 94.

49. Boratav, *İktisat*, 45–62; Hansen, *Turkey*, 319–37.

50. Alexander, *Personal*, 74.

51. Tekeli and İlkin, *Kadro*; Tekeli and İlkin, *Merkez Bankası*.

52. "Clearing" refers to government-to-government trade agreement with specific time and value limits. The value limits are usually expressed in a major currency, but each country's exporters are paid in their local currency. Free-trade advocates consider clearing agreements disruptive of free trade.

53. Tekeli and İlkin, *İktisat*, 3:175–340; Tekeli and İlkin, *Cumhuriyet*, 2:201–38 (İlkin, "Sovyet Uzmanlarının Rolü"), 239–79 (Tekeli, "Ege Bölgesi"), 281–362 (Tekeli and İlkin, "Modernleşme Çabaları"); Tezel, *İktisadi Tarih*, 247–60.

54. Kasaba, ed., *TMW*, 277–86 (Pamuk, "Economic Change"); Hansen, *Turkey*, 324–35; Boratav, *İktisat*, 54–62; Tezel, *İktisadi Tarih*, 247–67.

55. VanderLippe, *İnönü*, 66–85; Boratav, *İktisat*, 63–72; Hansen, *Turkey*, 335–37; Metinsoy, *Yaşam*.

56. Tekeli and İlkin, *İktisat*, vol. 3; Tekeli and İlkin, *Cumhuriyet*, 2:363–408 (Tekeli, "'Savaş Sonrası' Kalkınma"); VanderLippe, *İnönü*, 167–68, 172, 175–81, 186–87, 192, 203.

57. Turkey's potential to play a vanguard role was repeatedly emphasized by the writers in *Kadro*, although not necessarily in the same sense I emphasize: Tekeli and İlkin, *Kadro*, 153, 164, 173–74, 206, 218, 246–47, 293, 309–10, 315, 350, 360, 361, 363, 384, 401, 502–3.

58. Güvenç, *Türk Kimliği*, 12: "Türk Ulusu yoktu ki uyusun; uyumuyordu ki uyanmış olsun?"

59. Hale, *Development*, 23–24.

60. Shorter, "Independence," 417–41; Shorter, "Depression," 103–24; Tezel, *İktisadi Tarih*, 88–91; McCarthy, *Muslims and Minorities*, 115–21.

61. T[ürkiye] C[umhuriyeti] Başbakanlık Devlet İstatistik Enstitüsü, *Göstergeler*, 1923–1992, 74.

62. Tezel, *İktisadi Tarih*, 101, 233–34, 300–305, 394–97.

63. Bruinessen, *Kurdish*, 59–60; McDowall, *Kurds*, 196–202; Hirschon, ed., *Crossing*; Yıldırım, *Exchange*; Yıldırım, *Göç*.

64. Arat, "Turkish Women," 57–78; Durakbaşa, "Kemalism," 139–55; Kandiyoti, "End," 22–47; White, "State Feminism," 145–59; Arat, *Patriarchal*, 27–46; Bozdoğan and Kasaba, eds., *Rethinking*, 95–112 (Arat, "Modernity and Women"); Bozdoğan, *Modernism*, 79–88, 195–216.

65. Mango, *Atatürk*, 469; Üstel, *Vatandaşlık*, 215–22; Afetinan, *Emancipation*.

66. Arat, *Patriarchal*, 47–61.

67. Bozdoğan and Kasaba, eds., *Rethinking*, 198, an incident when Atatürk reportedly commanded people to dance: "Forward march! Dance!" (Nalbantoğlu, "Silent Interruptions"); personal communication from Paul Wittek (1894–1978), 1968, citing reminiscences of Albert Gabriel (1883–1972).

68. Zihnioğlu, *Kadınsız*; Libal, "Staging," 31–52.

69. Ağaoğlu, *Ölmeye Yatmak*, 7–18, 26, 34, 50, 73, 86; Duben and Behar, *Households*, 1; White, "State Feminism," 151.

70. Karaömerlioğlu, "Cult," 16–64; Karaömerlioğlu, *Orada*, 21–42; Toprak, "Narodnik," 69–81.

71. Enginün, *Halide Edib*, 62–65.

72. Karaosmanoğlu, *Yaban*. In this discussion, page numbers included in parentheses refer to this edition.

73. Karaosmanoğlu, *Yaban*, 130.

74. Karaömerlioğlu, "Cult," 212–24; Karaömerlioğlu, *Orada*, 161–72.

75. Findley, "Educational," 257–76.

76. Widmann, *Exil und Bildungshilfe*; Widmann, *Atatürk ve Üniversite*; Neumark, *Zuflucht*; Schwartz, *Notgemeinschaft*; Nicolai, *Moderne*; Apter, *Zone*, 41–64; Erichsen, "Frauen," 335–53; Konuk, "Philologists," 31–47; Reisman, *Modernization*; Akyüz, *Eğitim*, 310–12.

77. T[ürkiye] C[umhuriyeti] Başbakanlık Devlet İstatistik Enstitüsü, *Göstergeler*, 1923–1992, 6–7, 67–84.

78. Karaömerlioğlu, "Cult," 112–57; Karaömerlioğlu, *Orada*, 87–116; Akyüz, *Eğitim*, 338–45; Findley, "Rauf İnan," 77–82; Heper, *İnönü*, 140–41, 184–85; Öztürkmen, *Folklor*, 223–69.

79. Findley, "Rauf İnan," 77–82.

80. This section follows Vahide, *Islam*; Mardin, *Religion*; Yavuz, *Islamic Identity*, 151–78; van Bruinessen, *Agha*, 257–59, 276; Abu-Rabi', *Islam*; and Poyraz, "Reflections." I also owe thanks to Münevver Ayaşlı (personal communication, December 1967), the first person in Turkey who revealed to me that she was a Nurcu.

81. Vahide, *Islam*, 13, 29, 31, 33–63; Mardin, *Religion*, 77.

82. Vahide, *Islam*, 85–86, 105, 111–30, 349.

83. Mardin, *Religion*, 92–93; Vahide, *Islam*, 163–67.

84. Vahide, *Islam*, 180–82, 274, 305–48.

85. Touraine, *Modernity*, 39; Yavuz and Esposito, eds., *Turkish Islam*, 4; Khalid, *Politics*, 102; Mardin *Religion*, 155, 204.

86. Mardin, *Religion*, 202; Vahide, *Islam*, 330; Yavuz, *Islamic*, 168.

87. Vahide, *Islam*, 194, 202–5, 230, 246, 249, 259, 274–76, 408–10.

88. Mardin, *Religion*, 154–55.

89. Poyraz, "Reflections," 12; Algar and Voll, et al., eds., *Bediüzzaman*, 11 (Algar, "Yüzyılın Müceddidi").

90. Poyraz, "Reflections," 19; Nursî, *Lem'alar*, 420–52.

91. Yavuz, *Islamic Identity*, 159; Mardin, *Religion*, 194.

92. Tanpınar, *Beş Şehir*, 103–4.

93. The title of Timour Muhidine's French translation of the novel has been disfigured by a literal, back-translation from the Turkish: *L'Institut de remise à l'heure des montres et des pendules* (Paris: Actes-Sud, 2007). Tanpınar's title clearly refers to the Instituts de chronométrie of France and Switzerland. He would have been astonished to see any other title on a French translation of his novel.

94. Tanpınar, *SAE*, 27. Tanpınar's spelling and use of diacritical signs differs somewhat from the pattern generally followed in this book and is retained in discussing his text. Estate inventories back up the association between religiosity and the ubiquity of time-keeping devices among Muslims: Hanioğlu, *Brief History*, 29.

95. Kısakürek, *Bâbıâli*, 41–42, discussing two Istanbul coffeehouses of the mid-1920s, Meserret and İkbal, adding that İkbal's less distinguished customers were known as *esafil-i şark*, and the young Tanpınar was one of them.

96. Tanpınar, *SAE*, 350: "Yeniliği kendilerine ucu dokunmamak şartıyla seviyorlardı. . . . Fakat hayatlarında emniyetli ve sağlam olmayı tercih ediyorlar."

97. Bozdoğan and Kasaba, eds., *Rethinking*, 67 (Mardin, "Project as Methodology"), 96 (Arat, "Modernity and Women").

98. Özyürek, *Nostalgia*.

6. TURKEY'S WIDENING POLITICAL SPECTRUM

1. Eroğul, *Demokrat*, 55–96; Schick and Tonak, eds., *Transition*, 107–13 (Eroğul, "The Establishment of Multiparty Rule"); Ahmad, *Experiment*; Zürcher, *Turkey*, 221–30.

2. Kalaycıoğlu, *Dynamics*, 75, table 3.1, "National Election Results (1946–1957)."

3. Çoker, 6–7 *Eylül*; Güven, *Azınlık*; Kuyucu, "Unmixing," 361–80.

4. Eroğul, *Demokrat*, 119 (quoting İnönü in *Ulus*, 13 April 1956), 122 ("special motives"); Schick and Tonak, eds., *Transition*, 114 (Eroğul, "Establishment").

5. Quotation from Schick and Tonak, eds., *Transition*, 118 (Eroğul, "Establishment"); Kalaycıoğlu, *Dynamics*, 83–86.

6. Hale, *Foreign Policy*, 111–45; Brockett, "Legend," 109–42; VanderLippe, "Korean War," 92–102.

7. This observation goes back to my personal observations in Turkey, starting in 1967; see also Lerner and Robinson, "Swords," 19–44.

8. Birand, *Shirts*, trans. Paker and Christie, 83–96; Schick and Tonak, eds., *Transition*, 118–39 (Eroğul, "Establishment"), 147–78 (Ahmet Samim, "The Left").

9. Kalaycıoğlu, *Dynamics*, 93–95; Kili and Gözübüyük, *Anayasa*, 171–230.

10. Kalaycıoğlu, *Dynamics*, 95–99, 122–24.

11. Alpay, "'68 Kuşağı," 177, 179: emphasizing the collectivist concept of freedom in Marxism and thus linking its appeal to the weakness of individualism in Turkish political culture; Atılgan, *Yön*.

12. Schick and Tonak, eds., *Transition*, 193, 212, n. 77 (Ağaoğulları, "The Ultranationalist Right").

13. Schick and Tonak, eds., *Transition*, 155–73 (Samim, "The Left"); Alpay, "'68 Kuşağı," 169–70; Akın, "Polemikler," 86–103; McDowall, *Kurds*, 408–17.

14. McDowall, *Kurds*, 408–10.

15. Sarfati, "Rise," ch. 6.

16. Zürcher, *Turkey*, 258–63.

17. Hale, *Military*, 197.

18. Schick and Tonak, eds., *Transition*, 160–61 (Samim, "The Left").

19. Hale, *Military*, 215–45; Kalaycıoğlu, *Dynamics*, 97; Bozarslan, "Milicien," 185–90.

20. Schick and Tonak, eds., *Transition*, 147–49, 163–73 (Samim, "The Left"), 191–208 (Ağaoğulları, "Ultranationalist"); Hale, *Military*, 215–45.

21. Schick and Tonak, eds., *Transition*, 201 (Ağaoğulları, "Ultranationalist").

22. Hale, *Military*, 224–45; Bozarslan, "Milicien," 190–93, 207–8.

23. Bozarslan, "Milicien," 194–95, 234–43; McDowall, *Kurds*, 414, 420–23.

24. Compare Kalaycıoğlu, *Dynamics*, 88–89.

25. U.S. Department of State, *Foreign Relations of the United States, 1964–1968*, vol. 16, *Cyprus, Greece, Turkey*, document 54, Johnson to İnönü, 5 June 1964, consulted at http://www.state.gov/r/pa/ho/frus/johnsonlb/xvi/4757.htm; Hale, *Foreign Policy*, 133–62; Kalaycıoğlu, *Dynamics*, 99–101, 108–13.

26. Mallinson, *Cyprus*, 75–86; Salih, *Cyprus*; Göçek, "Politicized Past," 98–99.

27. Hale, *Foreign Policy*, 174–77; Arikan, *EU*, 61–69.

28. Kalaycıoğlu, *Dynamics*, 112–13; Göçek, "Politicized Past," 100–102.

29. Kasaba, ed., *TMW*, 266–300 (Pamuk, "Economic Change," followed in this section except as otherwise noted); Boratav, *İktisat*, 73–118; Hansen, *Turkey*, 338–82; Kazgan, *Ekonomi*, 77–120; Kepenek and Yentürk, *Ekonomi*, 80–175.

30. Kasaba, ed., *TMW*, 267 (table 10.1), 269 (graph 10.1; Pamuk, "Economic Change"); McDowall, *Kurds*, 401, tractorization in the southeast.

31. Kalaycıoğlu, *Dynamics*, 76–79; Karpat, "Mechanization," 83–103; Robinson, "Tractors," 451–62; Aktan, "Mechanization," 273–85.

32. Schick and Tonak, eds., *Transition*, 295 (Keyder, "Economic Development and Crisis"), 333–63 (Schick and Tonak, "The International Dimension: Trade, Aid, and Debt").

33. Buğra, *Business*; Heper, Öncü, and Kramer, eds., *Turkey*, 176–98 (İlkin, "Businessmen"); 199–218 (Nilüfer Göle, "Engineers").

34. Öğüt, "Car Ownership," 233–48; Akar, "Travel Reduction," 36 (fig. 3.14 and table 3.4).
35. Poem about the Anadol by Ali Rıza Özer found on the personal Web site of Can Kıraç: http://www.cankirac.com/m1.asp?id=75; on the construction of the first Bosphorus bridge, see also http://wowturkey.com/forum/viewtopic.php?t=12604; thanks to Yiğit Akın for these references.
36. Arikan, *EU*, 64, 68–69.
37. Hansen, *Turkey*, 379, table 11.10.
38. Schick and Tonak, eds., *Transition*, 295, 297 (Keyder, "Economic").
39. Kasaba, ed., *TMW*, 267 (table 10.1), 270 (graph 10.2; Pamuk, "Economic Change").
40. Schick and Tonak, eds., *Transition*, 192, 211, n. 67 (Ağaoğulları, "Ultranationalist").
41. T[ürkiye] C[umhuriyeti] Başbakanlık Türkiye İstatistik Kurumu, *İstatistik Göstergeler, 1923–2005*, various tables (online at http://www.tuik.gov.tr).
42. Buğra, "Poverty," 43; Danielson and Keleş, *Urbanization*.
43. Buğra, "Poverty," 44; Karpat, *Gecekondu*; Karpat, "Genesis" (http://www.ejts.org/document54.html); Erman, "Squatter," 983–1002; Kalaycıoğlu, *Dynamics*, 119–22.
44. Tekeli and Okyay, *Dolmuş*; Aslan, *1 Mayıs*.
45. Kasaba, ed., *TMW*, 189–98 (Kirişci, "Migration"); 199–225 (Soysal, "Turks in Germany"); Horrocks and Kolinsky, eds., *Turkish German*; Yerasimos, ed., *Turcs* (Kastoryano, "Les émigrés," 96–99); White, "Turks," 754–69; Argun, *Deutschkei*; Ewing, *Honor*.
46. Ağaoğlu, *Hayır . . .* , 36, 89, 102, 117, 142, 184.
47. Buğra, "Poverty," 41; McDowall, *Kurds*, 413.
48. Data from http://www.yok.gov.tr/egitim/raporlar/mart98/bolum2.html.
49. Bozarslan, "Milicien," 214–21; McDowall, *Kurds*, 413.
50. McDowall, *Kurds*, 403–4, 413.
51. Kasaba, ed., *TMW*, 273 (Pamuk, "Economic Change").
52. Brockett, "Print Culture."
53. Information from Yiğit Akin, September 2008, reporting from family members.
54. Bozdoğan and Kasaba, eds., *Rethinking*, 211–32, quotations in this paragraph, 211, 215, 225 (Özbek, "Arabesk Culture"); Kalaycıoğlu, *Dynamics*, 119; Özbek, *Gencebay*; Stokes, *Arabesk*.
55. Schick and Tonak, eds., *Transition*, 160, 161 (Samim, "The Left," italics in original).
56. Schick and Tonak, eds., *Transition*, 204 (Ağaoğulları, "Ultranationalist").
57. Bozdoğan and Kasaba, eds., *Rethinking*, 218–19 (Özbek, "Arabesk").
58. Compare Schick and Tonak, eds., *Transition*, 155–73 (Samim, "Left"); Şahin Alpay, "'68 Kuşağı," 169–70.
59. Helicke, "*Sebilürreşad*."
60. Helicke, "*Sebilürreşad*," 25, n. 86, quoting Eşref Edib, "Hükümetin Programı ve Ezan Meselesi," *Sebilürreşad*, 4, no. 80 (June 1950): 70.
61. Necip Fazıl Kısakürek, *Bâbıâli* (Istanbul: Büyük Doğu, 2001); "Kısakürek, Necip Fazıl," in *Türk Dili ve Edebiyatı Ansiklopedisi*, 5:329–33; www.necipfazil.com; Ahmet Izzet Bozbey, unpublished research reports on works of Necip Fazıl Kısakürek.
62. Kritzman, ed., *French Thought*, 7–9 (Rémond, "Action Française"), 363–74 (Kritzman, "The Intellectual"), 611–15 (Avni, "Charles Maurras"), 634–35 (Kéchichian, "Charles Péguy").

63. Menemencioğlu and İz, eds., *Verse*, 222–25; Akyüz, *Antoloji*, 934–79.

64. Kısakürek, *İdeolocya*, 314–15 ("cleansing" of minorities).

65. Kısakürek, *Bâbıâli*, esp. 254, 292.

66. Kemal, *Bereketli*, 173; www.orhankemal.org.

67. Kemal, *Bereketli*, 143, 166–69 (three times), 393, repetitions with variations.

68. Kemal, *Bereketli*, 264, 334 ("atın aptalı rahvan adamın aptalı pehlivan").

69. Kemal, *Bereketli*, 66. The term *oynaş* comes from a root that literally signifies mutual play—in this case, not in the childish sense of the word.

70. Kemal, *Bereketli*, 118–22 (the abduction), 135 (*zorlu avrat*).

71. Kemal, *Bereketli*, 154–66. The labor boss's title, *taşeron*, obviously derives from the French *tâcheron*. The translation as "labor boss" refers to his apparent role in the book as the man who hires the workers for the construction site and who is described as the "contractor's [sub-]contractor" (*müteahhidin müteahhidi*, 107).

72. Kemal, *Bereketli*, 145: "Dolaşırım yirmibeş yıldır gurbette. . . . Lâkin çözmedim bir kerre bile uçkur harama!"

7. TURKEY AND THE WORLD

1. Kalaycıoğlu, *Dynamics*, 122, 125–37; Hale, *Military*, 231–75; Keyder, "Bell Jar," 65–84; Kaplan, *Pedagogical*, 73–95; Sarfati, "Rise," ch. 6.

2. Dodd, *Crisis*, 71–79, 96–130; Kili and Gözübüyük, *Anayasa*, 253–332.

3. Kili and Gözübüyük, *Anayasa*, 292; Dodd, *Crisis*, 114.

4. Özbudun, "Conservative Democracy," 550.

5. Kalaycıoğlu, *Dynamics*, 126 (table 5.1), 131; Çarkoğlu and Kalaycıoğlu, *Democracy*, 113–205.

6. Kalaycıoğlu, *Dynamics*, 126 (table 5.1: ANAP got 45.1 percent of the vote in 1983 and 53 percent of the assembly seats).

7. Hale, *Military*, 246–58, and Dodd, *Crisis*, 60–87, favorable interpretations; Kalaycıoğlu, *Dynamics*, 125–31, less favorable; Heper, Kazancıgil, and Rockman, *Institutions*, 234–42 (Özbudun, "Constitution Making," 234, "missed opportunity").

8. Hale, *Military*, 270 ("regimented and solidarist view"); McDowall, *Kurds*, 445 ("The National Security Council tried to freeze any organic evolution of the Turkish republic").

9. Heper, ed., *Democracy*; Heper, ed., *Local*; Sayarı and Esmer, eds., *Politics*; White, *Islamist*.

10. Yavuz, *Islamic Identity*, 122–28; Kaplan, *Pedagogical*, 45–50; Shankland, *Islam*, 26–28, 59–61.

11. Yavuz, *Islamic Identity*, 75–76.

12. Heper and Sayarı, eds., *Political Leaders*, 161–80 (Acar, "Özal"); Sarfati, "Rise," ch. 6.

13. Heper and Keyman, "Double-Faced State," 259–77; Hale, *Foreign Policy*, 195–99; Zürcher, *Turkey*, 291–306.

14. Heper and Sayarı, eds., *Political Leaders*, 199–216 (Cizre, "Tansu Çiller: Lusting for Power and Undermining Democracy").

15. Heper and Sayarı, *Political Leaders*, 127–146 (Özdalga, "Erbakan"); Çınar, "Transformation," 472; Yavuz, ed., *Emergence*, 212 (Öniş, "Political"); Yavuz, *Islamic Identity*, 207–38, 275–76; Shankland, *Islam*, 87–118, 204–8.

16. Findley and Rothney, *World*, 417–19, contemporary press coverage and e-mail from individuals who lost family members in the earthquake.

17. Özbudun, "Conservative Democracy," 546.

18. Özbudun, "Conservative Democracy," 547–49; Keyman and Öniş, "Social Democracy," 219–20; Mecham, "Ashes," 339–58; Yavuz, *Islamic Identity*, 239–64.

19. Özbudun, "Conservative Democracy," 555.

20. Heper and Toktaş, "Erdoğan," 157–85.

21. Tuğal, "Appeal," 264–68 (Refah Party hybridity); Buğra, "Poverty," 45–48.

22. Çarkoğlu and Kalaycıoğlu, *Democracy*, 51 (table 3.1), 121 (table 6.2), 122 (table 6.3), 125 (table 6.4), 214–21; Eligür, "Elections."

23. Çınar, "Transformation," 469–86 (Verheugen quotation, 470); Tuğal, "Appeal," 254 (Erbakan and radical Islamists); Tuğal, *Passive Revolution*; Kalaycıoğlu, *Dynamics*, 196.

24. Keyman and Öniş, "Social Democracy," 212–13 (quotations); Navaro-Yashin, *Faces*, 171–78; Robins, "Drugs," 630–50.

25. Kalaycıoğlu, *Dynamics*, 174–82; quotations and quantitative data in this section are from these pages.

26. Putnam, Leonardi, and Nanetti, *Democracy*.

27. Meeker, *Nation*, 318–71; McDowall, *Kurds*, 399, 402–3, 412, 421 (Abdullah Öcalan's enmity for the Bucak clan of Siverek, then supporting Turkey's Justice Party, c. 1979; Sedat Bucak was one of the principals in the 1996 Susurluk affair).

28. Kalaycıoğlu, *Dynamics*, 175 (quotation); Çarkoğlu and Kalaycıoğlu, *Democracy*, 17–18, 19 (table 1.2). Their discussion speaks of a "relatively rigorous [vigorous?] protest potential" and cites several historical examples (18); but table 1.2, to which that comment refers, shows low levels of participation in protests.

29. Yavuz, ed., *Emergence*, 216–17 (Öniş, "Political Economy").

30. McDowall, *Kurds*, 414.

31. Heper, *Kurds*, 36; Zürcher, *Turkey*, 316–21; Yeğen, *Kürt*.

32. Heper, *Kurds*, 6, 11–12, 83–143 (91: the point about the constitutions).

33. Kasaba, ed., *TMW*, 343–56 (Bozarslan, "Kurds"); McDowall, *Kurds*, 414–17; Bruinessen, *Kurdish*, 225–88; Natali, *Kurds*, 92–116; Heper, *Kurds*, 155–65.

34. Marcus, *PKK*, 49; Göçek, "Politicized Past," 91–98.

35. McDowall, *Kurds*, 420–54; Hale, *Foreign Policy*, 173–74, 199–205.

36. McDowall, *Kurds*, 431, 433, 437–38, 439 ("social earthquake"); Heper, *Kurds*, 8, 115, 128 (Özal's Kurdish mother).

37. MacDowall, *Kurds*, 446–49.

38. Göçek, "Political Past," 94; Marcus, *PKK*, 272–85.

39. McDowall, *Kurds*, 445–46; see also Heper, *Kurds*, 160–61, 164–65, 177–86.

40. McDowall, *Kurds*, 449; Heper, *Kurds*, 113–14, 116.

41. Shishkin, "Risks."

42. Tavernise, "Kurdish Rebels," 6; Göçek, "Politicized Past," 95 ("mobilization and assimilation"); Marcus, *PKK*.
43. Hale, *Foreign Policy*, 166–74, 218–28, 296–322; McDowall, *Kurds*, 372–76; Zürcher, *Turkey*, 325–28.
44. Hale, *Foreign Policy*, 167–69, 252–60, 265–66; Arikan, *EU*, 161–65.
45. Hale, *Foreign Policy*, 191, 252–60; Mallinson, *Cyprus*; Salih, *Cyprus*; Göçek, "Politicized Past," 98–99.
46. Balci, *Missionnaires*, 44–49, 53–85; Hale, *Foreign Policy*, 287–96.
47. The European Union has evolved from the European Economic Community (1957) to the European Community (EC, 1967) and finally the European Union (1992). To avoid confusion, this discussion will refer to it consistently as the EU.
48. Desmond Dinan ed., *European Union*, 273–75 (Michalski, "The Enlarging European Union"); Dinan, *Europe Recast*, esp. 280–83; http://www.auswaertiges-amt.de/diplo/en/Europa/Erweiterung/KopenhagenerKriterien.html.
49. Judt, *Postwar*, 713–36, 765–68; Hale, *Foreign Policy*, 177–79, 233–45; Arikan, *EU*; Gökalp and Ünsar, "Myth," 93–116; Lake, ed., *EU*.
50. http://ec. europa.eu/enlargement/turkey/eu_turkey_relations_en.html.
51. "Negotiating Framework," Luxembourg, 3 October 2005; available online at http://ec.europa.eu/enlargement/pdf/st20002_05_TR_framedoc_en.pdf; Gökalp and Ünsar, "Myth," 94. See also "Enlargement Strategy, 2009–2010," available online at http://ec.europa.eu/enlargement/press_corner/key-documents/reports_oct_2009_en.htm.
52. Çınar, "Transformation," 480–81.
53. Figures for GDP per person stated in terms of purchasing power parity (PPP) in 1990 U.S. dollars, from Kasaba, *TMW*, 267 (table 10.1; Pamuk, "Economic Change"); except as otherwise noted, this discussion follows Pamuk.
54. Alexander, *Personal*.
55. Bianchi, *Interest Groups*, 259, 264, 268–272; Buğra, *Business*; Kaplan, *Pedagogical*, 37–38, 46–49, 50–56, 163, 173.
56. The acronym MÜSİAD suggests *Müslüman* (Muslim) more readily than *müstakil* (independent). Yavuz, *Islamic Identity*, 88, 92–96, 192; Demir, Acar, and Toprak, "Tigers," 166–88.
57. Yavuz, ed., *Emergence*, 220–24 (Öniş, "Political Economy"); Buğra, "Associations," 521–39; Jak Kamhi, founder and board chairman of the Profilo Holding Company, known for its household appliances, reportedly said that he was already a member of the EU (personal communication from Stanford Shaw, 1992). A prominent member of the Turkish Jewish community, Kamhi (b. 1925) is a longtime TÜSİAD member and Turkey's first member (1991–2003) of the European Roundtable of Industrialists, a major interest group within the EU.
58. Kolars and Mitchell, *Euphrates*, esp. 25–30; Özok-Gündoğan, "Social Development," 93–111.
59. UN Human Development Program, *Turkey* 2004, available at http://www.undp.org.tr/docAndPucDocuments/NHDR2004engfinal.pdf, 10 (table 1.1), 64–71 (tables A1–A4); see also Buğra, "Poverty," 45–52.

60. Hütteroth and Höhfeld, *Türkei*, 251–96; TÜSİAD, *Bölgesel*; Keyder, "Globalization," 124–34; Özaslan, Dincer, and Özgür, "Regional Disparities," available at http://www. ersa.org/ersaconfs/ersao6/papers/858.pdf .

61. Türkoğlu, "ICT Sector," available at http://www.igeme.org.tr/Assets/sip/san/ICT.pdf; "Haber Bülteni, 2008 Yılı Hanehalkı Bilişim Teknolojileri Kullanımı Araştırması Sonuçları," no. 138, 27 Ağustos 2008, www.tuik.gov.tr.

62. TÜİK, *Yıllık*, http://www.tuik.gov.tr/yillik/yillik.pdf; TÜİK, *Göstergeler*, 1923–2005, http://www.tuik.gov.tr/yillik/Ist_gostergeler.pdf.

63. The age dependency ratio is the number of the young and the elderly per hundred of those in the economically productive fourteen-to-sixty-four age bracket.

64. Data for 1982 from http://www.yok.gov.tr/egitim/raporlar/mart98/bolum2.html; data for 2006 from http://www.yok.gov.tr/hakkinda/fak_yuk_ens_2006.xls.

65. Keyder, "Globalization," 125, 129; statistical data from Greater Istanbul Municipality Web site: http://www.ibb.gov.tr/IBB/DocLib/pdf/bilgihizmetleri/yayinlar/istatistikler/ demografi/t211.pdf.

66. TÜİK, *Yıllık*, 78–80 (table 4.15).

67. I am indebted to Ayfer Karakaya Stump for advice about the Alevis. Published sources include Olsson, Özdalga, and Raudvere, eds., *Alevi*, 79–84 (Çamuroğlu, "Alevi Revivalism"); Krämer and Schmidtke, *Speaking*, 269–94 (Dressler, "Modern Dede"); White and Jongerden, eds., *Enigma*, 93–109 (Vorhoff, "Discourses"); Shankland, *Alevis*; Gezik, *Alevi Kürtler*; Şahin, "Alevi"; http://www.alevi.com, www.alevihaber. org, www.aleviyol.com/de/.

68. McDowall, *Kurds*, 446: "the Alevi community, probably 15 million in number of whom up to one third is Kurdish," late 1990s.

69. McDowall, *Kurds*, 413 on Maraş [Kahramanmaraş] and Çorum.

70. Çarkoğlu, "Ideology," 317–44; Şahin Alpay, "22 Temmuz ve Aleviler," *Zaman*, 11 September 2007, available at http://www.zaman.com.tr/yazar.do?yazino=586908.

71. Kasaba, ed., *TMW*, 388–418 (Arat, "Women's Struggles"); Göle, *Modern*.

72. Yavuz, *Islamic Identity*, 179–205; Yavuz and Esposito, eds., *Turkish Islam*, 19–47 (Yavuz, "The Gülen Movement"); Balci, *Missionnaires*; Agai, *Bildungsnetzwerk*; Hermansen, "The Cultivation of Memory in the Gülen Community" (26 October 2007), available at http://en.fgulen.com/content/view/2444/53/.

73. Balci, *Missionnaires*, 96–103; Yavuz and Esposito, eds., *Turkish Islam*, 20 (Yavuz, "Gülen Movement"); Agai, *Bildungsnetzwerk*, 123–26; Sevindi, *Islamic*.

74. Balci, *Missionnaires*, 103–11, 128, Yavuz, *Islamic Identity*, 183–89; Fethullah Gülen's Turkish and English Web sites contain many of his writings (http://tr.fgulen.com/, http://en.fgulen.com/).

75. Yavuz and Esposito, eds., *Turkish Islam*, 33 (Yavuz, "Gülen Movement"); Agai, *Bildungsnetzwerk*, 246–54. Yavuz translates *ışık evi* as "lighthouse," but in English that term refers to the seafaring type of lighthouse (*fener* in Turkish); for that reason "house of light" seems preferable.

76. Balci, *Missionnaires*, 115–16, 120–21. If space permitted, it could be shown that various branches of the Nakşibendi-Halidi movement went through analogous developments,

setting up companies, foundations, and electronic and print media. The owners of the companies often joined MÜSİAD: Yavuz, *Islamic Identity*; Ulutaş, "Naqshbandiyya."

77. Balci, *Missionnaires*, 143–208; additional data from Helen Rose Ebaugh, December 2008.

78. Yavuz, *Islamic Identity*, 197; Tavernise, "Schools." The Abant Platform takes its name from a resort on Lake Abant, in Turkey, where the first conference was held. The 2004 Abant Platform convened in Washington, DC, at the Johns Hopkins University's School of Advanced International Studies (SAIS) on the theme "Islam, Secularism, and Democracy, the Turkish Experience"; I was one of several U.S. scholars invited to make presentations at the conference.

79. http://en.fgulen.com/content/view/1260/13/: "Covering of women is mentioned in the Qur'an, but it doesn't specify how or in what form this should be done. Dwelling on the form narrows Islam's broad horizon. In fact, it would be a mistake to make a religious costume. The same thing is true for covering the head. It's a mistake to make this into one of the main principles of Islam and faith. The headscarf isn't one of Islam's main principles or conditions. It's against the spirit of Islam to regard uncovered women as outside of religion. We have so many things in common; we shouldn't be divided by details. If we're going to quarrel with one another in the mosque, first let's make peace in the mosque courtyard by giving priority to the spirit or essence of something before its form" (20–29 July 1997). Yavuz, *Islamic Identity*, 197, 201–2; Yavuz and Esposito, eds., *Turkish Islam*, 85–114 (Özdalga, "Three Women Teachers").

80. Ağaoğlu, *Dar Zamanlar*, I, *Ölmeye Yatmak*; II, *Bir Düğün Gecesi*; III, *Hayır*. . . . Below, in sections devoted to one of these novels, page numbers included in the text in parentheses normally refer to the novel under discussion; where a different novel is intended, the three titles are abbreviated as ÖY, BDG, and H. The literal translation of the title *Bir Düğun Gecesi* would be "A Wedding Night." The actual event referred to is an evening reception, during which the civil wedding occurs. Considering that the English expression "wedding night" refers not to the wedding but to the new couple's first night together, I have preferred "An Evening Wedding" as the translation that unambiguously indicates the book's subject. See also Erol, "Sexual Discourse," 187–202; Esen and Köroğlu, eds., *Hayata Bakan*; Gümüş, *Adalet Ağaoğlu*; Akkıyal, "*Dar Zamanlar*." I thank Adalet Ağaoğlu for her comments on these pages (letter of 1 November 2007).

81. Parla, "Tempomorphoses," 33–44.

82. Kaplan, *Pedagogical*, 89–115: in one country town, girls of the 1990s still faced analogous problems.

83. Ağaoğlu, ÖY, 41 ("making even oneself forget that one is a human being [*insan*] even before being a woman"), 161 (Aysel's exchange with Engin), 187 (Aysel's parents need to realize that she is not just a girl but "a PERSON" [*bir KİŞİ*—the only word in all capital letters in the whole book]).

84. Ağaoğlu, BDG, 24. The bridge crossing is a literary license. Tezel actually could not have crossed the Bosphorus bridge on her way to the wedding. The first Bosphorus bridge was under construction at the time of the wedding in Ankara (26 November 1972); the bridge did not open until 30 October 1973. Adalet Ağaoğlu's husband,

Halim Ağaoğlu, a civil engineer, worked on the construction of the bridge (personal communication, 1998); consequently the Ağaoğlus would have known its chronology precisely. On the bridge, see http://wowturkey.com/forum/viewtopic.php?t=12604.

85. Ağaoğlu, *H*: more than seven years have passed since Ayşen's wedding, which implies a date of 1979 or later (54); more than two years earlier on a June morning, Aysel had to stand trial after the coup (1980) had occurred (44); the date on which the novel's action occurs is 22 December (5, 207), but the year is not stated.

86. Ağaoğlu, *H*, 82, 122, 244; the statement that the lines come from Dylan Thomas's play *Under Milk Wood* (122) is incorrect; these are the first and third lines from Thomas's poem on the death of his father, of which the first line serves as the title; from Dylan Thomas, *The Poems*, published by J. M. Dent.

87. Ağaoğlu, *H*, 42, 222, 227, 238 with slight variations:

HER DURUMDA ÖZGÜR KİMLİĞİMİZİ KORUYABİLMEK ANCAK EDİMLE SÖYLENEBİLECEK ŞU İKİ SÖZCÜĞE BAĞLI: YİNELEMEYE HAYIR.

AYNILAŞMAYA HAYIR. AYNILIĞA HAYIR.

After a space, the condensed version follows (222): HER DURUMDA ÖZGÜR KİMLİĞİMİZİ KORUYABİLMEK ANCAK EDİMLE SÖYLENEBİLECEK ŞU TEK VE SON SÖZE BAĞLI: HAYIR.

88. Ağaoğlu, *Üç Beş Kişi*; Ağaoğlu, *Curfew* (trans. Goulden); notable films about the 1980 coup include Önder and Gülmez, *Beynelmilel* (The International, 2006) and Uğur, *Eve Dönüş* (Homecoming, 2006).

CONCLUSION

1. This phrase (*sahnedeki ihtilal*) forms the title of ch. 18: Pamuk, *Kar*, 153. Page numbers in references to the novel are those of the Turkish edition. The pagination of the English edition is almost identical: Pamuk, *Snow*.

2. An upsurge in the female death rate, variously analyzed as suicide or murder, occurred after 2000 in Batman; the causes are still being debated. Discussing this novel in an interview, Pamuk said that he transported the female suicides from Batman to Kars and combined them in his novel with the political struggle about the headscarf: "Orhan Pamuk: Batman'ı anlayamadık," http://www.kurdistan-post.com/News-file-article-sid-7351.html. For further information on Batman: İnci Hekimoğlu, "Batman'da kadınlar ölmüyor, öldürülüyor!" http://www.radikal.com.tr/ek_haber.php?ek=r2&haberno=2639, and Tutkun Akbaş, "İntihar değil Cinayet," http://www.tempodergisi.com.tr/toplum_politika/03966/. My thanks to Özgen Felek for these references.

3. Arsu, "Coup Plot," quoting Professor Midhat Sancar; Tavernise and Arsu, "Court."

4. Tanpınar, *Beş Şehir*, 103–4.

5. Judt, *Postwar*, 830 (quoting Yosef Hayim Yerushalmi). Judt's closing pages offer profound reflections on history and memory with specific reference to Europe. See also Göçek, "Nationalism," 168–80.

BIBLIOGRAPHY OF PUBLISHED SOURCES

Abdülaziz Bey. *Osmanlı Âdet, Merasim ve Tabirleri: Âdât ve Merasim-i Kadime, Tabirât ve Muamelât-ı Kavmiye-i Osmaniye* [Ottoman customs, ceremonies, and expressions]. Ed. Kâzım Arısan and Duygu Arısan Günay. 2 vols. Istanbul: Tarih Vakfı Yurt Yayınları, 1995.

Abrahamian, Ervand. *Iran Between Two Revolutions*. Princeton: Princeton University Press, 1982.

Abu-Manneh, Butrus. "A New Look at the Rise and Expansion of the Khalidi Sub-Order." In *Sufism and Sufis in Ottoman Society*, ed. Ahmed Yaşar Ocak, 279–314. Ankara: Turkish Historical Society, 2005.

———. "Salafiyya and the Rise of the Khalidiyya in Baghdad in the Early Nineteenth Century." *Die Welt des Islams* 43, no. 3 (2003): 349–72.

———. *Studies on Islam and the Ottoman Empire in the 19th Century (1826–1876)*. Istanbul: Isis, 2001.

———. "Transformation of the Naqshbandiyya, 17th–20th Century: Introduction." *Die Welt des Islams* 43, no. 3 (2003): 303–8.

Abun-Nasr, Jamil M. *A History of the Maghrib in the Islamic Period*. Cambridge: Cambridge University Press, 1987.

Abu-Rabi', Ibrahim M., ed. *Islam at the Crossroads: On the Life and Thought of Bediuzzaman Said Nursi*. Albany: State University of New York Press, 2003.

Adam, Volker. *Russlandmuslime in Istanbul am Vorabend des Ersten Weltkrieges: Die Berichterstattung osmanischer Periodika über Russland und Zentralasien*. Frankfurt: Peter Lang, 2002.

Adanır, Fikret, and Bernd Bonwetsch, eds. *Osmanismus, Nationalismus und der Kaukasus: Muslime und Christen, Türken und Armenier im 19. und 20. Jahrhundert*. Wiesbaden: Reichert Verlag, 2005.

Adıvar, Halide Edib. *Ateşten Gömlek* [Shirt of flame]. 1922. Reprint, Istanbul: Özgür, 1997.

———. *The Clown and His Daughter*. London: George Allen and Unwin, 1935. [English original of novel also published in Turkish as *Sinekli Bakkal*]

———. *Sinekli Bakkal*. 1935. Reprint, Istanbul: Atlas Kitapevi, 1996. [See also original English edition, *The Clown and His Daughter*]

Afetinan, A. *The Emancipation of Turkish Women*. Paris: UNESCO, 1962.

Agai, Bekim. *Zwischen Netzwerk und Diskurs; Das Bildungsnetzwerk um Fethullah Gülen (geb. 1938): Die flexible Umsetzung modernen islamischen Gedankenguts*. Schenefeld: EG-Verlag, 2004.

Ağaoğlu, Adalet. *Bir Düğün Gecesi* [An evening wedding]. Vol. 2 of *Dar Zamanlar*. 1979. Reprint, Istanbul: Yapı Kredi Yayınları, 1994.

———. *Curfew*. Trans. John Goulden. Austin: Center for Middle Eastern Studies, University of Texas at Austin, 1997.

———. *Hayır . . .* [No . . .]. Vol. 3 of *Dar Zamanlar*. 1987. Reprint, Istanbul: Yapı Kredi Yayınları, 1994.

———. *Ölmeye Yatmak* [Lying down to die]. Vol. 1 of *Dar Zamanlar*. 1973. Reprint, Istanbul: Yapi Kredi Yayinları, 1994.

———. *Üç Beş Kişi* [A few people]. Istanbul: Remzi, 1984. [English translation published as *Curfew*]

Ağaoğlu, Ahmet. *İhtilal mi, Inkılap mı?* [Revolution or reform?]. Ankara: Alaeddin Kıral Basımevi, 1942.

Ahmad, Feroz. *The Making of Modern Turkey*. London: Routledge, 1993.

———. "Ottoman Perception of the Capitulations, 1800–1914." *Journal of Islamic Studies* 11, no. 1 (2000): 1–20.

———. *The Turkish Experiment in Democracy, 1950–1975*. London: C. Hurst for the Royal Institute of International Affairs, 1977.

———. *The Young Turks: The Committee of Union and Progress in Turkish Politics, 1908–1914*. Oxford: Clarendon Press, 1969.

Ahmed, Leila. *Women and Gender in Islam: Historical Roots of a Modern Debate*. New Haven: Yale University Press, 1992.

Ahmed, Midhat. *Müşahedat* [Observations]. Istanbul: N.p. [Tercüman-ı Hakikat Matbaası?], 1308/1890–91.

———. *Müşahedat* [Observations]. Ed. Osman Gündüz. Ankara: Akçağ, 1997. [Latin-script edition]

Akar, Gülşah. "Automobile Travel Reduction in Urban Areas and City Centers, Case Study: Ankara." MA thesis, Ankara: Middle East Technical University, 2004.

Akarlı, Engin. *The Long Peace, 1861–1920*. Berkeley: University of California Press, 1993.

Akçam, Taner. *From Empire to Republic: Turkish Nationalism and the Armenian Genocide*. London: Zed, 2004.

Akkıyal, Berna. "Adalet Ağaoğlu'nun *Dar Zamanlar* Üçlemesinde 'Kimlik' Sorunluğu" [Identity issues in Adalet Ağaoğlu's trilogy *Dar Zamanlar*]. MA thesis, Ankara: Bilkent University, 2005.

Akın, Yiğit. "All Quiet on the Home Front? Politics and Everyday Life in Istanbul During World War I." PhD diss., Ohio State University, in progress.

———. *"Gürbüz ve Yavuz Evlatlar": Erken Cumhuriyet'te Beden Terbiyesi ve Spor* [Physical culture and sports in the early republic]. Istanbvul: İletişim, 2004.

———. *"Not Just a Game': Sports and Physical Education in Early Republican Turkey (1923–51)."* MA thesis, Istanbul: Boğazköy University, 2003.

——. "Reconsidering State, Party, and Society in Early Republican Turkey: Politics of Petitioning." *International Journal of Middle East Studies* 39, no. 3 (2007): 435–57.

——. "Uluslararası Etkileşim İçinde Solda Önemli Polemikler" [Important polemics on the left in international context]. In *Modern Türkiye'de Siyasi Düşünce* [Political thought in modern Turkey]. Vol. 8: *Sol Düşünce*, 86–103. Istanbul: İletişim, 2007.

Aksakal, Mustafa. *The Ottoman Road to War in 1914: The Ottoman Empire and World War I.* Cambridge: Cambridge University Press, 2008.

Aksan, Virginia. *An Ottoman Statesman in War and Peace: Ahmed Resmi Efendi, 1700–1783.* Leiden: Brill, 1995.

——. *Ottoman Wars, 1700–1870: An Empire Besieged.* Harlow, UK: Pearson Longman, 2007.

——. "Whatever Happened to the Janissaries? Mobilization for the 1768–1774 Russo-Ottoman War." *War in History* 5, no. 1 (1998): 23–36.

Akşin, Sina. *Turkey, from Empire to Revolutionary Republic: The Emergence of the Turkish Nation from 1789 to the Present.* Trans. Dexter H. Mursaloğlu. New York: New York University Press, 2007.

Aktan, Reşat. "Mechanization of Agriculture in Turkey." *Land Economics* 22, no. 4 (1957): 273–85.

Aktar, Ayhan. *Varlık Vergisi ve Türkleştirme Politikaları* [The capital levy and Turkification policies]. Istanbul: İletişim, 2000.

Akyıldız, Ali. *Ankanın Sonbaharı: Osmanlıda İktisadi Modernleşme ve Uluslararası Sermaye* [The Ottomans, economic modernization, and international capital]. Istanbul: İletişim, 2005.

Akyüz, Kenan. *Batı Te'sirinde Türk Şiiri Antolojisi* [Anthology of Turkish poetry under Western influence]. Ankara: Doğuş Matbaacılık, 1970.

——. *Ziya Paşa'nın Amasya Mutasarrıflığı Sırasındaki Olaylar* [Events during Ziya Paşa's governorship at Amasya]. Ankara: Ankara Üniversitesi Basımevi, 1964.

Akyüz, Yahya. *Türk Eğitim Tarihi (Başlangıçtan 1993'e)* [History of education]. Istanbul: Kültür Koleji Yayınları, 1994.

Alexander, Catherine. *Personal States: Making Connections Between People and Bureaucracy in Turkey.* Oxford: Oxford University Press, 2002.

Alexandris, Alexis. *The Greek Minority of Istanbul and Greek-Turkish Relations, 1918–1974.* Athens: Center for Asia Minor Studies, 1983.

Algar, Hamid, John Voll, et al., eds. *Bediüzzaman ve Tecdit* [Bediüzzaman and renewal]. Istanbul: Gelenek, 2002.

Ali Rıza Bey, Balıkhane Nazırı. *Eski Zamanlarda İstanbul Hayatı* [Istanbul life in olden times]. Ed. Ali Şükrü Çoruk. Istanbul: Kitabevi, 2001.

Alkan, Mehmet Ö., ed. *Tanzimat'tan Cumhuriyet'e Modernleşme Sürecinde Eğitim İstatistikleri, 1839–1924* [Education statistics from the Tanzimat to the Republic, 1839–1924]. Ankara: Devlet İstatistik Enstitüsü, 2000.

Alkan, Mustafa. "Hacı Bektaş-ı Velî Tekkesine Nakşibendî Bir şeyhin Tayini: Merkezî Bir Dayatma ve Sosyal Tepki" [On the appointment of a Nakşibendi şeyh at the shrine of Hacı Bektaş]. Paper presented at the Thirty-Eighth International Conference of Asian and North African Studies (ICANAS-38), Ankara, 2007.

Allen, W. E. D., and Paul Muratoff. *Caucasian Battlefields: A History of the Wars on the Turco-Caucasian Border, 1828–1921*. 1953. Reprint, Nashville, TN: Battery Press, 1999.

Alpay, Şahin. "'68 Kuşağı Üzerine Bir Deneme" [Essay on the '68 generation]. *Toplum ve Bilim* 41 (Spring 1988): 167–85.

Altınay, Ayşe Gül. *The Myth of the Military Nation: Militarism, Gender, and Education in Turkey*. New York: Palgrave Macmillan, 2004.

Anastassiadou, Meropi. *Salonique, 1830–1912: Une ville ottomane à l'âge des réformes*. Leiden: Brill, 1997.

And, Metin. *Culture, Performance and Communication in Turkey*. Tokyo: Daiwa, 1987.

——. *Geleneksel Türk Tiyatrosu, Köylü ve Halk Tiyatrosu Gelenekleri* [Traditional Turkish theater]. Istanbul: İnkilâp, 1985.

——. *Meşrutiyet Döneminde Türk Tiyatrosu, 1908–1923* [Turkish theater, 1908–1923]. Ankara: Türkiye İş Bankası Kültür Yayınları, 1971.

——. *Tanzimat ve İstibdat Döneminde Türk Tiyatrosu (1839–1908)* [Turkish theater, 1839–1908]. Ankara: Türkiye İş Bankası Kültür Yayınları, 1972.

Anderson, Benedict. *Imagined Communities: Reflections on the Origin and Spread of Nationalism*. 1983. Rev. ed. London: Verso, 1991.

Andrews, Walter G., Jr. *An Introduction to Ottoman Poetry*. Minneapolis: Bibliotheca Islamica, 1976.

Anscombe, Frederick F. *The Ottoman Gulf: The Creation of Kuwait, Saudi Arabia, and Qatar*. New York: Columbia University Press, 1997.

Apter, Emily. *The Translation Zone*. Princeton: Princeton University Press, 2006. [Contains two chapers on Auerbach in Istanbul]

Aracı, Emre. *Donizetti Paşa: Osmanlı Sarayının İtalyan Maestrosu* [Donizetti Paşa: The Ottoman palace's Italian maestro]. Istanbul: Yapı Kredi Yayınları, 2006.

Arat, Yeşim. *The Patriarchal Paradox*. Madison, NJ: Fairleigh Dickinson University Press, 1989.

——. *Rethinking Islam and Liberal Democracy*. Albany: SUNY Press, 2005.

Arat, Zehra F. "Turkish Women and the Republican Reconstruction of Tradition." In *Reconstructing Gender in the Middle East: Tradition, Identity, and Power*, ed. Fatma Müge Göçek and Shiva Balaghi, 57–78. New York: Columbia University Press, 1994.

Argun, Betigül Ercan. *Turkey in Germany: The Transnational Sphere of Deutschkei*. London: Routledge, 2003.

Arikan, Harun. *Turkey and the EU: An Awkward Candidate for EU Membership?* 2nd ed. Aldershot, UK: Ashgate, 2006.

Arsu, Şebnem. "Turkey Charges 86, Including Ex-Military Officers, in Coup Plot," *New York Times*, 15 July 2008, A9.

Aslan, Şükrü. *1 Mayıs Mahallesi: 1980 Öncesi Toplumsal Mücadeleler ve Kent* [The "1 May" neighborhood: social struggle and the city before 1980]. Istanbul: İletişim, 2004.

[Atatürk], Mustafa Kemal. *A Speech Delivered by Ghazi Mustapha Kemal, President of the Turkish Republic, October 1927*. Leipzig: K. F. Koehler, 1929.

[Atatürk], Mustafa Kemal, Gazi. *Nutuk*. Ankara: Türk Tayyare Cemiyeti, 1927. [The great thirty-six-hour speech]

Atay, Falih Rıfkı. *Çankaya*. Istanbul: Bateş, 1984. [Atatürk's life]

Atılgan, Gökhan. *Kemalizm ile Marksizm Arasında Geleneksel Aydınlar: Yön Devrim-Hareketi* [Traditional intellectuals between Kemalism and Marxism: The Yön-Devrim movement]. Istanbul: TÜSTAV, 2002.

Autheman, André. *The Imperial Ottoman Bank*. Trans. J. A. Underwood. Istanbul: Ottoman Bank Archives and Research Center, 2002.

Aybars, Ergun. *İstiklal Mahkemeleri, 1920–1927* [The independence tribunals, 1920–1927]. Izmir: Dokuz Eylül Üniversitesi, Atatürk İlkeleri ve İnkilâp Enstitüsü, 1988.

Aydemir, Şevket Süreyya. *Suyu Arayan Adam* [The man seeking water]. Istanbul: Remzi, 1993.

Aytürk, İlker. "The First Episode of Language Reform in Republican Turkey: The Language Council from 1926 to 1931." *Journal of the Royal Asiatic Society*, 3rd ser., 18, no. 3 (2008): 275–93.

——. "Turkish Linguists Against the West: The Origins of Linguistic Nationalism in Atatürk's Turkey." *Middle Eastern Studies* 40, no. 6 (2004): 1–25.

Baer, Marc D. *The Dönme: Jewish Converts, Muslim Revolutionaries, and Secular Turks*. Stanford, CA: Stanford University Press, 2009.

Balci, Bayram. *Missionnaires de l'Islam en Asie centrale: Les écoles turques de Fethullah Gülen*. Paris: Maisonneuve et Larose, 2003.

Banarlı, Nihâd Sâmî. *Resimli Türk Edebiyâtı Târihi* [History of Turkish literature]. Istanbul: Milli Eğitim, 1987.

Barlas, Dilek. *Etatism and Diplomacy in Turkey: Economic and Foreign Policy Strategies in an Uncertain World, 1929–1939*. Leiden: Brill, 1998.

Baron, Beth. *The Women's Awakening in Egypt: Culture, Society, and the Press*. New Haven: Yale University Press, 1994.

Behar, Büşra Ersanlı. *İktidar ve Tarih: Türkiye'de "Resmi Tarih" Tezinin Oluşumu, 1929–1937* [Power and history: The formation of the "Official History" thesis in Turkey, 1929–1937]. Istanbul: Afa, 1992.

Behar, Cem. *A Neighborhood in Ottoman Istanbul: Fruit Vendors and Civil Servants in the Kasap İlyas Mahalle*. Albany: SUNY Press, 2003.

Behar, Cem, ed. *Osmanlı İmparatorluğu'nun ve Türkiye'nin Nüfusu, 1500–1927* [The population of the Ottoman empire and Turkey]. Ankara: Devlet İstatistik Enstitüsü, 1996.

Bein, Amit. "A 'Young Turk' Islamic Intellectual: Filibeli Ahmed Hilmi and the Diverse Intellectual Legacies of the Late Ottoman Empire." *IJMES* 39, no. 4 (2007): 607–25.

Benoist-Méchin, Ja[c]ques. *Turkey, 1908–1938, the End of the Ottoman Empire: A History in Documentary Photographs*. Vaduz: Jeunesse, 1989.

Berkes, Niyazi. *The Development of Secularism in Turkey*. Montreal: McGill University Press, 1964.

Beşikçi, Mehmet. "The Organized Mobilization of Popular Sentiments: The Ottoman Navy League, 1909–1919." MA thesis, Istanbul: Boğaziçi University, 1999.

Beydilli, Kemal. *Türk Bilim ve Matbaacılık Tarihinde Mühendishâne, Mühendishane Matbaası, ve Kütüphanesi (1776–1826)* [The engineering academy, its press, and its library in the history of Turkish science and printing, 1776–1826]. Istanbul: Eren, 1995.

Bianchi, Robert. *Interest Groups and Political Development in Turkey*. Princeton: Princeton University Press, 1984.

Bingöl, Sedat. *Tanzimat Devrinde Osmanlı'da Yargı Reformu (Nizâmiyye Mahkemeleri'nin Kuruluşu ve İşleyişi, 1840–1876)* [Judicial reform in the Tanzimat, 1840–1876]. Eskişehir: Anadolu Üniversitesi Yayınları, 2004.

Birand, Mehmet Ali. *Shirts of Steel: An Anatomy of the Turkish Armed Forces*. Trans. Saliha Paker and Ruth Christie. London: I. B. Tauris, 1991.

Black, Jeremy. *Western Warfare, 1775–1882*. Bloomington: Indiana University Press, 2001.

Bloxham, Donald. *The Great Game of Genocide: Imperialism, Nationalism, and the Destruction of the Ottoman Armenians*. Oxford: Oxford University Press, 2005.

Bloxham, Donald, and Fatma Müge Göçek. "The Armenian Genocide." In *The Historiography of Genocide*, ed. Dan Stone, 344–72. London: Palgrave, 2008.

Blumi, Isa. *Rethinking the Late Ottoman Empire: A Comparative Social and Political History of Albania and Yemen, 1878–1918*. Istanbul: Isis, 2003.

Boratav, Korkut. *Türkiye İktisat Tarihi, 1908–1985* [Economic history of Turkey, 1908–1985]. Istanbul [?]: Gerçek, 1988.

Borgerhoff, Joseph L., ed. *Nineteenth Century French Plays*. New York: Appleton-Century-Crofts, 1959.

Bostan, Idris. *Beylikten İmparatorluğa Osmanlı Denizciliği* [Ottoman navigation]. Istanbul: Kitapyayınevi, 2006.

Bouquet, Olivier. *Les pachas du Sultan: Essai sur les agents supérieurs de l'état Ottoman (1839–1909)*. Paris: Peeters, 2007.

al-Boustany, Salah al-Din, ed. *The Journals of Bonaparte in Egypt*. 10 vols. Cairo: Al-Arab Bookshop, 1971.

Bozarslan, Hamit. "Le Mahdisme en Turquie: L''incident de Menemen' en 1930." *Revue du Monde Musulman et de la Mèditerranée* 91–94 (2000): 297–320.

———. "Le phénomène milicien: Une composante de la violence politique en Turquie des années 70." *Turcica* 31 (1999): 185–244.

Bozdoğan, Sibel. *Modernism and Nation Building: Turkish Architectural Culture in the Early Republic*. Seattle: University of Washington Press, 2001.

Bozdoğan, Sibel, and Reşat Kasaba, eds. *Rethinking Modernity and National Identity in Turkey*. Seattle: University of Washington Press, 1997.

Brockett, Gavin. "Betwixt and Between: Turkish Print Culture and the Emergence of Turkish National Identity, 1945–1954." PhD diss., University of Chicago, 2003.

———. "The Legend of 'the Turk' in Korea: Popular Perceptions of the Korean War and Their Importance to a Turkish National Identity." *War and Society* 22, no. 2 (2004): 109–42.

Brown, L. Carl. *International Politics and the Middle East: Old Rules, Dangerous Game*. Princeton: Princeton University Press, 1984.

———. *The Tunisia of Ahmad Bey, 1837–1855*. Princeton: Princeton University Press, 1974.

Bruinessen, Martin van. *Agha, Shaikh and State: The Social and Political Structures of Kurdistan*. London: Zed Books, 1992.

———. *Kurdish Ethno-Nationalism Versus Nation-Building States*. Istanbul: Isis, 2000.

Brummett, Palmira. *Image and Imperialism in the Ottoman Revolutionary Press, 1908–1911.* Albany: SUNY Press, 2000.

Buğra, Ayşe. "Class, Culture, and State: An Analysis of Interest Representation by Two Turkish Business Associations." *IJMES* 30, no. 4 (1998): 521–39.

——. "Poverty and Citizenship: An Overview of the Social-Policy Environment in Republican Turkey." *IJMES* 39, no. 1 (2007): 33–52.

——. *State and Business in Modern Turkey: A Comparative Study.* Albany: SUNY Press, 1994.

Can, Bilmez Bülent. *Demiryolundan Petrole Chester Projesi, 1908–1923* [The Chester project, 1908–1923]. Istanbul: Tarih Vakfı, 2000.

Cevdet, Ahmed. *Tarih-i Cevdet* [Cevdet's history]. 2nd ed. (*Tertib-i Cedid*) [Revised arrangement]. Istanbul: Matbaa-ı Osmaniye, 1309/1891–92.

Chatterjee, Partha. *The Nation and Its Fragments: Colonial and Postcolonial Histories.* Princeton: Princeton University Press, 1993.

Citino, Nathan J. "The Ottoman Legacy in Cold War Modernization." *IJMES* 40, no. 4 (2008): 579–97.

Cizre-Sakallıoğlu, Ümit. "Labour and State in Turkey: 1960–80." *Middle Eastern Studies* 28, no. 4 (1992): 712–28.

Clayer, Nathalie. *Aux origines du nationalisme albanais: La naissance d'une nation majoritairement musulmane en Europe.* Paris: Éditions Karthala, 2007.

Cleveland, William L. *A History of the Modern Middle East.* Boulder, CO: Westview, 1994.

Cole, Juan. *Colonialism and Revolution in the Middle East: Social and Cultural Origins of Egypt's 'Urabi Movement.* Princeton: Princeton University Press, 1993.

——. *Napoleon's Egypt: Invading the Middle East.* New York: Palgrave Macmillan, 2007.

Copeaux, Étienne. *Espaces et temps de la nation turque: Analyse d'une historiographie nationaliste, 1931–1993.* Paris: CNRS Éditions, 1997.

Criss, Bilge. *İşgal Altında İstanbul* [Istanbul under occupation]. Istanbul: İletişim, 1994.

Cuno, Kenneth. *The Pasha's Peasants: Land, Society, and Economy in Lower Egypt, 1740–1858.* Cambridge: Cambridge University Press, 1992.

Çadırcı, Musa. *Tanzimat Döneminde Anadolu Kentleri'nin Sosyal ve Ekonomik Yapıları* [Social and economic structure of Anatolian cities in the Tanzimat period]. Ankara: Türk Tarih Kurumu, 1991.

Çakır, Coşkun. *Tanzimat Dönemi Osmanlı Maliyesi* [Ottoman finance in the Tanzimat period]. Istanbul: Küre, 2001.

Çakır, Serpil. *Osmanlı Kadın Hareketi* [The Ottoman women's movement]. Istanbul: Metis, 1994.

Çarkoğlu, Ali. "Ideology or Economic Pragmatism? Profiling Turkish Voters in 2007." *Turkish Studies* 9, no. 2 (2008): 317–44.

Çarkoğlu, Ali, and Ersin Kalaycıoğlu. *Turkish Democracy Today: Elections, Protest and Stability in an Islamic Society.* London: I. B. Tauris, 2007.

Çavdar, Tevfik. *Türkiye Ekonomisinin Tarihi, 1900–1960* [Economic history of Turkey, 1900–1960]. Istanbul: İmge, 2002.

——. *Türkiye'nin Demokrasi Tarihi, 1839–1850* [History of democracy in Turkey, 1839–1850]. Istanbul: İmge, 2004.

Çayır, Kenan. *Islamic Literature in Contemporary Turkey: From Epic to Novel.* Houndmills, UK: Palgrave Macmillan, 2007.

Çelik, Hüseyin. *Ali Suavî ve Dönemi* [Ali Suavi and his period]. Istanbul: İletişim, 1994. *See also* Ebüzziya

Çetinkaya, Y. Doğan. *1908 Boykotu: Bir Toplumsal Hareketin Analizi* [The 1908 boycott: analysis of a social movement]. Istanbul: İletişim, 2004.

Çizgen (Özendes), Engin. *Photographer Ali Sami, 1866–1936.* Istanbul: Haşet, 1989. *See also* Özendes

Çınar, Menderes. "Turkey's Transformation Under the AKP Rule." *Muslim World* 96 (July 2006): 469–86.

Çoker, Fahri. *6–7 Eylül Olayları: Fotoğraflar—Belgeler, Fahri Çoker Arşivi* [Photographs of the events of 6–7 September 1955]. Istanbul: Tarih Vakfı, 2005.

Danielson, Michael N., and Ruşen Keleş. *The Politics of Rapid Urbanization: Government and Growth in Modern Turkey.* New York: Holmes and Meier, 1985.

Davison, Andrew. *Secularism and Revivalism in Turkey: A Hermeneutic Reconsideration.* New Haven: Yale University Press, 1998.

Davison, Roderic H. *Essays in Ottoman and Turkish History.* Austin: University of Texas Press, 1990.

——. *Reform in the Ottoman Empire, 1856–1876.* Princeton: Princeton University Press, 1963.

Dawisha, Adeed. *Arab Nationalism in the Twentieth Century: From Triumph to Despair.* Princeton: Princeton University Press, 2003.

Delanty, Gerard. *Modernity and Post-Modernity: Knowledge, Power and the Self.* London: Sage, 2000.

Demir, Ömer, Mustafa Acar, and Metin Toprak. "Anatolian Tigers or Islamic Capital: Prospects and Challenges." *Middle Eastern Studies* 40, no. 6 (2004): 166–88.

Demir, Yavuz. *Zaman Zaman İçinde, Roman Roman İçinde: Müşâhedât (Bir Üstkurmaca Olarak Müşâhedât)* [Müşahedat as a critical novel]. Istanbul: Dergâh, 2002.

Demirel, Ahmet. *Birinci Meclis'te Muhalefet* [Opposition in the First Grand National Assembly]. Istanbul: İletişim, 1994.

Deringil, Selim. *Turkish Foreign Policy during the Second World War: An "Active" Neutrality.* Cambridge: Cambridge University Press, 1989.

——. *The Well-Protected Domains: Ideology and the Legitimation of Power in the Ottoman Empire.* London: I. B. Tauris, 1998.

Devereux, Robert. *The First Ottoman Constitutional Period: A Study of the Midhat Constitution and Parliament.* Baltimore: Johns Hopkins University Press, 1963.

Dinan, Desmond. *Europe Recast: A History of European Union.* Boulder, CO: Lynne Rienner, 2004.

Dinan, Desmond, ed. *Origins and Evolution of the European Union.* Oxford: Oxford Unioversity Press, 2006.

Dodd, C. H. *The Crisis of Turkish Democracy.* Beverly, UK: Eothen, 1983.

——. *Politics and Government in Turkey.* Berkeley: University of California Press, 1969.

Doumani, Beshara. *Rediscovering Palestine: Merchants and Peasants in Jabal Nablus, 1700–1900.* Berkeley: University of California Press, 1995.

Douwes, Dick. *The Ottomans in Syria: A History of Justice and Oppression.* London: I. B. Tauris, 2000.

Dragostinova, Theodora. "Between Two Motherlands: Struggles for Nationhood among the Greeks in Bulgaria, 1906–1949." PhD diss., University of Illinois at Urbana-Champaign, 2005.

Dresch, Paul. *Tribes, Government, and History in Yemen.* Oxford: Clarendon Press, 1993.

Druzhinina, E[lena] I[oasafovna]. *Kiuchuk-Kainardzhiiskii Mir 1774 Goda: Ego Podgotovka i Zakliuchenie* [The Küçük-Kaynarca Peace of 1774: its preparation and conclusion]. Moscow: Izd-vo Akademii nauk SSSR, 1955.

Duara, Prasenjit. *Rescuing History from the Nation: Questioning Narratives of Modern China.* Chicago: University of Chicago Press, 1995.

Duben, Alan, and Cem Behar. *Istanbul Households: Marriage, Family and Fertility, 1880–1940.* Cambridge: Cambridge University Press, 1991.

Dumont, Paul. "Said Bey: The Everyday Life of an Istanbul Townsman at the Beginning of the Twentieth Century." In *The Modern Middle East: A Reader,* ed. Albert Hourani, Philip S. Khoury, and Mary C. Wilson, 271–87. Berkeley: University of California Press, 1993.

Dumont, Paul, ed. *Turquie: Livres d'hier, livres d'aujourdhui.* Strasbourg: Centre de recherche sur la Civilisation ottomane et le domaine turc contemporain, 1992.

Dumont, Paul, and François Georgeon, eds. *Villes ottomanes à la fin de l'Empire.* Paris: L'Harmattan, 1992.

Durakbaşa, Ayşe. "Kemalism as Identity Politics in Turkey." In *Deconstructing Images of "The Turkish Woman,"* ed. Zehra F. Arat, 139–55. New York: St. Martin's, 1998.

Ebüzziya, Ziyad. *Şinasi* [Study of İbrahim Şinasi]. Ed. Hüseyin Çelik. Istanbul: İletişim, 1997.

Ekinci, Mehmet Uğur. "The Origins of the 1897 Ottoman-Greek War: A Diplomatic History." MA thesis, Ankara: Bilkent University, 2006.

Eksertzoglou, Haris. *Osmanlı'da Cemiyetler ve Rum Cemaati: Dersaadet Rum Cemiyet-i Edebiyesi, 1861–1912* [The Ottoman Greek community and the Greek Literary Society of Istanbul, 1861–1912]. Trans. Foti Benlisoy and Stefo Benlisoy. Istanbul: Türkiye Ekonomik ve Toplumsal Tarih Vakfı, 1999.

Eldem, Edhem. *A History of the Ottoman Bank.* Istanbul: Ottoman Bank Historical Research Center, 1999.

Eligür, Banu. "Turkey's March 2009 Local Elections." *Turkish Studies,* 10, no. 3 (2009): 469–96.

Ellison, Grace. *An Englishwoman in a Turkish Harem.* London: Methuen, 1915.

——. *An Englishwoman in Angora.* New York: Dutton, n.d. [1923?].

Elmacı, Mehmet Emin. *İttihat Terakki ve Kapitulasyonlar* [The Committee of Union and Progress and the capitulations]. Istanbul: Homer, 2005.

Elon, Amos. *The Israelis, Founders and Sons.* New York: Bantam, 1971.

Enginün, İnci. *Halide Edib Adıvar'ın Eserlerinde Doğu ve Batı Meselesi* [East and West in the works of Halide Edib]. Istanbul: Edebiyat Fakültesi Matbaası, 1978.

Erdem, Hakan. "Recruitment for the 'Victorious Soldiers of Muhammad' in the Arab Provinces, 1826–1828." In *Histories of the Modern Middle East: New Directions*, ed. Israel Gershoni, Hakan Erdem, and Ursula Woköck, 189–206. Boulder, CO: Lynne Rienner, 2002.

Ergin, Osman. *İstanbul Mektepleri ve İlim, Terbiye ve San'at Müesseseleri Dolayısıyla Türkiye Maarif Tarihi*. [History of education]. 5 vols. Istanbul: Osmanbey Matbaası, 1939–43.

Erichsen, Regine. "Das Türkische Exil als Geschichte von Frauen und Ihr Beitrag zum Wissenschaftstransfer in die Türkei von 1933 bis 1945." *Berichte zur Wissenschaftsgeschichte* 28 (2005): 337–53.

Erickson, Edward J. *Defeat in Detail: The Ottoman Army in the Balkans, 1912–1913*. Westport, CT: Praeger, 2003.

———. *Ordered to Die: A History of the Ottoman Army in the First World War*. Westport, CT: Greenwood, 2001.

———. *Ottoman Army Effectiveness in World War I*. London: Routledge, 2007.

Erman, Tahire. "The Politics of Squatter (*Gecekondu*) Studies in Turkey: The Changing Representations of Rural Migrants in the Academic Discourse." *Urban Studies* 38, no. 7 (2001): 983–1002.

Eroğul, Cem. *Demokrat Parti (Tarihi ve İdeoloji)* [Democrat Party, history and ideology]. Ankara: İmge, 1990.

Erol, Sibel. "Sexual Discourse in Turkish Fiction: Return of the Repressed Female Identity." *Edebiyât* 6 (1995): 187–202.

Esen, Nüket, and Erol Köroğlu, eds. *Hayata Bakan Edebiyat: Adalet Ağaoğulu'nun Yapıtlarına Eleştirel Yaklaşımlar* [Literature that looks at life: critical approaches to the works of Adalet Ağaoğlu]. Istanbul: Boğaziçi Üniversitesi Yayınevi, 2003.

Evin, Ahmet Ö. *Origins and Development of the Turkish Novel*. Minneapolis: Bibliotheca Islamica, 1984.

Ewing, Katherine Pratt. *Stolen Honor: Stigmatizing Muslim Men in Berlin*. Stanford, CA: Stanford University Press, 2008.

Eyice, Semavi. "İstanbul'un Kaybolan Eski Eserlerinden: Fatma Sultan Camii ve Gümüşhaneli Dergâhı" [The Fatma Sultan Mosque and the Gümüşhaneli Meeting Hall]. *İstanbul Üniversitesi İktisat Fakültesi Mecmuası (Prof. Dr. Sabri F. Ülgener'e Armağan)* 43, no. 1–4 (1984–85): 475–511.

Fahmy, Khaled. *All the Pasha's Men: Mehmed Ali, His Army and the Making of Modern Egypt*. Cambridge: Cambridge University Press, 1997.

Faroqhi, Suraiya. *Der Bektaschi-Orden in Anatolien*. Vienna: Institut für Orientalistik der Universität Wien, 1981.

Faroqhi, Suraiya N., ed. *The Later Ottoman Empire, 1603–1839*. Vol. 3 of *The Cambridge History of Turkey*. Cambridge: Cambridge University Press, 2006.

Fatma Aliye. *Muhazarat* [Debates]. Istanbul: Matbaa-ı Ebüzziya, 1309/1891–92.

Fawaz, Leila Tarazi. *Merchants and Migrants in Nineteenth-Century Beirut*. Cambridge, MA: Harvard University Press, 1983.

Fewster, Kevin, Vecihi Başarın, and Hatice Hürmüz Başarın. *Gallipoli: The Turkish Story*. Crows Nest, Australia: Allen and Unwin, 2003.

Feyizoğlu, Turan. *Türkiye'de Gençlik Hareketleri Tarihi (1960–1968)* [Youth movements in Turkey, 1960–1968]. Istanbul: Belge Uluslararası Yayıncılık, 1993.

Findley, Carter Vaughn. "The Advent of Ideology in the Islamic Middle East (Part II)." *Studia Islamica* 56 (1982): 147–80.

——. "Ahmed Midhat'in *Sevda-yı Say-ü-Amel'*i" [Ahmed Midhat on free enterprise]. Trans. Boğaç Ergene. *Tarih ve Toplum*, November 2000, 23–29.

——. *Bureaucratic Reform in the Ottoman Empire: The Sublime Porte, 1789–1922*. Princeton: Princeton University Press, 1980.

——. "Ebu Bekir Ratib's Vienna Embassy Narrative: Discovering Austria or Propagandizing for Reform in Istanbul?" *Wiener Zeitschrift für die Kunde des Morgenlandes* 85 (1995): 41–80.

——. "The Evolution of the System of Provincial Administration as Viewed from the Center." In *Palestine in the Late Ottoman Period: Political, Social and Economic Transformation*, ed. David Kushner, 3–29. Jerusalem: Yad Izhak Ben-Zvi, 1986.

——. "État et droit dans la pensée politique ottomane: Droits de l'homme ou *Rechtsstaat*? À propos de deux relations d'ambassade." *Études Turques et Ottomanes, Documents de Travail* 4 (December 1995): 39–50.

——. "Osmanlı Siyasal Düşüncesinde Devlet ve Hukuk: İnsan Hakları mı, Hukuk Devleti mi?" [Human rights or *Rechtsstaat*? State and law in Ottoman political thought]. In *XII. [Onikinci] Türk Tarihi Kongresi*, 1195–202. Ankara: Türk Tarih Kurumu, 2000.

——. *Ottoman Civil Officialdom: A Social History*. Princeton: Princeton University Press, 1989.

——. "An Ottoman Occidentalist in Europe: Ahmed Midhat Meets Madame Gülnar, 1889." *American Historical Review* 103, no. 1 (1998): 15–49.

——. "Problems of Educational Democratization in an Era of Explosive Population Growth." *Journal of the Japan-Netherlands Institute* 6 (1996): 257–76.

——. "Rauf İnan'ı Anarken" [Remembering Rauf İnan]. *Kebikeç* 2, no. 3 (1996): 77–82.

——. "La soumise, la subversive: Fatma Aliye, romancière et féministe." *Turcica* 27 (1995): 153–76.

——. "Subjectivity and Society: Ahmed Midhat and Fatma Aliye." Unpublished paper, 2001.

——. *The Turks in World History*. New York: Oxford University Press, 2005.

——. "Writer and Subject, Self and Other: Mouradgea d'Ohsson and His *Tableau Général de l'Empire Othoman*." In *The Torch of the Empire: Ignatius Mouradgea d'Ohsson's Tableau Général de l'Empire othoman in the Eighteenth Century*, 23–57. Istanbul: Yapı Kredi Yayınları, 2002.

Findley, Carter Vaughn, and John Alexander Murray Rothney. *Twentieth-Century World*. 5th ed. Boston: Houghton Mifflin, 2002.

Finkel, Caroline. *Osman's Dream: The Story of the Ottoman Empire, 1300–1923*. New York: Basic Books, 2005.

Finn, Robert P. *The Early Turkish Novel, 1872–1900*. Istanbul: Isis, 1984.

Fleming, Katherine E. *The Muslim Bonaparte: Diplomacy and Orientalism in Ali Pasha's Greece*. Princeton: Princeton University Press, 1999.

Foley, Sean. "Shaykh Khalid and the Naqshbandiyya-Khalidiyya, 1776–2005." PhD diss., Georgetown University, 2005.

Fortna, Benjamin. *Imperial Classroom: Islam, the State, and Education in the Late Ottoman Empire.* Oxford: Oxford University Press, 2002.

Frey, Frederick W. *The Turkish Political Elite.* Cambridge, MA: MIT Press, 1965.

Frierson, Elizabeth. "Unimagined Communities: State, Press, and Gender in the Hamidian Era." PhD diss., Princeton University, 1996.

Fromkin, David. *A Peace to End All Peace: Creating the Modern Middle East, 1914–1922.* New York: Henry Holt, 1989.

Galip, Şeyh. *Beauty and Love.* Trans. and ed. Victoria Rowe Holbrook. New York: Modern Language Association, 2005.

Gawrych, George. *The Crescent and the Eagle: Ottoman Rule, Islam and the Albanians, 1874–1913.* London: I. B. Tauris, 2006.

Genç, Mehmet. *Osmanlı İmparatorluğunda Devlet ve Ekonomi* [State and economy in the Ottoman Empire]. Istanbul: Ötüken, 2000.

Georgeon, François. *Abdulhamid II, le sultan calife.* Paris: Fayard, 2003.

———. *Aux origines du nationalisme Turc: Yusuf Akçura (1876–1935).* Paris: Éditions ADPF, 1980.

———. *Des Ottomans aux Turcs: Naissance d'une nation.* Istanbul: Isis, 1995.

Georgeon, François, and Paul Dumont, eds. *Vivre dans l'Empire ottoman: Sociabilités et relations intercommunautaires (XVIIIe–XXe siècles).* Paris: L'Harmattan, 1997.

Gerber, Haim. *Ottoman Rule in Jerusalem, 1890–1914.* Berlin: Klaus Schwarz, 1985.

Gezik, Erdal. *Dinsel, Etnik ve Politik Sorunlar Bağlamında Alevi Kürtler* [The Alevi Kurds in the context of religious, ethnic, and political questions]. Ankara: Kalan, 2000.

Giddens, Anthony. *Modernity and Self-Identity: Self and Society in the Late Modern Age.* Stanford, CA: Stanford University Press, 1991.

Gingeras, Ryan. "Notorious Subjects, Invisible Citizens: North Caucasian Resistance to the Turkish National Movement in Northwestern Anatolia, 1919–23." *IJMES* 40, no. 1 (2008): 89–108.

Goldschmidt Jr., Arthur. *Modern Egypt: The Formation of a Nation-State.* Boulder, CO: Westview, 1988.

Göçek, Fatma Müge. "Furor Against the West: Nationalism as the Dangerous Underbelly of Modern Turkey." In *Nationalism and European Integration,* ed. I. Pawel Karolewski and A. Marcin Suszycki, 168–80. New York: Continuum, 2007.

———. *Rise of the Bourgeoisie, Demise of Empire: Ottoman Westernization and Social Change.* New York: Oxford University Press, 1996.

———. "Through a Glass Darkly: Consequences of a Politicized Past in Contemporary Turkey." *Annals of the American Academy of Political and Social Science* 617, no. 1 (2008): 88–106.

———. "Turkish Historiography and the Unbearable Weight of 1915." In *Cultural and Ethical Legacies of the Armenian Genocide,* ed. Richard Hovannisian, 337–67. New Brunswick, NJ: Transaction, 2006.

———. "What Is the Meaning of the 1908 Young Turk Revolution? A Critical Historical Assessment in 2008." *İstanbul Üniversitesi Siyasal Bilgiler Fakültesi Dergisi* 38 (2008): 179–214.

Göçek, Fatma Müge, ed. *Social Constructions of Nationalism in the Middle East*. Albany: SUNY Press, 2002.

Göçgün, Önder. *Namık Kemâl'ın Şairliği ve Bütün Şiirleri* [Namık Kemal and his complete poems]. Ankara: Atatürk Kültür Merkezi, 1999.

Gökalp, Deniz, and Seda Ünsar. "From the Myth of European Union Accession to Disillusion: Implications for Religious and Ethnic Polarization in Turkey." *Middle East Journal* 62, no. 1 (2008): 93–116.

Gökalp, Ziya. *Turkish Nationalism and Western Civilization*. Ed. and trans. Niyazi Berkes. New York: Columbia University Press, 1959.

———. *Türkleşmek, İslâmlaşmak, Muasırlaşmak* [On becoming Turkish, Islamic, and modern]. 1918. Reprint, ed. Kemal Bek. Istanbul: Bordo Siyah, 2004.

Göle, Nilüfer. *Modern Mahrem: Medeniyet ve Örtünme* [Modernity and veiling]. Istanbul: Metis, 1991.

Grant, Jonathan. "The Sword of the Sultan: Ottoman Arms Imports, 1854–1914." *Journal of Military History* 66, no. 1 (2002): 9–36.

Greene, Molly. *A Shared World: Christians and Muslims in the Early Modern Mediterranean*. Princeton: Princeton University Press, 2000.

Güçlü, Yücel. *Eminence Grise of the Turkish Foreign Service: Numan Menemencioğlu*. Ankara: Grafiker, 2002.

Gümüş, Semih. *Adalet Ağaoğlu'nun Romancılığı* [Adalet Ağaoğlu as a novelist]. Istanbul: Adam Yayınları, 2000.

Güran, Tevfik. *19. [Ondokuzuncu] Yüzyıl Osmanlı Tarımı Üzerine Araştırmalar* [Studies on nineteenth-century Ottoman agriculture]. Istanbul: Eren, 1998.

———. *Osmanlı Devleti'nin İlk İstatistik Yıllığı, 1897* [The first statistical yearbook of the Ottoman Empire, 1897]. Ankara: Devlet İstatistik Enstitüsü, 1997.

Güran, Tevfik, ed. *Osmanlı Dönemi Tarım İstatistikleri, 1909, 1913 ve 1914* [Ottoman agricultural statistics, 1909, 1913, and 1914]. Ankara: Devlet İstatistik Enstitüsü, 1997.

Gürüz, Kemal, Erdoğan Şuhubi, A. M. Celal Şengör, Kazım Türker, and Ersin Yurtsever. *Türkiye'de ve Dünyada Yükseköğretim, Bilim ve Teknoloji* [Higher education, knowledge, and technology in Turkey and the world]. Istanbul: Türk Sanayicileri ve İşadamları Derneği, 1994.

Güven, Dilek. *Cumhuriyet Dönemi Azınlık Politikaları Bağlamında: 6–7 Eylül Olayları*. [The republic's minority policy and the events of 6–7 September 1955]. Istanbul: Tarih Vakfı, 2005.

Güvenç, Bozkurt. *Türk Kimliği: Kültür Tarihinin Kaynakları* [Turkish identity: sources of cultural history]. Ankara: Kültür Bakanlığı, 1993.

Hale, Charles A. *The Transformation of Liberalism in Late Nineteenth-Century Mexico*. Princeton: Princeton University Press, 1989.

Hale, William. *The Political and Economic Development of Modern Turkey*. New York: St. Martin's, 1981.

———. *Turkish Foreign Policy, 1774–2000*. London: Frank Cass, 2000.

———. *Turkish Politics and the Military*. London: Routledge, 1994.

Hanioğlu, M. Şükrü. *A Brief History of the Late Ottoman Empire*. Princeton: Princeton University Press, 2008.

———. *Preparation for a Revolution: The Young Turks, 1902–1908.* New York: Oxford University Press, 2001.

———. *The Young Turks in Opposition.* New York: Oxford University Press, 1995.

Hansen, Bent. *Egypt and Turkey.* Oxford: Published for the World Bank by Oxford University Press, 1991.

Hanssen, Jens. *Fin de Siècle Beirut: The Making of an Ottoman Provincial Capital.* Oxford: Clarendon Press, 2005.

Hathaway, Jane, with contributions by Karl Barbir. *The Arab Lands Under Ottoman Rule: 1516–1800.* Harlow: Longman, 2008.

———. *The Politics of Households in Ottoman Egypt: The Rise of the Qazdağlıs.* Cambridge: Cambridge University Press, 1997.

Heinzelmann, Tobias. *Heiliger Kampf oder Landesverteidigung? Die Diskussion um die Einführung der allgemeinen Militärpflicht im Osmanischen Reich, 1826–1856.* Frankfurt: Peter Lang, 2003.

Helicke, James C. "Islam, National Identity, and Modernity: The Revival of the 'Turkish-Muslim' Journal *Sebilürreşad* in Turkey's Multiparty Period." Seminar paper, Ohio State University, 2006.

Heper, Metin. *Historical Dictionary of Turkey.* Metuchen, NJ: Scarecrow, 1994.

———. *İsmet İnönü: The Making of a Turkish Statesman.* Leiden: Brill, 1998.

———. *The State and Kurds in Turkey: The Question of Assimilation.* Houndsmill, UK: Palgrave Macmillan, 2007.

Heper, Metin, ed. *Democracy and Local Government: Istanbul in the 1980s.* Beverly, UK: Eothen, 1987.

———. *Local Government in Turkey: Governing Greater Istanbul.* London: Routledge, 1989.

Heper, Metin, Ali Kazancıgil, and Bert A. Rockman, eds. *Institutions and Democratic Statecraft.* Boulder, CO: Westview, 1997.

Heper, Metin, Ayşe Öncü, and Heinz Kramer, eds. *Turkey and the West: Changing Political and Cultural Identities.* London: I. B. Tauris, 1993.

Heper, Metin, and Sabri Sayarı, eds. *Political Leaders and Democracy in Turkey.* Lanham, MD: Lexington Books, 2002.

Heper, Metin, and Fuat Keyman. "Double-Faced State: Political Patronage and the Consolidation of Democracy in Turkey." In *Turkey Before and After Atatürk, Internal and External Affairs,* ed. Sylvia Kedourie, 259–77. London: Frank Cass, 1999.

Heper, Metin, and Şule Toktaş. "Islam, Modernity, and Democracy in Contemporary Turkey: The Case of Recep Tayyip Erdogan." *Muslim World* 93, no. 2 (2003): 157–85.

Hermansen, Marcia. "The Cultivation of Memory in the Gülen Community," 2007. Available at http://en.fgulen.com/content/view/2444/53/.

Hirschon, Renée. *Heirs of the Greek Catastrophe: The Social Life of Asia Minor Refugees in Piraeus.* New York: Berghahn Books, 1998.

Hirschon, Renée, ed. *Crossing the Aegean: An Appraisal of the 1923 Compulsory Population Exchange Between Greece and Turkey.* New York: Berghahn Books, 2003.

Hobsbawm, E. J. *Nations and Nationalism since 1780: Programme, Myth, Reality.* 2nd ed. Cambridge: Cambridge University Press, 1992.

Hodgson, Marshall G. S. *The Venture of Islam: Conscience and History in a World Civilization.* Vol. 2: *The Expansion of Islam in the Middle Periods.* Chicago: University of Chicago Press, 1974.

Holbrook, Victoria Rowe. *The Unreadable Shores of Love: Turkish Modernity and Mystic Romance.* Austin: University of Texas Press, 1994. *See also* Galip

Horrocks, David, and Eva Kolinsky, eds. *Turkish Culture in German Society Today.* Providence, RI: Berghahn, 1996.

Hourani, Albert. *A History of the Arab Peoples.* Cambridge, MA: Belknap Press of Harvard University Press, 1991.

Hourani, Albert, Philip S. Khoury, and Mary C. Wilson, eds. *The Modern Middle East: A Reader.* Berkeley: University of California Press, 1993.

Hulkiender, Murat. *Bir Galata Bankerinin Portresi: George Zarifi (1806–1884)* [Portrait of a Galata banker: George Zarifi, 1806–1884]. Istanbul: Osmanlı Bankası Arşiv ve Araştırma Merkezi, 2003.

Hurewitz, J. C., ed. *The Middle East and North Africa in World Politics: A Documentary Record.* 2 vols. New Haven: Yale University Press, 1975–1979.

Hütteroth, Wolf-Dieter, and Volker Höhfeld. *Türkei.* Darmstadt: Wissenschaftliche Buchgesellschaft, 2002.

Hyland, Steven. "Margins of the *Mahjar:* Arabic-Speaking Immigrants in Argentina, 1880–1946." PhD diss., Ohio State University, 2010.

İhsanoğlu, Ekmeleddin, and Mustafa Kaçar, eds. *Çağını Yakalayan Osmanlı! Osmanlı Devleti'nde Modern Haberleşme ve Ulaştırma Teknikleri* [The Ottoman who caught up with his times! Modern communication and transportation technologies in the Ottoman Empire]. Istanbul: İslam Tarih, Sanat ve Kültür Araştırma Merkezi (IRCICA), 1995.

İnal, Mahmud Kemal. *Son Asır Türk Şairleri* [Late Ottoman poets]. Istanbul: Milli Eğitim, 1969.

İnalcik, Halil, and Donald Quataert, eds. *An Economic and Social History of the Ottoman Empire, 1300–1914.* Cambridge: Cambridge University Press, 1994.

İnalcık, Halil. *Tanzimat ve Bulgar Meselesi* [The Tanzimat and the Bulgarian problem]. Istanbul: Eren, 1992.

İnan, M. Rauf. *Bir Ömrün Öyküsü* [Memoirs]. Ankara: Öğretmen Yayınları, 1988.

İslamoğlu, Abdullah. *II. Meşrutiyet Döneminde Siyasal Muhalefet (1908–1913)* [Political opposition during the Second Constitutional Period, 1908–1913]. Istanbul: Gökkubbe, 2004.

Issawi, Charles. *An Economic History of the Middle East and North Africa.* New York: Columbia University Press, 1982.

al-Jabarti, 'Abd al-Rahman. *Napoleon in Egypt: Al-Jabartī's Chronicle of the French Occupation, 1798.* Trans. Shmuel Moreh. Princeton: Markus Wiener, 1993.

Jelavich, Barbara. *History of the Balkans.* Vol. 1: *Eighteenth and Nineteenth Centuries.* Cambridge: Cambridge University Press, 1987.

Judt, Tony. *Postwar: A History of Europe Since 1945.* London: Penguin, 2005.

Jusdanis, Gregory. *The Necessary Nation.* Princeton: Princeton University Press, 2001.

Kabacalı, Alpay. *Ahmet İhsan Tokgöz'ün Matbuat Hatıralarım* [A. I. Tokgöz's memoirs of printing and publishing]. Istanbul: İletişim, 1993.

———. *Cumhuriyet Öncesi ve Sonrası Matbaa ve Basın Sanayii* [The printing industry, before the republic and under it]. Istanbul: Cem Ofset, 1998.

Kalaycıoğlu, Ersin. *Turkish Dynamics: Bridge Across Troubled Lands.* New York: Palgrave Macmillan, 2005.

Kamp, Marianne. *The New Woman in Uzbekistan: Islam, Modernity, and Unveiling Under Communism.* Seattle: University of Washington Press, 2006.

Kandiyoti, Deniz. "End of Empire: Islam, Nationalism and Women in Turkey." In *Women, Islam, and the State,* ed. Deniz Kandiyoti, 22–47. Philadelphia: Temple University Press, 1991.

Kandiyoti, Deniz, and Ayşe Saktanber, eds. *Fragments of Culture: The Everyday of Modern Turkey.* New Brunswick, NJ: Rutgers University Press, 2002.

Kansu, Aykut. *Politics in Post-Revolutionary Turkey, 1908–1913.* Leiden: Brill, 2000.

———. *The Revolution of 1908 in Turkey.* Leiden: Brill, 1997.

Kaplan, Sam. *The Pedagogical State: Education and the Politics of National Culture in Post-1980 Turkey.* Stanford, CA: Stanford University Press, 2006.

Karakaya-Stump, Ayfer. "Debating Progress in a 'Serious Newspaper for Muslim Women': The Periodical *Kadın* of the Post-Revolutionary Salonica, 1908–1909." *British Journal of Middle East Studies* 30, no. 2 (2003): 155–81.

Karakışla, Yavuz Selim. *Women, War and Work in the Ottoman Empire: Society for the Employment of Ottoman Muslim Women (1916–1923).* Istanbul: Ottoman Bank Archives and Research Center, 2005.

Karal, Enver Ziya. *Selim III'ün Hat-tı Hümayunları: Nizam-ı Cedit 1789–1807* [The "New Order": decrees of Selim III, 1789–1807]. Ankara: Türk Tarih Kurumu, 1988.

Karaosmanoğlu, Yakup Kadri. *Panorama.* Ed. Attila Özkırımlı. 1953–54. Reprint, Istanbul: İletişim, 1987.

———. *Yaban* [The stranger]. 1932. Reprint, ed. Atilla Özkırımlı. Istanbul: İletişim, 1993.

Karaömerlioğlu, M. Asım. "The Cult of the Peasant: Ideology and Practice, Turkey, 1930–1946." PhD diss., Ohio State University, 1999.

———. "Helphand-Parvus and His Impact on Turkish Intellectual Life." *Middle Eastern Studies* 40, no. 6 (2004): 145–65.

———. *Orada Bir Köy Var Uzakta: Erken Cumhuriyet Döneminde Köycü Söylem* [Early republican discourse about the villages]. Istanbul: İletişim, 2006.

———. "Turkey's 'Return' to Multi-Party Politics: A Social Reinterpretation." *East European Quarterly* 40, no. 1 (2006): 89–107.

Karpat, Kemal H. "The Entry of the Ottoman Empire into World War I." *Belleten* 68, no. 253 (2004): 687–733.

———. *The "Gecekondu": Rural Migration and Urbanization.* Cambridge: Cambridge University Press, 1976.

———. "The Genesis of the Gecekondu: Rural Migration and Urbanization (1976)." *European Journal of Turkish Studies,* Thematic Issue no. 1, Gecekondu (2004). Available at http://ejts.org/document54.html.

———. *Ottoman Population, 1830–1914: Demographic and Social Characteristics.* Madison: University of Wisconsin Press, 1985.

——. *The Politicization of Islam: Reconstructing Identity, State, Faith, and Community in the Late Ottoman State.* New York: Oxford University Press, 2001.

——. "Social Effects of Farm Mechanization in Turkish Villages." *Social Research* 27 (1960): 83–103.

——. *Turkey's Politics: The Transition to a Multi-Party System.* Princeton: Princeton University Press, 1959.

Kasaba, Reşat, ed. *Turkey in the Modern World.* Vol. 4 of *The Cambridge History of Turkey.* Cambridge: Cambridge University Press, 2008.

Kayalı, Hasan. *Arabs and Young Turks: Ottomanism, Arabism, and Islamism in the Ottoman Empire, 1908–1918.* Berkeley: University of California Press, 1997.

Kayoko, Hayashi, and Mahir Aydın, eds. *The Ottoman State and Societies in Change: A Study of the Nineteenth Century Temettuat Registers.* London: Kegan Paul, 2004.

Kazgan, Gülten. *Tanzimat'tan 21. Yüzyıla Türkiye Ekonomisi* [Turkey's economy from the Tanzimat to the twenty-first century]. Istanbul: Bilgi Üniversitesi Yayınları, 1999.

Keddie, Nikki. *Modern Iran: Roots and Results of Revolution.* New Haven: Yale University Press, 2003.

——. *Sayyid Jamāl al-Dīn "al-Afghānī": A Political Biography.* Berkeley: University of California Press, 1972.

Kemal, Orhan. *Bereketli Topraklar Üzerinde* [On these bounteous lands]. 1954. Reprint, Istanbul: Tekin, 2003.

Kepenek, Yakup, and N. Yentürk. *Türkiye Ekonomisi.* [Turkish economy]. 6th rev. ed., Istanbul: Remzi, 1994.

Keyder, Çağlar. "Globalization and Social Exclusion in Istanbul." *International Journal of Urban and Regional Research* 29, no. 1 (2005): 124–34.

——. "The Turkish Bell Jar." *New Left Review* 28 (July–August 2004): 65–84.

Keyman, E. Fuat, and Ziya Öniş. "Globalization and Social Democracy in the European Periphery: Paradoxes of the Turkish Experience." *Globalizations* 4, no. 2 (2007): 211–28.

Khalid, Adeeb. "Backwardness and the Quest for Civilization: Early Soviet Central Asia in Comparative Perspective." *Slavic Review* 65, no. 2 (Summer 2006): 231–51.

——. *The Politics of Muslim Cultural Reform: Jadidism in Central Asia.* Berkeley: University of California Press, 1998.

Khater, Akram Fouad. *Inventing Home: Emigration, Gender, and the Middle Class in Lebanon, 1870–1920.* Berkeley: University of California Press, 2001.

Khoury, Dina Rizk. *State and Provincial Society in the Ottoman Empire: Mosul, 1540–1834.* Cambridge: Cambridge University Press, 1997.

Khoury, Philip S. "Syrian Urban Politics in Transition: The Quarters of Damascus During the French Mandate." *IJMES* 16, no. 4 (1984): 507–40.

——. *Urban Notables and Arab Nationalism: The Politics of Damascus, 1860–1920.* Cambridge: Cambridge University Press, 1983.

Kili, Suna. *Kemalism.* Istanbul: Robert College, 1969.

Kili, Suna, and A. Şeref Gözübüyük. *Türk Anayasa Metinleri, Senedi İttifaktan Günümüze* [Comstitutional texts]. Ankara: Türkiye İş Bankası, 1985.

Kırımlı, Hakan. *National Movements and National Identity Among the Crimean Tatars (1905–1916).* Leiden: Brill, 1996.

Kısakürek, Necip Fazıl. *Bâbıâli* [Memoirs]. Istanbul: Büyük Doğu, 2001.

——. *İdeolocya Örgüsü* [The weave of ideology]. Istanbul: Kayseri Yüksek İslam Enstitüsü Talebe Derneği, 1968.

Kocabaşoğlu, Uygur. *Şirket Telsizinden Devlet Radyosuna: TRT Öncesi Döneminde Radyonun Tarihsel Gelişimi ve Türk Siyasal Hayatı İçindeki Yeri* [History of radio before the creation of TRT, Turkish State Radio]. Ankara: Ankara Üniversitesi Siyasal Bilgiler Fakültesi, 1980.

Koçak, Cemil. *Belgelerle İktidar ve Serbest Cumhuriyet Fırkası* [The Free Republican Party]. Istanbul: İletişim, 2006.

——. "CHP-Devlet Kaynaşması (1936)" [The fusion of the state and the Republican People's Party, 1936]. *Toplumsal Tarih* 118 (2003): 74–79.

Kolars, John F., and William A. Mitchell. *The Euphrates River and the Southeast Anatolia Development Project*. Carbondale: Southern Illinois University Press, 1991.

Konuk, Kader. "Jewish-German Philologists in Turkish Exile: Leo Spitzer and Erich Auerbach." In *Exile and Otherness: New Approaches to the Experience of the Nazi Refugees*, ed. Alexander Stephan, 31–47. Bern: Peter Lang, 2005.

Köroğlu, Erol. *Ottoman Propaganda and Turkish Identity: Literature in Turkey During World War I*. London: I. B. Tauris, 2007.

Kostopoulou, Elektra. "The Muslim Millet of Autonomous Crete: An Exploration into its Origins and Implications." PhD diss., Boğaziçi University, 2009.

Kramer, Heinz. *A Changing Turkey: The Challenge to Europe and the United States*. Washington, DC: Brookings Institution, 2000.

Krämer, Gudrun, and Sabine Schmidtke, eds. *Speaking for Islam: Religious Authorities in Muslim Societies*. Leiden: Brill, 2006.

Kritzman, Lawrence D. *The Columbia History of Twentieth-Century French Thought*. New York: Columbia University Press, 2006.

Kuniholm, Bruce R. *The Origins of the Cold War in the Near East: Great Power Conflict and Diplomacy in Iran, Turkey, and Greece*. Princeton: Princeton University Press, 1980.

Kushner, David, ed. *Palestine in the Late Ottoman Period: Political, Social and Economic Transformation*. Jerusalem: Yad Izhak Ben-Zvi, 1986.

Kuyucu, Ali Tuna. "Ethno-Religious 'Unmixing' of 'Turkey': 6–7 September Riots as a Case in Turkish Nationalism." *Nations and Nationalism* 11, no. 3 (2005): 361–80.

Kütükoğlu, Mübahat S. "Osmanlı Sosyal ve İktisadî Tarihi Kaynaklarından Temettü Defterleri." *Belleten* 39, no. 225 (1995): 395–417.

——. *Osmanlı-İngiliz İktisâdî Münâsebetleri, II (1838–1850)* [Ottoman-English economic relations]. Istanbul: Edebiyat Fakültesi Basımevi, 1976.

Lake, Michael, ed. *The EU and Turkey: A Glittering Prize or a Millstone?* London: Federal Trust for Education and Research, 2005.

Langensiepen, Bernd, and Ahmed Güleryüz. *The Ottoman Steam Navy*. Ed. and trans. James Cooper. Annapolis, MD: Naval Institute Press, 1995.

Langensiepen, Bernd, Dirk Nottelmann, and Jochen Krüsmann. *Halbmond und Kaiseradler: Goeben und Breslau am Bosporus, 1914–1918*. Hamburg: E. S. Mittler und Sohn, 1999.

Laut, Jens Peter. *Das Türkische als Ursprache? Sprachwissenschaftliche Theorien in der Zeit des erwachenden türkischen Nationalismus.* Wiesbaden: Harrassowitz, 2000.

Lerner, Daniel, and Richard D. Robinson. "Swords and Ploughshares: The Turkish Army as a Modernizing Force." *World Politics* 13, no. 1 (1960): 19–44.

Levy, Avigdor. "The Military Policy of Sultan Mahmud II." PhD diss., Harvard University, 1968.

Lewis, Bernard. *The Emergence of Modern Turkey.* London: Oxford University Press, 1961.

Lewis, Geoffrey. *The Turkish Language Reform: A Catastrophic Success.* Oxford: Oxford University Press, 1999.

Libal, Kathryn. "Staging Turkish Women's Emancipation: Istanbul, 1935." *Journal of Middle East Women's Studies* 4, no. 1 (2008): 31–52.

Lifchez, Raymond, ed. *The Dervish Lodge: Architecture, Art, and Sufism in Ottoman Turkey.* Berkeley: University of California Press, 1992.

Litvak, Meir. *Shi'i Scholars of Nineteenth-Century Iraq: The 'Ulama' of Najaf and Karbala'.* Cambridge: Cambridge University Press, 1998.

Lutfi, Ahmed. *Tarih-i Lutfi* [Lutfi's History]. 8 vols. Istanbul: Mahmud Bey Matbaası, 1290–1328/1873–1910.

McCarthy, Justin. *The Arab World, Turkey, and the Balkans (1878–1914): A Handbook of Historical Statistics.* Boston: G. K. Hall, 1982.

———. *Death and Exile: The Ethnic Cleansing of Ottoman Muslims, 1821–1922.* Princeton: Darwin, 1995.

———. *Muslims and Minorities: The Population of Ottoman Anatolia and the End of the Empire.* New York: New York University Press, 1983.

McCarthy, Justin, Esat Arslan, Cemalettin Taşkıran, and Ömer Turan. *The Armenian Rebellion at Van.* Salt Lake City: University of Utah Press, 2006.

McDowall, David. *A Modern History of the Kurds.* London: I. B. Tauris, 2005.

Mahmud Şevket Paşa. *Osmanlı Teşkilât ve Kıyafet-i Akeriyesi: Osmanlı Ordusunun Bidâyet-i Teessüsünden Zamanımıza Kadar* [Ottoman military institutions and uniforms]. Istanbul: Mekteb-i Harbiye Matbaası, 1325/1909–10.

Majd, Mohammad Gholi. *Iraq in World War I.* Lanham. MD: University Press of America, 2006.

Makdisi, Ussama. *The Culture of Sectarianism: Community, History, and Violence in Nineteenth-Century Ottoman Lebanon.* Berkeley: University of California Press, 2000.

Mallinson, William. *Cyprus: A Modern History.* London: I. B. Tauris, 2005.

Mandel, Neville J. *The Arabs and Zionism Before World War I.* Berkeley: University of California Press, 1976.

Mango, Andrew. *Atatürk.* London: John Murray, 1999.

Mantran, Robert, ed. *Histoire de l'Empire ottoman.* Paris: Fayard, 1989.

Marcus, Aliza. *Blood and Belief: The PKK and the Kurdish Fight for Independence.* New York: New York University Press, 2007.

Mardin, Şerif. *The Genesis of Young Ottoman Thought: A Study in the Modernization of Turkish Political Ideas.* Princeton: Princeton University Press, 1962.

———. "Religion and Secularism in Turkey." In *The Modern Middle East: A Reader*, ed. Albert Hourani, Philip S. Khoury, and Mary C. Wilson, 347–74. Berkeley: University of California Press, 1993.

———. *Religion and Social Change in Modern Turkey: The Case of Bedüzzaman Said Nursi*. Albany: SUNY Press, 1989.

———. "Super Westernization in Urban Life in the Ottoman Empire in the Last Quarter of the Nineteenth Century." In *Turkey: Geographical and Social Perspectives*, ed. Peter Benedict, Erol Tümertekin, and Fatma Mansur, 403–46. Leiden: Brill, 1974.

Marufoğlu, Sinan. *Osmanlı Döneminde Kuzey Irak (1831–1914)* [Northern Iraq under Ottoman Rule, 1831–1914]. Istanbul: Eren, 1998.

Masters, Bruce. *Christians and Jews in the Ottoman Arab World: The Roots of Sectarianism*. Cambridge: Cambridge University Press, 2001.

Matz, Jesse. *The Modern Novel: A Short Introduction*. Oxford: Blackwell, 2004.

Mazower, Mark. *Salonica, City of Ghosts: Christians, Muslims, and Jews, 1430–1950*. New York: Knopf, 2005.

Mecham, R. Quinn. "From the Ashes of Virtue, a Promise of Light: The Transformation of Political Islam in Turkey." *Third World Quarterly* 25, no. 2 (2004): 339–58.

Meeker, Michael. *A Nation of Empire: The Ottoman Legacy of Turkish Modernity*. Berkeley: University of California Press, 2002.

Menemencioğlu, Nermin, in collaboration with Fahir İz, eds. *The Penguin Book of Turkish Verse*. Harmondsworth, UK: Penguin Books, 1978.

Meriwether, Margaret L. *The Kin Who Count: Family and Society in Ottoman Aleppo, 1770–1840*. Austin: University of Texas Press, 1999.

Metinsoy, Murat. *İkinci Dünya Savaşı'nda Türkiye: Savaş ve Gündelik Yaşam* [Turkey in World War II]. Istanbul: Homer, 2007.

Miller, Ruth Austin. "From Fikh to Fascism: The Turkish Republican Adoption of Mussolini's Criminal Code in the Context of Late Ottoman Legal Reform." PhD diss., Princeton University, 2003.

Moran, Gerna. *Türk Romanına Eleştirel Bir Bakış: Ahmet Mithat'tan A. H. Tanpınar'a* [The Turkish novel]. Istanbul: İletişim, 1987.

Moreau, Odile. *L'Empire ottoman à l'âge des réformes: Les hommes et les idées du "Nouvel Ordre" militaire, 1826–1914*. Paris: Maisonneuve et Larose, 2007.

Nagata, Yuzo. *Muhsinzade Mehmed Paşa ve Ayanlık Müessesesi* [Muhsinzade Mehmed Paşa and warlordism]. Izmir: Akademi Yayınevi, 1999.

Nakash, Yitzhak. *The Shi'is of Iraq*. Princeton: Princeton University Press, 2003.

Namık Kemal. *İntibah, Ali Bey'in Sergüzeşti* [Awakening, or the Adventures of Ali Bey]. Istanbul (?): n.p., 1875 (?).

———. *İntibah, Ali Beyin Sergüzeşti* [Awakening, or the Adventures of Ali Bey]. Ed. Seyit Kemal Karaalioğlu. Istanbul: İnkilâp, 1993.

———. *Makalat-ı Siyasiye ve Edebiye* [Political and literary articles]. Istanbul: Selanik Matbaası, 1327/1911.

———. *Müntahabat-ı Tasvir-i Efkar* [N.K.'s Selected Articles from *Tasvir-i Efkar*]. Istanbul: Matbaa-ı Ebüzziya, 1304/1885–86.

——. *Vatan yahut Silistre* [Fatherland, or Silistria]. Istanbul (?): N.p., 1307/1889–90.

——. *Vatan-yahut-Silistre* [Fatherland, or Silistria]. Ed. Şemsettin Kutlu. Istanbul: Remzi, 1993.

Natali, Denise. *The Kurds and the State.* Syracuse, NY: Syracuse University Press, 2005.

Navaro-Yashin, Yael. *Faces of the State: Secularism and Public Life in Turkey.* Princeton: Princeton University Press, 2002.

Nazır, Bayram. *Macar ve Polonyalı Mülteciler: Osmanlı'ya Sığınanlar* [Polish and Hungarian Refugees among the Ottomans]. Istanbul: Yeditepe, 2006.

Neumark, Fritz. *Zuflucht am Bosporus: Deutsche Gelehrte, Politiker und Künstler in der Emigration, 1933–1953.* Frankfurt: Knecht, 1980.

Nicolai, Bernd. *Moderne und Exil: Deutschsprachige Architekten in der Türkei, 1925–1955.* Berlin: Verlag für Bauwesen, 1998.

Northrop, Douglas. *Veiled Empire: Gender and Power in Stalinist Central Asia.* Ithaca, NY: Cornell University Press, 2004.

Nuri, Osman. *Abdülhamid-i Sani ve Devr-i Saltanatı: Hayat-ı Hususiye ve Siyasiyesi* [Abdülhamid II and his reign, private and political life]. 3 vols. Completed by A. R. Istanbul: Kitaphane-i İslam ve Askeri, 1327/1909.

Nursî, Said. *Risale-i Nur Külliyatından Lem'alar.* Istanbul: Yeniasya, 2007.

Ochsenwald, William. *The Hijaz Railroad.* Charlottesville: University Press of Virginia, 1980.

——. *Religion, Society and the State in Arabia: The Hijaz Under Ottoman Control, 1840–1908.* Columbus: Ohio State University Press, 1984.

d'Ohsson, Ignatius Mouradgea. *Tableau général de l'Empire othoman.* 3 vols. Paris: Imprimerie de Monsieur, 1787–1820.

Okay, Orhan. *Batı Medeniyeti Karşısında Ahmed Midhat Efendi* [Ahmed Midhat faces Western civilization]. Istanbul: Milli Eğitim, 1991.

——. "İntibah Romanı Etrafında." [On the novel İntibah]. In *Ölümünün 100. [Yüzüncü] Yılında Namık Kemal* [Namık Kemal on the centennial of his death], 127–47. Istanbul: Edebiyat Fakültesi Basımevi, 1988.

Olsson, Tord, Elisabeth Özdalga, and Catharina Raudvere, eds. *Alevi Identity: Cultural, Religious, and Social Perspectives.* Istanbul: Swedish Research Institute in Istanbul, 1998.

Ortaylı, İlber. *Avrupa ve Biz* [Europe and us]. Ankara: Turhan Kitabevi, 2007.

——. *İmparatorluğun en Uzun Yüzyılı* [The empire's longest century]. Istanbul: Hil, 1987.

Owen, Roger. *The Middle East in the World Economy, 1800–1914.* London: I. B. Tauris, 1993.

Owen, Roger, and Şevket Pamuk. *A History of the Middle East Economies in the Twentieth Century.* Cambridge, MA: Harvard University Press, 1999.

Öğüt, Kemal Selçuk. "Modeling Car Ownership in Turkey Using Fuzzy Regression." *Transportation Planning and Technology* 29, no. 3 (2006): 233–48.

Ökçün, A. Gündüz, ed. *Osmanlı Sanayii: 1913, 1915 Yılları Sanayi İstatistikleri* [Ottoman industrial census of 1913–1915]. Ankara: Devlet İstatistik Enstitüsü, 1997.

Önder, Sırrı Süreyya, and Muharrem Gülmez, dir. *Beynelmilel* [The international]. Film featuring Özgü Namal, Cezmi Baskın, Nazmi Kırık, Umut Kurt, and Meral Okay. Istanbul [?]: BkM Film, 2006.

Özaslan, Metin, Bülent Dincer, and Hüseyin Özgür. "Regional Disparities and Territorial Indicators in Turkey: Socio-Economic Development Index (SEDI)." European Regional Science Association. Volos (Greece), 2006. Available at http://www.ersa.org/ersaconfs/ersa06/papers/858.pdf.

Özbek, Meral. *Popüler Kültür ve Orhan Gencebay Arabeski* [Popular culture and Orhan Gencebay's Arabesk]. Istanbul: İletişim, 1991.

Özbek, Nadir. *Osmanlı İmparatorluğunda Sosyal Devlet: Siyaset, İktidar ve Meşrutiyet (1876–1914)* [The "Social State" in the Ottoman Empire, 1876–1914]. Istanbul: İletişim, 2003.

———. "Policing the Countryside: Gendarmes of the Late 19th-Century Ottoman Empire (1876–1908)." *IJMES* 40, no. 1 (2008): 47–67.

Özbudun, Ergun. "From Political Islam to Conservative Democracy: The Case of the Justice and Development Party in Turkey." *South European Society and Politics* 11, nos. 3–4 (2006): 543–57.

Özçelik, Ayfer. *Kimliğini Arayan Meşrutiyet* [Constitutionalism in search of its identity]. Istanbul: İlgi Kültür Sanat, 2006.

Özdalga, Elisabeth, ed. *Late Ottoman Society: The Intellectual Legacy.* London: Routledge Curzon, 2005.

Özendes, Engin. *Photography in the Ottoman Empire, 1839–1919.* Istanbul: İletişim, 1995. *See also* Çizgen (Özendes)

Özok-Gündoğan, Nilay. "'Social Development' as a Governmental Strategy in the Southeastern Anatolia Project." *New Perspectives on Turkey* 32 (2005): 93–111.

Özön, Mustafa Nihat. *Namık Kemal ve İbret Gazetesi* [Namık Kemal and the newspaper *İbret*]. Istanbul: Yapı Kredi Kültür Yayınları, 1997.

Öztuncay, Bahattin. *James Robertson, Pioneer of Photography in the Ottoman Empire.* Istanbul: Eren, 1992.

———. *The Photographers of Constantinople: Pioneers, Studios and Artists from 19th Century Istanbul.* 2 vols. Istanbul: Aygaz, 2003.

Öztürkmen, Arzu. *Türkiye'de Folklor ve Milliyetçilik* [Folklore and nationalism in Turkey]. Istanbul: İletişim, 1998.

Özyürek, Esra. *Nostalgia for the Modern: State Secularism and Everyday Politics in Turkey.* Durham, NC: Duke University Press, 2006.

Palairet, Michael. *The Balkan Economies, c. 1800–1914: Evolution without Development.* Cambridge: Cambridge University Press, 1997.

Pamuk, Orhan. *Kar* [Snow]. Istanbul: İletişim, 2002.

———. *Snow.* Trans. Maureen Freely. New York: Alfred A. Knopf, 2004.

Pamuk, Şevket. *19. Yüzyılda Osmanlı Dış Ticareti* [Ottoman foreign trade in the nineteenth century]. Ankara: Devlet İstatistik Enstitüsü, 1995.

———. "The Evolution of Financial Institutions in the Ottoman Empire, 1600–1914." *Financial History Review* 11, no. 1 (2004): 7–32.

——. "Institutional Change and the Longevity of the Ottoman Empire, 1500–1800." *Journal of Interdisciplinary History* 35, no. 2 (2004): 225–47.

——. *İstanbul ve Diğer Kentlerde 500 Yıllık Fiyatlar ve Ücretler, 1469–1998* [Prices and wages in Istanbul and other cities, 1469–1998]. Ankara: Devlet İstatistik Enstitüsü, 2000.

——. *A Monetary History of the Ottoman Empire*. Cambridge: Cambridge University Press, 2000.

——. *The Ottoman Empire and European Capitalism, 1820–1913: Trade, Investment, and Production*. Cambridge: Cambridge University Press, 1987.

——. "Prices in the Ottoman Empire, 1469–1914." *International Journal of Middle East Studies* 36, no. 3 (2004): 451–68.

Parla, Jale. *Babalar ve Oğullar: Tanzimat Romanının Epistemolojik Temelleri* [Fathers and sons: epistemological bases of Tanzimat novels]. Istanbul: İletişim, 1993.

——. "Tempomorphoses: Tick-Tocks of the Clock and Tactics of the Novel." *Journal of Turkish Literature* 1 (2004): 33–44.

Parla, Taha. *Atatürk'ün Nutuk'u* [Analysis of Atatürk's Great Speech of 1927]. Vol. 1 of *Türkiye'de Siyasal Kültürün Resmî Kaynakları*. Istanbul: İletişim, 1991.

——. *Atatürk'ün Söylev ve Demeçleri* [Analysis of Atatürk's other speeches]. Vol. 2 of *Türkiye'de Siyasal Kültürün Resmî Kaynakları*. Istanbul: İletişim, 1991.

——. *Kemalist Tek-Parti İdeolojisi ve CHP'nın Altı Ok'u* [The Single-party ideology and the "Six Arrows"]. Vol. 3 of *Türkiye'de Siyasal Kültürünün Resmî Kaynakları*. Istanbul: İletişim, 1992.

——. *The Social and Political Thought of Ziya Gökalp, 1876–1924*. Leiden: Brill, 1985.

——. *Ziya Gökalp, Kemalizm ve Türkiye'de Korporatizm* [Ziya Gökalp, Kemalism, and corporatism in Turkey]. Ed. Füsun Üstel and Sabir Yücesoy. Istanbul: İletişim, 1989.

Parla, Taha, and Andrew Davison. *Corporatist Ideology in Kemalist Turkey: Progress or Order?* Syracuse, NY: Syracuse University Press, 2004.

Parlatır, İsmail. *Tanzimat Edebiyatında Kölelik* [Slavery in Tanzimat literature]. Ankara: Türk Tarih Kurumu, 1992.

Pınarcıoğlu, Melih, and Oğuz Işık. *Nöbetleşe Yoksulluk, Gecekondulaşma ve Kent Yoksulları: Sultanbeyli Örneği* [Impoverishment by turns: shantytown urbanization and the urban poor in Sultanbeyli]. Istanbul: İletişim, 2001.

Poulton, Hugh. *Top Hat, Grey Wolf and Crescent: Turkish Nationalism and the Turkish Republic*. New York: New York University Press, 1997.

Poyraz, Serdar. "Preliminary Reflections on Bediüzzaman Said Nursi and the Nurcu Movement." Unpublished seminar paper, Ohio State University, 2003.

——. "Science Versus Religion: The Influence of European Materialism on Turkish Thought, 1860–1960." PhD diss., Ohio State University, 2010.

Putnam, Robert, with Robert Leonardi and Raffaella Y. Nanetti. *Making Democracy Work: Civic Traditions in Modern Italy*. Princeton: Princeton University Press, 1993.

Quataert, Donald. *Manufacturing and Technology Transfer in the Ottoman Empire, 1800–1914*. Istanbul: Isis, 1992.

——. *Miners and the State in the Ottoman Empire: The Zonguldak Coalfield, 1822–1920*. New York: Berghahn Books, 2006.

——. *The Ottoman Empire, 1700–1922.* Cambridge: Cambridge University Press, 2005.

——. *Ottoman Manufacturing in the Age of the Industrial Revolution.* Cambridge: Cambridge University Press, 1993.

——. *Social Disintegration and Popular Resistance in the Ottoman Empire, 1881–1908: Reactions to European Economic Penetration.* New York: New York University Press, 1983.

Rafeq, Abdul-Karim. *Tarikh al-Jami'at al-Suriyya, al-Bidaya Wa'l-Numuww, 1901–1946, Awwal Jami'at Hukumiyya fi'l-Watan al-'Arabi* [History of the University of Syria, beginning and growth, 1901–1946, the first government university in the Arab lands]. Damascus: Maktabat Nobel, 2004.

Raimondo d'Aronco in Turchia (1893–1909), Progetti della Galleria di arte moderna di Udine; Udine Çağdaş Sanat Galerisi Koleksiyoundan Raimondo d'Aronco'nun Türkiye Yılları (1893–1909). Istanbul: Güzel Sanatlar Matbaası, 1995.

Raymond, André. *Grandes villes arabes à l'époque ottomane.* Paris: Sindbad, 1985.

Reed, Christopher A. *Gutenberg in Shaghai: Chinese Print Capitalism, 1876–1937.* Honolulu: University of Hawai'i Press, 2004.

Reilly, James A. *A Small Town in Syria: Ottoman Hama in the Eighteenth and Nineteenth Centuries.* Oxford: Peter Lang, 2002.

Reinkowski, Maurus. *Die Dinge der Ordnung: Eine vergleichende Untersuchung über die osmanische Reformpolitik im 19. Jahrhundert.* Munich: R. Oldenbourg, 2005.

Reisman, Arnold. *Turkey's Modernization: Refugees from Nazism and Ataturk's Vision.* Washington, DC: New Academia, 2006.

Robins, Philip. "Back from the Brink: Turkey's Ambivalent Approaches to the Hard Drugs Issue." *Middle East Journal* 62, no. 4 (2008): 630–50.

Robinson, Richard D. *The First Turkish Republic: A Case Study in National Development.* Cambridge, MA: Harvard University Press, 1963.

——. "Tractors in the Village." *Journal of Farm Economics* 34 (1952): 451–62.

Rodrigue, Aron. *French Jews, Turkish Jews: The Alliance Israélite Universelle and the Politics of Jewish Schooling in Turkey, 1860–1925.* Bloomington: Indiana University Press, 1990.

Rogan, Eugene. *Frontiers of the State in the Late Ottoman Empire: Transjordan, 1850–1921.* Cambridge: Cambridge University Press, 1999.

Rumpf, Christian. *Das Rechtsstaatsprinzip in der türkischen Rechtsordnung.* Bonn: Bouvier, 1992.

Sabev, Orlin. *İbrahim Müteferrika ya da İlk Osmanlı Matbaa Serüveni (1726–1746): Yeniden Değerlendirme* [Ibrahim Müteferrika and the first Ottoman press, 1726–1746]. Istanbul: Yeditepe Yayınevi, 2006.

Şahin, Şehriban. "The Alevi Movement: Transformation from Secret Oral to Public Written Culture in National and Transnational Social Spaces." PhD diss., New School for Social Research, 2001.

Said, Edward. *Culture and Imperialism.* New York: Vintage Books, 1994.

Salih, Halil Ibrahim, *Cyprus: Ethnic Political Counterpoints.* Baltimore: University Press of America, 2004.

Sancar, Erdinç. *21. [Yirmi Birinci] Yüzyıl Stratejilerinde Türk Denizcilik Tarihi* [Turkish naval history]. Istanbul: IQ Kultursanat Yayınları, 2006.

Şanizade, Ataullah. *Tarih-i Şanizade* [Şanizade's history]. 4 vols. Istanbul: N.p., n.d.

Saraçoğlu, Ahmet Cemaleddin. *Unutulan Meşhurlarımızdan Mizancı Murad Bey* [Biography of Mizancı Murad]. Ed. İsmail Dervişoğlu. Istanbul: Şema, 2005.

Saraçoğlu, Safa. "Letters from Vidin: A Study of Ottoman Governmentality and Politics of Local Administration, 1864–1877." PhD diss., Ohio State University, 2007.

Sarfati, Yusuf, "The Rise of Religious Parties in Israel and Turkey: A Comparative Study," PhD diss., Ohio State University, 2009.

Sayarı, Sabri, and Yılmaz Esmer, eds. *Politics, Parties, and Elections in Turkey.* Boulder, CO: Lynne Rienner, 2002.

Sayer, Derek. *Capitalism and Modernity: An Excursus on Marx and Weber.* London: Routledge, 1991.

Schick, Irvin Cemil. "Osmanlı Döneminde Matbuat Kapitalizmi" [Print capitalism during the Ottoman period]. *Virgül* 126 (January–February 2009): 58–63.

Schick, İrvin Cemil, and Ertuğrul Ahmet Tonak, eds. *Turkey in Transition: New Perspectives.* New York: Oxford University Press, 1987.

Schwartz, Philipp. *Notgemeinschaft: Zur Emigration Deutscher Wissenschaftler nach 1933 in die Türkei.* Ed. Helge Peukert. Marburg: Metropolis, 1995.

Sevindi, Nevval. *Contemporary Islamic Conversations.* Ed. Ibrahim M. Abu-Rabi', trans. Abdullah T. Antepli. Albany: SUNY Press, 2008.

Seyitdanlıoğlu, Mehmet. *Tanzimat Devrinde Meclis-i Vâlâ (1838–1868)* [The Supreme Council in the Tanzimat period]. Ankara: Türk Tarih Kurumu, 1994.

Shankland, David. *The Alevis in Turkey: The Emergence of a Secular Islamic Tradition.* London: RoutledgeCurzon, 2003.

——. *Islam and Society in Turkey.* Huntingdon, UK: Eothen, 1999.

Shaw, Stanford J. *Between Old and New: The Ottoman Empire Under Sultan Selim III, 1789–1807.* Cambridge, MA: Harvard University Press, 1971.

——. *From Empire to Republic: The Turkish War of National Liberation, 1918–1923: A Documentary Study.* 5 vols. Ankara: Türk Tarih Kurumu, 2000.

——. *The Ottoman Empire in World War I.* Ankara: Türk Tarih Kurumu, 2006.

Shaw, Stanford J., and Ezel Kural Shaw. *History of the Ottoman Empire and Modern Turkey.* Vol. 2: *Reform, Revolution, and Republic: The Rise of Modern Turkey, 1808–1975.* Cambridge: Cambridge University Press, 1977.

Shields, Sarah. *Mosul Before Iraq, Like Bees Making Five-Sided Cells.* Albany: SUNY Press, 2000.

Shishkin, Philip. "For Turks, Risks Abound: Incursion into Iraq May Undercut U.S., End Turkish Boom." *Wall Street Journal,* 17 October 2007.

Shissler, A. Holly. *Between Two Empires: Ahmet Ağaoğlu and the New Turkey.* London: I. B. Tauris, 2003.

Shorter, Frederic C. "The Crisis of Population Knowledge in Turkey." *New Perspectives on Turkey* 12 (Spring 1995): 1–31.

——. "The Population of Turkey After the War of Independence." *IJMES* 17, no. 4 (1985): 417–41.

——. "Turkish Population in the Great Depression." *New Perspectives on Turkey* 23 (Fall 2000): 103–24.

Shorter, Frederic C., and Miroslav Macura. *Trends in Fertility and Mortality in Turkey, 1935–1975.* Washington, DC: Committee on Population and Demography, U.S. National Academy of Sciences, 1982.

Şimşek, Veysel. "Ottoman Military Recruitment and the Recruit: 1826–1853." MA thesis, Ankara: Bilkent University, 2005.

Şinasi, İbrahim. *Şair Evlenmesi.* Ed. Şemsettin Kutlu. Istanbul: Remzi, 1982.

———. *The Wedding of a Poet: A One-Act Comedy (1859).* Trans. Edward Allworth. Whitestone, NY: Griffon House, 1981.

Smith, Charles D. *Palestine and the Arab-Israeli Conflict.* 5th ed. Boston: Bedford St. Martin's, 2004.

Sohrabi, Nader. "Global Waves, Local Actors: What the Young Turks Knew About Other Revolutions and Why It Mattered." *Comparative Studies in Society and History* 44, no. 1 (2002): 45–79.

———. "Historicizing Revolutions: Constitutional Revolutions in the Ottoman Empire, Iran, and Russia, 1905–1908." *American Journal of Sociology* 100 (1995): 1383–1447.

Somel, Selçuk Akşin. *The Modernization of Public Education in the Ottoman Empire, 1839–1908: Islamization, Autocracy and Discipline.* Leiden: Brill, 2001.

Sönmez, Banu İşlet. *II. [İkinci] Meşrutiyette Arnavut Muhalefeti* [Albanian opposition in the Second Constitutional Period]. Istanbul: Yapı Kredi Yayınları, 2007.

Stoddard, Philip Hendrick. "The Ottoman Government and the Arabs, 1911 to 1918: A Preliminary Study of the Teşkilât-ı Mahsusa." PhD diss., Princeton University, 1963.

Stokes, Martin. *The Arabesk Debate: Music and Musicians in Modern Turkey.* Oxford: Clarendon Press, 1992.

Sunar, İlkay. *State, Society and Democracy in Turkey.* Istanbul: Bahçeşehir University, 2004.

Suny, Ronald Grigor, *Looking Toward Ararat: Armenia in Modern History.* Bloomington: Indiana University Press, 1993.

Sürsal, Hilâl. *Gülten Akın: A Pioneering Turkish Woman Poet.* Bloomington: Ottoman and Modern Turkish Studies of Indiana University, 2006.

Swietochowski, Tadeusz. *Russia and Azerbaijan: A Borderland in Transition.* New York: Columbia Universtiy Press, 1995.

Tabak, Faruk. *The Waning of the Mediterranean, 1550–1870: A Geohistorical Approach.* Baltimore: Johns Hopkins University Press, 2008.

Tabakoğlu, Ahmet. *Gerileme Dönemine Girerken Osmanlı Maliyesi* [Ottoman finance entering the period of regression]. Istanbul: Dergâh, 1985.

Tanör, Bülent. *Türkiye'de Kongre İktidarları, 1918–1920* [Rule by congresses in Turkey, 1918–1920]. Istanbul: Yapı Kredi Yayınları, 1998.

Tanpınar, Ahmet Hamdi. *Beş Şehir* [Five cities]. 1946. Reprint, Istanbul: Dergâh Yayınları, 1998.

———. *Saatleri Ayarlama Enstitüsü* [The chronometric institute]. 1961. Reprint, Istanbul: Yapı Kredi Yayınları, 2004.

———. *Sahnenin Dışındakiler* [Those offstage]. 1950. Reprint, Istanbul: Dergâh Yayınları, 1990.

———. *XIX. [Ondokuzuncu] Asır Türk Edebiyatı Tarihi* [History of nineteenth-century Turkish literature]. Istanbul: Çağlayan Kitabevi, 1967.

Tavernise, Sabrina. "In the Rugged North of Iraq, Kurdish Rebels Flout Turkey." *New York Times*, 29 October 2007, 1, 6.

——. "Turkish Schools Offer Pakistan a Gentler Islam," *New York Times*, 4 May 2008, 1, 10.

Tavernise, Sabrina, and Şebnem Arsu. "Court Declares Turkey's Ruling Party Constitutional but Limits Its Financing." *New York Times*, 31 July 2008, A6.

Taylor, Charles. *Sources of the Self: The Making of Modern Identity*. Cambridge: Cambridge University Press, 1989.

Teitelbaum, Joshua. *The Rise and Fall of the Hashemite Kingdom of Arabia*. New York: New York University Press, 2001.

Tekeli, İlhan, and Selim İlkin. *Bir Cumhuriyet Öyküsü: Kadrocuları ve Kadro'yu Anlamak* [On the journal *Kadro* and its contributors]. Istanbul: Tarih Vakfı, 2003.

——. *Cumhuriyetin Harcı: Köktenci Modernitenin Doğuşu* [The mortar of the republic: the birth of radical modernity]. 3 vols. Istanbul: İstanbul Bilgi Üniversitesi Yayınevi, 2003–4.

——. *Osmanlı İmparatorluğu'nda Eğitim ve Bilgi Üretim Sisteminin Oluşumu ve Dönüşümü* [The system of education and knowledge production in the Ottoman Empire]. Ankara: Türk Tarih Kurumu, 1993.

——. *Para ve Kredi Sisteminin Oluşumunda Bir Aşama, Türkiye Cumhuriyet Merkez Bankası* [History of the Central Bank]. Ankara: T. C. Merkez Bankası, 1981.

——. *Türkiye Belgesel İktisat Tarihi* [Documentary economic history]. 3 vols. Ankara: Orta Doğu Teknik Üniversitesi, 1981–83.

Tekeli, İlhan, and Tarık Okyay. *Dolmuşun Öyküsü* [Story of the dolmuş]. Ankara: Çevre ve Mimarlık Bilimleri Derneği, 1981.

Tezel, Yahya S. *Cumhuriyet Döneminin İktisadi Tarihi, 1923–1950* [Economic history of the early republic, 1923–1950]. Ankara: Yurt, 1986.

Therborn, Göran. *European Modernity and Beyond: The Trajectory of European Societies, 1945–2000*. London: Sage, 1995.

Thompson, Elizabeth. *Colonial Citizens: Republican Rights, Paternal Privilege, and Gender in French Syria and Lebanon*. New York: Columbia University Press, 1999.

Tibawi, A[bdul] L[atif]. *Anglo-Arab Relations and the Question of Palestine, 1914–1921*. London: Luzac, 1977.

Times of London. *The Times Atlas of the World*. Boston: Houghton Mifflin, 1967.

Timur, Taner. *Osmanlı Kimliği* [Ottoman identity]. Istanbul: Hil, 1994.

Todorova, Maria N. *Balkan Family Structure and the European Pattern: Demographic Developments in Ottoman Bulgaria*. Washington, DC: American University Press, 1993.

Toledano, Ehud R. *As If Silent and Absent: Bonds of Enslavement in the Islamic Middle East*. New Haven: Yale University Press, 2007.

——. *The Ottoman Slave Trade and Its Suppression, 1840–1890*. Princeton: Princeton University Press, 1982.

——. *Slavery and Abolition in the Ottoman Middle East*. Seattle: University of Washington Press, 1998.

Toprak, Zafer. *İttihad-Terakki ve Cihan Harbi: Savaş Ekonomisi ve Türkiye'de Devletçilik, 1914–1918* [Union and progress and the world war: war economics and statism in Turkey, 1914–1918]. Istanbul: Homer, 2003.

———. *İttihat-Terakki ve Devletçilik, Türkiye'de Ekonomi ve Toplum (1908–1950)* [Union-progress and statism]. Istanbul: Türkiye Ekonomik ve Toplumsal Tarih Vakfı, 1995.

———. *Milli İktisat—Milli Burjuvazi, Türkiye'de Ekonomi ve Toplum (1908–1950)* [National economics, national bourgeoisie]. Istanbul: Türkiye Ekonomik ve Toplumsal Tarih Vakfı, 1995.

———. "Osmanlı Narodnikleri: 'Halka Doğru Gidenler'" [Ottoman Narodniks, "Going to the people"]. *Toplum ve Bilim* 24 (Winter 1984): 69–81.

Touraine, Alain. *Critique of Modernity.* Trans. David Macey. Oxford: Blackwell, 1995.

Tucker, Judith E. *In the House of the Law: Gender and Islamic Law in Ottoman Syria and Palestine.* Berkeley: University of California Press, 1998.

———. *Women in Nineteenth-Century Egypt.* Cambridge: Cambridge University Press, 1985.

Tuğal, Cihan Z. "The Appeal of Islamic Politics: Ritual and Dialogue in a Poor District of Turkey." *Sociological Quarterly* 47 (2006): 245–73.

———. *Passive Revolution: Absorbing the Islamic Challenge to Capitalism.* Stanford, CA: Stanford University Press, 2009.

Tunaya, Tarık Zafer. *Türkiye'de Siyasal Partiler* [History of political parties in Turkey]. 3 vols. Ankara: Hürriyet Vakfı, 1984–89.

Tunçay, Mete. *Türkiye Cumhuriyeti'nde Tek-Parti Yönetimi'nin Kurulması, 1923–1931* [The founding of single-party government in Turkey, 1923–1931]. Ankara: Yurt Yayınları, 1981.

———. *Türkiye'de Sol Akımlar* [Leftist currents in Turkey]. 2 vols. in 3. Istanbul: BDS Yayınları, 1991–92.

Turam, Berna. *Between Islam and the State.* Stanford, CA: Stanford University Press, 2007.

T. C. Başbakanlık Devlet İstatistik Enstitüsü. *İstatistik Göstergeler, Statistical Indicators, 1923–1992.* Ankara: Devlet İstatistik Enstitüsü, 1994. [printed statistical annual of the Turkish government]

T. C. Başbakanlık Türkiye İstatistik Kurumu (TÜİK). *İstatistik Göstergeler, 1923–2005, Statistical Indicators.* Ankara: Türkiye İstatistik Kurumu, 2007. [annual, available from www.tuik.gov.tr]

———. *Türkiye İstatistik Yıllığı, Turkey's Statistical Yearbook, 2006.* Ankara: Türkiye İstatistik Kurumu, 2007. [annual, available from www.tuik.gov.tr]

Türk Dili ve Edebiyatı Ansiklopedisi [Encyclopedia of Turkish language and literature]. 7 vols. Istanbul: Dergâh, 1976–82.

Türkoğlu, Yusuf. "ICT Sector in Turkey." *IGEME—Export Promotion Center of Turkey* (2008). Available at http://www.igeme.org.tr/Assets/sip/san/ICT.pdf.

TÜSİAD. *Türkiye'de Bölgesel Gelişme Politikaları: Sektör-Bölge Yığınlaşmaları* [Regional development policies in Turkey]. Istanbul: TÜSİAD, 2005. Available at http://www.tusiad.org/tusiad_cms.nsf/LHome/0EE596CE7B609309C225733E0043C83E/$FILE/No6.pdf.

Uğur, Ömer, director. *Eve Dönüş* [Homecoming]. Film featuring Mehmet Ali Alabora, Sibel Kekilli, Altan Erkekli, Savaş Dinçel, and Cengiz Küçükayvaz. Istanbul [?]: Limon Yapım, 2006.

Ulutaş, Ufuk. "Homogenization of the Nation in the Turkish Republic: The *Aliyah* (Emigration) of the Turkish Jews to Israel." PhD diss., Ohio State University, in progress.

——. "Namık Kemal between Tradition and Modernity." Unpublished paper. Ohio State University, 2004.

——. "Naqshbandiyya: A History of Survival." Unpublished paper. Ohio State University, 2004.

——. "Religion and Secularism in Turkey: The Dilemma of the Directorate of Religious Affairs." Seminar paper. Ohio State University, 2006.

UN Human Development Program. *Human Development Report: Turkey 2004*, 2004. Available at http://www.undp.org.tr/docAndPucDocuments/NHDR2004engfinal.pdf.

U.S. Department of State. *Foreign Relations of the United States, 1964–1968*. Vol. 16: *Cyprus, Greece, Turkey*. Washington, DC: U.S. Government Printing Office, 2002. Available at http://www.state.gov/r/pa/ho/frus.

Uşaklıgil, Halid Ziya. *Kırk Yıl* [Memoirs of his early life]. Istanbul: İnkilâp ve Aka, 1969.

Uyar, Hakkı. *Tek Parti Dönemi ve Cumhuriyet Halk Partisi* [The single-party period and the Republican People's Party]. Istanbul: Boyut, 1998.

Uzun, Ahmet. *Tanzimat ve Sosyal Direnişler: Niş Isyanı Üzerine Ayrıntılı Bir İnceleme, 1841* [The Tanzimat and local resistance: a detailed study of the Niş Rebellion, 1841]. Istanbul: Eren, 2002.

Ülgener, Sabri F. *İktisadî İnhitat Tarihimizin Ahlâk ve Zihniyet Meseleleri* [Issues of ethics and mentalities in the history of our economic decline]. Istanbul: Akgün Matbaası, 1951.

Ülker, Erol. "Contextualizing 'Turkification': Nation-Building in the Late Ottoman Empire, 1908–1918." *Nations and Nationalism* 11, no. 4 (2005): 613–36.

——. "Empires and Nation Building: Russification and Turkification Compared." MA thesis, Budapest: Central European University, 2004.

Ünsaldı, Levent. *Türkiye'de Asker ve Siyaset* [Soldiers and politics in Turkey]. Istanbul: Kitapyayınevi, 2008.

Üstel, Füsun. *"Makbul Vatandaş"ın Peşinde: II. Meşrutiyet'ten Bugüne Vatandaşlık Eğitimi* [Education for citizenship]. Istanbul: İletişim, 2004.

——. *Türk Ocakları (1912–1931): İmparatorluktan Ulus-Devlete Türk Milliyetçiliği* [The Turkish hearth societies]. Istanbul: İletişim, 1997.

Vahdat, Farzin. *God and Juggernaut: Iran's Intellectual Encounter with Modernity*. Syracuse, NY: Syracuse University Press, 2002.

Vahide, Şükran. *Islam in Modern Turkey: An Intellectual Biography of Bediuzzaman Said Nursi*. Albany: SUNY Press, 2005.

VanderLippe, John M. "Forgotten Brigade of the Forgotten War: Turkey's Participation in the Korean War." *Middle East Studies* 36, no. 1 (2000): 92–102.

——. *The Politics of Turkish Democracy: İsmet İnönü and the Formation of the Multi-Party System, 1938–1950*. Albany: SUNY Press, 2005.

Vassiliev, Alexei. *The History of Saudi Arabia*. New York: New York University Press, 2000.

Veinstein, Gilles, ed. *Salonique, 1850–1918: La "ville des Juifs" et le réveil des Balkans*. Paris: Editions Autrement, 1992.

Visser, Reidar. *Basra, the Failed Gulf State: Separatism and Nationalism in Southern Iraq*. Münster: LIT Verlag, 2005.

Volkan, Vamık D., and Norman Itzkowitz. *The Immortal Atatürk: A Psychobiography.* Chicago: University of Chicago Press, 1984.

Wallach, Jehuda L. *Anatomie einer Militärhilfe: Die Preussisch-Deutschen Millitärmissionen in der Türkei, 1835–1919.* Düsseldorf: Droste Verlag, 1976.

Walsh, Robert. *Constantinople and the Scenery of the Seven Churches of Asia Minor.* 2 vols. London, 1838.

Weiker, Walter F. *The Modernization of Turkey: From Ataturk to the Present Day.* New York: Holmes and Meier, 1981.

White, Jenny B. *Islamist Mobilization in Turkey: A Study in Vernacular Politics.* Seattle: University of Washington Press, 2002.

———. "State Feminism, Modernization, and the Turkish Republican Woman." *NWSA Journal* 15, no. 3 (2003): 145–59.

———. "Turks in the New Germany." *American Anthropologist* 99, no. 4 (1997): 754–69.

White, Paul J., and Joost Jongerden, eds. *Turkey's Alevi Enigma: A Comprehensive Overview.* Brill: Leiden, 2003.

Widmann, Horst. *Atatürk ve Üniversite Reformu* [Atatürk and university reform]. Trans. Aykut Kazancı and Serpil Bozkurt. Istanbul: Kabalcı, 2000.

———. *Exil und Bildungshilfe: Die Deutschsprachige Emigration in die Türkei Nach 1933.* Bern: Herbert Lang, 1973.

Wilhite, Vincent. "Guerrilla War, Counterinsurgency, and State Formation in Yemen." PhD diss., Ohio State University, 2003.

Woodward, Ralph Lee, ed. *Positivism in Latin America, 1850–1900: Are Order and Progress Reconcilable?* Lexington, MA: D. C. Heath, 1971.

Yalman, Ahmed Emin. *Yakın Tarihte Gördüklerim ve Geçirdiklerim* [Memoirs]. 2 vols. Istanbul: Pera Turizm ve Ticaret, 1997.

Yanıkdağ, Yücel. "'Ill-Fated' Sons of the 'Nation': Ottoman Prisoners of War in Russia and Egypt, 1914–1922." PhD diss., Ohio State University, 2002.

Yaramış, Ahmet, and Mehmet Güneş, ed. *Askerî Kânûnnâmeler, 1826–1827* [Military regulations, 1826–1827]. Ankara: Asil Yayın Dağıtım, 2007.

Yavuz, M. Hakan, ed. *The Emergence of a New Turkey: Democracy and the AK Parti.* Salt Lake City: University of Utah Press, 2006.

———. *Islamic Political Identity in Turkey.* New York: Oxford University Press, 2003.

Yavuz, M. Hakan, and John L. Esposito, eds. *Turkish Islam and the Secular State: The Gülen Movement.* Syracuse, NY: Syracuse University Press, 2003.

Yeğen, Mesut. *Devlet Söyleminde Kürt Sorunu* [The Kurdish question in official discourse]. Istanbul: İletişim, 1999.

Yerasimos, Stéphane, ed. *Les Turcs: Orient et Occident, Islam et laïcité.* Paris: Editions Autrement, 1994.

Yeşil, Ahmet. *Türkiye Cumhuriyeti'nde İlk Teşkilâtlı Muhalefet Hareketi, Terakkiperver Cumhuriyet Fırkası* [The Progressive Republican Party]. Ankara: Cedit, 2002.

Yıldırım, Onur. *Diplomacy and Displacement: Reconsidering the Turco-Greek Exchange of Populations, 1922–1934.* New York: Routledge, 2006.

———. *Diplomasi ve Göç: Türk-Yunan Mübadelesinin Öteki Yüzü* [Diplomacy and displacement ...]. Istanbul: İstanbul Bilgi Üniversitesi Yayınları, 2006.

Yılmaz, Hakan. "Islam, Sovereignty, and Democracy: A Turkish View." *Middle East Journal* 61, no. 3 (2007): 477–93.

Young, George. *Corps de droit ottoman.* 7 vols. Oxford: Oxford University Press, 1905–6.

Zahlan, Antoine B. "The Impact of Technology Change in the Nineteenth-Century Arab World." In *Between the State and Islam,* Charles E. Butterworth and I. William Zartman, 31–58. Cambridge: Cambridge University Press, 2001.

———. *Science and Science Policy in the Arab World.* London: Croom Helm, 1980.

Zihnioğlu, Yaprak. *Kadınsız İnkılap: Nezihe Muhiddin, Kadınlar Halk Fırkası, Kadın Birliği* [Revolution Without Women: Nezihe Muhiddin, the Women's People's Party, and the Women's Union]. Istanbul: Metis, 2003.

Zürcher, Erik J. *Turkey: A Modern History.* 3rd ed. London: I. B. Tauris, 2004.

———. *The Unionist Factor: The Rôle of the Committee of Union and Progress in the Turkish National Movement, 1905–1926.* Leiden: Brill, 1984.

Zürcher, Erik J., ed. *Arming the State: Military Conscription in the Middle East and Central Asia, 1775–1925.* London: I. B. Tauris, 1999.

INDEX

Abbas Hilmi I (governor of Egypt), 85–86
Abbas Hilmi II (khedive of Egypt), 212
Abbasid caliphate, 28
Abdülaziz, 83, 88, 107, 129, 147, 153
Abdülhamid I, 31
Abdülhamid II, 83–85, 88, 90, 93, 94, 105,
    197, 417; culture under, 184–90,
    286; economics under, 165–74;
    politics under, 133, 146–65, 180–81;
    society under, 175–84; Young Turks'
    opposition to and deposing of, 146,
    160–65, 190–91, 196, 418
Abdullah (son of Sharif Husayn), 217
Abdülmecid I, 44, 48, 88, 146
Abdülmecid II, 224
abortion, 63, 68, 175, 183, 241. *See also*
    birth control; fertility
Abraham (Kur'anic figure), 8
acquis-communautaire, 371–73
Action Army, 196, 197
Action Française, 340
Acuner, Selma, 382
Adana, 158, 171–73, 197, 210, 223, 341, 343, 380
Aden, 192
Adıvar, Halide Edib, 135, 193, 239–44, 280
adultery, 383
Aegean Army Corps, 322

Aegean issues, 369–70
al-Afghani, Jamaleddin, 149
Afghanistan, 264, 324, 368
Agâh, Yusuf, 104, 118
Ağaoğlu, Adalet, 255, 351, 390–403
Agop, Güllü, 129
Agricultural Bank, 111, 166, 170, 229, 232, 307
agriculture: in Abdülhamid II period,
    158, 170–71; during Democrat
    Party's rule, 307; in early Turkish
    republic, 272–75, 277; in Egypt, 38,
    60; since 1980, 374, 377; in reigns of
    Selim III and Mahmud II, 53–56;
    in Second Republic, 307, 325–27,
    331; in Tanzimat period, 94, 106,
    109–11, 132; taxes on, 267, 268;
    "tractorization" of, 275, 307, 325;
    in World War I, 209, 231–32. *See also*
    landowners; migration: rural-urban;
    pastoralism; peasants; provinces
al-Ahd (Arab secret society), 203
Ahmed Fevzi Paşa, 48
Akın (The raid) (Çamlıbel), 255
AK Party. *See* Justice and Development
    Party
aksiyon, 340, 386
Aksiyon (newspaper), 386, 387

AKUT, 358

Albanians, 38, 40, 161, 198, 201, 202, 205, 206, 341, 374

Alemdar. *See* Bayrakdar Mustafa

Aleppo, 62, 171, 174, 210, 215, 217

Alevi Muslims, 7, 142, 304; among Kurds, 250–51; population of, 381; rights movement for, 381–82; as secular republic's supporters, 9, 382; and Sunnis, 320–22, 338, 382; WPT's appeals to, 315

Alexander II (of Russia), 147

Alexandretta. *See* Hatay

Alexandria, 48, 63, 87

Algeria, 30, 136

Ali, Sabahattin, 283

Âli Paşa, Mehmed Emin, 88, 89, 94, 102–5

Ali Paşa (of Yanina and Tepelen), 30, 35–37

Alliance Israélite Universelle, 141

Alp, Tekin (Moise Kohen), 227

alphabet reform. *See* Turkish language

Anatolia: agriculture in, 55; Armenians in, 142–44, 154, 157, 209–11, 233–34, 250, 407; censuses and population in, 42, 62, 63, 182, 184, 233; climate of, 53; in Crimean War, 81–82; crown estates in, 170; ethnic cleansing in, 47, 209–11, 245; famine in, 83, 108; Germany's influence in, 205; Greek claims to parts of, 217, 219, 221, 223, 234; guilds in, 65; manufacturing in, 172, 173, 376, 378, 388, 418; Muslims in, 62, 211, 226; National Struggle in, 221, 222, 280; population exchanges in, 204–5, 226; railways in, 153, 157, 158, 168, 169, 208, 210; seen as homeland of Ottoman Empire and Turkish republic, 4, 40, 151, 202, 205, 215, 245; Syrian exiles in, 203; tax issues in, 97, 164, 165; Treaty of Sèvres on, 219; as Turkish core from

1913 on, 205; warlords in, 36, 47, 48; in World War I, 205, 208–9. *See also* migration: rural-urban

"Anatolian tigers," 376, 378, 388, 418

Anderson, Benedict, 10–11, 19

Anglo-Ottoman Commercial Treaty (1838), 43–44, 46–48, 51, 61, 71, 139

Ankara, 53, 157, 158, 168, 271, 354; as National Struggle headquarters, 222–24; shantytowns in, 321; superurbanization in, 331, 354, 380; as Turkey's new capital, 248–51, 259

Annan, Kofi, 370

"anticolonial nationalism," 10, 11–13

antiestablishment alignments. *See* leftists: in the 1960s

Arabesk music, 336, 337, 342

Arabic language, 94, 202–3, 252, 306, 381; script of, 253, 288–90

Arab lands: caliphates in, 149, 217; challenges to Abdülhamid II from, 137; climate of, 53; crown estates in, 170; and Gülen movement, 386; Janissaries guarding, 61; military schools in, 156; Muslims in, 62; and 1916 Arab revolt, 214–15, 217–18; oil in, 217; as Ottoman Empire's new center of gravity, 151, 202–4, 245; as Ottoman periphery, 205–6, 226; people from, as non-Turkish Muslims, 204; population of, 62, 116–17; railways in, 153, 168; trade of, 120; Treaty of Sèvres on, 219; Wahhabi religious movement in, 38, 70, 181; women writers in, 178; and Young Turk Revolution, 194, 201. *See also* Arabic language; *specific Arab countries*

Arab revolt (World War I), 214–15, 217–18

architecture, 259–60

Ardahan, 85, 218, 265

Argentina, 259

Armed Forces Union, 312

Armenian(s), 47, 62, 65, 85, 100, 101, 108, 116, 129, 223; anti-Turkish terrorism by, in 1970s, 324; attacks on, 141–44, 154, 157, 161, 189, 197, 203, 205, 209–11, 221, 226, 250; as characters in Ottoman novels, 185–86, 189; and OIB incident, 139; as Ottoman Empire emigrants, 177; Ottoman land owned by, 171; population of, in Ottoman Empire, 175, 177, 233–34; property of, 221; Treaty of Sèvres on, 219, 223; among Young Turks, 201

Armenian language, 203

Armenian Secret Army for the Liberation of Armenia, 324

Army Engineering School, 33, 41, 67, 90

Arvasi, Abdülhakim, 340

ASALA, 324

Aşkale labor camp, 266

associations law, 201–2

Atatürk, Mustafa Kemal, 124, 354; assassination attempt on, 251; birthplace of, 308; civilian rule by, 261–62, 309; death of, 261; dictatorial power of, 257, 262; family of, 264, 278–79; legacy of, 261–62, 303–4; in literature, 391, 392–93; in National Struggle, 219, 221–23, 261; and Nursi, 287; opposition to, 223–24, 249–53; personality cult of, 262, 304, 418; tomb of, 288; as Turkish republic leader, 247, 248–62, 271, 303; Western orientation of, 371, 372; in World War I, 209, 212, 214, 215

Ateşten Gömlek (Shirt of flame) (Adıvar), 193, 240, 241–44

Athens, 39

audiocassettes, 336, 386

Australasia, 17, 212, 389

Austria, 23, 24, 26, 31, 47, 48, 59, 71–74, 107. *See also* Austria-Hungary

Austria-Hungary, 85, 102, 111, 205, 207, 230, 232

authoritarianism: continuity of, in Ottoman and Turkish politics, 4, 6, 24, 36, 133, 137, 145, 146–48, 190, 198, 223–24, 245, 252, 257, 258, 270, 303, 340, 416; in Germany, 74; vs. "law state," 94; and single-party rule, 195–201, 266–70, 284, 287. *See also* centralization; factionalism

autocracy. *See* authoritarianism

automobiles, 327, 341

Avcıoğlu, Doğan, 313

ayan. See warlords

Azerbaijan, 209, 265, 370–71

Bâbiâli (Fazıl), 340–41

Baghdad, 69, 99, 196, 213–15, 217, 218; population of, 62, 116; railways in, 157–58, 168; schools in, 154; warlordism in, 30–31

Baghdad Pact (1955), 310

Balcı, Bayram, 386

Balfour Declaration, 217, 218

Balkan Defense Pact (1955), 310

Balkan Pact (1934), 264

Balkans (Rumelia), 26, 27, 29, 47, 62, 175, 278; agriculture in, 109, 111; climate of, 53; crises in, during Tanzimat, 80–85; crises in, under Abdülhamid II, 135; Gülen movement in, 386; in Ottoman-Russian wars, 25, 61; Ottoman territory lost in, 23, 25, 26, 75, 76, 134, 151, 170, 174, 175, 202, 206, 211; population and censuses of, 42, 61–62, 116, 202; railways in, 153; Russian military in, 47;

Balkans (Rumelia) *(continued)*
  separatist nationalism in, 24, 202; tax
  collection in, 97; as true homeland
  of many Turks, 4, 40, 202; warlords
  in, 29–30, 36; Young Turk
  Revolution begins in, 194. *See also*
  Balkan Wars; *specific places in*
Balkan Wars, 4, 108, 134, 145, 198, 200–202,
  205, 206–7, 211, 226–28, 239, 245, 286
Bank of Industry and Mines, 272
Basra, 30–31, 168, 213, 217, 218
Batum, 85, 218, 223
Bayar, Celâl, 268
Bayrakdar Mustafa, 35–36
"Becoming Turkish, Islamic, and Modern"
  (Gökalp), 17–18, 237, 238, 246,
  386, 416
bedouin, 40, 138, 204
Beethoven, Ludwig von, 343
Beirut, 116, 169–70, 206, 324
Bektaşi religious order, 40, 71, 381
Belgium, 200
Belgrade, 36, 165
Bengal, 13
Bereketli Topraklar Üzerinde (On these
  bounteous lands) (Orhan Kemal),
  305, 307, 341–49
Berkes, Niyazi, 1
Bessarabia, 85
Bethlehem, 81
bey (defined), 29
Beyoğlu (Istanbul neighborhood), 25, 186,
  188, 243
Bieberstein, Marschall von, 157
Bir Düğün Gecesi (An evening wedding)
  (Ağaoğlu), 390, 394–98
birth control, 183. *See also* abortion;
  fertility
Bismarck, Otto von, 85
Bitlis, 209, 210, 234, 385
Black Sea, 25, 26, 82, 83, 208

boarding schools, 178, 183
Bolivia, 315
Bosnia, 80, 83, 85, 99, 205, 364
Bosphorus bridges, 228, 328–29
bourgeoisie: conservatives among, 165;
  CUP as representing, 229, 276; in
  Egypt, 87; emergence of Ottoman
  Muslim, 103, 117–23, 132, 169, 174,
  179–81, 184, 186, 191, 227–29, 236,
  245; increase in, in Turkey, 307;
  "national," 13, 204, 229, 275, 327,
  376; as Ottoman notables, 29–31, 33,
  35, 36, 53, 56, 80, 87, 97, 111, 114, 122,
  138, 142, 149, 151, 162, 164, 195–96,
  203, 221, 222, 232; proto-, 19, 175,
  376, 417; in RPP, 257; in Salonica,
  227; spousal choice as critical issue
  for, 68, 118, 181; "state feminism" as
  affecting, 279–80; tax revolts by, 164;
  Turkish efforts to form and mobilize
  a, 13, 275, 417; as Turkish notables,
  252, 257–58, 269, 280; after World
  War II, 267. *See also* landowners;
  merchants
Braudel, Fernand, 21, 54
Brazil, 161, 259
Bretton Woods agreement, 275
Britain: and Baghdad Pact, 310; in
  Crimean War, 81, 82; and Cyprus,
  85, 219, 322, 323; and Egypt, 27, 43,
  47, 48, 78, 85, 86–87, 136–37, 212,
  219; and Greek Revolution, 39;
  imperialism of, 205; involvement
  of, in Ottoman Empire, 86–87,
  108, 111, 112, 142, 166, 168, 214,
  217–19; and Iraq, 205, 208, 210,
  213–14, 217–19, 262–63; in Kars,
  407; pan-Islamic fears in, 149; and
  partitioning of Ottoman Empire,
  214, 217–19; and slavery, 96; and
  Turkish National Struggle, 223; as

Turkish republic's ally, 264, 265; in World War I, 200, 204, 207–8, 210, 212–15. *See also* Anglo-Ottoman Commercial Treaty; Convention of London

Bucak, Sedat, 362, 365

Büchner, Ludwig, 163

Bugün (Islamic newspaper), 315

Bulgaria, 100, 144, 145; agriculture in, 109; in Balkan Wars, 202, 206, 207; under Berlin Treaty, 85; declares independence from Ottoman Empire, 205; fertility in, 184; insurrections in, 80, 83, 135; protoindustries in, 59, 113, 120; Russo-Turkish War in, 84; separation of ethnic groups in, 205; Soviets in, 265; tax collection in, 110; Turkey's boundary with, 245; Turks expelled from, 369; in World War I, 200, 207, 208, 212, 215

Bulgarian language, 203

Burç FM, 387

bureaucracy. *See* civil officials

Bursa, 112, 114, 132, 150, 170, 172, 277, 380

Büyük doğu (journal), 340

Cahit, Hüseyin, 195

Cairo, 62, 116

caliphates: Abbasid, 28; abolition of, 226, 248, 250, 252; Arab, 149, 217; Ottoman sultans as heads of, 25–26, 148–49, 190, 202, 243; spiritual vs. political authority of, 25–26, 148–49, 190, 202. *See also* sultans

Çamlıbel, Faruk Nafiz, 255

Capital Levy (wealth tax), 266, 275

capitulations, 25–26, 33, 43, 51, 59, 60, 139, 224, 227

carpet industry, 171–73

Catherine II (of Russia), 26

Caucasus, 25, 26, 30, 61, 81, 116, 181; Armenians in, 143; Muslim refugees from, 175; and National Struggle, 221; World War I in, 208–9, 215

Cavid, Mehmet, 199, 226–27, 251

Çayan, Mahir, 316

Celaleddin, Ahmed, 162–63

Celaleddin, Mahmud, 162

Cemal Bey (later, Paşa), 198–99, 203, 204, 212, 214, 232

censorship: under Abdülhamid II, 160, 177, 178, 194; under Democrat Party, 307–8; under early Turkish republic, 251, 258; in Europe, 125; 1961 constitution's lifting of, 311; of press, 96, 104, 160; under Second Republic, 336; of theater, 129; under Third Republic, 353; Turkish language's reform as a kind of, 256, 257, 289

censuses: of 1830–31, 42, 62; of 1840s, 97, 98; of 1881–93, 150, 156, 174, 181; of 1906–7, 150, 174; of 1927, 234, 277. *See also* population

CENTO (Central Treaty Organization), 310

Central Asia: Gülen movement in, 386, 388–89; and ideas about Turkish origins, 255–56, 338; languages in, 255–57; republics in, 252, 253, 361, 368, 370–72, 403. *See also specific places in*

Central Bank (Turkey), 273

centralization: in Egypt, 59–61; during Hamidian period, 145–60; push for, under Selim III and Mahmud II, 23–75; during Tanzimat era, 88–106; during Young Turk period, 201, 203. *See also* authoritarianism; decentralization central planning, 247, 273–75, 312, 313, 325, 326–27

Ceride-i Havadis (newspaper), 104

Çeşme, 25

Cevdet Paşa, Ahmed, 89, 94, 103, 184, 187

Cezzar Ahmed Paşa, 27

charity. *See* foundations (charitable)

Chatterjee, Partha, 10, 11–12

Chechens, 364

childbirth, 68

child labor, 173, 343–44

China, 13, 192, 315

Christians: on Crete, 78; divisions among, 65, 81, 100, 101, 141, 142; in Egypt, 27; European support for, in Ottoman Empire, 26, 65, 79–81, 83, 116, 141, 211, 243; European Union as "club" for, 372; in Lebanon, 78, 80, 141; massacres of, in World War I, 209–11; Muslims exchanged for, 204–5, 226, 278; as Ottoman Empire emigrants, 177; in Ottoman novels, 185–6; in Ottoman trade, 120, 169; population of, in Ottoman Empire, 62, 174, 177, 205; status of, in Ottoman Empire, 8–9, 25, 64–65, 99–100; and Treaty of Küçük Kaynarca, 26. *See also* Armenian(s); Greeks; missionaries; non-Muslims

"Chronometric Institute" (*Saatleri Ayarlama Enstitüsü*) (Tanpınar), 247–48, 291–303

Churchill, William, 104

Çiller, Tansu, 357–58

Circassians, 116, 161, 201, 204, 409

citizenship. *See* civil society

civil code, 279, 288, 383

civil officials (bureaucrats): under Abdülhamid II, 133, 150, 151, 153, 154, 158–61, 190–91; under Mahmud II, 41–42, 98, 418; as mediators between Ottomans and Europeans, 46, 61; non-Muslims among, 89, 92, 99, 102, 103, 120; during Tanzimat, 88–90, 94–99, 102–3, 120–23, 146. *See also* government

Civil Officials Commission, 159

civil society (citizenship), 363, 364, 381, 390–91, 417

clans, 365–66

class. *See* hierarchical order

climate (of Ottoman Empire), 53

clock: metaphors of, 76, 248, 291–303; Western, adopted by Turkish republic, 252

The Clown and His Daughter (*Sinekli Bakkal*) (Adıvar), 193, 240–44

coalition governments (in Turkey), 312, 317–18, 357–58, 386–87

coinage. *See* monetary system

"commando" training camps (1960s), 315, 316, 320

commercial treaty. *See* Anglo-Ottoman Commercial Treaty

Committee of Union and Progress (CUP), 161, 162, 164, 226; and Armenian massacres, 211, 221; bourgeoisie represented by, 229; economic policies of, 226–28; forms a party, 197–98; guardian role of, 165, 195, 221, 245; ideologist of, 199, 236–39; and National Struggle, 224, 234; opposition to, 198; Sublime Porte coup of, 198, 206, 227; Turkish republic's show trials against, 251; after World War I, 221; Young Turk Revolution, role in, 194–201. *See also* Young Turks

communal autonomy (of non-Muslims in Ottoman Empire), 8–9, 25, 64–65, 92, 99–100 communism: accusations of, in Turkey, 268, 284, 306, 308; Atatürk as avoiding, 262. *See also* Marxism; Soviet Union

Comte, Auguste, 161

Concert of Europe, 73, 75, 83

concubinage, 8, 30, 68, 127, 128

constitution(s) (Ottoman), 35–36; Abdülhamid II's restoration of, 164, 165, 190, 194–95; Abdülhamid II's suspension of, 158, 163, 190; amendments to, 197, 248; CUP as guardian of, 200, 245; of 1876, 84, 89, 92–94, 105, 146, 148, 158, 190, 248, 419; of religious millets, 92, 93, 100–101; Young Ottomans' calls for government based on, 104–6, 118, 123, 160; Young Turks' restoration of, 194. *See also* constitution(s) (Turkish)

constitution(s) (Turkish): demands for full implementation of, 268; extremists not willing to abide by, 306, 312, 313; Fundamental Organization Law seen as, 224, 248; National Defense Law as giving İnönü powers beyond, 266; 1960 amendments to, 311; of 1961, 311–15, 328, 334–36, 352, 354, 365; of 1961, amendments to, 316; of 1983, 351, 352–54, 365; of 1924, 248, 252, 257, 311, 312, 365; voiding of, by 1980 military coup, 351

constitutionalism, 163, 239, 270, 286; of 1876 and 1908, 104–6, 118, 123, 146, 160, 165, 194, 195–96, 313, 418. *See also* constitution(s) (Ottoman and Turkish)

constitutional monarchy, 146, 197

constitutional sultanate, 200

Convention for the Elimination of All Types of Discrimination Against Women (CEDAW), 383

Convention of London (1840), 48, 74

cooperatives, 229

Copenhagen criteria (for EU admission), 371, 373

core vs. periphery issues, 201, 205, 285

corporatism: of early Turkish republic, 66, 270, 271; Gökalp on, 237, 239, 313; of National Action Party, 320; after 1960 military coup, 311

corruption, 357, 359, 362–65, 375

Çorum, 320, 382

cosmopolitanism (of Ottoman Empire), 1, 9, 15, 23, 61, 64, 81, 190, 192, 201–2, 211, 245, 256, 292, 293–94, 416, 420; destruction of, 4, 144, 201–2, 209–11, 250, 276–78, 308. *See also* ethnic cleansing; Ottoman Empire: territory lost by

cotton, 38, 54, 60, 86, 171–73

Council of Ministers, 41, 158

Council of State, 158

courts: civil, during Tanzimat, 92, 94, 96, 99, 138; constitutional, 311–12, 316, 357, 384; Erdoğan in, 360; Menderes and other Democrats in, 312; after 1980 military coup, 352, 354; Nursi in, 287, 290; religious, 234–35, 252; state security, 316; Turkish republic's show trials in, 251. *See also* law; prison

Crete, 39, 47, 78, 93, 135–36, 144, 175, 205

Crimea, 23, 25, 26, 75, 76. *See also* Crimean War

Crimean War, 75, 76, 81–83, 90, 108, 116

Croatia, 374

crown estates, 170–71

Çırpan, Satı, 280

culture. *See* folk culture; literature; print capitalism; Turkish language

CUP. *See* Committee of Union and Progress

customs duties, 43, 51, 141, 173, 272. *See also* tariffs

customs union, 370, 372, 373, 375

Cyprus: British occupation of, 85, 219; and EU, 370, 373; as issue between Greece and Turkey, 308, 310, 313, 322–24, 348, 368, 369–70; partitioning of, 323, 370; Turkey's invasion of, 317, 323, 336

Czechoslovakia, 264, 315

Damascus, 69, 196, 204, 217; and Arab revolt, 214, 215; Cemal Paşa in, 203; population of, 62, 116; religious conflict in, 80; schools in, 154

La Dame aux camélias (Dumas fils), 125, 128–29

dam projects, 366–69

Dardanelles, 156, 212, 231, 264, 265

D'Aronco, Raimondo, 147

Dar Zamanlar (Hard times) (Ağaoğlu), 351, 390–403

Dashnak Party, 143, 144, 205

decentralization (of Ottoman Empire), 28–36, 50, 66, 202

"deed of agreement" (1808), 35–36

Defense of National Rights Societies, 221, 224, 248–51

Demirel, Süleyman, 313–18, 320, 329, 357, 366

Democratic Left Party, 358

Democrat Party (DP), 266–70, 287, 305–13, 324, 325–26, 337

Dersim, 251

Derviş, Kemal, 358, 375

dervish orders, 40, 65–66, 70–71, 196, 252, 258–59, 288, 381

Description de l'Égypt, 27

d'Espérey, Franchet, 215

developing countries: Turkey as, in twentieth century, 305, 325, 330, 374; Turkey as model for, 276; Turkish republic as, 247, 259, 279, 378

The Development of Secularism in Turkey (Berkes), 1

Devrim (journal), 313

Directorate for Women's Status and Problems, 382–83

Directorate of Religious Affairs (Turkish republic), 20, 252, 382–83, 419

diseases, 63, 116, 138, 209, 234

divorce (Islamic), 67, 235, 383

Diyarbakır, 164, 174, 210, 367

DP. *See* Democrat Party

dress reform: under CUP, 235; under Mahmud II, 40; some feminists' rejection of, 383; under Turkish republic, 252–53, 279, 286, 297, 304. *See also* women: veiling and unveiling of Muslim

Druzes, 78–80, 141

Duara, Prasenjit, 10, 13

Dumas, Alexandre (fils), 125, 127, 128–29

Durkheim, Émile, 236–39, 313

Durmuş, Osman, 358

Düstur, 92, 160

earthquakes, 358, 370, 373, 380

"Eastern Question," 24–28, 85

Ecevit, Bülent, 314, 316–18, 323, 358

economics: under Abdülhamid II, 139, 159, 160–61, 165–74; under AK Party, 361; under Democrat Party, 306–9, 325–26; under early Turkish republic, 270–76; as a focus of this book, 2–3; since 1980, 351, 374–79, 403; under 1961 constitution, 312; Ottoman and Turkish state's involvement in, 38, 43–44, 50–53, 58, 247, 257, 271, 273–75, 312, 313, 325–27, 387; print capitalism's connection to, 11, 19; under Second Republic, 310, 316, 321, 324–30, 334–35, 349; under Selim III and Mahmud II, 49–61; statist policies on, 247, 259, 272–76, 292, 304, 305, 323, 325, 327, 329, 374–76; during Tanzimat, 106–15, 120–23, 132; themes of, in Turkey's history, 415; under Third Republic, 354; Turkish republic's involvement in, 230–31, 247; under Young Turks, 193, 195, 276. *See also* central planning; government: finances of; manufactures; merchants; monetary system; monopolies; "national economy" policy; print capitalism; trade

Edirne, 62, 166, 198, 206–7, 245, 277, 385, 386

education: CUP reform of, 235; under early Turkish republic, 255, 283–84; for girls and women, 67–69, 117, 126, 178, 183–84, 227, 235, 239–40, 280, 283, 355–56, 380, 389; of Greeks in Epirus, 36; by Gülen movement, 387, 388–89; Islamist involvement in, 20, 149, 190; Jewish, 141, 201; legislation on, 153, 154; medreses for Islamic, 7, 67, 83, 143, 196, 234, 286; of Muslim children, 67, 68–69, 91, 117, 141, 153–54, 179, 387–89; for Muslim religious leaders (*imam-hatip* schools), 355–56, 359; new institutions for, 90–91, 96, 105, 117, 132, 138, 152, 153–54, 178, 227, 235, 284, 355, 380, 418; after 1980, 378, 380; non-Muslim, in Ottoman Empire, 36, 92, 102, 141, 153–54, 201; of political elites in Ottoman Empire, 90–92; and "print capitalism," 11;

religious, and civil service, 89; and rise of bourgeoisie, 87, 117–18; in rural areas, 110, 153, 280, 283–84, 341–42; under Second Republic, 334–35; under Third Republic, 355–56; after World War I, 277. *See also* literacy; *names of specific specialized schools*

Edward VII (of Britain), 164

EEC. *See* European Economic Community

Egypt, 33, 85–87, 104, 113, 135, 174, 417; Britain and, 27, 43, 47, 48, 78, 85, 86–87, 136–37, 212, 219; cotton in, 38, 54, 60, 86; ejection of French from, 37–39; elites in, 39, 49, 60, 87; mamluk warlords in, 26–28, 30, 35–40, 42–50, 54, 59–61, 63, 78, 83, 85–87, 104, 212; military service in, 38–39, 60, 63; Napoleon's invasion of, 23, 24, 26–28, 34, 73, 75, 202; nationalism in, 87, 136–37; 1919 revolution in, 192; Ottoman rivalry with, 46–49; Ottoman war with, 76, 78; population of, 62, 116; railways in, 86, 166; revolt against Ottoman Empire in, 204; state bankruptcy of, 109; tribute to Ottoman sultan from, 47, 48, 78, 86, 111; women writers in, 178; in World War I, 208, 212. *See also* Convention of London; *specific rulers in*

Ekoloji, 387

electronic media, 20, 379, 386

elites: background of Ottoman, 49, 102; business, 277–78; in Egypt, 39, 49, 60, 87; imperial, as sultan's slaves, 30, 46, 53, 66, 74, 75, 159; in Lebanon, 78–79; military, in Turkish republic, 190–91, 197, 309–11, 348–49; nationalist, 13;

elites: background of Ottoman (*continued*)
opposition to Tanzimat reforms
from, 102–6; as political leaders, 19;
political split among, under İnönü,
266–69; as Tanzimat political
leaders, 78, 88–91, 132; training
of civil, 41; as Turkish republic
political leaders, 165, 195–96,
276, 303. *See also* civil officials;
hierarchical order; notables;
patronage; *specific individuals*
Elizabeth (of Austria), 147
Elrom, Ephraim, 316
The Emancipation of the Turkish Woman
(İnan), 279
Emergence of Modern Turkey
(Lewis), 1, 2
Emrullah Efendi, 235
English language, 240
Enlightenment ideas, 34, 75, 163. *See also*
free trade; individualism; liberalism;
modernity; scientific materialism;
secularism
Entente Libérale, 198
Enver Bey (later, Paşa), 198–200, 202,
206–10, 212, 213, 221, 261
Erbakan, Necmettin, 315, 317, 322, 357–61,
372, 382, 386–87, 389
Erdoğan, Recip Tayyip, 351, 354–55, 359–61,
368, 369, 383, 415, 418, 419
Ergenekon, 415
Erim, Nihat, 316
Erzurum, 164, 209, 210, 222, 234, 266,
385, 386
Esad (sufi leader), 259
esham, 52–53
Eskişehir, 223
ethnic cleansing, 47, 78, 116, 202, 209–11,
234, 245, 340. *See also* ethnicity:
efforts to separate populations on
basis of

ethnicity: differences of, in nation-states,
14–15, 364; and divisions among
Ottoman bourgeoisie, 120–21;
efforts to separate populations on
basis of, 79–80, 143, 202, 204–5,
209–11, 219, 226, 232, 245, 278,
323; of Egypt's foreign elites, 49,
60, 87; increasing homogeneity
in early Turkish republic's, 276,
278; internal conflicts based on,
turned into foreign policy issues,
248, 256, 368; in Macedonia, 144,
145; as major divisive issue in
Ottoman Empire, 256; multiplicity
of, among Muslims, 364–65, 368,
369, 409; in Ottoman Balkans,
61, 65; as part of national culture,
18; as part of Turkish identity,
238–39; politicization of identities
based on, 74, 76, 81, 101–2, 132,
142, 178–79, 320–21, 337–38,
364–68, 416; separatism based on,
not allowed under Young Turks,
201–2. *See also* ethnic cleansing;
specific ethnic and national groups
Etibank, 273
Euphrates River, 53, 367, 368–69, 377
Europe: anticolonialist nationalism as
opposing imperialism of, 11–13, 105–
6; banning of literary works in, 125;
eastern, as EU members, 372–73;
"Eastern Question" of, 24–28, 85;
1848 revolutions in, 81; imperialism
of, as threat to Ottoman Empire,
9, 24–28, 30, 136, 139, 141–42, 190,
205–6, 416; industrial revolution in,
111, 112; influence of, on Ottoman
Empire, 9, 19, 72–76, 78, 83, 85, 88,
91, 95, 99, 134–42, 146–47, 156–58,
162–63, 166, 168, 183, 199–200, 207,
227–28, 232, 234; influence of, on

Turkish republic, 252–53, 255, 256, 259–60, 262, 290–91; migration of Turkish laborers to, 305, 321, 323–25, 327, 328, 332–34, 337, 338, 363, 372, 381, 403; modernity's origins in, 17–18; most Muslims as living under rule of, in 1800s, 148, 149; multiple religions in, 74; Nationalist Action Party in, 320, 321; Ottoman diplomats in, 34, 41, 43, 47, 61, 71–75, 417, 420; Ottoman Empire as briefly losing nearly all its territory in, during Balkan Wars, 206; politicized culture in, 15; population in, 116, 175; protection for non-Muslim religious communities from, 26, 65, 79–81, 83, 116, 141, 211, 243; soldiers from, as Egyptian military leaders, 49; soldiers from, as Ottoman military leaders, 208, 212–14; sultans' visits to, 88, 146–47; taxes in, 107; World War I's economic effects on, 229–30. *See also* Enlightenment ideas; European Union; foreign intervention; free trade; liberalism; modernity; *specific countries and institutions in*

European Commission on Human Rights, 356

European Court of Human Rights, 384

European Economic Community (EEC), 73, 305, 323, 329, 356. *See also* European Union

European Union (EU): conventions of, on human rights and torture, 356; and Cyprus, 370, 373; Turkey's interest in joining, 18, 350, 351, 359, 361, 362, 364, 367–69, 371–74, 377, 382, 403, 417, 420

European Women's Lobby, 382

"An evening wedding" (*Bir Düğün Gecesi*) (Ağaoğlu), 390, 394–98

Evren, Kenan, 351, 353

exile, 104; under Abdülhamid II, 84, 160–63; Dashnaks sent into, 144; early Turkish republic as sending opposition into, 249; by Entente for Ottoman Turks, 222; of Gülen, 387; of Janissaries, 37, 42; limits placed on sultan's rights regarding, 197; after 1960 military coup, 311; novels with characters sent into, 240, 241; pardoning of people sent into, 195; Young Ottomans choosing, 104, 124, 129; Young Ottomans sent into, 105, 129

export-led growth strategies, 325, 351, 354, 374–75

Exposition Universelle (Paris), 146–47

factionalism (personality-centered), 19, 37, 46, 49, 76, 89–91, 102, 103, 123, 161. *See also* patronage

Falkenhayn, Erich von, 214

family law reform, 234–35. *See also* marriage

fascism: corporatism's association with, 237; in Germany, 238, 262, 264; of Nationalist Action Party, 318, 320, 338; as threat to Turkish republic, 248; Turkish republic's rejection of, 262

al-Fatat (Arab secret society), 203

fatherland. *See vatan*

"Fatherland, or Silistria" (*Vatan yahud Silestre*) (Namık Kemal), 129–32, 211, 243, 411

Fatma Aliye, 126, 133, 178, 184, 187–90, 240, 417

Faysal (Sharif), 214, 217

Fazıl Paşa, Mustafa, 104, 161

Federation of the Revolutionary Youth of Turkey (Dev-Genç), 315

Felicity Party, 315, 359

feminism: Islamic, 383–84; since 1980, 379, 382–84; in Ottoman Empire, 8, 235; "state," 276, 278–80, 382; under Young Turks, 195. *See also* patriarchy

Fergan, Eşref Edib, 339

fertility, 181–84, 279–80, 335; declines in, due to fears of military conscription, 39, 63, 68, 175; declines in, due to violence and warfare, 144, 202, 203. *See also* abortion; birth control; population

fetvas, 234

fez, 40, 252, 253

First Constitutional Regime, 84, 133, 194

fiscalism, 50, 52, 58, 59–60

Flaubert, Gustave, 124

folk culture, 284, 381

foreign intervention: in early Turkish republic, 248, 275; in Egypt, 86–87; European protection for specific Ottoman religious communities as form of, 26, 65, 79–81, 83, 116, 141, 211, 243; as not needed after earthquake, 358; patterns of, in Middle East, 28, 136, 202; as threat to Ottoman Empire, 98, 139–42. *See also* Europe; imperialism; Russia

foundations (charitable), 20, 38, 58, 59, 95, 228, 234, 252, 320, 387, 388

The Fountain (newspaper), 387

France: in Crimean War, 81, 82; and Egypt, 23, 24, 26–28, 34, 48, 73, 75, 78, 86–87, 202; and Greece, 47; head scarves in, 384; imperialism of, 136, 157, 205; influence of, on Ottoman Empire, 93–94, 99, 108, 139, 141, 166, 168, 177, 228; and Lebanon, 80; and Ottoman Imperial Bank, 108, 166, 228;

Ottoman school in, 90; Ottoman trade with, 111; 1968 student uprising in, 315; and Syria, 168, 205, 217–19, 264; Treaty of Sèvres and, 219; Turkish labor in, 333; and Turkish National Struggle, 223; as Turkish republic's ally, 264, 265; Turks educated in, 280–81, 339; women's suffrage in, 279; in World War I, 200, 207, 208, 215, 219, 233; Young Ottomans and Young Turks in, 104, 124–25, 129, 161–63. *See also* French language; French Revolution

Franco, Francisco, 314, 340

"freedom," 27, 106, 123, 296

Freedom Party, 308

Freedom Society (Kurdish), 250

Free Republican Party, 258, 259

free trade (in Ottoman Empire), 43–44, 51, 57, 61, 112, 139, 171, 195, 226, 227, 276

French language, 42, 71, 89–91, 118

French Revolution, 23, 26, 31, 34

Fuad Paşa, Keçecizade, 76, 88, 102, 105

Fundamental Organization Law, 224, 248

Galatasaray Lycée, 91, 153, 154

Galib, Mehmed Said, 37

Galip, Şeyh, 34

Gallipoli, 207, 210, 212–13

GAP (Southeast Anatolia Project), 366–70

Garfield, James, 147

Gaza, 33

gecekondu. See shantytowns

Gencebay, Orhan, 337

gender: and boy-meets-girl themes in Ottoman literature, 126–32, 185, 189–90, 240–41; disparities in, due to war, 277; divisions between, 337, 338; and Gülen movement, 389; Kur'an and gender difference, 7, 65; literacy gaps related to, 129, 283, 335,

378; mixing of, 129, 297, 381, 391–92; modernity's challenges to Islamic norms regarding, 8, 9, 123–32, 177–78, 185, 235, 279–80, 417; and Muslim identity formation, 66–67, 131; of nationalist elites, 13, 19; and voting, 195, 235, 253, 279, 383. *See also* feminism; patriarchy; women

General Revolutionary Organization of the Islamic World, 221

Georgia (Caucasus), 26, 30, 209

Germany, 72–74; and early Turkish republic, 274; exiles from, in Turkey, 259–60, 283; fascism in, 238, 262; imperialism of, 205; and Ottoman Empire, 156, 157–58, 168, 199–200, 207–8, 211, 212–14, 218, 230, 232, 234; rule of law in, 73, 94, 364; soldiers from, as Ottoman military leaders, 208, 212–14; and Turkey in World War II, 264–65; Turkish labor in, 332–34; Turkish Nationalist Action Party in, 320; in World War I, 200, 207–8, 211, 212–14, 218, 219, 233

Gezmiş, Deniz, 316

Ghulam Ali, 69

Gladstone, William, 142

globalization: and Gülen religious movement, 384–90; identity and difference under, 380–84; vs. localism, 1, 350–51, 362, 405, 420; modernity as part of, 17–20; of 1960s radicalism, 314, 337–38, 365; of Turkish diaspora, 403

Gökalp, Ziya, 313, 339; "Becoming Turkish, Islamic, and Modern" by, 17–18, 237, 238, 246, 386, 416; CUP ideology developed by, 199, 236–39; and "national economy" policy, 227, 229; poem by, 360; "Principles of Turkism" by, 238

Gökçek, Melih, 354

Gökçen, Sabiha, 264

government (state): as asserting its right to legislate personal status issues, 235; authoritarianism under Ottoman and Turkish, 4, 6, 24, 36, 133, 137, 145, 146–48, 190, 198, 223–24, 245, 252, 257, 258, 270, 303, 340, 416; central planning by, 247, 273–75, 312, 313, 325, 326–27; finances of, 33, 58–61, 75, 83, 88, 106–9, 132, 134–35, 165–66, 193, 197, 230; military as unelected power center of Turkish, 200, 306, 415; purges of officials in, by Young Turks, 196; reform of, during Tanzimat, 88–106; reform of, under Mahmud II, 41–42; "state purchase" by, 52, 60, 109, 275; state services from, 268, 313, 334, 363–64; Young Ottomans' calls for constitutional, 104–6; Young Turks' calls for constitutional, 104–6, 118, 123. *See also* civil officials; constitution(s); economics; factionalism; monetary system; Ottoman Empire; parliaments; patronage; petitions; politics; sultans; taxes; Turkey; Turkish republic; *specific political parties, leaders, and rulers*

Grand Chancery, 148

Grand National Assembly, 222, 224, 257, 309, 357, 361, 368; architecture of, 259; becomes Turkish republic's parliament, 248; declares Turkey a republic, 226; Democrat Party's hold on, 307–8; Kurdish political parties in, 366, 368; military coup suspends, 351, 353; Senate for, 311, 353; women in, 279, 280, 383

grand vezir: Abdülaziz's, 88, 89;
Abdülhamid II's, 84, 181;
headquarters of, 76; Husrev Paşa as,
48; Mahmud II's, 34, 47; Mahmud's
abolition of, 42; Mahmud Şevket
Paşa as, 198; Said Halim Paşa as,
208; Young Turks' rules about, 197.
See also specific grand vezirs
grapes, 54
"gray wolves," 320, 337
Great Depression, 247, 259, 270, 272–77,
280, 283, 304
Greece, 144, 206; civil war in, 265;
earthquake in, 358, 370; and Egypt,
46–47; independence of, 64, 78,
101; loss of Ottoman territory to, 134;
1967 military coup in, 317, 322–23;
Ottoman population exchange
with, 204–5, 226, 278; in Ottoman-
Russian wars, 25, 29; Ottoman
war against, 136, 144–45, 156; parts
of Ottoman Empire claimed by,
217, 219, 221, 223, 234, 242–44, 262;
revolution in, 36, 39, 41, 63, 71,
142; Turkey's boundary with, 245;
Turkish Defense Pact with, 310;
Turkish friendship treaty with,
263–64; unites with Crete, 205.
See also Cyprus; Greek language;
Greeks
Greek language, 36
Greeks: in Balkan Wars, 202; Christians
among, 66, 100; in Istanbul
at World War I's end, 215;
nationalism of, 36, 70, 100, 101, 135,
215; 1913–14 boycott against, 228; as
Ottoman Empire emigrants, 177,
204–5; population exchanges of,
204–5, 226, 278; population of, in
Ottoman Empire, 62, 175, 234;
property of, 171, 221; 1955 riots

against, in Turkey, 308, 310; among
Young Turks, 201
Guevara, Ché, 315
guilds (in Ottoman Empire), 50, 57, 59,
65–66, 87, 112, 113, 227, 230, 293, 345
Gül, Abdullah, 361
Gülen, Fethullah, 3, 20, 21, 351, 371,
384–90, 403, 419
Gülhane decree (1839), 40, 42, 65,
71, 417; as charter for political
reform, 44, 46–49, 62, 74, 92, 93,
97; as conforming to sharia, 94,
419; effects of, 79–80; extends its
guarantees to all Ottoman subjects,
45, 79, 92, 99–100; on *vatan*, 45, 101
Gürsel, Cemal, 312
Güvenç, Bozkurt, 255

hadiths, 6, 69, 183
Hakimiyet-i Milliye (newspaper), 222
Halet Efendi, 37
Halid, Mevlana (Khalid al-Naqshbandi), 3,
19–21, 69–70, 250, 285, 287, 289, 418,
419. *See also* Halidiye-Nakşibendiye
Halide Edib [Adıvar], 239–44, 246, 280
Halidiye-Nakşibendiye, 19, 40, 44, 46,
69–71, 75, 123, 180–81, 250, 259,
285, 356, 357, 360, 365, 388, 418;
Religious Affairs Directorate's
"colonization" by, 20, 252,
382–83, 419
Halil Paşa [Kut], 213
Hamas, 357
Hamidiye cavalry, 143, 366
"Hard times" (*Dar Zamanlar*) (Ağaoğlu),
351, 390–403
Hasan Paşa, 31
Hashemites, 138
Hatay (Alexandretta), 224, 264, 278, 369
Hayır … (No …) (Ağaoğlu), 390, 398–403
Hearths of Ideals, 315

Hegel, G. W. F., 409
Hergün (NAP newspaper), 320
Herzegovina, 83, 85, 205
hierarchical order: based on class vs.
     tribe, 70; Chatterjee on, 13; in early
     Turkish republic, 334; in Egypt, 27,
     39, 49, 60, 87; of Istanbul's imperial
     household, 30; Kur'an on, 7–8;
     in Ottoman Empire, 65–66, 103;
     in provincial protoindustries, 114;
     revolts against, in Ottoman Empire,
     79–80; and skin tone, 360; and
     Turkish managerial-technocratic
     elite, 227, 275, 327–28, 376–77, 417;
     and working-class consciousness,
     168, 173, 179, 190, 195. *See also*
     bourgeoisie; clans; elites; notables;
     peasants; sultans; urbanization: and
     the poor
Higher Education Law, 352
Hijaz, 47, 136, 138–39, 149–50, 203–4, 217,
     219. *See also* Hijaz railway; Mecca;
     Medina
Hijaz railway, 139, 148, 150, 166, 168, 204
Hilmi, Şehbenderzade Ahmed, 195
Hilmi Paşa, Hüseyn, 145
history: as also made by excluded groups,
     304; literature as more astute about,
     than scholarly studies, 2–3, 338, 341,
     415, 421; role of, in nation-building,
     13, 273, 300, 421; in Turkish
     nationalist curriculum, 4, 13, 122,
     253, 255–56, 273, 352, 372, 421
Hitler, Adolf, 261, 340
Hnchak Party, 143
holding companies, 273, 327
honor, 45–46, 382, 383
Hotin siege, 25
"houses of light," 387, 388
human development index, 63, 68, 274,
     330, 335, 349, 374–76, 378–79

human rights, 92, 93, 100; AK Party on,
     359; and EU admission, 372; 1980
     military coup's violations of,
     352–54; Sadık Rifat on, 73–74;
     violations of, by Turkish state,
     363, 366–67. *See also* ethnic
     cleansing
Hungary, 81
Husayn ibn Ali, 204, 214, 217, 218
Husaynid dynasty, 136
Husayn Kamil, 212
Husayn-McMahon correspondence,
     217, 218
Hüseyin Paşa, Ağa, 37
Hüseyinzade Ali, 17–18
Husrev Paşa, 37–38, 40–41, 47, 48, 88

Ibrahim Paşa, 39, 47–49, 79, 85, 113
"idealists," 320, 337
identity (Ottoman and Turkish): Balkan
     Wars as creating a divide in, 201;
     and challenges of reconciling
     difference and equality, 314, 350–51,
     416–21; ethnicity as essential part
     of Turkish, 238–39; formation
     of, in period of Selim III and
     Mahmud II, 66–69; Gökalp on,
     238–39; Islam as essential part of,
     7, 18, 61, 204, 238–39, 338, 420;
     political, 101–2; politicization
     of religious and ethnic, 74, 76,
     78–81, 99–102, 132, 141, 178–79, 193,
     320–22, 351, 364–68, 416; Turkish
     language as marker of, 6, 7, 18,
     175, 278; of Turkish migrants in
     Germany, 333; Turkish republic's
     speculations about, 255–56. *See
     also* ethnicity; gender; identity
     politics; individualism; nationalism;
     religion(s)
identity papers, 174

identity politics: in Europe, 372; globalism
    and localism in, 1, 350–51, 362, 414,
    420; Kurdish, 364–68; lessons about,
    from 1960s, 314, 333–38; during
    Second Republic, 315, 337–38,
    348; during Third Republic,
    354. *See also* identity; religion(s);
    secularism
Idrisi, Muhammad, 204
"imagined community," 10–12
imam-hatip schools, 355–56, 359
IMF. *See* International Monetary Fund
imperialism: Afro-Eurasian struggles
    against, 192; European, as threat to
    Ottoman Empire, 9, 24–28, 30, 136,
    139, 141–42, 190, 205–6, 416. *See also*
    Ottoman Empire
import-substitution industrialization (ISI),
    58, 171, 247, 272–76, 305, 325–27,
    329, 349, 351, 354, 374
İnan, Afet, 279
indemnities: of Ottoman-Russian War,
    26, 52, 53; of Russo-Turkish War,
    85, 134–35. *See also* Public Debt
    Commission
independence tribunals, 251, 253
Independent Industrialists' and
    Businessmen's Association
    (MÜSİAD), 376–77, 417
India, 168, 192, 212, 378
individualism: Turkish champions of, 226;
    Western notions of, 16–17, 45, 297,
    381, 394
industry. *See* manufactures
İnönü, Erdal, 357
İnönü, İsmet, 261, 264–70, 306, 308, 309,
    311–13, 316, 322. *See also* İsmet Paşa
Institut d'Égypt, 27
International Court of Justice, 263
International Monetary Fund (IMF), 275,
    326, 329, 374, 375

Internet, 379, 386
İntibah (Namık Kemal), 125–31
Iran, 121, 149, 163, 192, 209, 214, 217, 264,
    310, 324, 357, 366, 368, 369
Iran-Iraq War, 368
Iraq: and Britain, 205, 208, 210, 213–14,
    217–19, 262–63; climate of, 53;
    and CUP, 203; in Iran-Iraq War,
    368; Kurds in, 366, 368, 369;
    1918–20 revolution in, 192; 1958
    revolution in, 309, 310; oil in,
    217, 263; Ottoman Empire's rule
    over, 36, 149, 151, 153; Persian Gulf
    War in, 369; Turkish Defense
    Pact with, 310; water issues in,
    368–69; after World War I, 217–19;
    in World War I, 208, 210, 213–14,
    232–33
İş Bankası, 271
ISI. *See* import-substitution
    industrialization
Islam: Abdülhamid and, 148–50, 179–81;
    activists embracing, 305, 315, 317,
    322, 323, 338, 356, 357; Anatolian
    businesses linked to, 376–77, 388,
    418; approaches to modernity based
    on, 3, 19–21, 24, 69–71, 75, 126, 133,
    139, 175, 184–90, 247, 285, 286,
    288–91, 350–51, 354, 359–61,
    383–90, 418–19; constitutionalism
    advocated in terms of, 105–6, 163;
    converts to, in novels, 186–87,
    241; CUP's reform of institutions
    associated with, 234–35; dialectic
    between secularism and, 15–16,
    18–22, 122–23, 416; elements of, 6–7,
    28, 64; as essential part of Turkish
    identity, 7, 18, 61, 204, 238–39, 338,
    420; as establishing uniformities
    across Ottoman Empire, 64, 239,
    250; Gülen's religious renewal

movement in, 3, 20, 21, 351,
384–90, 419; as inspiration for
martial sacrifice, 126, 129, 132,
156; jurisprudence (*fiqh*) of, 7;
Mevlana Halid's religious renewal
movement in, 3, 19–21, 44, 69–71,
75, 180–81, 285, 390, 418, 419; 1960s
political groups associated with,
315; no longer the state religion
under Turkish republic, 252; Nursi's
religious renewal movement in, 3,
20, 21, 284–91, 304, 339, 340, 384–86,
390, 419; as official Ottoman
religion, 7, 9, 26, 62, 64, 70, 133,
141, 142, 153, 174, 175, 214, 247, 256;
Ottoman sultans as caliphs of,
25–26, 148–49, 190, 202, 243; print
culture of, 20, 69, 195, 286, 288–89,
305, 336, 338–41, 419; religious
scholars of, under Mahmud II,
37; resurgence of, after Turkish
republic, 1; sectarian differences
within, 7, 142; similarity between
European standards and, 73; status
disparities under, 7–9, 45, 64, 65,
67–68; Young Ottomans' embrace
of, 105–6, 163. *See also* caliphates;
jihad; Kur'an; laicism; Muslims;
pan-Islamism; secularism; sharia;
specific groups and orders of
Islamic Society to Promote the
Employment of Ottoman
Women, 230
Ismailiyya, 212
Ismail Paşa (khedive of Egypt), 85,
86–87, 104
İsmet Paşa, 223, 224. *See also* İnönü, İsmet
Israel, 151, 316, 323, 369
Istanbul: Alevi neighborhood in, 382;
Armenian crises in, 143–44, 210;
and Capital Levy, 266; as capital of
Ottoman Empire, 29, 149, 150, 196;
Erdoğan's association with, 359–60;
grain supply in, 33; as Greater
City Municipality, 354; imperial
household in, 30; Janissaries in,
34, 37; manufacturing in, 172;
Muslim refugees in, 83, 84, 145,
202, 331, 367; 1955 anti-Greek riots
in, 308, 310; 1909 insurrection
in, 196; population of, 62, 116,
181–84, 277, 380; purged of Young
Turks, 163; purging of government
employees in, by Young Turks,
196, 197; railways in, 153, 157, 158,
166, 168, 169, 271; residents of, as
exempt from military service and
taxes, 95, 107; shantytowns in, 321,
331–32; students in, 37, 196, 316;
tailors in, 113; 1977 Taksim Square
demonstration in, 317; Treaty of
Sèvres on, 219; warlords summoned
to, 35; and World War I, 215, 222,
230–31, 243
Istanbul Chamber of Commerce, 226, 227
Istanbul University, 154, 235, 252, 315, 316
Italy, 111, 136, 203, 205–6, 215, 218, 219;
fascism in, 238, 262, 264; and
Turkish National Struggle, 223
Izmir, 172, 223, 229, 242–44, 251, 271,
385–87, 418; 1955 anti-Greek riots in,
308; as Greater City Municipality,
354; population of, 62, 116, 277, 380;
Treaty of Sèvres on, 219
Izmir Economic Congress, 271
Izmit, 358
Izzet Holo al-Abid, 149

Janissaries, 24, 29, 33, 36, 42, 66; and
guilds, 57–59; numbers of,
61; Selim's reforms for, 31, 34;
suppression of, 37, 39–40, 49, 71, 381

Japan, 163, 165, 192, 247; militarists in, 238, 259, 262, 276

Jerusalem, 215

Jesus, 8

Jews and Judaism, 7; as loyal to Ottoman Empire, 101; and "national economy" policy, 227; in Ottoman trade, 169; in Palestine, 175; population of, in Ottoman Empire, 62; in Salonica, 144; status of, in Ottoman Empire, 8–9, 64, 65, 92, 99–100; during World War II, 266; among Young Turks, 201. *See also* non-Muslims

jihad, 6, 73, 137, 149, 208, 214

Johnson, Lyndon, 322

Jordan, 151, 214, 217, 218

JP. *See* Justice Party

Jusdanis, Gregory, 10, 13–15

Justice and Development Party (AK Party), 315, 359–62, 364, 375–77, 382, 384, 415

Justice Party (JP), 312–18, 320, 356, 357

Kadro (journal), 258, 273

Kahramanmaraş, 320, 321, 382

Kamil, Mustafa, 137

kanun, 44, 55, 93, 94

Kar (Snow) (Pamuk), 338, 405–17

Karabük Steel Mill, 274, 275

Karakol, 221

Karaosmanoğlu, Yakup Kadri, 280

Karbala, 151, 159

Kars, 82, 84, 85, 218, 265, 405–15

Kartal battle, 25

Kastamonu, 164, 253

Kazakhstan, 370–71

Kâzim Karabekir, 222, 223

Kemal, Kara, 199, 230–31

Kemal, Mustafa. *See* Atatürk, Mustafa Kemal

Kemal, Namık, 77, 105–6, 123–32, 146, 149, 160, 211, 243, 411, 417

Kemal, Orhan, 283, 305, 307, 341–49

Kemal, Ziya, 105

Kemalism, 236, 237–38, 258

Kenya, 358, 367

Khalid al-Baghdadi. *See* Halid, Mevlana

Khalidiyya-Naqshbandiyya. *See* Halidiye-Nakşibendiye

khedive (Egyptian title), 86, 87, 212

Kıray, Mübeccel, 330

Kırşehır, 40

Kısakürek, Necip Fazıl, 20, 339–41, 386, 419

Kissinger, Henry, 323

Koç, Vehbi, 327

Koç group, 327

Konya, 47, 154, 158, 168, 210, 380

Köprülü, Fuat, 268, 308

Koraltan, Refik, 268

Korean War, 265, 305, 309

Kosovo, 144

Kotku, Mehmet Zahit, 360

KUK (National Liberators of Kurdistan), 321

Kur'an, 6, 69, 149; and the Gülen revival movement, 384–86; and interfaith relations, 8; as Nursi's master, 287, 290, 291; precepts of, 148; status disparities in, 7–9, 65, 67–68; teaching of, in Muslim schools, 67, 68, 91, 117; Young Ottomans advocate constitutionalism by reference to, 105, 106

Kurd(s), 40, 315, 341, 346, 362, 364–68; associations for, 201–2; cultural freedom for, 361; in CUP, 161; deportation of, 278, 287, 366, 367; divisions among, 364, 365; divisions between Turks and, 338, 351, 357, 364–68, 377, 378, 381;

feminists among, 383; Mevlana Halid as, 69–71; as minority group in Turkey, 278; as nomads preying on agrarian populations, 117, 142, 143, 210–11; as non-Turkish Muslims, 204, 365; political divisions among, 321, 363; population of, 250, 278, 364; as rebels against the Turkish republic, 20, 250–52, 256–58, 278, 287, 304, 351, 356, 364–68, 375, 377, 419; Sunni Muslims among, 250, 321, 365; under Third Republic, 356; Treaty of Sèvres on, 219; Özal's background as, 366

Kurdish language, 250, 278, 335, 353, 356, 365, 366, 383

Kurdistan Workers' Party (PKK), 321, 363, 365–69, 375

Kut, Halil Paşa, 213

Kuwait, 369

Kvergič, Hermann, 255

Kyrgyzstan, 370–71

labor unions, 328, 353

lace making, 171, 173

laicism: as Turkish republic's official policy, 1, 9, 18, 19, 21, 122, 239, 247, 252–253, 256, 258, 268, 356, 360, 382, 416–418. *See also* secularism

Land Law of 1858, 94, 110, 111, 122, 151, 417

landowners, 55–56; Agricultural Bank as benefiting, 229; conservatism of Muslim, 20; as heading organizations representing workers and peasants, 271; and Islamic revival movements, 70; Kurdish, 251, 363; Kurdish, and PKK, 365–67; as part of Ottoman bourgeoisie, 121–23; during Tanzimat era, 80, 109, 114; World War I as benefiting, 221; during World War II, 267

land surveys, 59–60, 94, 97–98, 111

land tenure: and crown estates, 170–71; distributions of unused land under, 267, 268, 274, 307, 325, 417; since 1980, 377; in Selim III and Mahmud II's era, 55–56; Tanzimat codes on, 94, 96, 110, 111, 114, 122, 151, 417

language(s): differences of, in nation-states, 14–15; multiple, in single religious millet, 101; regional cleavages and differences in, 321; in schools, 202; vernacular, 11, 13, 19. *See also* Turkish language

law: civil, 279, 288, 383; customary, 24, 68; equality before, 16, 45, 79, 92, 99–100; European influence on, 48–49, 91, 95, 96, 99; external vs. internal public, 74, 91–92; family, 234–35 (*see also* marriage; impact of secular, on interfaith relations, 8–9; and Islamic jurisprudence, 7; penal, 93, 253, 373, 383; rule of, 45, 73–74, 91, 93, 94, 364, 375, 415; state, as conforming to sharia, 44, 64; sultan's decrees as, 24, 93, 102, 158, 199; on surnames, 253, 342; three sources of, in reform-era Ottoman Empire, 24. *See also* constitution(s); courts; legislation; prison; sharia; *specific laws and decrees*

Law for the Encouragement of Industry, 272

Law for the Maintenance of Order, 251, 253, 339

Law for Unification of Instruction, 252–53

Law of Fundamental Organization, 224, 248

Law of National Defense, 266, 274–75

Law on Associations, 201–2

Law on Higher Education, 352

Law on Provincial Administration, 99, 151, 197, 202

Law to Transfer Land to the Peasants, 268
Lazes, 204, 341, 345
League for Private Initiative and
    Decentralization, 162–63
League of Nations, 218, 262–63
Lebanon: emigration from, 177; famine
    in, 232, 233; Kurds in, 365;
    Ottoman crises with, 78–80, 95,
    96, 100, 135, 141, 143; Ottoman
    provincial administration in, 151;
    silk production in, 54; statutes on
    regimes for, 93; taxes in, 107; U.S.
    intervention in, 309; after World
    War I, 217–18, 233
leftists: in the 1960s, 305, 313–16, 318, 320,
    324, 336–38, 365, 393–94, 398, 400.
    See also specific left-wing groups
legislation: during Abdülhamid II's reign,
    151, 158; for emancipating women
    in Turkish republic, 247; under
    İnönü, 266; following 1980 coup,
    352–54; under Mustafa Kemal, 224,
    251–53; under "national economy"
    policy, 228, 231; during the
    Tanzimat, 91–94, 98–102, 132, 138,
    153, 154, 158; during Young Turks
    period, 197, 201–2. *See also* law;
    specific laws
Lesseps, Ferdinand de, 86
Lewis, Bernard, 1, 2
liberalism: authoritarianism behind
    discourse of, 303; and
    constitutionalism, 270; in Democrat
    Party's economic policy, 306–9;
    economic, and Second Republic,
    325–26; expressed in Islamic terms,
    105–6; impact of European, on
    Ottoman rulers, 43–45, 61, 237; vs.
    "national economy" policy, 226; of
    Progressive Republican Party, 250;
    under Third Republic, 354; Young

Turks' differences with, 165. *See also*
    free trade
"liberty," 27, 106, 123–24
Libya, 30, 62, 357
List, Friedrich, 227
literacy: in early Turkish republic, 283–84,
    304; in eastern Anatolia, 367;
    gender gaps in, 129, 283, 335, 378;
    increase in, and "print capitalism,"
    11, 19, 117–18, 132, 178, 289–90; lack
    of, among "regimental" soldiers,
    41; new teaching methods for, 91;
    and rural migrants, 341–43; under
    Second Republic, 334–49; in 2005,
    378; after World War I, 277. *See
    also* literature; print capitalism;
    readers
literature: under Abdülhamid II, 184–90;
    as conveying deeper insights into
    Turkish realities than scholarly
    studies, 2–3, 338, 341, 415, 421;
    during early republic, 284–303;
    impact of Turkish language reforms
    on, 256–57; during National
    Struggle, 236–44; in nation-
    building, 13, 14–15, 18; new forms of,
    11, 19, 105, 124–25, 132, 185, 189, 390;
    since 1980, 384–403, 405–15;
    pre-Tanzimat, 71–75; print
    capitalism's connection to, 11, 19;
    satirical, 103–4; during Second
    Republic, 325, 336–48; during
    Tanzimat, 77, 123–32; transformative
    aspects of, 183, 190; Turkish, as
    highly politicized, 417. *See also*
    poetry; print capitalism; theater;
    specific authors and titles
Lüfti, Muhammad, 385
Lutfullah Bey, 162
"Lying down to die" (*Ölmeye Yatmak*)
    (Ağaoğlu), 390–94

Macedonia, 113, 141; in Balkan Wars, 206, 207; crisis in, 144–45, 154; CUP's base in, 196; nationalism in, 144–45, 164; Ottoman Empire population exchange with, 204

al-Madani, Muhammad Zafir, 136, 147, 149

magazines and journals, 20, 42, 195, 235, 313; for women, 117, 178, 184, 195, 235. *See also* censorship

al-Mahdi, Muhammad Ahmad, 137

Mahmud II, 76, 78; economy under, 49, 53, 57; politics under, 23, 24, 31, 35–43, 46–49, 56, 59, 75, 88, 146, 418; provincial administration under, 98; society under, 61, 70, 71

Makarios, Archbishop, 322, 323

malikâne system, 51–52, 58. *See also* tax-farming

Malta, 222

mamluks, 26–27, 30–31, 38. *See also* warlords; *specific rulers*

manufactures: under Abdülhamid II, 171–74, 179; of early 1800s, 54, 57–59; during early Turkish republic, 272–74, 277; laws encouraging, 272; during Second Republic, 327–29; since 1980, 375, 376–77; during Tanzimat period, 106, 112–15, 120–21, 132. *See also* import-substitution industrialization; trade unions

manuscript culture, 19, 20, 41, 289–90, 339, 419. *See also* scribal corps

Maoism, 316, 318

Mardin, Şerif, 303

marriage: civil, 235; and freedom to choose one's spouse, 68, 118, 181; Muslim, 67–68, 129, 181–84, 190; to reintegrate larger family relationships, 188. *See also* adultery; concubinage; divorce; polygyny

Marshall Plan aid, 265, 275, 325

Marxism, 16–17, 237, 313–14, 321, 336. *See also* communism

Masonic lodges, 258

materialism. *See* scientific materialism

Maupassant, Guy de, 280, 281

Maurras, Charles, 339–40

McKinley, William, 147

McMahon, Henry, 214, 217, 218

Mecca, 168; Özal's pilgrimage to, 356; pilgrimages to, and disease, 63, 138; semiautonomous status of, 203; sultan as protector of, 138–39, 149–50; in World War I, 214

Mecelle, 94

Medeni Bilgiler (İnan), 279

Medina, 168, 196, 203–4, 214; sultan as protector of, 138–39, 149

medreses, 7, 67, 83, 143, 196, 234, 252, 286

Megiddo battle, 215

Mehmed (dervish), 258–59

Mehmed Ali Paşa (governor of Egypt), 104, 212; economy under, 50, 54, 59–61; politics under, 28, 35–40, 42–49, 78, 83, 85–87; society under, 63

Mehmed IV, 72

Mehmed the Conqueror, 215

Mehmed V Reşad, 196, 286

"Memorandum of the Four," 268

Menderes, Adnan, 267, 268, 306, 308–9, 325, 326

Menemen, 258

merchants: Anatolian, 376–77, 388, 418; conservatism of Muslim, 20; foreign, and Ottoman Empire, 25, 26, 33, 43, 51–52, 59, 60, 139, 224, 227; and Islamic revival movements, 70; Muslim, in Ottoman territories, 33; among Ottoman bourgeoisie, 120–21, 169, 174, 184, 186, 227–29; Ottoman women as, 231; in RPP,

merchants: Anatolian *(continued)*
257; World War I as benefiting, 221,
277–78; after World War II, 267. *See
also* trade
Mexico, 192, 276
Midhat, Ahmed (writer-publisher), 133,
146, 184–89, 241, 417
Midhat Paşa (grand vezir), 84, 89, 93, 99
migration: in early Turkish republic, 278;
forced, of Kurds, 251; of Greeks out
of Ottoman Empire and Turkey,
177, 204–5, 308, 322; of Muslim
refugees to Ottoman Empire and
Turkey, 83, 109, 116, 144, 145, 156,
158, 175, 182, 190, 202, 204, 236,
278, 368, 369; rural-urban, 116,
181, 204, 325, 331–32, 337, 338,
341–49, 364–67, 381; as transforming
composition of Ottoman and
Turkish population, 174, 190; of
Turkish laborers to Europe, 305,
321, 323–25, 327, 328, 332–34, 337,
338, 363, 372, 381, 403
Military Academy, 41, 67, 90, 91, 124, 148,
151, 156, 178
military forces: and Aegean Army
Corps, 322; Atatürk's legacy
regarding politics and, 261–62,
309; civil officials rather than
Ottoman, as filling power gap,
88–89; in early Turkish republic,
264, 266; Egypt's, 38–39, 47–49,
59, 60; Islam as inspiration
for sacrifice by, 126, 129, 132,
156; Muslim women in, 231; in
National Struggle, 221; 1980 coup
by, 305, 306, 321–22, 324, 330,
337, 348, 351–54, 390, 398–403;
1997 political intervention by,
357–58, 386; 1971 coup by, 305,
306, 316–17, 320, 336, 348, 390,
394–98; 1960 coup by, 305, 306,
309–11, 326, 348; Ottoman, in
World War I, 207–16; Ottoman
Empire's, 24–25, 29, 39–41, 46–49,
59, 61, 72–73, 75, 78, 107, 137–38,
147, 156, 206–16, 245; refugees
in Ottoman, 156; sultans' reform
of, 31–33, 37, 39–40, 88, 154,
156–57, 190, 418; as taking control
of politics, 190–91, 193, 305,
306, 309, 310, 351–54; tensions
between "school men" and
"regimentals" in Ottoman, 41, 90,
156, 196; as Turkish government's
unelected power center, 200,
306, 415; worldview of officers
in, 309–11, 348–49; Young Turk
propaganda in, 163. *See also*
elites; Janissaries; mamluks;
military service; warlords
Military Medical School, 41, 90, 161
military service: criticism and revolts over
conditions in, 129–32, 139, 156,
159, 164; in Egypt, 38–39, 60, 63;
as falling on Muslim rural males,
63, 95–96, 156, 170, 175, 203, 231,
266–67; Hijaz residents as exempt
from, 138; Istanbulites as exempt
from, 95, 107; and non-Muslims,
9, 40, 49, 63, 92, 197, 201; paid
substitution for, 40, 92, 201;
population declines attributed to
fear of conscription for, 39, 63, 68,
175; reform of, by CUP, 199–200
millets, 64–65, 92, 93, 100, 101–2, 124, 142
Ministry of Justice, 95, 252
Ministry of War, 42, 95, 198
missionaries: Christian, 65, 70, 79, 141,
202; Islamic, 149
Missolonghi, 39
Mizan (CUP newspaper), 162

modernity: as challenging Islamic gender
norms, 8, 9, 123–32, 177–78, 185,
235, 279–80, 417; constitutionalism
as symbol of, 270; description of,
15–18, 238; developing countries as
still preoccupied with, 2; dialectic
between secular and religious
approaches to, 18–22, 122–23, 129–30,
158, 190–91, 338, 360–61, 386–87,
405, 414–21; effects of, on interfaith
relations, 8–9, 209–11; in Egypt, 27,
87; ethnic cleansing as byproduct
of, 202; EU admission as test of,
373–74; global scope of, 17–18,
350–51; Islamic approaches to, 3,
19–21, 24, 44–46, 69–71, 75, 126,
133, 139, 175, 184–90, 247, 285, 286,
288–91, 350–51, 354, 359–61, 383–90,
418–19; literature's connection
with, 3, 123–32; modernization
theory as differing from present-
day understandings of, 1–2, 15; and
the nation-state, 13–15; Ottoman
diplomats' explanations of, 72–75;
as part of Turkish identity, 238;
pluralism as need of late, 16, 17,
420–21; print capitalism's impact
on, 103–6; tension between
rationalization and subjectivity
as characteristic of, 36, 153–54,
158, 161, 190, 288, 420–21; Turkish
republic's emphasis on, 247–60;
war as Ottoman experience of, 229.
See also globalization; identity;
liberalism; nation-state; print
capitalism; rationalization; science;
scientific materialism; secularism;
subjectivity
modernization theory, 1–2, 15
Moldavia (principality), 25, 30, 80–81, 83
Moleschott, Jacob, 163

Monastir, 144, 164
monetary system: adjusted to U.S. dollar,
275; bimetallic standard for, 107–8,
165–66, 230; debasing of, under
Mahmud II, 49, 53, 107; 1958
devaluation of, 326; gold standard
for, 165, 230; paper money in, 108,
230; 2001 crisis in, 375
monopolies: Commercial Treaty on, 43,
44; defined, 43; elimination of,
109; and guilds, 57–58; state, 38,
43–44, 52, 257, 271, 274, 387; of
warlords, 60
Montenegro, 83, 85, 116, 206
Montreux, 264
Morea, 25, 29, 39
Morocco, 218, 378
Mosul, 30, 213, 215, 262–63
Motherland Party, 354, 356–59
Mount Ararat, 251
Mount Lebanon, 62, 78, 80, 98–99,
112, 172
Muhammad (prophet), 6, 8, 39, 64, 183,
381. *See also* hadiths; Kur'an
Muhammadan Union, 196, 286
Muhazarat (Fatma Aliye), 133, 184,
187–90
muhtar, 42, 280
Mujaddidiyya-Naqshbandiyya, 69–71
Murad, Mızancı, 162
Murad V (sultan), 83, 147
Muş, 209
Müşahedat (Ahmed Midhat), 133,
184–87
MÜSİAD, 376–77, 417
Müşfik Efendi, Hafız, 103–4
Muslims: banks exclusively for, 228;
Christians exchanged for, 204–5,
226, 278; conservative, as Young
Turks' opposition, 196; on Crete, 78;
dissatisfaction of, after World

Muslims: banks exclusively for (*continued*)
War II, 266–67; as financing Hijaz
railway, 150, 166, 168; identity
formation among, 66–69, 131;
increase in population of, in
Anatolia, 226; majority of, as
living under European rule in
1800s, 148, 149; massacres of,
in World War I, 210; multiple
ethnicities among, 364–65,
368, 369, 409; as part of Ottoman
commercial bourgeoisie,
120–21, 169, 174, 184, 186, 227–29;
population of, in Ottoman Empire,
62, 174, 202, 233–34; population
of, in Turkish republic, 278; as
refugees, 83, 109, 116, 144, 145,
156, 158, 175, 182, 190, 202, 204,
236, 278, 368, 369. *See also* Alevi
Muslims; Islam; Kurd(s); non-
Muslims; Shi'i Muslims; Sunni
Muslims
Mussolini, Benito, 261, 264
Mustafa III, 31
Mustafa IV, 34–36
Mustafa Suphi, 224

Nablus, 113–15, 120–22, 132, 170, 215
Najaf, 151, 159
Nakşibendis. *See* Halidiye-Nakşibendiye
NAP. *See* Nationalist Action Party
Napoleon: and Egypt, 23, 24, 26–28,
34, 73, 75, 202; Russia's invasion
by, 36
al-Naqshbandi, Khalid. *See* Halid,
Mevlana
Nasiruddin (of Iran), 147
National Credit Bank, 228
National Defense Law, 266, 274–75
National Development Party, 268
National Economy Bank, 230

"national economy" policy, 193,
226–29, 236, 245, 270–71, 273,
276, 417
nationalism: "anticolonial," 10, 11–13; Arab,
203, 204; Armenian, 101, 143–44,
209–10; cultural, 104–5, 123–32;
Egyptian, 87, 136–37; Greek, 36,
70, 100, 101, 135, 215; as ideology,
14, 17, 18, 236–39; Kurdish, 321,
365–68; Macedonian, 144–45,
164; militaristic, 123, 129–32; non-
Ottoman, and CUP, 161; Nursi's
opposition to, 287; question of
Young Turks', 201–5; scholarship
on, 10–15; as threat to Ottoman
Empire, 1, 9, 21, 23, 24, 70, 83,
98, 101–2, 190, 416; Turkish, 212,
256, 259–60, 262, 268, 270, 284,
381, 385, 386, 389; in Turkish
historical curriculum, 4, 122,
273. *See also* identity; "imagined
community"; imperialism;
National Struggle (Turkish);
nation-state; Turkification;
ultranationalism
Nationalist Action Party (NAP), 236,
314, 317, 318, 320, 321–22,
356, 358
Nationalist Front government, 317
nationalization, 271–75
National Liberators of Kurdistan
(KUK), 321
National Order, 315
National Outlook movement, 315
National Pact, 222, 224
National Salvation Party, 305, 315, 317, 322,
338, 356, 357
National Security Assembly, 351,
353, 354
National Security Council (Turkish),
311–12, 316, 357, 361, 367

National Struggle (Turkish), 20, 192,
219–26, 245–46, 248, 249, 271,
295, 303, 334, 417; beginning of,
215, 219, 267; economics during,
226–33; foreign support for, 262;
legacy of, 337, 367–68, 420;
literature during, 126; national
resistance societies supporting, 200,
221, 224; 1926 trials and veterans of,
251; novels about, 240, 241–44, 280;
Nursi's support for, 287; women in,
235, 280
National Turkish Student
Union, 315
National Unity Committee, 311
The Nation and Its Fragments
(Chatterjee), 13
nation-state: as ethnically and/or
religiously homogeneous, 145,
245, 276–78; implications of term,
248; and modernity, 13–15; Turkish,
and sugar beets, 273; Turkish, as
replacing Ottoman Empire, 64,
237–39, 245. *See also specific*
states
NATO (North Atlantic Treaty
Organization), 265, 305, 309, 310,
322, 348, 369, 371
Navarino, 47
Navy Engineering School, 31, 41,
67, 90
Nazi-Soviet Non-Aggression Pact
(1939), 264
Nazım, Dr., 163, 199
The Necessary Nation (Jusdanis),
13–15
Nelson, Horatio, 27
New Order (Selim III's). *See* Nizam-ı
Cedid
newspapers: assertiveness of, under İnönü,
267; censorship of, 96, 104, 160;

criticism of Kemal regime in, 249;
ethnic prejudice in, 266; Gülen
movement's, 386, 387–88; 1980
military coup's suspension of, 352;
nationalism's link to rise of, 10–11,
87; relative freedom of Egyptian,
137; after restoration of the 1876
constitution, 195; rise of, 103, 104,
117; of Young Turks, 161, 162. *See*
also censorship; magazines and
journals; print capitalism
Nicholas II (of Russia), 164
Nightingale, Florence, 82
Nile River, 53
Niyazi Bey, 164
Nizam-ı Cedid (New Order), 31, 33–35, 38,
40, 72–73, 75, 76, 91
Nizib, 47, 49, 78
"No ..." (*Hayır ...*) (Ağaoğlu), 390,
398–403
nomads, 117, 142, 143, 210–11. *See also*
bedouin; Kurd(s)
non-Muslims, 304; as barred from Hijaz,
138, 168; Capital Levy's effects on,
266, 275; early Turkish republic
as almost devoid of, 277; Gökalp's
overlooking of, 239; legal treatment
of, 45, 79, 85, 92–93, 95, 99–100,
235; and military service, 9, 40,
49, 63, 92, 197, 201; as Ottoman
bankers, 108; in Ottoman civil
service, 89, 92, 99, 102, 103, 120;
in Ottoman literature, 126, 185–86;
Ottoman taxes on, 9, 51, 92, 98; in
Ottoman trade, 112, 120, 121, 169,
178–79, 227–29, 231; population
of, in Ottoman Empire, 61–62;
status of, in Ottoman Empire,
8–9, 25, 64–65, 92, 99–100. *See*
also Christians; Jews and Judaism;
specific ethnic groups

North Africa, 53, 62. *See also* Egypt; Libya; Tunisia

North Atlantic Treaty Organization. *See* NATO

notables: Ottoman, 29–31, 33, 35, 36, 53, 56, 80, 87, 97, 111, 114, 122, 138, 142, 149, 151, 162, 164, 195–96, 203, 221, 222, 232; Turkish, 252, 257–58, 269, 280

Nursi, Said, 3, 20, 21, 71, 195, 247, 284–91, 304, 339, 340, 419; successors to, 384–88

Öcalan, Abdullah, 321, 358, 365, 367, 368

Odian, Krikor, 100

OIB. *See* Ottoman Imperial Bank

oil: in Aegean Sea, 370; 1973 crisis in, 305, 310, 324–25, 329, 377; states with, 217, 263

Okyar, Fethi, 258

olives, 54

Ölmeye Yatmak (Lying down to die) (Ağaoğlu), 390–94

"On these bounteous lands" (*Bereketli Topraklar Üzerinde*) (Orhan Kemal), 305, 307, 341–49

Orbay, Rauf, 250

Organization for Economic Cooperation and Development, 326

"Oriental Railway," 165

Ottoman Empire, 83; "backwardness" of, 50, 76, 88, 121, 123, 179, 186, 276, 292; cosmopolitanism's destruction in, 4, 144, 201–2, 209–11, 250, 276–78, 308 (*see also* ethnic cleansing); debts of, paid by Turkish republic, 271, 272; elites in, 19; Europe's influence on, 72–76, 78, 83, 85, 88, 91, 95, 99, 134–42, 146–47, 156–58, 162–63, 166, 168, 183, 199–200, 207, 227–28, 232, 234; First Constitutional Regime in, 84, 133, 194; geography and climate of, 4, 5, 9–10, 53, 62–63, 233; Islam (Sunni) as official religion in, 7, 9, 26, 62, 64, 70, 133, 141, 142, 153, 174, 175, 214, 247, 256; as multiethnic, multinational empire, 1, 9, 15, 23, 61, 64, 81, 190, 192, 201–2, 211, 245, 256, 292, 293–94, 416, 420; nationalism as threat to, 1, 9, 21, 23, 24, 70, 83, 98, 101–2, 190, 416; as never colonized, 9, 192; partitioning of, after World War I, 214, 217–19, 245; religious conservatives' power under, 21; Second Constitutional Government in, 194; as "sick man of Europe," 1, 23, 77, 85, 193; solidarism of, 57, 65–66, 100–101, 154, 229, 237, 292, 295, 297, 363; sovereignty of, 9, 51, 79, 83, 136, 137, 218–19; state bankruptcy of, 83, 88, 108–9, 134–35; territory lost by, 9–10, 23, 25–28, 36, 62, 75, 76, 83, 116, 132, 134, 135, 145, 151, 169, 174, 202, 206–7, 217–19, 223; Turkish republic as replacing, 19, 21; wars' effects on, 63, 74–75; in World War I, 192, 199–200, 204–5, 207–19, 228–33, 245, 261, 267. *See also* caliphates; civil officials; guilds; hierarchical order; Istanbul; military forces; Muslims; non-Muslims; Ottomanism; population; print capitalism; railways; slavery; trade; Turkey; Turkish republic; *specific places, sultans, wars and treaties of*

Ottoman Freedom Society, 163–64

Ottoman-Greek War, 136, 144–45, 156

Ottoman Imperial Bank (OIB), 108, 139, 144, 145, 166, 228, 273

Ottomanism (*Osmanlılık*), 99–102, 106, 107, 117, 201–2, 211, 239

Ottoman Liberals' Party, 196

Ottoman revivalism (architecture), 259–60
Ottoman-Russian wars, 23, 24–25, 28, 29, 31, 36, 40, 47, 53, 61, 63; Russo-Turkish War, 75, 76, 84–85, 108, 116, 132, 134, 156, 157. *See also* indemnities; Treaty of Küçük Kaynarca
Ottoman Turkish language. *See* Turkish language (Ottoman and modern)
Özal, Turgut: economic policy under, 321, 329–30, 374–75, 386; and EU admission, 372; Kurdish mother of, 366; religious orientation of, 20, 356, 418, 419; as Third Republic leader, 351, 354–57, 359, 369, 375, 386

Pakistan, 310, 389
Palestine, 27, 113–15, 175, 192, 201, 203, 204, 214, 217–19, 314, 357, 369
Pamuk, Orhan, 338, 405–17
pan-Islamism, 149, 157, 206
pan-Turkism, 221, 262, 338, 370–71
paper money. *See* monetary system
parliaments (of Ottoman Empire), 84, 93, 99, 103, 146, 222; and CUP, 197–99; reestablishment of, under Young Turks, 194–97, 245; survival of, ensured by CUP, 165. *See also* Grand National Assembly
Parvus (Israel Alexander Helphand), 227
Paşa (defined), 29
pastoralism, 53–55, 67, 110, 142
Pasvanoğlu, Osman, 30
patriarchy: Atatürk's, 279; other hierarchies linked to, 65; patrimonial sultanate likened to, 30, 163, 190; patronage related to, 362–63; resistance to, in Ottoman families, 184; resistance to, in Ottoman novels, 188–89; in Turkish

republic's law, 279, 383; Western vs. Ottoman versions of, 8
patriotism. *See* Ottomanism; *vatan*
patronage: under Abdülhamid II, 160, 162, 196; contemporary, 362–63; in early Turkish republic, 257–58, 267, 298; in Lebanon, 79, 80; literary, 123; between shantytown inhabitants and politicians, 332; during Tanzimat, 89, 103, 104, 114, 118, 119; of warlords, 30, 31. *See also* factionalism
PDA. *See* Public Debt Administration
Peasantist Society, 280
peasants, 55–56, 60, 67, 72, 79, 80, 109, 110, 114, 119, 236; changes in women's lives among, 280; on crown estates, 170–71; forced labor of, 266; illiteracy among, 284, 304; as majority of early republic's population, 277–78; military service as falling on, 95–96, 156, 170, 175, 203, 231, 266–67; vs. nomads, 117, 142, 143, 210–11; number of, in Second Republic, 331; political unreliability of, 243–44. *See also* agriculture; landowners; migration: rural-urban; "populism"; provinces
Peasants' Association, 232
Peker, Recep, 268
penal codes, 93, 253, 373, 383. *See also* prison
People's Houses, 254–55, 280
People's Liberation Army of Turkey, 316
People's Liberation Party-Front of Turkey, 316
People's Party, 224, 248. *See also* Republican People's Party
People's Rooms, 254–55
Persian Gulf War, 369
Persian language, 253, 381

Pertev Paşa, 37, 46, 199
petitions, 258, 286, 363, 383
photography, 83, 159, 177, 184
physical culture, 260–61
Pious Foundations Bank, 228
PKK (Kurdish Workers' Party), 321
plays. *See* theater
poetry, 103, 123–25, 360, 381, 407
"A Poet's Marriage" (Şinasi), 118–19
Poland, 15, 25, 26, 81, 372
Polatkan, Hasan, 312
politics: under Abdülhamid II,
    134–65; vs. administration, 146;
    authoritarianism in Ottoman and
    Turkish, 4, 6, 24, 36, 133, 137, 145,
    146–48, 190, 198, 223–24, 245, 252,
    257, 258, 270, 303, 340, 416; in early
    Turkish republic, 248–70; as a focus
    of this book, 2–3; Gülhane decree as
    charter for reform of Ottoman, 44,
    46–49, 62, 74, 92, 93, 97; military
    forces as taking charge of, 190–91,
    193, 305, 306, 309, 310, 351–54 (*see
    also* military forces: coups by); and
    nation-state, 14–15; participation
    in, 102–6; personality-centered
    factionalism vs. issue-based, 19,
    37, 46, 49, 76, 89–91, 102, 103, 123,
    161; polarization of, during Second
    Republic, 305, 312, 313–20; print
    capitalism's connection to, 11, 19;
    and religious-secular dialectic, 22;
    Second Republic mobilization
    around, 305–49; under Selim III
    and Mahmud II, 24–49; during
    Tanzimat, 77–87; themes of, in
    late Ottoman and Turkish history,
    415–16; transition to multi-party,
    267; in Turkey 1950–80, 306–24;
    under Young Turks, 194–226. *See
    also* factionalism; government;
    patronage; *specific leaders and
    politicians*
polygyny, 30, 67–68, 182, 279
population: declines in, due to fears of
    military conscription, 39, 63, 68,
    175; declines in, due to violence
    and warfare, 4, 134, 144, 174–77,
    193, 202, 203, 209–11, 278; of early
    Turkish republic, 277–78, 331;
    explosion of Turkey's, in twentieth
    century, 305, 312–14, 330–32, 334,
    349, 351; of Kurds, 250, 278, 364;
    low density of, before twentieth
    century, 54–55, 59, 61, 62, 109,
    110, 175, 274; of Muslims living
    under European rule in 1800s,
    148, 149; nation-states' assumption
    about homogeneity of, 16, 145,
    245, 276–78; since 1980, 379–80,
    403; occupations of, in early 1800s,
    53–54; in Ottoman Empire, 61–62,
    174, 175, 177, 202, 233–34; during
    Tanmizat era, 109, 110, 112, 115–16;
    urban vs. rural in Ottoman Empire,
    112; World War I Ottoman Empire
    losses of, 233–34, 276. *See also*
    censuses; ethnic cleansing; fertility;
    migration; *specific ethnic and
    religious groups*
"populism" (in Turkish republic), 247, 258,
    272, 276–84
post coaches, 29, 42, 72
"postcolonialism," 10
postmodernity, 2
Pressel, Wilhelm von, 157
"Principles of Turkism" (*Türkçülüğün
    Esaslan*) (Gökalp), 238
print capitalism, 10–11, 19; development
    of, in Ottoman Empire, 31, 91, 96,
    103–6, 117–18, 132, 177–79, 190,
    418; French, in Egypt, 27; Islamic,

20, 69, 195, 286, 288–89, 305, 336, 338–41, 419; and rise of bourgeoisie, 87, 117–18, 123, 132; secularist intellectuals' use of, 179, 181. *See also* censorship; literacy; magazines and journals; manuscript culture; newspapers; readers; Turkish language

prison, 210, 420; Erdoğan in, 360–61; 1960s radicals in, 312, 316, 324, 336–37; novels about, 393, 394, 396, 401, 414; PKK leaders in, 367; religious figures in, 259, 286–88; sultans in, 35, 147; war-related, 232; writers in, 340. *See also* penal codes

privatization, 374–76

Privy Treasury, 148, 149, 170

Progressive Republic Party, 250, 251

Prosperity Party. *See* Refah Party

prostitutes, 126–29

protectionism. *See* tariffs

protoindustries, 58–59, 110, 112–13, 120

provinces: Alevis in, 381–82; civil officials as administrators in, 89, 90, 97–99, 105, 150; councils for administration of, 95, 97–99, 103, 121–22, 146; education in, 110, 153; laws on administration of, 99, 151, 197, 202; manufacturing in, 376; military conscription in, 63, 95–96, 156, 170, 175, 203, 231, 266–67; Muslim religious teachers sent to, 149; National Struggle in, 221; protoindustries in, 58–59, 110, 112–13, 120; state and party merged in, under Turkish republic, 257–58; violence in, 29–30, 36, 39, 42, 56, 59, 63, 109, 110, 116–17, 144, 145, 154, 197, 365–68; women's organizations in, 382; Young Turks exiled to, 163. *See also* agriculture; landowners;

notables; pastoralism; peasants; warlords

provisionism, 50–52, 58, 59–60, 230

Prussia, 31, 48

psychoanalysis, 295–97

Public Debt Administration (PDA), 108–9, 135, 139, 165, 170, 181, 226

Public Debt Commission (in Egypt), 86

public works, 151–53, 169, 190, 228, 266, 307. *See also* railways

Pugachev Rebellion, 25

Qaddafi, Muammar, 357

Qadiri religious order, 69, 70

quarantines, 39, 63, 96, 138

Quiemada (film), 409

radio, 257, 280, 307, 311, 336, 379

railways: in Egypt, 86, 166; in the Hijaz, 139, 148, 150; nationalization of Turkish, 271–72, 274; in Ottoman Empire, 110, 151–53, 156, 157–58, 166–70, 177, 190, 208, 210

Ratib Efendi, Ebu Bekir, 71–72

rationalization: of economy, 50; as modernity's essence, 34; state policy as imposing, on the people, 16, 17, 256; tension between subjectivity and, 36, 153–54, 158, 161, 190, 288, 420–21

readers (new), 11, 91, 103, 104–5, 117–18

reading groups (*dershane*), 289, 387, 388

Red Sea, 214

Refah Party (Prosperity Party), 315, 354–55, 357–58, 360, 361, 376, 383

Reform decree of 1856, 92, 93, 100, 102

refugees: Muslims as, 83, 109, 116, 144, 145, 156, 158, 175, 182, 190, 202, 204, 236, 278, 368, 369

Régie des tabacs, 139, 170, 172, 272

registry offices, 42, 97, 122

religion(s): attempts to separate groups on basis of, 47, 78, 79–80, 116, 202, 204–5; conditions of early 1800s, 66–67, 69–71; dialectic between approaches to modernity based on secularism and, 15–16, 18–22, 122–23, 129–30, 158, 190–91, 338, 360–61, 386–87, 405, 414–21; differences among, in nation-states, 15, 109; European protection for specific, in Ottoman Empire, 26, 65, 79–81, 83, 116, 141, 211, 243; Gökalp on, 238–39; increasing homogeneity of, in early Turkish republic, 276–78; Islamic, as essential part of Turkish identity, 7, 18, 61, 204, 238–39, 338, 420; mixing of, in Ottoman Empire, 57, 64, 92, 120–21, 142, 144, 170; modernity's effects on, 8–9, 15–16, 70; politicization of identities based on, 74, 76, 78–81, 99–102, 132, 141, 178–79, 320–21, 337–38, 364–68, 416; as primary identity marker in Ottoman Empire, 61, 62, 64–66, 119; separatism based on, not allowed under Young Turks, 201–2; states identified with specific, 9, 18; Turkish republic as forbidding political use of, 251. See also Christians; ethnic cleansing; Islam; Jews and Judaism; laicism; Muslims; secularism

religious brotherhoods (Islamic), 7, 20, 71, 287–89, 381, 419. See also dervish orders; sufism; specific religious brotherhoods

Republican People's Party (RPP), 313, 316, 337, 358; Alevi support for, in 2007, 382; Atatürk's speech before, 251–52, 256; coalition governments by, 312, 317–18, 359; after Democrat Party won office, 306–9; elements from, in Motherland Party, 356; establishment of, 250; as moving to the left in 1966, 314; as only party in early Turkish republic, 266–70, 279, 284, 287; as opposing civil liberties crackdown by Erim, 316–18; opposition to, under İnönü, 266–69, 275; state's merging with, 257–59, 266; Turkish Hearth associations merged with, 254

Republican Women's Party, 279

Republic of Armenia, 47. See also Armenian(s)

Republic of Cyprus, 370. See also Cyprus

Reşid Paşa, Mustafa, 37, 46, 61, 74, 89, 102

Resmi Efendi, Ahmed, 73

revenue. See taxes

Revolutionary Workers' Unions, 317

revolution vs. transformation, 194, 237–38, 243, 294

Rifat Paşa, Sadık, 71–75, 89, 91

rightists: of the 1970s, 315–16, 318–19, 324, 336–38. See also specific right-wing or ultranationalist groups

Risale-i Nur (Treatise of Light) (Nursi), 287–91, 384, 386

Rıza, Ahmed, 161

road development, 325, 326, 382

Romania, 80–81, 83, 85, 93, 98, 100, 116, 207, 264, 372. See also Moldavia; Wallachia

Roosevelt, Franklin, 262

Rousseau, Jean-Jacques, 15

RPP. See Republican People's Party

Rumelia. See Balkans

rural areas. *See* provinces

Rusçuk (Bulgaria), 34

Russia, 107; and Anatolia, 168, 407; anti-
Muslim policies of, 47, 78, 116;
and Armenians, 205; and claims
to protect Orthodox Christians in
Ottoman Empire, 26, 65, 141; in
Crimean War, 81–82; and Egypt,
48; 1833 Ottoman alliance with, 47,
248; and Greece, 47; 1918–20 civil
war in, 192; 1905 revolution in, 163,
192; 1917 revolution in, 209, 214,
218; Nursi as prisoner of, 286–87;
and Poland, 15; population of, 175,
177; territory gained by, 85, 121; as
threat to Ottoman Empire, 24–25,
218; and Turkish National Struggle,
221, 223; and Turkish republic,
248; Wallachia and Moldavia
occupied by, 80–81; in World War
I, 200, 205, 207–10. *See also* foreign
intervention; Ottoman-Russian
wars; Soviet Union; *specific wars*

Russo-Japanese War, 163, 192, 199

Russo-Turkish War, 75, 76, 84–85, 108, 116,
132, 134, 156, 157

Saadabad Pact (1937), 264

Saatleri Ayarlama Enstitüsü
(Chronometric Institute)
(Tanpınar), 247–48, 291–303

Sabahaddin Bey, 162–63, 196, 226

Sabancı group, 327

Saddam Husayn, 369

al-Sadik, Muhammad, 136

Safvet Paşa, 84

Şahin, Abdülfettah. *See* Gülen, Fethullah

Said (governor of Egypt), 85, 86

Said, Edward, 2

Said, Küçük, 150, 153

Said Halim Paşa, 208

Said of Palu, 250–51, 257, 287

sailcloth factories, 58

Sakarya River, 223, 244

Şakir, Bahaeddin, 163, 199

salam (*salem*) contracts, 113–14

Salonica, 144, 145, 164, 166, 177; Atatürk's
birthplace in, 308; in Balkan Wars,
206; CUP headquarters in, 199,
202, 227; loss of, 227; manufacturing
in, 172–73; modernization of, 151;
population of, 63, 184; schools in,
154; in World War I, 215

Samanyolu TV, 387

Sami, Şemseddin, 160

Sanders, Liman von, 212

San Stefano, 84–85

Sanusiyya sufi order, 136

Sarıkamış, 208–9

Sasun, 143

ibn Saud, Abd al-Aziz, 204

Saudi Arabia, 217

Saudis, 214, 217

al-Sayadi, Abulhuda, 149

Saydam, Refik, 266, 267

School of Civil Administration, 91, 150,
151, 153, 154

schools. *See* education

science: Gülen on, 387; and modernity, 15,
27, 238–39; Nursi on, 20, 286, 287

scientific materialism, 10, 11–13; as
belief system, 16; in early Turkish
republic, 253, 259, 290; Nursi's
refutations of, 20, 290–91; reception
of, by Ottoman elites, 9, 19, 20, 161;
Young Turks' embrace of, 163, 238,
313, 416, 418

scribal corps, 41, 50, 61, 71, 90. *See also*
manuscript culture

Scutari, 206

Sebilürreşad (journal), 20, 195, 339, 419

Second Constitutional Government, 194

Second Republic, 305, 306, 310–22
secularism: of Ağaoğlu's fiction, 390–403;
    Democrat Party's support for,
    306; as designed to place religion
    under state control, 239, 252, 339;
    as destined to eliminate religion,
    9, 290; dialectic between religion
    and, in Turkish history, 15–16, 18–22,
    122–23, 129–30, 158, 190–91, 386–87,
    405, 414–21; Islamic challenges to,
    between 1950 and 1980, 306, 339,
    417; of modern law, 8–9; Nursi's
    challenges to, 285, 288–91, 304;
    in Tanzimat reforms, 80, 94, 106;
    as Turkish republic's governing
    principle, 1, 9, 18, 19, 21, 122, 239,
    247, 252–53, 256, 258, 268, 356, 360,
    382, 416–18; of Young Turks, 163,
    165, 179, 191, 193, 245, 268; of Young
    Turks, opposition to, 196. *See also*
    religion(s); *specific religions and
    religious figures*
Selim III, 23, 24, 42, 49, 72, 73, 76, 88;
    centralization under, 31–34, 75,
    146, 418; economy under, 49, 50,
    57; Janissaries as deposing, 29, 33,
    34; murder of, 34; as a poet, 103;
    reforms under (*Nizam-ı Cedid*), 31,
    33–35, 38, 40, 91
Seniha Sultan, 162
Serbia, 36, 64, 70, 83, 85, 113, 116, 144,
    206, 207
Sèves (French colonel), 49
Şevket Paşa, Mahmud, 196–98
Şeyhülislam (defined), 37, 252
Shahin, Tanyus, 79
Shahname (Firdawsi), 409
shantytowns, 321, 331–32, 336, 337
sharia (Islamic law): application of, to
    Muslims and non-Muslims, 70;
    courts of, 94, 252, 253;

Halidiye-Nakşibendiye's observance
    of, 70, 181; land tenure under, 55;
    Mecelle as codification of, 94; as
    one source of Ottoman Empire
    legal authority, 24, 44; opposition
    to Turkish state based on, 361;
    Ottoman state law as conforming
    to, 44, 64; as part of Islam, 6–7, 27;
    status disparities in, 6–9, 45, 64, 65,
    67–68, 100; sultans and, 25, 45, 46,
    93; Young Ottomans' citing of, 106;
    Young Turks and, 196, 234–235
Shi'i Muslims, 7, 137–38, 149,
    151, 153
"Shirt of Flame" (*Ateşten Gömlek*)
    (Adıvar), 193, 240, 241–44
Siberia, 286–87
Siirt, 360, 361
Silistria, 25, 43, 81, 129–30, 411
silk production, 54, 171–73
Şinasi, İbrahim, 104, 105, 118
Sincan, 357
Sinekli Bakkal (*The Clown and His
    Daughter*) (Adıvar), 193,
    240–44
Singapore, 149
sipahis (cavalry), 31, 33, 41, 110
Sırat-ı Müstakim (journal), 20, 195,
    339, 419
Sirhindi, Ahmad, 69, 70, 287
Sivas, 222, 277, 343
"six arrows" ideology, 238, 258, 262
siyaset, 46
Sızıntı, 387
Skopje, 165
slavery: abolition of, 9, 96, 159; Kur'anic
    provisions on, 7, 65; of Ottoman
    elites by sultan, 30, 46, 53,
    66, 74, 75, 159; in Ottoman
    empire, 8, 26–27, 30–31, 38, 46;
    in Ottoman literature, 127, 188.

See also concubinage; "liberty";
mamluks
Slovakia, 378
"Snow" (*Kar*) (Pamuk), 338, 405–17
soap production, 113–15, 120–22, 132, 170
Social Democrat Populist Party, 357
society: under Abdülhamid II, 174–84;
conditions of, in early 1800s, 61–69;
in early Turkish republic, 276–84;
as a focus of this book, 2–3; during
National Struggle period, 233–36;
print capitalism and change in,
11, 19; under Second Republic,
330–38; since 1980, 379–89; in
Tanzimat era, 115–23; themes of, in
late Ottoman and modern Turkish
history, 415–21. *See also* population;
special aspects of
sociology, 10, 17, 163, 178, 229, 236–39, 303,
330, 394, 401
Sofia, 165
Soil Products Tax, 267, 268, 275
solidarism (in Ottoman Empire), 57,
65–66, 100–101, 154, 229, 237, 292,
295, 297, 363. *See also* corporatism;
Ottomanism
Souchon, Wilhelm, 208
South Africa, 149
Southeast Anatolia Project (GAP),
366–69, 377
Soviet Union, 261, 262, 310; Afghanistan
invasion by, 324, 368; Central Asian
policies of, 252, 253; collapse of,
338, 370, 372, 388; Czech invasion
by, 315; and early Turkish republic,
262–65; five-year plans in, 274; as
threat to Turkey, 305, 309, 321, 322,
370; Turkic successor states to, 351,
368, 370–72, 388–89, 403. *See also*
Russia
Spain, 314, 340, 415

Spanish Tragedy (Kyd), 412
Special Organization, 200, 210–11, 221
spies, 141, 159–60, 162–63
spirituality, 11, 13. *See also* religion(s)
SPO. *See* State Planning Organization
sports, 260–61
Stalin, Josef, 261
state. *See* government
State Planning Organization (SPO),
312, 326–27, 329. *See also* central
planning
"state purchase," 52, 60, 109, 275
state services, 268, 313, 334, 363–64
statist economic policies: privatization
and, 374–76; in Turkey, 247, 259,
272–76, 292, 304, 305, 323, 325,
327, 329
status disparities (in Islam), 7–9, 45, 64,
65, 67–68
"The Stranger" (*Yaban*) (Karaosmanoğlu),
280–83
Suavi, Ali, 105
subjectivity: under Abdülhamid II, 177–79,
190; collective, 16–17; Islamic vs.
secular explorations of, 351, 383–84,
414; modernity's transformation of,
16, 256; under Second Republic,
336–37; during Tanzimat, 103,
117–23, 132; tension between
rationalization and, 36, 153–54, 158,
161, 190, 288, 420–21; in works of
Ağaoğlu, 390–403. *See also* identity;
identity politics; individualism
Sublime Porte, 41, 43, 71, 83, 340–41;
under Abdülhamid II, 158, 181;
CUP coup at, 198, 206, 227; reform
initiatives from, 76, 77, 88, 90,
95–96, 98, 132, 146; under Young
Turks, 195
Sudan, 38, 137
Suez Canal, 86, 138, 172, 214

sufism, 69–71, 136, 181, 250, 252, 259, 288, 289, 340, 345, 356, 365, 381, 385. *See also specific movements*
Süleyman Paşa, 49
sultans: abolition of, 224, 248; as caliphs of Islam, 25–26, 148–49, 190, 202, 243; elites as slaves of, 30, 46, 53, 66, 74, 75, 159; factionalism under, 19, 37, 46, 49, 76, 89–91, 102, 103, 123, 161; hierarchical relations of, 30, 119; powers of, 24, 35–36, 88, 93, 102, 121, 133, 146, 148–49, 158–60, 197, 212; as protector of the Hijaz, 138, 149–50; titles of, 25; wealth of retinue of, 66, 88, 107. *See also* caliphates; grand vezir; politics; Topkapı Palace; Yıldız Palace; *specific sultans*
Sümerbank, 273
"Sun Language Theory," 255, 256
Sunni Muslims, 7, 304; and Alevis, 320–21, 338, 382; among Kurds, 250, 321, 365; and religious politics, 7, 9, 26, 62, 64, 70, 133, 141, 142, 153, 169, 174, 175, 214, 247, 256, 382
supply agencies, 230–31
Supreme Council of Judicial Ordinances, 43
surname law, 253, 342
Susurluk scandal, 362, 365, 415
Sweden, 333
Switzerland, 279, 333
Sykes-Picot agreement (1916), 217–18
Syria, 205; Cemal Paşa in, 203, 204, 214, 232; climate of, 53; Egypt's occupation of, 45, 47–49, 79; emigration from, 177; famine in, 203, 232, 233; France's influence in, 168, 205, 217–19, 264; geography of, 78; Kurds in, 365–69; 1919–20

revolution in, 192; Ottoman crown estates in, 171; Ottoman provincial administration in, 151; population of, 233; Tanzimat violence in, 95, 100; warlords in, 36; water issues in, 369

Tabriz, 209
taife, 64, 65
Tajiks, 371
Takvim-i Vekayi (newspaper), 42, 160
Talat Bey (later, Paşa), 164, 198–99, 221
Tanin (newspaper), 195
Tanpınar, Ahmet Hamdi, 247–48, 291–303, 417, 419, 421
Tanzimat, 20, 76–78, 88–106, 138, 146, 150, 153, 268, 361, 417
tariffs (protectionism), 58, 226, 227, 270–74. *See also* customs duties
Tarsus, 173
Tasvir-i Efkâr (newspaper), 118
Tatars, 25, 116
Tatlıses, Ibrahim, 337
Tawfiq (khedive of Egypt), 85, 87
taxes (revenue): from agrarian products, 106–7; Capital Levy as, 266; collection of Ottoman, 51, 55–56, 97–98, 107, 109, 110, 139; Egyptian tribute to Ottoman sultan as form of, 47, 48, 78, 86, 111; evasion of, 58, 364; French, on Egyptians, 27; Gülhane decree reform of, 42, 45; Istanbulites as exempt from, 95, 107; on Ottoman non-Muslims, 9, 51, 92, 98, 156; religious foundations' immunity from, 38; revolts against, 27, 98, 164, 165, 169, 180, 417; size of, in Ottoman Empire, 106–7; on soil products, 267, 268; Tanzimat reform of, 92, 95, 97–98. *See also* military service: paid substitution for; tax-farming

tax-farming: abolition of, 38, 59, 97, 107, 272; defined, 29; denunciation of, 44; evolution of, 51–52, 55–56, 98, 107, 113–14

Tehran, 209

telegraph, 83, 151, 153, 156, 159, 164, 222

telephones, 379

television, 311, 336, 337, 354, 358, 379, 387, 414–15

Tercüman-ı Ahval (newspaper), 104, 118

textile manufacturing, 58–59, 112–14, 120, 132, 171–74, 343–47

theater (plays), 11, 118, 123, 126, 129–32, 211, 240, 255, 412–14

Third Republic (Turkey), 351–74

Thomas, Dylan, 399

Thrace, 145, 204, 208, 211, 215, 222–24

Thunderbolt Army Group, 213–15

Tigris River, 53, 367, 377

Tito, Marshall, 310

TOBB (Turkish Union of Chambers of Commerce and Exchanges), 327, 367

Tokat, 58–59

Tola, Tahsin, 288

Topkapı Palace (Istanbul), 39, 43, 77, 88, 107, 132, 146, 153

Townshend, Charles, 213

Trabzon, 29, 164, 209, 363

"tractorization," 275, 307, 325

trade: under Abdülhamid II, 169–70; in early Turkish republic, 270–72; free, in Ottoman Empire, 43–44, 51, 57, 61, 112, 139, 171, 195, 226, 227, 276; non-Muslims in Ottoman, 112, 120, 121, 169, 178–79, 227–29, 231; between Ottoman Empire and foreign merchants, 25, 26, 33, 43, 51–52, 59, 60, 139, 224, 227; Ottoman ministry of, 95; during Tanzimat period, 111–12, 120–21, 132. *See also*

customs duties; export-led growth strategies; import-substitution industrialization; tariffs

trade unions, 328, 353

traditionalism (in Ottoman economic policy), 50, 61

transformation vs. revolution, 194, 237–38, 243, 294

Transjordan, 170, 217, 219

Translation Office (Sublime Porte), 41, 90–91

"Treatise of Light" (*Risale-i Nur*) (Nursi), 287–91, 384, 385

Treaty of Berlin (1878), 85, 134, 142, 174

Treaty of Brest-Litovsk, 218

Treaty of Küçük Kaynarca, 23, 25–26, 51, 52, 148

Treaty of Lausanne, 219, 224, 226, 227, 249, 262, 264, 270–71, 278

Treaty of Paris (1856), 75, 83

Treaty of Sèvres, 218–19, 223, 226, 250, 262

trials. *See* courts

Tribal School, 151

True Path Party, 352, 357

Truman, Harry, 265

Truman doctrine, 265

Tunis, 62, 93, 136

Tunisia, 30, 62, 135, 136, 157

Türkçülüğün Esasları (Principles of Turkism) (Gökalp), 238

Türkeş, Alparslan, 311, 314, 317, 318, 320, 321–22

Turkey: Armenian terrorism against, 324; and authoritarian political history, 4, 6, 24, 36, 133, 137, 145, 146–48, 190, 198, 223–24, 245, 252, 257, 258, 270, 303, 340, 416; borders of, 245, 250; coalition governments in, 312, 317–18, 357–58, 386–87; defined in relation to Ottoman Empire, 4, 6; difference and equality as

Turkey: Armenian terrorism *(continued)*
continuing issues for, 314, 350–51,
416–21; earthquake in, 358, 370,
373, 380; first official usage of term,
222; history curriculum in, 4, 13,
122, 253, 255–56, 273, 352, 372, 421;
interest of, in joining European
Union, 18, 350, 351, 359, 361, 362,
364, 367–69, 371–74, 377, 382, 403,
417, 420; 1997 military ultimatums
in, 357–58, 386; multiparty politics
in, 305–6, 313, 324, 327; 1980 coup
in, 305, 306, 321–22, 324, 330, 337,
348, 351–54, 390, 398–403; 1971
coup in, 305, 306, 316–17, 320, 336,
348, 390, 394–98; 1960 coup in, 305,
306, 309–11, 326, 348; recognition
of, as independent nation, 226;
Second Republic in, 305, 306,
310–22; Third Republic in, 351–74;
U.S. military bases in, 309, 369;
Western orientation of, 19, 88,
103, 252–53, 255, 256, 262, 288, 289,
305, 306, 309–10, 322, 340–41, 348,
357, 361, 369, 371, 372, 374, 416–18,
420. *See also* Ankara; developing
countries; economics; government;
human rights; identity; Islam;
migration; modernity; National
Struggle; Ottoman Empire;
politics; population; religion(s);
Turkification; Turkish language;
Turkish republic; urbanization
Turkification, 201, 203, 204, 221, 284.
See also ethnicity; Islam; Turkish
language
Turkish Hearth associations, 204,
254–55, 258
Turkish Historical Society, 255–56
Turkish Industrial Development
Bank, 207

Turkish Industrialists' and Businessmen's
Association (TÜSİAD), 327, 367,
376–77, 417
Turkish Journalists and Writers
Foundation, 387–89
Turkish language (Ottoman and
modern): and alphabet reform,
21, 118, 247, 253, 256–57, 283, 288,
290, 419; for call to prayer, 252;
continuing changes in, 21, 101–2,
255–56; differences between Turkic
languages and, 371; Egyptian elites'
use of Ottoman, 39; government
requiring use of, in business, 227;
as marker of Turkish identity, 6,
7, 18, 175, 278; novelists writing in,
240; as part of Ottomanism, 201–2;
politicization of, under Turkish
republic, 255–56, 365, 416; print
capitalism and change in, 11–13,
19–20, 103–6; reform of, 247, 253,
255–57, 283, 419; reform of, as
form of censorship, 256, 257, 289;
Tanzimat legislation published in,
94; in the theater, 129
Turkish Language Society,
254, 255–57
Turkish Radio and Television Authority,
311, 316
Turkish republic: Abdülhamid II's
laws published under, 160;
authoritarianism in, 6, 165;
corporatism of, 66; as developing
nation, 247; economic aspects of,
58, 230–31, 247, 259; establishment
of, 192, 226, 248; Europe's influence
on, 252–53, 255, 256, 259–60, 262,
290–91; geography of, 4, 206;
laicism as official policy of, 1, 9,
18, 19, 21, 122, 239, 247, 252–53, 256,
258, 268, 356, 360, 382, 416–18;

legitimacy for, 248–49; opposition to, 251, 258–59; as Ottoman Empire's heir, 245; as parliamentary constitutional government, 200; political polarization in, 337; religious brotherhoods suppressed under, 7, 20, 71, 287–89, 381, 419; single-party regime of, 247, 248, 257–59, 266–70, 284, 287; social scientists' interest in, 1–2; struggle to establish, 10, 21; and surname law, 253, 342; Treaty of Lausanne as recognizing, 219; women's emancipation under, 247, 278–79, 304, 382. *See also* Directorate of Religious Affairs; economics; government; National Struggle; Ottoman Empire; politics; Second Republic; Third Republic; Turkey; Turkish language; *specific rulers, organizations, and politicians*

Turkish Republic of Northern Cyprus, 370

Turkish-Soviet Friendship Treaty (1921, 1925), 248, 262, 265

Turkish Teachers Foundation, 388

Turkish Union of Chambers of Commerce and Exchanges (TOBB), 327, 367

Turkish Women's Federation, 279

Türkleşmak, İslamlaşmak, Muasırlaşmak (Gökalp). *See* "Becoming Turkish, Islamic, and Modern"

Turkmenistan, 370–71

Turkmens, 369

Türk Yurdu (journal), 204

"turnkey" projects, 60

TÜSİAD. *See* Turkish Industrialists' and Businessmen's Association

"Twelfth of July Declaration" (İnönü), 268

Ukraine, 26

ultranationalism, 305, 311, 314–18, 320–22, 324, 337, 338, 370, 415. *See also* Nationalist Action Party

Ulum-ı İktisadiye ve İctimaiye Mecmuası, 226–27

Ulusu, Bülend, 321

Union and Progress Party (Unionists). *See* Committee of Union and Progress (CUP)

United Nations, 265, 323, 369, 370

United States: aid to Turkey from, 265, 275, 309, 325, 348; Civil War in, 86, 111, 171; on Cypus tensions, 322, 323; emigration to, from Ottoman Empire, 177; and EU admission standards, 373; Gülen movement in, 389; Iraqi invasion by, 368; military bases of, in Turkey, 309, 369; New Deal policies in, 276; and Turkish anti-American activism, 316; Turkish investments from, 271; in Vietnam War, 314–15

unity: Islamic, 123–24, 132, 149; of Ottomanism, 99–102, 106, 107, 117, 201, 211, 239

'Urabi Bey, Ahmad, 87, 136–37

urbanization: and fertility, 184; of Kurds, 364–67; since 1980, 379–80; and the poor, 119; during Second Republic, 331–32, 349; and shantytowns, 321, 331–32, 336, 337; during Tanzimat era, 116; under Third Republic, 354–55; in Turkey, 305, 379

Uzbekistan, 370–71

vaccinations, 63

Van, 164, 209–10, 234, 286, 287

vatan (fatherland), 45, 101, 106, 123, 129–32, 363, 411

Vatan yahud Silistre (Namık Kemal). *See*
    "Fatherland, or Silistria"
Vekayi-i Misriye (newspaper), 42
Verdi, Giuseppi, 125, 128
Verheugen, Günter, 361
Vietnam War, 314–15
"village guards," 366
Village Institutes, 284, 304
violence: population declines due to,
    4, 134, 144, 174–77, 193, 202, 203,
    209–11, 278; in provinces, 29–30, 36,
    39, 42, 56, 59, 63, 109, 110, 116–17,
    144, 145, 154, 197, 365–68. *See also*
    ethnic cleansing; *specific wars*
Virtue Party, 315, 358, 359
Vogt, Karl, 163
von der Goltz, Colmar, 156, 199, 213
voting: cynicism about, 362; two-stage
    system of, 195, 250, 268; for women,
    195, 235, 253, 279, 383

Wahhabi religious movement, 38, 70, 181
Wallachia (principality), 25, 30, 80–81, 83
Wangenheim, Hans von, 208
warlords (ayan), 26–31, 33, 35–39, 56,
    59–60, 109. *See also names of*
    specific warlords
wealth tax (Capital Levy), 266, 275
wheat, 53–54
Wilhelm II (of Germany), 157, 200
Wilson, Woodrow, 221
women: with careers, 186–88, 264, 378,
    382, 383, 392–94; education for girls
    and, 67–69, 117, 126, 178, 183–184,
    227, 235, 239–40, 280, 283, 355–56,
    380, 389; emancipation of, during
    Turkish republic, 247, 278–79, 304,
    382; foreign, in Ottoman literature,
    126; French soldiers' treatment of,
    27; magazines for, 117, 178, 184,
    195, 235; Muslim, as novelists, 126;

178, 239–44; in Nursi's reading
    groups, 289; rights of Muslim vs.
    European, 8, 67, 187; in Turkish
    politics, 357–58, 360, 382; veiling
    and unveiling of Muslim, 67, 131,
    177, 235, 241, 252, 360, 361, 383 384,
    389, 392, 408, 410, 411, 413, 415;
    voting for, 195, 235, 253, 279, 383;
    work done by, 60, 112, 172, 173, 179,
    231–32, 245–46, 277, 343–45. *See also*
    feminism; gender; patriarchy
Workers Party of Turkey (WPT), 313, 315
World Bank, 275, 358, 374, 375
World War I, 141, 168, 273, 280, 295,
    304; as byproduct of modernity,
    202; Ottoman Empire in, 192,
    199–200, 204–5, 207–19, 228–33, 245,
    261, 267
World War II, 248, 261–62, 274–75;
    dissatisfaction after, 266–68;
    Turkey's neutrality in, 264–65, 305
WPT (Workers' Party of Turkey),
    313, 315

Yaban (Karaosmanoğlu), 280–83
Yahya (imam), 137, 205
Yanina, 35, 36–37
Yavuz, Hakan, 386
Yemen, 135, 137–38, 154, 164, 181, 205
Yeni Ümit, 387
Yıldız Palace (Abdülhamid II's), 146–47,
    157, 158, 184, 195
Yılırım Ordular Grubu, 213–15
Yılmaz, Mesut, 357–58
Yön (journal), 313
Young Ottomans, 160, 161, 418; exiling
    of, 129; on government finances,
    107; Islamic engagement of, 163;
    literature by, 123–32; as opposing
    Tanzimat reforms, 104–6, 118; as
    provincial administrators, 122

Young Turks, 20; constitutionalism of, 133, 237, 262; constitutional rule under, 133, 262; goals of, 164–65, 275; ideology of, 194, 238, 258, 262; and nationalism, 201–5; 1908 revolution of, 145, 192–94, 286, 417, 418; in novels, 241; opposition of, to Abdülhamid II, 146, 160–65, 190–91, 418; opposition to, 196–97, 339; "populism" under, 280; regime of, 138, 245, 276; rise of, 137, 160–65; scientific materialism of, 163, 238, 313, 416, 418; secularism of, 163, 165, 179, 191, 193, 245, 268

youth activism (1960s). *See* leftists; rightists; ultranationalists; *names of specific leaders and groups*

Yugoslavia, 264, 310, 374. *See also names of states and regions in*

Zaman (newspaper), 387, 388

Zaydi sect (of Shi'is), 137–38, 181, 205

Zeki Paşa, 143

Zionists, 175, 192, 201, 203, 218

Ziya Bey (later, Paşa), 122

Ziya Hurşit, 251

Zohrab, James, 138

Zola, Émile, 185

Zorlu, Fatin Rüştü, 312